Keep this book. You will need it and use it throughout your career.

About the American Hotel & Motel Association (AH&MA)

Founded in 1910, AH&MA is the trade association representing the $85.6 billion lodging industry in the United States. AH&MA is a federation of state lodging associations throughout the United States with 11,000 lodging properties worldwide as members. The association offers its members assistance with governmental affairs representation, communications, marketing, hospitality operations, training and education, technology issues, industry research, and more. Members have the opportunity to network and share knowledge with other hospitality industry professionals through the association's many committees and through national conventions and leadership forums.

About the Educational Institute of AH&MA (EI)

An affiliate of AH&MA, the Educational Institute is the world's largest source of quality training and educational materials for the lodging industry. EI develops textbooks and courses that are used in more than 1,200 colleges and universities worldwide, and also offers courses to individuals through its Distance Learning program. Leading hotel chains, management companies, and independent properties rely on EI for training resources that focus on every aspect of lodging operations. Industry-tested videos, CD-ROMs, seminars, and skills guides prepare employees at every skill level to succeed in hospitality. EI also offers professional certification for the industry's top performers.

About the American Hotel Foundation (AHF)

An affiliate of AH&MA, the American Hotel Foundation provides financial support that enhances the stability, prosperity, and growth of the lodging industry through educational and research programs. The foundation has awarded hundreds of thousands of dollars in scholarship funds for students pursuing higher education in hospitality management. AHF has also funded research projects on topics of importance to the industry, including occupational safety and health, environmental action, turnover and diversity, and best practices in the U.S. lodging industry.

SECURITY and LOSS PREVENTION MANAGEMENT

Educational Institute Courses

Introductory

INTRODUCTION TO THE HOSPITALITY INDUSTRY
Fourth Edition
Gerald W. Lattin

AN INTRODUCTION TO HOSPITALITY TODAY
Third Edition
Rocco M. Angelo, Andrew N. Vladimir

TOURISM AND THE HOSPITALITY INDUSTRY
Joseph D. Fridgen

Rooms Division

FRONT OFFICE PROCEDURES
Fifth Edition
Michael L. Kasavana, Richard M. Brooks

HOUSEKEEPING MANAGEMENT
Second Edition
Margaret M. Kappa, Aleta Nitschke, Patricia B. Schappert

Human Resources

HOSPITALITY SUPERVISION
Second Edition
Raphael R. Kavanaugh, Jack D. Ninemeier

HOSPITALITY INDUSTRY TRAINING
Second Edition
Lewis C. Forrest, Jr.

HUMAN RESOURCES MANAGEMENT
Second Edition
Robert H. Woods

Marketing and Sales

MARKETING OF HOSPITALITY SERVICES
William Lazer, Roger Layton

HOSPITALITY SALES AND MARKETING
Third Edition
James R. Abbey

CONVENTION MANAGEMENT AND SERVICE
Fifth Edition
Milton T. Astroff, James R. Abbey

MARKETING IN THE HOSPITALITY INDUSTRY
Third Edition
Ronald A. Nykiel

Accounting

UNDERSTANDING HOSPITALITY ACCOUNTING I
Fourth Edition
Raymond Cote

UNDERSTANDING HOSPITALITY ACCOUNTING II
Third Edition
Raymond Cote

BASIC FINANCIAL ACCOUNTING FOR THE HOSPITALITY INDUSTRY
Second Edition
Raymond S. Schmidgall, James W. Damitio

MANAGERIAL ACCOUNTING FOR THE HOSPITALITY INDUSTRY
Fourth Edition
Raymond S. Schmidgall

Food and Beverage

FOOD AND BEVERAGE MANAGEMENT
Third Edition
Jack D. Ninemeier

QUALITY SANITATION MANAGEMENT
Ronald F. Cichy

FOOD PRODUCTION PRINCIPLES
Jerald W. Chesser

FOOD AND BEVERAGE SERVICE
Second Edition
Ronald F. Cichy, Paul E. Wise

HOSPITALITY PURCHASING MANAGEMENT
William P. Virts

BAR AND BEVERAGE MANAGEMENT
Lendal H. Kotschevar, Mary L. Tanke

FOOD AND BEVERAGE CONTROLS
Fourth Edition
Jack D. Ninemeier

General Hospitality Management

HOTEL/MOTEL SECURITY MANAGEMENT
Second Edition
Raymond C. Ellis, Jr., David M. Stipanuk

HOSPITALITY LAW
Third Edition
Jack P. Jefferies

RESORT MANAGEMENT
Second Edition
Chuck Y. Gee

INTERNATIONAL HOTEL MANAGEMENT
Chuck Y. Gee

HOSPITALITY INDUSTRY COMPUTER SYSTEMS
Third Edition
Michael L. Kasavana, John J. Cahill

MANAGING FOR QUALITY IN THE HOSPITALITY INDUSTRY
Robert H. Woods, Judy Z. King

CONTEMPORARY CLUB MANAGEMENT
Edited by Joe Perdue for the Club Managers Association of America

Engineering and Facilities Management

FACILITIES MANAGEMENT
David M. Stipanuk, Harold Roffman

HOSPITALITY INDUSTRY ENGINEERING SYSTEMS
Michael H. Redlin, David M. Stipanuk

HOSPITALITY ENERGY AND WATER MANAGEMENT
Second Edition
Robert E. Aulbach

SECURITY and LOSS PREVENTION MANAGEMENT

Second Edition

Raymond C. Ellis, Jr.
David M. Stipanuk

EDUCATIONAL INSTITUTE
American Hotel & Motel Association

Disclaimer

This publication is designed to provide accurate and authoritative information in regard to the subject matter covered. It is sold with the understanding that the publisher is not engaged in rendering legal, accounting, or other professional service. If legal advice or other expert assistance is required, the services of a competent professional person should be sought.
—*From the Declaration of Principles jointly adopted by the American Bar Association and a Committee of Publishers and Associations*

The authors, Raymond C. Ellis, Jr., and David M. Stipanuk, are solely responsible for the contents of this publication. All views expressed herein are solely those of the authors and do not necessarily reflect the views of the Educational Institute of the American Hotel & Motel Association (the Institute) or the American Hotel & Motel Association (AH&MA).

Nothing contained in this publication shall constitute a standard, an endorsement, or a recommendation of the Institute or AH&MA. The Institute and AH&MA disclaim any liability with respect to the use of any information, procedure, or product, or reliance thereon by any member of the hospitality industry.

© 1999
By the EDUCATIONAL INSTITUTE of the
AMERICAN HOTEL & MOTEL ASSOCIATION
2113 N. High Street
Lansing, MI 48906–7221

The Educational Institute of the American Hotel & Motel Association is a nonprofit educational foundation.

All rights reserved. No part of this publication may be reproduced, stored in a retrieval system, or transmitted, in any form or by any means—electronic, mechanical, photocopying, recording, or otherwise—without prior permission of the publisher.

Printed in the United States of America
 2 3 4 5 6 7 8 9 10 03 02 01 00

Ellis, Raymond C.
    Security and loss prevention management / Raymond C. Ellis, Jr., David M. Stipanuk. — 2nd ed.
    p. cm.
    Includes bibliographical references and index.
    ISBN 0–86612–178–1
    1. Hotels—Security measures. 2. Hotel management. I. Stipanuk, David M. II. Title.
TX911.3.S4E45   1999
647.94'068'4—dc21   99–33105
                                CIP

Editors: Robert Bittner
          Jennifer Smith

Contents

Congratulations xi
Preface xiii
About the Authors xv
Study Tips xvii

1 **Security and the Lodging Industry** 3

   A Growing Concern 3
   Developing the Security Program 4

   The Need for Effective Management • Areas of Vulnerability • Security Requirements

   Setting Up the Security Program 6

   The Importance of Law Enforcement Liaison • Security Staffing

   The Elements of Security Training 15

   Who Is Responsible? • The Authority of a Security Officer • The Team Concept

   Security and the Law 24
   Legal Definitions 28

   The Connie Francis Case • Societal Concerns • Recommended Reading

   Endnotes, Key Terms, Review Questions, Internet Sites 33
   Case Study: Steve's Royal Problem 36
   Case Study: Doughnuts and Dilemmas 39
   Appendix: Selected Court Cases 44

   Wenninger v. Motel 6, Inc. • Peters v. Holiday Inns, Inc. • Fortney v. Hotel Rancroft, Inc. • Phillips Petroleum Co. v. Dorn • Reichenbach v. Days Inn of America, Inc. • Orlando Executive Park, Inc. v. P.D.R. • Matt et al. v. Days Inns of America, Inc. • Robertson v. Sixpence Inns of America, Inc. • Malone et al. v. Courtyard by Marriott Limited Partnership et al.

   Review Quiz 99

2 **Security Equipment** 103

   Physical Security and Perimeter Control 104

   Perimeter Barriers • Lighting • Parking Areas • Glass Protection

   Surveillance 122

   Closed-Circuit Television

Communication Systems 125
Alarm Systems 130
    Local Alarms • Contact Alarms • Remote Alarms • Safety Alarms

Safety Equipment 133
    Smoke Detectors • Fire Extinguishers • Carbon Monoxide Detectors • Sprinkler Systems • Accident Prevention Signs

Guestroom Security 137
    Locks • Biometrics • Secondary Access–Limiting Devices • Viewports • Room Communications • In-Room Security Information

Endnotes, Key Terms, Review Questions, Internet Sites 154
Case Study: Lights…Camera…Action? 157
Review Quiz 161

3 Security Procedures Covering Guest Concerns 165

Key and Keycard Control 165
    Electronic Access Systems

Surveillance and Access Control Procedures 174
    Patrols

The Presence of Unauthorized Persons 176
    Drug Dealers

Safe Deposit Box Procedures 179
    Keys and Key Control • Access Procedures • Special or Unusual Access

The In-Room Safe 186
Lost and Found Procedures 186
Endnotes, Key Terms, Review Questions, Internet Sites 191
Case Study: The Safe Deposit Box That Wasn't 193
Appendix: Sample Room Notices 199
Review Quiz 203

4 Departmental Responsibilities in Guest and Asset Protection 207

Losses Affecting All Departments 207
    Responding to Employee Theft

The Human Resources Department 211
    Exit Interviews • Violence in the Workplace • Alcohol and Drug Use and Abuse

The Engineering Department 217

Contents **vii**

    The Rooms Division 219
        Front Service • The Housekeeping Department

    Purchasing and Receiving 225
    Storage and Issuing 228
    The Food and Beverage Department 228
        Spoilage and Pilferage • Alcohol Storage, Issuing, and Service • Point-of-Sale (POS) Systems

    The Recreation Department 232
        Swimming Pools • Health Clubs and Jogging Trails

    Casino and Gaming Security 238
    Report Writing and Recordkeeping 240
    Special Guests and Events 243
        Guests with Disabilities • VIP Guests • Youth Groups • Conventions, Meetings, and Exhibits

    Endnotes, Key Terms, Review Questions, Internet Sites 249
    Case Study: Soccer and Spice and Everything Chaotic 251
    Case Study: Is It Getting Hot in Here? 255
    Review Quiz 257

5 The Protection of Funds **261**

    Accounting Control Procedures 261
        Inventory Control • Payroll Procedures and Concerns • Sequential Numbering Systems • Bank Deposits

    Physical Protection of the Accounting Function 263
    Cashiering Procedures 264
    Establishing Credit Policies and Procedures 265
        Credit Cards • Checks • Denying Credit to a Guest • Guest Registration and Check-out

    Computer Security 274
        Accountability • Auditability • System Integrity • Cost Effectiveness • Ease of Implementation • Policy Compliance

    An Internal Audit Program 280
    Key Terms, Review Questions, Internet Sites 283
    Case Study: Points of Internal Control at the Eastwick Resort 284
    Review Quiz 287

6 Emergency Management **291**

    Developing an Emergency Management Program 291
    Bombs and Bomb Threats 295

Fire 297
Hurricanes 299

    Hurricane Watch • Hurricane Warning • Waiting • Direct Hit • Conclusion

Tornadoes 303
Floods 303
Earthquakes 304
Blackouts 305
Robberies 306
Medical and Dental Emergencies 307
Terrorism 313

    Sabotage • Kidnappings and Hostage Situations • Riots and Civil Disturbances

Media Relations 316

    What to Tell the Media • Dealing with Group Disturbances

Endnotes, Review Questions, Internet Sites 321
Case Study: Terrorist on the Telephone 322
Review Quiz 325

7 Risk Management and Insurance 329

The Risk Management Process 329

    Identification of Risk • Assessment of Potential Losses • Selection of Proper Risk Management Instruments • Studying the Plan and Implementing Decisions

Contributions of Risk Management to a Business 334
Direct and Indirect Contributions 335
Insurance 336

    Insurance Purchase • Industry Regulation • Insurance Coverage

Commercial Package Policy 339

    Commercial Property Coverage • Commercial General Liability Coverage • Commercial Crime Coverage • Boiler and Machinery Coverage • Inland Marine Coverage • Commercial Automotive Coverage

Additional Types of Coverage 347

    Flood Coverage • Umbrella Coverage • Legally Mandated Coverage

Claims Management 348
Establishing a Safety Committee 350

    The Value of Communication • The Roles of the Safety Committee • Safety Committee Duties

Endnotes, Key Terms, Review Questions, Internet Sites 354

          Case Study: Slipping Up—A Committee Catches Careless Acts 358
          Review Quiz 362

Appendix:
A Guide to OSHA Regulations for the Lodging Industry 365

Index **439**

Congratulations...

You have a running start on a fast-track career!

Developed through the input of industry and academic experts, this course gives you the know-how hospitality employers demand. Upon course completion, you will earn the respected American Hotel & Motel Association certificate that ensures instant recognition worldwide. It is your link with the global hospitality industry.

You can use your AH&MA certificate to show that your learning experiences have bridged the gap between industry and academia. You will have proof that you have met industry-driven learning objectives and that you know how to apply your knowledge to actual hospitality work situations.

By earning your course certificate, you also take a step toward completing the highly respected learning programs—Certificates of Specialization, the Hospitality Operations Certificate, and the Hospitality Management Diploma—that raise your professional development to a higher level. Certificates from these programs greatly enhance your credentials, and a permanent record of your course and program completion is maintained by the Educational Institute.

We commend you for taking this important step. Turn to the Educational Institute for additional resources that will help you stay ahead of your competition.

Preface

TRAVELERS EXPECT AND demand secure and safe experiences at the lodging properties they choose to visit. Owners and investors expect and demand that a property will be operated as efficiently and profitably as possible. A property that implements a security and loss prevention program that fulfills the wishes of these groups begins each day with a competitive edge. This textbook looks at several areas that may be of concern to security–conscious managers and employees.

The first point to be made is that the security and loss prevention needs of different properties vary. Recent decades have witnessed a great diversification within the lodging industry. New and different types and styles of lodging properties have been developed, each adding a significant element to the industry's ability to serve its various markets effectively. This diversification, coupled with a rising crime rate, has also resulted in more diversified security needs. Although certain properties' needs may be similar, each property is ultimately unique.

The security function at various lodging properties may be performed by people with many different titles. Smaller properties often assign the security function to a manager with other responsibilities. Larger properties may decide to maintain a full–fledged security department with its own department head. Regardless of who is in charge of the security effort, that person should be considered part of the management team at the property level. Security is a consideration in many of the management team's decisions; direct input from an executive–level security director can improve communications, which may help to increase the effectiveness of the security program.

Over the years since the initial publication of this book, the lines have become increasingly blurred between security and loss prevention management. Some major hotel corporations have designated a loss prevention function that incorporates safety, security, and fire protection. These disciplines have become sufficiently important that a vice president designation is often provided in the corporate organizational chart.

This textbook is designed to accomplish four main goals: (1) to help a lodging property develop its security and loss prevention programs, (2) to serve as a reference for topics and issues to review if a security or loss prevention incident should occur, (3) to help employees become aware of security and loss prevention concerns, and (4) to provide security and loss prevention information to students who are entering the industry.

Chapter 1 looks at initial concerns and concepts relating to security. It traces the recent history of lodging security and loss prevention, outlines the general areas a security and loss prevention program should consider, examines the legal requirements associated with protecting guests and property, and discusses several elements involved in setting up a security and loss prevention program. The Appendix at the end of Chapter 1 presents and briefly discusses nine legal cases involving the lodging industry.

Chapters 2 through 5 look at security equipment and procedures as they relate to physical security, internal control, and the overall protection of guests and assets. Security and loss prevention responsibilities are broken down by department, with special attention given to the protection of funds through effective accounting control procedures, credit procedures, and computer security. Chapter 6 includes a discussion of emergency management, highlighting important procedures for handling emergency situations themselves while providing guidelines for maintaining a positive media presence.

Chapter 7 examines the risk management process and insurance details from a lodging perspective. As previously noted, the lines have become indistinct between the safety, fire protection, and security aspects of loss prevention. Nevertheless, it is important that there be a distinct and separate review of the safety and fire protection disciplines and their effect upon the bottom line. In the fire protection and safety areas, extensive federal legislation exists. This chapter looks at general safety and fire protection issues, then turns to a discussion of many federal safety regulations that apply to lodging properties.

The importance of security and loss prevention for today's lodging industry should not be overlooked or underestimated. There are too many ways in which a property that is inattentive to such concerns can be victimized. Managers and employees who understand the nature of potential security problems are better able to help protect themselves, their property, and their guests.

The authors wish to thank the following people for their contributions to the development of this resource: Earl J. Bleser, CFE, President, Hospitality Safeguards; Chad Callaghan, CPP, CLSD, Senior Director of Loss Prevention, Marriott International; William G. Cox, CPP, CHA, CLSD, Security Consultant; Thomas G. Davis, CLSD, President, Hospitality Risk Controls, and consultant to the AH&MA Loss Prevention Committee; and Mark Hamilton, CHE, CHTP.

Raymond C. Ellis, Jr.
Houston, Texas

David M. Stipanuk
Ithaca, New York

About the Authors

Raymond C. Ellis, Jr.

Raymond C. Ellis, Jr., MBA, CHE, CHTP, CLSD, has spent 39 years with the American Hotel & Motel Association (AH&MA), 22 of them as a consultant. During that time, his work emphasized security, operations, and research. He is currently an Adjunct Professor at Conrad N. Hilton College of Hotel and Restaurant Management, University of Houston, where his focus is on facilities management and loss prevention management. He is the founder and director of the Loss Prevention Management Institute (LPMI) and is a regular contributor to *Lodging* magazine's monthly bulletin *Lodging Law*. He was elected to the Hospitality Financial and Technology Hall of Fame (1989) and awarded AH&MA's 1999 Lamp of Knowledge for Outstanding Educator.

David M. Stipanuk

David M. Stipanuk is an Associate Professor of Property Asset Management at the School of Hotel Administration at Cornell University. His teaching responsibilities include hospitality risk management, facilities management, development and construction, and sustainable development. He is co-author of *Hospitality Facilities Management and Design* and co-editor of *Water Resources for Lodging Operations*, both published by the Educational Institute.

Study Tips for Users of Educational Institute Courses

Learning is a skill, like many other activities. Although you may be familiar with many of the following study tips, we want to reinforce their usefulness.

Your Attitude Makes a Difference

If you want to learn, you will: it's as simple as that. Your attitude will go a long way in determining whether or not you do well in this course. We want to help you succeed.

Plan and Organize to Learn

- Set up a regular time and place for study. Make sure you won't be disturbed or distracted.
- Decide ahead of time how much you want to accomplish during each study session. Remember to keep your study sessions brief; don't try to do too much at one time.

Read the Course Text to Learn

- *Before* you read each chapter, read the chapter outline and the competencies. If there is a summary at the end of the chapter, you also want to read it to get a feel for what the chapter is about.
- Then, go back to the beginning of the chapter and *carefully* read, focusing on the material included in the competencies and asking yourself such questions as:

    —Do I understand the material?

    —How can I use this information now or in the future?

- Make notes in margins and highlight or underline important sections to help you as you study. Read a section first, then go back over it to mark important points.
- Keep a dictionary handy. If you come across an unfamiliar word that is not included in the key terms, look it up in the dictionary.
- Read as much as you can. The more you read, the better you read.

Testing Your Knowledge

- Test questions developed by the Educational Institute for this course are designed to reliably and validly measure a student's ability to meet a standard of knowledge expressed by the industry-driven competencies.

- End-of-the-chapter Review Quizzes help you find out how well you have studied the material. They indicate where additional study may be needed. Review Quizzes are also helpful in studying for other tests.
- Prepare for tests by reviewing:
    —competencies
    —notes
    —outlines
    —questions at the end of each assignment
- As you begin to take any test, read the test instructions *carefully* and look over the questions.

We hope your experiences in this course will prompt you to undertake other training and educational activities in a planned, career-long program of professional growth and development.

Chapter 1 Outline

A Growing Concern
Developing the Security Program
    The Need for Effective Management
    Areas of Vulnerability
    Security Requirements
Setting Up the Security Program
    The Importance of Law Enforcement Liaison
    Security Staffing
The Elements of Security Training
    Who Is Responsible?
    The Authority of a Security Officer
    The Team Concept
Security and the Law
Legal Definitions
    The Connie Francis Case
    Societal Concerns
    Recommended Reading
Case Studies
Appendix: Selected Court Cases
    Wenninger v. Motel 6, Inc.
    Peters v. Holiday Inns, Inc.
    Fortney v. Hotel Rancroft, Inc.
    Phillips Petroleum Co. v. Dorn
    Reichenbach v. Days Inn of America, Inc.
    Orlando Executive Park, Inc. v. P.D.R.
    Matt et al. v. Days Inns of America, Inc.
    Robertson v. Sixpence Inns of America, Inc.
    Malone et al. v. Courtyard by Marriott Limited Partnership et al.

Competencies

1. Explain the key issues in developing and setting up a security program, including law enforcement liaisons and security staffing. (pp. 3–15)

2. Identify the elements of security training that are critical to an effective security program. (pp. 15–24)

3. List and describe the legal concepts and societal concerns related to security issues and court cases, and summarize the importance of the Connie Francis case to the lodging industry. (pp. 24–33)

1

Security and the Lodging Industry

LODGING PROPERTY MANAGERS have many responsibilities, one of which is security. Providing **security** in a hotel or motel is the broad task of protecting people—guests, employees, and others—and assets. Crimes involving the theft of assets usually result in greater losses to lodging properties than crimes against persons, but crimes against persons have a greater effect on public relations (and therefore occupancy) and may generate high legal expenses.

Lodging property security efforts may involve such areas of concern as guestroom security, key control, locks, access control, perimeter control, alarm systems, communication systems, lighting, closed-circuit television, safe deposit boxes, inventory control, credit and billing procedures, computer security, staffing, preemployment screening, employee training, responsible service of alcoholic beverages, emergency procedures, safety procedures, record keeping, and more.

It must be stated, however, that each lodging property is different and has differing security needs; the material included in this book should not be construed as recommending any industry standard.

A Growing Concern

The industry's concern with security has increased greatly as a result of the continuing crime rate against both assets and people and the rapidly growing number of lawsuits filed against innkeepers and even individually named employees for failure to provide adequate security. While crimes against guests may raise moral and ethical questions, innkeepers and potential innkeepers do not need a textbook to explain that such issues are involved in providing safe and secure accommodations. Rather, it is the legal implications of this fact and the various actual security systems and procedures available that must be studied. Such information is never gained through intuition.

In most states, innkeepers have a legal duty to provide "reasonable care" (which will be discussed later) for the protection of guests and guests' invitees. Innkeepers may be held responsible for injuries to guests caused by their employees in the course of their employment. Innkeepers sued for negligence in allegedly not providing reasonable care for someone who was injured or victimized on their premises are losing millions of dollars every year in court judgments and out-of-court settlements.

Even if financial considerations were the only concern in providing security (which they certainly are not), the urgency of considering a security program if one is not already in place is obvious.

Developing the Security Program

Some important points relating to the development of a security program need to be made at the outset. First, a security program should stress the prevention of security problems. It is far more desirable to keep security incidents from occurring than it is to catch a criminal after a crime has been committed. Certain actions and procedures, properly implemented, may help to prevent or discourage such incidents. Nonetheless, it must be recognized that *not all crime is preventable*.

A facility's security program, therefore, should be designed to train its staff to prevent the preventable security incidents and to react quickly, appropriately, and effectively, whenever possible, to any unpreventable security incidents.

Each property should continually review its security procedures. Whenever necessary, the property should update its procedures to meet its changing security needs. The following list indicates general areas that should be considered for inclusion in a property's security program:

- Locks, key control, and electronic or mechanical card access control
- Guestroom security
- Control of persons on premises
- Perimeter control
- Protection of assets (money on hand, guests' assets, equipment, inventories)
- Emergency procedures
- Communications
- Security records

In addition, a property's design and layout can greatly affect its security program. For lodging establishments still at the planning stage, security concerns should be considered at the architectural level.

The Need for Effective Management

Providing appropriate security for any lodging establishment is a never-ending activity. In a climate of increased crime against guests, employees, lodging properties, and the assets of each, management is continually challenged to develop and support an effective security program. Without continuous awareness at the management level, a property's security may suffer.

In the development of security guidelines for an individual property, all members of the management and supervisory team of the property should be involved. The special needs of the particular hotel or motel must be incorporated in the procedures. While in draft, the materials should be reviewed by legal counsel. Upon approval, the information should be provided to all employees. If prepared for each individual department, the data can be provided on a job-by-job basis. There is a greater likelihood that employees will review the material if the format addresses specific assignments without detailing the total security operations of the property. Turnover and changes in job assignments necessitate a regular review program to keep all employees aware of their security responsibilities.

While recognizing the need for protection of the guests, the employees, and the assets of each, management must also recognize that guests and employees may themselves create security problems by stealing property and services from the hotel or motel.

Security should be recognized and used as a management tool. Whether the size of the property requires a large security staff or allows for the security function to be assigned to one or several on-premises supervisory staff, the security role should be clearly defined and implemented. The protection of guests, employees, and assets requires managers (and, indeed, all employees) to be constantly alert to possible security breaches.

Areas of Vulnerability

A more mobile America, the criminal derivatives of the drug culture, and a continuing crime rate combined to create new security problems for hotels and motels. Earlier, the security problem had related essentially to room thefts—assaults or rapes were almost unheard of. Recently, however, hotels and motels have gained an unfortunate visibility with regard to criminal incidents that can include assault, arson, and armed robbery. Crimes against the guest, even if few in number, can generate adverse publicity, can seriously damage the reputation of the property, and may be extremely costly during subsequent litigation.

One problem in designing a security program to deal with such crimes is that the security effort must take into consideration the property's image. The lodging industry is, after all, a service industry. A hotel or motel markets an image of hospitality as its main product. Security procedures that virtually invoke martial law may be good for security, but they will probably be bad for hospitality. Poorly thought-out security procedures may offend or inconvenience guests and drive them away altogether.

Another area of asset vulnerability results from the use of inadequate procedures for checking and giving credit. Such procedures may lead to losses by permitting the unauthorized or fraudulent use of credit cards, personal checks, and travelers checks. This type of incident is less visible to the general public than personal crime and is therefore less likely to greatly affect public relations efforts. Nonetheless, when establishing credit procedures to protect a property from incurring losses through bad debts, care must again be taken to avoid offending one's guests.

A high degree of vulnerability exists in the protection of the physical assets of a lodging establishment. All too often, these expenses are ignored and written off as a cost of doing business. Very little effort may be spent in trying to control the loss of tableware, ashtrays, linens, and towels—to name but a few of the items whose theft results in a monetary loss to the organization; however, when an organized crime team is concentrating on stealing color television sets from the rooms of a hotel or motel, the extent of the dollar loss becomes immediately evident.

Whether dealing with an organized crime effort or with the theft of assets by guests or employees, management has a responsibility to take preventive action.

Studies by the U.S. Small Business Administration have indicated that business failures can often be directly related to employee theft, which may appear in numerous forms within the hotel or motel and may combine to constitute a major concern.

Security Requirements

Unfortunately, providing adequate security has become more difficult since there has not only been a significant crime rate (even though at a decreasing rate in the last years of the 1990s) but also due to the growing number of lodging establishments throughout the United States. The growth of the automobile industry and the mobility of the American people have brought lodging facilities to the highways in the form of motor courts, inns, and lodges. In addition, resorts, resort condominiums, conference centers, and all-suite and airport properties have proliferated. Each new concept or expansion of a successful format for serving the traveling public has added to both the variety of lodging properties and the variety of communities in which lodging properties are located. Such diversity is clearly one of the strengths of the lodging industry, but it also provides some of the industry's profoundest challenges. This is perhaps nowhere truer or more evident than in the area of hotel and motel security.

No two hotels or motels have identical security requirements. National security standards are not feasible for such a varied industry. The ever-growing diversity of lodging operations, locations, layout, staff, functions, and clientele makes it impossible to develop any standard that could reasonably apply to all properties. Because each property is different, something which is a required security procedure for one property may or may not be of value to another.

Occasionally, organizations, agencies, and schools attempt to introduce plans for the initiation of security standards for the lodging industry. While such efforts are undoubtedly well-intentioned, the lodging industry quite reasonably tends to view them as unrealistic and ultimately counterproductive. The material in this book attempts to outline those aspects of security that may need to be considered by lodging properties as they develop their own individual security programs; the material should not be construed as recommending any industry standard.

It is highly unlikely that any single property would ever have to implement every security procedure or use every device that is discussed. Rather, note those items that are applicable to your property and then consider how to correct any of your property's existing or potential security exposures. If necessary, seek outside assistance from local law enforcement agencies or a qualified lodging industry security consultant.

Setting Up the Security Program

A lodging property's management should consider many factors in evaluating its property's security requirements and in determining whether a special security presence is warranted. If it is, management must decide how that presence may best be integrated with the operation of the hotel or motel. A management team's commitment to the concept of security as a vital function within its hotel or motel is necessary in order to integrate security into the day-to-day operation and administration of the property.

Setting up such an integrated security system is a process that involves many elements. These may include establishing working relationships with local law enforcement agencies, choosing whether to use in-house or contract security personnel, and creating an appropriate and effective security training program for all personnel.

The Importance of Law Enforcement Liaison

Because hotels and motels are affected by the communities in which they are located, a property's management may gain insight into potential security problems by looking at the crime rate and past experiences of the property and surrounding community. Liaisons with police authorities and neighboring lodging properties can help management gain an understanding of the nature and extent of local crime problems. Review with local law enforcement agencies the crime experience, trends, and current problems of your property's locale.

Developing such liaisons often results in clear benefits. In some residential communities, local organizations have developed community crime watch programs in their areas; such programs attempt to promote neighborhood or block activities to develop an awareness of suspicious persons or actions. Some lodging properties have adopted a similar concept that involves developing a telephone network that notifies both police and participating lodging properties when a crime has happened. Each property notified, in turn, may call other properties in the network. Some properties find that such a program may aid the security efforts of the participating lodging establishments. However, such a program should be cleared with local counsel to ensure that the information disseminated does not violate Federal Trade Commission regulations or other federal or local laws, or result in a suit for defamation or libel.

Public safety is, of course, the specific responsibility of law enforcement agencies. In conjunction with a property's security program, its management should cultivate and maintain close and cooperative liaison with the local branch of these agencies. Inform them of your concern and interest in the security of your property, your guests, and your employees. Invite the appropriate law enforcement personnel to visit your property so they can become familiar with it. If possible, review security procedures with the local authorities. Be sure to request police guidance in crime prevention and always document such efforts.

A good relationship with local law enforcement agencies can often encourage a prompt response to security incidents and will probably result in your property benefitting from more frequent police patrols. Police presence can also be a deterrent to certain crimes; measurable reductions in total crimes have been noted in some cases in which liaison relationships have been developed. Good relationships may also be very helpful and much appreciated following a security incident or during an emergency.

Frequently, community police budget limitations within a jurisdiction do not permit an evaluation of crime as it relates to a specific hotel or motel. Where a crime unit does exist within a law enforcement agency, a full review of community and lodging industry crime experience may be available. Such a report will usually include data on homicide, rape, robbery, assault, burglary, theft, auto theft, and a general category of other.

The liaison relationship may also overcome the problem of guests reporting incidents to the police but not to the management of the hotel or motel. This results in discrepancies in the reports of incidents on the premises and hampers the security program because employees may be unaware of some incidents. In a close working relationship, it is more likely that the police will alert management when they are called directly regarding a guest complaint. This permits management to respond to the guest and to be aware of areas where corrective action may be required. It also prepares management for possible litigation and facilitates the preparation of necessary information for legal and insurance review.

A Potential Problem. Unfortunately, law enforcement agencies and private security personnel have not always cooperated well with each other. Police have sometimes viewed private security efforts as staffed with poorly trained older (or retired) personnel who are largely ineffective and even fairly apathetic. In today's changing security scene, this stereotype often does an injustice to a lodging property's security personnel or function as private security has become more professional and sophisticated. Better communication is the key to educating local law enforcement agencies about the broad scope of a lodging property's security program and about the growing professionalism of the industry's security personnel.

The most effective cooperation results when both the police and the property understand the needs of the other. The police should know enough about a property and its security program to be able to offer appropriate assistance in a given situation. They should be informed of any special events or visitors (for example, political or entertainment figures) that may involve an unusual security risk at the property. On the other hand, the property's staff should have a basic understanding of police procedures so that they can be of greatest assistance to the police once they arrive. Local law enforcement authorities will be able to explain the type of assistance they would find most helpful. This information should be included in a property's ongoing security training program.

In one positive development, some police departments have gone so far as to assign a number of detectives to work directly with hotel and motel security directors. These detectives can teach a property's personnel about police procedures and needs, offer guidance to the staff about what to watch for, and share information about any crime patterns in the area that may affect the property. At the same time, they learn about the property and its security system, improving the likelihood of effective police response in times of need.

Security Staffing

In developing a security program, a hotel or motel will need to consider whether to hire staff as full-time personnel, to contract with a local security company, to

AT YOUR RISK

ANTHONY MARSHALL

Hotel Security Should Wear Appropriate Uniforms

Frank J. Moran plays the snare drum for the Law Enforcement Emerald Society of South Florida Pipe and Drum Band. As the security manager for Wackenhut Corp., he is putting his weight behind getting hoteliers to properly uniform their security officers.

"Anyone who believes that a uniformed security officer isn't a deterrent to crime is nuts," he said.

Moran, a security professional, told me a "blazer" story. Recently, at an urban, city hotel in Miami, the property's 16 full-time security officers were dressed in dark blue blazers, gray flannel pants, and white button-down shirts. No security emblems or badges adorned the uniforms. The security officers looked very preppie—instead of looking like security officers.

Unfortunately, the hotel had a problem—criminal acts against property and guests were on the rise. In an attempt to lower the crime rate, the director of security decided to abandon the "soft" dress code and go "high profile" instead. He wanted his security officers visible and dressed to be seen. His rationale was most criminals prefer to do their business at hotels where there are no security officers watching them.

Finally, the officers looked like security officers. Moran told me all of the security officers liked looking more like a law enforcement official rather than taken for reception desk personnel.

Hotel guests expressed their comfort to management for the visible security presence. From the guests' standpoint, the more para-military looking, the better. Today's hotel guests do not want to become another hotel crime statistic; guests want competent security protection.

Lastly and most importantly, in the first 90 days after the introduction of the new uniforms, the hotel's crime rate plummeted. Crimes of distraction, such as stolen luggage from the lobby and briefcases from the restaurant, abruptly stopped. Other types of hotel crime significantly decreased, too.

I asked Moran to describe to me an ideal hotel security officer's uniform. He said it would consist of a military-style light colored shirt with epaulets and button-flap chest pockets. He suggested long sleeves for formality. He recommends a conservative, dark, single-colored clip-on-tie (the tie should pull off during an altercation rather than becoming a choking hazard).

Moran said security officer designation arm patches should appear on both sleeves. An officer's identification name tag should be attached over the right side pocket. Moran suggested a security badge be worn over the left shirt pocket, and he likes large, wide-brimmed Stetson cowboy hats or the traditional "Smoky the Bear" style ones.

"I don't like baseball hats on security officers," Moran said. "They lack command appearance and aren't professional."

Pants, he says, should be dark in color and have no cuffs to get tangled up in during an altercation or chase. Military-style, pant-leg piping, he claimed, adds

(continued)

At Your Risk *(continued)*

> additional command appearance. He recommends plain black belts and socks, and shoes with rubber soles.
> "Blue blazers are great for hosts greeting guests, but not security officers greeting criminals," Moran said.
> "What about mace or other sprays?" I asked.
> "Never!" said Moran. "Sprays are chemical weapons and require training before use, and, in hotels, the likelihood of spraying guests as well as criminals is too high of a risk to take."
> "What about a radio?" I asked.
> "An excellent communication device, enabling the officer to communicate with his superiors as well as other appropriate authorities, is an essential part of an officer's uniform," Moran said.
> Understand, Moran said, the uniform is one of the tools that enable security officers to successfully accomplish their tasks.
> Once the hotel's director of security had issued for his security officers the new uniforms, he then ordered an electric golf cart as part of his crime reduction program. Today, a uniformed security officer patrols the hotel's outside property seven days a week, 24 hours a day. The results: No criminal activity. Will it last forever? No, but it works like magic now.
> Uniformed hotel security officers are a deterrent to crime. Don't deter your deterrent with improper uniforms.

Courtesy of *Hotel & Motel Management*, June 1, 1998. Used with permission.

arrange for part-time protection with local off-duty police personnel, or to use any combination of these or other options.

Because of a facility's size and organizational structure, it may be appropriate to assign security responsibility to a member of the management staff, such as a resident or assistant manager, a chief engineer, or the human resources director. If management decides the property needs a security department, it must determine whether the department should be a proprietary unit with in-house staff functions or a security program run through a reputable, licensed contract security company. In some situations, it may be feasible to employ off-duty police to cover certain hours of operation while the property's staff provide daytime coverage as one of their responsibilities. If the security department or function is integrated into the property, additional considerations include determining whether the staff will wear uniforms, whether certain or all members of the security staff will be armed, and whether there are shifts on which security personnel need not be assigned. (Unless mandated by a local or state jurisdiction, the senior security executives of the lodging industry are unanimously opposed to the use of firearms by security staff. The rare instance where an armed security officer would have been of value in a specific security incident is far outweighed by the insurance costs and the potential for accidental injury or death of innocent bystanders in a shoot-out.)

All decisions concerning security deserve careful thought and should be discussed with legal counsel. Each option has its adherents.

Contract Security. The proponents of contract security organizations argue that such organizations can provide sophisticated services at considerable savings. In addition, they assert that a reputable contract security company will provide thoroughly screened, tested, and trained personnel. It may also provide consulting services, including in-depth surveys of hotel or motel security requirements, electronic audio countermeasure sweeps (a debugging tactic), data processing security, and assistance in contingency planning for bomb threats and natural disasters. Finally, they contend that an in-house security staff may become too familiar and friendly with the other employees. If a guard catches a friend stealing, he or she might hesitate to report that friend. Some people believe that this situation may be less likely to occur if the security personnel are supplied by an outside agency.

In selecting a security company, make sure that extensive guard training, geared specifically to each facility, is provided. Review contract and insurance requirements (i.e., named insured clauses and requirements for proof of insurance) with legal counsel. If your state or community requires such agencies to be certified, verify that the agency you choose meets this legal requirement. Be clear and specific regarding the services to be provided by the contract organization. Require the security firm to conduct frequent unannounced inspections, day and night, by supervisory personnel to ensure that its guards are in compliance with company regulations. Determine whether the security service can provide a sufficient number of personnel on short notice in the case of a large-scale emergency. Insist that security officers be required to file daily and unusual incident reports. Determine the percentage of the security firm's hotel and motel customers retained on an annual basis; rates of retention are an excellent indication of a company's service level.

Carefully construct the contract so there will be no misunderstanding as to the supervision of the contract security officers; supervision should be provided by the contract security organization while the contract staff is on the premises. The management of the lodging facility should carefully establish exactly what the contract employee is to do under most conceivable circumstances.

When hotel management gives orders or instructions to the contract employee, a different relationship is established. The responsibility for the actions of the contract security office becomes blurred, and there are instances in which the contract employee has been considered as a workers' compensation case for the property rather than for the contract security company. Contract companies have held and prevailed that the instructions from the hotel or motel executive may have placed the contract employee in jeopardy and may have been contributory to the workers' compensation incident. In other instances, the contract employee has turned to his or her company for the workers' compensation relief, but has sued the lodging establishment under general comprehensive liability, which affords the opportunity for a much greater settlement than would be available through workers' compensation only.

A contract security organization will almost always be willing to perform an in-depth security survey for a property if the property has not already performed one for itself or had one performed by another agency. Remember, however, that a contract security organization is selling services. This fact may sometimes lead such an organization to overstate a property's security needs, which can pose an unfortunate problem for an innkeeper. Suppose a property implements some (perhaps even most) of a contract security organization's recommendations, yet despite such efforts, a security incident occurs on the premises. It is possible that a plaintiff might subpoena and use the security organization's written recommendation in court as evidence of the innkeeper's knowledge of alleged "inadequate security." Even if the recommendation overstated the needs, if the innkeeper failed to implement every suggestion, a jury *may* be more likely to judge the innkeeper negligent.

In-House Security. Proponents of proprietary or in-house security departments point out a number of advantages to this system. They emphasize the fact that the hotel or motel has greater control over security officers or staff members without intermediate outside supervision. They also argue that training for in-house security staff members can be much more directly related to the lodging industry. They believe that the peculiarities and special needs of the industry are more effectively addressed by those within the industry than by those in a contractual relationship with the industry. In addition, they emphasize that the quality of personnel is under the direct control of the hotel or motel in a proprietary system, rather than under the control of the contract security company, and that the director and staff of an in-house department are more effectively integrated with the other departments and personnel of the property. Serious consideration should be given to including the security director as a member of the property's executive committee, an action that would not be possible with a contract staff and supervision. Finally, they point out that a greater sense of loyalty may be developed among an in-house staff since career paths can be established that move security personnel into other roles in the organization.

Off-Duty Police. Some properties use off-duty police officers for their security staff. There are certain benefits associated with this practice. Such officers have superior training in reacting to and dealing with crimes and other emergencies, they understand the law, they are used to dealing with people, they may be better able to identify known criminals, they are immediately recognized as authorities, and they often do in fact have more authority than ordinary citizens (as a deputized individual, they are not limited to a "citizen's arrest"). In addition, police liaison and response may be enhanced. However, there may be potential drawbacks as well. First, police officers may be oriented more toward apprehension functions than toward prevention. Second, some jurisdictions require off-duty officers to be armed and this may not be desirable (if they are armed and injure somebody, the property may be liable). In addition, off-duty officers may not be permitted to wear uniforms in some jurisdictions. Finally, an officer may be working at the hotel or motel following a full-duty police shift and the fatigue factor must be considered.

Personnel Practices. Security concerns should be addressed during the selection and hiring of all employees. Personnel screening is a critical consideration in hiring a member of the security department, given that this individual is responsible for the protection of persons and assets on the property. The use of an authorization statement and affidavit should be considered, if approved by legal counsel. Such a

AT YOUR RISK

ANTHONY MARSHALL

Senseless Shooting Shows Danger of Armed Security Guards

Abraham Oliden was shot in the chest and stomach on Friday afternoon, January 2, 1998. Oliden was killed by Miguel Valdes, over an argument in the parking lot.

Witnesses said that Valdes, an armed security guard, lost his temper when Oliden, a delivery man, blocked some parking spaces with his van. Irrational? Absolutely. Negligent? Sure.

"It's one of those things that happens in this world that you never expect," said Valdes' mother.

It's illogical to never expect that a shooting misadventure can occur where armed security guards are involved. It's not farfetched: The arming of security guards always involves risks of an accidental or irrational shooting.

Hoteliers owe it to themselves to consider all the implications of taking such a step in their hotels. To arm hotel security guards is to risk misadventure, devastating publicity, and millions of dollars in lawsuits for the shooting of a hotel employee or guest.

Today's hoteliers must focus on security to win today's customers. It's a fact of life. Travelers want a safe haven, and many travelers ask reservation agents if the hotel is safe.

Security questions often make hoteliers squirm, but they shouldn't. The common law requires hoteliers to exercise "reasonable care" for the security of their guests. The law doesn't require "best care" or "the finest care."

Reasonable care is that care that a reasonable hotelier would exercise after prudent consideration of the size, type, and location of the hotel, as well as the history of criminal activity at or in the vicinity of the hotel.

Reasonable security practices include having a good key-control system. One such system issues each registrant a new key, invalidating all previously used ones. All security experts expect hotels to provide guestroom doors with peepholes, chain or bar guards, and sturdy bolt locks.

It always is a plus to have brightly illuminated public areas, walkways, hallways, and parking lots. Enclosed and secured guestroom hallways are becoming common, and the presence of visible, uniformed security guards is always favorable.

Don't arm hotel security guards with firearms, grenades, and flame-throwers. That's the stuff of movies—not real life. Do dress security guards in military-style police uniforms, however, as a flashy deterrent to crime. It's common sense: Most criminals don't commit crimes in front of witnesses, especially uniformed security officers.

The law does not require—nor do guests have the right to expect—hotels to become armed fortresses. Common law simply requires hotels to exercise reasonable care for their security.

Hiring uniformed, armed, off-duty policemen as security guards is one option.

One advantage to this is that they arrive qualified for security work. Their training and experience cannot be successfully challenged in court by complaining plaintiffs in a lawsuit.

(continued)

At Your Risk *(continued)*

> One disadvantage, however, is that some off-duty police officers lack the diplomacy and tactfulness to interact well with hotel guests. They may take the Rambo approach with guests: too tough and rough.
>
> Some hotels may employ off-duty police officers in security as well as non-security related jobs, but there's a catch to that. Hotel managers may be unaware that many police departments throughout the United States require off-duty police to carry their weapons. I was once introduced to an off-duty police officer, in civilian clothes, wearing a concealed ankle holster with his loaded pistol in it. I felt uncomfortable.
>
> When should off-duty police officers, employed by the hotel, leave their guns at home? That's a policy issue for management to establish and enforce. While I like the badge and the honorable men and women wearing it, I don't like off-duty officers' guns in hotels.
>
> An off-duty police officer working for a hotel is classified as a hotel employee, and the hotel would be liable for that officer's negligent acts.
>
> Valdes shot Oliden in a fit of temper for which his employer may have to pay dearly. Imagine the horror if this asinine shooting had occurred at your hotel—surrounded by reporters and television cameras trying to answer the unanswerable.
>
> Perhaps you would hear yourself say: "It's one of those things that happens in this world that you never expect!"
>
> That's not a thoughtful, nor a sufficient, answer to such a senseless tragedy.

Courtesy of *Hotel & Motel Management*, February 16, 1998. Used with permission.

statement, signed by the job applicant, allows the property to more easily investigate the applicant's background. Bonding (insuring for protection from employee theft) through an insurance company permits more effective screening of applicants and is certainly warranted in the case of security staff members who, by virtue of their function, have access to most areas of the hotel or motel.

Scheduling security staff on the property is another important consideration. During daytime operations, involving all employees as the "eyes and ears" of the property may make it possible to reduce the security staff to a few key persons able to respond to a security-related call from an employee. In setting schedules, special programs and activities that may affect the number of security staff needed during a particular work shift should be taken into consideration. In many properties, additional security staff members are assigned during the nighttime hours.

Supervision. Supervision of the security function is a critical element in the successful administration of the lodging establishment's program. The security director or manager may have other responsibilities such as the resident or assistant manager, chief engineer, or human resources director, but in larger properties it may be more effective to assign a full-time director to the security department. As previously noted, the director of security should be a member of the management or executive planning committee in order to provide maximum cooperation and exchange of information. To do otherwise may allow problems to arise that could

A Typical Day

A typical day's schedule for a security officer might look like this:

- Sign in at your department or with the manager on duty
- Pick up your equipment
- Check for activities from the previous shift that might need your attention
- Check daily function sheets for upcoming events
- Begin your patrol, covering guestroom areas, public and recreation areas, perimeter, parking lot, and service areas
- Repeat patrols hourly
- Complete your patrol log at regular intervals
- Check employee packages
- Monitor employee time clocks
- Investigate guest claims
- Respond to emergencies
- Investigate disturbances
- Report suspected controlled substance abuse
- Complete daily log and report incidents that may need attention on the next shift
- Return equipment
- Sign out with manager on duty

A security officer might complete numerous rounds of the property during an eight-hour shift.

Source: *Lodging Security Officer Training* (East Lansing, Mich.: Educational Institute of the American Hotel & Motel Association, 1995).

have been anticipated and prevented—concerning, for example, the arrival of a special group, exhibit, convention, or conference.

The supervisor of the security function must take special care to prevent possible collusion between the security staff and other members of the hotel or motel staff. This problem is usually addressed by rotating the security staff through various assignments throughout the hotel or motel on a regular basis.

The Elements of Security Training

Training for security personnel is critical to an effective security program, regardless of the source of the security staff on the premises. Although a contract security guard is usually trained by the contract security company, he or she still needs an orientation to the philosophy and special service needs of the particular hotel or motel. Orientation is also necessary for off-duty police officers since they are shifting from an apprehension role to a prevention role. Also, a careful analysis must be undertaken of the limits of an on-premises security officer's authority under the local codes and regulations of the jurisdiction. Procedures to follow in a citizen's arrest, the arrest authority of a deputized security guard, and the legal limits placed upon an off-duty police officer are all factors to review in such an analysis.

In addition, since every employee of a lodging facility may act as an integral part of its security program, all employees should be given a thorough security orientation at the time they are hired and should be regularly exposed to an ongoing security education program throughout their term of employment. Such continuing security education programs can occur in conjunction with departmental or staff meetings. Records of attendance and minutes of such meetings should be maintained and preserved for possible future reference.

Training should be comprehensive and should include all aspects of the protection of guests, the general public, employees, and the assets of guests, employees, and the property. Depending upon a particular facility's needs, training may be expanded to include the special concerns of emergency management and interconnections with the other departments in the hotel or motel.

The key point is that the differing needs of every property call for the development of individually designed security systems and individualized security training programs. Of course, this is not to say that no two lodging properties will ever have security systems with common elements. Though never identical, the security needs of various properties are sometimes similar. Common elements are likely to arise from the common potential problems faced by lodging properties.

A training program, including training documents such as a security manual or employee handbook, should be developed to meet very specific needs. While security textbooks are important training documents in their own right—they can point out problems common to the lodging industry and can discuss the various ways different properties have dealt or may deal with them—they cannot offer a specific series of steps that will invariably solve all properties' security problems. They cannot relieve management of its responsibility to investigate and determine its property's unique security requirements. Discussions such as this create a general awareness that must then be applied to a specific situation or property. The practical insights gained from a careful examination of the security needs of a given property should be included in that property's security training program.

Insights that have an impact on training may also be gained when security personnel keep abreast of the latest thinking and developments in the security field by reading the various security publications available. Because new security equipment is regularly being introduced and approaches to security are constantly being refined, such periodicals can provide important supplemental information that may help management keep its particular security program up-to-date. Exhibit 1 lists several of these publications.

A training program might cover such topics as the nature and role of private security, the nature and extent of crime, and an examination of the criminal justice system. It should deal with such specific topics as the legal powers of and limitations on security personnel in their property's jurisdiction. It should also inform

Exhibit 1   Selected Security and Law Enforcement Publications

Hospitality Law
747 Dresher Road
P.O. Box 980
Horsham, PA 19044-0980
(215) 784-0860

Hotel/Motel Security and Safety Management
Rusting Publications
402 Main Street
Port Washington, NY 11050
(516) 883-1440

The Police Chief
International Association of Chiefs of Police
515 N. Washington Street
Alexandria, VA 22314-2357
(703) 836-6767

Research in Brief
National Institute of Justice
Office of Justice Programs
810 7th Street, NW
Washington, DC 20531
(202) 307-2942

Security Letter
166 East 96th Street
New York, NY 10128
(212) 348-1553

Security Management
American Society for Industrial Security
1655 North Fort Meyer Drive
Arlington, VA 22209
(703) 522-5800

Security Technology & Design
Locksmith Publishing Corp.
850 Busse Highway
Park Ridge, IL 60068
(847) 692-5940

Security World
Cahners Publishing Company
Cahners Plaza
1350 East Touhy Avenue
Des Plaines, IL 60018
(847) 635-8800

employees about patrol techniques, access control procedures, report writing, fire prevention, alarm systems, communication systems, and any other specific information that they should know in order to perform their jobs effectively.

It is unfortunate when a manager does not realize the importance of implementing a well-planned training program. Having a trained security staff can play a part in protecting a hotel against certain lawsuits; being able to prove that security staff were trained can go a long way with a jury attempting to determine negligence or reasonable care. In numerous lodging cases, the presentation of an effective and well-organized security program has been persuasive to both the jury and the court. As previously noted, not all crimes are preventable. The proof of a sincere effort to combat such criminal incidents has been a significant element in a judgment favorable to the defense. Though security is the focus here, the lack of security training may sometimes be part of an overall lack of training in a property. The manager of such a property may have accepted certain myths about training which need to be dispelled. The myths include the following:

- "Positions turn over so fast, it doesn't pay to train." High turnover is sometimes used to argue against implementing an extensive training program. The problem with this kind of thinking is that the lack of a training program, or the ineffectiveness of an existing training program, may itself be one cause of the high turnover.

- "Experienced employees don't need training." Not all experience is good experience. Some experienced applicants may have been poorly trained and may have developed poor work habits. Also, it is difficult to evaluate experience. An applicant with ten years of experience may in reality have one year of experience repeated ten times.
- "Training is simple. Anybody can do it." Managers or supervisors who have been promoted from the same job for which they are now training others often feel that they know everything about the job and that they can teach others spontaneously or as the need arises. This kind of hit-and-miss training may produce haphazard results.
- "Employees always resist training." Employees do not resist training. They resist when their trainers are poorly prepared, when the training is poorly presented, and when their training is never followed up by performance appraisals or on-the-job coaching.

Admittedly, it takes time—and therefore money—to develop an effective security training program. Management needs to carefully examine its operation and premises to discover potential security exposures. It then must decide how to best use its resources (systems, procedures, and personnel) to deal with the exposures. Every aspect of management's plan that relies on the performance of personnel then needs to be explained through training to the affected personnel.

Nevertheless, the cost of developing a security training program should be seen as an investment in the future of an operation that will reap significant benefits. An operation in which all employees are attuned to security concerns can create a safer environment for its guests, visitors, and employees, as well as a more profitable operation. Guests and their visitors will respond positively to the feeling of safety and security experienced on the premises. The employee turnover rate may drop both because effective training generally reduces turnover and because fears of being assaulted or victimized will be alleviated. The operation may become more profitable as the costs associated with high employee turnover drop, and losses due to criminal activity are reduced. Legal costs may also fall, since every prevented crime represents an averted potential lawsuit. Employee awareness of an organized security effort may also reduce employee theft.

An important part of preparing a security training program is determining not only what should be learned, but also who should learn it. The training for security department personnel in a large property will probably be more extensive than the security training for personnel in that property's other departments. A room attendant or bellperson may not need to know the design of the entire security system. Rather than unnecessarily overloading all employees with security information they will not need (which can discourage and alienate them), trainers should focus their efforts on providing employees with the information the employees need to know in order to operate more effectively in their jobs.

Another important point is that each property should write down its security standards and procedures in a security manual that can be used to help train employees. A carefully written manual helps ensure consistency in employee training and performance. Just as important, actually having to write the manual forces management to think carefully and to organize its thoughts about security in a way that often does not happen if managers and trainers are allowed to rely merely on their memories and on oral instruction. The formats of security manuals can vary; regardless of the format used, the contents of a security manual should cover the broad range of its property's security concerns in *specific* terms.

In addition, with the input of many of the lodging industry's corporate security executives, the Educational Institute (EI) of the American Hotel & Motel Association (AH&MA) developed a very effective training program for security officers. Successful completion of *Lodging Security Officer Training* provides the individual with a "certificate of completion."[1]

Who Is Responsible?

When a property uses an in-house security staff, it is obvious to all concerned that the property is responsible for the actions of its staff. The property cannot evade this responsibility merely by using off-duty officers or a contract security service, because these security officers are usually considered to be the hotel or motel's agents. If the security officers are negligent, the property may be held liable. Such services do not relieve a property of its legal responsibility to provide reasonable care.

One legal case that deals with this topic is *Vacation Village v. Burns International Security Service*. Vacation Village hired Burns International Security Service to provide security officers for its 44-acre hotel complex. Early one morning, four armed men used a master key to enter a guestroom. The men sexually assaulted a woman and her teenage daughter while holding the husband and teenage son at gunpoint. Responding to a noise complaint, the sole Burns security officer knocked on the door, causing the assailants to flee.

The victims filed suit against Vacation Village and Burns for failure to provide adequate security. The plaintiffs settled out of court for $1 million, which was paid entirely by Vacation Village. Vacation Village had also filed against Burns for negligence, contending among other things that Burns had promised to provide fully trained and supervised security officers, when in fact it had provided untrained and largely unsupervised personnel with little security background. Burns defended itself by contending that Vacation Village knew it was missing master keys but did not want to spend money to re-key the property; that Vacation Village had a bad attitude about security, revealed by its repeated refusals to discuss security problems with Burns personnel; and that any negligence on Burns's part was not the proximate cause (defined later in this chapter) of the plaintiffs' injuries. The jury voted that Burns was negligent, but decided that this negligence was not the proximate cause of the incident. Vacation Village had to pay the entire $1 million out-of-court settlement.

The use of off-duty police officers poses certain potential legal problems as well. If an off-duty officer uses his or her legal authority to arrest someone who then proves that the arrest was inappropriate and unwarranted, whose agent is the officer: the community's or the property's? In some cases, the officer is considered

> **Guns and Security Officers**
>
> Although security officers in some industries carry firearms or other weapons, few in the lodging industry do so. Lodging directors of security say there are many reasons why lodging security officers should not be armed. Chief among these reasons:
>
> - Weapons lead to more injuries among lodging security officers. If criminals see that the security officer is armed, they are more likely to use a weapon if they have one. Or security officers could injure themselves. For example, one security officer accidentally shot himself while practicing "fast draws" during his coffee break.
>
> - Weapons could increase the property's liability or damages awarded if courts deem officers have used unreasonable force. One security officer apprehended an intruder, put a gun to his head, and marched him off toward the manager's office. Before they got to the office, however, the gun went off and killed the intruder.
>
> - Lodging properties are often crowded places where passers-by could be easily caught in cross-fire. An accidental shooting of an innocent bystander could be a disaster for the officer, the bystander, and the property.

Source: *Lodging Security Officer Training* (East Lansing, Mich.: Educational Institute of the American Hotel & Motel Association, 1995).

the property's agent. This means the property could be held liable for false arrest and false imprisonment. Similar liability could result if an armed officer inappropriately injures someone.

The Authority of a Security Officer

The presence of a uniformed security officer may connote to some people the image of a public law enforcement officer. In fact, some security officers—once outfitted with a uniform, badge, and, at times, weaponry—sometimes wrongly believe themselves to possess the authority of public law enforcement officers. This attitude must be changed if the police, the public, and the individual security officer are to understand and accept the role and authority of the private security officer in crime prevention. The right of a property owner to protect his or her property and the role of the security officer as his or her agent is a key principle behind the security officer's authority.

A hotel or motel security officer, in the absence of any special commission, deputization, ordinance, or state statute, possesses no greater authority than any other private citizen. However, because the security officer can be involved in protective functions on a daily basis, he or she may be in position to use certain powers more than most other private citizens. The exercise of these powers may involve nothing more than simply stopping undesired conduct, or it may involve making a citizen's arrest. In *all* actions that interfere with the rights of others, the security officer should endeavor to obtain consent and voluntary cooperation from the person being interfered with.

Most security officers will, at some point in their careers, be faced with situations in which they must determine the appropriate legal action to be taken, such as calling the police, questioning a suspect, or making a citizen's arrest. To prevent improper acts which could result in a liability suit against the security officer and/or the employer, an officer must understand what constitutes a crime according to the appropriate criminal law so that he or she may be more specific in relaying information to and working with public law enforcement agencies.

Criminal statutes set limits on the behavior of lodging security officers. Activity beyond these limits may result in criminal charges being filed for assault, battery, manslaughter, or other crimes. **Tort law**, which provides bases for actions permitting one person to remedy a wrong committed against him or her by another, also restricts the actions of the security officer. Tort law permits an injured party to bring a lawsuit for damages against the security officer, as well as the employing property, for such unreasonable conduct as false arrest, false imprisonment, malicious prosecution, defamation, slander, and other tortious acts. Individuals charged with responsibility for security should be familiar with applicable state and local laws regulating private security, particularly those relating to citizen's arrest.

Citizen's Arrests. Most states, through state statutes, judicial pronouncements, or common law, permit citizen's arrests by private citizens under certain circumstances. There is considerable variation among states concerning the privileges conferred and restraints imposed in a citizen's arrest.

A **citizen's arrest** occurs when an individual is *lawfully* deprived of his or her freedom. Normally, the task of arresting criminal offenders is one for a sworn police officer. Even where the law permits a security officer to make a citizen's arrest, he or she should do so only if a sworn police officer cannot respond in time and good judgment requires prompt action on the part of the hotel or motel. Non-security personnel should not attempt to make a citizen's arrest.

It is essential that each security officer be familiar with the statutory arrest authority of private citizens as set forth in the applicable statutes and judicial pronouncements of the state in which he or she is employed. In New York, for example, a private citizen may make an arrest for a felony only when the suspect has in fact committed it; merely having reasonable grounds for believing the suspect committed a felony is insufficient grounds for making a citizen's arrest. In other states, the felony must be committed in the presence of the citizen making the arrest. Some states do not permit a citizen's arrest for the commission of a misdemeanor of any type, while in other states, such as New York, a citizen's arrest for a misdemeanor is permitted, provided the offense is in fact committed in the presence of the citizen making the arrest. In any event, hotels and motels in all states should check with local counsel before instituting any procedures for detaining persons on their premises.

Moreover, security officers cannot exercise lawful arrest power for any purpose other than to turn the individual arrested over to the proper authorities.

An arrest made without proper legal authority may constitute false arrest and false imprisonment, and could result in civil and criminal liability on the part of the security officer and civil liability on the part of the lodging property. Except for a felony or misdemeanor arrest when and where permitted under state law, or except as provided for in some areas by state statutes relating very specifically to shoplifting, no other involuntary detention or confinement should be attempted. Any person who voluntarily consents to being detained must clearly understand that he or she is free to leave at any time.

Even situations in which sworn police officers, responding to a hotel or motel's complaint, make an arrest may present the lodging property with a potential problem. If a guest or patron is arrested without justification at the instigation of the hotel or motel, the property might be faced with a suit for malicious prosecution.

Search. When a security officer makes a legal citizen's arrest for a felony or misdemeanor, the right of self-defense may in some states justify a search for an offensive weapon under certain circumstances. Individual properties, however, should check with local counsel to determine what circumstances, if any, would justify a search by a private citizen incidental to a lawful arrest. If a person consents voluntarily to a search, the consent should be obtained by the security officer in writing if at all possible and should be witnessed by at least one other individual.

Interrogation. There is no prohibition against security officers asking questions. It must be remembered, however, that the person being questioned is under no obligation to answer. Moreover, if a guest is wrongfully accused of criminal activity in the presence of others, even by the form of the questions, the lodging property might be sued for slander. Generally, routine questioning should be conducted quietly in public areas so that there can be no subsequent allegation of false imprisonment or defamation. In-depth interrogation of suspects conducted in private is best conducted by two employees.

There should be no use of physical force or threats of force to coerce answers. Such actions might result in criminal charges being filed against the security officer and a civil suit against the hotel or motel.

Private security officers generally are not required to give prior Miranda warnings to persons suspected of crimes (that is, that they have the right to remain silent; that anything said can be used against them in court; that they have the right to an attorney; and if they cannot afford an attorney, one will be provided). However, sworn police officers who may be working while off duty as security officers should give such warnings prior to interrogating a person on whom an investigation has focused and who is suspected of a crime.

Use of Force. Generally speaking, a private citizen may only use such force as is reasonably necessary to effect a lawful arrest or to prevent the escape of a person from custody who has been lawfully arrested. If excessive or unreasonable force is used, the security officer may be subject to criminal action by the state, and both he or she and the lodging property may be subject to a civil action for damages by the person against whom force was used.

No employee should use any force calculated to cause death or serious bodily harm unless there is a threat to his or her personal safety or the personal safety of another person. Deadly force may never be used to protect property.

The Team Concept

An important goal of a training program is to turn an entire staff into a protection team. The development of the team concept may have considerable benefit for a hotel or motel in providing protection to guests, employees, and the property itself. In the team approach, all department heads and supervisors regard security as an aspect of their jobs. While they usually are not directly involved in routine security assignments, they can be invaluable in maintaining the security of the property. Similarly, each employee has a responsibility to assist in a security capacity. It is essential, for example, that room attendants call the security office or the property's management when they notice a suspicious person in the guestroom area or back in the service areas of the property. Such alertness on the part of employees has been instrumental in many cases in the prevention of incidents and in the arrest of criminals on the premises of hotels and motels. Whether the security role is incorporated in the activities of an assistant manager, a resident manager, or an owner-manager at the small property level, or in the role of a full-time director of security in the large property, the team concept is still valid. Employees in properties of any size can, for example, be instructed to:

- Be alert to and report any suspicious activities or persons anywhere on the property.
- Avoid confronting a suspicious individual. Instead, the employee should step into a secured area (guestroom, locked linen room, or other space containing a phone), lock the door, and call the office designated to receive such emergency calls.
- Report any drug paraphernalia or other suspicious items that may be exposed to public view when working within a guestroom. (Never search through a guest's luggage or property.) In one case, a jewel thief was arrested when a room attendant noticed an open case filled with jewelry. The thief stayed at one hotel while breaking into the other hotels and motels in the community. In another case, a thief left a case of burglar tools open.
- Alert security when rooming guests with large but empty pieces of luggage.
- Check on the proper posting of innkeeper laws, as may be required for the jurisdiction in which the hotel or motel is located.
- Check to make sure that any information cards or tent cards provided for the guest's information on security are in their proper locations.

This list contains only a brief selection from the wide range of activities a training program can prepare a staff to perform. Every property will be able to construct its own list to deal with its unique security concerns.

In 1993, the "Traveler Safety Campaign" was introduced by the American Hotel & Motel Association to inform the traveling public of safety/security concerns and enlist them as members of the lodging security team. The initiative included the following participating members:

- American Automobile Association (AAA)
- American Association of Retried Persons (AARP)
- American Society of Travel Agents (ASTA)
- National Crime Prevention Council and its mascot, McGruff The Crime Dog

Millions of "Traveler Safety Tips" cards (see Exhibit 2) were distributed and variously displayed in guestrooms. Some hotel chains incorporated the ten suggestions on the key folder. A videotape was also made available for review by guests on the information channel in each guestroom.

There have been instances where crimes have been prevented when the guests have followed the campaign's recommendation of calling the front desk to report a suspicious person or incident.

Security and the Law

Every state has its own statutes and court rulings on innkeeper laws. These laws deal with the rights and responsibilities of innkeepers and can be fairly extensive. Although such laws almost invariably deal with the same general topics, they can differ from state to state. Lodging management and security personnel should read the innkeeper statutory laws of their state. The understanding gained from this information can contribute to the development of a more effective security program.

Also, in determining what elements might be included in a particular security program, it may be wise to review recent court and jury decisions that deal with hotel and motel security matters. Many recent cases have addressed one or more of the following issues: locking systems, key control, security personnel on the premises, lighting, door viewports, police liaison, foreseeability or prior notice, crime in the community, security efforts tailored to the needs of a specific property, and the involvement of employees as the hotel or motel's "eyes and ears" with regard to the security function. These areas of concern are frequently stressed in depositions by expert witnesses for the plaintiff.

Several significant cases dealing with hospitality industry security are presented at the end of this chapter. Before we examine any cases, however, it is important to gain a basic understanding of the workings of the American legal system. In *Understanding Hospitality Law*, Jack P. Jefferies provides a brief explanation of this system:

> The laws governing hotels and motels in the United States are myriad. They include many common law rules that have evolved from early English judicial decisions and social customs. The common law system was developed in England during the Middle Ages as courts sought to resolve disputes between individuals by applying generally accepted rules and principles of justice. As society evolved from the feudal to the industrial era, courts under the common law system continued to apply many of the rules and principles enunciated by courts in earlier, similar

Exhibit 2 Traveler Safety Tips Card

TRAVELER SAFETY TIPS
American Hotel & Motel Association

1. Don't answer the door in a hotel or motel room without verifying who it is. If a person claims to be an employee, call the front desk and ask if someone from their staff is supposed to have access to your room and for what purpose.

2. When returning to your hotel or motel late in the evening, use the main entrance of the hotel. Be observant and look around before entering parking lots.

3. Close the door securely whenever you are in your room and use all of the locking devices provided.

4. Don't needlessly display guest room keys in public or carelessly leave them on restaurant tables, at the swimming pool, or other places where they can be easily stolen.

5. Do not draw attention to yourself by displaying large amounts of cash or expensive jewelry.

6. Don't invite strangers to your room.

7. Place all valuables in the hotel or motel's safe deposit box.

8. Do not leave valuables in your vehicle.

9. Check to see that any sliding glass doors or windows and any connecting room doors are locked.

10. If you see any suspicious activity, please report your observations to the management.

We Support the National Citizens' Crime Prevention Campaign.
TAKE A BITE OUT OF CRIME

Printed on recycled paper
Copyright 1993 by
The American Hotel
& Motel Association
1201 New York Avenue, N.W.
Washington, D.C. 20005-3931

Source: American Hotel & Motel Association, Washington, D.C.

Nominated by The Webby Awards as one of the best five Politics & Law sites on the Internet (1998), FindLaw (http://www.findlaw.com) offers a variety of free services designed to make legal and government information easy to find online.

cases. Within this developing common law system, special common law rules regarding the rights and liabilities of innkeepers and their guests also evolved. This special body of rules applicable to innkeepers under the common law resulted from the public nature of the occupation. . . .

Examples of old common law rules uniquely applicable to innkeepers are: (i) innkeepers as operators of public places must as a general rule provide available accommodations to travelers who are willing and able to pay for such accommodations, and (ii) an innkeeper under common law would be liable as an insurer for the loss of guests' property brought to the inn, with certain exceptions.

Throughout the years, the common law rules governing innkeepers [in all states except Louisiana, where the Louisiana Civil Code is based on the Code Napoleon] have, however, been refined by court decisions, and modified by federal, state, and municipal legislation and administrative agency rules and regulations, which, in turn, have then been further defined by federal, state, and municipal court decisions and administrative agency rulings.

In addition, hotels and motels today are subject to numerous statutes, rules, and regulations governing a multitude of subjects never covered by common law. These governing statutes, rules, and regulations have, in turn, been further defined by other court decisions and rulings. . . .

It is important for the layperson to note . . . that since the United States is a federation of states, each state through its state court system develops its own case law and judicial precedent on issues involving state laws. State courts generally decide issues involving local and state laws and disputes between citizens of the state. In this respect each state court system is independent of other state jurisdictions. Thus, for example, the decision of the highest state court in California may be binding on lower courts in California, but is not binding on the courts in another state, such as New York. This is true even though a New York court in interpreting a New York State statute could indeed look at a California State court decision interpreting a similar California statute, and find the California court decision reasoning to be "persuasive" or "interesting" or "of no effect whatsoever" in New York. It is thus that a New York court can reach a different result from California courts on the same general issue.

The layperson should also be aware that the federal court system includes 94 district courts and a court of appeals for each of 13 judicial circuits, and the Supreme Court of the United States. . . . Federal courts generally decide disputes involving federal laws and disputes between citizens from different states (subject to certain jurisdictional requirements). One federal circuit court of appeals may reach a decision different from that of another federal circuit court of appeals on the same type of legal problem. It is left to the U.S. Supreme Court to determine which of the circuit courts is correct (or to decide to leave the different decisions of both circuit courts standing).

This is an oversimplification in your introduction to the laws governing hotels, motels, and restaurants, but it is intended to help you understand why a decision in California may differ from a court decision in New York, Iowa, or Hawaii, and to understand why two federal circuit courts render what appear to be directly contrary decisions on apparently the same question when the courts are both part of the same federal court system.

It is important that the layperson also recognize that the law is a continually changing body of rules and cannot be viewed as frozen in time and space. For example, common law rules established a standard of absolute liability of the hotel operator for the loss of a guest's property. The state legislatures in most states then limited this common law liability, often to $500. In some states, the legislatures then increased the amount of this liability to more than $500. Moreover, some state courts today appear to exercise a quasi-legislative function in redefining and modifying the meaning of said statutes with the effect of increasing liability. Many other laws (common law, statutory, and regulatory) affecting hotel and motel operators are also undergoing constant evolution and change over the years.

Thus, from both a historic and national perspective, the laws affecting hotels and motels present a slowly changing kaleidoscope of legislation, regulations, rules, and court and administrative decisions affecting the legal rights, responsibilities, and liabilities of hotel and motel operators.[2]

The frequency of all types of lawsuits is increasing annually, and hotels, motels, inns, clubs, restaurants, and resorts are not immune from this danger. Management cannot afford to ignore the financial ramifications associated with costly settlements. The hospitality industry, with its special emphasis on people and personal services, represents an area where the possibility for litigation is very great.

Legal Definitions

Generally, in a suit alleging negligence, the plaintiff must show that the defendant innkeeper had a duty to use reasonable care to protect the plaintiff or victim from foreseeable acts; that the defendant failed to perform this duty; that this failure was the proximate cause of the incident; and that the plaintiff actually suffered loss or injury.

The central legal issue is that innkeepers owe a duty of care to all persons on their properties. Failure to meet this duty may result in security-related liability. In most states, the innkeepers' duty or standard of care is legally defined as taking reasonable care to protect against foreseeable acts. There is probably no concept that has affected the lodging industry more than the court interpretation of **reasonable care**. Unfortunately for the innkeeper, there is no concise and clear-cut determination of what a court or jury may consider to be reasonable care in any given case. Whether reasonable care is exercised depends on the facts and circumstances in each case. Because such an uncertain legal climate exists, this text considers various cases which may have long-term implications (sometimes contradictory) for the industry.

Like reasonable care, **foreseeability** is an imprecise term. Courts and juries may consider certain consequences to be foreseeable at some properties and not at others. Factors that may help determine foreseeability at a given property include the prior incidence of that type or similar types of crime on the premises, the prior incidence of all types of crime on the premises, and (in an increasing number of cases) the crime rate of the surrounding community. The practical result of many court and jury decisions as they relate to foreseeability has been to expand the innkeeper's duty to include being aware of criminal activities both on- and off-premises. For example, if certain crimes are taking place in a community, a court or jury might decide that a reasonable innkeeper should foresee the possibility of a similar crime happening on-premises; if such a crime does indeed occur on-premises and the victim alleges negligence on the innkeeper's part in not taking reasonable steps to prevent such a crime, it may be difficult for the innkeeper to plead successfully that he or she did not know about the crimes in the community if they were generally known.

Simply failing in a duty does not in itself establish liability for negligence. The breach of a duty to exercise reasonable care must be shown to be the underlying

proximate cause of an incident. Proximate cause, sometimes called **legal cause**, is usually defined as that primary moving predominating cause from which an injury follows as a natural, direct, and immediate consequence, and without which the injury would not have occurred. It is not sufficient that the defendant's conduct has been one of the causes of the plaintiff's injury. It must be the proximate cause, which is sometimes said to depend on whether the conduct has been so significant and important a cause that the defendant should be legally responsible. A proximate cause of an incident need not be its only cause.

Foreseeability is again a factor. **Negligence** involves a foreseeable risk, a threatened danger of injury, and an injury that is caused by conduct unreasonable in proportion to the foreseeable danger. For example, if someone carelessly leaves a can of gasoline near an open flame and the gas then explodes, causing injury, a jury might find that such an act created a foreseeable risk of harm and that the injury was caused by conduct unreasonable in proportion to the foreseeable risk.

Suits alleging negligence request that the defendant be required to pay **damages**. There are two types of damages: compensatory and punitive. **Compensatory damages** are awarded to compensate the plaintiff for pain and suffering, loss of income during a period of absence from work, medical and hospital expenses, and recuperative facility or home-service expenses. Compensatory damages may sometimes be covered, perhaps after the payment of a deductible, by an individual's or corporation's liability insurance policy. In recent years, there has been a trend within the courts for juries to assess punitive damages in addition to compensatory damages. **Punitive damages** are damages awarded against a person to punish him or her for outrageous conduct. The chief purpose of punitive damages is to inflict punishment as an example and a deterrent to similar conduct. Some courts have allowed insurance coverage for punitive damages under certain circumstances, while other courts have disallowed insurance coverage of punitive damages as a matter of public policy. The size of punitive damage awards can be substantial, sometimes totaling several million dollars.

The court in which a suit or case is first tried is often called the **trial court**. The suit is filed by the **plaintiff** against the **defendant**. At the commencement of a lawsuit, the defendant can ask for dismissal of the complaint. If the allegations in the plaintiff's complaint fail to establish a valid legal claim or the defendant has an absolute affirmative defense, the complaint should be dismissed. After each party has had an opportunity to discover the facts of the case, but before the case is tried, either the plaintiff or the defendant can ask for a **summary judgment**. A defendant can be granted summary judgment if, upon undisputed facts, the plaintiff fails to meet the factual and legal requirements to establish its case. A plaintiff can be granted summary judgment if, upon undisputed facts, the defendant's liability is absolute, that is, the plaintiff has a valid legal claim supported by the facts and no defense is possible. The jury will then deliberate only the amount of damages to be awarded.

After the close of proofs offered in evidence, either the plaintiff or defendant can ask for a **directed verdict**. The defendant can contend that it should be granted a directed verdict because the plaintiff failed to prove its cause of action. The plaintiff can request a directed verdict claiming that the defendant has been unable to establish a defense. Directed verdicts are rendered by judges, not juries.

If the case goes to the jury and the jury returns a decision, the losing party can ask for **judgment n.o.v. (notwithstanding the verdict)** and/or a new trial. In granting judgment n.o.v., the trial judge overrules all or part of the jury verdict. The judge can also grant a new trial.

Whichever party loses the suit can appeal the decision. The party appealing is the **appellant**; the party appealed against is the **appellee** or **respondent**.

The Connie Francis Case

A landmark legal case relating to lodging security is the 1976 *Garzilli v. Howard Johnson's Motor Lodges, Inc.*, commonly known as the "Connie Francis Case." The case is a landmark for innkeepers not for any important legal precedent it set regarding the legal duty of innkeepers, or the type or amount of damages awarded (though they were substantial), but rather because the fame of the plaintiff focused the attention of the national media and the nation on the topic of hotel and motel security for the first time. Ms. Francis, one of the most popular and successful singers of the 1950s and 1960s, contended that her 1974 assault and rape were due to the inadequate security of the motel at which she was staying. She showed that the type of sliding glass door through which her assailant entered could be opened quite easily from the outside and that the defendant knew of this fact—the motel had been burglarized four times already that year by people entering in this manner. The motel had in fact ordered auxiliary locks, but a United Parcel Service strike had delayed their delivery.

Ms. Francis was awarded $2.5 million in compensatory damages for pain, suffering, and lost income. Her husband was awarded $150,000 for deprivation of the society, companionship, and services of his wife, whose psychological trauma was severe. The defendant asked the judge to overrule or reduce the jury verdict or to grant a new trial. The judge reduced the husband's award to $25,000 but refused the defendant's other requests. In denying these requests, he summarized certain important points.

> [I]n the early morning hours of November 8, 1974, ... Connie Francis was criminally assaulted by an unknown man who came through one of the sliding glass doors of her rooms. The doors gave the appearance of being locked, but the testimony showed they were capable of being unsecured from the outside without much difficulty.
>
> In addition to the pain and suffering which accompanied and immediately followed the assault and the fear, anxiety and depression which ensued thereafter, the proof showed that Connie Francis continued to suffer from a significant depressive reaction and a traumatic neurosis which was manifested by depression, social and sexual withdrawal and traumatic phobia. It was the opinion of one of her psychiatrists who testified that she would have significant difficulty in ever trying to resume her professional career for at least the next ten years. Connie Francis herself testified that she could no longer appear before an audience because of her feeling of shame and humiliation, and she could no

longer stay in a hotel or motel room which would be necessary for her to do if she were to fulfill her engagements....

Plaintiffs' counsel made, and set forth in his brief, various calculations based on the testimony in the case showing that the jury could have projected a ten year loss in earnings for the plaintiff of an amount between $5,330,000 and $11,950,000. Even if the jury had taken an average of her earnings in the last three years in which she worked prior to her partial retirement [from which she was emerging at the time of the crime] (i.e., 1968–1970), Connie Francis' projected loss of earnings for the ensuing ten years would have been $2,585,000 and this would have made no allowances for the substantial cost-of-living increases which occurred between 1969 and 1974. In addition, of course, none of such calculations makes any allowance whatsoever for the criminal assault, the horrendous results which ensued therefrom and the pain, suffering, mental anguish and humiliation which followed.

To an outsider, unfamiliar with all the facts in the case, the verdict undoubtedly seems quite extraordinary. There is no question but that it is substantial. Nonetheless, in the Court's opinion, given all of the facts herein and particularly the professional standing of the plaintiff, it cannot be said to be so excessive as to warrant the intervention by a court.[3]

The case was settled for $1,475,000 during pendency of the appeal.

Societal Concerns

Hospitality managers need to be aware of their responsibility and understand their roles in shaping societal perceptions of security and safety issues in the media. Managers must also recognize that these concerns, which they must address, are expressed through both the legal and political systems as well as media attention.

At the legal and political system levels, the manager needs to be aware of the possible changes to items such as building codes, workers compensation and Occupational Safety and Health Administration (OSHA) regulations, and even legally mandated insurance provisions which can affect the business. Most of these changes represent the input of individuals and groups to the political process. Groups such as the American Hotel & Motel Association (AH&MA) and state and local lodging associations provide the means for managers to be aware of current concerns as they are being expressed in the political arena.

Since attitudes and beliefs may be strongly influenced by the media, knowing what the media are focusing upon—and being prepared to deal with those issues—is important. With immediate industry response, the resulting concerns can be reduced and impact on the industry lessened. For example, a major TV investigative news program once ran a feature on hotel security; they interviewed victims of hotel crime and showed how easy it was to gain access to guestroom floors and even to get guestroom keys. This show prompted the lodging industry to launch a major program that addressed the resulting societal concerns about hotel security.

Hotel fires are another example of a widespread concern that resulted in positive code and regulation change. Outraged at the number and extremity of hotel fires, customers were instrumental in the initiation of changes to fire codes and

Exhibit 3 Fires in Residential Properties Other than Homes

[Line chart titled "Numbers in thousands" showing three series from 1977 to 1994:

Total (dashed): 1977=26.5, 1978=25, 1979=24, 1980=23.5, 1981=22, 1982=22, 1983=17.5, 1984=16, 1985=16, 1986=15, 1987=14, 1988=15, 1989=13.5, 1990=12.5, 1991=13, 1992=13, 1993=12, 1994=13

Hotel/Motel (black): 1977=14, 1978=12, 1979=13.5, 1980=12, 1981=11.5, 1982=11.5, 1983=10.5, 1984=9, 1985=9, 1986=8.5, 1987=8, 1988=8, 1989=8.5, 1990=6.5, 1991=7, 1992=7, 1993=6, 1994=6.5

Other Residential (gray): 1977=12.5, 1978=12, 1979=11.5, 1980=11.5, 1981=10.5, 1982=7, 1983=8.5, 1984=7.5, 1985=8, 1986=7, 1987=6, 1988=6.5, 1989=6, 1990=6.5, 1991=6, 1992=6.5, 1993=6.5, 1994=6.5]

Reprinted with permission from *NFPA Journal®* (Vol. 90, No. 4), ©1996, National Fire Protection Association, Quincy, MA 02269.

industry practices that resulted in a great reduction in the number of hotel fires (see Exhibit 3), the amount of property damage, and the loss of life. These reductions prompted the National Fire Protection Association (NFPA) to change their survey reporting protocols for U.S. fire experiences, eliminating the lodging category entirely. NFPA's original 1977 study divided fire loss into two categories—hotels and motels and other residential properties. This practice of separate reporting lasted until 1995, when hotels and motels were included in the "other" category. This modification of categories is "a milestone in the dramatic and remarkable progress of fire safety in the lodging industry."[4]

Recommended Reading

The Appendix for this chapter contains nine cases that deal with the various important legal concepts we have discussed in this chapter, especially duty of reasonable care and foreseeability. For example, *Reichenbach v. Days Inn of America, Inc.*[5] is a decision finding a motel not liable for an attack on the plaintiff in the motel's parking lot because "[t]here was no evidence that this incident was foreseeable or that the motel had any practical or reasonable method to protect its guest from or prevent this unprovoked hit and run attack." Two cases that discuss the varying security needs of different properties are *Peters v. Holiday Inns, Inc.*[6] and *Orlando Executive Park v. P.D.R.*[7] *Peters* states, "[A]n innkeeper's standard of care in providing security will vary according to the particular circumstances and location of the hotel." *Orlando Executive Park* agrees, stating, "Obviously, a six-unit, one building 'Mom and Pop' motel will not have the same security problems as a large high rise, thousand room hotel, or [as] a three hundred room motor lodge spread out over six buildings. Each presents a peculiar security problem of its own." *Malone et al.*[8] looks at the liability that may result from not responding appropriately to a reported security incident.

Endnotes

1. For more information on this program, contact the Educational Institute of the American Hotel & Motel Association, 2113 N. High Street, Lansing, MI 48906, 1-800-349-0299, or see *Lodging Security Officer Training Program* (East Lansing, Mich.: Educational Institute of the American Hotel & Motel Association, 1995).

2. Jack P. Jefferies, *Understanding Hospitality Law,* Third Edition (East Lansing, Mich.: Educational Institute of the American Hotel & Motel Association, 1995), pp. 3–6.

3. Excerpted from *Garzilli v. Howard Johnson's Motor Lodges, Inc.*, U.S. District Court, E.D. New York, No. 75 C 979, Sept. 20, 1976.

4. John R. Hall, Jr., "A Tale of Fire Safety Programs That Work—Two Decades of Hotel/Motel Fires," *NFPA Journal*, (Vol. 90, No. 4), July/August 1996.

5. 401 So.2d 1366 (Fla. Dist. Ct. App., 5th Dist. 1981), *petition denied*, 412 So.2d 469 (Fla. 1982).

6. 89 Wis.2d 115 (1979), 278 N.W.2d 208.

7. 402 So.2d 442 (Fla. Dist. Ct. App., 5th Dist. 1981).

8. 74 Ohio St.3d 440, 659 N.E.2d 1242.

Key Terms

appellant—The party appealing a previous court decision.

appellee—The party appealed against. Also known as respondent.

citizen's arrest—Common law in most states, a citizen's arrest permits arrests by private citizens when an individual is *lawfully* deprived of his or her freedom. It should be done only if a sworn police officer cannot respond in time and good judgment requires prompt action.

compensatory damages—Damages awarded to compensate the plaintiff for pain and suffering, loss of income during a period of absence from work, medical and hospital expenses, and recuperative facility or home-service expenses.

damages—Monetary awards paid by the defendant to compensate the plaintiff, to punish the defendant, or both.

defendant—The side the suit is brought against.

directed verdict—An immediate decision rendered by a judge after the close of evidence, because either side failed to prove its cause.

foreseeability—The reasonable likelihood that a specific future incident could have been foreseen—and, therefore, prevented—based on knowledge of past similar incidents on the premises or in the surrounding community.

judgment n.o.v (notwithstanding the verdict)—A judgment by a trial judge that overrules all or part of the jury verdict.

legal cause—The primary or predominating cause from which an injury follows as a natural, direct, and immediate consequence, and without which the injury would not have occurred. Also known as proximate cause.

negligence—Failure to exercise the care that a reasonably prudent person would exercise under like or similar circumstances.

plaintiff—The side that initiates and files the suit.

proximate cause—The primary or predominating cause from which an injury follows as a natural, direct, and immediate consequence, and without which the injury would not have occurred. Also known as legal cause.

punitive damages—Damages awarded against a person as punishment for outrageous conduct which also acts as a deterrent to similar conduct.

reasonable care—Taking actions that are ordinary or usual to protect against a foreseeable event—the central legal issue being that innkeepers owe a duty of care to all persons on their property. Failure to meet this duty may result in security-related liability.

respondent—The party appealed against. Also known as appellee.

security—Protecting people and assets. Security efforts may involve such areas of concern as guestroom security, key control, locks, access and perimeter control, alarm and communication systems, lighting, closed-circuit television, safe deposit boxes, inventory control, credit and billing procedures, computer security, staffing, pre-employment screening, employee training, responsible service of alcoholic beverages, emergency and safety procedures, and record keeping.

summary judgment—A judgment granted (1) to the defendant when the plaintiff fails to meet the factual and legal requirements to establish its case or (2) to the plaintiff when a valid legal claim exists supported by the facts with no possible defense.

tort law—Provides bases for actions permitting one person to remedy a wrong committed against him or her by another. It permits an injured party to bring a lawsuit for damages against the security officer and the employing property for such unreasonable conduct as false arrest, false imprisonment, malicious prosecution, defamation, and slander.

trial court—The court in which a suit or case is first tried.

Review Questions

1. What are the general areas that should be considered for inclusion in a property's security program?

2. What are the main areas of vulnerability that create security problems for hotels and motels?

3. Why is it important to cultivate a law enforcement liaison?

4. What are the various types of security staffing, and what are the advantages and disadvantages of each?

5. Why is training critical to an effective security program? What specific elements should be incorporated into a training program? What are some of the myths about training?

6. Should security guards be armed? Why or why not?

7. What is the extent of a security officer's authority? What types of behavior can the officer legally engage in? What activities could result in civil and criminal liability?

8. What does the "team concept" refer to in a security training program? What are some things that all employees can be instructed to do?

9. How can courts in different states come to different conclusions regarding similar issues?

10. Why is *Garzilli v. Howard Johnson's Motor Lodges, Inc.* considered a landmark legal case?

Internet Sites

For more information, visit the following Internet sites. Remember that Internet addresses can change without notice.

American Hotel & Motel Association (AH&MA)
http://www.ahma.com

American Society of Travel Agents (ASTA)
http://www.astanet.com/

Educational Institute of the AH&MA
http://www.ei-ahma.org

FindLaw: Internet Legal Resources
http://www.findlaw.com

International Association of Chiefs of Police
http://www.theiacp.org

International Association of Professional Security Consultants
http://www.iapsc.org

International Foundation for Protection Officers
http://www.ifpo.com

Legal Online
http://www.legalonline.com

Loss Prevention Management Institute
http://www.hrm.uh.edu

National Crime Prevention Council
http://www.ncpc.org

National Fire Protection Association (NFPA)
http://www.nfpa.org/

National Institute of Justice
http://www.ojp.usdoj.gov/nij/

RiskNet: Safety Forum
http://www.rnsf.com

U.S. Department of State, Overseas
Security Advisory Council (OSAC)
http://www.ds.state.gov/osacmenu.cfm

Case Study

Steve's Royal Problem

Steve Tritsch was enjoying his first month as a full-fledged GM. He'd enjoyed his previous position at a large, downtown property in Philadelphia. In fact, his GM there had been a valuable reference for his new job. But it was exciting to now be out on his own. Although the Royal Court was a smaller property, with 198 rooms, it was still a full-service hotel with numerous strengths: it was in a prime location just off the expressway, it was a well-known brand with a national reputation, and it seemed to have an excellent, well-trained staff. The only real problem was financial. Apparently, the previous GM had not been able to turn those strengths into a sufficient number of bookings. Steve's job was to keep expenses down, increase revenue as much as possible, and turn the Royal Court around. After 30 days on the job, he was well on his way to turning those goals into realities.

Then the letter from Lawhead, Alexander, and Fisk arrived. Apparently, a female guest had her purse snatched in the hotel's parking lot three months ago, on June 4. Now her attorneys were threatening to file suit unless the Royal Court made restitution. They requested payment of $25,000 as compensation for their client's loss of property, multiple injuries, and pain and suffering.

Steve took a deep breath. He knew what writing a check for $25,000 would do to his property's struggling bottom line: $25,000 represented an awful lot of room nights—especially when his insurance deductible was twice that amount. But he also wondered if the letter might be nothing more than an empty threat. He had to get the facts.

First, he checked the previous GM's files for any record of the incident. Although he did find one folder labeled "On-Premises Security," it only contained a form letter of dismissal that had apparently been sent to all of the hotel's security staff this past March, six months ago. He also paged through the previous GM's planner and found no notations regarding a June 4 incident. Increasingly frustrated, he dialed his executive housekeeper, a 15-year veteran who seemed to have an almost infallible memory. "Ginnie, do you remember anything about a purse snatching earlier this year?" Steve asked.

"You'll have to be more specific than that, Steve," she said. "There was one in late winter that happened in the corridor upstairs, and there was another one in June. That was out in the parking lot."

"So, it's true," Steve said. "A guest got injured during a purse snatching on our property."

"Well, there were injuries," Ginnie began, "but I seem to remember that she wasn't exactly a guest. I'd want to check on that."

"Thanks. I'll take care of it," ended Steve.

Steve picked up the letter and walked down to the front desk. Malia Etoise, another long-time staff member, was working this afternoon. "Hi, Malia. I need to find out if," he glanced down at the letter, "a Lauren Heidegger was a guest here on June third or fourth."

Malia entered the necessary information into her computer terminal. "Hmm," she began, "I'm not showing a Lauren Heidegger or any Heideggers for those dates. But for some reason that name's ringing a bell."

"She's claiming to have been the victim of a purse snatching on June 4," Steve prompted.

"Oh, I remember that," Malia said, nodding her head. "It was awful. She came running in here and her knees were bleeding and her dress was torn. Once all the other women heard about it, there was total chaos for a while."

"All the other women?" Steve asked.

"Mrs. Heidegger was here for a women's luncheon of some kind. I don't remember all the details. But once the word spread, women just streamed out of the Briar Room and filled the lobby wanting to know everything that happened, wanting us to call the police."

"Which you did, of course," Steve stated in a matter-of-fact tone.

Malia paused for a moment. "Yes, that time I'm sure we did call the police."

"That time? So, there were other incidents when you didn't call the police?" Steve asked.

Malia rolled her eyes and nodded. "Not my choice. But the way it was explained to me was that all police calls show up in the newspaper, and your predecessor didn't want that kind of publicity."

Steve returned to his office and fell into his chair, not certain what his next step should be. It certainly sounded as if the incident had occurred on Royal Court property and that there were witnesses to that fact. But Mrs. Heidegger wasn't a guest after all; maybe the property wasn't liable. Besides, the previous GM hadn't even felt the incident warranted a written record. At Steve's former job, the hotel was large enough to afford a full-time security staff and he hadn't paid much attention to their work. Now, it seemed the responsibility for security rested firmly on his shoulders, but he was stymied. "Maybe Carson has some advice for me," Steve thought, recalling how his former boss had gone out of his way to be a mentor for him. He picked up the phone.

"That's a tough spot," Carson agreed. "But I'm sure you'll handle it fine."

"Great," Steve said, sounding less than confident. "Where do I go from here?"

"I'll lay it out for you," Carson replied. "First, call the legal department at the corporate office. Let them know about the letter and that you're researching the matter. They may ask a lot of questions you can't answer yet, but you'll get the answers as you continue the investigation."

"To me the only real question is: do we settle or go to court?" Steve remarked curtly.

Carson calmly replied, "But you can't answer that until you know how strong your position is. You need to find out whether your operation has taken 'reasonable care.' There aren't any hard-and-fast rules about what that is—it can vary from community to community. You need to find out what reasonable care means for your location.

"First, contact the police department and get a computer print-out of all the calls made to your address. They can probably do it while you wait. Now, some incidents on that list may not really involve your hotel at all—maybe there was a car accident on the street and the driver came in to use the phone, that kind of thing. You'll need to go through the list and find out which incidents do apply.

"Next, I'd call up the local newspaper and ask them to search their morgue for all of the stories with the name of your hotel in it. Chances are, any problems that would generate a police call would also show up in the newspaper. There might even be some mentions in the paper that didn't involve the police. Give the newspaper's librarian a couple of days to get the information you need.

"While you're waiting, though, I'd recommend talking to some of the other GMs in your area. Ask them what types of crime problems they've had or are having. Some might not want to talk specifically about their own operation—you know, nobody wants to give the impression that their place isn't as safe as can be—but you should be able to get a good feel about what kind of neighborhood you're in.

"You've already started talking to your staff, and that's good. I'd suggest that you do more of that. Just walk around and ask your people what incidents they might remember, what their overall impression is of hotel security and crime in the area."

"Carson," Steve interrupted, "you and I both know that perceptions aren't always accurate. They're subjective."

"That's true," Carson replied. "But, accurate or not, do you want a dozen members of your staff on the witness stand telling a jury that they didn't feel safe at the Royal Court Hotel? I don't think so. Better to find out sooner than later."

"I understand," Steve sighed.

"One last thing," Carson added. "Drive around your neighborhood and try to see it through the eyes of a plaintiff's attorney who wants to prove negligence. Is yours the only property without a fence? Without security lighting? In other words, does it look as if you care about security?"

The next few days proved both valuable and anxiety-filled.

The police call sheet only noted the June purse snatching, not the late-winter incident that Ginnie remembered. But it also listed three car burglaries in the parking lot, one break-in during a wedding reception (in which the bride and groom's wedding gifts and honeymoon luggage were stolen), some vending machine vandalism, and two calls in response to guestroom parties that resulted in property damage. All during the last 12 months.

The first local GM Steve called began the conversation by thanking his predecessor. "If he hadn't let those three security officers go," she said, "I'd still be reviewing résumés." She went on to explain that a rise in criminal activity throughout the area had led most of the other hotels to actually increase their security. As far as she knew, Royal Court was the only property to eliminate staff—and she had immediately added two of them to her payroll. Another property down the road had hired the third security officer. "I think a lot of us felt he was just shooting himself in the foot," she admitted. "Sure, he saved some money up front—and I know things have been tight for everybody—but…" She didn't have to finish the sentence. Steve was beginning to understand.

Other incidents surfaced once Steve began chatting with his staff. Some tires were slashed by vandals. Some fights erupted in the bar. Malia recalled that there had even been rumors that the Royal Court recently had a reputation as a favored place to buy drugs for dealers who wanted fast interstate access. That activity had diminished, though, when the Carriage Bridge Hotel across the street started offering doughnuts and coffee to the police working the night shift; the close proximity of a squad car was enough to scare the dealers away—at least at night. Unfortunately, that didn't completely convince the staff at the Royal Court. Some employees continue to ask not to work the night shift and others only enter and leave the hotel in pairs.

The newspaper search only confirmed what Steve had already learned: the Royal Court had seen more than its share of security problems. Apparently, he'd just been lucky in not seeing any new incidents during his first 30 days on the job. He realized that luck was not good enough. Not only did he have to present the facts of his investigation to the corporate legal department along with his recommendation, he also had to implement an effective security program immediately.

With his notes in front of him, Steve picked up the telephone and placed a call to the corporate office.

Discussion Questions

1. What evidence can Steve share with the corporate legal department that would support a recommendation either to settle for $25,000 or to take the case to court?

2. What steps can Steve and his staff take to effectively reduce the number of security incidents at the Royal Court, while still working to keep expenses to a minimum?

Case Number: 3871CA

The following industry experts helped generate and develop this case: Wendell Couch, ARM, CHA, Director of Technical Services for the Risk Management Department of Bass Hotels & Resorts; and Raymond C. Ellis, Jr., CHE, CHTP, CLSD, Professor, Conrad N. Hilton College, University of Houston, Director, Loss Prevention Management Institute.

Case Study

Doughnuts and Dilemmas

Phil Watson, the general manager of the Bluestone Hotel, was just settling down to some early morning paperwork when the buzzer on his intercom sounded. He pushed the speaker button: "Yes, Jean?"

"There's a Douglas Koneval on line two. He wants to know if you've still got 'Calamity Jane' in your 'bag.' He said you'd know what he's talking about."

Phil chuckled. "Put him through, put him through." Phil waited for the muffled click, and then said: "Doug!"

"Phil! You still trying to make putts with that beat up old putter of yours!?"

"Hey, that putter was good enough to send you back to the clubhouse a broken and defeated man! How've you been? I haven't heard from you in a while."

"Actually, I've been pretty busy," Doug said. "You heard I'm at the Wellington now, right?"

The Wellington was an independent hotel upstate. "No, I didn't know that."

"Yes, I took the GM job a couple of months ago."

"Your first job as a general manager! That's great! How's it working out for you?"

"Well, that's why I'm calling. Things have been going pretty smoothly so far—there's a good staff here, and I've got ideas for improving some things, but something happened yesterday that got me thinking about security issues here at the hotel. It was nothing major—we had a loud guest get a little belligerent when we asked him to quiet down—but it hit me that I don't have a contact at the local police department yet and I really don't know how to go about making one. You've been at the Bluestone for a lot of years, and I know you have an excellent relationship with the police. I was hoping I could pick your brain a bit this morning and get some ideas on how I can establish a good relationship with the police here in my little community."

Phil laughed. "Well, I don't know that I've got anything spectacular to offer, but I can share some basics with you that just about any general manager would probably try."

"That's just what I need."

"Well," Phil began, "the first thing I'd do is arrange to have lunch with the police chief. I can't remember—does the Wellington have F&B?"

"Yes, we have a nice little restaurant on-site."

"Well, I'd invite him to the restaurant. Is the police chief a 'him' or a 'her,' by the way?"

"It's a 'him,'" Doug replied. "Malcolm Ramsey is his name. I've never met him, but I've heard he's an okay guy to deal with."

"Invite Malcolm to the restaurant, have a nice lunch, and just introduce yourself and get to know him a little. If he has the time, ask him to walk around the property with you after lunch and point out any security concerns you should be aware of."

"Great idea! I could even have him write something up for me, a report that I could—"

"Whoa, stop right there!" Phil interjected. "You do not want anything in writing from Malcolm."

"I don't? Why not? He might come up with some great suggestions that would really make the property safe."

"Yes, he might, but he might also come up with suggestions that you could never afford to implement. If you have a written report lying around with some security advice in it that you didn't act on and something happens at the hotel—" Phil shrugged. "You could be in serious trouble if that report winds up in court."

"Good point. Okay, nothing in writing. What else should I do?"

"Well, let Malcolm know that you're interested in a good relationship with his department and that you're willing to do what you can to accommodate his officers. Let him know that officers out on patrol are welcome to stop by and use the hotel's restrooms, for example. If the officers are tired of writing out police reports with their clipboards balanced on their knees or on steering wheels, they can come by and use a table in the employee breakroom. And they're welcome to just stop by for coffee and pastries."

"Doughnuts still work," Doug laughed.

"Yes, they do," Phil agreed. "And little courtesies can pay big dividends when something happens at your property. Three weeks ago we had a 'domestic situation' occur in one of our rooms. Our front desk got a call around midnight—'Hey, there's a racket going on next door, I can't sleep'—and Sylvia at the front desk says, 'Okay, I'll take care of it.' She calls the room—410, I think it was—and asks them to pipe down. She gets a response like: 'Oh, no problem. Sorry,' et cetera, et cetera. A few minutes later, the phone rings again—'Hey, they're still going at it in Room 410; now some woman's crying in there'—so Sylvia contacts the security guard and the manager on duty, Bret Russell. The two of them go up to the room and knock on the door. 'What's going on? Is everyone okay?' 'Yeah, yeah,' the man inside says, 'we're just arguing a little bit.' 'Open the door, please.' So the door opens and this guy is standing there in his underwear, the desk lamp's turned over, and a woman's standing on the other side of the bed in a nightshirt, a hand cupped over one eye. 'Ma'am, are you okay?' 'Yeah, I'm okay, we're just having a little disagreement, that's all. Everything's cool.' 'Are you sure?' 'Yeah, we're done.' 'We'll pay for the damages,' the guy says, so Bret says, 'All right, we'll leave, but take it easy in here, okay?' 'Sure thing, we're sorry,' the guy says. So Bret and the security guard leave the room and they don't even get all the way down the hall to the elevator before they hear the guy start yelling again and another lamp go over. 'That's it,' Bret says, 'we're calling the police.'

"And the officers were great. Two squad cars were at the hotel within five minutes, and ten minutes later the husband was in one of them, on his way to jail. The other officer stayed with the wife while she packed and went to the front desk to pay the bill, then he took her to a shelter for battered women. The whole thing was over in 20 minutes and they handled it beautifully. Real quiet. None of the other guests even knew the officers had been there."

"That's the kind of cooperation I'm looking for," Doug said. "What about hiring off-duty police officers for hotel security work? Is that a good idea?"

"Two words," Phil replied. "'No guns.'"

"'No guns'?"

"That's right. Off-duty officers can be good additions to your staff—if you tell them that you don't want guns on your property. It's a liability issue. Even though these officers are on the city's police force, when you hire them, they're working for you. If they accidentally shoot an innocent bystander, the hotel is on the hook, not the city."

"That's good to know," Doug said. "Should I just approach the officers individually with offers?"

"I'd ask the chief about it during your lunch with him. Just tell him what you are considering, and ask him what his policy is. Some police departments don't allow their officers to do free-lance security work. On the other extreme, some departments have a sergeant in charge of evenly distributing that kind of work among the officers. Other departments let individual officers cut their own deals."

"You've given me a lot to think about," Doug said, in that tone of voice people get when they are winding down their phone call. "I really want to get started on the right foot with Malcolm. A good relationship with the police is really important."

Doug took his cue to sum up. "Well, the thing to do first is to set up a lunch with Malcolm and let him know that you want to do what it takes to have a positive working relationship with his department."

"Hey, thanks for the time, Phil. I gotta run, but I really appreciate your ideas. I'll let you know how things work out."

"Do that, Doug, and best of luck to you. I know you'll do well."

Phil no sooner hung up the telephone when the intercom buzzer sounded again. "Yes, Jean?"

"Lieutenant Foster is here to see you."

What a coincidence, Phil thought. "Send him in, please."

The office door opened and Jean showed in one of the lieutenants on the local police force. Phil came around from behind his desk and shook his hand warmly. "Hi, Glenn, nice to see you again. What brings you out our way?"

"Good morning, Phil." Glenn took a seat in one of the two chairs in front of Phil's desk. Phil, rather than sit behind his desk, sat in the other.

"I got a problem that maybe you can help me with," Glenn continued. "The FBI called me a few minutes ago, looking for—," Glenn paused to pull a notebook out of the inside pocket of his sport coat—"looking for a 'Ruben Drosha.' I guess this guy's really bad news. We need to know if he's at the hotel, what phone calls he's made, and his credit card number. They're trying to track where he's been. You know the drill."

Phil shifted in his seat uncomfortably. "Do you have subpoenas for any of that stuff, Glenn? Because if you don't, you know the only thing I can legally tell you is whether he's registered at the hotel."

Glenn snorted. "Get real, Phil, this is a Saturday. All the judges are up north getting their fishing boats out about now. Like I said, the FBI just called me. I was hoping we could keep this on an informal, friendly basis."

Phil shook his head. "Sorry, Glenn, but I just can't do it. I can tell you if he's here or not, and I can put a call through to his room if you want to talk to him, but that's as far as I can go without a court order."

"I'm sorry you feel that way." Glenn stood up, signaling an end to the discussion. Phil stood up, too. "The chief will be disappointed. He thought you'd be more cooperative," Glenn said quietly. "But I guess you gotta do what you gotta do. Let's go check reservations and see if Drosha's here. It's not much, but at least I won't go back to the FBI entirely empty-handed."

Discussion Questions

1. In addition to the things Phil mentioned to Doug, what other things can Doug do to promote a good relationship with his local police department?

2. The "domestic situation" that occurred at Phil's hotel could have turned out much worse. What are some of the things that could have gone wrong, had it been handled less effectively by hotel staff members?

3. Despite Phil's advice to Doug about establishing a good working relationship with the police, and despite Phil's wish to preserve his relationship with his own local police force, Phil turned down Lieutenant Foster's request for information about a man wanted by the FBI. Why did Phil refuse to give Foster all of the information he wanted?

Case Number: 3871CB

The following industry experts helped generate and develop this case: Wendell Couch, ARM, CHA, Director of Technical Services for the Risk Management Department of Bass Hotels & Resorts; and Raymond C. Ellis, Jr., CHE, CHTP, CLSD, Professor, Conrad N. Hilton College, University of Houston, Director, Loss Prevention Management Institute.

Appendix

Selected Court Cases

It is unfortunate that security personnel are often relatively or entirely unaware of what is involved in legal proceedings. This Appendix presents several cases that deal with fundamental issues relating to lodging security.

One of the difficulties that sometimes confronts innkeepers is the existence of legal decisions that seem to contradict each other or that at least point in different directions. We will look at a number of decisions concerning the duty of reasonable care owed to guests and others by innkeepers and at the treatment of a closely related topic, foreseeability. As you read, you will notice that many cases deal with more than one issue.

Wenninger v. Motel 6, Inc.

We first look to a lodging case in a trial court document from the United States District Court for the Northern District of Texas. The case, *Wenninger v. Motel 6, Inc.*, is included here because, by containing the judge's instructions to the jury and the jury's verdict, it essentially presents an opportunity to view these elements of the legal system in action. Notice that the charge of the court in this case carefully explains to the jurors several important legal concepts as used by that Court in that particular state. Notice also that, in the verdict, the jurors deal with very specific questions. Following this judgment, Wenninger accepted a settlement of $165,000. Although an older case, it set the stage for a vast overhaul of guestroom access lock and control systems.

Wenninger v. Motel 6, Inc.
No. CA 4-80-176-E (U.S. Dist. Ct. N.D. Tex., 1981)

MAHON, Judge.
JUDGMENT

On the 20th day of April, 1981, came on to be heard the above styled and numbered cause, wherein CAROL A. WENNINGER is Plaintiff and MOTEL 6, INC. is Defendant. All parties, by and through their respective attorneys of record, appeared and announced ready for trial.

A jury of twelve good and lawful persons was duly impaneled and sworn to try this case. After having heard the evidence, argument of counsel and charge of the Court, the jury did return, in open court, its unanimous verdict in which all twelve jurors concurred upon each and every finding. In response to the special interrogatories, definitions and explanatory instructions submitted to the jury by the Court in its charge, all twelve jurors did find as follows:

(1) That, on the occasion in question, the Defendant, Motel 6, Inc., was negligent.

(2) That such negligence was a proximate cause of the occurrence in question.

(3) That the total compensatory damages sustained by Plaintiff, Carol Wenninger

amounted to the sum of One Hundred Thirteen Thousand, Two Hundred Seventy-Five and no/100 Dollars ($113,275.00).

(4) That Plaintiff should be additionally awarded the sum of Seventy-Five Thousand and no/100 Dollars ($75,000.00) as punitive or exemplary damages.

The same being submitted to the jury by the Court on the 22nd day of April, 1981, the jury returned into open court its verdict on the same day, which verdict was received and accepted by the Court.

It is therefore, ORDERED, ADJUDGED and DECREED that Plaintiff, Carol A. Wenninger, recover the sum of One Hundred Eighty-Eight Thousand, Two Hundred Seventy-Five and no/100 Dollars ($188,275.00) from Defendant, Motel 6, Inc., with interest on said sum at the rate of nine percent (9%) per annum from the date of judgment until date paid.

It is further ORDERED, ADJUDGED and DECREED that all costs herein are hereby taxed against the Defendant, Motel 6, Inc., for which let execution issue if not timely paid.

* * *

CHARGE OF THE COURT
Members of the Jury:

Now that you have heard the evidence and the argument, it becomes my duty to give you the instructions of the Court as to the law applicable to this case.

It is your duty as jurors to follow the law as stated in the instructions of the Court, and to apply the rules of law so given to the facts as you find them from the evidence in the case.

You are not to single out one instruction alone as stating the law, but must consider the instructions as a whole.

Neither are you to be concerned with the wisdom of any rule of law stated by the Court. Regardless of any opinion you may have as to what the law ought to be, it would be a violation of your sworn duty to base a verdict upon any other view of the law than that given in the instructions of the Court; just as it would be a violation of your sworn duty, as judges of the facts, to base a verdict upon anything but the evidence in the case.

Justice through trial by jury must always depend upon the willingness of each individual juror to seek the truth as to the facts from the same evidence presented to all the jurors; and to arrive at the verdict by applying the same rules of law, as given in the instructions of the Court.

At the outset, I am sure you understand by this time that all parties to this litigation, whether individual or corporation, or whatever their character, must be treated alike insofar as their rights are concerned. This case should be considered and decided by you as an action between persons of equal standing in the community, of equal worth, and holding the same or similar stations in life. A corporation is entitled to the same fair trial at your hands as a private individual. The law is no respecter of persons; all persons, including corporations, stand equal before the law, and are to be dealt with as equals in a court of justice. You should not have any personal feelings or preferences as between individuals and corporations.

A corporation may only act through natural persons, who are known as its agents. In general, any agent or representative of a corporation possessing adequate authority may bind the corporation by his acts, declarations and omissions.

Do not let bias, prejudice, sympathy, resentment, or any such emotion play any part in your deliberations, and do not speculate on matters not shown by the evidence. Keep constantly in mind that it would be a violation of your sworn duty to base a verdict upon anything but the evidence in the case. You will carefully and impartially consider all the evidence in the case, follow the law as stated by the Court, and reach a just verdict, regardless of the consequences.

This case is submitted to you on special issues, propounded to you in the form of questions, which you will answer from a preponderance of the evidence submitted to you under the rulings of the Court, answering the questions by unanimous consent of the jury through your foreman and writing your answers in the space provided therefor following each question. It is necessary that the jury be advised of, and understand, certain legal terms which play such a large part in the determination of this sort of litigation, so at the outset, I will give you some definitions and explanations.

In a civil action such as this the burden is on the plaintiff to prove every essential element of his case by the preponderance of the evidence. If the proof should fail to establish any essential element of plaintiffs' claim by a preponderance of the evidence of the case, the jury should find for the defendant.

By the term "preponderance of the evidence," as used in this charge, is meant the greater weight or degree of credible evidence in the case. To "establish by a preponderance of the evidence" means to prove that something is more likely so than not so. In other words, a preponderance of the evidence in the case means such evidence as, when considered and compared with that opposed to it, has more convincing force, and produces in your minds belief that what is sought to be proved is more true than not true. It does not necessarily mean the greater volume of evidence or the greater number of witnesses, but it means that when you sift from all the evidence of this case that which you consider credible or worthy of belief, you take the evidence on each side and the side that has greater weight, that tips the scale, that is the one that preponderates. In determining whether any fact in issue has been proved by a preponderance of the evidence in the case, the jury may, unless otherwise instructed, consider the testimony of all witness[es], regardless of who may have called them, and all exhibits received in evidence, regardless of who may have produced them. So, the preponderance of the evidence merely means the greater weight or degree of the credible testimony.

You, as jurors, are the sole judges of the credibility of the witnesses and the weight their testimony deserves.

You should carefully scrutinize all the testimony given, the circumstances under which each witness has testified, and every matter in evidence which tends to show whether a witness is worthy of belief. Consider each witness's intelligence, motive and state of mind, and demeanor and manner while on the stand. Consider the witness's ability to observe the matters as to which he has testified, and whether he impresses you as having an accurate recollection of these matters. Consider also any relation each witness may bear to either side of the case and the extent to which, if at all, each witness is either supported or contradicted by other evidence in the case.

Inconsistencies or discrepancies in the testimony of a witness, or between the testimony of different witnesses, may or may not cause the jury to discredit such testimony. Two or more persons witnessing an incident or a transaction may see or hear it differently; and innocent misrecollection, like failure of recollection, is not an uncommon experience. In weighing the effect of a discrepancy, always consider whether it pertains to a matter of importance or an unimportant detail, and whether the discrepancy results from innocent error or intentional falsehood.

After making your own judgment, you will give the testimony of each witness such credibility, if any, as you may think it deserves.

The rules of evidence ordinarily do not permit witnesses to testify as to opinions or conclusions. An exception to this rule exists as to those whom we call "expert witnesses." Witnesses who, by education and experience, have become expert in some art, science, profession, or calling, may state their opinions as to relevant and material matters, in which they profess to be expert, and may also state their reasons for the opinion.

You should consider each expert opinion received in evidence in this case, and give it such weight as you may think it deserves. If you should decide that the opinion of an expert witness is not based upon sufficient education and experience, or if you should conclude that the reasons given in support of the opinion are not sound or if you feel that it is outweighed by other evidence, you may disregard the opinion entirely.

In the final analysis, it is the responsibility of the jury to make its own independent decision as to ultimate facts in this case and to reach that opinion based on all of the evidence, regardless of the source from which it came.

There are two types of evidence that may be introduced as to the facts of a case. One is direct evidence, such as the testimony of an eyewitness; the other is indirect or circumstantial evidence, the proof of a chain of circumstances pointing to the existence or non-existence of certain facts. A fact is established by circumstantial evidence when the fact sought to be established may be fairly and reasonably inferred from all other facts and circumstances proved in the case. In order to establish a theory, conclusion or hypothesis by circumstantial evidence, the proved facts and circumstances must be such as to make that theory, conclusion or hypothesis more probable, not merely possible, than any other theory, conclusion, or hypothesis based upon those facts and circumstances. In other words, the fact to be proved is established as an inference from proven circumstances. A fact is established by circumstantial evidence only if its existence is more probable than any other fact that can be reasonably inferred from all of such evidence.

As a general rule, the law makes no distinction between direct and circumstantial evidence, but simply requires that the jury find the facts in accordance with the preponderance of all of the evidence in the case, both direct and circumstantial. In other words, the finding of a fact cannot be based on mere surmise or speculation.

In the late evening hours on November 15, 1979, or the early morning hours on November 16, 1979, plaintiff arrived and registered at the "Motel 6" located in Haltom City, Texas, which is owned and operated by defendant. Plaintiff claims that before she went to sleep she locked the push-button lock on the door knob. Plaintiff claims that she awoke when an unknown male entered her room. Plaintiff further claims that the unknown male forced her to submit to sodomy and forced her to submit to sexual intercourse. Plaintiff claims the male then stole a sum of money and her watch and that he thereafter fled the room.

Plaintiff claims that defendant was negligent in not providing adequate protection for its guests at this particular motel against the intentional wrongful acts of third persons. In particular plaintiff claims that defendant was negligent in the following respects.

1. The push-button lock on the motel's door knob was inadequate to prevent entry from outside the room.

2. Failure to have a deadbolt or other suitable lock on the motel room door.

3. Failure to have a night latch on the motel room door.

4. Failure to provide its guests with a telephone.

5. Failure to have an employee on duty to watch for and protect against unauthorized individuals on the motel premises.

Plaintiff claims that as a proximate result of defendant's negligence, if any, she suffered physical pain, mental anguish and loss of personal property. You are instructed that *mental anguish* means intense mental suffering including, but not limited to, intense humiliation, intense embarrassment or intense fear. To constitute mental anguish, there must be something more than ordinary worry, vexation, disappointment, anger or resentment. You are further instructed that mental anguish concerning the filing, conduct or outcome of the lawsuit shall not be considered for any purpose.

Defendant denies that it was negligent in any respect, in providing proper protection for its guests.

You are instructed that plaintiff has the burden to prove from a preponderance of the evidence that defendant is liable for plaintiff's damages. To find defendant liable, you must find from a preponderance of the evidence the following three essential elements:

1. Defendant acted or failed to act as alleged by plaintiff;

2. Such actions or failure to act by defendant constitutes negligence; and

3. Such negligence, if any, of defendant was a proximate cause of the damage, if any, to plaintiff.

You are instructed that *negligence* is the failure to use ordinary care. *Ordinary care*, with reference to the conduct of defendant, means that degree of care which a reasonable and prudent motel owner or operator would have used under the same or similar circumstances to protect its guests from intentional injuries caused by third persons. However, you are instructed that a motel owner or operator has the duty to use such ordinary care only if it has reason to know that such acts are likely to occur, either generally or at some particular time. Liability for injuries may arise from the failure of the proprietor to exercise reasonable care to discover that such acts by third persons are occurring, or are likely to occur, coupled with the failure to provide reasonable means to protect his patrons from the harm or to give a warning adequate to enable the patrons to avoid the harm. A motel owner or operator is not an insurer of the safety of its guests, but such owner or operator is responsible to exercise ordinary or reasonable care in conformity with the principles which have just been discussed.

Proximate cause means that cause which, in a natural and continuous sequence, produces an event, and without which cause such event would not have occurred; and in order to be a proximate cause, the act or omission complained of must be such that a person using ordinary care would have foreseen that the event, or some similar event, might reasonably result therefrom. There may be more than one proximate cause of an event.

If you find from a preponderance of the evidence that plaintiff is entitled to an award of damages, defendant claims that plaintiff was negligent herself and that such negligence should reduce her damages.

Defendant claims that plaintiff was negligent in the following respects:

1. Failure to use the push-button locking mechanism on her door;

2. Failure to cry out at the time she realized that the intruder was in her room; and

3. Failure to offer any resistance to the intruder.

You are instructed that defendant has the burden to prove from a preponderance of the evidence that plaintiff was negligent. To find plaintiff negligent, you must find from a preponderance of the evidence the following three essential elements:

1. Plaintiff acted or failed to act as alleged by defendant;

2. Such acts or failure to act by plaintiff constitutes negligence; and

3. Such negligence, if any, of plaintiff was a proximate cause of injury, if any, to plaintiff.

You are reminded that *negligence* is the failure to use ordinary care. *Ordinary care* in reference to plaintiff means that degree of care which would be used by a person of ordinary prudence under the same or similar circumstances.

In other words negligence, in reference to plaintiff, means failure to use ordinary care; that is to say, failure to do that which a person of ordinary prudence would have done under the same or similar circumstances, or doing that which a person of ordinary prudence would not have done under the same or similar circumstances.

In reference to plaintiff, *proximate cause* has the same meaning as hereinbefore defined in this Charge.

You are the exclusive judges of the facts proved, the credibility of the witnesses, and the weight to be given their testimony; but you are bound to receive the law from the Court as stated herein and be governed accordingly.

Now, bearing in mind the foregoing instructions, as well as further directions later given in this charge or orally, you will return herein answers to the following interrogatories, or to such of them as may be necessary, according to specific explanations in connection with said interrogatories.

* * *

VERDICT OF THE JURY

We, the Jury, return our answers to the following interrogatories as our verdict in this case.

QUESTION NO. 1:

A. Do you find from a preponderance of the evidence that on the occasion in question defendant had a push-button lock on its door knob which was inadequate to prevent entry from outside the room?

ANSWER:
(x) Yes
( ) No

If you answered "Yes" to part A, then answer part B; otherwise do not answer parts B or C.

B. Do you find from a preponderance of the evidence that such conduct was negligence?
ANSWER:
(x) Yes
( ) No

If you answered "Yes" to part B, then answer part C; otherwise do not answer part C.

C. Do you find from a preponderance of the evidence that such conduct was a proximate cause of the occurrence in question?
ANSWER:
(x) Yes
( ) No

QUESTION NO. 2:
A. Do you find from a preponderance of the evidence that on the occasion in question defendant failed to have a deadbolt or other suitable lock of sturdy construction on the motel room door?
ANSWER:
(x) Yes
( ) No

If you answered "Yes" to part A, then answer part B; otherwise do not answer parts B or C.

B. Do you find from a preponderance of the evidence that such failure was negligence?
ANSWER:
(x) Yes
( ) No

If you answered "Yes" to part B, then answer part C; otherwise do not answer part C.

C. Do you find from a preponderance of the evidence that such failure was a proximate cause of the occurrence in question?
ANSWER:
(x) Yes
( ) No

QUESTION NO. 3:
A. Do you find from a preponderance of the evidence that on the occasion in question defendant failed to have a night latch on the motel room door?
ANSWER:

(x) Yes
( ) No

If you answered "Yes" to part A, then answer part B; otherwise do not answer parts B or C.

B. Do you find from a preponderance of the evidence that such failure was negligence?
ANSWER:
(x) Yes
( ) No

If you answered "Yes" to part B, then answer part C; otherwise do not answer part C.

C. Do you find from a preponderance of the evidence that such failure was a proximate cause of the occurrence in question?
ANSWER:
(x) Yes
( ) No

QUESTION NO. 4:

A. Do you find from a preponderance of the evidence that on the occasion in question defendant failed to provide its motel guest with a telephone which might be used in the event of an emergency?
ANSWER:
(x) Yes
( ) No

If you answered "Yes" to part A, then answer part B; otherwise do not answer parts B or C.

B. Do you find from a preponderance of the evidence that such failure was negligence?
ANSWER:
(x) Yes
( ) No

If you answered "Yes" to part B, then answer part C; otherwise do not answer part C.

C. Do you find from a preponderance of the evidence that such failure was a proximate cause of the occurrence in question?
ANSWER:
(x) Yes
( ) No

QUESTION NO. 5:

A. Do you find from a preponderance of the evidence that on the occasion in question defendant failed to have an employee on duty to watch for and protect against unauthorized individuals on the motel premises?
ANSWER:
(x) Yes
( ) No

If you answered "Yes" to part A, then answer part B; otherwise do not answer parts B or C.

B. Do you find from a preponderance of the evidence that such failure was negligence?
ANSWER:
(x) Yes
( ) No

If you answered "Yes" to part B, then answer part C; otherwise do not answer part C.

C. Do you find from a preponderance of the evidence that such failure was a proximate cause of the occurrence in question?
ANSWER:
(x) Yes
( ) No

If you have answered "Yes" to *any* of the following questions: 1C, 2C, 3C, 4C *or* 5C, then answer Questions 6 and 7. If you have answered "No" to *all* of the following questions: 1C, 2C, 3C, 4C, and 5C, then answer no further questions.

QUESTION NO. 6:

What sum of money, if any, if now paid in cash, do you find from a preponderance of the evidence would fairly and reasonably compensate plaintiff, Carol Wenninger, for her injuries, if any, which you find from a preponderance of the evidence resulted from the occurrence in question?

Answer separately in dollars and cents, if any, to each of the following elements. Do not reduce the amount of your answers because of the negligence, if any, of the plaintiff.

(a) Physical pain, if any, that plaintiff has sustained from the date of the occasion in question until the date of this trial.
Answer in dollars and cents or none.
ANSWER: *$7,500*

(b) Mental anguish, if any, that plaintiff has sustained from the date of the occasion in question until the date of this trial.
Answer in dollars and cents or none.
ANSWER: *$30,000*

(c) Mental anguish which, in reasonable probability, plaintiff will suffer in the future beyond the date of this trial.
Answer in dollars and cents or none.
ANSWER: *$75,000*

(d) Reasonable value of plaintiff's personal property lost.
Answer in dollars and cents or none.
ANSWER: *$350.00*

QUESTION NO. 7:

Find, from a preponderance of the evidence, the reasonable expenses, if any, for necessary medical and hospital care received by plaintiff, Carol Wenninger, in the past for treatment of her injuries resulting from the occurrence in question.

Do not reduce the amount of your answer because of the negligence, if any, of the plaintiff.

Answer in dollars and cents or none.
ANSWER: $425.00

QUESTION NO. 8:

8A. Do you find from a preponderance of the evidence that on the occasion in question, plaintiff failed to use the push-button locking mechanism with which her door was equipped?
ANSWER:
( ) Yes
(x) No
If you answered "Yes" to part A, then answer part B; otherwise do not answer part B or C.

B. Do you find from a preponderance of the evidence that such failure was negligence?
ANSWER:
( ) Yes
( ) No
If you answered "Yes" to part B, then answer part C; otherwise do not answer part C.

C. Do you find from a preponderance of the evidence that such failure was a proximate cause of the occurrence in question?
ANSWER:
( ) Yes
( ) No

QUESTION NO. 9:

A. Do you find from a preponderance of the evidence that the plaintiff failed to cry out at the time she realized that the intruder was in her room?
ANSWER:
(x) Yes
( ) No
If you answered "Yes" to part A, then answer part B; otherwise do not answer parts B or C.

B. Do you find from a preponderance of the evidence that such failure was negligence?
ANSWER:
( ) Yes
(x) No
If you answered "Yes" to part B, then answer part C; otherwise do not answer part C.

C. Do you find from a preponderance of the evidence that such failure was a proximate cause of the occurrence in question?
ANSWER:
( ) Yes
( ) No

QUESTION NO. 10:
A. Do you find from a preponderance of the evidence that the plaintiff failed to offer any resistance to the intruder?
ANSWER:
(x) Yes
( ) No
If you answered "Yes" to part A, then answer part B; otherwise do not answer parts B or C.

B. Do you find from a preponderance of the evidence that such failure was negligence?
ANSWER:
( ) Yes
(x) No
If you answered "Yes" to part B, then answer part C; otherwise do not answer part C.

C. Do you find from a preponderance of the evidence that such failure was a proximate cause of the occurrence in question?
ANSWER:
( ) Yes
( ) No
If you have answered "Yes" to *any* of the following questions: 8C, 9C, or 10C, then answer Question No. 11; otherwise proceed to Question No. 12.

QUESTION NO. 11:
In answering this question you should consider only the negligence of plaintiff and defendant that you have found to be a proximate cause of the occurrence in question; therefore, the percentage should total 100%.

What percentage of the negligence that caused the occurrence in question do you find from a preponderance of the evidence to be attributable to each of the parties found by you to have been negligent?

The percentage of negligence attributable to a party is not necessarily measured by the number of acts or omissions found.

Answer by stating the percentage, if any, opposite each name.
ANSWER:

Motel 6, Inc.	_____ %
Carol Wenninger	_____ %
Total	100 %

If you have awarded plaintiff any money in your answer to either Question No. 6 or Question No. 7, then answer Question No. 12; otherwise do not answer Question No. 12.

QUESTION NO. 12:
In addition to the damages you have awarded plaintiff in Question 6 or 7, the law permits the jury, under certain circumstances, to award the injured person punitive and exemplary damages, in order to punish the wrongdoer for some extraordinary misconduct, and to serve as an example of warning to others not to engage in such conduct.

In this case, you must decide whether the negligence of defendant constitutes "gross negligence." "Gross negligence" is that entire want of care which raises the belief that the act or omission complained of is the result of conscious indifference to the rights or welfare of the person or persons to be affected by such act or omission.

Whether or not to make any award of punitive and exemplary damages, in addition to those damages you have found for plaintiff in Question 6 or 7, is a matter exclusively within the province of the jury, if the jury should unanimously find, from a preponderance of the evidence in the case, that the defendant's acts or omissions which proximately caused damage to the plaintiff constituted "gross negligence"; but the jury should also bear in mind, not only the conditions under which, and the purposes for which, the law permits an award of punitive and exemplary damages to be made, but also the requirement of the law that the amount of such extraordinary damages, when awarded, must be fixed with calm discretion and sound reason, and must never be either awarded, or fixed in amount, because of any sympathy, or bias, or prejudice with respect to any party to the case.

What sum of money, if any, do you find from a preponderance of the evidence should be awarded to plaintiff as punitive and exemplary damages?

Answer in dollars and cents or none.
ANSWER: $75,000

Peters v. Holiday Inns, Inc.

In the next case, *Peters v. Holiday Inns, Inc.*, the Wisconsin Supreme Court discussed "ordinary care" and recognized the importance of circumstances in determining whether a specific security procedure or type of equipment is necessary in a given situation. Asserting that "an innkeeper's standard of care in providing security will vary according to the particular circumstances and location of the hotel," the Court cited a number of relevant factors to consider in deciding whether a lodging property has exercised ordinary care. The Court listed several security procedures and devices which may be needed, depending on the particular circumstances, but—as the Court pointed out—this does not mean that such procedures and devices are necessary or invaluably useful to any particular hotel or motel. Over the years, there has been no significant change in the court evaluation and ruling, as noted in the following case.

Peters v. Holiday Inns, Inc.
89 Wis.2d 115 (1979), 278 N.W.2d 208

COFFEY, Justice.
Appeal is taken from a summary judgment entered in favor of the defendant-respondent Holiday Inns, Inc., a Tennessee corporation. The defendant wholly owns

the stock of M.H.I. Inc., a Wisconsin corporation that operates a motel known as the Holiday Inn West located at 201 North Mayfair Rd., Wauwatosa, Wisconsin. In the early morning hours of December 31, 1975, the plaintiff-appellant Francis J. Peters, a motel guest, was assaulted and robbed in his room. Peters commenced this action alleging the motel was negligent in permitting two intruders access to his room that resulted in his being beaten and robbed. The plaintiff and defendant concede the facts leading up to and culminating in the assault on Peters, although the plaintiff presented additional facts to the court at a summary judgment hearing.

Shortly before 3:00 A.M. on December 31, 1975, a car containing four males parked in front of the motel's entrance. The four men sat in the car for a short time before one of the car's occupants entered the motel lobby. The lobby is in the motel's main building, while the plaintiff's room, No. 185, is located in a separate but adjacent structure. The assailant, a former employee of the motel, was known as Elvis to the employees on duty. Upon entering the motel, he asked whether "Uncle George" was working that night and after being told he was not scheduled to work, "Elvis" left the lobby. Rather than exiting the building, the assailant entered the motel's kitchen area where he stole one of the bellboy shirts.

The activities of the four men were observed by a Wauwatosa policeman who was routinely patrolling the defendant's premises in an unmarked squad car. The officer became suspicious after seeing the man who departed earlier from the car return and then observed the auto proceed to the rear of the parking lot near adjacent the motel rooms. The patrolman then entered the motel and questioned the two employees on duty concerning their conversation with "Elvis." The employees informed him that a short time ago the patrons of Room 143 had phoned the desk to report that a man knocked on their door claiming their room phone was out of order and that he had a message for them from the desk. The patrolman, upon receipt of this information, alertly suspecting something unusual, called headquarters and requested the aid of additional squads that arrived at the scene shortly thereafter.

The imposter "messenger," after being denied entrance to Room 143, apparently proceeded to Peters' room, No. 185. The man knocked on the door and repeated the same *modus operandi*, informing Peters his phone wasn't working and that he had a message for him from the desk. The plaintiff-appellant explains that he looked through the door's one-way viewer and saw a man in the hallway wearing a bellboy's white shirt, the type worn by Holiday Inn personnel. Peters opened the door, believing the message was the 6:30 A.M. "wake-up call" he had requested. Two men pushed their way into the room and held the plaintiff at gunpoint while one of the assailants searched Peters' pants and room. They found approximately $700 in cash and a set of keys to the plaintiff's bowling alley. The intruders forced Peters to accompany them, apparently intending further criminal activity. The plaintiff was pushed into his own car and at this time the police converged upon the vehicle and the four men were apprehended at the scene.

At the time of the assault, the outside entrance to the separate structure housing Rooms 143 and 185 was neither locked, monitored by closed circuit television, nor manned by motel staff or security personnel. Further, it is not necessary to pass through the lobby before entering the building. The only security provided by the motel was a dead bolt lock on each room as well as a chain lock and a one-way viewer. It is pointed out that the hallway outside Rooms 143 and 185 was well lighted at the time of the assault. It was established by affidavit that the Inn did not employ security guards, as in the past five years there had been few incidents requiring calls to the police for help and that the police routinely patrol the motel entrance and parking lot.

On December 13, 1976, following a hearing on the defendant's motion for summary judgment, the trial court granted the motion based upon the affidavits submitted by the parties and additional evidentiary facts presented to the court at the hearing. The trial court expressed its reasoning for the decision in the following language:

> Now, plaintiff argues that he has a right to present this evidence to the trier of the fact. That is true only if the evidence, if presented to the trier of the fact, drawing all reasonable inferences in favor of it, would sustain a verdict in favor of the plaintiff. I cannot find that it would. I find to the contrary, that it would not, and that under the circumstances present at the time and place, no more diligent or effective circumstances could have existed for the preservation, care and protection of the plaintiff than in fact existed on the occasion in question. Had the police department not been fortuitously on the premises, I could view the plaintiff's complaints with a different point of view. I think unquestionably, absent the presence of the police officers on the occasion in question, and the report of the phone call by the desk clerk to the police department, there would be presented to the jury a question of reasonable diligence.

The presence of the police is described as "fortuitous" as they were on the scene during a routine patrol of the premises. Further, their investigation was not initiated by a report from the motel personnel, but rather because of the suspicious circumstances personally observed by the Wauwatosa patrolman in the parking lot area.

Throughout this opinion we will refer to the residents of the Holiday Inn as guests of a motel or hotel interchangeably.

Issues:

1. What degree of care is required of a hotel or innkeeper in providing security measures to protect the personal safety of its guests?

2. Did the trial court err in granting summary judgment for the defendant based upon the conceded and additional facts presented, as well as the parties' affidavits and briefs presented?

In this case, the court is called upon to establish the standard of care to be imposed upon an innkeeper to provide adequate security measures for the safety of his guests. Prior to this decision, the court considered a restaurateur's duty to protect his customers from bodily injury as a result of a third party's assaultive conduct. In *Weihert v. Piccione*, 273 Wis. 448, 78 N.W.2d 757 (1956), a restaurant patron was injured when an altercation broke out between other customers. *Weihert* held that a restaurant owner owes his customers the following duty of care in protecting them against bodily injury:

> ... the proprietor of a place of business who holds it out to the public for entry for his business purposes (including a restaurant) is subject to liability to members of the public while upon the premises for such a purpose for bodily harm caused to them by the accidental, negligent, or intentionally harmful acts of third persons, if the proprietor by the exercise of reasonable care could have discovered that such acts were being done or about to be done, and could have protected the members of the public by controlling the conduct of the third persons, or by giving a warning adequate to enable them to avoid harm. *supra* at 456, 78 N.W.2d at 761.

In our mobile society, travellers carry sums of money because of necessity and the problems caused by the lack of adequate identification for cashing checks in areas away from home. Thus, innkeepers should foresee that necessarily large amounts of monies and credit cards are carried by their guests and consequently increased security is required in these days of rapidly increasing assaultive crimes. Certainly hotel patrons can expect that reasonable security will be provided, combined with the friendliness, hospitality and graciousness so widely advertised by modern hotels.

In *Osborne v. Montgomery* 203 Wis. 223, 242-43, 234 N.W. 372, (1971), it was noted that once a legal duty has been imposed, the standard of care to be exercised is defined in the following language:

> ... the degree of care which the great mass of mankind ordinarily exercises under the same or similar circumstances. A person fails to exercise ordinary care when, without intending to do any wrong, he does an act or omits a precaution under circumstances in which a person of ordinary intelligence and prudence ought reasonably to foresee that such act or omission will subject him or his property, or the person or property of another to an unreasonable risk of injury or damage.[1]

Thus, the conduct of hotel innkeepers in providing security must conform to the standard of ordinary care. In the context of the hotel-guest relationship, it is foreseeable that an innkeeper's failure to maintain adequate security measures not only permits but may even encourage intruders to rob or assault hotel patrons. Therefore, we hold that a hotel has a duty to exercise ordinary care to provide adequate protection for its guests and their property from assaultive and other types of criminal activity. [citations omitted]

* * *

[I]n meeting its standard of ordinary care a hotel must provide security commensurate with the facts and circumstances that are or should be apparent to the ordinarily prudent person. In other words, an innkeeper's standard of care in providing security will vary according to the particular circumstances and location of the hotel.[2]

Accordingly, as the degree of care that an innkeeper must exercise will vary in relation to the attendant circumstances, relevant factors in deciding whether a hotel has exercised ordinary care in providing adequate security are: industry standards,[3] the community's crime rate,[4] the extent of assaultive or criminal activity in the area or in similar business enterprises,[5] the presence of suspicious persons,[6] and the peculiar

---

[1] From Wisconsin Jury Instruction—Civil, Part I, 1005 adopting the language of *Osborne v. Montgomery*.

[2] *Dean v. Greenwich Corp.*, 21 Misc.2d 702, 193 N.Y.S.2d 712 (1959).

[3] In *Yamada v. Hilton Hotel Corp.*, 60 Ill.App.3rd 101, 17 Ill.Dec. 228, 376 N.E.2d 227 (1977) a trial court's judgment in favor of the defendant hotel owner was reversed and remanded for a new trial. The appellate court found it was error for the trial court to refuse to permit the hotel security chief from testifying as to the security measures taken by other downtown Chicago hotels.

[4] *Id.*

[5] *Rosier v. Gainesville Inns Assoc., Ltd.*, Fla. App. (1st Dist.), 347 So.2d 1100 (1977) refused a directed verdict in favor of the motel noting that it was a jury question as to whether the room door locks provided by the hotel were adequate in light of prior hotel robberies within the past 5 months.

[6] *Jenness v. Sheraton-Cadillac Properties, Inc.*, 48 Mich.App. 723, 211 N.W.2d 106 (1973).

security problems posed by the hotel's design. A hotel's liability depends upon the danger to be apprehended and the presence or absence of security measures designed to meet the danger. The particular circumstances may require one or more of the following safety measures: a security force, closed circuit television surveillance, dead bolt and chain locks on the individual rooms as well as security doors on hotel entranceways removed from the lobby area.

Consequently, we apply the ordinary care standard to the facts of this case in determining whether the defendant motel was entitled to summary judgment. The plaintiff's primary contentions are that the motel was negligent in: (1) allowing suspicious persons to roam about the premises unsupervised during the early morning hours; (2) permitting the suspicious person to gain access to the Holiday Inn uniforms thus enabling the man to pose as a hotel employee; (3) as it is not necessary to pass by the motel lobby, the motel failed to provide security personnel, television monitoring equipment or other security devices, including locks on the outside doors leading to the hallways in the separated motel building where Rooms Nos. 143 and 185 were located so as to prevent ingress to all but motel patrons. The trial court described these contentions as "potentially valid" but nonetheless concluded the evidentiary facts did not raise competing inferences which would sustain a verdict in favor of the plaintiff. The trial court's rationale is stated in the following language:

> The fortuitous presence of the police department, however, establishes the fact that the plaintiff in fact was protected by the most effective means that could have prevailed; that if in fact the defendants were less than diligent with regard to the security installation, such as the stolen indicia, the security force and the building locks, in fact then, that was not causal of the plaintiff's loss because it was supplanted by the effectiveness of the fortuitous presence of the police department, and the motion for summary judgment in favor of the defendant is granted.

* * *

We hold, based upon the applicability of the established duty of ordinary care imposed on a hotel to provide security, and the facts and circumstances presented by the parties, reasonable persons could draw competing inferences as to whether the defendant motel provided adequate security. The present case raises a jury question as to whether or not the presence of the assailant in the motel lobby, not for purposes of renting a room, but looking for a certain motel employee at 3:00 A.M. was suspicious circumstance requiring the motel staff to monitor the intruder's whereabouts.

* * *

Further, in this case a jury may draw different conclusions over whether the motel was compelled to have locks, security personnel or television monitoring equipment in the entranceway to the separated structure, even though the affidavits indicate the police have been sparingly called because of past security problems. It is conceivable that a jury may conclude these precautions were necessary since the presence of unauthorized persons in the separated building cannot be discovered from the lobby desk. *Brewer v. Roosevelt Motor Lodge*, Me., 295 A.2d 647 (1972) involved a hotel guest who was raped and robbed by men entering her room through an open screened window. She alleged the hotel was negligent and that jury questions were raised as to the following:

> ... the defendant's failure to provide locking devices on the screens of its motel rooms or bars on the windows, to fence off its establishment from easy access by members of the general public, to install the most modern television monitoring system inside the hallways of the motel as well as on the outside of the complex, to maintain guards on the adjacent grounds, or in the alternative, its omission to give notice to its patrons of these alleged security inadequacies, . . . *Id.* 295 A.2d at 651
>
> The *Brewer* court affirmed the verdict in the hotel's favor noting that the hotel's security omissions were not causal of her attack, since the entry of the assailants through an open window could have been prevented by the victim if she had used the safety latch provided on the window. Thus, the attack and illegal entry could not be foreseen or anticipated by an innkeeper exercising reasonable (ordinary) care. However, in the present case, the assault and robbery could have been prevented had the intruders been denied access to the motel's hallways, or observed in the process of entering the separated motel building. The presence of security personnel, outside door locks or television monitoring equipment, we believe, would certainly discourage criminal activity within the motel.
>
> We do not agree with the trial judge that the "fortuitous presence" of the Wauwatosa police, as a matter of law, supplants the causal relation between the absence of other security measures and the plaintiff's assault. A hotel's duty to provide reasonable security requires that preventative safety measures must be taken under certain circumstances. The police were present before and during the attack, yet this did not prevent the occurrence. This fact necessarily raises a triable issue regarding whether the fortuitous presence of the police in plain clothes and unmarked cars was the most effective security alternative commensurate with the size of the area to be protected. A jury may consider it more persuasive that security personnel in uniform patrolling the motel premises would have discouraged the assailants.
>
> * * *
>
> The proof at trial may very well establish that the lower court's decision was correct. The issues in this case were sufficiently complex to raise reasonable doubts of uncertainty and a jury should have been given an opportunity to return a verdict. Hotel liability cases requiring a plaintiff to prove the innkeeper's failure to exercise ordinary care commensurate with the circumstances are difficult cases which will present our trial courts with many matters of complex factual proof that usually cannot be decided on the basis of affidavits in support of summary judgment.
>
> Judgment reversed and cause remanded for proceedings consistent with this opinion.

Fortney v. Hotel Rancroft, Inc.
Phillips Petroleum Co. v. Dorn

The next two cases bear an interesting relationship to each other. Both deal with the duty of care owed by innkeepers to guests assaulted in their own rooms. In *Fortney v. Hotel Rancroft*, the Illinois Appellate Court initially called for a "very high degree of care" to be exercised. After receiving Hotel Rancroft's petition for rehearing claiming that the duty of care required by the Court was too high, the

Court changed its requirement from "a very high" to "a high" degree of care, though it called these relative terms. A Florida trial court in *Phillips Petroleum Co. v. Dorn* relied on *Fortney* for its terminology in instructing the jury that the hotel was under a duty to exercise a high degree of care to protect its guests and was reversed on appeal for that reason. The appellate court in *Phillips* saw *Fortney* as demanding a higher degree of care than is required by law.

Fortney v. Hotel Rancroft, Inc.
5 Ill. App. 2d 327 (1955), 125 N.E. 2d 544

FEINBERG, Justice.

Plaintiff sues to recover for injuries, resulting from an assault upon him while he was a guest of the defendant hotel. There was a jury trial, and at the close of the plaintiff's case, no defense being offered, defendants' motion to direct a verdict was sustained. The jury returned a verdict of not guilty, and judgment was entered upon the verdict. To reverse this judgment, plaintiff appeals.

The evidence discloses that defendants owned and operated the Hotel Rancroft in Chicago, to which the general public was invited as guests. Plaintiff admittedly was a guest of the hotel and had occupied room 404 on the fourth floor of the hotel for approximately eight years prior to the occurrence in question. The entrance to the hotel is from Randolph Street. Leading from the entrance is a long, narrow lobby to the elevators, the staircase and the hotel clerk's office and desk. The desk is located at the west wall. Three elevators leading to the upper floors are at the east wall, opposite the clerk's desk. Immediately to the south of the clerk's desk is the stairway leading to the upper floors of the hotel.

The only entrance to plaintiff's room was through a door, which had a Yale lock. The key to his room was issued to him when he became a guest of the hotel and bore an identification tag marked "Hotel Rancroft." He was directed by the management to leave the key at the desk with the clerk whenever he left the hotel. He always followed the direction, never leaving the hotel without turning the key in at the desk, even if he only went out for a newspaper.

On the night of the occurrence, James Quinn was on duty at the clerk's desk, apparently in charge of the hotel during his hours of duty. He took charge of the guests' keys left at the desk, took care of the telephone and ran the elevators.

On Sunday, February 19, 1950, plaintiff left the hotel around midnight. He was taken down in one of the elevators operated by Quinn. On leaving his room, he pulled the door shut and heard the tumbler click, and the door was locked. He left the key with Quinn at the desk on the lobby floor and went to the tavern next door. Nothing unusual occurred during his stay at the tavern. He left there and visited another tavern on North Clark Street. He returned to the hotel, arriving there at approximately 4:00 o'clock in the morning. During the entire evening, he testified, he had not engaged in any arguments or fights with anybody and was not intoxicated. Arriving at the hotel, he entered the lobby, and the only person present was Quinn. He was behind the desk. Quinn gave him his key and took plaintiff in the elevator to the fourth floor. Upon arriving at his room, plaintiff unlocked the door and entered the room. All of the lights were off, and he reached around the side of the room to turn the switch for the ceiling lights. Upon turning on the lights, he took off his coat and hat and hung them in the closet. He turned toward the bed, and as he did, someone appeared to step out of the bathroom and hit him across the side of the face, knocking him unconscious. He did not regain consciousness until Tuesday afternoon, when he found himself lying across the bed. The houseman and maid were bathing his face. They remained with him approximately an hour. On Wednesday following the attack, blood was observed on the north wall of the room at the right-hand side of the bed and on the bedclothes.

Plaintiff remained in his room all day Wednesday. He telephoned the desk clerk on duty that he was in need of a doctor. He was advised that a doctor had been called, but no medical assistance arrived until Thursday afternoon about 3:00 o'clock. The doctor was accompanied by defendant Rubenstein. He was advised by the doctor to go to Roosevelt Hospital and went there in a cab. He was examined there Thursday afternoon, and at the suggestion of the attending doctor, Dr. Udell, an eye specialist, was called in for consultation. They administered shots of penicillin to plaintiff. Sometime thereafter his left eye was removed, due to the injury to the eye resulting from the assault. He remained at the hospital seventeen days.

The relationship of innkeeper and guest imposed a duty upon the defendants to use a "very high degree of care" to secure the safety of the guest. [citations omitted] In Vol. 43, C.J.S., Innkeepers, §22, p. 1175, it is stated:

> The innkeeper must protect his guest, while in the inn, against injury at the hands of third persons whether they are guests or strangers, where it is within his power or that of his servants to do so.

The ruling of the court in directing a verdict for the defendants presents to us the question whether the evidence, and every reasonable inference which can be drawn from it, tends to prove the charge of negligence in the complaint. If it does, then the court was in error in directing a verdict.

We think that the circumstances disclosed by the evidence called for some explanation from the defendants as to how the stranger, who assaulted plaintiff, could gain entrance to plaintiff's room at the early hour of the morning in question without a key; or how it was possible for the stranger to reach the fourth floor of the hotel, whether by use of the elevator or staircase, without being noticed by the night clerk in charge of the desk. There was no such explanation forthcoming, since no evidence was offered by the defendants.

In the absence of such explanation, we think the evidence presents two reasonable inferences: the first, that the stranger who assaulted plaintiff was entrusted with a key to plaintiff's room; or, secondly, the key, where usually kept at the night clerk's desk, was left unguarded and thereby made accessible to a stranger. The facts we have detailed and the reasonable inferences we are forced to draw from them, in our opinion, establish prima facie, a breach of defendants' duty, and entitle plaintiff to a jury's determination of the facts. Directing a verdict for the defendants in the instant case denied to plaintiff the constitutional right of trial by jury. [citations omitted]

Defendants rely on *Walden v. Chelsea Hotel Co.*, 337 Ill.App. 292, 85 N.E.2d 861 (Abst.). That case and others cited by defendants are not applicable. In the Walden case an employee, entrusted with a key to perform his usual duties as a porter, invaded the guest's room with use of his key, when he was off duty, and assaulted her. He was not then in the discharge of any duty entrusted to him. There was no showing that defendant was negligent in hiring the employee or was aware that he was an immoral character. The factual distinction is obvious.

* * *

The judgment is reversed and the cause remanded for a new trial.
Reversed and remanded.
KILEY, P.J., and LEWE, J., concur.

Upon Petition for Rehearing:
FEINBERG, Justice.
Defendants, in their petition for rehearing, contend that our holding, that the circumstances in the instant case imposed upon defendant as an innkeeper the duty to use a "'very high degree of care'", went beyond the rule established by the cases in Illinois and elsewhere. They contend that the only duty an innkeeper owes to his guest is to use ordinary care for the safety of the guest. Defendants rely upon [several cases (citations omitted)] which support the rule of "ordinary or reasonable care."

* * *

None of the cases relied upon by defendants present the special circumstances present in the instant case. Whether the rule of duty requires a "very high degree of care" or a "high degree of care," we do not regard as vital. They are relative terms.

We have concluded to modify the statement in our opinion as to the degree of care required, and hold the defendants in the instant case to the exercise of a high degree of care. We think that the application of such a rule of duty is warranted in the instant case, under the special circumstances, as a necessary protection for a guest. A guest, who is either asleep in his room or about to enter his room, should not be subjected to the risk of an assault by a stranger. A guest has a right to rely upon the innkeeper doing all within his power to avoid or prevent such an assault, and to that end should be required to exercise a high degree of care. This rule of duty finds support in the statement in 43 C.J.S. Innkeepers, §22, p. 1175, and cases therein cited, quoted in our opinion.

The petition for rehearing is therefore denied.
KILEY, P.J., and LEWE, J., concur.

Phillips Petroleum Company of Bartlesville, Oklahoma v. Dorn
292 So.2d 429 (Fla. App. D4, 1974)

DOWNEY, Judge.
Appellant, Phillips Petroleum Company of Bartlesville, Oklahoma, is the owner and operator of a hotel in Fort Lauderdale, Florida, known as "Pier 66," and appellees, Shirley Dorn and Philip Dorn, her husband, were registered guests therein. Immediately after returning to their room one evening they were set upon by three men who had somehow gained entrance to their room. Mrs. Dorn refused to take the situation lying down and was beaten up for her efforts. The intruders took a small amount of jewelry and cash, bound and gagged the appellees and departed.

Appellees' complaint charged appellant with negligence in failing to use reasonable care for the safety of its guests in that appellant (a) failed to provide adequate security personnel in the hotel to protect its guests, and (b) permitted unknown persons to have access to room keys. Appellant responded with a general denial and the defense of contributory negligence.

Appellees requested the court to instruct the jury that appellant was required to exercise a high degree of care for the protection of its guests. Appellant objected to such an instruction, arguing that the appellees were business invitees, to whom the duty owed was reasonable care. The court overruled the objection, and after instructing the jury that negligence is the failure to use reasonable care and that reasonable care is that degree of care which a reasonably careful person would use under like circumstances, the court stated:

> However, a guest who is either asleep in his room or is about to enter his room should not be subjected to the risk of assault by a stranger. A guest has a right to rely upon the innkeeper doing all within his power to avoid or prevent such an assault, and to that end should be required to exercise a high degree of care.

The jury returned a verdict for the husband for $3,000, and "no award" for the wife. A final judgment was entered February 6, 1973, for the husband for $3,000 and costs. Appellant and the appellee wife each filed motions for new trial. On March 22, 1973, appellant's motion was denied but appellee wife's motion was granted. Appellant's notice of appeal filed on April 13, 1973, was directed solely to the aforesaid final judgment in favor of the husband.

* * *

With reference to the judgment for the husband, it is our view that the trial court's quoted instruction to the jury imposed upon appellant a standard of care more onerous than required by law, and that the judgment in favor of the husband must therefore be reversed.

A registered guest in a hotel is a business invitee to whom the hotel owes a duty of reasonable care for their safety. See cases cited at 17 Fla.Jur., Hotels, Restaurants, and Motels, §24; 40 Am.Jur.2d, Hotels, Motels, and Restaurants, §111. While most of the Florida cases announcing the innkeeper-guest standard of care involve a hotel's common rooms and other facilities which are available for the use of all hotel guests in common, we see no reason to require a higher degree of care for protection of a guest in the confines of the particular room assigned to him upon registration, than in the common areas. As pointed out by the Supreme Court in the recent case of *Wood v. Camp*, Fla.1973, 284 So.2d 691, persons entering the premises of another fall into one of three categories, trespassers, licensees, or invitees. Each category has a standard of care ascribed to it by law which constitutes a guideline by which to test the negligence vel non of the possessor of the land, and the standard of care owed to an occupant of a hotel room (an invitee) is reasonable care. 284 So.2d at 694.

The instruction under consideration was lifted verbatim from the Illinois case of *Fortney v. Hotel Rancroft*, 5 Ill.App.2d 327, 125 N.E.2d 544, 548 (1955). The authorities cited therein do not appear to justify the language used, and a subsequent Illinois case citing Fortney indicates the standard in that state is reasonable care. [citations omitted] A few other cases do refer to an innkeeper's duty to his guests as requiring a high degree of care, or a very high degree of care. See cases cited at 43 C.J.S. Innkeepers §22, page 1174, note 13. However, the majority view does not appear to support that extreme standard. [citations omitted]

Appellees' complaint alleges that appellant was negligent in failing to use reasonable care for their safety. Yet the instruction complained of advises the jury that a guest has a right to rely upon the innkeeper doing "all in his power" to avoid or prevent an assault by a stranger. Does this mean the jury could find that a large corporation like Phillips Petroleum Company was able to employ a guard for every room in the hotel and that it should have done so? Phillips no doubt has the power to do so. But as the authorities cited above indicate, it did not have the duty to do so since since such a requirement is clearly unreasonable. Thus, the instruction complained of misinformed the jury as to the standard of care which appellant was required to exercise in protecting the appellees, and therefore it constitutes reversible error. [citation omitted]

Finally, the court's instruction that a guest who is either asleep in his room or is about to enter his room should not be subjected to the risk of assault by a stranger could well leave the jury with the impression that the court felt appellant was in fact negligent in not preventing the assault from happening....

In all events, the court's instruction imposed upon appellant a higher duty than was required by the pleadings, the evidence, or more importantly, the law. This was error. [citation omitted]

Accordingly, the judgment for the appellee, Philip Dorn, is reversed and remanded for a new trial.

Reichenbach v. Days Inn of America, Inc.
Orlando Executive Park, Inc. v. P.D.R.

The next two cases, which were both decided by the Florida District Court of Appeal, present interesting—and, at least according to one judge involved in both cases, conflicting—opinions dealing with the closely related issues of duty of care and foreseeability. *Reichenbach v. Days Inn of America, Inc.* affirmed a summary judgment holding a motel *not* liable for an assault that took place in a parking lot on its premises. *Orlando Executive Park, Inc. v. P.D.R.* (which named the franchisor, Howard Johnson Company [HJ], in addition to the franchisee, Orlando Executive Park, Inc. [OEP]) affirmed a verdict holding the defendant innkeepers liable for an assault that took place in a hallway on their motel's premises.

In looking at the question of adequate security in terms of the foreseeability of the assaults, these cases, especially the dissenting and concurring opinions of Judge Cowart, point out some of the difficulties and differences of opinion involved in determining an innkeeper's duty of care and whether given events are foreseeable. Judge Cowart's rather narrow definition of foreseeability in *Orlando Executive Park*—under which he would require the plaintiff to show that precautions not taken by the innkeeper *would*, not *might*, have prevented the plaintiff's injury or loss—is fairly atypical. Some courts accept it, many others do not.

You will notice that *Orlando Executive Park* deals with several important issues, not merely reasonable care and foreseeability. It is a case that commands our attention for a number of reasons—its treatment of apparent agency, the judge's decision not to assess punitive damages, and the role of patrolling guards. Note the Court's approval of the statement from *Peters v. Holiday Inns, Inc.* dealing with the standard of ordinary care imposed upon innkeepers.

Reichenbach v. Days Inn of America, Inc.
401 So. 2d 1366 (Fla. Dist. Ct. App., 5th Dist. 1981),

petition denied, 412 So. 2d 469 (Fla. 1982)

UPCHURCH, Judge.

This is an appeal from a summary final judgment holding a motel not liable for an assault on one of its guests. We affirm.

Appellant, Alfred E. Reichenbach, was a guest at appellee's motel. At approximately 10:00 P.M., he parked his car in the parking lot and proceeded to step out of the car. At this point, an assailant came up and stated: "Don't do anything foolish." Reichenbach responded, "what" and was immediately shot twice. The assailant fled. The incident occurred so quickly that appellant could not identify or describe the assailant. A bus driver, the only eyewitness, was present with a charter group as a guest of the motel. Just before the shooting he had noticed a security guard making his rounds in the area where the event took place. Another employee was also patrolling. A few minutes after seeing the guard he saw a young, white male on the walkway. They greeted each other and he noticed "nothing unusual whatever" about the man and nothing to indicate he was armed. The bus driver walked upstairs onto the breezeway overlooking the parking lot. He then noticed appellant drive into the parking lot. As appellant got out of the car, the young man ran up to him, shot twice, ran to another car in the parking lot and left.

An innkeeper may be liable if he fails to take reasonable precautions to deter the type of criminal activity which resulted in a guest's injury. See *Orlando Executive Park v. P.D.R.*, Case No. 79-1743/T4-706 (Fla. 5th DCA July 15, 1981). In the case before us, there was no evidence that the innkeeper could have deterred or prevented appellant's injury by reasonable precautions which were not taken. There was no evidence that this incident was foreseeable or that the motel had any practical or reasonable method to protect its guest from or prevent this unprovoked hit and run attack.

AFFIRMED.

COBB, Judge, concurs.

COWART, Judge, concurs specially.

* * *

COWART, Judge, concurring specially:

I specially concur with the majority opinion but write to point up what I perceive as an aberration of existing tort principles.

A registered guest of a motel is entitled to receive from the innkeeper the degree of care owed a business invitee. [footnote omitted] Generally, an innkeeper stands in such a special relation to guests that the innkeeper has a duty to take reasonable action to protect them against unreasonable risks of physical harm and this duty can include the obligation to exercise control over the conduct of third persons and to prevent a third person from criminally assaulting a guest. [footnotes omitted]

The duty of an innkeeper to protect guests from the danger of a criminal assault by a third person presents an interesting problem relating to the concept of foreseeability. Appellants maintain that the location or particular character of a specific motel business, or past experience, should cause the innkeeper to reasonably anticipate that criminal assaults are likely to endanger the safety of guests.[4] It is contended that ability to generally foresee such danger creates a duty on the innkeeper to take affirmative action to deter persons intent on such wrongful conduct and to warn guests of prior criminal activity.[5] From these broad premises it is argued that a specific criminal assault on a guest by a third person was the proximate cause of, or resulted from, the failure of the innkeeper to meet this duty.

That motel guests will be criminally assaulted in the future is not only foreseeable —it is a certainty. This will occur not because the innkeepers do not protect guests but because crime will continue and citizens generally will continue to be criminally assaulted and motel guests will be no exception. However, the general foreseeability of the risk of a criminal assault upon a guest by a third person only permits such precautionary measures as will deter crime generally. Employing security guards, and installing closed-circuit video cameras and lights may *deter* crime generally but cannot reasonably be expected to *prevent* all crime or any one specific criminal act.[6] This is evident from the fact that, although society takes action to deter crime generally, law enforcement[7] rarely prevents a crime and then only when, by

---

[4]The motel in the instant case was undisputedly the location of prior criminal acts. Prior to this assault there had been one rape complaint, two armed robberies of motel guests in their rooms, two robberies of the gas station on the premises, and numerous instances of police response to complaints of unidentified activity in and around the motel. However, the innkeeper had no prior warning or notice that Dr. Reichenbach might be harmed or that the assailant might harm any guest.

[5]It is hard to envision just what type of warning would be appropriate. Must the prudent innkeeper maintain highway signs and placards at the registration desk warning potential customers that if they become guests of his motel they may be criminally assaulted by unknown third persons?

[6]To deter is to inhibit, to turn aside or to discourage and the success of efforts to deter depends on the person sought to be deterred. To prevent is to stop, to obstruct or to deprive another of the power to act regardless of his will or desire to act. The success of an effort to prevent depends largely on the opportunity, means and ability of the one who seeks to prevent an act or result. The difference in these terms illustrates the innkeeper's plight and the fallacy in the argument that a failure to deter criminal acts generally is evidence of the breach of a duty to prevent a threatened assault. Only law-abiding citizens and timid would-be offenders are deterred. Bold determined robbers, rapists, murderers, and other criminal assailants are not deterred and are rarely thwarted. As a practical matter their failures result from the inadequacy of their own abilities and efforts and not from the intervention of others. This unhappy truth should be obvious to all who are experienced in the criminal justice system, or who have contemplated the history of assassinations, or who observed Jack Ruby shoot Lee Harvey Oswald. Indeed, since the oral argument in this case, two staggering events have occurred. First, on March 30, 1981, a man attempted to assassinate President Ronald Reagan, possibly the most intensely protected individual in the United States. Barely a month and a half later, a similar assassination attempt was made on the life of Pope John Paul II. Although no one would contend these events resulted from the negligence of the property owner, it is interesting to note that President Reagan's assassination attempt occurred as he was exiting from a hotel, the entity involved in both this case and Orlando Executive Park v. P.D.R., Case No. 79-1743/T4-706 (Fla. 5th DCA July 15, 1981).

[7]It should also be noted that, in the performance of its duties, law enforcement has certain immunities and rights to use force that citizens do not have.

chance or by specific information relating to a threatened or planned crime, there is opportunity to take specific action to prevent a particular crime. Innkeepers should not be legally required to do that which organized society cannot do.[8] No reasonable standard of care should require one to be ever on guard, ever present, ready and able, to prevent an unforeseeable personal criminal attack upon another. [footnote omitted] Although crime is foreseeable, generally an innkeeper, as well as others, may, under ordinary circumstances, reasonably assume that third persons will not violate the criminal law and will not intentionally cause harm to guests. Since the innkeeper is not an insurer of the guest's safety and is not liable, strictly or otherwise, for the acts of third persons,[10] he is under no duty to exercise any care to warn or to take preventive action[11] until he knows, or has reason to believe, that a third person is acting, or is about to act, in a manner as will, or is likely to, cause harm to a guest. [footnote omitted] By their very nature assaults usually occur suddenly and without warning and without giving an opportunity to defend. Therefore, to prevent an assault by one person upon another requires an opportunity arising from some specific knowledge, notice or warning.[13]

---

[8]The Florida Crime Index released by the Florida Department of Law Enforcement on November 13, 1980, shows that violent assaultive crimes (murder, rape, robbery and aggravated assault) comprised 11.7 percent of all reported index offenses for the first nine months of 1980 and reflected a 28.9 percent increase over the same period in 1979. Certainly bank robbery is the one assaultive crime most easy to anticipate and to prevent, yet in the 10 years following the Bank Protection Act of 1968, bank robberies increased fourfold and last year reached 7,037 nationwide. Employees of motels, along with those of convenience stores and service stations, are themselves prime victims of robberies and other assaults.

[10]Perspective requires one to bear constantly in mind that the assaultive act of the criminal assailant is the legal efficient, or proximate, cause of a victim's injuries. This is not a case where the assailant's acts and the innkeeper's acts join together to contribute to a guest's injuries. We are here only concerned with an innkeeper's duty to take steps to prevent an injury which he in no way affirmatively causes or to which he contributes.

[11]The argument will be made that the failure to impose liability on the innkeeper under the facts of this case will result in motels foregoing all precautions to protect their guests. I do not believe this will result. There is an economic incentive to provide general deterrent measures. With a growing concern for crime, a traveler will choose the safest accommodations available. In an industry peculiarly dependent upon goodwill, it is in an innkeeper's own interest to employ general deterrent measures to enhance its good name and reputation. Secondly, the innkeeper must be reasonably prepared to meet his duty to prevent assaults on guests when he has an adequate opportunity and it is reasonably possible for him to do so.

[13]Generally, criminal acts have been found foreseeable, creating a duty to prevent them, only when a defendant with a duty knew or should have known that a specific person was likely to assault someone. [citations omitted] *Cf. Relyea* v. *State*, 385 So.2d 1378 (Fla. 4th DCA 1980) (no liability was found when the wrongdoers were complete strangers to the landowner and to the victims, and where the incident occurred precipitously). In the absence of actual or constructive knowledge of the particular risk and a reasonable opportunity to protect from that harm by preventing the act, duties have not been imposed. [citations omitted] See also *Worth* v. *Stahl*, No. 79-1505, 79-1841, (Fla. 4th DCA Sept. 24, 1980)[1980 F.L.W. 1804](holding that a tavernkeeper having no knowledge of the violent character of the patron who assaulted another patron had no duty to take action because he had inadequate notice of the need and an inadequate opportunity to act to prevent the harm).

Additionally, even where an innkeeper has reason to believe a third person is likely to assault a guest, an innkeeper's duty should be coextensive with his ability to meet that duty. This means the innkeeper should not be held responsible for an assault by a third party on a guest unless the innkeeper, acting reasonably, could have feasibly prevented it. There are severe limitations on the capability of anyone to prevent an assault on another person by a third party. First, it is in the nature of things that mobile or free moving objects are difficult to protect and secure. It is for this reason that more vehicles are stolen than other less mobile chattels and that valuable objects are kept in vaults, safety boxes and other various stationary places. Motel guests, like other free citizens, go and come at their pleasure. Also, persons intent on making a criminal assault, especially those not acting on impulse or merely upon an opportunity or perceived necessity, have the advantage of surprise and select the time, place, method and circumstances, rarely giving the victim, the police or an innkeeper an opportunity to prevent that particular assault.[14] Additionally, in earlier times innkeepers were required to accept the public generally but could with some impunity reject or eject persons considered disorderly, intoxicated, dangerous or undesirable. However, now in Florida, motels are not entirely free to exclude guests [footnote omitted] or persons who visit guests[16] or other members of the public who come to use facilities and services which are customarily available to the public. [footnote omitted] Thus, the character of a motel is essentially that of a public place and innkeepers lack the usual possessor's peculiar ability to exercise control over third persons using his property. This "open door policy" extends to all public areas and, while it impairs security, it is a necessary consequence of a free society and of motels and other public and semi-public places. Considering these circumstances, even when there is reason to be apprehensive of potential risk of harm to guests from an assault by a particular individual, the innkeeper must act reasonably and lawfully toward everyone, including third persons who may appear to be suspicious. Unless the circumstances not only give reasonable opportunity but also demand immediate action, when criminal acts are threatened the reasonable prudent present-day innkeeper can normally only call the police.[18]

Lastly, even if the innkeeper realizes, or should realize, that an assault is probable and circumstances do not permit police to be summoned, yet give the innkeeper a reasonable opportunity to act, the innkeeper should have a reasonable ability and method to prevent the assault before he is held liable for not doing so. An innkeeper who personally resorts to physical force risks harm to himself and legal consequences in the form of compensation and punitive damages. Even when physical force is justified, the innkeeper and his employees may not be able to physically restrain a strong,

---

[14]Man's best efforts to control a potential assailant are impotent. On July 16, 1980, Richard Sherman "Bush Ax" Williams, a Florida State Prison inmate, fatally stabbed a fellow inmate through the bars of his cell. Since then, Thomas Knight, a death row inmate, fatally stabbed his prison guard, Richard Burke.

[16]"[B]y the very nature of the business, the operator of the hotel is bound to anticipate that a registered guest is apt to have business and social callers." *Steinberg v. Irwin Operating Co.*, 90 So.2d 460, 461 (Fla. 1956).

[18]This reasonable and proper action creates police reports suggesting criminal activity in the area which, as here, is used as evidence against the innkeeper.

violent or dangerous third person. What if, as here, the assailant is armed? An unarmed innkeeper is no match for an armed assailant. If the innkeeper had been standing at alert beside Dr. Reichenbach when this assault with a firearm occurred, as a practical matter exactly what could the innkeeper have done to have protected his guest? There are no limitations on the assailant, but the innkeeper's right to arm himself is severely limited, and there is great penalty if the legal restrictions are disregarded. [footnotes omitted]

This is not a case where an innkeeper[21] or an employee or other person within the control of the innkeeper [footnote omitted] commits an assault on a guest. Nor does this case involve an innkeeper who neglected to take action after learning of the potential need of a particular guest for protection from some threatened harm. [footnote omitted] Nor does this case involve a cause of action based on express or implied contract. [footnote omitted] Neither does this case involve locking devices or other security measures relating to a private room which not only deter crime but, under some circumstances, might be capable of physically preventing access by members of the public generally, thereby preventing an assault. [footnote omitted] This case involves an alleged neglect of a duty of the innkeeper to prevent a third person from doing intentional harm to a guest in a public area where there was only general knowledge of the possibility of criminal assault but nothing is claimed to have given the innkeeper foresight that a particular person might assault some guest or that a particular guest might be assaulted by someone.

In order for an innkeeper to be liable for breach of his duty to take affirmative action to protect guests from the unlawful assaults of third parties, I would require that specific facts be alleged and proved that would put a reasonable innkeeper on notice that a particular person was likely to assault some guest or that a particular guest was likely to be assaulted by some assailant and, also, specific facts would be required to detail circumstances that afforded the innkeeper a reasonable and feasible opportunity and ability to prevent the particular attack. I would hold here that an innkeeper is not responsible to a guest for a sudden violent criminal assault by a third person which occurred in a public area without warning and under circumstances giving the innkeeper no reason to anticipate the particular assault, no opportunity to act and no reasonable way to prevent it.

---

[21] Of course in such event the innkeeper would be liable not for negligence but for the intentional tort.

Orlando Executive Park, Inc. v. P.D.R.
402 So. 2d 442 (Fla. Dist. Ct. App. 1981)

ORFINGER, Judge.

In an action for damages brought by appellee against the appellants, Orlando Executive Park, Inc. (OEP), and Howard Johnson Company (HJ), the jury returned a verdict for the appellee in the amount of $750,000 as compensatory damages against both defendants jointly, and awarded punitive damages in the amount of $500,000 against each defendant separately. Upon defendants' post-trial motions for directed verdict, the trial judge directed verdicts in favor of the defendants on the punitive damage claims, but denied a motion for new trial, remittitur or directed verdict on the claim for compensatory damages. The defendants have appealed the final judgment for compensatory damages, and the plaintiff has cross-appealed the order directing verdict on the punitive damage claim.

The factual circumstances giving rise to this litigation, viewed in the light most favorable to the plaintiff, follow: Plaintiff, a 33 year-old married woman, and the mother of a small child, was employed as a supervisor for a restaurant chain. Her duties required that she travel occasionally to Orlando and because of the distance from her home, she stayed overnight in the Orlando area on those occasions.

On October 22, 1975, she was in Orlando performing the duties of her employment. She telephoned the Howard Johnson's Motor Lodge involved in this action at approximately 9:30 P.M. and made a room reservation.[1] Approximately ten minutes later she left the restaurant and drove directly to the motor lodge. When she arrived, she signed the registration form which had already been filled out by the desk clerk and was directed to her room which was located on the ground level in building "A", the first building behind the registration office. Plaintiff parked her car, went to her room and left her suitcase there. She then went back to her car to get some papers and when starting back to her room, she noticed a man standing in a walkway behind the registration office. Having reentered the building and while proceeding back along the interior hallway to her room, she was accosted by the man she had seen behind the registration office, who struck her very hard in the throat and on the back of her neck and then choked her until she became unconscious. When consciousness returned, plaintiff found herself lying on the floor of the hallway with her assailant sitting on top of her, grabbing her throat. Plaintiff was physically unable to speak and lapsed into an unconscious or semi-conscious state. Her assailant stripped her jewelry from her and then dragged her down the hallway to a place beneath a secluded stairwell, where he kicked her and brutally forced her to perform an unnatural sex act. He then disappeared in the night and has never been identified.

Plaintiff's action for damages was based on her claim that defendants owed her the legal duty to exercise reasonable care for her safety while she was a guest on the premises. And she alleged that this duty had been breached by, [among other things] allowing the building to remain open and available to anyone who cared to enter, by failing to have adequate security on the premises either on the night in question or prior thereto so as to deter criminal activity against guests which had occurred before and which could foreseeably occur again, failing to install TV monitoring equipment in the public areas of the motel to deter criminal activity, failing to establish and enforce standards of operation at the lodge which would protect guests from physical attack and theft of property, and failure to warn plaintiff that there had been prior criminal activity on the premises and that such activity would or might constitute a threat to her safety on the premises.

There was evidence submitted tending to show serious physical and psychological injury as a result of this assault which was susceptible of the conclusion that within a year following the assault, plaintiff lost her job because of memory lapses,

---

[1] She had stayed at this same motor lodge approximately one week earlier. Arrangements had been made for the billing of her room charges directly to her employer.

mental confusion and inability to tolerate and communicate with people. There was evidence from which the jury could conclude that this injury was permanent and that she would require expensive long-term medical and psychiatric treatment, and that she had suffered a great loss in her earning capacity.

The motor lodge is a part of a large complex known as "Howard Johnson's Plaza" located just off Interstate 4. The complex includes a Howard Johnson's Restaurant, the Howard Johnson's Motor Lodge, a pub, an adult theater, and five office buildings. The motor lodge contains approximately three hundred guest rooms in six separate buildings, plus a registration office, and it was owned and operated by defendant Orlando Executive Park, Inc., under a license agreement with the parent company, Howard Johnson Company. The restaurant, the pub and the adult theater on the property were operated by the defendant, Howard Johnson Company. Approximately 75% of the Howard Johnson motor lodges throughout the country are owned and operated by licensees. The Howard Johnson Company never established any standards or procedures to be followed by licensees relating to the matter of guest security, although it has established such procedures for the lodges which it owns and operates. Each licensee handled that problem as it deemed best.

There was no regular security force at the motor lodge, nor were there other security devices such as TV monitors in hallways or other common areas. One security guard was employed from time to time, on a sporadic basis. For the six-month period prior to the incident in question, management of the motor lodge was aware of approximately thirty criminal incidents occurring on the premises. While most of these involved burglary, some of them involved direct attacks upon the guests. Following one of the attacks, approximately ten weeks prior to the incident in question, the motor lodge owners had hired a full-time security guard, but he was terminated a short time later. Anticipating high occupancy, one security guard had been employed for the evening in question commencing at 10:00 P.M. While it is not clear whether the attack occurred during the period this guard was on duty, the jury could have concluded that he was not on duty at the time, although he was on the premises becoming familiar with the layout because he had never been on the property before. Additionally, the evidence indicated that the guard had been employed to patrol the parking areas, and not the motor lodge buildings. The security service which provided the guards from time to time had recommended the employment of two to three guards on a full-time basis. Plaintiff's security expert testified that three guards on staggered shifts would be necessary to deter criminal activity, although he agreed that there were no industry standards for security guards and that it was impossible to say that the assault would not have occurred if three guards had been on the premises. He did, however, testify that in his opinion, a proper security force would serve as a deterrent to this type of activity and the chance of this happening would be slight.

I. LIABILITY OF ORLANDO EXECUTIVE PARK, INC.

It seems clear that in Florida registered guests in a hotel or motel are business invitees to whom the hotel or motel owes a duty of reasonable care for their safety. [citation omitted] While recognizing this principle and conceding this duty, appellants say, nevertheless, that there is no evidence of a breach of their duty, since the injury to appellee was caused by the criminal act of a stranger, thus acting as an intervening efficient cause for which they are not responsible.

The evidence clearly shows numerous criminal activities on the premises in the six-month period immediately prior to this occurrence.[2] The testimony of a security expert produced by plaintiff indicated adequate security at this motor lodge required the presence of at least three full-time security guards. Thus the question becomes one of foreseeability. Could a jury, under the facts of this case, reasonably conclude that the absence of adequate security would lead to the robbery and attack here?[3] Such is ordinarily a question for the jury. [citation omitted]

Several courts in similar or analogous situations have discussed the questions raised here. In *Holley v. Mt. Zion Terrace Apartments, Inc.*, 382 So. 2d 98 (Fla. 3d DCA 1980), the plaintiff's decedent was raped and murdered while a tenant in defendant's apartment complex. The crime was committed by an intruder, believed to be a co-tenant. The basis of plaintiff's action against the landlord was it alleged negligent failure to provide reasonable security measures in the building's common areas. There, as here, the defendants argued that they were not responsible for the results of criminal conduct of third persons. In reversing a summary judgment for the defendant, the court said:

> Particularly in view of the evidence concerning the past record, and therefore the future foreseeability of violent crime at its premises, a jury could properly find that a discharge of the landlord's duty to keep the common areas reasonably safe required that a guard or other security measures be provided at the complex, in order to prevent just such a tragic incident as the one involved in this case.

* * *

> Under our system, it is peculiarly a jury function to determine what precautions are reasonably required in the exercise of a particular duty of due care.

* * *

> We first reject, as entirely fallacious, the defendant's claim that the brutal and deliberate act of the rapist-murderer constituted an "independent intervening cause" which served to insulate it from liability. It is well-established that if the reasonable possibility of the intervention, criminal or otherwise, of a third party is the avoidable risk of harm which itself causes one to be deemed negligent, the occurrence of that very conduct cannot be a superseding cause of a subsequent misadventure. As said in *Restatement (Second) of Torts*, §449 (1965):

---

[2] Although aware of a formal request by plaintiff's attorneys to produce records of criminal incidents pre-dating this six-month period, after the trial court ordered production of these records, defendant's agent admitted that she had ordered them to be destroyed. The court instructed the jury that they could infer from this action that the evidence suppressed would have been unfavorable to the party who destroyed it. While appellants appeal the giving of this instruction, we do not consider this point because it was not properly preserved for review.

[3] This question, one of causation, should be distinguished from a plaintiff's initial burden of demonstrating a duty to take reasonable measures against foreseeable criminal activity. If the criminal activity is not foreseeable, no duty arises. [citation omitted] Defendants in this case stipulated that they were on notice of criminal activity, admitting the duty to take reasonable measures against this type of attack.

> If the likelihood that a third person may act in a particular manner is the hazard or one of the hazards which makes the actor negligent, such an act whether innocent, negligent, intentionally tortious, or *criminal* does not prevent the actor from being liable for harm caused thereby. (emphasis supplied.)
>
> See also, W. Prosser, Torts, supra, §44, at 275, nn. 20-21. The application of this principle to the case at bar is obvious. *Since Mt. Zion is liable, if at all, for only failing to protect its tenant from a criminal attack, it cannot escape responsibility because the attack has actually taken place.* (emphasis supplied).

Id. at 101. In a suit for damages arising out of a robbery and rape in a hotel room, the court in *Nordmann v. National Hotel Company*, 425 F.2d 1103 (5th Cir. 1970), summarized its holding thusly:

> The evidence was ample to support the jury's verdict. For its twelve hundred rooms, and with a large ball in progress, the hotel had on duty at the time of the robbery and assault only one security officer, one room clerk and one bell boy. The jury could, with reason, determine that defendants had failed to perform their general duty to protect their guests.

Id. at 1107.

Appellant continues, however, with its argument that there was no evidence that security was inadequate or more to the point, that any specific quantity of security guards or other measures would have prevented this robbery and attack. They say that since there are no standards for security in the motel industry, there is no way for a jury to determine the reasonableness (or unreasonableness) of any particular security measure. The absence of industry standards does not insulate the defendants from liability when there is credible evidence presented to the jury pointing to measures reasonably available to deter incidents of this kind, against which the jury can judge the reasonableness of the measures taken *in this case*.

Obviously, a six-unit, one building "Mom and Pop" motel will not have the same security problems as a large highrise thousand room hotel, or [as] a three hundred room motor lodge spread out over six buildings. Each presents a peculiar security problem of its own. How the means necessary to fulfill the duty of care varies with the peculiar circumstances of each case is explained by the Wisconsin Supreme Court in *Peters v. Holiday Inns, Inc.*, 89 Wis.2d 115, 278 N.W. 2d 208 (1979) in the following language which we approve:

> Thus, in meeting its standard of ordinary care a hotel must provide security commensurate with the facts and circumstances that are or should be apparent to the ordinarily prudent person. In other words, an innkeeper's standard of care in providing security will vary according to the particular circumstances and location of the hotel.
>
> Accordingly, as the degree of care that an innkeeper must exercise will vary in relation to the attendant circumstances, relevant factors in deciding whether a hotel has exercised ordinary care in providing adequate security are: industry standards, the community's crime rate, the extent of assaultive or criminal activity in the area or in similar business enterprises, the presence of suspicious persons, and the peculiar security problems posed by the hotel's design. A hotel's liability depends upon the danger to be apprehended and the presence or absence of security measures designed to meet the danger. The particular circumstances may require one or more of the following safety measures: a security force, closed-circuit television surveillance, dead bolt and chain locks on the individual rooms as well as security doors on hotel entranceways removed from the lobby area.

Id. at 212. [citation omitted]

The reference to these standards is not to be interpreted as an opinion of this court that the absence of any of the mentioned security measures will result in a finding of liability of the innkeeper, because this is not the test. We only intend to say that the jury may consider competent evidence of the need or effect of any of these security measures or combination thereof in the context of the circumstances and evidence before it, in determining whether the innkeeper has met his duty of providing his guest with reasonable protection for his safety.

Here, the jury had the right to consider the size and layout of the complex, its various accessory uses and the apparent ease of entrance into the motel buildings, and could have concluded that these factors required *some* security measures. They could also conclude from the evidence that the type of activity within the complex increased the security risk and that no security was provided at the time of this attack.

And while appellant suggests plaintiff was required to show the attack would have been prevented had reasonable measures been taken, this is not the test. Causation, like any other element of plaintiff's case, need not be demonstrated by conclusive proof:

> and it is enough the (plaintiff) introduces evidence from which reasonable men may conclude that it is more probable that the event was caused by the defendant, than that it was not. The fact of causation is incapable of mathematical proof, since no man can say with absolute certainty what would have occurred if the defendant had acted otherwise.

W. Prosser, *Law of Torts*, §41 at 242 (4th Ed. 1977). Plaintiff adduced evidence that reasonable measures were not taken. Expert testimony, as well as reasonable inferences from the suggested measures, allowed a conclusion that the chance of this attack was "slight" had reasonable measures been taken. Thus the question of whether defendant's negligence was the proximate cause of plaintiff's injury was properly a jury question. [citations omitted]

Plaintiff also proved that the area under the stairwell where she was dragged was dark and secluded and was in itself a security hazard which should have been boarded up as had other similar stairwells in the motel. OEP management actively discouraged criminal investigations by sheriff's deputies, minimizing any deterrent effect they may have had. Thus, the totality of the circumstances presented a jury question regarding causation. See *Rosier v. Gainesville Inns Assoc. Ltd.*[4] It cannot be said that there was a complete absence of probative facts to support the jury's conclusion. [citation omitted]

Appellants rely on cases such as *Worth v. Stahl*, 1980 FLW 1804 (Fla. 4th DCA, September 24, 1980), *Burnsed v. ABC Liquors, Inc.*, 1980 FLW 1986 (Fla. 1st DCA October 15, 1980) and *Relyea v. State* 385 So.2d 1378 (Fla. 4th DCA 1980), but they are all

---

[4]In agreeing that a jury question was presented on the security issue, the court re-stated the traditional rule on intervening cause:

"While the question of proximate cause in a negligence action is one for the court where there is an active and efficient intervening cause, [citation omitted], still if such intervening cause is either foreseeable or might reasonably have been foreseen by the defendant, his negligence may be considered the proximate cause of the injury notwithstanding the intervening cause."

347 So.2d at 1102

distinguishable. In *Worth*, unlike the case [now under consideration], there was no proof that the violent acts were foreseeable. *Burnsed* was a [very brief] decision with no opinion. The dissent gives us a clue as to the facts, but no insight into the reasons for the majority opinion. From the facts in the dissent, the case could very well have turned on the issue of foreseeability and proximate cause. Likewise, *Relyea* turned on the absence of proof that any prior, similar criminal acts had ever occurred on the campus so as to create an issue as to the foreseeability of the attack in question. Thus, these cases are all inapposite.

Appellants next contend that the verdict for compensatory damages is excessive and that the trial court erred in not granting its motion for remittitur. Where the trial court denies a motion for remittitur, this strengthens the presumption of correctness of the jury verdict and the trial court can be reversed on appeal only for an abuse of discretion. [citation omitted] When ordering a remittitur, the amount of excess must be clearly determinable from facts in the record, [citation omitted] or there must be an apparently high verdict coupled with extrinsic evidence of improper influence. [citation omitted] Here, there was evidence that plaintiff's future medical expenses would be incurred, there was testimony that plaintiff's future loss of earnings could be in excess of $600,000, which, coupled with evidence of the injury itself and plaintiff's pain and mental anguish, supports the jury's verdict. There is no showing that the award exceeds the maximum limit of the reasonable range within which a jury may operate. [citation omitted]

II. LIABILITY OF HOWARD JOHNSON COMPANY

Appellant Howard Johnson Company contends that the trial court erred in not granting its motion for directed verdict. Appellee proceeded against this appellant on the theory of apparent agency. Appellant argues strongly that the evidence fails to show any control or right of control by HJ over the operation of the motel, but while this argument may be relevant to a claim of *actual* agency, it has no relevance to the theory of *apparent* agency. Appellee sought damages against HJ solely on the apparent agency doctrine, and the jury was so instructed.

The doctrine of apparent agency, sometimes referred to as agency by estoppel, consists of three primary elements: (1) a representation by the principal; (2) reliance on that representation by a third person; and (3) a change of position by the third person in reliance upon such representation to his detriment. The principal is estopped to deny the authority of agent, because he had permitted the appearance of authority in the agent and thereby justified the third party in relying on that appearance of authority as though it were actually conferred upon the agent. [citation omitted][5] Put another way,

> Where a principal has, by his voluntary act, placed an agent in such a situation that a person of ordinary prudence, conversant with business usages and the nature of the particular business, is justified in presuming that such agent has authority to perform a particular act, and therefore deals with the agent, the principal is estopped, as against such third person, from denying the agent's authority.

---

[5] It is important to note that the doctrine rests on appearances created by the principal rather than on appearances created by the agent. [citation omitted]

T. G. Bush Grocery Co. v. Conely, 61 Fla. 131, 55 So. 867, 869 (1911); *Hertz International, Ltd. v. Richardson*, 317 So.2d 824, 827, (Fla. 3d DCA 1975).

HJ attacks the verdict of the jury by arguing that (1) there was insufficient evidence of representations by it, and (2) there was insufficient evidence of reliance by plaintiff. We will address both issues.

Appellant asserts that the only representations of HJ to be considered are the sign announcing the lodge as a "Howard Johnson's," and the distinctive color scheme. Appellant correctly points out that gas station signs alone do not make a gas station operator a general agent of the oil company. [citation omitted] The reason for this is that it is common knowledge that gas station operators are independent contractors, and "these signs and emblems represent no more than notice to a motorist that a given company's products are being marketed at the station." [citations omitted] Thus, the "representation" made by service station signs is only that a certain kind of gasoline is sold, not that the operator is an agent for the oil company with respect to any standard of service,[6] car repair,[7] or maintenance of premises.[8] In *Cawthon [v. Phillips Petroleum Co.*, 124 So. 2d 517 (Fla. 2d DCA 1960)], Phillips' advertisements (for products sold at "Phillips" gasoline stations) did not subject Phillips to liability for a station operator's negligent brake repair, because

> There appeared in the advertisement no statement that mechanical or repair services were solicited or offered by the oil company to its employees or agents; neither did the advertisement indicate agency.

124 So.2d. at 521.

While OEP might not be HJ's agent for all purposes, the signs, national advertising, uniformity of building design and color schemes allow the public to assume that this and other similar motor lodges are under the same ownership.[9] A HJ official testified that it was the HJ marketing strategy to appear as a "chain that sells a product across the nation." Additionally, the license agreement between HJ and OEP clearly gives HJ the right to control the architectural design and the "standards of operation and service . . . and the licensee agrees at all times to conform to such standards."[10]

---

[6]*B.P. Oil Corp. v. Mabe*, 370 A.2d 554 (Md.App. 1977) (operator negligently fills radiator).

[7]*Crittendon v. State Oil Co.*, 22 N.E. 2d 561 (Ill.App. 1966) (signs might allow belief that "State Oil" products are sold, but do not warrant assumption that station operator was agent in repairing and driving plaintiff's car).

[8]*Apple v. Standard Oil, Div. of American Oil Co.*, 307 F. Supp. 107 (N.D. Cal. 1969) (American Oil not liable when station operator's dog bites plaintiff).

[9]Even in service station cases some courts have found the existence of apparent agency where the representations involved more than advertising the product being sold, as e.g., *Gizzi v. Texaco, Inc.*, 437 F.2d 308 (3d Cir. 1971), dealing with Texaco's "you can trust your car to the man who wears the star" slogan.

[10]The agreement also provides that in the event of termination, licensee will discontinue use of signs and other indicia of operation as a Howard Johnson Motor Lodge and will discontinue use of the color scheme and remove the cupola and all orange tile from the buildings or structures "effectively to distinguish the same from its former appearance as a designation of a 'Howard Johnson's Motor Lodge' . . ."

Florida has adopted section 267 of the *Restatement (Second) of Agency* (1958), which says:

> One who represents that another is his servant or other agent and thereby causes a third person justifiably to rely upon the skill of such apparent agent is subject to liability to the third person for harm caused by the lack of care or skill of one appearing to be a servant or other agent as if he were such.

[citation omitted]

There was sufficient evidence for the jury to reasonably conclude that HJ represented to the traveling public that it could expect a particular level of service at a Howard Johnson Motor Lodge. The uniformity of signs, design and color scheme easily leads the public to believe that each motor lodge is under common ownership or conforms to common standards, and the jury could find they are intended to do so.[11] [citations omitted]

On the question of reliance, the jury had a right to conclude that appellee believed exactly what appellant wanted her to believe, i.e., that she was dealing with Howard Johnson's, "a chain that sells a product across the nation." Appellee testified that when she realized her need for a room, she called the Howard Johnson Motor Lodge. She had stayed there once before. Thus, she was calling a specifically identified establishment, not just any motel. She also testified that she was not aware that any of the HJ motels were individually owned, but assumed "they were Howard Johnson's". While more could have been presented, we believe that this, coupled with the evidence of the extensive efforts of HJ to market a uniform product, presented an issue to the jury on the question of reliance which they obviously resolved in appellee's favor. In *Economy Cab v. Kirkland*, 127 Fla. 867, 174 So. 222 (1937), a passenger in a taxicab was injured and sued the company whose name was carried on the cab. The passenger had telephoned this company, and a cab bearing the colors and insignia of the company responded. The suit was defended on the ground that this taxicab, like some others, was in reality owned and operated by a third party, hence the company was not liable. Justice Terrell, in speaking for the court, said:

> Under such state of facts the law will presume as to the public generally and the plaintiff that defendant cab and driver were a common carrier for hire *and in the service of the company whose name it bore*. One of the first principles of hornbook law we were taught in the law school was that for every wrong the law provides a remedy. If the law is to be circumvented by litigants as proposed here, then we were taught a futile lesson. They should not be permitted to parade under a flag of truce to garner a profit and then raise the black flag when called on to make restitution for damage perpetrated. (emphasis added)

---

[11] A vice president of HJ testified:
Q. Well, do you consider the Howard Johnson name to be a valuable name?
A. Yes, we do.
Q. *Do you consider the name to imply* cleanliness and *safety* and all of those good things?
A. *Yes,* we do. (R-893). (emphasis supplied)

* * *

Third parties who happen to own a cab and use it in the name of the company at the call of the company and under the colors of the company will be treated as the company.

174 So. at 224. [citation omitted]

Appellant's remaining points on appeal have been considered and are without merit.

Appellee cross appeals the action of the trial court in granting appellant's motion to set aside the punitive damage award. The trial court found that the evidence and reasonable inferences therein, viewed in the light most favorable to appellee, were insufficient to support the award to punitive damages against either defendant. We do not find the conduct of defendants to be of such egregious nature as to support a punitive damage award. [citations omitted]

The judgment appealed from is AFFIRMED.
UPCHURCH, Judge, concurs.
COWART, Judge, dissents with opinion.

* * *

COWART, J., dissenting:

The majority opinion effectively imposes a form of strict liability upon landowners and business. It is axiomatic that a person's duty should not be greater than his ability to meet that duty. Security measures in businesses and homes may increase a potential assailant's perception of his risk of apprehension and thereby discourage or deter some persons *sometimes;* however, they do not, and cannot, *prevent* a particular assault made without warning by a determined assailant in an area commonly open to the public. Therefore, any duty of care should be likewise limited. By imposing liability for failing to take reasonable security precautions without requiring that the assault would have been (not *might* have been) prevented by taking those precautions, the majority has effectively eliminated any real requirement of proximate cause and foreseeability in actions of this type.

The majority opinion is applicable far beyond the facts of this case. Since *all* landowners owe a general duty of care to their invitees, the existence of prior criminal activity of an assaultive nature on their property, or in the area, under the majority view, makes a similar assault on every invitee reasonably foreseeable and thereby subjects every landowner to liability if "reasonable precautions" were not taken regardless of whether the precautions would have prevented the assault. Simple justice is for the assault victim to be paid; for the assailant to pay; and for the innkeeper to *not* have to pay. To hold landowners, lessees and franchisors liable for injuries which they did not have the opportunity or power to prevent in the hope that society generally will benefit from frantic but futile attempts to buy "security" to meet this impossible duty goes beyond mere fallacy and is both legally and morally wrong. See the special concurring opinion in *Reichenbach v. Days Inn, Inc.*, Nos. 80-300, 80-603 (Fla.

5th DCA July 15, 1981).[12]

---

[12] I find this case factually indistinguishable from the situation presented in *Reichenbach* where this court held precautions taken by the motel were as a matter of law sufficient to avoid liability. Both cases involve a motel's liability for the result of criminal conduct of an assaultive nature by unknown third persons; both motels had been the location of prior similar criminal activity, both motels had one security guard on the premises at the time of the assault and neither motel had taken any other significant security measures (i.e. TV monitors).

Matt et al. v. Days Inns of America, Inc.

The next case looks at foreseeability in relation to prior instances of criminal acts on the premises of the defendant, as well as the experience of other properties in the vicinity of the defendant at the Harts Field Airport in Atlanta, Georgia. In *Matt et al. v. Days Inns of America, Inc.*, the trial court granted Days Inns' motion for summary judgment. Upon appeal by plaintiff Matt, the Supreme Court of Georgia reversed the trial court's grant of summary judgment to Days Inns. While determining that the proprietor is not the insurer of the invitee's safety, the court did find "the proprietor had reason to anticipate a criminal act..."

Matt et al. v. Days Inns of America, Inc.
212 Ga. 792 (1994), 443 SE2d 290

BIRDSONG, Presiding Judge.

Richard and Kellee Matt appeal the grant of summary judgment to Days Inns of America, Inc. The Matts sued Days Inns for damages sustained after Richard Matt was shot in a robbery attempt at the Atlanta Airport Days Inn. The Matts contended that Days Inns' negligence was the proximate cause of Richard Matt's injuries because it failed to provide adequate security and failed to take reasonable precautions to protect him from reasonably foreseeable criminal acts of third persons.

Subsequently, Days Inns moved for summary judgment contending that it was not liable as Richard Matt's injuries were caused by the unforeseeable criminal conduct of a third person. More specifically, Days Inns asserted that although there had been crimes against property in this parking lot and two robberies by force sometime earlier, there had been no substantially similar armed robbery on its premises which would give notice of the possible occurrence of the kind of event that caused Richard Matt's injuries. Ultimately, the trial court granted Days Inns' motion for summary judgment because it found Days Inns had established that there was no genuine issue of material fact on the issue of foreseeability.

On appeal, Matts contended that the trial court erred because they introduced evidence that there were 82 crimes committed at the hotel in the three years preceding the attack on Richard Matt. The records show that one robbery occurred in a guest room and 81 other crimes were committed in this Days Inn's parking lot, including one purse snatching one year prior and a robbery by force without the use of a weapon some three years earlier.

In addition, the Matts introduced evidence showing that there are three other airport hotels within a one-quarter mile radius of the Days Inn, and that at one hotel there were 184 parking lot crimes, including five armed robberies, one strong-arm robbery, two rapes, ten assaults, and one kidnapping; another of the hotels had 257 parking lot crimes, including four armed robberies, one strong-arm robbery, one rape, and 26 assaults; and at the other hotel, three total parking lot crimes including two assaults and one kidnapping. The evidence showed that Days Inns' procedures required that it monitor criminal activity within the area of each Days Inn and adapt its crime prevention plan accordingly.

After their marriage in another state the day before, the Matts drove to Atlanta and, upon their travel agent's recommendation, checked into the Days Inn with plans to take a honeymoon flight to Mexico very early the next morning. The evidence showed that the Matts had never spent the night in an Atlanta hotel before.

The evidence presented showed the shooting occurred in the early morning hours in the first row of cars parked very near the front door of the Inn and that a security guard was seated in a vehicle some 40–50 feet from the place of the shooting. The security guard saw the crime taking place and notified the front desk to call the police because a robbery was in progress.

Testimony from the security guard and Richard Matt showed that the robbery attempt happened very quickly. While Richard Matt opened the trunk of his car to remove some luggage, another car came up behind him. When someone in the car demanded Matt's wallet and Matt did not comply immediately, he was shot. The car then sped away.

The Matts contend that Days Inns failed to exercise its responsibility to protect them on its premises, and that under Days Inns' security procedures, the guard should not have been seated in the car, but should have been patrolling the premises. Further, an expert witness for the Matts, a former chief of security for Days Inns, testified that under the facts known to Days Inns prior to the shooting, a crime such as the one which resulted in the injury to Richard Matt was foreseeable. The trial court found, however, that for criminal activity to be foreseeable, there must have been previous substantially similar criminal acts, and that the "test of 'substantial similarity' is stringent and is met only where the injured party can demonstrate that the prior criminal acts took place in a like manner and under similar conditions as the criminal act in issue." The trial court found that the previous criminal activity at the Days Inn was not substantially similar under this test and, consequently, granted summary judgment. The Matts appealed under OCGA § 9-11-56 (h).

Held: Under our law, Days Inns has an obligation as an innkeeper to exercise ordinary care to keep its premises safe for its guests. [citation omitted] Days Inns, however, relies upon *Savannah College of Art &c. v. Roe*, 261 Ga. 764 (409 SE2d 848) and *Lau's Corp. v. Haskins*, 261 Ga. 491 (405 SE2d 474), for the propositions that before a landowner may be liable for a third party's criminal act there must have been at least one prior substantially similar incident, and further the fact that a security guard is present does not increase the standard of care.

Although an innkeeper is not an insurer of the safety of the guests, it is bound to exercise ordinary care to protect its guests from unreasonable risks of which the innkeeper has superior knowledge, and if an innkeeper has reason to anticipate criminal acts, it has the duty to exercise ordinary care to guard against injury caused by dangerous characters. [citation omitted] "[O]rdinary diligence is that degree of care which is exercised by ordinarily prudent persons under the same or similar circumstances." OCGA § 51-1-2. "Exactly what constitutes 'ordinary care' varies with the circumstances and the magnitude of the danger to be guarded against. Since it is impossible to prescribe definite rules in advance for every combination of circumstances which may arise, the details of the standard must be filled in each particular case. But, to be negligent, the conduct must be unreasonable in light of the recognizable risk of harm." (Citations and punctuation omitted.) *Lau's Corp.*, supra 493. The Matts, however, may not rely upon Richard Matt's injuries as evidence that Days Inns failed to take reasonable measures to protect him against injury. *Lau's Corp.*, supra at 494.

Additionally, the Matts produced evidence from Days Inn's security guard that he did not feel safe patrolling the premises and prior to Matt's shooting had requested permission to carry a weapon, wear a bullet-proof vest, and carry a portable telephone. He had also requested that a gate controlling access to the parking lot be installed. Further, there is evidence that a Days Inns security audit conducted some years prior to the Matt shooting had recommended increased security patrols in the parking lot.

Knowledge that the premises subjected its guests to an unreasonable risk of criminal attack is a prerequisite to recovery under OCGA § 51-3-1 and such knowledge may be demonstrated by evidence of the occurrence of prior substantially similar incidents. *Savannah College of Art*, supra at 765. Moreover, under *Lau's Corp.*, supra at 493, evidence of criminal activity in the area in which the hotel is located may be considered on this issue.

Therefore, the question is whether the prior robberies by force in the Days Inn parking lot are substantially similar to the armed robbery in which Richard Matt was shot. Substantially similar does not mean identical, and it is not a question whether a weapon was used, but whether prior crimes should have put an ordinarily prudent person on notice that the hotel's guests were facing increased risks. "All that is required is that the prior [incident] be sufficient to attract the [hotel's] attention to the dangerous condition which resulted in the litigated [incident]." *Pembroke Mgmt. v. Cossaboon*, 157 Ga. App. 675, 677 (278 SE2d 100).

Thus, the test is whether the prior criminal activity was sufficiently substantially similar to demonstrate the landowner's knowledge that conditions on his property subjected invitees to unreasonable risk of criminal attack so that the landowner had reasonable grounds to apprehend that the present criminal act was foreseeable.

Consequently, it cannot merely be stated that because none of the prior offenses at the Days Inn was an armed robbery with a firearm that none of the events were substantially similar. To reach that result would require the conclusion that a hotel somehow would safeguard its guests differently to protect them from robberies by force and violence than from armed robberies, or protect them differently from armed robbers with firearms than those with knives, or protect guests differently from assaults than from armed robberies. We do not find that the Supreme Court intended such a result in *Savannah College of Art*. Indeed, in *Savannah College of Art* the prior offenses were not crimes of violence against the persons of any of the dormitory residents, but offenses against property or public morals which would not put the college on notice that it was reasonable to expect a sexual attack on a dormitory resident.

In this appeal, however, the record of criminal activity in the parking lots of nearby hotels, including serious crimes against persons, when coupled with the record of criminal activity in its own parking lot (a crime about once every two weeks) was sufficient to create a genuine issue of material fact on whether Days Inns was put on notice that criminal conduct against its guests was foreseeable.

Moreover, although a landowner does not become an insurer of safety by taking some security precautions on behalf of invitees and undertaking some measures to protect patrons does not heighten the standard of care or ordinarily constitute evidence that further measures might be required [citation omitted], neither does providing security insulate the landowner from liability when the security measures proved to be inadequate. [citation omitted] Consequently, we find genuine issues present on whether Days Inns' security measures were adequate or whether they were performed in a negligent manner.

The dissent by Judge Blackburn addresses the issue of whether Days Inn was negligent and it concludes that Days Inn cannot be liable in this case because it could not have prevented this crime. Issues of negligence, however, are for the jury, except in plain and palpable cases in which reasonable minds cannot differ. [citation omitted] This is not such a case. First, a jury might find that an innkeeper is not limited to actions that might prevent guests from being injured once a crime is in progress. Thus, it is possible a jury might find that the visible presence of a security guard in the parking lot (as Days Inns' own security procedures required) could have prevented this robbery. Further, a jury also might find negligence in that the unarmed security guard remained safely in his vehicle while allowing Richard Matt to face alone the dangers of the parking lot that prompted the security guard to request increased protection for his personal safety. Moreover, a jury might also find that Days Inn was negligent in not maintaining an armed security force, given the dangers in this hotel parking lot, and a jury might also conclude that Days Inn was negligent in not installing a security gate that could have prevented this drive-through robbery attempt. Both of these measures were recommended to Days Inn management by its security guard prior to Richard Matt's shooting, but were then rejected.

Further, pretermitting whether our law allows knowledge of high crime areas to be charged to the public in general, it is hard to conclude that such knowledge could be attributed to a visitor from another state. Moreover, we reject the conclusion that this court is authorized to decide whether Days Inn could do no more to protect its guests, including Richard Matt.

Accordingly, as we find the Matts carried their burden as respondents to Days Inns' motion for summary judgment under the standards announced in *Lau's Corp. v. Haskins*, the trial court erred by granting summary judgment to Days Inns of America.

Judgment reversed. Pope, C.J., McMurray, P.J., Beasley, P.J., Cooper and Smith, J.J., concur. Andrews, Johnson, and Blackburn, J.J., dissent.

ANDREWS, Judge, dissenting.

The trial judge correctly granted summary judgment in favor of Days Inns.

The gravamen of Matt's suit for damages is not that someone attempted to rob him in the Days Inn parking lot but that during the attempt he was shot. Under *Savannah College of Art &c. v. Roe*, 261 Ga. 764, 765 (409 SE2d 848) (1991), liability for damages resulting from the shooting depends on whether Days Inn knew or should have known that conditions on its premises subjected Matt to an unreasonable risk of being shot. The requisite knowledge "may be demonstrated by evidence of the occurrence of prior substantially similar incidents." Id. At 765. Accordingly, in theabsence of any evidence in this case that Days Inn otherwise knew about the present incident, in order to prove that Days Inn had the requisite knowledge, the evidence must show the occurrence of prior substantially similar incidents on the premises. Id.; [citation omitted].

The record in this case shows that, prior to the present shooting, there had been two previous unarmed robberies and some unspecified crimes against property on the Days Inn premises. Conceding that there were no prior shootings or even armed robberies on the premises, the majority, nevertheless, concludes that the present attempted armed robbery and shooting was "substantially similar" to the prior unarmed robberies. Instead of focusing on the obvious dissimilarities between the prior unarmed robberies and the present shooting, the majority analyzes *Savannah College of Art's* "substantially similar" requirement by focusing instead on "whether the prior crimes should have put an ordinarily prudent person on notice that the hotel's guests were facing increased risks," and by relying on a pre-*Savannah College of Art* case for the proposition that "'[a]ll that is required is that the prior (incident) be sufficient to attract the (hotel's) attention to the dangerous condition which resulted in the litigated (incident).'" The majority concludes that "the record of criminal activity in the parking lots of nearby hotels, including serious crimes against persons, when coupled with the record of criminal activity in its own parking lot (a crime about once every two weeks) was sufficient to create a genuine issue of material fact on whether Days Inns was put on notice that criminal conduct against its guests was "foreseeable."

The "substantially similar" test set forth in *Savannah College of Art* involves a straightforward, direct comparison of any prior crimes on the premises to the present criminal incident. In establishing a clearly stated (if not always easily implied) limit to liability, *Savannah College of Art* attempts to lend at least some degree of predictability to the duty of a premises owner to protect invitees from the intervening criminal acts of third persons. The majority has expanded the limits of potential liability under the *Savannah College of Art* test by finding "substantial similarity," not by direct comparison of the prior crimes on the premises to the present incident, but by a sort of totality of the circumstances test stated in terms of whether the prior unarmed robberies and other crimes at the Days Inn, located in a "high crime" area where armed robberies had occurred at other businesses, were sufficient to show that Days Inn knew or should have known of an unreasonable risk that Matt might be shot in an attempted armed robbery.

The focus should be on a direct comparison of any previous criminal acts on the premises to the present criminal incident. *Savannah College of Art* makes absolutely clear that a premises owner's knowledge that his business is located in a "high crime" area, where crimes have been committed at other locations, does not establish a duty to protect invitees from similar crimes that might be committed on the owner's premises. The fact that numerous crimes similar to the present criminal attack may have been committed at other locations in the area is irrelevant if there is no evidence of prior substantially similar crimes on the Days Inn premises. [citation omitted] Under *Savannah College of Art*, if the prior crimes on the Days Inn premises were not "substantially similar" to the present criminal incident, Days Inn is presumed not to have the requisite knowledge and there would be no liability for his injuries. Directly compared, the two unarmed robberies and other crimes against property occurred on the Days Inn premises, were not "substantially similar" to the present shooting.

This test should be strictly applied as a necessary limit to a premises owner's duty to protect invitees from the intervening criminal acts of third persons. Unless this duty is strictly defined and limited, business owners will be burdened with the uncertain duty of preventing criminal activity against their patrons, which government and law enforcement have been unable to prevent. A proprietor is not the insurer of his invitees' safety and, despite the dangerous area in which his business is located, it is not the proprietor's duty to provide to invitees what amounts to police protection from violent crime in the area.

As to the claim that security was inadequate, knowledge of a dangerous condition giving rise to the present shooting "would be necessary, in order to show the existence of even an initial duty on the part of [Days Inn] to provide preventive security measures." *Bishop v. Mangal Bhai Enterprises*, 194 Ga. App. 874, 877 (392 SE2d 535) (1990). Since there were no prior "substantially similar" attacks on the premises, there was no such knowledge and no duty to provide security adequate to protect against this kind of attack. [citation omitted] Additionally, "[t]here was no evidence that any security efforts undertaken by [Days Inn] were otherwise below a reasonable standard of care, made the situation worse by increasing the danger, misled [Matt] into the belief that the danger had been removed, or deprived [Matt] of the possibility of help from other sources." Id. [citation omitted]

Accordingly, Days Inns was entitled to summary judgment in its favor.

I am authorized to state that Judge Johnson joins in this dissent.

BLACKBURN, Judge, dissenting.

In the present case, the robbery attempt and shooting happened very quickly. The perpetrator pulled up to the victim in the hotel parking lot and shot the victim without getting out of the car. The security guard was seated some 40–50 feet from the location of the incident. It was an unfortunate incident, but it was "not of such a nature as to reasonably allow the proprietor to intercede, warn its invitees, or otherwise act to prevent injury to [the victim]." *Taylor v. Atlanta Center, Ltd.*, 208 Ga. App. 463, 466 (430 SE2d 841) (1993). The concept of foreseeability necessarily requires that Days Inn have such knowledge that it could reasonably anticipate that *the subject crime* would likely occur, and given that, the anticipated crime must be of such a nature that they could have reasonably prevented same. Liability must be based on fault, and there could be no fault absent the presence of both of these elements. To say otherwise is to make the proprietor the insurer of the injured party, which the law does not allow. [citation omitted] Therefore, I support the trial court's grant of Days Inns' motion for summary judgment.

The evidence presented tended to show that the Atlanta Airport Days Inn is located in a high crime area with which knowledge plaintiff would be charged as a member of the general public. Days Inn had no greater ability or duty to anticipate *specific* intentional criminal acts by unknown persons than did the plaintiff. The presence of a security guard in the parking lot within 40 feet of the crime scene who did not have time to intercede clearly shows that Days Inn was prevented from protecting the plaintiff by the speed and nature of the attack, which it could not have reasonably anticipated. If the security guard, as provided, was not adequate, then at what density must the proprietor staff the premises? Absent a one-on-one ratio of security guard to invitee, how could Days Inn have prevented this incident? Presidents, with scores of armed secret service agents, have been assassinated by determined assailants. Surely we cannot require a heightened security for each guest at a hotel. This requirement would be unreasonable as a matter of law, would make the cost of providing hotel services prohibitive, and would result in a total abandonment of large geographic areas by businesses of every description.

DECIDED MARCH 18, 1994—RECONSIDERATION DENIED APRIL 1, 1994

Robertson v. Sixpence Inns of America, Inc.

This case in the Supreme Court of Arizona established an obligation for the property to inform (duty to inform) a security contractor (or any other independent contractor) of any dangers on the property. The court considered the action of the trial court and the court of appeals in the fatal shooting of an off-duty police officer who was acting as an independent contract-security officer. The higher court reversed and remanded the case for further proceedings consistent with the following opinion.

Robertson v. Sixpence Inns of America, Inc.
No. CV-89-0170-PR

Court of Appeals, No. 2 CA-CV 88-0364, Maricopa County, No. C-561942

(As presented in 55 Ariz. Adv. Rep. 11)

GORDON, Chief Justice

Police officer John A. Robertson was shot and killed by an armed robber while working as an off-duty security guard at the Sixpence Inns in Phoenix, Arizona. His wife, Evorah Faye Robertson (plaintiff), sought damages from Sixpence Inns (defendant) for its alleged negligence. The trial court granted partial summary judgment in favor of defendant on all but one claim, and granted a directed verdict on the remaining claim of negligent failure to warn. The court of appeals affirmed the trial court in a memorandum decision.

Plaintiff petitioned this court for review of the court of appeals decision affirming both the summary judgment and directed verdict. We granted review on only the directed verdict.

Because plaintiff presented sufficient evidence of negligent failure to warn to take the issue to jury, we vacate the court of appeals decision and reverse and remand to the trial court for further proceedings consistent with this opinion.

FACTS AND PROCEDURAL HISTORY

The granting of a directed verdict indicated that the court believed reasonable minds could not differ on the outcome of the case on the evidence presented. See *Chambers v. Western Arizona CATV*, 130 Ariz. 605, 607, 638 P.2d 219, 221 (1981). Because we disagree with the courts below and believe reasonable minds could reach different inferences and conclusions on the evidence presented in this case, we set out that evidence in some detail.

John A. Robertson was a full-time police officer who also worked part-time as an off-duty security guard for Sixpence Inns. The security guard duty was assigned through his precinct and Robertson was equipped with his full Phoenix police uniform, weapon, and hand-held two-way radio when working at the motel.

On the night of November 17, 1984, while working at Sixpence Inns, Officer Robertson stopped Randy J. Harris on suspicion of trespass. After asking for identification, the officer used his radio to request a warrant check on Harris. Before Robertson received a reply, however, someone from the motel yelled to him that the man he stopped had just robbed a motel guest. Robertson told Harris not to leave and turned toward the voice. When Robertson turned his back, Harris shot him in the neck, fatally wounding him.

Officer Robertson's widow and children filed a worker's compensation claim for death benefits against the City of Phoenix and Sixpence Inns. In the Industrial Commission hearing, all parties stipulated that Robertson was killed in the line of duty as a Phoenix police officer. That status arose just before the shooting, when the person called to the officer about the robbery. The administrative law judge also determined that when Robertson was not acting as a police officer, he was an independent contractor of Sixpence Inns. The City of Phoenix, therefore, was found liable for the entire worker's compensation claim. The employment status findings were affirmed in *City of Phoenix v. Industrial Comm'n*, 154 Ariz. 324, 742 P.2d 825 (App.1987).

Plaintiff then sued defendant Sixpence Inns, alleging negligence in failing to furnish a safe place to work and in failing to warn Robertson of the armed robber on the premises. The court granted partial summary judgment to defendant, but preserved the issue of failure to warn for trial.[1]

At trial, motel manager Clifford Kaiser testified to the events leading up to the shooting. At some undisclosed time in the evening of November 17, 1984, a man, later identified as Randy J. Harris, entered Room 220 of the Sixpence Inns and robbed two men at gunpoint. Harris stripped the men, bound them, and threatened one of them by placing a gun in the victim's mouth. He also tore the telephone off the wall before leaving the room. Some time later, the victims freed themselves and reported the robbery to the desk clerk in the motel office. The clerk then reported the robbery to Kaiser. Because neither the motel clerk nor the victims testified at trial, no evidence was presented establishing the length of time between the robbery and the report to Kaiser.

Kaiser testified that upon hearing of the robbery, he ran to the victim's room, where he learned that the robber was armed and had threatened one victim with a gun. After noticing that the phone was ripped from the wall, Kaiser went to the room next door and used the phone to call the desk clerk, before returning briefly to the victim's room. Although the desk clerk assured Kaiser that she had already called the police, she apparently had not done so. According to the testimony of a communications supervisor for the Phoenix police department, the police first heard about the robbery when the motel clerk phoned in information about Robertson's shooting.

Conflicting testimony was presented about Kaiser's actions after he left the victims' room the second time. Kaiser testified at trial that after viewing the room where the robbery occurred, he ran outside to the west and north sides of the motel looking for Robertson. He stated that when he could not find Robertson, he returned to his apartment and watched television for a moment until he heard a shot. In a pretrial disposition used at trial, however, Kaiser gave no indication that he conducted a search for Officer Robertson before returning to his apartment.

---

[1] In denying Sixpence Inns' motion for summary judgment on the issue of failure to warn, the judge explained:

The Court thinks that a reasonable jury could conclude that the defendant motel did not tell the police department, before the decedent officer was shot, that an armed robbery had occurred; that there was sufficient time before the officer was shot for the motel staff to tell the police department of the robbery and for the police department to so advise the officer; that, if the officer had been so advised, he would have taken significant precautionary measures to prevent himself from being shot; and, that, under all circumstances, the motel staff should have told the police department of the robbery in sufficient time for the department to relay the robbery report to the officer.

A different judge, however, heard essentially the same evidence at trial and granted the directed verdict.

Plaintiff's security expert, Kevin Parsons, Ph.D., testified that, in his opinion, the motel owed a duty to warn Robertson immediately of the armed robbery and the failure to warn fell below the required standard of conduct. He stated that Robertson would have been informed of the robbery almost immediately if the motel had called the police promptly. Moreover, had Robertson been forewarned of an armed robber on the premises, he would have reacted differently when he encountered Harris. The testimony of two of Robertson's police coworkers supported the expert's opinions. They stated that if Robertson had been forewarned he would not have approached Harris as he did and that he likely would have taken additional steps to protect himself.

At the close of plaintiff's evidence, the trial judge granted defendant's motion for directed verdict, finding that plaintiff failed to present sufficient evidence of defendant's negligence to present the issue to the jury.

The court of appeals affirmed both the summary judgment and the directed verdict. With respect to the directed verdict, the court noted that the only duty defendant owed to Robertson was the duty to warn of known perils on the premises. The court found that plaintiff presented no evidence that defendant knew or had reason to know that the robber remained on the premises. It found important the lack of evidence with respect to the time delay between the robbery and the notification of Kaiser. Relying on an estimated time delay, the court found that "common sense alone dictates that the likelihood of an armed robber remaining at the site diminishes significantly with every tick of the clock." [citation omitted] Thus, the court held, plaintiff failed to establish that defendant owed any duty to warn Officer Robertson. In addition, the court stated that, on the whole, plaintiff failed to establish a *prima facie* case of negligence.

Discussion

A. Standard for Directed Verdict

The issue before us is whether the trial court correctly granted defendant's motion for directed verdict. When considering a motion for directed verdict, a trial court must decide, as a matter of law, whether the moving party's evidence is sufficient. A motion for directed verdict admits the truth of the evidence offered by the opposing party, and cannot be granted if reasonable minds can differ as to the inferences or conclusions drawn from the evidence. Moreover, it is the jury's function to select which of the conflicting inferences or conclusions is the most reasonable. [all citations omitted]

B. Prima Facie Case of Negligence

The trial judge listed five reasons for granting defendant's motion for directed verdict: (1) no evidence of negligence by the motel clerk or Kaiser; (2) no evidence that defendant knew the armed robber was still on the premises; (3) no evidence that the failure to warn Robertson was the cause of his death; (4) the conduct of Harris was an intervening superseding cause; and (5) any increased alertness that plaintiff postulated would have resulted from a warning did in fact exist because Robertson was informed of the robbery and had requested a warrant check. The first four reasons and a reading of the record indicate that the trial court believed the plaintiff failed to prove the elements of duty, breach of duty, and causation as required to establish a *prima facie* case of negligence. The rationale behind the fifth reason is unclear, although the statement appears to imply that the trial court viewed Officer Robertson's own actions as somehow relieving defendant of the duty to warn.

The court of appeals, quoting *Markowitz v. Arizona Parks Bd.*, 146 Ariz. 352, 354, 706 P.2d 364, 366 (1985), correctly noted that plaintiff must show defendant owed "a duty or obligation, recognized by law, which requires the defendant to conform to a particular standard of conduct in order to protect others against unreasonable risks of harm" to withstand a motion for directed verdict in a negligence action. [citation omitted] However, the court then upheld the directed verdict, finding that defendant owed no duty unless sufficient evidence was presented that defendant knew the robber was still on the premises, and that plaintiff failed to establish a *prima facie* case of negligence.

We believe that both lower courts misinterpreted the law of negligence as it applies to the facts of this case. We therefore, once again, review Arizona law dealing with the elements of a *prima facie* case of negligence as it applies to the facts of this case.[2]

1. Duty

a. Overview

The existence of a duty is a question of law to be determined by the court. [citation omitted] "Duty" arises from the recognition that certain relations between individuals impose on one a legal obligation for the benefit of another. [citations omitted]

Both the trial court and the court of appeals apparently believed plaintiff failed to establish that defendant owed Robertson any duty because plaintiff presented no evidence that defendant knew the robber was still on the motel premises. We disagree with that analysis. We believe both courts erroneously equated the issue of existence of *any* duty with the specific details of the required standard of conduct. [citation omitted]

In an earlier and separate proceeding before the Industrial Commission, the administrative law judge determined that Robertson acted as an independent contractor up to the time he was alerted of the robbery. [citation omitted] The parties have not contested that finding throughout the proceedings or in this appeal. Indeed, arguments by both parties throughout the proceedings indicate they apparently agreed with the finding.

Whether defendant knew the robber was still on the premises is certainly one factor to consider in determining whether defendant breached the required standard of care. However, we cannot state as a rule of law that a contractee is relieved of all duty to independent contractors simply because the contractee does not know whether a hazard still exists on the property. Because Robertson was still acting as an independent contractor when defendant learned of the robbery, the first inquiry on the motion for directed verdict was whether defendant owed any duty to warn Robertson *as an independent contractor*. If a duty is found to exist, only then does the issue arise as to whether defendant breached the required standard of conduct.

b. Duty owed to independent contractor

---

[2] Although proof of injury or damages is also an element of a *prima facie* case of negligence, that element is not contested here and therefore we do not discuss it. We also note that only the trial court specifically addressed the issue of causation in this case. Although the court of appeals stated generally that plaintiff failed to prove a *prima facie* case of negligence, it did not make any specific findings regarding causation.

Generally, an independent contractor and the contractor's employees are included in the category of business invitees for the purpose of determining the duty owed by the contractee. [citation omitted] The general rule of liability for an owner or occupier to business invitees requires one "to discover and correct or warn of hazards which the possessor should reasonably foresee as endangering an invitee." *Markowitz*, 146 Ariz. At 355, 706 P.2d at 367 (citing Restatement (Second) of Torts §343 (1965)).

This duty to protect invitees includes the obligation to warn invitees of any danger of which the occupier knows or should know and of which the invitee is unaware and unlikely to discover. [citations omitted] The warning must allow the invitee to decide intelligently whether to accept an invitation to enter the property and, if the invitee chooses to do so, protect himself against any danger. [citation omitted] Therefore, the owner/occupier or contractee owes a duty "to an independent contractor and to his employees to turn over a reasonably safe place to work, or to give warning of any dangers." [citations omitted]

In the context of this case, we may say as a matter of law that defendant, as a contractee, owed a duty of reasonable care to its independent contractor, Officer Robertson, to warn of certain hazards, much like the duty an owner/occupier owes to business invitees. That duty remained constant, although the conduct required to fulfill that duty was determined by the circumstances. Because a duty existed in this case, we must address whether plaintiff presented sufficient evidence such that reasonable minds could differ on whether defendant's actions were negligent.

2. Standard of Conduct

The general test for whether a defendant's conduct breached the standard of care is whether a foreseeable risk of injury existed as a result of defendant's conduct. [citation omitted] Where reasonable people could differ as to whether an injury was foreseeable, the question of negligence is one of fact left to the jury. [citations omitted]

Various conditions may alter the standard of conduct required to satisfy the duty arising in the contractee-independent contractor relationship. For example, courts generally will find that a contractee is not liable to an independent contractor where injury occurs because of a condition the independent contractor was hired to correct. [citation omitted] In addition, courts usually will find that a contractee "is not liable for death or injury of an independent contractor or one of his employees resulting from dangers which the contractor, as an expert, has known, or as to which he and his employees 'assumed the risk.'" [citation omitted] In such situations, the contractee still owes a general duty of reasonable care to the independent contractor. [citation omitted] However, if the contractor was hired to correct a hazardous condition or assumed the risk of the condition, circumstances may indicate that the contractee's duty was satisfied even though the contractee did not warn the independent contractor of that condition on the premises. [citation omitted]

In some situations, however, a contractee must still protect an independent contractor from known dangers or provide adequate warning of their existence. Such an obligation exists, for example, where the circumstances indicate that the contractee should anticipate harm to the independent contractor despite the contractor's knowledge of the danger... [citations omitted]

We believe reasonable people could disagree about whether defendant took adequate precautions to protect Officer Robertson. In fact, the evidence could support many conclusions about what conduct would have been reasonable under the circumstances and we do not believe any of those conclusions apply as a matter of law. Viewing the evidence in the light most favorable to plaintiff, defendant could have anticipated the harm to Officer Robertson. Plaintiff asserted that the motel was located in a high crime area, indicating that defendant should have been alerted to potential criminal conduct. In addition, Kaiser learned that the robber was armed and knew that Robertson was patrolling the motel premises. Plaintiff at least arguably established that Kaiser should have anticipated Robertson's encounter with Harris on the motel property. Although Robertson may have had a "heightened sense of awareness," that would not relieve defendant of his obligation as a matter of law. Whether the surrounding circumstances were sufficient to render defendant's conduct a breach of its duty to Robertson should have been presented to the jury to decide.

3. Proximate Cause

The trial court stated that plaintiff presented no evidence that defendant's conduct caused Robertson's death, and dismissed the testimony of plaintiff's expert and Robertson's coworkers as speculation. Apparently, the trial court believed that even if plaintiff presented sufficient evidence of duty and breach of the standard of conduct, a directed verdict was required on the issue of proximate cause. Although the court correctly stated the general principles, we believe it improperly applied the law to the facts of the case.

In a cause of action for negligence, plaintiff must show some reasonable connection between defendant's act or omission and plaintiff's damages or injuries. [citation omitted] Thus, plaintiff bears the burden of proof on the issue of proximate cause, which Arizona courts unvaryingly define as follows:

> The proximate cause of an injury is that which, in a natural and continuous sequence, unbroken by any efficient intervening cause, produces an injury, and without which the injury would not have occurred. [citations omitted]

The defendant's act or omission need not be a "large" or "abundant" cause of the injury; even if defendant's conduct contributes "only a little" to plaintiff's damages, liability exists if the damages would not have occurred but for that conduct. [citation omitted] Plaintiff need only present probable facts from which the causal relationship reasonably may be inferred. [citation omitted].

Ordinarily, the question of proximate cause is a question of fact for the jury. Only when plaintiff's evidence does not establish a causal connection, leaving causation to the jury's speculation, or where reasonable persons could not differ on the inference derived from the evidence, may the court properly enter a directed verdict. [citations omitted] In this case, plaintiff presented sufficient evidence from which reasonable persons could infer that defendant's conduct contributed at least "a little" to Robertson's shooting. The failure to warn Robertson of the armed robbery arguably left him at a disadvantage when he confronted Harris. Reasonable persons could conclude that if Robertson had been forewarned he would have taken added precautions.

Defendant also asserted in the motion for directed verdict that Harris's act of shooting Robertson was an intervening superseding cause, claiming the act was unusual, unforeseeable, and violent in nature. Apparently, both courts below agreed with defendant's assertion. We disagree, however, because Harris's act reasonably could be found to have been within the scope of the risk created.

An intervening cause is an independent cause that intervenes between defendant's original negligent act or omission and the final result and is necessary in bringing about that result. [citations omitted] Not all intervening acts are superseding causes, however. A superseding cause, sufficient to become the proximate cause of the final result and relieve defendant of liability for his original negligence, arises only when an intervening force was unforeseeable and may be described, with the benefit of hindsight, as extraordinary. [citations omitted]

In appropriate cases, the scope of the risk created by defendant's original negligence may include the criminal conduct of a third person. [citations omitted] An appropriate case typically involves a special relationship between defendant and another, such as occupier-invitee, where defendant's original conduct created or increased the risk of harm through the misconduct of another, even when that misconduct is intentional or criminal in nature. [citation omitted]

Defendant relied on *Hebert v. Club 37 Bar* (Arizona 1984) to support the motion for directed verdict on the issue of superseding cause. In *Hebert*, the court of appeals held that a tavern owner could not be held liable for selling alcohol to an alcoholic who shot and killed another patron outside the bar. [citation omitted] As defendant correctly pointed out, the court in *Hebert* noted that the tavern owner knew the man was intoxicated and carried a gun in his car. However, defendant failed to point out that the court also found that the plaintiff presented no evidence the tavern owner knew of the man's violent propensity or had any indication of the events prior to their occurrence. In fact, the man had exhibited little or no violent tendencies before the events took place. Thus, the court held, the man's intervening actions could not be foreseen by the tavern owner and became the superseding cause of the patron's death. [citation omitted]

The facts of the case before us are distinguishable from the facts in *Hebert*. In this case, reasonable persons could find that Robertson's shooting was foreseeable. Defendant knew an armed robbery had taken place, indicating other violence might occur. Thus, reasonable persons could find that defendant should have foreseen that failing to warn Robertson of the robbery would expose him to possible criminal conduct. Arguably, the shooting was within the scope of the risk created by defendant's conduct, and the issue should have been left to the jury to decide.

C. Conclusions and Disposition

After reviewing the record in this case, we find that plaintiff presented evidence that, if taken as true for purposes of the motion, would have caused reasonable persons to differ, precluding a directed verdict.

As determined in the Industrial Commission hearing, and not contested throughout these proceedings, Robertson was still acting as defendant's independent contractor when defendant learned of the robbery. Thus, defendant owed the duty to warn Officer Robertson of any dangers of which defendant was aware and of which Robertson was unaware. The robbery constituted such a danger and the duty to warn Robertson about its occurrence arose when defendant first discovered the robbery. That duty was not eliminated by the mere passage of time.

Once it was established that defendant owed a duty to Officer Robertson, plaintiff needed to present evidence sufficient to permit reasonable jurors to find in plaintiff's favor on the elements of breach and causation. We believe plaintiff satisfied that burden. Plaintiff's expert testified that the failure to call the police promptly breached the standard of care and that the negligence continued until after Robertson was shot. Two of Robertson's coworkers testified that Robertson would have acted differently had he been forewarned of the robbery. This testimony, combined with other evidence, could give rise to varying inferences and conclusions. The evidence indicates that the motel failed to call the police about the robbery until after Robertson had been shot; it supports the inference that had the motel reported the robbery promptly, Robertson could have been forewarned by the police dispatcher. If Robertson had been forewarned, he arguably would have acted more cautiously when he encountered a suspicious person.

Because reasonable minds could reach various conclusions on the evidence offered in this case, the jury should have been allowed to choose which conclusion to draw. Whether defendant was negligent in failing to warn Robertson was an issue of fact for the jury to decide, as were the questions whether defendant's failure to warn was a cause of Robertson's shooting or whether the passage of time made Harris's act a superseding cause.

We hold that the trial court erroneously granted the directed verdict in this case. The court of appeals memorandum decision is vacated and the case reversed and remanded for further proceedings consistent with this opinion.

FRANK X. GORDON, JR. Chief Justice

CONCURRING:

STANLEY G. FELDMAN Vice Chief Justice
JAMES DUKE CAMERON Justice
JAMES MOELLER Justice
ROBERT J. CORCORAN Justice

Malone et al. v. Courtyard by Marriott Limited Partnership et al.

A critical issue in this case is the nature of the response to the several reports by guests that it appeared that guests (the plaintiffs) were being assaulted. It was claimed that the negligence of the defendant warranted punitive damages in view of a conscious disregard for the safety of the plaintiff.

Malone et al. v. Courtyard by Marriott Limited Partnership et al.
74 Ohio St.3d 440, 659 N.E. 2d 1242

Source: (Copr. © West 1997 No claim to orig. U.S. govt. works.)

Hotel guests who were raped by another guest sued hotel on claim of negligence and request for punitive damages based on defendant's conscious disregard for plaintiff's safety. The Court of Common Pleas, Franklin County, granted directed verdict for defendant on punitive damages claim, and after verdict for one plaintiff and for defendant as to other plaintiff, defendant was granted new trial. Plaintiffs appealed. The Court of Appeals, Tyack, J., reversed decision for directed verdict and new trial, and defendant sought discretionary appeal. The Supreme Court, Wright, J., granted appeal and held that: (1) punitive damages based on conscious disregard malice were not warranted absent defendant's knowledge of danger posed to plaintiffs, and (2) order for new trial was not abuse of discretion.

On July 21, 1989, Lolita Malone and Karen Linda Meador arrived at a Courtyard by Marriott at approximately 11:30 P.M. and were assigned Room 249. They were in town for a national jazz festival, and the hotel atmosphere that night has been described as being like a college dorm party. The two women later met a man at the elevator who identified himself as Vincent Michael (his real name was Vincent Gatewood). Gatewood went with the two women to their guestroom, talked for a few minutes, and offered to go get some drinks. Around 12:30 A.M., while the three were talking and drinking in the room, Marriott security guard Christopher Letkiewicz knocked on the guestroom door and indicated that he had received complaints about the noise. A little later, Malone and Meador asked Gatewood to leave the room so they could get dressed to go out. Gatewood agreed. He returned around 1:30 A.M. and offered to show them around to the local clubs. The women agreed. Gatewood led them in a separate car.

Upon returning to the hotel around 3:30 A.M., Gatewood again accompanied the women to their room and opened their door after Meador handed him the key. The women told Gatewood that they were tired, but he insisted on getting them more drinks. The women reluctantly agreed. However, when they later asked Gatewood to leave, he was resistant. After several brief arguments, during which Malone believed he might become violent, the women were able to get Gatewood outside the guestroom. Meador then discovered she didn't have the guestroom key and was afraid Gatewood had it. When Malone cracked the door to ask if Gatewood had the key, he became angry and pushed through the door, entering the women's room and strangling Malone. When Meador tried to assist her friend, Gatewood struck her across the face. Malone escaped the room and ran for the elevator at the end of the hall. Gatewood pursued her and shoved her into his nearby guestroom. Meador ran into the hallway screaming for help. Gatewood struggled with her at the doorway to his room, then pulled her into his room and threw her against the wall.

The women had told a different version of these events to Jean Reed, a social worker with whom they met on July 22, 1989. According to Reed's testimony, neither woman had mentioned anything about the assault that had occurred in their room. Malone and Meador had told her that Gatewood left their room, shouted profanities in the hallway, and returned to his own room. Then, when Malone went down the hall to the elevator, Gatewood pulled her into his room. Meador saw the assault and ran to help.

Inside Gatewood's guestroom, they began screaming and pleading with Gatewood to let them go. He told them to be quiet, and he threatened to kill them if they did not do what he said. When they refused to undress, he tore their clothes off. Over the next three hours, Gatewood repeatedly raped both women. He allowed the women to leave his room at 7 A.M. after they convinced him that they were planning to meet friends that morning, and the friends would be suspicious if they didn't arrive. Before they left, however, Gatewood warned the women to tell no one about the incident, or else they would be found and punished. The women immediately went to the front desk to get a new key then briefly returned to their guestroom before going to a local hospital where they were examined and interviewed.

On September 18, 1990, Malone and Meador filed suit against both Courtyard by Marriott and Gatewood (although Gatewood was later dropped), alleging that Marriott personnel negligently failed to respond to reports by other hotel guests of an "abusive situation" and that Marriott's alleged failure to respond to those calls was "willful, wanton, and reckless, and demonstrated a conscious disregard for the safety and well being of Malone and Meador when a great probability of harm existed." As a result, Malone and Meador sought punitive damages.

At trial in 1993, several people who had been staying in guest rooms close to Malone and Meador's testified that they had heard screaming and yelling, slamming doors, and thumps in the early morning hours and had made several calls to the front desk staff to send someone up to investigate the noises.

Marriott moved for a directed verdict on all claims. Judge Beverly Pfeiffer granted Marriott's motion to dismiss the claims for punitive damages, but the compensatory claims pertaining to the charge of negligence went to the jury. The jury granted a general verdict in favor of Marriott and against Malone, finding her 51 percent negligent, and that her negligence directly caused her injuries. The jury also found Meador negligent, but determined her negligence was not the cause of her injuries and awarded her $300,000 in compensatory damages.

Marriot moved for judgment n.o.v. or else a new trial or remittitur. The motion for judgment n.o.v. was denied, but the court sustained the motion for a new trial on the grounds that the verdict for Meador was not supported by the evidence and that the damage award was excessive.

Meador and Malone appealed. The Franklin County Court of Appeals reversed the trial court both on the punitive damages issue and on the granting of a new trial. In the opinion of the appeals court, trial testimony had established sufficient evidence of Marriott's conscious disregard for Malone and Meador's safety to create a question for the jury on the issue of punitive damages. The court reinstated Meador's jury award and concluded that the trial court's order for a new trial was erroneous, and the case was sent back to the trial court on the punitive damages issue.

WRIGHT, Justice

At its core, this case presents two questions for our consideration. First, was the trial court's grant of Marriott's motion for a directed verdict on the issue of punitive damages in error? Second, was the judge's order for a new trial on Meador's negligence claim in error? We answer these queries in the negative.

[1] The directed verdict on the question of punitive damages should have been affirmed by the court of appeals. In determining whether to direct a verdict, the trial court does not engage in a weighing of the evidence, nor does it evaluate the credibility of the witnesses. [citation omitted] Rather, the court is confronted solely with a question of law: Was there sufficient material evidence presented at trial on this issue to create a factual question for the jury? [citation omitted] A motion for directed verdict may be granted when "the trial court, after construing the evidence most strongly in favor of the party against whom the motion is directed, finds that upon any determinative issue reasonable minds could come to but one conclusion upon the evidence submitted and that conclusion is adverse to such party, the court shall sustain the motion and direct a verdict for the moving party as to that issue." [citation omitted]

[According to Ohio law,] Malone and Meador were obligated to present evidence of malice on the part of Marriott before their claim for punitive damages could proceed to the jury.

[2] Our case law defines malice as (1) that state of mind under which a person's conduct is characterized by hatred, ill will or a spirit of revenge, or (2) a conscious disregard for the rights and safety of other persons that has a great probability "of causing substantial harm." [citations omitted]

Appellees argued, however, that sufficient evidence had been introduced at trial to create a question for the jury on the second definition of malice. Specifically, appellees' counsel pointed to the testimony of one witness who stated that she contacted the front desk twice between 4:00 and 4:20 A.M. because she had heard an argument coming from Gatewood's room. Appellees contend that Marriott's failure to respond to Williams's complaints constituted a conscious disregard for the safety of Malone and Meador, and created a great probability of harm to them. As a matter of law, this portrayal of Marriott's response is inaccurate.

[3] Marriott's alleged nonfeasance cannot be characterized as malice because the information provided to its employees was too ambiguous. In two telephone calls to the front desk, the witness complained only of someone "fighting and making a lot of noise," and she requested that the front desk "send someone up." She did not provide the front desk with information on the nature of the disturbance, and in her deposition testimony she characterized the noise from Gatewood's room as a domestic quarrel.

[4] The apparent miscommunication between the witness and the front desk staff is significant because of this court's pronouncements on the "conscious disregard" theory of malice. An award of punitive damages based on conscious disregard malice requires "a positive element of conscious wrongdoing. [citation omitted] This element has been termed conscious, deliberate or intentional. It requires the party to possess knowledge of the harm that might be caused by his behavior." [citation omitted]

In other words, Marriott, through its agents, must have actually known of the threat to its guests. Absent such proof of a defendant's subjective knowledge of the danger posed to another, a punitive damages claim against the defendant premised on the "conscious disregard" theory of malice is not warranted. Since nothing in the witness's calls to the front desk provided Marriott personnel with information about the physical threat confronting appellees, a charge to the jury on punitive damages would have been unjustified. Accordingly, the trial court's decision to direct the verdict was appropriate.

[5] It is significant to note that even if punitive damages were warranted in this case, Malone could not recover them because the jury did not award her compensatory damages. As we have held time and time again, punitive damages may not be awarded when a jury fails to award compensatory damages. [citation omitted]

The appellees attempt to circumvent this bar to Malone's recovery of punitive damages by pointing out that Malone failed to recover compensatory damages under the negligence theory only because the jury found that she had been 51 percent comparatively negligent. Since comparative negligence is not available as an affirmative defense for an action based on recklessness, appellees theorize that Malone could have recovered compensatory damages on a recklessness theory. Such an award would also allow Malone to overcome the bar to punitive damages that was articulated elsewhere.

Appellees then assert that the allegation of recklessness in count three of their complaint actually constituted a claim for both punitive and compensatory damages. The trial court's decision to direct a verdict on the third count of their complaint thus prevented the jury from addressing recklessness as a basis for compensatory damages as well as punitive damages. If the directed verdict on that issue were to be reversed, appellees contend that Malone could still attempt to recover compensatory and punitive damages.

Although the court of appeals found this argument persuasive, it is flawed in one vital respect: there is absolutely no indication in the pleadings, including the complaint amended after the close of evidence, that appellees ever pursued a compensatory damages claim based on recklessness. In the first two counts of their amended complaint, Malone and Meador asserted negligence on the part of appellants and enumerated the harms for which they were seeking damages. In the third count of the amended complaint, the appellees alleged that Marriott had engaged in "willful, wanton, and reckless" behavior and had shown "conscious disregard for the safety and well being of Malone and Meador when a great probability of harm existed, and as such, [Malone and Meador were] entitled to punitive damages." In no reasonable way can the appellees' complaint be read as advancing a claim for compensatory damages based on recklessness. Consequently, the jury was not deprived of an opportunity to determine the merits of such a claim, and Malone is not entitled to a new action based on recklessness.

The trial court's decision to order a new trial on Meador's negligence claim was not erroneous, and the court of appeals' reversal of that order was unfounded. The order was predicated on two subsections of Civ.R. 59(A) which state:

> A new trial may be granted to all or any of the parties and on all or part of the issues upon any of the following grounds: (4) Excessive or inadequate damages, appearing to have been given under the influence or passion or prejudice;... (6) The judgment is not sustained by the weight of the evidence...

[6][7][8] In evaluating the propriety of the trial court's decision premised on the weight of the evidence, we must note that a reviewing court can reverse such an order for a new trial only upon a finding of an abuse of discretion. [citation omitted] "Abuse of discretion" connotes "an unreasonable or unconscionable attitude upon the part of the court." [citations omitted] In addition, the abuse of discretion standard requires a reviewing court to "view the evidence favorably to the trial court's action rather than to the original jury's verdict." [citation omitted] This deference to a trial court's grant of a new trial stems in part from the recognition that the trial judge is better situated than a reviewing court to pass on questions of witness credibility and the "surrounding circumstances and atmosphere of the trial." [citation omitted]

[9] It is also important to note that the order of a new trial does not terminate a case; instead, it simply grants a new trial. Unlike directed verdicts and judgments notwithstanding the verdict, an order for a new trial does not dispose of litigation; instead, its purpose is to prevent "miscarriages of justice which sometimes occur at the hands of juries" by presenting the same matter to a new jury. [citations omitted]

[10] In light of the standard of review and the policies underlying it, the trial court's order for a new trial based upon the weight of the evidence does not appear to be arbitrary or capricious, given the evidence presented at trial and the seemingly contradictory verdicts rendered by the jury. As stated in the decision, no proof of pecuniary loss to Meador was offered at trial. The most compelling consideration in support of the trial judge's order, however, was the jury's incongruous determinations regarding Meador's and Malone's comparative negligence.

The jury interrogatory forms indicate that both appellees were found negligent, but only Malone's negligence was found to have caused her injuries. Such a disparate set of outcomes is difficult to understand when, as the trial judge noted, both Malone and Meador "invited Gatewood ... to their room, had drinks with him, went out to several bars, and upon return again allowed him in their room." The trial court went on, recalling that "there were several opportunities for [Meador] to have called either hotel security or other law enforcement for assistance. For example, Gatewood took Malone to his room leaving Meador outside free to return to her room and phone for assistance or knock on doors of other hotel guests for help."

A reasonable person confronted by such a set of facts could validly conclude that the jury's verdict for Meador was against the manifest weight of the evidence. We therefore find no abuse of discretion on the part of the trial court in its determination that the verdict was not supported by the weight of the evidence. Accordingly, it is unnecessary for us to address the trial court's conclusion that the verdict was excessive. We reverse the judgment of the court of appeals and reinstate both the trial court's directed verdict and its order for a new trial for Meador.

Judgment reversed.
MOYER, C.J., and PFEIFER and COOK, JJ., concur.

REVIEW QUIZ

When you feel you have covered all of the material in this chapter, answer these questions. Choose the *best* answer.

1. Which of the following is a true statement about security?

    a. Protection of physical assets is an important part of a security program.
    b. Once a property has determined its security procedures, they should never be changed.
    c. Most hotels belong to a single franchised chain and have virtually identical security requirements.
    d. Experienced employees do not need security training.

2. Industry–wide security standards are:

    a. the most important consideration for a property's security program.
    b. recommended by this text.
    c. not feasible.
    d. defined by laws which vary from state to state.

3. Which of the following is a benefit of law enforcement liaisons?

    a. They prepare management for possible litigation.
    b. They may encourage a prompt response to security incidents.
    c. They lead to a reduction in the amount of employee theft.
    d. They guarantee heightened security around a property.

4. A security officer has the authority to:

    a. search a guest's luggage in his or her absence.
    b. arrest a person for loitering.
    c. shoot a person caught breaking into an empty room.
    d. ask questions.

5. A primary goal of a security training program is to:

    a. offer security advice to local neighborhood groups.
    b. attract security conventions.
    c. make the staff a "protection team."
    d. attract off–duty police officers to the property.

6. Punitive damages are awarded:

    a. for pain and suffering.
    b. for hospitalization expenses.
    c. in order to deter outrageous conduct.
    d. for all of the above.

REVIEW QUIZ (continued)

7. A concept involved in all lodging security negligence cases is:
   a. the amount of punitive damages awarded.
   b. proximate cause.
   c. plea bargaining.
   d. length of sentence.

Answer Key: 1-a-C1, 2-c-C1, 3-b-C1, 4-d-C2, 5-c-C2, 6-c-C3, 7-b-C3

Each question is linked to a competency. Competencies are listed on the first page of the chapter. An answer reading 3-b-C4 translates to:

   3: the question number
   b: the correct answer
   C4: the competency number

Chapter 2 Outline

Physical Security and Perimeter Control
    Perimeter Barriers
    Lighting
    Parking Areas
    Glass Protection
Surveillance
    Closed-Circuit Television
Communication Systems
Alarm Systems
    Local Alarms
    Contact Alarms
    Remote Alarms
    Safety Alarms
Safety Equipment
    Smoke Detectors
    Fire Extinguishers
    Carbon Monoxide Detectors
    Sprinkler Systems
    Accident Prevention Signs
Guestroom Security
    Locks
    Biometrics
    Secondary Access-Limiting Devices
    Viewports
    Room Communications
    In-Room Security Information

Competencies

1. Identify critical elements of and concerns related to physical security and perimeter control equipment. (pp. 104–125)

2. Explain the importance of communication systems for security, describing the types of equipment available and the key considerations when evaluating such systems. (pp. 125–129)

3. Explain the features and benefits of various alarm systems. (pp. 130–133)

4. Describe various types of safety equipment and how they can help protect lodging properties and their staff and guests. (pp. 133–137)

5. Identify potential elements of guestroom security and describe their uses. (pp. 137–146)

2
Security Equipment

AT THE MOST basic level, an effective security program comprises three elements: security personnel, equipment, and procedures. Personnel and equipment are physical resources. Procedures specify the ways these resources are to be used in order to achieve organizational goals. Everything relating to security deals with at least one of these elements. Training, for example, involves teaching personnel about equipment and procedures.

As is true in all businesses with limited capital, choices must be made about which investments will bring the best return. In terms of security, individual properties have to decide what sort of balance they desire between personnel and equipment. Some properties opt for elaborate equipment which they believe will better meet their needs than a larger security staff. Other properties determine that personnel better address their needs than elaborate equipment. These decisions, as with all decisions relating to security, have to be made based on the specific requirements of each hotel or motel property.

Regardless of the balance chosen, however, management determines the amount and type of security equipment to be used at a property. Equipment can range in complexity from the simplest window latch to the most complex alarm systems. The presence of equipment at a property does not alter the property's need for security procedures—even properties with complex equipment rely on their staffs to operate and respond to it—but it can alter the nature of those procedures. And although some properties do not use much equipment, no property is entirely without it—room locks, originally introduced in 1829 by the Boston Tremont as a luxury, are now omnipresent.

A property's management should understand the uses and limitations of any given type of security equipment before authorizing its installation. A comprehensive review of need and feasibility should be completed by objective experts to determine whether the system is appropriate for the property (a survey or audit provided at no charge by the representative of a product or system may contain a seller's natural bias). Even when choosing *not* to purchase a particular type of equipment, management should be prepared to demonstrate that in this situation the equipment would not have significantly improved its property's security. This is important because many lawsuits filed against lodging properties cite the lack of certain types of security equipment (for example, closed-circuit television) as evidence of negligence. The property that carefully considers even its rejected equipment options may be better able to answer such charges of negligence.

Modern technology holds many potential benefits for the lodging industry, but care must be taken to select equipment and systems that are practical and that have proven effective within the industry. Before making a purchase, request a list of other properties within the lodging industry using a particular item or system to determine whether it is effective for lodging establishments and if it would be effective for your particular property. Management should also consider the ability of the security staff (supplemented by the maintenance staff) to do the necessary preventive maintenance to keep the system working. Finally, a reputable organization with experience substantiated by successful installations should be selected to supply equipment or systems.

This chapter examines some of the types and uses of security equipment in the lodging industry today, but does not constitute an endorsement of any equipment discussed.

Physical Security and Perimeter Control

Since transient guests do not have the sense of territory or the ability to easily recognize intruders *as* intruders that neighbors in a residential community have, effective physical security is needed to reduce their vulnerability. **Physical security** involves the protection of the building and grounds and the building's contents (although it is distinguished from the security program that deals with control over and accountability for the contents). It covers such diverse factors as layout, design, lighting, fences and gates, hardware, closed-circuit television, and alarms.

Physical security control is most easily integrated into the architectural design of a building at the conceptual stage. It is more difficult (but no less important) for security elements to be retrofitted into already existing properties. Crime Prevention Through Environmental Design (CPTED) has become a recognized tool for the architect and developer in the construction of a lodging or hospitality facility. The basic principles of CPTED include **target hardening** (controlling access to neighborhoods and buildings and conducting surveillance on specific areas to reduce opportunities for crime to occur) and **territorial reinforcement** (increasing the sense of security in settings where people live and work through activities that encourage informal control of the environment).

Some CPTED considerations for a lodging facility might include:

- Ability to see persons on an elevator at lobby level from the front desk.
- Entrances well-lit and designed so as to eliminate areas in which a person might hide.
- Guestroom corridors well-lit and without areas in which a person might hide.
- Lighting on the exterior of the structure that will not be screened-out by landscaping or building features—again, an avoidance of hiding places.
- Pool and health club locations where a ready check might be made by staff passing in the vicinity of the facility.
- In general, a layout that will maximize the sense of openness and awareness of persons in the territory (territorial reinforcement).[1]

In designing or redesigning the physical security of a hotel or motel, a number of factors should be taken into consideration. Exhibit 1 provides a checklist of

Exhibit 1   Physical Security Checklist

Perimeter
1. Will a fence help protect the premises?
2. If there is a fence in place, is the fence too high to climb or protected with barbed wire?
3. Is the fence in good repair?
4. Is the fence designed so no one can crawl under it?
5. Are materials such as trash containers, incinerators, etc., that could be used in scaling the fence placed a safe distance away?
6. Are the gates solid and in good repair?
7. Are the gate hinges in good repair?
8. Are there flammable materials in the receiving area which should be removed?
9. Is there a frequent trash pickup?
10. Is adequate lighting provided for the entire area?

Doors
1. Are all unused doors secured?
2. Are door frames strong and securely in place?
3. Is the glass in back doors and similar locations protected by wire-glass or bars?
4. Are all doors designed so the lock cannot be reached by breaking glass or a light sash panel?
5. Are the hinges designed and located to prevent the pulling or breaking of the pins?
6. Is the lock bolt designed and placed to prevent easy displacement with a "jimmy" or other instrument?
7. Is the lock designed or the door frame placed so the door cannot be pried open by spreading the frame?
8. Is the bolt protected or constructed so it cannot be cut?
9. Is the lock securely mounted so it cannot be pried off?
10. Are the locks on the door in good working order?
11. Are the keys in the possession of trusted personnel and are they secured when employees leave the premises?
12. Are padlock hasps constructed so the screws cannot be removed?
13. Are the hasps heavy enough?
14. Are all doors locked and/or barred during non-operating hours? Is emergency evacuation capability maintained at all times on such doors?
15. In non-operating hours, are access locations properly checked by security staff and/or central station or proprietary protection systems?

Windows
1. Are easily accessible windows protected by gratings, bars, or other access-limiting devices?
2. Are unused windows permanently locked?
3. Are windows which are not protected by bars locked?
4. Are there unneeded windows at lower floors or other areas which could be replaced by glass blocks or other less vulnerable alternatives?
5. Are the windows and locks so designed or located that they cannot be opened by simply breaking the glass?

Other Openings
1. Are unnecessary skylights (which may be subject to hurled objects) protected or have they been eliminated?

(continued)

Exhibit 1 *(continued)*

  2. Are accessible skylights protected with bars, etc.?
  3. Are roof hatches properly secured?
  4. Are the doors to the roof or elevator penthouses in good condition and securely locked?
  5. Are laundry and trash chutes provided with locks?
  6. Are all ventilator shafts and vent openings protected?
  7. Are entrances to sewers and service tunnels protected?
  8. Are fire exits and escapes designed to permit easy exit but to limit illegal entry?

Building Construction
  1. Are the walls of the building(s) of frame construction and fire-resistive or capable of being made so?
  2. Is the roof fire-resistive and secure?

Safes
  1. Is the safe fire-resistive?
  2. Is the safe fastened securely to the floor or wall, ceiling, and floor, set in concrete, or appropriately alarmed?
  3. If a vault is used, are the walls as well as the door secure?
  4. Is cash on hand kept to a minimum?

Security Officers
  1. Is it feasible to have an in-house security staff? Or, is it more appropriate to employ a contract security service or off-duty police?
  2. Do the security officers receive proper screening, training, and supervision, whether they are in-house or contract?
  3. If security personnel are armed, are they properly armed and proficient in the use of such arms?
  4. If there are full-time security personnel, are they free from "extra duties" so they are able to perform their protective duties fully?
  5. If a commercial security service is employed, is the service checked to confirm that it has the ability to provide full services?
  6. Would it be beneficial to conduct emergency drills?
  7. If available, has complete central station or proprietary supervisory service been considered in addition to standard security services?
  8. Has closed-circuit television or a similar monitoring device been investigated as a means of increasing effective surveillance by your security force?

Public Protection
  1. Is proper liaison maintained between the hotel or motel and the police and fire departments?
  2. Do the police and fire departments have the phone number of key personnel and vice versa?

Electronic Data Processing
  1. If there is a computer on the property, have proper steps been taken to ensure computer integrity with proper off-premises backup capability?
  2. Is the computer facility in a secure location?
  3. Is the computer room protected from the danger of hurled objects, flood, or fire?

Communications Equipment
  1. Is the communication center (telephone room, etc.) located in a secure place?
  2. Is adequate protection provided for wires and cables, etc.?
  3. Has an emergency communications plan been developed?

Exhibit 2 Sample Self-Inspection Form

1. What problems are created by the community in which the property is located?
2. What is the potential for civil disorder, vandalism, or similar security incidents?
3. Does the traffic pattern around the property create special problems?
4. Are there areas or zones for control of traffic when deliveries are being made, bus tours are loading or unloading, guests begin arriving in their own vehicles, cabs, etc.?
5. Are there problems of loitering, begging, or solicitation outside pedestrian entrances to the hotel?
6. Is there easy access to major roadways which could permit a robber to make a quick escape by high-speed roadways?
7. What is the ease of access for police? The fire department? Guests? Employees?
8. Are driveways provided?
9. Do one-way streets adjacent to the property permit easy routing of traffic to and from the location?
10. Are underground access routes available?
11. Is there adequate illumination in all exterior areas including streets, passageways, walkways, alleys, delivery areas, and employee and guest access locations?
12. Is there an adequate supply of water in the event of a fire emergency?
13. Is there auxiliary pumping capacity in the event of failure within the local water system or loss of power on the property?
14. Is there easy access to a water source for the fire department?
15. Is there danger of illegal entry into the property through underground service routes, tunnels, sewers, subways, manholes, and basement areas?
16. Is adequate protection provided for incoming utilities, gas, electric, phone, water service, and sewage disposal lines? Be aware of the special vulnerabilities of these locations. Know all emergency cut-offs for such services.
17. Could there be access from adjacent buildings over the roof or through adjacent windows?
18. Are windows and doors secured between the hotel or motel and adjacent structures?
19. What is the use and occupancy of the adjoining buildings?
20. Is there a fire danger from the neighboring structures?
21. What dangers are present for arriving or departing employees?
22. What transportation facilities are available to employees in addition to private motor vehicles?
23. Are parking facilities adequate and safe for serving the needs of the employees and guests?
24. Is there an adequate guard service, police service, or surveillance system to protect the guests and employees using parking facilities?
25. Are safe employee entrances and receiving areas provided?
26. Are appropriate security personnel and/or systems provided?
27. Are there dangers for guests arriving at the door by taxi or other public transportation?

factors to examine. In addition, an effort should be made to develop a self-inspection or survey form tailored to the property. A sample of such a form is included as Exhibit 2.

Many hotel and motel properties have been caught in community transitions which have created or aggravated the crime problems within their immediate vicinities or in adjacent communities. A change in the surrounding neighborhood may mean that a criminal can make a strike and then quickly disappear into an area of either commercial or residential high-density buildings. When this occurs, it may be necessary to re-evaluate existing physical systems to determine whether they respond to new circumstances.

Even in communities where a minimum of crime exists, it is important to periodically review physical security systems and operations in relation to the surrounding community. Adjoining buildings and neighborhoods and nearby restaurants, entertainment, or other facilities attractive to guests are elements to consider in structuring a physical security program. When local attractions result in guests going to and from the property at varying times throughout the evening and early morning hours, consider controls on access to the property.

There are several elements worthy of consideration in establishing the space or perimeter for a lodging property that will be subject to a security system. Design features within the structure define the degree to which the occupants and staff may monitor activities occurring in the residential space. Secured space may extend beyond the guestrooms to hallways, lobbies, and grounds. The use of reasonable care is of central importance; by recognizing what might reasonably be secured, the perimeter of the property may be established.

Remember that the standard of reasonable care can be variously interpreted. One case that deals with the duty of care owed to guests at a property's perimeter is *Banks v. Hyatt Corporation*, in which Hyatt was found liable for the death of one of its guests who was shot on a public sidewalk outside the hotel. In this case, the plaintiffs sued the hotel operators as well as the operators of a shopping mall that was part of the same building complex in which the hotel was located. The action was a derivative claim brought by the family of the guest who was murdered in a robbery attempt as he was returning to the hotel after walking through sections of New Orleans. The assault occurred on a public sidewalk only four feet from entrance doors that led to the shopping mall and the hotel. On appeal, the Fifth Circuit Court of Appeals affirmed the lower court's decision in holding the defendant hotel operators liable for damages of $975,000 while absolving the shopping mall operator from any liability.

Banks v. Hyatt Corporation
722 F.2d 214 (CA5 La, 1984)

reh den 731 F.2d 888 (CA5 La)

WISDOM, Circuit Judge.

This appeal presents the issue whether a landowner or an innkeeper can be liable to a business invitee or guest, respectively, for a criminal assault by a third party that occurs just outside the entrance doors to the hotel on property owned by the landowner but serving as a public sidewalk.

At 9:30 P.M. on April 12, 1979, an armed robber shot Dr. Robert Banks a few feet from the Loyola Avenue entrance to the Hyatt Hotel and the Poydras Plaza Mall in New Orleans. Dr. Banks was a registered guest of the hotel. He and a friend, Dr. John Hakola, were returning from dinner in the French Quarter. They had walked back and were "approximately at the door of the hotel," according to Dr. Hakola, when they were confronted by two young men, one of whom had a gun. Dr. Hakola managed to enter the building, but Dr. Banks was not so fortunate. He was shot and fell dead on the sidewalk, his head thirty feet from the street curb of Loyola Avenue and his feet only four feet from the glass doors at the entrance way to the Hyatt Hotel and the Poydras Plaza Mall.

Dr. Banks's widow and children brought this diversity action for wrongful death against Hyatt Corporation, lessee and operator of the hotel, and Refco Poydras Hotel Joint Venture, owner and operator of the Poydras Plaza Mall and owner of the hotel. The plaintiffs charged the defendants with negligently (1) failing to provide adequate security to protect the decedent from assaults by third persons, and (2) failing to warn him of the danger of being assaulted near the Loyola Avenue entrance to the hotel and mall. After extensive discovery the parties tried the matter from April 27 through May 1, 1981. The jury returned a verdict, on written interrogatories, finding both Hyatt and Refco negligent and awarding damages totalling $975,000 for all the plaintiffs.

Hyatt and Refco filed motions for judgment notwithstanding the verdict or, alternatively, for a new trial. After a hearing, the district court denied Hyatt's motions, but granted Refco's motion for a judgment n.o.v. Hyatt appealed from the judgment in favor of Refco as well as from the judgment in favor of the plaintiffs. The plaintiffs appealed from the judgment in favor of Refco. We affirm.

I. FACTS

On the facts, this case is sui generis [one of a kind]. Because we could find no controlling Louisiana decisions and no common law decisions specifically on point, we certified certain questions to the Louisiana Supreme Court. [footnote omitted] That Court was "of the opinion that once the relevant facts are determined, the case can be decided on existing, established principles of Louisiana law." It therefore denied the certification. *Banks v. Hyatt Corp.*, La. 1983, 436 So.2d 1171.

A. "The Relevant Facts" Are Not in Dispute

The plaintiffs begin their brief with the statement that the "essential facts of this case are undisputed." Hyatt and Refco make the same statement in their briefs, and we agree. The dispute is over the inferences to be drawn from the facts. The troublesome problem is whether the killing occurred in circumstances and at a place in which the jury could properly find Hyatt liable for breach of the innkeeper's duty of care to a guest and Refco liable for breach of an owner's duty of care to an invitee.

The trial court rejected Hyatt's proposed charge to the jury:

> An innkeeper, such as Hyatt Corporation, has no duty to protect its guests from assaults by third persons committed *outside the environs* of the hotel and, more particularly, it has no duty to protect its guests from assaults by third parties in areas where such protection is commonly owed by a Municipal Police Department, such as on public sidewalks.

2 Record 338 (emphasis added). In his instructions to the jury, the trial judge did not use the word "premises" nor the broader term "environs" that Hyatt had suggested. As appears from the pertinent charge quoted in the margin, the trial judge did not

limit the physical area in which an innkeeper owes a duty of care to a guest for acts of a third person.[2]

If the charge is taken literally, Hyatt is correct in arguing that the hotel would be liable to a guest for any harmful act occurring any place, as long as the hotel "could have discovered" the act and protected the guest "by controlling the conduct of the tortfeasor or by giving adequate warning." Such is not the law of Louisiana or of any other state. The instructions must be construed in the light of common sense. As we read the charge and as the jury must have read the charge, the trial judge intended the jury to consider—and apparently the jury did consider—all the physical facts relating to the killing and all the circumstances involving Hyatt's responsibility, and not just that Dr. Banks was killed at a location beyond the legal description of the hotel property and in an area serving as a public sidewalk, title to which was in Refco subject to a public servitude of passage. The instructions imply that an innkeeper's duty of care to a guest extends to the environs of a hotel, that is, an area immediately outside of a hotel's entrance or an area that a reasonable jury might consider to be part of the entrance. Here, the jury undoubtedly inferred that the location of the killing was within an area where Hyatt was responsible for security.

Perhaps because the trial judge considered that an innkeeper owes a higher duty of care to a guest than a possessor of land owes to an invitee, he limited the liability of Refco by charging as follows:

> In order to hold defendant, REFCO, liable, you must first find from the evidence that defendant, REFCO, was the *owner of the property at the location* of the death of decedent. Should you so find, then you are instructed that an owner must use ordinary care to protect patrons against the wrongful acts of third persons, who may be *in or upon the premises*, where he has reasonable cause to anticipate the wrongful act and the probability of injury.

2 Record 391 (emphasis added). This charge indicates that the trial judge concluded that the jury could find Refco to be "the owner of the property at the location of the death of the decedent." As in its consideration of Hyatt's liability, and not unreasonably, the jury necessarily inferred that Refco's area of invitation to invitees included the immediate access to the premises. Nevertheless, the trial judge granted the judgment n.o.v. in favor of Refco.

---

[2] The trial judge charged:

"Although a proprietor of an inn or hotel is not an insurer of the safety of his guests or patrons against tortious or improper acts or conduct of other guests, patrons, or third persons, he is bound to exercise reasonable care in this respect for their safety. Such a proprietor is liable for injuries to guests or patrons caused by intentionally harmful acts of third persons, if, by the exercise of reasonable diligence, he could have discovered that such acts were being done or were about to be done and could have protected his guests or patrons by controlling the conduct of the tortfeasor or by giving adequate warning to enable the guest to avoid him.

"In this regard, the proprietor is not bound to anticipate and guard against the unusual or abnormal, or against something which reasonable care, skill, or foresight could not have discovered or prevented. There is no duty imposed on the proprietor to warn of obvious dangers created by a third person unless he has knowledge of such dangers or unless knowledge may be inferred from the surrounding circumstances. While the standard of care is that of an ordinarily prudent person, it must be realized that reasonable care is a relative term in that the degree of care must be commensurate with the risks and dangers attending the activity being pursued and changes with the facts and circumstances of each particular case." 2 Record 390.

B. The Physical Layout of the Hotel and Mall

Besides the property leased to Hyatt Corporation, Refco owned and operated the Poydras Plaza Shopping Mall. Refco had title to the location where the killing occurred, subject to a servitude of passage. The servitude, which Refco's predecessor in title had granted to the City of New Orleans, extended from the curb of Loyola Avenue through the mall to an elevated walkway to the Superdome.

Poydras Plaza Mall is a two-story rectangular structure with the long sides perpendicular to Loyola Avenue. It is located in the middle of the block between Poydras and Girod Streets. Directly behind it and contiguous to it is the Hyatt Hotel, the residential portion of which is a tall tower. On the front wall of the mall on an overhang that goes straight up for two floors are large letters reading "Poydras Plaza." Three sets of glass doors are recessed under the overhang and lead to the mall, the hotel, and ultimately the Superdome. A person a few feet in front of the doors would therefore be under the second floor of the building and within the entrance way. The photographs admitted into evidence clearly demonstrate this fact. "Hyatt Regency" is lettered on the middle set of doors, "Poydras Plaza" on the left-hand doors, and "Superdome" on the right-hand doors, as one faces the building. On one side of the building next to the doors is a sign saying "Regency Conference Center," and on the other side of the building is a sign saying "Imperial Palace Regency." The hotel is advertised and frequently referred to as the Hyatt Regency Hotel. There is only one other entrance to the hotel, the motor lobby at the rear of the building. The mall now has stores and offices on each of its two levels, but in 1979 the only businesses open to the public were located on the second level.

An unobstructed passageway, subject to the servitude of passage previously mentioned, enables one to walk from the Loyola Street entrance through the Poydras Plaza to the Superdome. Three quarters of a block from Loyola Avenue, the mall divides and passes around a set of elevator banks, a stairwell, and escalators leading to the portions of the hotel tower occupied by Hyatt and the lower level reception and registration area of the hotel. The two halves rejoin and continue in the form of an elevated walkway to the Superdome, one block from the hotel tower.

The street level portion of the passageway ends abruptly behind and beneath the second set of stairs from the Loyola Avenue entrance. The ground level right of passage is blocked by a solid wall. To reach the second level of the shopping mall and to continue through the structure, one must ascend one of the two sets of stairs or use escalators adjacent to the set of stairs nearest the mall entrance of Loyola Avenue. To proceed further, one must go through the atrium area of the hotel tower. This entire mall area is open to the public and, of course, to hotel guests.

C. Evidence of Previous Criminal Incidents

The plaintiffs introduced evidence to show that the Hyatt-Poydras Plaza complex and its environs had been the scene of a number of crimes. Some of the evidence was in the form of "incident reports" and "security log" entries prepared by Hyatt security guards detailing each criminal incident that the guards investigated and reported. These reports described incidents occurring both on and off the premises. In the three month period preceding the Banks killing, there were eleven armed robberies and five simple robberies within the immediate surroundings of the hotel. Dr. Banks was the second person to be shot at the Loyola Avenue entrance, and the fifth victim of armed robbery at the entrance, since the date of the hotel's opening in 1976.

At trial, the Hyatt Director of Security, Joseph Murry, reviewed twenty-one Hyatt Security Department Incident Reports describing incidents at the Loyola Avenue entrance or in the near vicinity of that entrance. The incidents occurred between December 17, 1976, and April 6, 1979, only six days before the death of Dr. Banks. Twelve of those incidents involved weapons. Murry also reviewed Hyatt Security logs detailing approximately fifty additional incidents occurring between September 1976 and April 1979. Of these incidents, at least fourteen involved weapons.

Murry's own correspondence reflected no less than seven "serious criminal violations" on or about the Hyatt premises between February 5, 1979, and March 6, 1979. The correspondence showed that the prime hours of crime incidence were between 6:00 P.M. and 2:00 A.M. and, specifically, that increased patrols were required on the Loyola Avenue corridor between Girod and Poydras Streets.

A representative of Property Management Systems, Inc., a national management corporation that contracted with Refco to supply management services for the mall, testified that he had recommended to Refco that a security guard be stationed at the Loyola Avenue entrance to the mall between the hours of 8:00 P.M. and 4:00 A.M. He also said that he had made the recommendation because that entrance to the mall was his "area of responsibility."

D. Provisions for Security

In April 1979, Refco operated the mall through Property Management Systems. Earlier, in the 1976 lease to Hyatt, Refco had agreed to provide normal and customary upkeep and security at no cost to Hyatt. In 1978 Refco, through Property Management Systems, contracted with Hyatt for the hotel to hire men, trained and employed by Hyatt, to provide security in the mall area from the Loyola Avenue entrance through and including the shopping area on the second level. Hyatt's Chief of Security supervised the security personnel, but Refco dictated security policy by issuing instructions through Hyatt's Chief. Each mall officer prepared a report at the end of his shift, which went to Property Management Systems. Hyatt paid the mall officers' salaries and billed Refco for the total cost of these payments. Security officers wore Hyatt blazers and carried Hyatt radios so that they could alert the hotel to any danger in the mall that might threaten guests in the hotel. Hyatt's former general manager testified that [Hyatt] participated in the security measures so that it "would, in fact, have at no cost to Hyatt our man with a visible presence in the shopping plaza so that [Hyatt] would know of any activity in that area before it might affect the operation of the hotel." Testimony of Thomas R. Gaskill, 5 Record 194.

Early in 1979, before Dr. Banks's death, Hyatt, Refco, and three other property owners in the square became concerned about the increase in crime in and around their property. They requested the New Orleans Police Department to detail additional police patrols to the area. The department denied this request. The five property owners then hired off-duty, uniformed, armed police officers to patrol the perimeter of the property including the parking area on each side of the mall, although none of the five had leased that area. The "perimeter patrol" started three weeks before the Banks incident. It was a large area for one man to patrol. At the time of the killing, the officer providing perimeter protection was in the motor lobby, at the opposite end of the complex.

II. ISSUES ON APPEAL

Hyatt contends on appeal that the district court's instructions regarding the duty of an innkeeper to protect guests represent a "novel, unprecedented and unwarranted extension" of that duty. Hyatt also contends that the district court erred (1) in refusing to instruct the jury on contributory negligence and assumption of risk, and (2) in granting the judgment n.o.v. in favor of Refco.

Refco argues that the owner of a building owes no duty to protect third parties from crimes occurring on a public sidewalk outside the building. If a duty of reasonable care is due, Refco maintains, it complied with that duty.

The defendants properly preserved these points in the trial court.

Because we find no evidence of contributory negligence or assumption of risk on the part of Dr. Banks,[3] we affirm the district court's refusal to instruct the jury on those defenses. Thus, the primary issue concerns the duty of care that Hyatt and Refco owed Dr. Banks.

III. DUTY OF CARE

A. The Nature of Defendants' Respective Duties

Although the Restatement of Torts maintains that landowners and innkeepers owe the same duty of care towards business invitees and guests, respectively, [footnote omitted] Louisiana law recognizes a distinction in this regard. The owner or operator of a business owes a duty to invitees to exercise reasonable care to protect them from injury. This duty does not extend, however, to unforeseeable or unanticipated criminal acts by an independent third person. "Only when the owner or management of a business has knowledge, or can be imputed with knowledge, of a third person's intended criminal conduct which is about to occur, and which is within the power of the owner or management to protect against, does such a duty towards a guest arise." *Davenport v. Nixon*, La.App. 1 Cir. 1983, 434 So.2d 1203, 1205 (citing cases). [citations omitted] Because there is no evidence in this case that Refco employees knew, or can be imputed with the knowledge, that Dr. Banks and his companion were about to be assaulted at the [Loyola Avenue] entrance to the mall, Refco cannot be held to have violated its duty of care to Dr. Banks. We therefore affirm the district court's decision to grant judgment n.o.v. in favor of Refco.

The Louisiana Supreme Court has recently held that innkeepers owe their guests a duty of care higher than ordinary or reasonable care:

> An innkeeper does not insure his guests against the risk of injury or property loss resulting from violent crime. The innkeeper's position vis-a-vis his guests is similar to that of a common carrier toward its passengers. Thus, a guest is entitled to *a high degree of care and protection. The innkeeper has a duty to take reasonable precautions against criminals.*

---

[3]In *Roberts v. Tiny Tim Thrifty Check*, La.App. 4 Cir.1979, 367 So.2d 64, the court held that a business invitee who initiated a physical struggle with an armed assailant was guilty of contributory negligence and assumption of risk. *See id.* at 66. There is absolutely no evidence in this case that Dr. Banks initiated a struggle with his assailant. The investigating detective proffered his unsubstantiated opinion that there had been a struggle between Dr. Banks and his assailant, but the detective did not indicate who had initiated the struggle. 4 Record 95.

Kraaz v. La Quinta Motor Inns, Inc., La.1982, 410 So.2d 1048, 1053 (emphasis added; citations omitted).[5] This distinction between innkeepers and other businesses is not unique in American jurisprudence. This Court has noted in dictum that some cases require innkeepers to exercise "a higher degree of care"[6] than "ordinary or reasonable care to protect their guests against injury by third persons." *Nordmann v. National Hotel Co.,* 5 Cir. 1970, 425 F.d 1103, 1107. Florida law recognizes the same distinction. An ordinary business cannot be liable for a third-party assault against an invitee unless the business has actual or imputed knowledge of the impending assault and the opportunity to prevent it. [citations omitted] An innkeeper, however, "may be liable if he fails to take *reasonable precautions to deter* the *type* of criminal activity which resulted in a guest's injury." *Reichenbach,* 401 So.2d at 1367 (emphasis added). The distinction is no doubt rooted in the belief that business patrons of innkeepers, like those of common carriers and unlike those of other businesses, have entrusted their personal security to the innkeeper.

In the present case, the trial court instructed the jury to use the standard of "reasonable care," "that of any ordinarily prudent person." As is apparent from the above discussion, this instruction is inaccurate, but in a manner favorable to Hyatt. Under *Kraaz,* innkeepers owe a high degree of care which embraces a duty to take reasonable precautions against criminal assaults on guests. Thus, the trial court did not commit reversible error in its instruction concerning the *nature* of Hyatt's duty.

B. The Physical Extent of Hyatt's Duty

The question remains whether Hyatt is entitled to judgment as a matter of law because the assault on Dr. Banks occurred outside of the entrance doors to the hotel, on a sidewalk subject to a servitude of passage. After examining general tort doctrine, the relevant caselaw, and the policies underlying tort liability, we find ourselves unwilling to create an immunity based on a distance of four feet.

1. General Tort Doctrine

With certain exceptions, none applicable in the instant case, the Louisiana law of delicts is substantially similar to the common law of torts. Louisiana courts have frequently quoted and cited with approval the first and second Restatements of Torts, Corpus Juris, American Jurisprudence, Prosser, and Harper & James. Article 2315, the generally governing statutory provision, is broad enough to allow Louisiana courts to develop delictual responsibility along common law lines.[7] Indeed, the

---

[5]The court in *Davenport* questioned, but did not decide, whether the *Kraaz* court meant to subject innkeepers to a more demanding duty of care than that required of other businesses. *See Davenport,* 434 So.2d at 1205. We find it clear from the language quoted in text that the Louisiana Supreme Court did intend to recognize such a distinction.

[6]"A high degree of care" is the language used by the courts in a number of cases in describing the standard of care in the innkeeper-guest relation. *See, e.g., Mrzlak v. Ettinger,* 1975, 25 Ill. App.3d 706, 712,323, N.E.2d 796, 800; *Fortney v. Hotel Rancroft., Inc.,* 1955, 5 Ill.App.2d 327,335,125 N.E.2d 544,548.

[7]Article 2315 of the Louisiana Civil Code provides that "[e]very act whatever of man that causes damage to another obliges him by whose fault it happened to repair it." La.Civ.Code Ann.art. 2315 (West Supp. 1982).

doctrine of contributory negligence, followed for many years in Louisiana, is an import from the common law incompatible with the spirit of the civil law. [footnote omitted]

The Restatement of Torts sets forth the duties to aid or protect another that arise out of special relations existing between the actor and the person to be aided or protected. The general rule, as stated in section 314 of the first Restatement of Torts (1934), is that one person's realization that action on his part is necessary to protect another person does not in itself impose a duty to take such action. [footnote omitted] Section 314A, added in the second Restatement of Torts (1965), states the following exceptions to the rule:[10]

> Special Relations Giving Rise to Duty to Aid or Protect
> (1) A common carrier is under a duty to its passengers to take reasonable action
> (a) to protect them against unreasonable risk of physical harm, …
> …
> (2) An innkeeper is under a similar duty to his guests.
> (3) A possessor of land who holds it open to the public is under a similar duty to members of the public who enter in response to his invitation.

Comment c of this section limits this duty of care to the premises of the innkeeper or possessor of land.

> The rules stated in this Section apply only where the relation exists between the parties, and the risk of harm, or of further harm, arises in the course of that relation. A carrier is under no duty to one who has left the vehicle and ceased to be a passenger, nor is an innkeeper under a duty to a guest who is injured or endangered while he is away from the premises. Nor is a possessor of land under any such duty to one who has ceased to be an invitee.

Comment e of section 332, defining "invitee," states: "The possessor of land is subject to liability to another as an invitee only for harm sustained while he is on the land within the scope of his invitation."

The Restatement unquestionably states the general rule correctly. If we were to apply the rule strictly, giving a literal reading to the two comments quoted above, we might be compelled to reverse the judgment against Hyatt. But as Professor Prosser, the first reporter for the Second Restatement of Torts, has said:

> This area of invitation will of course vary with the circumstances of the case. It extends to the entrance of the property and to a safe exit after the purpose [of the visit] is concluded; and it extends to all parts of the premises to which the purpose may reasonably be expected to take him.

W. Prosser, *Law of Torts* §61, at 392 (4th ed. 1975).

We find Professor Prosser's gloss on the Restatement persuasive. We therefore conclude that the general law of torts, as reflected in the Restatement and in Prosser,

---

[10] The Restatement of Torts holds landowners and innkeepers to the same duty of care towards invitees and guests, respectively. As noted in Section A, Louisiana law distinguishes between the duty of care owed by landowners and that owed by innkeepers by holding innkeepers to a higher degree of care. The Restatement is discussed here only for its relevance to the physical extent of the innkeeper's duty of care.

does not preclude recovery against Hyatt for injury occurring in the entrance way to the defendants' premises.

2. The Relevant Caselaw

There are no relevant Louisiana codal articles or statutes. The parties have been unable to find any cases directly on point, and this Court has done no better. The appellants and the appellees have directed our attention to cases on the fringe of the issue.

Hyatt, Refco, and the American Hotel and Motel Association (amicus curiae), rely particularly on *Mitchell v. Archibald & Kendall, Inc.*, 7 Cir.1978, 573 F.2d 429; *Kline v. 1500 Massachusetts Avenue Apartment Corp.*, D.C.Cir.1970, 439 F.2d 477; and *Semmelroth v. American Airlines*, E.D.Ill.1978, 448 F.Supp.730.

* * *

We are not persuaded by the defendants' citations; the plaintiffs' cases are closer in point and closer home. *Cothern v. LaRocca*, 1970, 255 La. 673, 232 So.2d 473, involved a restaurant abutting a motel. A patron of the restaurant had parked his automobile half on the restaurant's property and half on the motel's property. As the patron's wife left the car on the motel's property, she twisted her leg in an open hole. The Louisiana Supreme Court held that, in the factual circumstances of this case, the restaurant owner owed no duty to its invitee:

> LaRocca, the restaurant owner, did not know that invitees of the restaurant sometimes parked on the motel property. No invitation, either implied or expressed, had been extended to his invitees to use the abutting premises. He did not know of the existence of the uncovered hole on the adjacent premises and could not, even with reasonable inspection from his own premises, have readily, if at all, discerned the hole in the tall grass. We conclude that under these facts LaRocca owed no duty to protect Mrs. Cothern from this unknown defect on the adjoining property.

Id. at 687–88,232 So.2d at 478. The necessary implication is that, had the owner invited his patrons to use the adjacent property, or known that they sometimes did, and knew or should have known of the dangerous condition, the court would have found that the owner owed a duty of care to the invitee.

In *Lowe v. Thermal Supply, Inc.*, La. App.2 Cir.1970, 242 So.2d 351, the court found such a duty. *Lowe* involved a refrigeration supply store located in front of a vacant lot. The lot was owned by an unnamed third party. The evidence showed that on several occasions the defendant would leave refrigeration parts in the rear of its place of business to be picked up by its customers. The only way to reach this area was to go through the vacant lot. While proceeding through the lot to pick up some parts, the plaintiff's feet became entangled in the grass and she was injured. The court held that the plaintiff was an invitee and that the defendant therefore owed the plaintiff a duty to correct hidden defects or to warn the plaintiff of the defects. *Id*. at 352. The court held for the defendants, however, on the ground that the plaintiff was contributorily negligent.

Chief Justice (then Judge) John Dixon pointed out in dissent:

> There is a recent case involving injury on nonowned property which indicates that there might be liability if the dangerous condition to which a customer is exposed is known to the business inviting the customer, even though the dangerous

condition is not on land owned or leased by the business establishment. See *Cothern v. LaRocca*, 255 La. 673, 232 So.2d 473 (1970).

The evidence is sufficient to show that the employees of Thermal Supply knew about the high grass. I am convinced that the tall, thick grass caused Mrs. Lowe to fall, and the defendant did not carry the burden of proving her contributory negligence.

Id. at 353 (Dixon, J., dissenting).

These two decisions suggest that Louisiana courts take a broad view of the duty of care owed to an invitee by an owner or possessor of land when the danger to the invitee is located on adjacent land, at least when injury occurs on the access to the owner's business. A similar perspective is suggested in *Rozelle v. Employers' Liability Assurance Corp.*, La.App. 2 Cir.1972, 260 So.2d 757, *writ denied*, 261 La. 1068, 262 So.2d 45. In that case, which involved a slip-and-fall injury occurring in the entrance way to a store, the court held that a business's duty of reasonable care to invitees "extends to the entrance way of a store as well as to the interior of the store." 260 So.2d at 759. It is likely that the Louisiana Supreme Court had these cases in mind when it denied certification in the present case.

Decisions from other jurisdictions have gone far in applying the duty of care to invitees. In *Shields v. Food Fair Stores, Inc.*, Fla.App.1958, 106 So.2d 90, *cert. denied*, Fla.1959, 109 So.2d 168, the court addressed the liability of a store for an injury occurring in the entrance way to the store's parking lot. The trial court dismissed the complaint. The appellate court reversed, holding that:

> The duty owed to invitees by an occupier of premises to maintain them in a reasonably safe condition includes and extends to approaches to the premises which are open to invitees in connection with their business on the premises, and which approaches are so located and constituted as to represent an invitation to visit the place of business and to use such means of approach.

Id. at 92 (citations omitted).

In *Tarshis v. Lahaina Investment Corp.*, 9 Cir.1973, 480 F.2d 1019, the guest of an Hawaiian resort beach hotel sued the hotel for a swimming injury that occurred in the ocean surf in front of the hotel. Reversing the district court's summary judgment of dismissal, the Court of Appeals held that the hotel had a duty to warn its guests and patrons of the dangerous conditions in the ocean along its beach frontage "which were not known to [the plaintiff] or obvious to an ordinarily intelligent person and either were known or in the exercise of reasonable care ought to have been known to the [hotel]." *Id*. at 1020.

Finally, in *Great Atlantic & Pacific Tea Co. v. Pederson*, 1 Cir.1957, 247 F.2d 4 (per curiam), the Court refused to upset a jury verdict finding the defendant liable for injuries to the plaintiff that occurred when the plaintiff fell on an unlighted ramp that was not part of the defendant's premises. The court stated that:

> We are satisfied that this was a routine case where the issues of negligence and contributory negligence were properly left to the jury. It was of course unimportant that the concealed ramp, into which the plaintiff fell, was not in occupation and control of the defendant as lessee. As the Supreme Judicial Court stated in *Carleton v. Franconia Iron & Steel Co.*, 1868, 99 Mass. 215, 217:
>
> "The owner or occupant of land is liable in damages to those coming to it, using due care, at his invitation or inducement, express or implied, on any business to be transacted with or permitted by him, for an injury

occasioned by the unsafe condition of the land *or of the access to it*, which is known to him and not to them, and which he has negligently suffered to exist and has given them no notice of."

247 F.2d at 5 (emphasis added).

Though we have not located any case on all fours with the case at bar, we find that the cases lend greater support to the plaintiffs' position than they do to the defendants' position. We are convinced that, at least under Louisiana law, the duty of a business to protect invitees can extend to adjacent property, particularly entrances to the business premises, if the business is aware of a dangerous condition on the adjacent property and fails to warn its invitees or to take some other reasonable preventive action. As an innkeeper, Hyatt is potentially liable not only for dangerous physical conditions, but also for foreseeable criminal assaults by third persons. Hyatt clearly was aware of the risk of criminal assault that its guests faced in the immediate area surrounding the hotel, especially at the [Loyola Avenue] entrance. Hyatt did take preventive action, although the jury found, not irrationally, that Hyatt did not do enough. The caselaw supports the conclusion that there is no legal bar to finding Hyatt liable for Dr. Banks's death. This conclusion is supported also by the policies underlying tort liability, to which we now turn.

3. Policies of Tort Liability

The law of torts has never stood still. Section 314 of the first Restatement of Torts, stating the law as the American Law Institute perceived it in 1934, laid down the rule that an "actor" is under no duty to act to protect another even though such action could and may be necessary to prevent injury to the other. Thirty years later, a culture aware of the increasing complexity of society and the concomitant increasing interdependence of social actors could no longer tolerate that rule. The ALI added section 314A to the Restatement, which recognizes three important exceptions to the general rule.

The essence of section 314A of the Restatement is the recognition that a duty to protect may arise out of a special relation between one actor and another. "If the conduct of the actor has brought him into a human relationship with another, of such character that sound social policy requires either some affirmative action or some precaution on his part to avoid harm, the duty to act or take the precaution is imposed by law." Harper & Kime, *The Duty To Control the Conduct of Another*, 43 Yale L.J. 886, 886 (1934). As is not unusual, and as Harper and Kime point out, Justice Cardozo led the way:

> Given a relation involving in its existence a duty of care ... , a tort may result as well from acts of omission as of commission in the fulfillment of the duty thus recognized by law. What we need to know is not so much the conduct to be avoided when the relation and its attendant duty are established as existing. What we need to know is the conduct that engenders the relation. It is here that the formula, however incomplete, has its value and significance.

Moch Co. v. Rensselaer Water Co., 1928, 247 N.Y. 160, 167, 159 N.E. 896, 898.

Because an innkeeper's duty to protect its guests is relational, it follows that the duty should exist only when the relation exists and when the risk of injury arises in the course of the relation. This rationale underlies the Restatement's limitation of the duty to the premises of the innkeeper. *See* Restatement (Second) of Torts §314 comment c (1965). We find this limitation to be an artificial legal boundary, and decline to adopt it.

Tort law has become increasingly concerned with placing liability upon the party that is best able to determine the cost-justified level of accident prevention. [citations omitted] Holding a negligent innkeeper liable when there is a third-party assault on the premises is sensible, not because of some abstract conceptual notion about the risk arising within "the course of the relation," but because the innkeeper is able to identify and carry out cost-justified ("reasonable") preventive measures on the premises. If the innkeeper has sufficient control of property, the innkeeper should not be immune from liability when his failure to take such actions results in an injury to a guest. As between innkeeper and guest, the innkeeper is the only one in the position to take the reasonably necessary acts to guard against the predictable risk of assaults. He is not an insurer, but he is obligated to take reasonable steps to minimize the risk to his guests within his sphere of control.

The security measures adopted by Hyatt, especially the "perimeter patrol," demonstrate the Hyatt had the power to take preventive action within the immediate surrounding area. As noted above, the jury found that Hyatt did not go far enough. Allowing the jury's finding of negligence to stand should induce Hyatt to determine and to put in effect cost-justified preventive measures covering both the premises of the hotel and such adjacent areas as are sufficiently within its control to permit reasonable preventive action.

IV. CONCLUSION

Our decision in this case is strongly influenced by the peculiar facts with which we are presented. Dr. Banks's death occurred only four feet from the entrance doors to the mall and hotel, underneath an overhang that is actually the second floor of the complex. The defendants were aware of the crime problem in the plaza complex and its immediate environs, and were capable of taking reasonable action to reduce the risk of guests and invitees in these areas.

We affirm the judgment n.o.v. in favor of Refco, because that defendant's duty of care to invitees does not include a duty to adopt precautionary measures to reduce the general risk of criminal assault. Hyatt's duty to its guests, however, does embrace a responsibility to take reasonable precautionary measures. We reject Hyatt's argument that its duty cannot, as a matter of law, extend to the location of Dr. Banks's death. Dr. Banks did not make it through the entrance doors to the complex. We refuse to transform those doors into an impregnable legal wall of immunity.

The judgment of the district court is AFFIRMED.

In discussing the geographic area for which the hotel could be found liable for inadequate security, the court indicated that such area would extend only to the hotel's own premises and the area immediately surrounding its entrance. The court indicated that it was not prepared to say that a hotel had a duty to provide security beyond this limited area or to warn guests of crime hazards in other parts of the city.

In establishing the perimeter of a property, a number of questions may be posed.

- Are there physical systems which could enhance the response capability of security personnel?
- At what location would the personnel response capability be maximized?
- Is it necessary and feasible to monitor a particular physical system on a 24-hour basis? Are there alternative schedules which might be acceptable? For example, the presence of employees in a receiving area may minimize the necessity for constant monitoring of closed-circuit television until the receiving area closes. It may be advisable, however, to monitor the receiving area from time to time during working hours to reduce thefts by employees or delivery personnel.
- Should perimeter protection be extended to include pools, recreational facilities (i.e., tennis courts, squash courts, jogging paths, cycling paths, boating areas, etc.), and other hotel entertainment facilities remote from the main lodging building? If so, how may it be done effectively?

Perimeter Barriers

It is common that a lodging establishment's perimeter access be restricted by fencing or barriers that separate the property from wooded areas, busy thoroughfares, industrial and commercial complexes, or apartment complexes. Such areas might present security problems or risks to the lodging facility and its guests. Under certain conditions, it may be desirable to restrict perimeter access to a property by planting shrubbery. In such a case, care should be taken to keep the shrubbery from serving as a hiding place for unwanted intruders or unauthorized persons.

Lighting

Because criminals like to work in the dark, appropriate lighting for the property is a critical aspect of security in the physical protection program. It is also one of the least expensive security measures to implement. Efforts may need to be made to eliminate dark areas in the property where someone could hide prior to accosting a guest or employee. Attention should be focused on lighting for entranceways, corridors, steps, walkways, recreational areas, and parking facilities. Outdoor lighting should be reviewed for each specific hotel or motel relative to its special needs. The source of light is very important. Placing the lighting source on a building to illuminate the immediate surroundings may have the advantage of partially blinding an intruder; it may also make the intruder unsure of whether he or she can be observed from the building. However, it may also partially blind those personnel responsible for securing the property. Consequently, it is suggested that care be taken in order to properly place lighting sources.

With regard to energy conservation, many lighting units are available which use minimum energy but provide maximum light. A lighting engineer or specialist may determine the amount of lighting needed, the best location for lighting, and various other considerations resulting in its most effective utilization as a security tool.

> **Parking Facility CPTED Security Features**
>
> - The single most important CPTED security feature is lighting. Lighting codes should meet the standards of the Illuminating Engineering Society of North America.
> - Elevator lobbies and stairs in open parking garages should be open to parking areas except at roof levels where glass enclosures may be provided for weather protection.
> - Access control and perimeter security should always be considered in the initial design stage. Even if the potential site for the parking facility is low risk, the risk level could change in the future.
> - Emergency communications such as panic buttons and closed-circuit television cannot compensate for a lack of CPTED. However, they can enhance CPTED in high-risk facilities, and all facilities should be designed so such enhancements can be easily installed.

Source: Mary Smith, "Crime Prevention through Environmental Design in Parking Facilities," *The National Institute of Justice Research in Brief,* April 1996.

In addition to the normal lighting system, a standby system of emergency lighting may be provided for backup in the case of a power failure. With the possibility of brownouts and blackouts, the ability to provide backup lighting in critical locations may be important to security management planning.

Another frequently overlooked protection feature is locks for electric switch boxes and control boxes. If an outsider is able to gain access to the switch control for a crowded function room, he or she may gain an important advantage in his or her ability to commit crimes against guests or the property.

Parking Areas

Providing safe parking facilities is another important aspect of physical security on the lodging premises. Whether in a separate structure, attached to the hotel or motel, in a lot surrounding the hotel or motel, or adjacent to the guestrooms, parking facilities should be analyzed with respect to protection for guests, invitees, and employees.

Factors to consider with regard to parking facilities include adequate lighting, proper directional markings to ensure smooth traffic flow, employee observation, monitored entrances, and other access-limiting systems. Roving vehicle or foot patrols may also be considered. If patrols are warranted, they should be irregularly timed to prevent establishing a patterned routine. Parking security is one area best handled through cooperative efforts with local police authorities. Whenever possible, arrangements should be made for occasional police car patrols through the parking facility. *Peters v. Holiday Inns, Inc.* is a case in which a police patrol played a central role in apprehending four criminals. In this case, four suspicious men were observed and apprehended by a police officer who was routinely patrolling the premises in an unmarked squad car.

Glass Protection

There are a number of glass protection items important to the security of the property. Prior to the 1970s, most glass was single pane that broke easily and caused serious injuries. Today, a common requirement in all jurisdictions is the specification of either tempered safety glass or a glass containing a central plastic element that would reduce the problem of severe injuries from glass shards when a panel is accidentally broken. In order to warn guests that a glass panel is in place, further mandates include precautionary placement of window decals, a planter, or an article of stationary furniture, such as a bench, attached to the floor. These items can help prevent the severe injury that can occur when a person accidentally walks through an "invisible" glass panel.

Energy conservation programs have also made a difference in the type of glass that is installed in lodging establishments. The introduction of double glazing (using argon gas as an insulator between two panels of glass) provided a tinted glass that made it less likely to be mistaken for an opening to or from a location. "Super smart" glass windows (which contain three argon-filled layers) maximize both energy control and protection against accidental breakage by "walk through" incidents.

As vandalism and violence are growing problems, enhanced plastic products can provide windows with the strength to withstand anything from a hurled brick to the swing of an axe; the application of special films to existing glass can even make the panels resistant to bullets. However, in considering the use of such protection, evaluate the likelihood of a guest having to escape from an area where the window may be the only escape path.

Surveillance

Surveillance plays a role in most aspects of guest and property protection, including perimeter control. It is a function that typically relies on personnel, but also one that may potentially be enhanced or supplemented by the use of various types of equipment. For example, in the lobby area, if possible, the front desk person should be able to observe the property's entrances and elevators. Elevators can be programmed to stop and open their doors at lobby level in order to allow their occupants to be observed. Using mirrors to observe persons on the elevators may also be feasible. Of course, elevators are sometimes located where it is not possible to monitor them from a control center such as a front desk, assistant manager's desk, or concierge's desk. However, where such a control capability does exist, consideration should be given to having the elevator stop at a monitored location during certain hours of the night.

With the development of *tower* or *club* floors, a number of hotels and motels are introducing elevator key controls which require a guest key to make the elevator stop at the restricted floor. Other properties program elevators to go only from the lobby to club floors; such properties usually place someone at the club floor elevator to ensure that those people trying to reach the floor are allowed to be there. Where a single elevator lobby is located on the ground level, some properties have placed a security officer and desk at the entrance to the bank of elevators.

In some hotels, only registered guests with keys and their invitees are permitted to pass that point. The use of glass-enclosed elevators on the outside wall of the building in atrium properties and in some high-rise facilities permits monitoring by staff in the vicinity of the elevator. Some high-rise properties turn off some elevators at night.

Escalators may be feasible in areas of the property where people are continuously moving to meeting or other function rooms or concourse shopping areas. Observation of the escalators involves both security and safety considerations. Personnel should be instructed in procedures for stopping the escalators in an emergency. Escalators should be turned off when not in use.

Closed-Circuit Television

Closed-circuit television (CCTV) can sometimes be used effectively as a surveillance tool in multiple-entry properties. It must be remembered, however, that a CCTV system is only as effective as the monitoring system and the property's ability to respond reasonably to what may be observed. Exhibit 3 lists some available features of CCTV systems. Usually, monitors are located in a control center and employees are assigned to respond promptly and appropriately when an incident is noted on the CCTV.

Although CCTV is of some value in controlling employee areas for protection of assets, it may be of limited use in the viewing of public areas. Because observed activities often do not lend themselves to an accurate evaluation of what is actually taking place, CCTV is most effective in areas where there should be no movement. In addition, the lighting found in some areas of a property may be too dim for the most efficient use of CCTV. One must also consider the guest's and employee's right of privacy when evaluating the installation of CCTV. For example, it may be considered an invasion of privacy to place CCTV cameras in a property's restrooms. Local counsel should be consulted concerning such questions.

The placement of CCTV in elevators has generally reduced vandalism and crimes against individuals. Placement of a camera in a corner of the cab will, with wide-lens capability, provide 100 percent coverage of the cab's interior. A durable housing should be provided to minimize vandalism; a covert camera may be installed if vandalism becomes a problem. Some innkeepers have even installed CCTV cameras that were not in fact hooked up or operational. The rationale for this has been that the presence of the cameras would be sufficient to deter criminals who would not realize that they were not actually being observed. Some courts and juries, however, have found the use of such "dummy" cameras to be inappropriate because it implies a degree of protection which is not in fact present. Such an implication may have unfortunate consequences. A person being victimized, for example, may base his or her behavior on the belief that the scene is being witnessed by someone in the CCTV control room and that help is certainly on the way.

Involve a reputable consultant, engineer, and a systems supplier with a hospitality industry track record prior to CCTV installation. In using CCTV, hotel and motel management may wish to consider adding an intercom capability to the area being monitored. Time-lapse photography or time-lapse videocassette recorders

Exhibit 3 Features of Closed-Circuit Television (CCTV) Systems

	Cameras
Features	**Description and Consideration**
Fixed	One camera mounted in a stationary position which presents a constant view. Relatively inexpensive—you can install three fixed-lens cameras for the cost of one pan/tilt/zoom camera.
Pan/tilt or pan/tilt/zoom (PTZ)	A motorized camera that pans back and forth or up and down. "Auto pan" means the camera moves in a constant back and forth motion. An operator with a joystick can zoom in on scenes or move the camera in a desired direction. More advanced PTZ models can be individually programmed by the operator to move in a desired pattern and to pan faster or slower as they scan certain areas. Activity can be missed while a camera is panning away from a scene. Programmable units are considered superior.
Lenses	During installation it's best to have your supplier try out different lenses at each spot where cameras will be mounted so you can see which lenses give you the view you want.
Switching or sequencing	Images being viewed (and recorded) switch from camera to camera every few seconds. With this approach, important activity in the field of one camera can be missed while other cameras in the sequence are taking shots. This technology is considered outmoded.
Quad	A four-camera system: activity in the field of each camera is picked up and recorded almost simultaneously. When watching the monitor you can either look at all four images at the same time—one in each quadrant—or pull up one image to fill the screen.
Two-page quad	Uses up to eight cameras. The monitor shows views from the first four cameras, then flips to show views from the second four. Other configurations are possible: if you use only six cameras, for example, the views from two key cameras can stay on the screen all the time while the views from the other four flip back and forth.
Multiplexer	A system using 16 cameras: activity in the field of each camera is picked up in a sequence so rapidly it is practically simultaneous. You can view all 16 images on the monitor at once or pull up one image for close examination. When playing back recorded film, you can specify which camera's images you want to see.
Overt	Cameras out in plain view serve as a deterrent to crime.
Covert	Hidden cameras are useful for detecting employee problems such as theft. Some experts say cameras in pool areas should be concealed so guests do not assume someone else is watching out for the safety of their children.
Black and white	In general, black and white cameras produce higher resolution than color cameras and are less expensive.
Activity detection	In a multiple-camera system, an activity detection feature prompts one camera to shoot more pictures if activity is occurring in its field of view. When the activity stops, the cameras return to their preset mode.
Video motion detection	These systems have external triggers that set off an alarm or perform some other action (shutting a gate, calling 911, putting a message on a computer screen) if motion is detected in a camera's field of view.

Exhibit 3 *(continued)*

Features	Recorders — Description and Consideration
Time lapse	Records a series of pictures with brief intervals in between so viewer sees each motion in a jerky manner similar to that in old-time silent movies. Industrial time-lapse recorders are designed to run 24 hours a day 365 days a year, unlike VCRs for home use.
Real time	Captures so many frames per second that it flows smoothly on the monitor.
Digital	Digital recorders save video information on the hard drive of a computer, allowing users to store more information in less space and to search and manipulate the information in ways not available on standard time-lapse VCRs.
Alarm	Some recorders allow you to fast-forward to activity that has triggered an alarm, so you don't have to scan the entire tape.
Time/date generator	Industrial time-lapse VCRs have a built-in feature that marks the time and date on the film. This feature is not included on VCRs for home use.
Panic button	A unit the size of a cigarette pack that can be portable (carried by bellhops or parking attendants, for example) or mounted in parking garages and other strategic spots. When the button is pushed, an alarm sounds. The closest PTZ camera can swing in the direction of the button and zoom in, if the camera and lens are capable of preset positioning.

Source: Vicki Meade, "CCTV: A Key Element in the Security Equation," *Lodging*, December 1995, p. 54.

may also be integrated with CCTV systems. If deemed appropriate, this technique may be of value in monitoring cashier functions, receiving docks, storage areas, and other sensitive locations where a potential for security incidents exists. Within casino operations, CCTV and time-lapse photography are essentially mandated by state authorities. CCTV can also provide coverage of the pool and its entrance(s), serving the dual function of protecting guests while they are in the pool and protecting the entrance(s) from intruders.

Since on-site monitoring is often difficult to implement, an alternative service potential has been developed. In the late 1990s, remote monitoring from off-premises locations became an option. The televised image is beamed via satellite to a location that could be 1,000 or more miles from the site being monitored. The agent monitoring the site has direct voice capability to that location, with the further ability to immediately initiate a 911 call within the community being monitored. In one incident, the agent viewed a hold-up of a cashier at gunpoint. He immediately called 911, reporting the robbery in progress and the location for response. When the perpetrator stepped behind the counter and began to pistol-whip the cashier, the agent moved to verbal intercession stating, "Security has noted your presence, and the police have been called and are on their way." The robber immediately fled from the scene.

Communication Systems

In order to respond promptly to a security need, a communication system may be required that facilitates the quick notification of the employee or employees

> **CCTV Tips from the Experts**
>
> - If you choose to have CCTV, get a good system. Avoid going with the lowest bidder; if you're called into court you need to show you hired the best company, not the cheapest.
>
> - Before cameras are installed, make sure the supplier lets you see the image from the proposed camera positions using different lenses. Does the camera do what you want? You may think you want a wide-angle view, for example, but could discover it doesn't give you the detail you need, or you may find there's too much glare in the place you'd intended to mount a camera.
>
> - If possible, have security personnel watch your video monitors around the clock to catch problems as they happen. At the very least, record everything so you'll have evidence in case of a crime or accident.
>
> - When your CCTV equipment is first installed, make a master tape, label it with the date, and store it away. Every so often compare it with new images to see if the camera is wearing out.
>
> - Do not record more than 24 hours on a tape, even if your system allows you to fit many more. Recording 48 hours, for example, means you get half as many shots of a specific activity. In a 96-hour mode you could miss an important action entirely.
>
> - Do not automatically re-record the same tape every 24 hours. Instead, archive the tapes for at least 14 days before recycling them. Designate one staffer to be responsible for archiving, and have that person clearly label each tape with the date it covers.
>
> - Use only industrial videotapes in industrial time-lapse recorders, and do not use them beyond their life expectancy. Never use tapes designed for home VCRs.

Source: Vicki Meade, "CCTV: A Key Element in the Security Equation," *Lodging*, December 1995, p. 56.

responsible for the security function. When choosing such systems and equipment, a property's management should consider the size and configuration of its property. The communications system should be able to contact all areas of the property where there may be a need for personnel to be reached.

One type of communications equipment sometimes used by lodging properties is the paging system in which the security officer carries a pager on rounds so the desk clerk or other appropriate personnel can then contact the security officer at any time. Some types of pager units even allow the caller to speak to the security officer for a few seconds through the officer's unit (even though the officer cannot speak to the caller).

Two-way radios operating on protected channels allow the security officer and the front desk to communicate directly without the lag time that may be associated with paging systems. In properties with more than one security officer, such radios also allow security officers, who may be moving about the premises, to communicate with one another.

Communication systems have been extended to also include the guest and the public. Some properties have installed "duress" systems, which permit the monitoring of a scream or higher decibel sound (indicating a possible call for assistance) at a recording location anywhere throughout a property. Even if it is an "unwanted alarm" activated by screams from children at play, it is better to investigate and determine the cause for the high decibel response. In more advanced systems, there is the capability of two-way communication. This system is particularly valuable in parking facilities, remote entrances, stairwells, or other locations where protection seems advisable.

One legal case that included in its charge of negligence the lack of adequate and prompt response to a security need is *Nordmann v. National Hotel Company*. The assault on the plaintiffs in this case was reported to hotel personnel very near its beginning, but was not responded to for almost an hour, at which time Mrs. Nordmann escaped screaming, causing the assailant to flee. The delay was allegedly due in part to an ineffective means of communication between the front desk personnel who received the report and the security officer on duty at the property. Although the case occurred a number of years ago, it focuses on a continuing need to properly instruct *all* employees to promptly respond whenever an emergency is reported. The police should be notified immediately, then a follow-up effort should be made to contact on-premises security staff.

Nordmann v. National Hotel Company
425 F.2d 1103 (CA5 La, 1970)

RIVES, Circuit Judge.

Mr. and Mrs. Nordmann sued the National Hotel Company for damages which resulted from a robbery and assault committed upon them in a Jung Hotel room in New Orleans between 12:10 A.M. and 1:10 A.M. on October 18, 1965. The Nordmanns, accompanied by a friend and business associate, William Mixon, registered into the hotel as paying guests the previous afternoon. That evening, with several other friends, they attended a ball in the hotel ballroom. The hotel contains some twelve hundred guest rooms, and there were some twelve to fourteen hundred people at the ball. Shortly after midnight, when the Nordmanns left the ball and started up to their room, they entered a self-serving, automatic type elevator. They were followed by the man who later robbed and assaulted them. When they left the elevator they did not notice that this man followed until Mr. Nordmann put the key in the door. At that time the man thrust a gun in Nordmann's back and pushed them into the room and on the bed. He took such money as Nordmann had in his wallet, fifty dollars, forced him to lie down on the bed, had Mrs. Nordmann get a razor blade from the bathroom and cut a section of a venetian blind cord with which he tied Nordmann's hands behind his back. He announced that "It's not just the money I want, that's not all I want." He proceeded to make indecent advances to Mrs. Nordmann, repeatedly slapping and hitting her, and forced her to mix him two drinks. Finally, on her plea to let her mix him another drink or get water for her husband, Mrs. Nordmann was permitted to go back into the bathroom. She described the conclusion of the assault thus:

"So, when I got into the bathroom I turned my head, and as I turned my head I could see that he walked over to my husband and pulled his collar loose, and when he did, I don't know what came over me, but the bathroom door was close enough to the knob of the main door, that I said, 'Dear, God don't let that chain be on that door,' because I reached out and I turned that knob and I opened the door and I ran screaming down the hall. That's all that I remember as far as that episode was concerned."

The assailant fled down an inside fire escape and has never been captured.

This appeal is from a judgment entered on a jury's verdict for $16,000 in favor of Mrs. Nordmann and for $5,000 in favor of Mr. Nordmann. Six grounds are urged for reversal. We find no merit in any of them and affirm.

* * *

The appellants ... argue that "the verdict of the jury is contrary to law and the evidence." This contention is almost frivolous. The law imposes upon innkeepers *at least* ordinary or reasonable care to protect their guests against injury by third persons, [footnote omitted] and some cases call for the exercise of a higher degree for care. [footnote omitted] In this case the court, by its instructions, held the defendants to a standard of ordinary or reasonable care to protect the hotel's guests from injury by third persons.

The complaint charged the defendants with negligence in the following particulars:

1. Permitting criminals, sex deviates and vagrants to wander indiscriminately about the hotel;
2. Failure to maintain a competent staff of employees;
3. Failure to maintain adequate security personnel;
4. Failure to summon the police immediately; and
5. Failure to have the hotel security officer investigate the incident as soon as it was reported to a hotel employee.

The evidence was ample to support the jury's verdict. For its twelve hundred rooms, and with a large ball in progress, the hotel had on duty at the time of the robbery and assault only one security officer, one room clerk and one bellboy. The jury could, with reason, determine that the defendants had failed to perform their general duty to protect their guests. The evidence of the defendants' negligence after the incident was reported is much stronger.

The occupant of the adjoining room was David DuCharme, an insurance adjuster, who happened to be working on some of his papers when his attention was distracted by the happenings. He heard in a male voice the demand for a knife, for a razor blade, and a woman's voice in response, then "the man who had directed the demand for the knife told the woman to cut down the venetian blind cord."

Mr. DuCharme continued to describe in detail just what he had been able to hear of what was happening in the next room. He became convinced that a robbery and assault were taking place. Taking the telephone, he got under the bed covers to prevent his own report from being heard, and got the telephone operator to whom he stated in substance: "I said, 'This is Dave DuCharme in Room 1048. There is a hold-up or there is a robbery and attempted rape'—I believe were very near the words I used—'going on in the room next to mine.' * * * I said, 'This is an emergency.

Call the police immediately. This is an emergency.' And I repeated myself, 'There is a robbery and attempted rape going on in the next room to me. It is an emergency. Call the police immediately.'" Instead of taking action herself, the operator responded that, "I will connect you with the room clerk." When the room clerk answered, Du-Charme repeated substantially the same report: "I said, 'I have just told the operator, and I am telling you.' I said, 'This is an emergency. I want you to call the police immediately.' And I identified myself again. I said, 'This is Dave DuCharme in Room 1048. There is a robbery and attempted rape going on in the room next to mine.' And I repeated myself two or three times again, and stated, 'This is an emergency. Call the police immediately.'" The room clerk's response was "well, you know, it takes the police 15 or 20 minutes to get here," and DuCharme replied: "I didn't ask you any questions about time. I told you this was an emergency and to call the police immediately." DuCharme estimated it took approximately 5 minutes in which even to report the robbery and assault.

That was only the beginning of the delay. The room clerk admitted that he did not immediately call the police. There were policemen on duty in the ballroom, but they were never summoned. Instead, the room clerk started looking for the security officer or house detective. The jury could have found from the evidence that the police were not actually called until more than 40 minutes after Mr. DuCharme notified the telephone operator and the room clerk of the "emergency" and "robbery and attempted rape." When the police finally were called at 1:11 A.M., according to the time precisely stamped by time clock, patrolmen arrived at the hotel within 4 minutes but long after the assailant's escape. Indeed, Mr. DuCharme confronted the room clerk with a demand for the reason the police were not notified earlier and met only the desultory response, "We were real busy at the time and we can't be calling the police for everybody that calls down here." There was ample evidence to support the jury's verdict.

* * *

In the light of the evidence as to the suffering, mental anguish, shock and injury to the nervous system of Mr. and Mrs. Nordmann, we cannot hold the district court in error for failing to grant a motion for new trial or to require a remittitur of damages. Indeed, we agree with the appellees' counsel that the damages awarded were modest. The judgment is Affirmed.

Though we raise this case in the context of the need for communication systems, the inability of the room clerk to find the security officer was clearly only part of this defendant hotel's security problem. In their unreasonable refusal to immediately call the police or offer other appropriate aid to the plaintiffs after learning of the assault, the hotel's personnel call to mind the alleged inadequate response of the employees in *Boles v. La Quinta Motor Inns,* in which the motel was found not liable for an attack on one of its guests, but was found liable for the way in which it reacted after it learned of the crime. Other than notifying police, the motel employees—even its managers—refused to offer any assistance to the victim, who was still bound and panic-stricken in her room. The inadequate response resulted in greater injury to the victim and a damages award totaling $78,000.

> **The High Price of a Poor Response**
>
> In 1992, a South Carolina jury awarded $10.1 million to members of the rock band Sons of the South after the band sued a Walterboro hotel for invasion of privacy. The band's attorney, E. Paul Gibson, presented evidence that the 172-room hotel had as many as 100 peepholes. The $10.1 million verdict was subsequently settled for $500,000, but the jury's attitude was obvious in its verdict.
>
> After the case, the band's lawyer picked up many Peeping Tom cases. Talking about one such case, he was quoted in *The New York Times*:
>
> "I was certain that the hotel would acknowledge the problem, blame it on some rogue employee and take steps to improve things. Saying you're sorry is a powerful defense...
>
> "The day [the hotel] announces they have a problem and are taking steps to stop it, that's the last they'll hear of Paul Gibson. But until that day, as long as they deny everything and call decent people liars, I will continue to dog them."
>
> Gibson's comment suggests a point that is often overlooked: An innkeeper's initial handling of guest injuries or problems—physical, emotional, or mental—clearly influences any subsequent course of events, including litigation decisions. In case after case, lawyers representing both plaintiffs and hotels have told *Hospitality Law* that many lawsuits could have been avoided if the injured guests hadn't been insulted by the hotel's treatment of them.
>
> Perhaps because of the obvious physical risks involved, ski resorts have generally set a good example in their adept avoidance of lawsuits by injured guests. Given the nature and number of skiing accidents, ski resorts are sued far less often than one might suspect.
>
> The reason: "Friends don't sue friends," sums up Linda Meyers Tiklasky, a former Olympic skier who is a risk management consultant to more than 150 ski areas. In collaboration with her husband, Tiklasky conducted studies that found that the way hotel or resort personnel react to accidents or injuries shapes the subsequent behavior of victims. She says simple gestures make a big difference:
>
> "You have to follow up. Express your sympathy. That's what people want. Send cards. Send flowers. Find out what you can do to help."

Source: *Hospitality Law*, LRP Publications. Used with permission.

Alarm Systems

There is a growing use of alarm systems in some hotels and motels. Alarm systems may sometimes be invaluable for the many entrances and emergency exits found throughout a hotel or motel and for perimeter control.

Access to hotel and motel corridors and guestrooms can be controlled through keys or cards which control admission to both the locked corridor areas and the guestroom. The integrity of the door control system may be enhanced through the use of panic hardware for emergency exits. If feasible, the door may be fitted with an alarm which will sound at a control center if an entrance door is violated. This is critical where a fire door must be secured against illegal entry but still be available for exit.

In some hotels, the telephone room can serve as a control center for all property alarms if it is properly located. Generally, this room should be physically accessible only to authorized persons. It may receive alarm signals from cashiers, safes, or emergency door locations, in addition to being a communications control point.

There are three basic types of alarm systems—local alarms, contact alarms, and remote alarms.

Local Alarms

Local alarms (that is, those not hard-wired to a central monitoring location) may serve as deterrents. A typical example is the local alarm that is integrated with the panic hardware on a fire exit. When the exit door is opened, the circuit is broken and the alarm sounds.

Contact Alarms

Contact alarms (systems which *are* hard-wired to a central point) can be monitored and appropriate action may be taken when the alarm goes off. **Silent alarms** are always hardwired to a central point and may be considered for cashier areas, storerooms, and other areas. From such a point, the alarm can be silently transmitted to the telephone room, police department, or private security company; both the police and the on-premises security personnel can be alerted. An example of a contact alarm sometimes used in cashier areas that is helpful during robberies involves using a money clip that cannot be removed from a cash register without tripping a silent alarm. Some properties record the serial numbers of the money in this clip, which is usually not used for normal transactions, to make it easier to trace.

Restaurants, cocktail lounges, ballrooms, and other function rooms attract members of the public who are not registered guests of the hotel or motel. Unfortunately, there is no one best location for alarms in such facilities. Consequently, protection may include silent alarms at the cashier's locations with security personnel assigned for major functions, conventions, or programs that will attract a large number of non-registered individuals.

Remote Alarms

Remote alarm systems typically rely on some sort of transmission—for example, the more elaborate microwaves, radio waves, seismic detection, and photoelectric light and infrared radiation beams.

Microwave detectors—active units which transmit and receive electromagnetic energy—are designed to detect motion. Perimeter protection with microwaves is used in some properties due to its long-range capabilities; its potential for stability, once adjusted; and its virtually tamper-proof characteristics. This is best used in locations where unwanted movement should be detected.

Systems utilizing **radio frequency (RF) fields** trip an alarm when any intruder breaks the radio wave by moving into an RF field. As with the use of the microwave detector noted above, these systems are of greatest value in locations where there should be no motion. This system is best used as an intruder alarm.

The **seismic detector**, which registers pressure, is also used in a perimeter control function. Usually, the device is buried in the ground, thereby escaping detection by even the most sophisticated intruder. Though it can be used to help protect against Peeping Toms, its use is limited within the industry and is generally practical only for highly specialized protection needs such as in the referenced Peeping Tom problem.

Another perimeter control system is the **photoelectric light beam**. In this system, a filtered light beam passes between a sending and receiving unit; as is the case in RF field systems, any break in the beam sets off an alarm. This system is generally used for outside perimeter control, especially in resort properties.

Finally, **infrared radiation detection** is another limited use alarm system which is generally used in areas where only inanimate objects are found under normal circumstances (such as a locked storeroom). Since the system is set to accept a predetermined radiation level, if a person (who always has a higher radiation level) enters the area, the alarm is triggered. Again, such a system is generally used only to resolve a specific problem within a lodging establishment. For example, one large resort uses infrared detection to monitor a rooftop which could provide access to guestroom windows; it also protects entryways to the convention center when it is not in use.

The decision for alarms must be directed by the following considerations:

- What is the response capability for reacting to a local alarm on premises throughout 24 hours of each day? Would there be an increase in false (unwanted) alarms response by a contract agency or the local police if the alarm is connected to a security service or the police? Is the sounding of the alarm likely to deter a criminal act?

- Is the contact alarm relayed to an on-site location which has a person assigned to each work shift, 24 hours each day? What will the delay interval be in calling for the police? How quickly are they likely to be able to respond? If the community provides a direct alarm network, would it be feasible for the contact alarms to be directly linked? Where such linkage does not exist, are there contract security services that could receive the initial alarm, relay it to the police, and then proceed as a back-up to the police response?

- The silent alarm, similar to the contact alarm, provides the capability of warning that a crime is in progress. Sounding of the alarm within the hearing range of the perpetrator could possibly endanger the lives of other persons who are victims of the criminal act. In what locations would such alarms be best utilized? Will there be sufficient time for possibly intercepting the criminal—as in stealing product from a back-of-the-house storage facility?

Safety Alarms

While the use of some alarm systems is usually optional, fire alarm systems are generally required by local fire codes. The Occupational Safety & Health Act (OSHA) also requires alarms to alert employees to fires or other emergency conditions. Thus, every lodging establishment must have a fire alarm system in operating condition that is tested at least every two months.

> ### The Hotel and Motel Fire Safety Act of 1990
>
> In 1990, the Hotel and Motel Fire Safety Act was enacted in the United States as an amendment to the Federal Fire Prevention and Control Act of 1974. Its purpose is to "save lives and protect property by promoting fire and life safety in hotels, motels, and all places of accommodation affecting commerce." The Act requires government employees traveling on business to stay in accommodations that adhere to the life safety requirements in the legislation guidelines—guestroom smoke detectors and automatic sprinkler systems. Section 29 of the Act requires installation of a hard-wired, single-station smoke detector in each guest room, and all properties with four or more stories must install an automatic sprinkler system in accordance with National Fire Protection Association (NFPA) standards. Members of the AH&MA Safety & Fire Protection Group and the AH&MA Governmental Affairs Department have monitored the application and implementation of this law.
>
> The various code groups—NFPA, International Building Code (IBC), American National Standard Institute (ANSI), and Underwriters Laboratories (UL)—and most jurisdictions have always mandated that full smoke detection systems and automatic sprinkler systems be installed in all lodging establishments, regardless of the height of the structure.
>
> Many existing facilities that would not be required to install an automatic sprinkler system have found it expedient to make such a renovation. Additionally, the potential for litigation on the part of travel agents, meeting planners, and corporate travel offices—should they place clients in a property without adequate fire protection—has resulted in the voluntary installation of smoke detection and sprinkler systems by many establishments, regardless of the volume of federal employee business.

With arson being a continuing problem within the lodging industry, increasingly sophisticated systems are vital. In addition to providing an audible alarm in the relevant area, it is important to evaluate the advantage of installing a central console at the front desk or other location where 24-hour coverage is available. This permits prompt notification of local fire authorities. Review local code specifications on monitoring system requirements. If an alarm can be directly relayed to a fire station in the community, this possibility should be carefully evaluated. In any event, the fire department should be immediately notified of the alarm. No delays should be made to determine the nature and extent of the fire before calling for professional assistance. OSHA mandates that delays in transmitting alarms should not exceed 30 seconds. In communities where a volunteer fire service is provided, this may create a major problem and a variance may be necessary. Similarly, in a large city the fire authorities may prefer a verification period in excess of 30 seconds to avoid answering unwanted smoke alarms. An unwanted alarm, as distinguished from a false alarm, may result from the correct functioning of a smoke alarm in reporting a concentration of smoke in, for example, an area of heavy cigarette, cigar, or pipe smoke, even though a fire danger is not immediately present.

Safety Equipment

The basic safety equipment a lodging establishment should have and be aware of includes such things as smoke detectors, fire extinguishers, sprinkler systems, and

Exhibit 4   Major Fire Safety Issues Covered by the Life Safety Code

- **Means of Egress.** Adequate, protected exits must be available in a fire or other emergency. Number of exits, exit width, exit placement, emergency lighting, exit signs, and maximum travel distance to an exit are all covered.

- **Protection Against Fire Spread.** The construction of a building should help prevent the spread of smoke and fire. Floor/ceiling assemblies, stairwells, and building service shafts are all required to be fire-rated to help contain smoke and fire to its floor of origin. Stairwell doors should be self-closing.

- **Protection of Hazardous Areas.** Areas of the hotel with a significantly higher chance of fire or explosion than the rest of the hotel should be separated from the rest of the building with fire-rated walls and self-closing doors, and be protected with a sprinkler system.

- **Floor, Wall, and Ceiling Finish Flammability.** Because of the high flammability and smoke toxicity of some fabrics and finishes, acceptable flame spread and toxicity ratings allowed in various parts of the hotel are regulated. Improper materials could greatly speed fire or produce highly toxic smoke.

- **Fire Detection and Alarm Systems.** A building fire alarm system is required in all hotels and motels except existing buildings up to three stories high with exterior access in all rooms. Components include smoke or heat detectors and automatic sprinkler systems.

- **Fire Hose Standpipe Systems.** Building codes generally require fire protection standpipe systems in hotels above specific heights. The type required is determined by the applicable code, building height, and the presence or absence of sprinklers.

- **Fire Sprinkler Systems.** Sprinkler systems are required on all existing high-rise hotels except those with exterior exits for all guestrooms. The system design depends on the occupancy classification.

- **Room and Corridor Isolation.** Because a simple closed door can contain smoke and fire to the room of their origin—leaving the corridor usable for exiting—20-minute rated doors with self closers are required for all new and existing guestrooms. Walls between corridors and guestrooms are also required to be fire rated.

Source: William J. Beasland, "Fire Safe Hospitality," *The Construction Specifier*, December 1993.

accident prevention signs. The major fire safety issues covered by the Life Safety Code are listed in Exhibit 4.

Smoke Detectors

Smoke or heat detection units are required by an increasing number of local jurisdictions. Regulations vary from those only requiring smoke and/or heat detectors in corridors, storerooms, and under stairways to those requiring full systems that provide protection in every guestroom, guest bathroom, public area, and back-of-the-house location. Smoke and heat detection units also vary in their characteristics;

some have the ability to report a heat buildup prior to evidence of smoke or flame, while others respond only to smoke and other products of combustion.

Single-station hard-wired smoke detectors require that the unit be on electric wiring as opposed to battery power. In some cases where the sounding of a unit can put the building into general alarm, a public address system can advise guests and staff within the property accordingly. Annunciated systems, which integrate all smoke detectors in each location with a master panel, permit staff to immediately determine where a smoke detector has activated and to respond accordingly. There are also battery back-up systems for use during power failures (which frequently occur in a fire scenario) that may be installed as a third level back-up when auxiliary power generation activates at the time of a primary electric source interruption. Many local jurisdictions enacted regulations requiring fully annunciated smoke detector systems in all new construction and the retrofitting of smoke detectors for all lodging establishments.

Fire Extinguishers

There are four classes of fires that a lodging property should be prepared for. Class A fires involve ordinary combustibles, Class B fires involve flammable liquids, Class C fires involve electrical equipment, and Class K fires involve cooking oils and fats. Exhibit 5 lists the various types of fire extinguishers and the classes of fire for which they are appropriate.

Although some jurisdictions will permit the elimination of fire extinguishers in a facility with a full sprinkler system, consideration should still be given to the use of extinguishers as they would permit the fighting of incipient fires rather than waiting for a fire to generate enough heat to activate an automatic sprinkler system.

Carbon Monoxide Detectors

Carbon monoxide is a dangerous by-product of a malfunctioning water heater, kerosene heater, coal boiler, or any other wood, coal, or petroleum product unit. (It is also the most critical toxic gas generated in any structural fire.) There have been tragic incidents in which carbon monoxide from such units has resulted in the death of a guest or staff. Since carbon monoxide is invisible and has no smell, it cannot be detected by natural means. As of this writing, a few jurisdictions have enacted legislation requiring the installation of carbon monoxide detectors in locations where the petroleum, coal, or wood-fired unit is present. It further requires installation of detectors on each floor of a structure for each 10,000 feet per floor. During the late 1990s, the National Fire Protection Association and the Underwriters Laboratories began developing installation, use, and testing standards.

Sprinkler Systems

Sprinkler systems are now mandated in an establishment four stories or higher, adhering to the Hotel and Motel Fire Safety Act of 1990. This requires a system covering back-of-the-house, public, and all guestroom locations. Most jurisdictions now require full sprinkler systems in the new construction of any commercial occupancy regardless of the height of the structure. Even in the few jurisdictions

Exhibit 5   Types of Fires and Extinguishers

CLASS	SYMBOL	TYPE OF FIRE	EXAMPLES
A		Common Combustibles	Wood, paper, cloth etc.
B		Flammable liquids and gases	Gasoline, propane and solvents
C		Live electrical equipment	Computers, fax machines
D		Combustible metals	Magnesium, lithium, titanium
K		Cooking media	Cooking oils and fats

TYPE	A	B	C	D	K
Foam	✓	✓		Not Normally Found in Hotels	
Water (Pump Tank) (Cartridge) (Pressurized)	✓				
Loaded Stream	✓	✓			
Dry Chemical		✓	✓		
Dry Chemical (A,B,C-Triplex)	✓	✓	✓		
Dry Chemical (Foam Compatible)		✓	✓		
Wet Chemical					✓
Carbon Dioxide		✓	✓		
Halon	✓	✓	✓		

Note: Halon is banned for refills under the Montreal Protocol and should gradually be replaced under that protocol and its time limits. Halon is being replaced in many establishments by traditional water sprinkler systems or water fogging or misting systems. (Courtesy of Sheraton Corporation and Badger Fire Protection) that have not addressed the problem, a property that is not required to have smoke detection or sprinklers will find it difficult, if not impossible, to defend against a plaintiff action. The plaintiff's attorney would note that smoke detectors and sprinklers are "state of the art." In other words, while they may not be a standard for a particular community, such protection is so widely used in the industry that a prudent business person would install such protection as a wise business investment.

Accident Prevention Signs

OSHA classifies accident prevention signs into three categories: danger signs, caution signs, and safety instruction signs.[2] Danger signs, which indicate immediate danger, should be posted to warn of specific dangers and to warn that special precautions may be necessary. Red should be the basic color for identification of all danger signs, which include restricted area, in case of fire, do not enter, and emergency exit signs.

Caution signs should only be used to warn against *potential* hazards or to caution against unsafe practices. The color yellow has been used to advantage for marking physical hazards on stairs in both back-of-the-house stairways and fire stairwells. Areas of construction or remodeling should have caution signs. Floor stand signs could warn guests of wet floors and to watch their step.

Safety instruction signs should be used only where there is a need for general instructions relative to safety measures. These signs are typically green with white lettering. Signs with green arrows, for example, could be used to note the path to follow between buildings or on trails.

The same type of sign can also be categorized differently depending on what type of precaution is necessary. For instance, an elevator sign may be a caution ("This elevator can hold 2,300 pounds"), a warning ("This elevator is out of order"), or a safety ("Please hold handrails as the elevator ascends and descends quickly").

All wording of the signs must be concise and easily read, must contain sufficient information to be easily understood, and must make a positive rather than a negative suggestion.

Guestroom Security

Guestroom security may be enhanced by the use of security equipment such as hotel/motel function locks, safety chains, and similar devices; secondary access-limiting devices on sliding glass, balcony, and connecting room doors; access-limiting devices for operational windows; a guestroom telephone or other communication device available for use 24 hours a day; a peephole in or window next to the guestroom door; and decals or notices detailing security information for the guest.

Locks

Guestroom locks can be a critical aspect of guest protection. Locks and locking systems are needed which lend themselves to the smooth and efficient operation of the property, but which are not easily compromised. If a property uses a master

AT YOUR RISK

ANTHONY MARSHALL

Stand Guard Against Potential Danger Zones

Butter belongs on bread, not on the floor, so when some rose-shaped butter patties fell off a food cart onto the hotel's floor, it meant trouble for a florist delivering a box of cut flowers for a hotel function. The florist didn't see the butter spill and stepped on it. He slipped and fell, suffering serious injuries.

A hotel steward had attempted to clean up the butter before the florist's arrival and subsequent injury. However, his attempt to make the delivery area safe failed; the cleaning efforts simply spread the butter around the floor.

The steward placed a safety-alert cone on the middle of the butter spill before he went looking for assistance. Unfortunately, while he was gone, someone moved the cone.

What did the steward do wrong? He abandoned a space made unsafe by his activities, knowing that it was in a dangerous condition. What should he have done? He should have stood guard, summoned assistance from passing employees and warned others to avoid the danger. He did the right thing in placing the safety cone where the spill occurred but failed by abandoning the danger area. And, as could have been foreseen, someone moved the safety cone.

What's the law? First, a hotel must exercise reasonable care to detect hazards. This was done when the steward spotted the spill. Second, a hotel must exercise reasonable care to remove the hazard or to warn persons of its existence. This was not done.

The steward didn't remove the hazard because the floor was still slippery. And, the warning was inadequate because he left the area, and someone moved the cone.

Readers of this column may recall the Opryland Hotel safety-training story about its annual award of excellence that was presented to an employee who stood still. The employee spotted a dangerous rip in the carpet. He asked a passing employee to dial the hotel's help line rather than abandon the area of danger. Understanding that the rip was a hazard and could trip guests, he stood on it until the maintenance crew arrived to repair it. He understood the danger and his duty toward others.

Opryland's safety-training program paid off. No guest or employee was injured by tripping on the ripped carpet—a job well done.

Shouldn't people look where they are going and avoid danger? Yes, where a danger is obvious, people are expected to use reasonable care to notice and avoid it. That is common sense and the law.

Where persons are aware of a danger created by a hotel's negligence, yet choose, voluntarily, to proceed, most courts deny recovery. The injured party assumed the risk. In other words, he took an unreasonable risk in encountering the danger. The hotel is off the hook.

The key legal word is "knowledge." To relieve a hotel of its duty to an injured person, proof that the person knew of the risk is the key, so it is important to have sufficient warnings.

At Your Risk (continued)

> **Offer specific warnings**
>
> Warnings that are vague and ambiguous aren't worth much. To avoid liability, the hotel must show that the injured party had knowledge of the risk he voluntarily encountered.
>
> For example, where a slippery floor exists, a "Danger—Slippery Floor" warning sign is better than simply placing a safety cone in the immediate danger area. Why? Because the sign conveys specific knowledge of the type of risk that exists. The cone, on the other hand, doesn't. People confronted by a safety cone can reasonably conclude different purposes for its presence.
>
> Here are two points about safety cones. First, in a court of law a safety cone may be found to be too ambiguous and vague to charge the injured party with knowledge of the risk voluntarily encountered. And, second, the mere placement of a safety cone in a danger zone may not discharge the hotel's duty to exercise reasonable care to warn persons of known dangers.
>
> Slips and falls can be expensive. Train employees to detect floor hazards and to eliminate them or adequately warn patrons of their existence. It pays to warn well.

Courtesy of *Hotel & Motel Management*, November 23, 1992. Used with permission.

keying system in which one key opens all or many of the property's doors, it should face the possibility that a master key may be lost or stolen. If this happens, every lock's code or combination (that is, the arrangement of tumblers in the core of the lock) may need to be changed. Depending on the type of locks used, this re-keying can be a relatively quick and inexpensive process or a long and costly one. (One of the best ways to avoid this situation is to follow effective key control procedures.)

There are five basic types of guestroom function locks: 1) locks with the key channel in the knob, 2) standard mortise locks, which generally include a face plate with the knob, a separate key channel on the corridor side of the door, and a deadbolt unit on the guestroom side of the door, 3) mortise locks with programmable cylinders for easily changed key combinations, 4) mortise locks with removable cores, and 5) electronic locks with random selection of new key combinations for each guest.

A number of systems have been introduced to add to the re-key and core-change capabilities of guestroom lock sets. Concurrent with this development has been the use by some hotels and motels of mortise locks. A growing number of fire authorities in various states are requiring that the deadbolt be integrated with the knob, so that turning the knob will automatically release the deadbolt as well as the basic latch. In 1993, the American Automobile Association added the specification to its inspection criteria requiring a deadbolt of at least one inch in length for all corridor and connecting-room doors; failure to provide such a deadbolt would eliminate the property from the approved facilities listings of the AAA.

Electronic locks were installed in over two million of the 3.8 million hotel rooms covered in a 1998 survey.[3] They provide an effective method for "locking out" cards previously issued and allowing admission to only the current guest.

Electronic systems may also employ a touch-pad system in which a special code is established for each guest during his or her stay. This usually requires a guest to enter a sequence of numbers known only to the guest in order to enter the guestroom. The control sequence of the prior guest is canceled and the lockset receives the communication to accept the new combination. This new series is "locked" into the mechanism for the duration of that guest's stay. When a new guest is roomed, a new combination is set. This system is less popular than the encoded electronic card systems which are in most of the two million-plus rooms noted above.

A variety of electronic systems are available; most include one or more of the following elements:

- A mortise lock integrated with an electronic card reader.

- A keycard which either communicates with the front desk computer and permits entry or which is compatible with the permission-level within the microchip in the lockset unit in the guestroom door. This establishes entrance capability either at the time the keycard is being produced or upon introduction to the door lock.

- A computer terminal at the front desk or adjacent area which produces the keycard and selects the code which will permit entry by a new keycard and will reject all prior units issued for that room.

- A computer capable of providing millions of combinations for entrance to a guestroom.

- A battery source and/or hard-wired system for energizing the lock system.

- A touch-pad system.

- The capability of "timing" the card so it no longer functions as of a set time, such as upon check-out.

With the use of electric and electronic locking systems, a standby source of emergency power generation should be considered for the operation of front office equipment. For immediate takeover in the event of a power failure, battery packs may be supported by an auxiliary generating source. That source may be extended to provide emergency lighting and other power use as may be appropriate to a given lodging establishment. Of course, the electronic locking systems with a power supply integrated into each lock will not require this backup.

Installing electronic or mechanical access-control systems for guestroom doors has been helpful for reducing room theft in some hotels and motels. Most systems can even keep a record of the number of guest entries, as well as those of employees. Not only does the sophisticated door control system deter the outsider, it also reduces room theft by employees. The employee who may be inclined to remove something from the room no longer has the excuse of claiming that a missing key must have been used by a criminal for illegal entry into the room. Also, with the vast number of possible combinations in electronic systems, there is very little possibility that a criminal will be able to duplicate an entry card.

The use of inadequate locks is often a point in lawsuits alleging negligence. The importance of using effective locks is illustrated by the following case in which a directed verdict in favor of the defendant hotel was reversed because testimony showed that the lock on the plaintiffs' room was of "the lowest grade, a normal residential lock" without a deadbolt.

Again, the elements in an older case continue to be valid, reminding management to stress the need for using the secondary locking devices such as deadbolts, chains, or bars. The following case portrays such a scenario.

> *Rosier v. Gainsville Inns Associates, Ltd.*
> 347 So.2d 1100 (Fla. Dist. Ct. App. 1977)
>
> ERVIN, Judge.
> The Rosiers, plaintiffs in this personal injury action, seek review of a final judgment directing verdict for appellees. We reverse.
> The Rosiers attended the University of Florida homecoming weekend in 1974. They were guests at the Gainesville Holiday Inn where they had two rooms, one for their children and one for them. Before retiring for the night, the Rosiers secured their children's room, locked their outside door but did not secure the chain latch. At about 1:30 A.M., they awoke to find a ski-masked burglar in the room at the foot of their bed. Mr. Rosier jumped from the bed and tackled the intruder. A struggle ensued, Mr. Rosier was stabbed twice, though not seriously, and Mrs. Rosier received a shattered right finger before the intruder escaped through the open outside door. While Mrs. Rosier was closing the door, she saw a key on a long leather strap on the floor. Mr. Rosier also saw the key strap. To her horror, Mrs. Rosier then saw the intruder return and as she pushed on the door to keep him out the intruder snatched the key from the floor and again fled.
> This negligence action was then brought. The complaint alleged a breach of duty by the motel in that: (1) A passkey was available to the assailant. (2) The locks provided for the room were inadequate. (3) No security guard was provided.
> During the presentation of their case, both Mr. and Mrs. Rosier identified the key strap used by the intruder as identical to keys worn by the motel maids around their necks. A security expert testified on behalf of the Rosiers that the type [of] lock used in the exterior door was the lowest grade, a normal residential lock. He testified the industrywide standard in 1974 was a mortise lock, which when locked from the inside, secured the door with a dead bolt, and could not be opened by a maid's passkey or a duplicate room key. Mortise locks were used in the newer units of the Gainesville Holiday Inn. The motel manager testified passkeys were distributed at the beginning of each day and returned at the end of the day and deposited in a safe overnight. At the time of this incident, no passkeys were missing.
> Following the presentation of Rosiers' case, the trial court directed a verdict for appellees. We need only consider one specific allegation of negligence on the part of the Gainesville Holiday Inn to find that a prima facie case has been made.
> The court stated the failure by the Gainesville Holiday Inn to use adequate locks could not reasonably be considered the cause of the Rosiers' injuries. He found that since the Rosiers failed to secure the chain latch to the outside door, one could not reasonably assume the Rosiers would have used the dead bolt latch had the mortise lock been available. Such a conclusion could only be reached by the jury.[1] It is clear
>
> ---
> [1] While the question of proximate cause in a negligence action is one for the court where there is an active and efficient intervening cause, [citation omitted] still if such intervening cause is either foreseeable or might reasonably have been foreseen by the defendant, his negligence may be considered the proximate cause of the injury notwithstanding the intervening cause. 23 Fla.Jur. *Negligence* §39 (1959).

> that upon a motion for directed verdict, all reasonable inferences are construed in favor of the nonmoving party. [citation omitted] Reasonable inferences could be drawn from the above facts to satisfy the "but for" test for causation set forth in Florida Standard Jury Instruction 5.1(a).
>
> There is of course the question of foreseeability. Could the motel reasonably foresee that the failure to use adequate locks would lead to the sort of injury sustained here? Here there was some evidence of illegal entries into unoccupied motel rooms. Indeed, the motel manager was questioned concerning a police incident report stating that persons unknown entered a nearby room of the motel, probably with the aid of a passkey. That report was made some five months before this incident. It is clear that the motel licensee had knowledge of prior burglaries of guests' rooms carried out in a manner similar to that shown by plaintiffs. A registered guest in a hotel or motel is a business invitee to whom the innkeeper owes a duty of reasonable care for his safety. [citation omitted]
>
> * * *
>
> Reversed and remanded for further proceedings not inconsistent herewith.
> MILLS, Judge, concurs.
> BOYER, Acting Chief Judge, dissents.
> BOYER, Acting Chief Judge:
> I respectfully dissent. In my view the learned trial judge did not err. I would affirm.

In another case, the plaintiff showed that the $3/8"$ deadbolt used in her room defectively had $1/8"$ of play and was given another $1/8"$ of play by the loose fitting door. The remaining $1/8"$ was not secure enough to withstand the forced entry which preceded the plaintiff's assault.[4]

Biometrics

A new and highly technical access control system involves **biometrics**. Such a system utilizes human characteristics which are unique to a specific individual. Just as one's fingerprints are not duplicated anywhere in the population, so there are unique attributes to be found in a voice; the retina or iris of an eye; and the size, shape, and print of a hand.

There are already some affordable products available for a variety of needs that can authenticate face shape, voice, signatures (by remembering the speed, shape, stroke, and pen pressure used), and irises. Future biometric applications could include a person's voice being recorded at check-in and immediately being transmitted to the door accessing a restricted guestroom corridor, guestroom, health club, point-of-sales locations throughout the premises, or any other facility which should be limited to guest access only.

Secondary Access-Limiting Devices

As noted under the American Automobile Association inspection requirements, the connecting doors between guestrooms must be capable of being secured with a

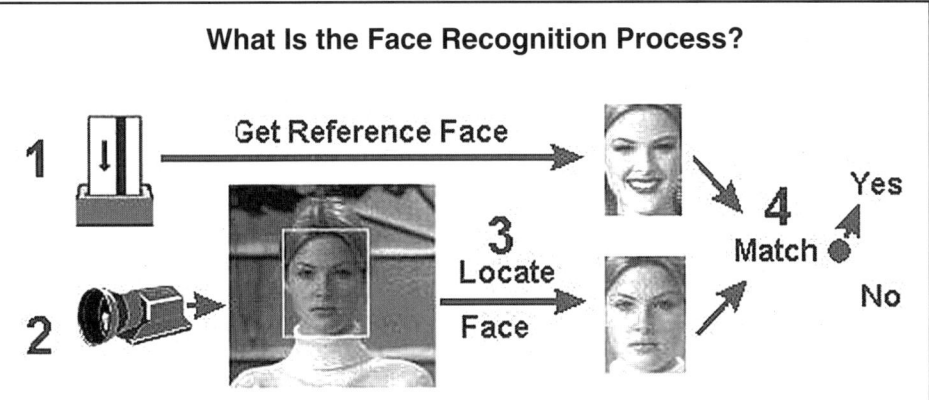

What Is the Face Recognition Process?

Face verification involves the steps of 1) getting the reference face with a PIN, password, card or digital certificate, 2) getting the live face image, 3) locating the live face, and 4) matching the live face with the reference face to determine whether they came from the same person. Face identification, which is a different mode of operation, matches the live face to a database of faces. It uses steps 2 and 3 and then cycles step 4 through the database.

Source: http://www.miros.com

deadbolt. Connecting doors only have a knob on the guestroom side of each door. In addition, a deadbolt security mechanism must be visible and should be capable of being activated by the guest. A chain or surface-mounted slide bolt is not acceptable.

Sliding glass doors are another consideration in establishing the security of a guestroom. A number of secondary access-restricting devices are currently available and should be examined as possible additions to the single latch provided with each sliding glass door. Hinged bars and metal and wood sections that can be placed in the sliding channel or additional lock units are sometimes used to add to the security of sliding glass doors. A metal peg may be inserted in a hole drilled through both the sliding door and the frame to prevent the sliding door unit from being lifted out of the channel and removed from the frame.

Windows which open may need secondary latching devices. If local fire codes permit, devices which limit how far windows can be opened may be installed to help prevent intruders from entering through ground floor or balcony windows and to reduce or eliminate the possibility of children or even adults falling out of open windows.

Viewports

Consider the need for the guest to be able to identify a caller before opening the door. A viewport (door viewer or peephole) is one device that can serve this purpose. Courts and juries in some jurisdictions have ruled that a window next to the door will satisfy the need to identify a caller. A wide-angle viewport maximizes

AT YOUR RISK

Anthony Marshall

Hotels without Peepholes Can Court Catastrophe

John and his wife, Mary, live in rural America where it is not uncommon to carry a firearm in one's car or truck. John had never been involved in a civil or criminal case in his life.

One evening John and Mary checked into a small roadside motel, typical of the thousands of older, usually independently owned motels that line this nation's highways. The door of their ground-floor guestroom opened onto the motel's parking lot. After checking in, they took their luggage into their room—along with a pistol they had been keeping in the glove compartment of their car.

That evening, when the couple was in bed, there was a knock at the door. They went to the door and asked who it was.

"The manager," came the reply.

This motel was different from most in that there was no peephole in the front door. Denied this basic security device—which costs only a few dollars to purchase and install—John did what most folks do when there is an unexpected knock on the door: He opened the door a crack to see who was there.

John was immediately shot in the stomach by one of three men who pushed their way into the motel room. Two of the assailants then began stabbing John in the chest, throat and arms as the third forced Mary to the rear of the room.

Before opening the door, John had picked up his pistol. He didn't realize that he had been shot and stabbed. When he did realize it, he started shooting.

The horror of this scene is captured in John's sworn deposition.

Q: Did you hit them?
A: Yes.
Q: And these would be the two men with the knives, correct?
A: Yes.
Q: What happened after you shot these two men?
A: One of them fell dead at the door.
Q: Do you know where you shot him?
A: In the chest, I think.
Q: And the other? In the shoulder and where else?
A: And in the face, I think.
Q: What was the third man doing at the time?
A: I don't remember.
Q: OK. What happened then?
A: I think I shot him, just grazed him in the side. And he picked up his brother, who was almost dead, and put him in the trunk and left.

Had John and Mary been afforded the opportunity to use a peephole in the motel-room door, they would have seen the three unknown men outside and likely would never have opened the door.

Was the motel negligent?

At Your Risk *(continued)*

> American common law mandates that hotel and motel guests are entitled to "reasonable care" in security. In determining what is reasonable, a variety of factors come into play: size, location, past history of crimes on the premises as well as adjacent areas.
>
> While what constitutes reasonable care in security is arguable in some circumstances, there are certain standards that are not open to dispute. For example, motel room doors should have a lock. (The type of lock may be arguable.)
>
> In my opinion, a peephole is a standard security device, the absence of which constitutes negligence. The fact that a property is small and has budget rates is no excuse for failing to provide reasonable care in security.
>
> Failure to provide a peephole is but one example of a breach of a motel's duty to provide reasonable care. Survey your property for security lapses—and eliminate them.

Courtesy of *Hotel & Motel Management*, October 7, 1991. Used with permission.

the view of the corridor adjacent to the guestroom door. Under the requirements of the Americans with Disabilities Act of 1990 (ADA), additional viewports should be positioned at a lower level in the door to accommodate guests in wheelchairs. If it is determined that viewports should be installed, lighting in the corridors should be arranged to prevent glare and to avoid placing faces in the shadows.

Room Communications

Management should consider placing a telephone or some other type of communication device in each guestroom. This telephone or device can be used by the guest to notify the property of emergencies or suspicious activities and by the property to notify the guest of emergencies (such as fires).

A few lodging properties are exploring the feasibility of using two-way interactive cable television to provide security for and emergency communication with the guest. The coaxial cable usually delivers entertainment and programming to the guestroom, but it also has the capacity to return communication via the same cable. This permits monitoring of guest medical alerts, burglar alarms, and fire alarms. With the growing number of senior citizens that are traveling, and a heightened concern for the disabled, there are an increasing number of two-way emergency communication systems being installed in lodging establishments.

In-Room Security Information

There has been a concerted effort on the part of the lodging industry to effectively involve the guest as a member of the security team for a property. In addition to participating in nationwide safety programs (such as the AH&MA's "Traveler Safety Campaign"), many hotels have expanded the idea through their own on-premises programs, including videotapes with security and fire protection instructions that can be viewed on one of the TV channels. This data is usually included on a channel which provides a review of the property's activity schedule for the day.

Many jurisdictions also require that a floor plan or an information card be provided which indicates the location of the guestroom in relation to fire stairwells. This information card also lists the steps to be taken by the guest in the event of a fire emergency.

In addition to fire protection data, consider including security data on the guestroom door. Decals or notices may be posted that:

- Inform the guest how to double lock the guestroom door
- Instruct the guest not to open the door without first identifying the person seeking entrance
- Explain any special guestroom security devices
- Point out the availability of safe deposit boxes at the front desk
- Contain any other information the property's management may decide to include

The presence of a decal containing security information on guestroom doors resulted in a favorable court decision for the lodging establishment in *Courtney v. Remler*.

Courtney v. Remler
566 F Supp 1225 (S.C. Dist. Ct. 1983)

HAWKINS, Judge.

This diversity action came on for trial before the court without a jury on February 22, 1983. The plaintiff was the victim of a brutal assault, robbery and rape while on her honeymoon on Hilton Head Island in Beaufort County, South Carolina. The incident occurred on October 1, 1979, while the plaintiff and her husband were spending the weekend at a motel owned by the defendants. The complaint alleged that the defendants negligently supervised and operated the motel in which the incident occurred, and such negligence was the proximate cause of the injuries, both physical and mental, sustained by the plaintiff.

The court, having heard all the evidence and having reviewed the briefs of counsel filed in this case, and having fully considered the applicable law, makes the following Findings of Fact and Conclusions of Law:

FINDINGS OF FACT

1. The plaintiff is a resident and citizen of the Town of Johnston, which is located in Edgefield County, South Carolina.
2. The individually named defendants are doing business as Hotel Investments, a limited partnership. The general partners are residents and citizens of the State of Georgia.
3. Hotel Investments, a Georgia Limited Partnership, was formed by Agreement and Certificate of Limited Partnership dated the 17th day of December 1975. The purpose of this limited partnership was to own the land and improvements involved in this litigation.

4. Quality Management Company was incorporated under the laws of the State of Georgia on the 13th day of February 1976, and was duly qualified to transact business in the State of South Carolina. The company was formed for the purpose of operating the motel in question.
5. Hotel Investments, as Owner, and Quality Management, Co., as Operator, entered into an Agreement dated the 1st day of September 1978, and pursuant thereto, Quality Management Company took control and possession of the entire property, including the motel operation of the Islander Inn. The Agreement, pursuant to its terms, terminated on the 28th day of February 1979, and the Agreement was not renewed.
6. On October 1, 1979, the plaintiff was brutally assaulted and raped while she and her husband were spending their honeymoon on Hilton Head Island, South Carolina, and staying at the Islander Inn.
7. The plaintiff is a Caucasian female born April 20, 1958. She grew up in a small-town, rural environment in Edgefield, South Carolina.
8. The plaintiff was married to Ronald H. Courtney on September 29, 1979, in Edgefield, South Carolina.
9. Ronald H. Courtney was a lifetime resident of Johnston, South Carolina. At the time of his marriage to the plaintiff, he was employed at a service station.
10. Prior to October 1, 1979, neither the plaintiff, nor her husband, nor any member of their respective families had been victims of a crime.
11. Criminal activity on Hilton Head Island had steadily increased each year since 1975.
12. There had been no assaults or any other crimes against any person occurring on the Islander Inn premises prior to the subject assault.
13. Although neither the plaintiff nor her husband had ever been to Hilton Head Island, they were aware of the reputation of the island as a luxury resort, but were unaware of any criminal activity occurring there.
14. The plaintiff's husband had stayed in motels on several occasions, but the plaintiff had only been a guest in a motel on one or two other occasions during her life.
15. The motel in question was originally designed and the plans and specifications were prepared by Mr. Terry Keane, a licensed architect who had previously designed other motels. Mr. Keane was originally hired by "Islander Associates," the original developers of the project.
16. Islander Associates obtained a franchise for the motel from Quality Inns International, Inc. ("Quality Inns"). The plans and specifications were approved by Quality Inns.
17. While under construction, the property was conveyed by Islander Associates to Hotel Investments, defendants herein, who completed construction of the motel pursuant to said plans. During completion of construction by defendants, Quality Inns inspected and approved the property pursuant to its franchise agreement. Hotel Investments subsequently determined to terminate the franchise agreement and the motel began operating as the Islander Inn, which was its designation at the time of the attack upon the plaintiff.

18. The plaintiff and her husband arrived at the Islander Inn during the early morning hours of September 30, 1979. Upon checking in, they noticed a uniformed security guard at the reception desk.
19. The Islander Inn complex consisted of a main building housing the lobby, reception area, restaurant and lounge. There were four (4) outlying buildings containing guest rooms. Each of the buildings containing guest rooms was rectangular in shape, two (2) stories in height, and had front and rear access doors. In addition, each ground level room had access to the outside via a sliding glass door.
20. Each guest room building had a long hallway down the center of the building separating the rooms on either side. The access doors to each building were not locked. Each guest room had a door leading into the hallway, and the hallway had a two and one-half (2.5) foot recessed area containing the entranceways to two rooms with an exact duplicate thereof across the hall.
21. Above each guest room door was a fluorescent light which provided the illumination of the hallways and the ability to see through the "observation port" located within the room side of the door. In front of each fluorescent light was a wooden valance to reflect the light rays directly up and down.
22. The motel room (Room 220) in which the assault occurred, as all rooms, had a fire-rated steel entrance door with a steel door frame. The steel door frame was constructed with a solid metal doorstop which prevented the opening of the door by the insertion of any object between the doorstop and the balance of the frame.
23. The doors were equipped with a door-latch with an automatic locking device. The door closed and locked automatically.
24. The doorknob on the door was a motel security type which required the use of a key to open the door from the hall. The exterior or hallway-side portion of the doorknob contained "security lips," a mechanism utilized to deter the possible picking of the lock. The interior or room-side portion of the doorknob contained a push button whereby, when engaged, the entire exterior locking mechanism of the doorknob was secured against the possible opening of the door with either a room key or an employee's master key. For emergency situations, the management did maintain an emergency key which could override this double locking mechanism.
25. The steel door contained a separate "dead bolt" security lock which was activated by a latch on the interior or room side of the steel door. On the exterior of the door a "room number" plaque was secured to the door and concealed an aperture in the door that allowed the "dead bolt" to be released from the hallway.
26. The doors contained an "observation port" whereby a guest in the room could look through the same and identify a person knocking outside the door or attempting to gain entrance. This observation port contained optics providing for magnification and wide vision when looking from the inside to the outside.
27. The door was not equipped with a chain lock or safety chain.
28. The steel door did not have warning or cautionary instructions reminding guests to keep their doors locked and not to open the door for a stranger.

29. The sliding glass door, which provided a second means of access to the outside, contained a locking mechanism which had to be locked manually from the interior. It was the policy of the management to have a sticker or decal affixed to the sliding glass door above the handle and locking mechanism warning all guests to keep doors locked for their protection. It was the further policy of management to have the maids, when cleaning a room, leave all drapes covering the sliding glass door halfway open to allow sunlight to enter the room, and, consequently, this warning decal could easily have been seen. The maids were also instructed by management to replace any decals that either wore off or were torn off.
30. Room 220, on the date and time complained of, also had a telephone located therein, which was in proper working order, with instructions on the phone indicating numbers to dial direct to the front desk, the manager, and other motel offices.
31. Quality Management Company had a planned, ongoing security system which included both "in-house" personnel, as well as the utilization of a private security patrolman.
32. On a twenty-four (24) hour basis, security was provided by "in-house" personnel, including specific staff members and a security conscious awareness program extending to all employees. Housekeeping employees were charged with the responsibility of cleaning guest rooms and checking to see that the rooms were in order.
33. Certain employees were permitted to reside in efficiency units located on the Islander Inn premises.
34. Exterior lighting on the premises originally consisted primarily of low level pathway lights. The main parking area was illuminated by high intensity mercury vapor lights. There were no exterior lights on the buildings themselves. In 1978, light poles were added around the perimeter of the premises and 150 watt light bulbs were used.
35. At the time of the rape incident, only Mr. Richard Kwaiser, the general manager of the motel, and Beverly Martin, his replacement as general manager, were assigned living quarters in the complex. Prior to the incident, as many as three to four people lived on the premises.
36. In addition to the employee security, a private security guard company, Preventor Security, was hired to provide extra security during nighttime hours. At the time of the incident, one Preventor Security uniformed guard was on duty from approximately 10:00 P.M. until 7:30 A.M.
37. Mr. Kwaiser began working in the motel business in 1972 when he was employed by the DeSoto Hilton in Savannah, Georgia. He underwent a company training program at that time. His primary functions were sales and securing conventions. In 1974, he was assigned to the Atlanta Hilton.
38. In 1975, Mr. Kwaiser joined the Hyatt Corporation and was assigned to the Hyatt Hotel on Hilton Head Island. His primary function initially was to book conventions into the hotel. He also began to perform management-on-duty functions and was acting manager at night and on weekends. In 1977, Mr. Kwaiser accepted employment at the defendants' motel.
39. Between 7:30 and 8:00 P.M. on October 1, 1979, the plaintiff and her husband were in their room, at which time they heard a knock at their motel door.

Having been told by friends at their wedding that they would visit them after they arrived on Hilton Head Island, the plaintiff's husband responded to the knock.

40. The plaintiff's husband received no response to his inquiry as to who was there and looked through the "observation port." Seeing no one, he opened the door.
41. Once the door was opened, two (2) black males, armed with pistols and wearing coverings over their heads, forced their way into the room. They bound and gagged the plaintiff and her husband, robbed them of their money, ransacked their luggage and room, and raped and assaulted the plaintiff.

CONCLUSIONS OF LAW

This court has jurisdiction since the uncontroverted evidence is that the plaintiff is a resident and citizen of the State of South Carolina and the defendants are residents and citizens of a state other than South Carolina, and the matter in controversy exceeds the sum of $10,000. [citation omitted]

* * *

We now turn our attention to the plaintiff's allegations that the motel was unreasonably supervised and operated, and such unreasonableness was the proximate cause of plaintiff's injuries. In the presentation of her case, the plaintiff raised a spate of conditions that could give rise to negligent conduct including negligent design of the premises and guest buildings, inadequate locking and safety mechanisms on the guest room doors, failure to give cautionary warning to guests, inadequate lighting on exterior of buildings and within the guest building hallways, and inadequate security to protect guests from criminal activity. In response to these arguments, the defendants contend they breached no duty owed to the plaintiff since the motel premises were reasonably safe for guest occupancy and the intervening criminal acts of third persons were not reasonably foreseeable.

The traditional formula for the elements necessary to establish a negligence cause of action may be stated briefly as follows:

1. A duty recognized by law, requiring the actor to conform to a certain standard of conduct, for the protection of others against unreasonable risks;
2. A failure on the part of the actor to conform to the standard required;
3. The breach of the duty must be the "proximate cause" of the injuries, and
4. Actual loss or damage resulting to the interest of others.

[citations omitted]

The first condition of the formula definitely exists. There can be no doubt that motel management owes to its guests a duty to conduct its business according to a certain standard of conduct. The standard of conduct required by law is that an innkeeper is under a duty to its guests to take reasonable action to protect them against unreasonable risk of physical harm. [citation omitted] Of course, the statement of the duty only begs the question. The real issue to be determined is whether the innkeeper, under the circumstances, has taken reasonable action to protect its guests. This issue is addressed in the second condition.

After establishing the existence of a duty, the plaintiff must next prove that the defendants breached their duty or failed to conform to the required standard. The defendants first contend that no duty was breached since the injuries to the plaintiff were caused by unforeseeable criminal acts of a third party.

When criminal acts are the actual cause of another's injuries, an innkeeper is not automatically exonerated from allegations of negligence. An act or an omission may be deemed negligent conduct if the actor realizes or should realize that his conduct involves unreasonable risks of harm to another through the conduct of a third person which is intended to cause harm, even though such conduct of the third person is criminal. [citation omitted] The Reporter's Notes immediately following Section 302 B elaborates on this point of law as follows:

> e. There are, however, situations in which the actor, as a reasonable man, is required to anticipate and guard against the intentional, or even criminal, misconduct of others. In general, these situations arise where the actor is under a special responsibility toward the one who suffers the harm, which includes the duty to protect him against such intentional misconduct. . . . The following are examples of such situations. . . .
>
> * * *
>
> B. Where the actor stands in such a relation to the other that he is under a duty to protect him against such misconduct. Among such relations are those of carrier and passenger, *innkeeper and guest*, employer and employee, possessor of land and invitee, and bailee and bailor. (emphasis added).

Restatement (Second) of Torts 302 B, Comment e(B) (1965).

The South Carolina Supreme Court has on numerous occasions addressed the problem where an actor stands in a special relationship with another requiring the actor to reasonably protect others from criminal activity.[1] [citations omitted] In *Shipes [v. Piggly Wiggly St. Andrews, Inc.*, 269 S.C. 479, 238 S.E. 2d 167 (1977)] the plaintiff had been shopping in the defendant's grocery store, and at approximately 7:30 he walked to his car in defendant's parking lot. He was then assaulted by several persons, none of them connected with Piggly Wiggly. Plaintiff brought suit alleging the defendant negligently failed to adequately light and supervise its parking lot, which negligence proximately caused plaintiff's injuries. The Court held that the defendant did not know or have reason to know of criminal attacks on its premise such as the one on the plaintiff. Thus, the defendant was not under a duty to protect against such attacks. [citation omitted] However, the Court cited approvingly the Tennessee case of *Cornpropst v. Slogan*, 528 S.W. 2d 188 (Tenn. 1975), which stated that if the owners of a shopping center knew or had reason to know of acts occurring or about to occur on its premises that posed imminent probability of harm to an invitee, a duty of reasonable care to protect against such act arises.

---

[1] Although the Supreme Court has never addressed this problem as it relates to the innkeeper-guest scenario, the law is analogous to the common carrier-passenger situation, employer-employee situation, and possessor of land-invitee situation, which the Court has addressed.

Based on the law stated above, the defendants in the present case argue they had no duty to protect their motel guests from criminal attacks since the assault and rape of October 1, 1979, could not be reasonably anticipated. The defendants argue that there had never been a crime against a person on the premises until the rape against the plaintiff, although vandalism incidents had been reported on a few occasions. On the other hand, there can be no question that crime had dramatically increased on Hilton Head Island over the four years preceding the rape attack. Even one of the defendants' witnesses, a County police officer, testified as to the dramatic increase in crime on the island. In addition, during the three month period immediately preceding the attack on the plaintiff, a rape was reported each month on Hilton Head Island, and there is no question that the Islander Inn manager, Mr. Kwaiser, was aware of these rapes. In fact, the Islander Inn added light poles around the perimeter of the premises after discussions about the other rape incidents. Presumably, the management added the lights to deter the type of criminal activity that was occurring elsewhere on the island.

The Islander Inn hired a private security guard in May 1979 to guard the premises during the hours of 10:30 P.M. to 7:00 A.M. According to Mr. Kwaiser, all employees were informed of the crime problems on the island and instructed how to react if confronted with a crime. These types of action by the Islander Inn [are] an indication of its awareness of the criminal activity on the island. The security guard was presumably hired to protect the guests from late night crimes. As evidenced by its own conduct, Islander Inn obviously foresaw the possibility of criminal attacks on its guests and made a determination to combat the attacks. Since the defendants knew or should have known [of] the possibility of criminal acts on their guests, they had a duty to exercise reasonable care to protect against such acts arising.

An innkeeper is not the insurer of safety for his guests. Rather, he owes to his guest the duty of exercising reasonable care to maintain in a reasonably safe condition those parts of his premises which a guest may be expected to use. [citations omitted] In the final analysis, the issue is whether, under all the circumstances, the innkeeper in this case provided for its guests reasonable protection against injuries from criminal acts. [citation omitted]

It is important to keep in mind that although criminal activity on the Islander Inn premises was foreseeable, only minor vandalism had occurred in the past, and there had been no criminal acts committed against a person. This fact is important when considering the amount of protection the Inn must afford its guests. Although Hilton Head Island was considered by many a "high crime" area, the Islander Inn management obviously did a fine job of keeping the criminal element off its premises until the time of the rape on October 1, 1979. However, it would be incorrect for this court to say the mere fact of a rape is conclusive evidence that security at the Inn was unreasonable. To do such would be to hold the Inn as an insurer of its guests' safety.

Mr. Kwaiser was hired to manage the hotel at Islander Inn's inception in 1977. Prior to becoming known as the Islander Inn in the spring of 1979, the Inn had a franchise with Quality Inns. The franchisor made monthly checks of the premises and gave suggestions to Mr. Kwaiser concerning more efficient operation of the motel. According to Mr. Kwaiser's testimony, the in-house security system was accepted by Quality Inns, and no other comments were made about security. There can be no doubt that armed guards in every building, twenty-four hours a day, would have provided the guests with more protection than the security system employed by Islander Inn. However, it must be remembered that the inn's function was as a luxury-island motel, not a prison. In considering the reasonableness of the security, the court must take into account the purpose and function of the business.

Based on the lack of criminal activity on the premises in the past, one uniformed guard during the nighttime hours is reasonable security for a guest at the motel. The motel is relatively small with 190 total guest rooms. One trained guard could adequately patrol the premises. When the guard left at 7:30 A.M., security was turned over to the employees. Maid services would go in and out of all the buildings. The maintenance force was busy throughout the day doing various chores on the premises. Guests at the motel were actively going in and out of their rooms and the restaurant area. The tennis facilities had a tennis pro throughout the day working on the premises. A few employees were allowed living accommodations on the premises. Before retiring for the evening, Mr. Kwaiser would walk the premises to ensure everything was operating smoothly. Then the night guard would arrive. The entire security program was reasonable under all the circumstances.

The plaintiff also alleges the buildings were negligently designed. This claim is based on the fact that the guest room doors were recessed and this made it difficult for one looking through the "observation port" to see visitors outside the door. Also, the recessed doorways made lighting in the hall inadequate, giving a shadow-effect throughout the hallway. There was testimony from the building architect that the hallways were designed in this fashion to avoid the dreary effect of long, straight hallways. Quality Inns had approved the design originally. The same type of design is prevalent throughout the industry. The recessed doors do not obstruct the view through the "observation port" if the visitor is standing at the door. The only view that is obstructed is if someone knocks at the door and steps a few feet away from the door. That should caution the guest that something suspicious is happening. Therefore, the design of the building is reasonable.

The lighting in the hallways, although dim, was adequate. The exterior lighting consisted of high intensity mercury vapor lights in the parking lot, light poles with 150 watt light bulbs around the perimeter of the premises, and low level pathway lights throughout the premises. This lighting was adequate.

The plaintiff next alleges that the doors to the guest rooms did not provide adequate protection for the guests. The essence of this charge is the failure of the doors to be equipped with "safety chains" or "chain locks." The architect for the motel testified that safety chains were deliberately excluded because they hindered management's entry into a room in case of emergencies. The doors had numerous locking and safety mechanisms which provided adequate protection for the guests. The dead bolt lock could be deactivated from the hallway by removing the room number plaque and inserting a finger, but this feature was intended to allow management easy access to the rooms in case of an emergency.[2] The guest room doors, with all their locking mechanisms, provided reasonable protection for the safety of the guests.

---

[2] There is no indication that the assailants knew the dead bolt lock could be deactivated from the hallway, and there is no question that they did not actually deactivate the dead bolt lock.

> The plaintiff also alleges that failure to have any warning or cautionary signs in Room 220, as is customary in the industry, was unreasonable on the defendants' part. The testimony is disputed as to whether Room 220 actually had a warning sign in it at the time of the rape, but it is undisputed that the Islander Inn had a policy to place decals on the sliding glass doors warning all guests to lock their rooms for their protection. Furthermore, the maids were instructed to check every room to make sure everything was proper, and the curtains were drawn after a clean-up so that the absence of a decal could be easily noticed. The warning system or procedure was reasonable.
>
> The Islander Inn, as a whole, was operated and supervised reasonably. The Inn obviously felt a need to protect its guests from criminal attacks by third persons, and measures were taken to ensure their safety. The measures were reasonable. The rape incident was a truly unfortunate and horrible experience, but the defendants cannot be held responsible. For this court to hold otherwise would be equivalent to making all motels the insurer of their guests' safety. Therefore, it is
> ORDERED, that this action be dismissed.

Endnotes

1. Mary Smith, "Crime Prevention through Environmental Design in Parking Facilities," *The National Institute of Justice Research in Brief*, April 1996.
2. Information in this section is taken from *OSHA: A Guide to Occupational Safety and Health Standards Compliance for the Lodging Industry* (Washington, D.C.: American Hotel Foundation), pp. 27–28.
3. The survey was conducted by Chervenak, Keane & Co., 307 E. 47th Street, New York, NY 10017, at the request of the Loss Prevention Management Institute, Conrad N. Hilton College, University of Houston.
4. *Kiefel v. Las Vegas Hacienda, Inc.*, 404 F.2d 1163 (7th Cir. 1968), *cert. denied* 395 U.S. 908 (1969).

Key Terms

biometrics—Security technology which utilizes an individual's unique characteristics, including fingerprint, eye, and voice recognition.

closed-circuit television (CCTV)—A security surveillance tool utilizing television monitors, usually located in a control center where employees are assigned to monitor and respond to incidents.

contact alarms—Alarm systems which are hard-wired to a central monitoring point, where action can be taken when the alarm goes off.

infrared radiation detection—A limited-use alarm system set to accept a predetermined radiation level and trigger an alarm if a person (who emits a higher level of radiation than an inanimate object) enters the area.

local alarms—Alarm systems not hard-wired to a central monitoring location; may serve as deterrents.

microwave detectors—A perimeter control system with long-range capabilities and tamper-proof characteristics that detects motion by transmitting and receiving electromagnetic energy.

perimeter control—Alarm systems designed to prevent and/or detect intrusion on a hotel or motel's property or grounds. The three basic types of alarm systems are local alarms, contact alarms, and remote alarms.

photoelectric light beam—A perimeter control system in which a filtered light beam passes between a sending and receiving unit; any break in the beam sets off the alarm.

physical security—The protection of the building, grounds, and the building's contents that covers such diverse factors as layout, design, lighting, fences and gates, hardware, closed-circuit television, and alarms.

radio frequency (RF) fields—An alarm system in which radio signals are used to detect motion; the alarm is tripped when an intruder breaks the radio wave by moving into an RF field.

remote alarm—Alarm system that typically relies on some sort of transmission such as microwaves, radio waves, or photoelectric light beams.

seismic detector—A perimeter control system, usually buried in the ground, which registers pressure; it's use is limited within the industry and is generally only for highly specialized protection needs.

silent alarms—A type of contact alarm always hard-wired to a central point; may be considered for cashier areas, storerooms, and other areas where the alarm can be silently transmitted to the telephone room, police department, or private security company.

target hardening—Controlling access to neighborhoods and buildings and conducting surveillance on specific areas to reduce opportunities for crime to occur.

territorial reinforcement—Increasing the sense of security in settings where people live and work through activities that encourage informal control of the environment.

Review Questions

1. What equipment is typically used for physical security at a hotel?
2. What are the benefits of closed-circuit television (CCTV)?
3. What issues should be considered when deciding to install alarm systems?
4. Where might silent alarms be most effective in a hotel?
5. What are the four classes of fires most likely at a lodging operation?
6. What role has the Hotel and Motel Fire Safety Act of 1990 played for hotels?
7. OSHA classifies accident prevention signs into what three categories?
8. What are the five basic types of guestroom locks?

9. What are some of the electronic locking systems available to lodging operations?

10. What guestroom security equipment features might be most important to guests with disabilities?

Internet Sites

For more information, visit the following Internet sites. Remember that Internet addresses can change without notice.

Advanced Safety Systems
http://www.advancedsafety.com

American Fire Sprinkler Association (AFSA)
http://www.sprinklernet.org

American Hotel & Motel Association (AH&MA)
http://www.ahma.com

American National Standards Institute (ANSI)
http://www.ansi.org

Business and Legal Reports (BLR)
http://www.safetyonilne.net/blr

CardKey
http://www.cardkey.com

Cerebus Division, Fire and Security Needs
http://www.cerbpyro.com

Computerized Security Systems (CSS)
http://www.cssmain.com

Digital Persona
http://www.digitalpersona.com

Gentex Fire Protection Products
http://www.gentex.com/fire

Government Institutes
http://www.govinst.com

Guest Access International
http://www.guestaccess.com

Ilco Unican
http://www.ilcounican.com

International Building Codes (IBC)
http://www.intlcode.org/codes/index.htm

IriScan
http://www.iriscan.com

LockTech, Inc.
http://www.hotelkeycard.com

Lodging Technology Corporation
http://www.lodgingtechnology.com

Loss Prevention Management Institute
http://www.hrm.uh.edu

National Association of Fire Equipment Distributors
http://www.nafed.org

National Burglar and Fire Alarm Association
http://www.alarm.org

National Fire Protection Association (NFPA)
http://www.nfpa.org

National Safety Council
http://www.nsc.org

National Standard Systems Network (NSSN)
http://www.nssn.org

Nexus Electronic Locking Solutions
http://www.nexus.tm

Securitron Magnalock Corporation
http://www.securitron.com

Sensar
http://www.sensar.com

Sensormatic Electronics Corporation
http://www.sensormatic.com

TESA
http://www.tesa.com

TimeLox
http://www.timelox.com

TrueFace (Miros)
http://www.miros.com

Underwriters Laboratories (UL)
http://www.ul.com

VeriVoice
http://www.verivoice.com

VingCard
http://www.vingcard.com

Visionics
http://www.faceit.com

 Case Study

Lights... Camera... Action?

Ted Kline, COO of Berryworth Inns, greeted the executive committee members as they entered the conference room for their monthly meeting. In attendance were the controller, director of security, and the VPs of operations, engineering, and sales.

"As you may know, this month marks the three-year anniversary of the chain-wide installation of electronic locking systems. After looking over our incident reports and claims for this area, I'm happy to report that the system has been a great success! Besides the number of lock-incident cases dropping to almost none, the cost of the few cases that did occur decreased dramatically—by 30 percent! Since this was a decision agreed on by all present, these statistics are something that we can all be proud of—so give yourselves a hand!"

As the smattering of applause died down, Ted continued, "Since this last investment was so successful, and we have definitely seen the payoff and reaped the benefits, I believe it's time to branch out and implement yet another security feature that can help minimize other security incidents—while reducing expenses, of course. Gerald, why don't you take it from here."

All eyes turned toward their security guru. "Thanks, Ted. Well, as I see it, there are two priorities we can choose to address—actually, they were numbers two and three on our list three years ago when we decided to go with the electronic locking systems, and I believe they are still critical today. I believe our next logical choice would be either updated lighting or a CCTV system. Each of these would help address problems we've been having in the parking lot, corridors, and stairwells."

Frank, the engineer, asked the obvious first question. "Well, what does each actually involve?"

"By lighting we mean both inside and outside lighting," Gerald responded. "We'd be replacing existing fixtures with energy efficient lamps, increasing wattage, and adding additional fixtures wherever necessary—keeping within the aesthetics of the properties, of course—we wouldn't want anything obnoxious."

"What do you mean by inside lighting? Are you talking about brighter corridors and stairwells and such?" asked Frank.

"Yes," Gerald continued. "Who here hasn't stayed at a hotel somewhere where it was just a tad difficult to look through that little peephole and clearly make out who was standing outside your door? Better lighting would make that identification process easier. Anyway, turning to CCTV now. That installation would involve the placement of numerous cameras throughout the property—both inside and out—and some sort of home base or control panel for monitoring."

Alan, the controller, raised his head, "There's obviously a cost involved for both ideas. What kind of investment are we looking at for each option? I'm sure each is quite hefty."

"Actually, Alan," Ted answered, "it's hard to justify one choice over the other if you look only at the financial aspect. There are many other factors that need to be taken into consideration in order to make the most beneficial decision. But we can start with financial concerns."

Alan continued, "What worries me is the initial purchase price of everything—new lamps and fixtures, along with any increased energy costs to maintain whatever new lighting system or level of lighting that is deemed appropriate—"

"—especially," interrupted Frank, "when before we've just changed the lamps or increased the wattage or cleaned the lenses."

"Those are valid concerns," said Gerald, "but research shows that the new high-tech lighting systems are actually more cost- and energy-efficient and will save money in the long run."

"So does that mean you're in favor of lighting as our next investment?" asked Alan.

"Now, don't go jumping to conclusions. Just because I can validate lighting as a potentially cost-efficient investment doesn't mean I don't have other concerns," answered Gerald.

Ted tried to clarify by asking, "So your choice would be CCTV?"

"Actually, yes," responded Gerald. "Why? Most of all, because it's an excellent deterrent of criminal activity. Chances are, if people see or know that their actions are being caught on tape, they will be less likely to commit their intended act. And if an incident did occur, we'd have a tape recording of it, and the suspect would be much easier to apprehend—something which police officers really like since they don't need to get a confession and they have immediate evidence."

Frank jumped in, "Well, the same thing can be said for lighting—it's also an excellent deterrent! The brighter it is, and the more lights there are around, the less likely criminals are going to invade that space. They'll move on to another property where it's darker."

Sandy, the VP of sales, finally spoke up, "Gerald, I agree with you—CCTV should be the choice. We can sell that! CCTV is a specific security feature that clients and prospects can immediately understand and see as providing better physical protection for them. On the other hand, it would be really hard for me or our sales staff to make the same point by saying, 'We have lots more lights now.' Lights won't seem to offer the same level of protection or sense of personal security that CCTV does. So, from a sales and marketing aspect, CCTV holds significantly more potential as a salable feature—especially when it comes to repeat customers associating security with our brand image."

Kamron, the VP of operations, finally broke in. "Those are all fine points, too, Sandy, but have you thought about the additional staffing that would be necessary for all those CCTV monitors that would be installed across our 30 properties? In order to be effective, those monitors should be under surveillance 24 hours a day, and some of our properties just couldn't handle that."

Gerald, knowing more about security options than the rest of the group, interjected, "Actually, there is a possibility of remote monitoring. It's new but seems to be catching on."

Ted spoke up, "I've never heard of that. What exactly is it—"

"—and how much does it cost? It sounds expensive," Alan finished.

"I'm not sure of the expense," answered Gerald. "The basic premise is that we install the monitors, link them through a satellite to a monitoring office somewhere else—say Texas or Michigan or something—and their staff watches our hotel. Voilá—no additional staff necessary."

"Like I said, that sounds expensive," repeated Alan.

"Look, all I'm saying is that it's something that would need to be investigated—it's another option if we didn't want to add staff," Gerald responded.

Ted broke in again. "Excellent point, Gerald. However, it reminds me of something I read recently—how failure to monitor your CCTV system could actually create additional liability. I mean, what happens if someone is being attacked in full view of a camera and nothing is done about it? That sounds like a budget-breaking lawsuit to me."

Kamron answered, "I agree. But it seems like that would only be a problem in properties that weren't sufficiently staffed. And of course we would take precautions to make sure we definitely weren't understaffed—even if we had to look into that satellite monitoring thing. But, if you think about it, the same negligence lawsuit could happen with lighting, too. You can have the best lighting in the world, but if there's no staff around—security or otherwise—to do anything about an attack, what's the point of that increased lighting?"

"Wait a minute," said Alan. "Okay, yes it's true that both CCTV and lighting can be seen as a deterrent to criminal activity. But, lighting makes more financial sense. Although the costs may be about equal up front, the lighting system could pay for itself in a few years while CCTV would mean a continuous drain on a hotel's labor costs. And what actually may be the most critical point—if our competition has recently increased their lighting systems, we need to do the same thing if we want to stay market competitive."

"You bet—and the same thing could be said about CCTV, too," added Gerald. "Keeping up with the Joneses, as they say."

Sandy shook her head. "Gentlemen, all this talk is well and good, but you're still missing my point. Sales can't use lighting as a selling point. Trust me on this. It would be like asking me to sell romance versus a dozen roses. We all know romance is there, but people can see and touch and feel and smell roses—making for a much easier sell. Sure, additional lighting in the parking lot might make the hotel seem more inviting to transient guests arriving at night, but what about the majority of our business? What about groups and meeting planners? I know for a fact that I can schedule more groups and tours with the added benefit of a CCTV security system. Why? Because I can show them the system. I can't show them lights. They take lights for granted—they might know it was bright, but they wouldn't connect that to increased security. Believe me, in the long run, the increased business brought in by the CCTV system would greatly outweigh the investment cost."

"Well people," Ted concluded, "it looks like we have a tough decision on our hands."

Discussion Questions

1. What are the advantages and disadvantages of choosing improved lighting as the security investment?
2. What are the advantages and disadvantages of choosing CCTV as the security investment?
3. Which investment would you recommend and why?

Case Number: 3872CA

The following industry experts helped generate and develop this case: Wendell Couch, ARM, CHA, Director of Technical Services for the Risk Management Department of Bass Hotels & Resorts; and Raymond C. Ellis, Jr., CHE, CHTP, CLSD, Professor, Conrad N. Hilton College, University of Houston, Director, Loss Prevention Management Institute.

REVIEW QUIZ

When you feel you have covered all of the material in this chapter, answer these questions. Choose the *best* answer.

1. Which of the following statements is *false*?

    a. Management determines the amount and type of security equipment to be used at a property.
    b. Elaborate security equipment will better meet the needs of any property than will a larger security staff.
    c. The presence of security equipment does not alter the property's need for security procedures.
    d. No property is entirely without some form of security equipment.

2. Closed-circuit television (CCTV) is most effective:

    a. for viewing public areas.
    b. when used in restrooms.
    c. when used in conjunction with dummy cameras to deter criminal conduct.
    d. in areas where there should be no movement.

3. Which of the following provides the most effective form of security communication?

    a. pagers
    b. duress systems
    c. two-way radios
    d. telephones

4. Which of the following alarm systems is most likely to be triggered by pressure?

    a. photoelectric light beam
    b. microwave detectors
    c. infrared radiation detection
    d. seismic detector

5. Decisions about security equipment should be made:

    a. by legal counsel.
    b. with a clear understanding of the equipment's uses and limitations.
    c. based on needs of other properties in the area.
    d. all of the above.

REVIEW QUIZ *(continued)*

6. Which of the following is *least* likely to be found in a guestroom?

    a. deadbolts
    b. security information decals
    c. microwave detectors
    d. window locks

7. Effective key control procedures can help reduce the need for:

    a. re-keying locks.
    b. magnetic card readers.
    c. computers at the front desk.
    d. the use of CCTV.

Answer Key: 1-b-C1, 2-d-C1, 3-c-C2, 4-d-C3, 5-b-C4, 6-c-C5, 7-a-C5,

Each question is linked to a competency. Competencies are listed on the first page of the chapter. An answer reading 3-b-C4 translates to:

- 3: the question number
- b: the correct answer
- C4: the competency number

Chapter 3 Outline

Key and Keycard Control
    Electronic Access Systems
Surveillance and Access Control Procedures
    Patrols
The Presence of Unauthorized Persons
    Drug Dealers
Safe Deposit Box Procedures
    Keys and Key Control
    Access Procedures
    Special or Unusual Access
The In-Room Safe
Lost and Found Procedures
Appendix: Sample Room Notices

Competencies

1. Identify various types of key control and their advantages and disadvantages. (pp. 165–169)

2. Explain how effective access control is achieved through surveillance and security patrols. (pp. 174–176)

3. Explain how to deal with the presence of unauthorized or undesirable persons. (pp. 176–178)

4. Implement effective safe deposit box security procedures and explain the hotel's liability for safe deposit boxes and in-room safes. (pp. 178–186)

5. Describe and implement lost and found procedures. (pp. 186–191)

3
Security Procedures Covering Guest Concerns

EVERY PROPERTY'S MANAGEMENT needs to establish procedures for its staff to follow that will help lead to the safe and secure functioning of the operation. All employees, not merely security personnel, should know the appropriate security procedures that will help protect the guests and the property from danger and loss at the hands of criminals operating on the premises.

Unfortunately, not all losses come at the hands of such criminals. Many security procedures are needed to control theft by guests and internal theft by employees. Other procedures address the potential for loss created by or during emergencies, including accidents. Asset protection procedures involve protecting the property from losses arising from any number of sources, both internal and external.

This chapter discusses a number of security procedures that help protect guests and the property from victimization, loss, and liability. We will look at key and keycard control, surveillance and access control, safe deposit boxes, in-room safes, and the lost and found function.

Key and Keycard Control

A system of key control is essential to the security of a lodging property. All keys—whether metal or electronic—should be adequately controlled. The best lock in the world may be unable to protect a property or its guests if poor key control allows a criminal to obtain a key to that lock.

Most lodging properties use at least three levels of keying. These levels typically include emergency keys, master keys, and guestroom keys. The **emergency key** opens all guestroom doors, even when they are double locked. It can be used, for example, to enter a room when the guest needs aid and is unable to reach or open the door. The emergency key should be highly protected and its use strictly controlled and recorded; it should never leave the property. One procedure for emergency keys is to have them locked in a safe or safe deposit box and signed out by the individual needing one. The log should be dated and signed by the individual taking the key.

A **master key** opens all guestrooms that are not double locked. Depending upon the need, the master key or keycard may be further established as a section master, a floor master, or a grand master. For example the section master may be used by a housekeeping supervisor who is providing a quality check on service of the room by the room attendant. If it is more practical for the entire floor to be supervised by one person, that individual would be provided with a floor master. The executive housekeeper and assistant housekeeper would have a grand master, permitting access to any guestroom. Similarly, the management should establish protocol on use of these levels of master keys or keycards for engineering and maintenance, room service, mini-bar replenishment and service, front and bell service, and security.

The need for careful control and accounting of all such master-level keys or keycards is apparent when one recognizes the numerous reasons for accessing a room while the guest may not be present. The most effective control of the master key is to have it signed in and out on a daily basis. This key, when not in use on the property, should be retained in a locked case and secured in a designated place of safe-keeping—by department in a larger property and at the front desk or executive office in a smaller facility. It should only be issued to authorized personnel based on their need to use the key, not simply on their status within the operation. A written record should be maintained that details which employees have received master keys. This record can be made a part of the employee personnel file or it can be a separate file maintained by a representative of management. Employee requests for additional or duplicate master keys should also be in writing. Master keys should be accounted for whenever employees resign, transfer, go on vacation, or leave the property or an area within a property for whatever reason. These keys should also never be removed from the property.

The guestroom key opens a single guestroom if the door is not double locked. Guestroom keys should be controlled by front desk personnel, who should always make sure the person receiving the guestroom key is the guest registered for that room. Appropriate identification should always be requested. An effort should always be made to retrieve keys from guests when they check out. For the convenience of, and as a reminder to, the guest, consider having well-secured key return boxes located in the lobby, at exit points of the hotel or motel, and in courtesy vehicles. In some resort areas, such as Hawaii, there have been secured key receptacles placed beyond security screening points in the airport terminal. A number of keys are retrieved in this manner as guests awaiting a flight are reminded, when they notice the receptacle, that they had failed to return the key at check-out.

Consider using keys that do not have the property's name, address, or logo on them. This practice makes it much more difficult for keys that have been lost to be traced to the appropriate property by whoever finds them. Even when only a post office box number is provided on the key or tag, studies have indicated that these keys sometimes get into the criminal community. The holder of the key may then learn which property is renting the box listed. Eliminating any sort of return address also eliminates the expense of return postage.

In a similar vein, most properties do not list the room number on the key. Instead, they code each room or room key to a master list at the front desk. Under this system, the number on the key refers to the list. The guest is provided with an identification card, folder, or some other method for identifying the room number. The guest should be reminded to keep the room number identifier separate from the key or keycard or the protection of the unidentified keycard will be compromised.

Some properties have successfully reduced the number of lost keys by requiring key deposits from the guest at the time of registration. This results in a higher number of keys being returned at check-out, since keys must be returned to recover the deposit.

Employees may play an important role in the control of keys and access to the guestrooms. Cashiers, door attendants, bellpersons, courtesy vehicle operators, and any other appropriate employees should be instructed to remind guests to return keys at check-out. Whenever a key has been left in a room by a departing guest, it should be secured. It should not be left on the top of a housekeeping cart or in any unsecured area. In order to ensure the security of section master, floor master, and grand master keys, they should be secured by employees at all times during the workshift and turned in prior to leaving the premises. Many organizations require that keys (from guestroom keys to the grand master) be returned to security and placed in a locked cabinet in a secured area of the hotel or motel. Keys should not be taken from the property by employees, regardless of their responsibilities or position on staff.

Keys issued on a temporary basis should be listed in a log that reflects the reason for the issue, the issue date, the time out, the time in, to whom issued, and by whom issued. All keys for which the general manager or other appropriate manager is responsible should be kept in a locked safe deposit box or other secure area when not in use. Every property should determine who will be responsible for room key blanks, control keys, master and submaster blanks, and so forth. These responsibilities are sometimes split up among various personnel such as the controller and the chief engineer. Consideration should be given to performing an annual audit of all keys in the possession of employees. Keys should be returned and shown to management for its verification and updating of records.

At properties that make their own metal keys, key-making machines should be secured at all times except when actually being used. If it is impossible to secure the key-making machine, remove the drive belt and secure that instead. All blanks and control keys under the supervision of the key-making function should be locked in a strong, wall-mounted key box.

Whenever there is any known or suspected compromise of any metal keys, a loss or theft, or an unauthorized entry by key, the affected lock(s) should be changed or rotated to another portion of the property. When master keys or emergency keys are involved, re-keying the entire area should be considered.

Electronic Access Systems

Electronic and computer locking systems greatly change the nature of and reduce the need for re-keying. The ability to change the data on an electronic keycard permits a level of control that has never been attained before. When the access code to a guestroom lock changes after the departure of every guest, lost keycards become a minor problem. Some properties even let the guest keep the card as a souvenir. If a master keycard is lost, the process of changing every room's access code is usually fairly easily accomplished, sometimes from a centrally located computer.

There are stand-alone systems that require a computer unit at the front desk or in the front office which contains the ranking of entries for each lockset on the property. The process of ranking ensures issuance of a card that is programmed to block the entry of a person who may have checked out and retained the keycard with the intention of re-entering illegally. It further establishes the legal entry of the new guest and protects that entry during the duration of the assigned stay. The lockset, containing a microchip, provides a "smart door" that can read the card and determine whether admission should be permitted. It also records all card entries to the room. Thus, in addition to the entries by the guest, there will be an indication of entries by room service, housekeeping, front service, engineering, etc. The lock may be interrogated as to what cards were used for entry. Unless there is evidence of a break-in, this is invaluable in the event of missing items from a guest room as it directly focuses on those employees who had access to the room. Many reputations have been restored and many a thankful employee has been cleared of suspicion due to the success of these products. Knowledge of these system capabilities may also serve as a deterrent to those less ethical.[1] Some systems also add a time control feature, in which the card's room access expires after check-out.

On-line electronic systems provide control (changing room access) from a remote center to the lockset through infrared, hard wire, or radio frequency technology. In the instance of the stand-alone system, the keycard communicates to the lockset upon insertion or swiping of the keycard in the lockset.

During the 1990s, many of the major chains mandated the installation of electronic card access systems for both corporate and franchised properties. This established card access as "state of the art" and makes it difficult to defend a case in which key control is a major issue and a property did not provide an electronic card access system.

Exhibit 1 provides a list of questions concerning key control. Though definitely not exhaustive, it makes a number of points that can help lodging property operators to reduce key control problems.

Key control procedures are often an issue in lawsuits filed against lodging properties. In *King v. Trans-Sterling, Inc.*, the plaintiff charged that she had been attacked and raped in her room at the Stardust Hotel in Las Vegas. The room showed no signs of forced entry and evidence showed that, although the hotel had lost as many as 500 keys a week, the rooms had not been re-keyed since the hotel opened 25 years earlier. No records had been kept that would indicate how many master keys had been lost or even which employees had keys to which rooms. The then-owners of the Stardust Hotel were ordered to pay $750,000 in compensatory damages and $2.5 million in punitive damages.

Another case was settled out of court following the visit of the plaintiff's attorney to the defendant hotel in the case. He approached the front desk and requested the key to the room which his client had been assigned at the time of the incident. The key was given to the attorney without any questions or any request for identification. Upon the attorney's return to court with the key, settlement was arranged in the judge's chambers.

Exhibit 1   Basic Key Control Questions

1. Are key records kept up-to-date by all departments controlling those records?
2. Are keys issued to employees on a basis of need rather than convenience or status?
3. Is there a standard policy for rotating all keys and locks at least once a year?
4. Are locks replaced promptly when master and emergency keys are lost or found missing?
5. How many master keys are available, and to whom are they issued? Would a system of submaster keys that restricted employees to specific areas be helpful to your property?
6. When did you last spot check to ensure that officials or employees actually had keys that were issued to them? Do your employees turn in their keys at the end of a shift?
7. Are extra keys maintained securely? Do you limit access to extra keys?
8. If you make your own replacement keys, what restrictions (if any) do you place on access to this equipment?
9. What restrictions do you make on duplicate keys?
10. How many keys leave the premises with guests over a six-month period? What percentage is returned and what is the replacement cost?
11. Do you have a policy requiring employees to inquire about the key at check-out time?

In the following case, *Kraaz v. La Quinta Motor Inns, Inc.*, an employee of the defendant gave a pass (or master) key to someone claiming to be a guest who had lost his key. The employee asked for no identification. The man used the key to enter the plaintiffs' room, where he and an accomplice assaulted and robbed them.

Kraaz v. La Quinta Motor Inns, Inc.
410 So. 2d 1048 (La. App., 1981)

WATSON, Justice.

The primary issue is the delictual liability of an innkeeper for an employee's negligence which is a substantial factor in the armed robbery of a guest. A secondary issue is the quantum of damages awarded plaintiffs.

Plaintiffs, Larry and Joyce Kraaz, are in an itinerant business: buying, selling, racing, and betting on horses. Their only permanent home is the residence of his parents in Chicago.

On December 31, 1978, Mr. and Mrs. Kraaz were attending the race meeting at the Fair Grounds and were staying at the La Quinta Motor Inn in Metairie, Louisiana. At approximately 4:00 A.M. the seventeen year old desk clerk, David Ulmer, was approached by two men. One of them identified himself as Benson in 233, who had lost his key. Since there was a Benson registered in 233 and no room key available, approached by two men. One of them identified himself as Benson in 233, who had lost his key. Since there was a Benson registered in 233 and no room key available, Ulmer gave the man a pass key to all rooms in the motel. This was contrary to company policy. Subsequently, Ulmer became apprehensive, discovered that Benson knew nothing about the key request, and observed two men coming from the direction of the Kraaz's room, one of them with a gun in his waistband.

In the interim, the two men had unlocked the door of the room occupied by Mr. and Mrs. Kraaz and broken the chain. They hog-tied Larry Kraaz, physically abused Joyce Kraaz, and took a package containing about $23,000 from Mrs. Kraaz's purse. They also took a .25 caliber Smith & Wesson automatic but overlooked another $15,000 in cash which was lying near the gun. The thieves also failed to find an additional $3,000 in the purse. The money was intended for the purchase of race horses. The testimony was that these are generally cash transactions.

Thomas Tomillo, a horse trainer, testified that he was training two horses for Kraaz in December of 1978 and working with him on the purchase of additional horses. Mrs. Kraaz gave him between $1,000 and $1,500 that day from the package which was stolen that night. It originally contained $25,000.

Larry Kraaz said he was knocked out of bed and pinned down on the floor by two men with a gun. His wife started screaming and got hit in the face. Kraaz feared he would be killed and his wife raped and killed. He heard the hammer clicking on a large caliber weapon being held against his head. After he was tied with wire and his mouth taped, they mauled his wife and put her in the bathtub. Then they came out of the bathroom, picked up her purse, emptied it out, grabbed the bundle of cash and ran. Kraaz broke the wire, threw his pants on and reached for his pistol, but it was gone. He got a .44 magnum from his car and tried unsuccessfully to intercept the thieves at the back door of the motel. While chasing them through the motel with his gun, Kraaz observed the elderly security guard sound asleep on the steps behind the office. Since the crime, Joyce Kraaz has become paranoid about motels and Larry has lost her companionship. She had previously travelled around the country with him ten months of the year. Now Joyce Kraaz feels more secure in Chicago, where there are other people and a dog in the house. After the [in]cident, he described her as "a complete basket case."

One of the two assailants wore a mask. Joyce Kraaz was convinced that she and her husband would be killed, because she could identify the man without the mask. Her mouth, leg, and hip were bruised and swollen. She remained in the room until her husband took her to the hospital that afternoon about 5:00 P.M. She could not walk and thought her hip might be broken. The emergency room doctor told her that the swelling was just a very bad bruise and would go away in time. She has been too frightened and uncomfortable to resume her former life and now takes sleeping pills and tranquilizers regularly. She has lost weight and has no appetite. Because she needs help, she intends to undergo therapy with a Chicago psychiatrist.

Dr. Terry E. Passman, a board certified psychiatrist, saw Joyce Kraaz shortly after the robbery on January 3, 1979. He described her as extremely frightened, apprehensive, and essentially unable to function. He gave her some medication to calm her down enough to converse. Dr. Passman diagnosed an acute traumatic neurosis. Despite her total incapacity, he decided hospitalization might aggravate the anxiety. Sodium Amytal, an extremely strong sleeping drug, was administered intravenously at a hospital emergency room to help her over the initial period of shock. According to Dr. Passman, Joyce Kraaz had experienced several traumatic incidents as an adolescent, which she had repressed.[1] The experience at the La Quinta

---

[1] At age thirteen, Joyce Kraaz saw her mother's jaw broken by her stepfather. The stepfather had made frightening sexual advances toward her.

broke down her defense mechanism and caused an exaggerated reaction to the situation. In Dr. Passman's opinion, Mrs. Kraaz could have lived a normal life except for this incident.

Dr. Passman saw Joyce Kraaz again on January 17 when she was still extremely upset, crying and fearful, with a feeling of impending doom. Another tranquilizer was prescribed. On January 22, she was less anxious, but still had problems at night. The incident had created a fear of rape which had adversely affected her sex life with her husband, previously a strong point in the marriage.

Dr. Passman next saw Joyce Kraaz on January 29. She had improved, but still had early morning awakening, a symptom of depression, fear, and guilt. She was still extremely anxious and her sex life unsatisfactory. When she next came to New Orleans, Dr. Passman could not fit her into his schedule. Dr. Passman advised Joyce Kraaz to continue psychotherapy.

Mr. Kraaz became convinced that the sessions with Dr. Passman were doing his wife more harm than good because she was so upset afterward. His solution was to let time take care of the problem, but this did not work. She went back to Dr. Passman. On March 18, 1980, Dr. Passman described Joyce as haggard and tense. Her marriage and sex life have been significantly impaired by the crime. On March 20, Larry Kraaz told Dr. Passman their sex life is terrible and the marriage is deteriorating. Dr. Passman discussed the need for future treatment with both Mr. and Mrs. Kraaz and recommended therapy at least twice a week for two years, possibly longer. He referred them to several psychiatrists in Chicago. According to Dr. Passman, his current fee is $65 a session and this is comparable to Chicago fees.

Detective Alfred Cantrell of the Jefferson Parish Sheriff's Department participated in the investigation. He confirmed that a key had been used to open the door, the chain lock was broken, and a large roll of cash remained on the night stand. The detective did not count the roll which Larry Kraaz said contained $15,000. Gary Croutcher, the manager of the motel, told Cantrell they had been having security problems.

An earlier incident at the motel involved W. L. Quattlebaum, Jr., an insurance company employee, who also owns, buys, and sells race horses. Someone knocked on his door the night before the Kraaz robbery and identified himself as the manager. Quattlebaum cracked the door and saw a man wearing a ski mask and gloves. He managed to push the door closed and reported the attempted robbery to the motel office. Although the desk clerk said he would take care of calling the police, the police never came.

A notice allegedly posted on the door of the Kraaz room quotes some "Louisiana Hotel Laws" in very small print. The entire notice measures approximately three inches by seven inches. The last two items are LSA-C.C. arts. 2968 and 2971.[2] C.C. art. 2968 reads as follows:

---

[2]LSA-C.C. art. 2971 provides:

"No landlord or innkeeper shall be liable under the provisions of the foregoing six articles to any guests or party of guests occupying the same apartments for any loss sustained by such guests or party of guests by theft or otherwise, in any sum exceeding one hundred dollars, unless by special agreement in writing with the proprietor, manager or lessee of the hotel or inn a greater liability has been contracted for.

"Provided that no guest shall be held bound by the limitation of the value established in this Article unless this Article is conspicuously posted in the guest room."

Every landlord or keeper of a public inn or hotel, shall be required to provide with an iron chest or other safe deposit for valuable articles belonging to his guests or customers, and each landlord or hotel keeper shall keep posted upon his doors and other public places in his house or entertainment, written or printed notices to his guests and customers that they must leave their valuables with the landlord, his agent or clerk, for safe keeping, that he may make safe deposit of the same in the place provided for that purpose.

When such a safe is provided and a notice to that effect is "conspicuously posted", liability is limited to $100. LSA-C.C. art. 2971. Significantly, Civil Code article 2969[3] exempts from this limitation losses which "occur through the fraud and negligence of the landlord, or some clerk or servant provided by him in such inn or hotel." *Laubie v. Sonesta International Hotel Corp.*, 398 So.2d 1374 (La., 1981) held that the limitation of liability in LSA-C.C. art. 2971 only applies to the innkeepers' contractual liability as a depositary. The innkeeper remains liable for damages resulting from fault on the part of him or his employees.

Neither the investigating officers nor the Kraazs saw the notice allegedly posted in the room. Joyce and Larry Kraaz both said they didn't know the La Quinta had a safe.

Gary Croutcher, the manager at La Quinta, testified that he checked the Kraaz room for damage between 9:00 and 10:00 A.M. the day after the [in]cident and observed a notice posted behind the door. Joyce Kraaz testified in rebuttal that Croutcher did not appear in her room that morning. According to Croutcher, the housekeeper is instructed to automatically replace any missing notices. The La Quinta has six safes. Croutcher admitted that he had not pointed out the notice to Mr. and Mrs. Kraaz or anyone else at the time of the crime and had not been asked about it until three or four weeks before trial. There is no sign at the registration desk advising that there is a safe for valuables. Croutcher's testimony was contrary to that of Detective Alfred Cantrell and other witnesses in many particulars.

The trial court concluded that La Quinta's employee was grossly negligent in providing a pass key to criminals and the motel was liable for the Kraazs' damages. Mrs. Kraaz was awarded $3,500 for physical injuries, $30,000 for traumatic neurosis, and future medical expenses of $13,000. Mr. Kraaz was awarded $2,500 for his physical and mental pain and suffering and $23,000 for the lost cash. The trial court was not satisfied that there was a notice posted on the motel door, but stated that, even if present, it was not sufficient to alert the Kraazs to the fact that a depositary was available for the protection of their valuables. The Court of Appeal affirmed. *Kraaz v. La Quinta*, 396 So.2d 455 (LaApp. 4 Cir. 1981). A writ was granted to review the judgment. 401 So.2d 992 (La., 1981).

---

[3]LSA-C.C. art. 2969 provides:

"Every landlord, hotel or inn keeper who shall comply with the requirements of the preceding articles (article), shall not be liable for any money, jewelry, watches, plate, or other things made of gold or silver, or of rare and precious stones, or for other valuable articles of such description as may be contained in small compass, which may be abstracted or lost from any such public inn or hotel, if the same shall not be left with the landlord, his clerk or agent, for deposit, unless such loss shall occur through the fraud or negligence of the landlord, or some clerk or servant employed by him in such inn or hotel; provided, however, that the provisions of this article, shall not apply to a wearing watch, or such other articles of jewelry as are ordinarily worn about the person."

Defendant relies heavily on LSA-C.C. art. 2970 which provides:

> He (the innkeeper) is not responsible for what is stolen by force and arms, or with exterior breaking open of doors, or by any other extraordinary violence.

The Court of Appeal held that Civil Code art. 2970 was not applicable because, even though the chain on the door was broken, the initial entry to the room was made with a pass key. *Laubie* also involved a forcible entry; a chain lock was severed. *Laubie* states that LSA-C.C. art. 2970, like LSA-C.C. art. 2971, relates only to the innkeeper's contractual obligations as a depositary. 398 So.2d 1377. If a forcible armed entry were unaccompanied by fault on the part of the innkeeper or his employees, there would be no liability. However, that is not the case. The elderly security guard was asleep. The seventeen year old boy on duty gave a pass key to the entire motel to two strangers. There was unquestionably negligence. Since the pass key was a key element in the robbery, Civil Code article 2970 does not exonerate the innkeeper from liability.

Defendant also relies upon *Robbins v. Ponchartrain Apartment*, 175 La. 278, 143 So. 263 (1932). In *Robbins*, the trial court's determination that the landlord's clerk was negligent was reversed. Leaving the safe unlocked at 3:00 A.M. was held to be "not negligence." 143 So.2d 265. That somewhat dubious conclusion distinguishes the matter from this one.

An innkeeper does not insure his guests against the risk of injury or property loss resulting from violent crime. [citation omitted] The innkeeper's position vis-a-vis his guests is similar to that of a common carrier toward its passengers. [citation omitted] Thus, a guest is entitled to a high degree of care and protection. [citation omitted] The innkeeper has a duty to take reasonable precautions against criminals. Safeguarding the room keys is a minimum requirement. The duty to avoid handing a pass key to any stranger is even stronger. Breach of this duty was a direct cause of plaintiffs' physical, emotional, and financial damages. La Quinta's employee, Ulmer, was at fault in giving the two armed robbers a pass key. The employer is liable for the resulting damages. [citation omitted]

The attitude of La Quinta's management toward the safety of its guests is emphasized by Quattlebaum's testimony about the lack of interest in the attempted robbery of his room. [citation omitted] In Quattlebaum's case, the thief's lack of a key enabled him to avoid being robbed.

Contributory negligence of the Kraazs in having the money with them is urged as a defense. Mere possession of money does not constitute negligence. The trial court was unconvinced that a notice about safe keeping was posted in the room. The trier of the fact was well justified in disregarding Croutcher's testimony to the contrary. Even if posted and adequate, the notice was certainly not conspicuous. The Kraazs could not foresee that assailants would open their room door with a pass key in the middle of the night, leaving them no time to defend themselves or call for help. They were not negligent.

There is no abuse of discretion in the award of damages. [citation omitted] The facts more than amply support the amounts awarded.

For the foregoing reasons, the judgment of the Court of Appeal is affirmed.
AFFIRMED.

Surveillance and Access Control Procedures

Personnel play a central role in watching for trouble and protecting the guests and property from loss and unauthorized access. All employees should be trained to watch for suspicious persons or situations. For example, desk clerks should, when possible, watch a property's entrances, elevators, and stairways. Surveillance equipment may allow the elevator to be programmed to stop at a certain floor for observation, but it is still up to personnel to actually observe it. Likewise, closed-circuit television is virtually pointless without personnel monitoring it.

The point is that even surveillance equipment relies on personnel understanding how to use it most efficiently and effectively to control access to a property. Effective access control calls for the development of procedures that deal with how to respond to the information gained through both surveillance equipment and observations of employees.

Patrols

One aspect of surveillance and access control that is frequently mentioned in lawsuits alleging negligence is the absence or inadequate number of patrolling security officers both inside the property and on the grounds. Patrolling security officers were an issue in *Wenninger v. Motel 6, Inc.*; *Orlando Executive Park, Inc. v. P.D.R.*; and *Banks v. Hyatt Corp.* A patrolling police officer played a major role in *Peters v. Holiday Inns, Inc.*

The patrol function is very important. Patrols should follow a varied pattern, in terms of both timing and area. Regularly timed patrols should be avoided since they establish a consistent pattern which criminals can observe and work around.

The two primary functions of patrolling are to deter and detect security and safety incidents and problems. Security officers who patrol a property should be trained in what to look for. Patrolling is much more than simply walking or driving around a property; it involves being alert to anything unusual and can call on the employee's sight, hearing, smell, and touch. Some properties develop a security patrol checklist which helps ensure that patrolling employees remember to check all areas and aspects of the operation.

Patrolling employees can deter crime in a number of ways. First, their visible presence may deter crime. Second, patrol personnel can note conditions that may result in potential security risks, such as lighting or access control equipment which is not functioning correctly. As part of the patrol function, the employee who discovers such conditions should report the discovery to the appropriate individual or department—immediately, if the situation warrants it. Third, patrol personnel can observe and investigate suspicious persons and situations. Each property develops its own procedures for its security personnel to follow when investigating a suspicious person or situation. Suspicious persons may include drunks and potential prostitutes; non-guests loitering in the lobby, on the grounds or parking lot, and on guestroom floors; and any persons (including employees) who are in areas they should not be in. Suspicious situations may include doors left unlocked or ajar, forced locks, broken windows, and automobiles left parked and/or with the motor running in inappropriate places.

AT YOUR RISK

ANTHONY MARSHALL

Trade Secrets of a Professional Unwanted Guest

"I think you should go to jail," Harris Rosen, President of Tamar Inns, Inc., suggested to me. "Michael Smith can teach you a lot about locks." Rosen spoke from experience. Michael had visited Tamar's Omni Hotel in Orlando often, but never as a registered guest....

Michael's story was a fascinating tale of desperation, survival and smarts. From age 16, when he left home, Michael exploited his cunning to live free at various hotels' expense. The secret to his success was easy access to the hotel's keys: guestroom keys, master keys—even safe deposit keys.

Michael soon learned that stealing a guest's safe deposit box key from his or her room opened the floodgate to cash, credit cards, and jewelry—all of which could be easily traded for drugs and the other necessities of his life at the time.

Once he had given the correct guest's name and room number to the front-desk associate, he often heard the following: "Please sign for the envelope on the signature line." Not once in 22 years was he ever asked for personal identification.

Michael learned that front desk associates almost always focus exclusively on getting the signature on the guest's safe deposit box envelope. That's what they'd been trained to do. Demanding personal identification was never part of their jobs.

Michael earned the equivalent of a master's degree in the hotel industry's history of keys. No lock or security technique could stop him. When Michael started at 16, most hotel keys he stole were standard metal keys with the room number stamped right on them. Room identification was a cinch. A few years later, when many hotels began to cross-code guestroom key numbers, he simply broke their codes.

"Most hotel codes were not too difficult to decipher," Michael explained. "They might renumber guestroom 215 to read 512 and that was about it."

Electronic locks eventually entered the market and the hotel industry focused on giving each new registrant a new key code. Security officers breathed a sigh of relief because they assumed key-control problems would vanish. They hoped room burglaries would stop—but that's not what happened.

Michael studied the new electronic locks. He discovered the deadbolt doesn't close on an electric lock when a guest exits their room. Armed only with a 14-inch industrial screwdriver, he could enter a guestroom in two seconds flat. Without a deadbolt, it was easy.

Rosen, like many hoteliers, thought electronic locks were the answer to guestroom security problems. After Michael was arrested, Rosen decided to tackle the problem. Working with his staff and the company that initially installed the locks, they found a solution. Today, all of Rosen's hotels have spring-activated deadbolts. Once guests leave their rooms, a large deadbolt automatically springs into place.

"We've locked out the Michael Smiths," Rosen said, insisting all Tamar's hotel rooms are now secure. Michael Smith has studied the new system and agrees. In fact, Michael is so impressed with the response to his previous trade secrets, he believes he can help Rosen or other hoteliers even more.

"I think I'd make a fine security officer with his company," Michael said....

(continued)

At Your Risk *(continued)*

> My interview with Michael provided a great deal of insight into the flaws of hotel security. If some of that information alerts hotels to their vulnerability and promotes improvements in security, then perhaps Michael's true rehabilitation has already begun.

Courtesy of *Hotel & Motel Management*, February 15, 1999. Used with permission.

The patrol function allows the security officer to move throughout all areas of a property. For this reason, training for patrols should emphasize an awareness of fire and safety in addition to security. A significant contribution may be made to a property's protection through this special training. Fire or smoke and unsafe conditions such as torn rugs, loose handrails, unsafe walking surfaces, missing fire extinguishers, obstructions in stairwells and emergency exits, burned out emergency exit lights, and so forth should be noted and promptly reported by patrolling employees.

Training should inform patrol personnel not only what to look for, but also how to respond to what is seen. Many properties require their patrol personnel to file a report at the end of their shift noting what they have seen, especially if it was unusual or called for some sort of action. In situations calling for immediate action from the employee, the employee needs to know which action his or her property's management considers appropriate or which action is required by applicable laws. In developing these guidelines to train patrol personnel, a property's management should consult local counsel.

The Presence of Unauthorized Persons

A lodging facility, although open to the public, is private property. An innkeeper has the responsibility to monitor and, when appropriate, to control the activities of persons on the premises. It is, however, imperative that any activities which limit the freedom of movement of any person or persons in the lodging facility be undertaken by the property's staff with the utmost discretion. Such actions should always be reasonable and appropriate. Recall that the authority of security officers may be limited, that the unauthorized restraint of an individual may cause the employee and the property to be liable for false arrest, and that some activities are best handled by local law enforcement officials if time permits.

Unauthorized or undesirable persons (as determined by management for each particular property) should be discouraged from visiting the property, but again, extreme discretion and tact should be used. When deciding whether to evict persons from the premises, great care should be taken to react to what they actually *do* as opposed to who they are or seem to be. For example, persons suspected of being prostitutes should be evicted with great care. It can be a costly and embarrassing error to question the character or reputation of an individual. Such questioning, if unfounded, can serve as a basis of legal action for slander. The eviction of persons from public space (such as the lobby and any restaurants) is governed by laws applicable to places of public accommodation. Management should review the statutes applicable to its location.

On the other hand, guestrooms and guest corridors are not deemed open to the public. No one other than guests, legitimate visitors of guests, and the property's employees should be in these areas. The normal laws of trespass apply in these areas and should be consulted. If employees see a suspicious person on a floor or in an elevator, they have the right to ask if he or she is a guest or a visitor. They can also ask to see the person's room key or accompany the person to the room he or she intends to visit. Unauthorized persons may be asked to leave the property and warned not to return. Such action should be documented and, if the person returns, the police should be notified.

The problem of prostitution is of particular concern to the security department or the individual responsible for security on the premises. In a number of cities, prostitution is also connected with theft and assault. The presence of prostitutes eventually affects the reputation of the property and can seriously affect future occupancy rates. Consequently, it is a problem that may involve the security staff, the local police, the property's management, and legal counsel. Determine what legal recourse exists within the community. Consult with legal counsel to determine if protection may be found under laws covering trespass, pandering, soliciting, loitering, or other local rulings on prostitution. This is a problem that requires close liaison with legal counsel and local police authorities and the commitment of management to prosecute. The security staff must also be aware of the possibility of organized prostitution activity on the property. In some cases, employees working in collusion with the front desk or even with security staff members have provided prostitutes to guests.

Unfortunately, legitimate guests sometimes invite undesirable persons (such as prostitutes) to their rooms. When this occurs, the property may be unable to keep such a person out. The property may need, however, to closely watch the appropriate guestroom so it can escort the undesirable person off the premises as soon as he or she emerges. If this precaution is not taken and the undesirable person assaults another guest before leaving the premises, the property may be found negligent since it knew of the presence of the person yet failed to take adequate action. After escorting an undesirable person off the premises, the security officer should record the circumstances. If the facts seem to warrant it, management should consider informing the police.

Drug Dealers

Sometimes a property has to deal with undesirable persons who are guests. One such type that deserves brief special attention is the drug smuggler. Smugglers sometimes stay at hotels and motels while waiting for drug shipments to arrive. Because of the unusual nature of their business, their behavior may be atypical of the property's regular guests. A property's employees can be trained to watch for certain suggestive signs.

Specifically, smugglers often pay cash for everything. One person may register and pay with cash for several people. Because of the uncertainty frequently involved in when a shipment will arrive, smugglers may stay for an indeterminate

178 *Chapter 3*

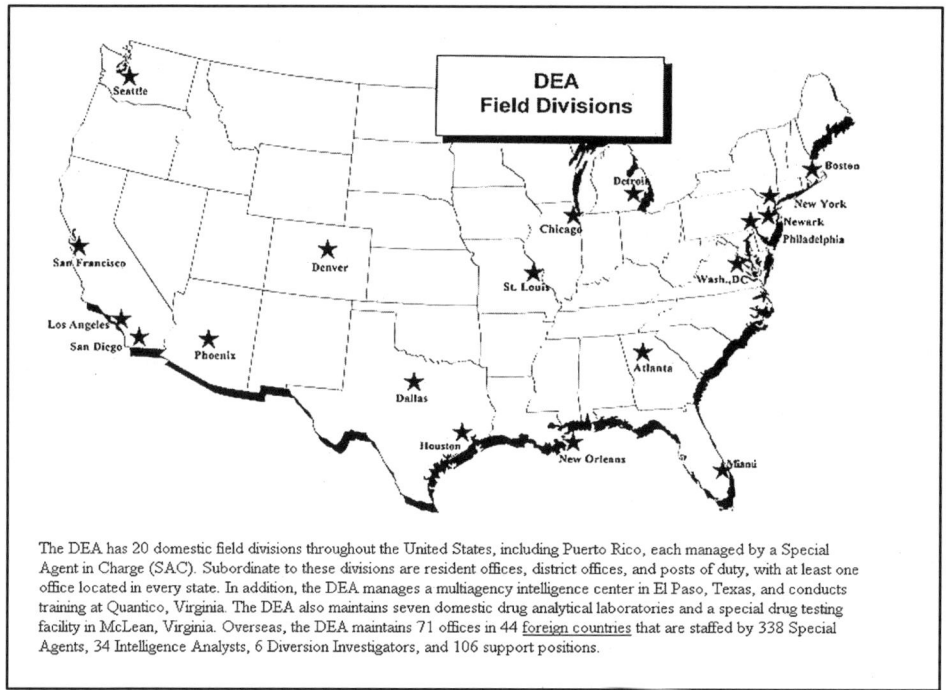

The DEA has 20 domestic field divisions throughout the United States, including Puerto Rico, each managed by a Special Agent in Charge (SAC). Subordinate to these divisions are resident offices, district offices, and posts of duty, with at least one office located in every state. In addition, the DEA manages a multiagency intelligence center in El Paso, Texas, and conducts training at Quantico, Virginia. The DEA also maintains seven domestic drug analytical laboratories and a special drug testing facility in McLean, Virginia. Overseas, the DEA maintains 71 offices in 44 foreign countries that are staffed by 338 Special Agents, 34 Intelligence Analysts, 6 Diversion Investigators, and 106 support positions.

The Department of Drug Enforcement Administration (DEA) office locations and telephone numbers can be found online at the U.S. Department of Justice website at http://www.usdoj.gov/dea/pubs/briefing/7.htm.

time, paying day by day. They may drive trucks, vans, campers, recreational vehicles (in other words, anything with large storage space), or even expensive late-model cars, and may, at registration, incorrectly or falsely report these vehicles' license plate numbers. They may make and/or receive many long-distance or room-to-room telephone calls.

Of course, many guests who are not smugglers may meet one or even a few of these conditions. And even if a guest meets several, that is not proof that the person is a drug smuggler. Still, when several of these signs and/or any other unusual behavior arouse the suspicions of the innkeeper, he or she should consider contacting the local law enforcement agency.

During the closing decades of the twentieth century, the problem of illegal drug labs began to involve hotel and motel rooms. These labs are used for the illegal manufacture of methamphetamines, a drug known on the street as *speed* or *crank*. The introduction of highly toxic and explosive drugs creates major health hazards, as well as potential damage to property. The greatest danger is the residue left from the manufacturing process. One authority notes that the fumes from the cooking process smell like dirty diapers; the fumes may also have a long-term effect on the lungs and liver.

When such an odor is detected by the staff when passing an occupied room, special care should be taken at the time of room cleaning to determine whether the room has been used for drug production. If there is obvious residue and other evidence that a room may have been used for drug manufacture, the room should immediately be sealed and the authorities should be called. Guests in adjoining rooms should be moved with the explanation that a guest spilled chemicals and they are being moved for their convenience and comfort; no further explanation should be given. The authorities responding to the incident should include the Department of Drug Enforcement Administration (DEA), the local office in the community which handles drug spills and removal of toxic wastes, and the local police and fire authorities. It is interesting to note that even though the end product may be a drug, the chemicals used in concocting the drug are the problem, hence the Occupational Safety & Health Administration (OSHA) becoming involved through "Hazardous Waste Operations and Emergency Response." Before an incident occurs, however, this matter should be reviewed with the above agencies in order to follow a procedure that will maximize the safety of those on premises, as well as those assigned to correct the problem. Such a room should not be returned to inventory for assignment until approved by the appropriate authorities.

Safe Deposit Box Procedures

In most states, there is a limit to a property's liability for the loss of a guest's valuables if the property has safe deposit boxes or a safe for the storage of the guest's valuables and the guest is notified of the availability of the safe or safe deposit boxes. The notice given to guests of such safekeeping facilities usually takes the form of public postings. The appendix to this chapter includes sample room postings from two states. By law, these postings typically must appear at several conspicuous places on the premises, often within the guestroom itself. Since the laws in this regard vary from state to state, legal counsel should be contacted to ensure that a property is in compliance with the applicable state laws concerning safes, safe deposit boxes, and the posting of notices. Exhibit 2 includes a review of requirements under the Innkeeper's Statutes for the 50 states and the District of Columbia. Properties should verify from time to time if there have been any amendments to a specific state's requirements.

You will note in the Receipts column that a number of states require that a receipt be issued. This creates a number of problems that should be reviewed by senior management with corporate counsel. For example, one problem would be the provision of a receipt for $100,000 in cash or jewelry. Has the property now abrogated the state limitation on liability to the limits shown in Exhibit 2? Has the property encountered a privacy issue since the guest must divulge the items and values if a receipt is to be issued? Pay particular attention to the Postings column as cases have been lost through failure to provide proper signage; in such incidents, the guest has not been provided with proper notice of the safe deposit box procedure.

The innkeeper's limited liability laws often also apply when a guest's property is lost or stolen from a safe deposit box, unless that property is lost or stolen through the negligence of the lodging operation. If a guest files suit over property missing from his or her safe deposit box, a court may inquire into the degree of

Chapter 3

Exhibit 2 Innkeeper's Statutes—Basic Requirements by State

STATE	LIABILITY LIMIT ($)	STATUTE	POSTINGS	RECEIPTS
Alabama	300	34.15.13	Guestrooms (rear of door, lobby)	Y
Alaska	1,000	08.56.050	3 or more conspicuous places	N
Arizona	500	33.302	Guestrooms or office (conspicuously)	N
Arkansas	300	20.26.302	10+ conspicuous places	Y
California	500	Secton 1859	Guestrooms or office (prominent place)	N
Colorado	5,000	24.44.106	Guestrooms, parlors & public rooms	N
Connecticut	500	44.1	Guestrooms & office	N
Delaware	0	1502	Guestrooms & other conspicuous places	N

Note: Delaware liability considered "zero" if safe deposit box is not used.

STATE	LIABILITY LIMIT ($)	STATUTE	POSTINGS	RECEIPTS
D.C.	1,000	34.101	Guestrooms (conspicuously) & public area	N
Florida	1,000 (money) 500 (clothing)	509.111	Clearly legible on receipt of deposit	Y
Georgia	750	43.21.10	Guestrooms (conspicuously)	N
Hawaii	500	486K.4	Guestrooms	Y
Idaho	500	39.1823	Office, lobby & public room, elevator or corridor	Y
Illinois	250/500	71.1	10+ conspicuous places	Y
Indiana	600	32.8.8.1	Registration desk or guestrooms	N
Iowa	500	671.2	Office or public room & guestrooms	Y
Kansas	250	36.402	Guestrooms	Y
Kentucky	300	306.020	Office, public rooms & parlors	N
Louisiana	500	2971	Door & other public places, guestrooms (conspicuously) & registration desk	N
Maine	300	2901	Not less than 10 conspicuous places	N
Maryland	1,000	15.104	Guestrooms	N
Mass.	1,000	140.10	Guestrooms	N
Michigan	250	427.101	Office, ladies' parlor & sitting room, bar-room, washroom & 5 other conspicuous places (not less than 10 total)	Y
Minnesota	1,000	327.71	Front desk & guestrooms	Y
Mississippi	500	75.73.5	Office or lobby	Y
Missouri	200	419.010	Suspended in office, barroom, saloon, reading, sitting & parlor rooms & guestrooms	Y

Exhibit 2 (continued)

Montana	500	70–6–501	Office or public room & guestrooms	N
Nebraska	500	41.208	Office or public room & guestrooms	N
Nevada	750	651.010	Personally or in office & guestrooms	N
New Hampshire	1,000	353.1	Posting a copy	N
New Jersey	5,000	29.2.2	Guestrooms (conspicuously)	N
New Mexico	1,000	49.6.1	Guestrooms (conspicuously)	N
New York	1,500	200	Office, public rooms & parlors	N
N. Carolina	500	72.3	Guestrooms & office	N
N. Dakota	300	60.01.29	10+ conspicuous places	Y
Ohio	500	4721.02	Office, ladies' parlor & sitting room, bar-room, washroom & 5 other conspicuous places (not less than 10 total)	Y
Oklahoma	300	503A	Office or public rooms or parlors or guestrooms (conspicuously)	N
Oregon	300	699.010	10+ conspicuous places (250+ rooms) or 5+ conspicous places (less than 250 rooms)	N
Pennsylvania	300	PL9.61	10+ conspicuous places	Y
Rhode Island	500	5.14.1	A public & conspicuous place & manner	N
S. Carolina	500 / 1,000 (jewelry)	45–1–40	Guestrooms	N
S. Dakota	300	43.40.1	10+ conspicuous places	Y
Tennessee	300	62.7.104	Guestrooms (conspicuously)	N
Texas	50	73.4592	Guestrooms (on inside of door)	Y
Utah	250	29.1.1	Office & guestrooms (conspicuously)	N
Vermont	300	83.3142	Office & public parlors	N
Virginia	500	35.1.28	Guestrooms & office	N
Washington	1,000	19.48.030	3 or more public rooms, elevator lobbies, public corridors or entrances, or in the public parlors	N
W. Virginia	250	16.6.22	Guestrooms, office & public reception room (conspicuous places)	N
Wisconsin	300	50.80.3	Guestrooms (conspicuous, large print)	N
Wyoming	0	33.17.101	Office & guestrooms on rear of door	N

Note: Wyoming liability considered "zero" unless negligence is substantiated.

care exercised in the safe deposit operation. Failure to use the degree of care which the law requires can result in liability on the part of the hotel or motel. Even in cases in which the hotel or motel is negligent, however, some states place limits on the innkeeper's liability. In turn, some lawsuits have begun challenging the validity of such laws.[2]

It is the responsibility of management to develop and monitor safe deposit procedures for its property. Due to the variety of properties using a variety of safe deposit facilities, a uniform procedure for all properties cannot be established. The following discussion presents guidelines that may be used to develop procedures. This discussion does not, however, examine every situation that may arise concerning the use of safe deposit boxes.

All employees with safe deposit responsibilities should be thoroughly trained in proper safe deposit procedures and be aware of the reasons for the various rules. Supervisors should impress upon safe deposit attendants the importance and seriousness of this responsibility, ask for an immediate report of any unusual incident, and require accurate, up-to-date records and complete compliance with procedures.

Safe deposit boxes should be located in an area to which there is limited access. Unauthorized persons, whether guests or employees, should not be permitted in the area. Such a location may be in the vicinity of the front desk, where the box may be secured while still visible to the guests.

Keys and Key Control

One of the fundamentals of sound protection is the control of unissued keys to prevent any unauthorized persons from having access to them. Strict control should apply to the storage, issue, and receipt of keys. Keys to unused boxes should be stored in a place not accessible to unauthorized employees or to guests; there should be no access to the unissued keys except by employees responsible for this function. When such employees receive the key to a surrendered box, they should immediately secure the key. Spare locks and locks out for repair should also be carefully controlled. An adequate record should be maintained of all losses of keys, all changes of locks and safe deposit boxes, and all forcings of safe deposit box doors.

Two keys should be required to open any safe deposit box. The control or **guard key**, which must be used in conjunction with the guest's key to open the box, should always be secured. Great caution should be exercised in the use of the control key. Only those persons authorized to grant access to boxes should ever have possession and control of this key. It should never be taken from the safe deposit area or left where it is accessible to guests or to unauthorized employees. It should be accounted for at each change of shift.

There should be only one guest key for each safe deposit box, even when more than one guest is using the same box. Under normal circumstances (that is, when one box is being used by one guest), the guest receives this key to his or her box. Under no circumstances should there be any duplicate keys for a guest's safe deposit box. If a key is lost, the box should be drilled open in the presence of a witness, the guest (or the guest's legally authorized agent), and someone from the property. Because no extra keys are kept, the safe deposit agreement signed by the guest should make it clear that the guest will be billed for all drilling and replacement costs that arise from the loss of the guest's key.

AT YOUR RISK

ANTHONY MARSHALL

Liability Notices: More Than Just Part of Guestroom Décor

It's attached to the back of most hotel guestroom doors, almost always in an inexpensive frame. The small print necessitates a magnifying glass for anyone who wishes to read it. As a room furnishing, it's unattractive. That's probably why hoteliers who don't understand the law often put the hotel's limited liability notice in such inconspicuous places.

I recently surveyed several local housekeepers as to the importance of having the posted notice in guestrooms. None of them knew much about it, other than that their supervisor had told them it belonged there.

In my opinion, if housekeepers are responsible to see that the notice is posted, management should take the time to explain it to them. Educated employees always do a better job.

Every state has some sort of limited-liability statute, though the titles often vary. These statutes modify the old Common Law rule that held innkeepers liable for the loss of guests' valuables. Strict compliance with the statute's specific requirements reward hoteliers with a legal windfall: limited liability for the loss of guests' valuables—very limited.

Most hotel interior decorators squirm at the ugliness of the limited liability signs posted at hotels. That's why they often conceal them or dispose of them during renovations. The signs vanish—and with them goes the hotel's most important protection in liability claims.

I have never understood why something so important can be treated so frivolously. In one hotel, during a recent stay, I found the liability notice attached to the back wall of a dark closet. In another, I located it inside a chest of drawers.

These errant designers need only read their state's innkeepers limited-liability statutes to understand the disservice they are doing to their clients. Concealing what the law requires to be conspicuous can needlessly expose the hotel to substantial liability.

States provide protection

State legislatures have provided hotels with an out in case of a loss of guests' valuables, but they can only do so if the hotel informs their guests properly. Therefore, should the notification not be in compliance with the statutory requirements, the hotel is left defenseless against any liability claims.

In New York state, for example, the business law limits the hotel's liability to $1,500, but the hotel is required to provide a safe for guests to use and to prominently notify guests of its availability. If a hotel is in full compliance with a statute, it cannot be held liable for a sum in excess of $1,500 unless otherwise agreed upon by the parties in writing.

As with so many other hotel-related issues, there is a training component to hotel liability. Don't allow an overzealous safe-deposit box attendant who, in an ill-conceived attempt to please the guest, erroneously commits the hotel to insuring the guests' valuables. Attendants should be properly trained to accept—or reject—the guests' valuables.

(continued)

At Your Risk (continued)

> I asked Bruce M. Young, the hotel liability expert with Kanterman & Taub in New York, if guests actually sue a hotel for $1,500.
> Young hesitated a moment, judiciously weighing his answer.
> "Yes, they do," he said. "But the guest is not after a mere $1,500!"
> He explained that the guest's lawyer has to sue for $1,500 to get the case into court. Once he's there, though, he wants to recover the full value of the loss. To do this, the plaintiff must prove that the postings of the notice were insufficient or that the hotel agreed to insure the valuables.
> As it is unlikely that any hotel manager agreed to insure the valuables, that leaves the posting of the notices to attack. A hotel that had not bothered to post the notices would obviously lose the battle.
> Young said that hoteliers should review their state's limited liability statute to determine if they are in compliance. In New York state, the statute requires "posting a notice... in a public and conspicuous place in the office and public rooms, and in the public parlors of such hotel, motel or inn..." The law here is simple: no notice, no benefits.
> Don't display the hotel's limited liability notices in portable picture frames. That runs contrary to the most famous Marshall's Law: Don't screw it up by not screwing it down. Securely attach the notices to the walls, because if they're carried off and aren't replaced, the hotel's liability blooms.
> Portable frames also tempt the wicked. As Young said, "Where portable, homestyle picture frames are used, it's a great motivation to steal."
> In other words, why make the presence or absence of the notice a question in a jury's mind for the price of a few screws you could buy at a hardware store for 10 cents?
> Notices do not have to be in multiple languages, but Young said hotels that exclusively book persons speaking a common language other than English might consider it. Why leave open any possibility for a lawsuit? Do whatever it takes.
> Hoteliers have been blessed by their various state legislatures with limits to their liabilities in cases where guests lose valuables.
> As hoteliers can't afford to lose these blessings, the "amen" of this story is to encourage full compliance with the requirements of the innkeepers' limited liability laws.

Courtesy of *Hotel & Motel Management*, June 16, 1997. Used with permission.

Access Procedures

Clearly, the primary goal in using effective safe deposit procedures is to prevent unauthorized access. Access control is the most vital of all safe deposit responsibilities. It is imperative that the identity of the guest be established before access is granted. One way of doing this is to require the guest to sign his or her name on a form requesting access. This signature is then compared with that on the agreement signed by the guest when the box was first issued. Some properties ask guests to include some other piece of information about themselves (such as a mother's maiden name) on the agreement, so that if there is doubt regarding the guest's signature during a request for access, the employee can ask for this other information.

Whatever procedure is used at a property, it should be followed for every access, regardless of the frequency and regardless of how well the attendant knows the guest. A wife or other member of a family or the boxholder's representative, regardless of how well known, should not be granted access to the box unless that person's signature is on the initial agreement. No exceptions should be made to this procedure.

After a guest's identity has been verified, the safe deposit attendant should accompany the guest to the safe deposit area and, in the clear sight of the guest, use the control key and the guest's key to open the box, always being careful that the guest sees his or her key and box. The attendant should give the box to the guest. Some properties then require their employee to step out of the area until the guest is finished, in order to provide the guest with privacy. Other properties require their employee to remain in the area, but without handling the contents of the box or taking notice of the amount or type of valuables in the box. In any event, the employee should *not* place items into or remove items from a guest's box. Only the guest should do this. Also, the guest should be with the employee at all times while the box is being opened or locked. The employee should never be alone with a guest's valuables. When the guest is finished, the attendant should re-lock the box and return the guest's key, making sure that the guest always has the opportunity to see the key and box while in the attendant's possession. Upon final release of the box and return of the guest's key, the guest and employee should sign the release notice, which should then be filed.

Because space considerations often preclude maintaining a safe deposit box for every room on a property, the demand for such boxes may sometimes exceed the supply. When this happens, alternative procedures may be needed. One method of dealing with excess demand is to allow guests the opportunity to place their belongings in a larger safe deposit box that contains the belongings of more than one guest. If the guest declines, some properties explore with the guest the possibility of using boxes at a nearby bank, sometimes at no cost to the guest.

If the guest agrees to share a larger box, his or her property needs to be placed in some sort of sealable container (such as an envelope) to keep it separate from the other guests' property. When the guest desires access, the attendant verifies the guest's identity and then gives the guest the appropriate container(s).

The key to the safe deposit box used to hold sealed containers containing the property of more than one guest should be maintained in a secure place together with a log. Each time the key is used to open the larger box, the entry should be recorded in the log. Some properties require this key to be kept by a member of management when not in use.

Special or Unusual Access

Safe deposit boxes are sometimes the subject of court orders. When court orders are received, they should be referred to the property's management. All right of access should be suspended until the property's rights and obligations are determined. Management should consult with legal counsel prior to granting box access, unless the property already has specific legal instructions in effect regarding compliance with this type of access.

Under no circumstances should access to a safe deposit box be allowed based solely on telephone, email, or fax authorization. A letter requesting access should not be recognized unless it is a proper legal authorization.

If a guest leaves a lodging property without properly surrendering a box and then mails the key to the property, the property should secure the key and ask the guest to sign a release form. The box should not be opened until this form is received. If, when the box is opened, it contains property, the box should be relocked, the key secured, and a notice sent to the guest requesting him or her to personally remove the contents and surrender the box or to forward a power of attorney for the guest's representative to do so.

If a departed guest returns a key by messenger, the messenger should be requested to return the key to the guest and request that the guest come in personally. If the guest cannot do so, he or she should sign a release form if the box is empty or forward a power of attorney if the box contains property.

When a guest does not surrender a box upon check-out, the property should send the guest a registered letter requesting surrender of the box. If the guest does not respond within the appropriate legal time limit, the hotel or motel should dispose of the contents of the box in accordance with state law and the advice of counsel. This same procedure is sometimes followed in cases in which the key is returned by a guest who will not follow the prescribed surrender procedures. Exhibit 3 lists a sample outline for safe deposit box procedures that could be adopted by an establishment.

The In-Room Safe

In-room safes for the protection of guests' items have been introduced by several lodging industry vendors. Such units can include key, keycard, digital keypad, or credit card reader opening systems.

The feasibility of such an installation should be reviewed with the security team and the property's management. Insurance and legal reviews should also be completed. Postings in the guestrooms should be made in all instances to make it clear to the guest that safe deposit boxes or a safe is provided in the offices for the storage of guest valuables, and that management is not responsible for valuables not placed there. Otherwise, a state's statutory limits of liability on valuables may not protect the lodging property.

Lost and Found Procedures

Clear procedures should be developed to deal with lost and found items. The personnel in charge of the lost and found function need to be aware of their state's laws concerning lost and found items so they can ensure that the property avoids any liability with respect to the disposition of such items. The lost and found function can be assigned to any number of departments. The selection of the department, however, does not affect the nature of the job.

All found items should be turned over to the lost and found function. Some properties require the employee finding the item to fill out a form stating where it

Exhibit 3   Sample Safe Deposit Box Procedures

A. Purpose
The following procedures will ensure that all properties are in compliance with state Innkeeper's Statutes as they relate to the use of safe deposit boxes by registered guests (boxes are not to be issued to non-registered individuals). Failure to comply with state requirements can result in the forfeiture of protection offered by these statutes. Any departure from these procedures must be reviewed by management.

B. Responsibility
The hotel manager is responsible for procedure implementation and training of front desk personnel. Periodic, documented audits of critical elements of the program are also required.

C. Safe Deposit Box Location
A protected area should be provided for guest activity with his/her box. If the area is enclosed, the door should be kept shut at all times. Entry should be by means of a key- or code-activated locking device. If the area is not enclosed, a location should be used that provides adequate security for this activity (i.e., back office, business center). Closed-circuit TV is recommended for enclosed rooms in order to detect someone who is not supposed to be there.

D. Limits of Liability
Each state's Innkeeper's Statute defines specific limits for monetary liability of a registered guest's property. Limits of liability for safe deposit boxes should be 1) in writing on the *Safe Deposit Box Agreement* card (along with the state statute reference number), 2) posted over the safe deposit boxes, and 3) placed on the inside lid of the safe deposit box tray. The dollar amount stated must be the same as the state statute.

E. *Safe Deposit Box Agreement* Card
See sample on next page. *Note: The information provided on the card is the minimum allowable. Never delete or change information without review by management.*

F. Safe Deposit Box Keys
Guest keys for boxes are to be kept in a locked key cabinet until issued. The key to this cabinet is to be on the MOD/designate key ring *at all times*. The property's control key is *not* to be kept 1) in a drawer, 2) in the door of an empty box, or 3) on a hook/ring behind the front desk. *Note: There is to be only one guest key for each box and one control key in existence.*

G. Procedures—Sign Up and Initial Use
1. The registered guest completes the *Safe Deposit Box Agreement*.
2. The front desk agent checks the card for completeness, fills in time and date of box issuance, and signs the card. The card is filed by box/key number.
3. The agent hands the box key to the guest and informs him/her about the "one-key policy" and the fee for drilling if a key is lost.
4. The guest is escorted to the safe deposit box area.
5. The agent unlocks the box by inserting the guest key and control key.
6. The box tray is removed by the agent and given to the guest along with his/her key. The guest places his/her property into the tray.
7. The guest returns the tray to the agent, along with his/her box key. After locking the box, the agent returns the guest key and secures the control key.

H. Procedures—Accessing the Box
When a guest wishes to access his/her box, the following procedures must be followed.
1. The guest shows his/her key and requests access. The front desk agent asks for the guest's name. The agent does not take the guest's key at this time.
2. The agent pulls the *Agreement* card and verifies the information to confirm the guest's identity. This includes room number, home address, and other information given on the card.

(continued)

Exhibit 3 *(continued)*

No   **SAFE DEPOSIT BOX AGREEMENT**

AM/PM

Key No.	Date Issued	Time

Front Desk Agent	Check-Out Date

As a condition of the receipt of such articles deposited by me in this safe-deposit box, I hereby agree that access to this safe-deposit box will be obtainable only through this signature and upon the presentation of this key in person, and for any failure so to present this key in person the HOTEL shall not be liable for any loss occasioned by such failure to personally present such key. And I hereby agree that, in the event I should not personally surrender this key and remove the contents of this box within ten (10) days after I shall cease to be a guest of the hotel, the HOTEL may force entrance to said safe-deposit box and remove the contents thereof, and while retaining the said contents, the HOTEL shall not be liable for any loss occasioned by my failure to remove such contents, and in any such event or in the event that the key is lost while in my custody, I hereby agree to pay the HOTEL for the cost of opening the safe-deposit box and replacing the key.

*PLACE YOUR STATE'S "INNKEEPERS STATUTE"
REFERENCE CODE NAME, NUMBER, AND
DOLLAR ($) LIMIT OF LIABILITY HERE*

Signature

Guest Name (Please Print)	Room No.

Home Address

City

State	Zip Code

Mother's Maiden Name

DETACH STUB BELOW AND GIVE TO THE DEPOSITOR AS THEIR RECEIPT

- -

DEPOSITOR'S RECEIPT   No

Name_____
                  Cashier to print clearly

Room No._____ Key No._____ Date Issued_____

The safe-deposit key must be turned in to the Front Desk before or at the time of departure.

Exhibit 3 *(continued)*

3. Upon confirmation of the guest's ID, the agent has the guest sign a *Safe Deposit Box Access* slip. The signature is checked against the original on the *Agreement* card.
4. If the signature is the same, the agent signs and dates the *Access* slip and staples it to the *Agreement* card. All subsequent *Access* slips are stapled to the card.
5. The process continues from "Sign Up and Initial Use" procedures, Step 4.

I. **Procedures—Surrendering Box**
The following procedures are to be followed whenever a guest wishes to surrender his/her box.
1. Follow the same procedures for box access up to and including the handing of the tray and guest key to the guest, Step 6.
2. After the guest empties the tray and returns it to the agent, the agent asks if the tray is empty. If the guest says "Yes," the agent visually checks the tray.
3. The agent places the tray back into the box, inserts both keys, locks it, and removes the control key.
4. The guest signs and dates the line on the back of the *Agreement* card for surrendering the box. The agent confirms this and signs and dates the card. The card is filed with the hotel registration card.

J. **Procedures—Guest Leaves without Surrendering Box**
The following procedures must be followed whenever a guest checks out of the hotel without emptying his/her box.
1. The guest must send a notarized letter indicating:
   - his/her request that the box be opened
   - the box's contents and value
   - how the contents are to be returned to the guest
   - if the guest will have a representative present when the box is opened
2. The MOD and one front desk agent must be present when the box is opened
3. The guest's letter is signed and dated by the MOD and agent, indicating that the written instructions were followed

K. **Procedures—A Warrant Is Presented for Box Contents**
Whenever a law enforcement officer presents a warrant for the contents of a safe deposit box, the following procedures must be followed:
1. The property retains a copy of the warrant.
2. The MOD is present when the box is opened and contents are inventoried.
3. The warrant is signed and dated by the MOD, indicating that the box was opened and all contents were delivered to the officer.

L. **Procedures—Abandoned Box**
The determination of whether property in a safe deposit box has been "abandoned" must be considered carefully in accordance with local laws. The process must involve the hotel manager, and complete documentation of all actions must be maintained.

M. **Procedures—Special Requirements**
1. Guest loses key—The property has the box drilled by a qualified locksmith or facilities engineer. This procedure is witnessed by the MOD, and proper documentation is maintained. The guest is charged for drilling according to the property's policy.
2. Property loses control key—To maintain the integrity of the safe deposit box system, a new control key must be made for all control locks replaced.
3. Record retention—Safe deposit box records (cards, guest letters, warrants, etc.) must be retained for seven (7) years.
4. Audits—Keys, cards, and boxes should be audited nightly by the night auditor. The hotel manager should conduct an audit of the safe deposit box program at least quarterly. All audits are to be documented.

AT YOUR RISK

Anthony Marshall

Finders Keepers, Losers Weepers—After 90 Days

When is the next flight to Miami? I asked the reservationist at the other end of the line. An hour? A glance at the clock in my guestroom convinced me I could make it. "Book me!" I said.

I threw my clothing into my suitcase, used express check-out, and raced to grab a cab at the front entrance. I barely made my flight home.

A couple of days later, I discovered that my favorite blue blazer was missing. It wasn't in the laundry or hanging in my closet. Could I have left my favorite jacket at the hotel? Inconceivable—I am not a careless person.

The next day, I went to Burn's clothing store. I told Mike, the proprietor, that my treasured blue blazer was missing. After selling me another one, Mike suggested that I call the hotel. Why not, I thought. If the hotel had it, I'd simply be the proud owner of two identical blazers.

I called the hotel and asked to be connected with the lost-and-found department. The operator told me there were two—one was for items left in guestrooms, the other for items left in public space. The housekeeping department was in charge of the former and the security department oversaw the latter.

"Where did you lose the jacket?" the telephone operator asked, anxious to connect me with the correct lost-and-found.

I maintained my composure and politely told her that I was sorry, but I did not know where I had lost my jacket.

Mislaid, legally speaking

Putting my legal hat on I realized that I had misspoken. I had not "lost" my jacket; to the law, I had "mislaid" it. Property is mislaid when its owner voluntarily puts it aside and forgets where it is. It's not lost, because the owner knows that it's missing. For property to be lost, the owner must have unintentionally parted with and forgotten about it. I never forgot about my blue blazer—I was sick about it.

Unfortunately, neither of the lost-and-found departments had my blazer. But I'm a good sport—I hope whoever is wearing my jacket enjoys it as much as I did.

According to the law, if I had "abandoned" my jacket, it would immediately belong to the finder. Legally, to abandon property the owner must voluntarily discard it with no intention of reclaiming it. I didn't do that. For abandonment to occur, I would have had to throw my jacket into the wastebasket with no intention of reclaiming it, like I've done with old shirts.

When does the finder of lost property get to keep it? It varies according to state law, but 90 days is common. In other words, many states have passed statutes that reward the finder for turning over lost property to the police. If it is not claimed by the owner in 90 days, it belongs to the finder. These laws are intended to encourage the return of found property to the proper authorities.

Hoteliers who require employees to turn over to the hotel, any property found in the hotel and to waive all rights to possession of it, don't get very much found property from their employees.

At Your Risk *(continued)*

> I called some local hotelier friends of mine to find out what treasures have turned up in their lost-and-found departments. Usually, it's the same old stuff: eyeglasses, old clothing, keys, junk jewelry. But a few hotels had some real treasures:
>
> Paul Breslin, executive assistant manager of Fountainbleau Hilton Resort & Towers in Miami Beach, had a $50,000 diamond ring turned over to him by a room attendant. It was returned to its owner; the attendant was given a reward.
>
> Tom Soule, director of security at the Omni Colonade Hotel in Coral Gables, said his hotel has found several sets of dentures. (Wouldn't you think people would want to have their teeth back?)
>
> Rich Hancock, G.M. of the Biscayne Bay Marriott in Miami, said his hotel's lost-and-found has lots of bathing suits, sunglasses, and one set of new handcuffs. Maybe the police had a training session at his hotel.
>
> What treasures does your lost-and-found harbor? Take a look—those treasures might be yours. Legally.

Courtesy of *Hotel & Motel Management,* October 2, 1995. Used with permission.

was found, a description of the item, the date, and the employee's name. Other properties have the lost and found personnel fill out such a form.

Some states require that an effort be made to return lost items to the owners. Articles found in guestrooms or those with addresses on them obviously make it easier to find the owner. Upon receipt of such items, a letter should be sent requesting the guest to contact the hotel or motel for proper identification and return of the item.

If a guest calls the property either to ask questions about a letter he or she has received concerning a found item or to report a lost item, the call should be directed to the lost and found personnel. This helps to avoid giving conflicting information to the caller—it can greatly upset a guest if one employee says a lost item has been found when it in fact has not, especially if the guest has returned to the property to claim his or her item based on the erroneous information. The employee who takes a call reporting a lost item should ask for all pertinent information, including a description of the item, the area in which it was lost (if known), the date it was lost, and the guest's name and address. Some properties keep an inquiry log for this information.

Upon receipt of a found item, lost and found personnel should log, bag, tag, and store the item. When the item is valuable, it should be secured. Some properties place wallets, jewelry, money, credit cards, and other valuables in a safe deposit box.

When an article is claimed, this fact should be recorded in the log. If the article was mailed to the owner, the date of the mailing should be noted.

Endnotes

1. Elizabeth Lauer, "The Evolving Electronic Lock," *The Hotel & Restaurant Technology Update,* Spring 1999.

2. For more information concerning innkeeper's laws and challenges to their validity, see Jack P. Jefferies, *Understanding Hospitality Law*, Third Edition (East Lansing, Mich.: Educational Institute of the American Hotel & Motel Association, 1995), chapter 8.

Key Terms

emergency key—Opens all guestroom doors, even when they are double locked. It should be highly protected and its use strictly controlled and recorded; it should never leave the property.

guard key—One of two keys required to open any safe deposit box, it must be used in conjunction with the guest's key to open the box; this key should always be secured.

master key—Opens all guestrooms that are not double locked. It should be highly protected and its use strictly controlled and recorded; it should never leave the property.

Review Questions

1. What are the three levels of keying that most properties use?
2. Why is key and keycard control essential to the security of a lodging property?
3. How do electronic and computer locking systems change the nature of key control? How do these systems reduce the need for re-keying?
4. What are the primary functions of patrolling? Why is patrolling an important part of surveillance?
5. Who might a hotel deem as unauthorized persons? Why should great care be taken when deciding whether to evict them from the premises?
6. What problems can occur with the manufacture of illegal drugs?
7. Why would the issuance of a safe deposit box receipt create problems?
8. What key control and access procedures are typically used for safe deposit boxes?
9. Are in-room safes safer than safe deposit boxes? Why or why not?
10. Why is it important to have the lost and found function assigned to only one department?

Internet Sites

For more information, visit the following Internet sites. Remember that Internet addresses can change without notice.

Amerisafe Industries, Inc.
http://www.ameriworld.com

Associated Locksmiths of America
http://www.aloa.org

Audit Security Bags
http://www.auditbags.com

CardKey
http://www.cardkey.com

CISA Security Products, Inc.
http://www.repla.com

Drug Enforcement Administration (DEA)
http://www.usdoj.gov/dea/

Guest Access International
http://www.guestaccess.com

Ilco Unican
http://www.ilcounican.com/

Loc International
http://www.loc-international.com

LockTech, Inc.
http://www.hotelkeycard.com

Securitron Magnalock Corporation
http://www.securitron.com

Case Study

The Safe Deposit Box That Wasn't

Amanda stood behind the front desk of the Metropolitan, a 376-room upscale hotel, and tried to ignore the butterflies in her stomach. It was just her second day on the job, and there was so much to remember! She glanced over at Ron, standing at the other end of the counter. It was comforting to have him working the shift with her—he had worked for the Metropolitan for two years and had been a big help yesterday whenever she got flustered or confused. Her first day was extremely busy because everybody was checking in for the annual aluminum siding trade show and convention that started today. In a way, it was good that her first day was so busy, because she hadn't had time to be nervous. But today, most of the hotel's guests were off attending the show at the convention center downtown and the Metropolitan was relatively quiet.

Amanda gazed across the opulent lobby at the bank of house phones. A middle-aged woman in a tight, leopard-print jumpsuit was speaking angrily into one of the telephones, her free arm, festooned with gold and black bracelets, waving in the air as she pounded home her points to the unfortunate soul on the other end of the line. At this distance Amanda could faintly hear the clicking of the bracelets but could not make out what the woman was saying. Finally the woman slammed the receiver down in its cradle and started looking frantically around the lobby. When her eyes settled on Amanda, the woman grabbed the gold vinyl suitcase at her feet and strode purposefully toward the front desk. "Oh, please," thought Amanda, "don't come over here, go talk to Ron!"

But the woman stayed on course, and Amanda had plenty of time to take in the big hair, the heavy makeup, and the wounded, self-righteous expression before the woman stopped in front of her and said: "There's something wrong with your phones!"

"Ma'am?"

"I can't get through to my husband's room. I kept dialing '326,' but I couldn't get through."

Ron stepped in smoothly. "Our house phones no longer connect directly to the guestrooms."

"Yeah, yeah, that's what the operator said. That's not very convenient, you know," the woman responded.

"We changed our system in order to provide more privacy and security for our guests," Ron continued. "Did the operator reach your husband for you?"

"No, she started explaining why dialing '326' wasn't working and I told her what I thought of her new system before I hung up on her."

From her training, Amanda remembered that you were never to put callers through to guestrooms if they only asked to be put through to a certain room number. You always had to ask whom the person was calling, so you could confirm that the person knew the guest and was not simply calling rooms at random. Thieves, for example, had been known to call room after room until they found one that was empty, then go ransack the room.

"What's your husband's name?" Amanda asked. "We can try to connect you here at the front desk."

"Virgil Jones," the woman responded.

Amanda moved to the computer and called up Virgil's reservations record. Yes, a Virgil H. Jones was registered in Room 326. "Mr. Jones checked in to Room 326 yesterday—let me try to reach him for you."

Amanda picked up the front desk telephone, dialed, and listened to the phone ring ten times. "Sorry, there's no answer."

"That's okay—just give me a key to the room then," ordered the woman.

Immediately a red flag went up for Amanda. New as she was, she was well aware that key control was an extremely important issue at the Metropolitan.

"I'm sorry, ma'am, but it's against our policy to give out keys to guests who are not registered. Mr. Jones is the only person registered for that room."

"But I'm his wife! Look," the woman rummaged through her handbag and came up with her driver's license, "here's my ID. I'm Sheila Jones. See? That's me there."

"I'm sorry, Ms. Jones," Amanda said. "Had your husband told us you were coming, we would have noted it in the reservations record and there'd be no problem. But we're not allowed to let unregistered guests into rooms." She glanced at Ron.

"That's right, Ms. Jones," Ron said. "We'd do the same thing for you. It's actually against the law to admit an unregistered guest to a room."

"My husband doesn't know I'm coming. I didn't think I would get off work, but my boss finally gave in." Sheila Jones put on an ingratiating smile. "Can't you break the rules just this once? I really want to surprise Virgil."

"I'm sorry," Amanda said, "we really can't." She looked at Ron again for support, and he nodded in agreement.

"Is your husband here for the big convention?" Amanda asked.

Sheila nodded sulkily.

"Then he's probably at the Grandthorpe right now—that's the big convention hotel downtown. That's where the trade show is."

"I'll never find him there," Sheila fumed.

"You're welcome to look around in our restaurant and lounge to make sure he's not still here."

"It would be a lot easier if you'd just let me in the room," Sheila grumbled. "I'm tired—it was a long drive."

Amanda tried to give Sheila her best empathetic smile. "I'm sorry. I'll tell you what—if you can't find him, let us know and we'll put you in another guestroom temporarily so you can freshen up."

"I suppose that'll have to do," Sheila said wearily. "I'm not gonna bother looking for him. I'm tired, and if he's not in his room he's probably at the convention like you said. Just give me a room."

After Sheila collected a key to Room 287 and left in a huff, Ron congratulated Amanda for a job well done. "You did the right thing. Her ID proves she's Sheila Jones, but it doesn't prove she's Virgil's wife. She probably really is his wife, and ninety-nine times out of a hundred probably nothing bad would happen if we let a wife or a husband or a brother or somebody into a room. But it's not worth taking a chance on violating the privacy or compromising the safety of our guests. It's that one time in a hundred that can lead to serious trouble."

Thankfully, Sheila did not make another appearance and the rest of the morning passed uneventfully. Just after Amanda returned to the front desk after lunch, a short, balding fellow in a shiny blue suit approached the desk and gave her a big smile. "Hi, I'm Virgil Jones, Room 326. Any messages or mail for me?"

"No, Mr. Jones, but someone was asking about you. A Ms. Sheila Jones was here. She said she was your wife and wanted to wait for you in your room, but we had to turn her down."

Virgil looked startled rather than pleased. "Where is she now?"

"We put her in another room so she could freshen up. Let me call her and let her know you're here." Amanda called Room 287 and in a few minutes Sheila appeared in the lobby.

"Hi, baby!" Virgil called out when he saw her, rushing up and giving her a bear hug.

Sheila looked at Amanda over Virgil's shoulder and tried to pull away. "That's enough, honey." She extracted herself and approached the front desk. "Thanks for the room," she said to Amanda. "I feel so much better after my shower."

"You're welcome."

"I forgot to bring my room key down with me. Can I return it later, or do you want it right away? I'll be moving over to Virgil's room now."

"Just leave it in the room, that's fine," Amanda said. "Do you need any help with moving your luggage? I can send a bellperson up."

Virgil shook his head. "We can handle it. Thanks."

The next day Amanda experienced her first time alone at the front desk. Ron had an early dental appointment and wouldn't be in until 11:00. Even though the front desk manager assured Amanda that he would be available in case things got busy, Amanda crossed her fingers and hoped for an uneventful morning.

It was just before nine o'clock when Sheila appeared in the lobby again, dressed slightly more conservatively in a tight purple jumpsuit. She smiled at Amanda and held up a safe deposit box key. "Good morning. I'd like to get into our safe deposit box, please."

Thank goodness I don't have to say no to her again, Amanda thought gratefully. "Yes, Ms. Jones, right this way, please." Quickly, Amanda mentally reviewed her training in how to handle safe deposit box requests as she led Sheila into the small safe deposit box room just to the right of the front desk. One side wall contained the bank of safe deposit boxes; the master key to all the boxes hung by a chain secured to the wall. Pushed against the opposite wall was a narrow table with a file box on it.

Let's see, Amanda mused, I'm supposed to ask for identification, pull the card, get the card signed, initial the card—okay, I can do this. "Can I see some identification, please?"

Sheila groaned. "Not this again," she grumbled. She opened her handbag and came up with her driver's license again.

"Thank you," Amanda said, and looked under the "J's" in the file box for the right card. There it was: Box 116, signed out by Mr. Virgil H. Jones.

"Will you sign the card, please? And I'll initial your signature." Amanda gave Sheila the card and a pen and indicated the narrow table. Sheila signed the card and gave the pen to Amanda; Amanda initialed the card and recorded the date and time.

"Thank you." Amanda put the card back in the file box. "Now I'll put my key in the box and turn it." Amanda found Box 116 and turned the master key in the appropriate lock. "And now your key."

Sheila stepped forward and turned her key in the second lock. Amanda swung the box door open, pulled the long, narrow drawer from the box, and handed the drawer to Sheila. "I'll be right outside—just let me know when you're finished."

"That won't be necessary," Sheila said—somewhat grimly, Amanda thought. "This will only take a second."

Amanda turned her back discreetly while Sheila placed the drawer on the table. Amanda heard the metallic creak of the lid lifting, then a sharp intake of breath from Sheila, and then something like a sob. Amanda resisted the impulse to turn around. It's none of our business, it's rude, and it might get us into trouble, she remembered Ron telling her, so never watch guests get into their safe deposit boxes. Amanda was thinking of quietly leaving the room when she heard the lid close and Sheila said, "Okay, I'm done, thank you."

Amanda turned around and took the box from Sheila. The lighting in the room made it hard to tell, but Amanda thought Sheila's eyes were redder and puffier than before. Amanda returned the drawer to its box, swung the box door shut, and turned both keys in their locks. She let the master key hang by its chain and handed the guest key back to Sheila. "Is there anything else I can do for you?"

"No, thanks," Sheila sniffed with a sad smile. "You've done quite enough."

The next day was Amanda's day off. Ron was at the front desk with another guest service representative named Dennis when Virgil Jones approached just after 8 A.M., looking puzzled. "This is going to sound like a strange question," he said, "but—have you seen my wife?"

"No, sir, not this morning," Ron replied.

"I didn't hear her get up, and her suitcase is gone." Virgil rubbed his chin for a moment, then shrugged. "I'm sure she'll turn up," he turned to go. "Like a bad penny," he said under his breath as he walked away.

About 20 minutes later, Virgil was back at the front desk, looking considerably more anxious than before. "I can't find my safe deposit box key," he said to Ron. "Do you have a spare? I need to check on something right away."

Ron shook his head. "I'm sorry, sir, but, for security reasons, we don't have spare keys to any of our boxes."

"What do we do now? I've got to get into that box!"

"Well, you have two options," Ron said. "One, we can call a locksmith. The firm we use is good about coming out right away. They're usually here between a half hour and an hour after we call—and I believe the last time they came out for this they charged around $80. Whatever the charge is, we will add it to your room bill. Or, two, I can call our maintenance department and have one of the staff 'punch' the lock for us. He can probably be up here in just a few minutes, but if you choose this option there's a $100 charge because we'll have to replace the lock."

"Call the maintenance guy," Virgil said grimly. "I'm not waiting no hour."

"Very well." Ron moved to the front desk phone and spoke a few words into it before returning to Virgil. "He'll be up right away. Do you remember your safe deposit box number?"

Virgil was churning his fingers through his hair, a worried expression on his face. "No," he said. "Maybe 110, 218? I don't know."

"Well, we can look it up in our files. Excuse me for a moment." Dennis was busy with another guest, so Ron answered the front desk telephone.

When Ron hung up, he smiled and waved to a young man just getting off one of the lobby elevators. "Ah, here's Ted already." Ted was in a gray maintenance uniform and carrying a box of tools. "Come with me, please," Ron said to Ted, and then, "Mr. Jones, right this way."

The three men entered the safe deposit box room. Ron opened the file box and turned to Virgil. "Can I see some ID, please?"

Virgil pulled out a fat wallet and gave Ron his driver's license.

"Thank you." Ron put the license on the table and flipped quickly to the "J's" in the file box. There was the card: Box 116, signed out by Virgil H. Jones. Ron compared the signature on the license to the signature on the card, nodded, and gave the license back to Virgil. Ron noticed that Virgil had not gotten into the box since he had first opened it up, but that Sheila Jones had signed for it yesterday. Ron looked at the initials alongside the signature: "A.M."—Amanda Muldinado—and shook his head. Rookies, he thought.

"It looks like you reserved box 116, Mr. Jones," Ron said. "Sign here, please, and we'll get it open for you right away." Ron pushed the card over to Virgil before turning to put the master key in the master-key lock for box 116 and turning it.

Virgil started to sign the card but stopped. "I see my wife's signature here. She got into the box yesterday?"

"Looks like it," Ron said. Behind them Ted set down his box of tools. After a couple of sharp blows, Ted said, "All set."

Ron pulled the long drawer out of box 116 and handed it to Virgil. "We'll leave you alone now, Mr. Jones," Ron said quickly, and motioned for Ted to exit. Ron was hardly back at the front desk before Virgil reappeared.

"Is everything all right, Mr. Jones?"

"No, everything is not all right," Virgil said in measured tones. "Something's missing."

Ron's heart started to pound. "Oh, no! What's missing? Can you describe it?"

"There was a solid gold ID bracelet in there with the name 'Mitzy' engraved on it," Virgil said grimly. "Now it's gone."

"Oh, no," Ron said again.

"And now my wife is gone," Virgil continued. "I hope this hotel makes a lot of money," he said with quiet fury, "because the Metropolitan's going to pay for my divorce."

Discussion Questions

1. Why does Virgil Jones think that he might have grounds to compel the Metropolitan to "pay for his divorce"? Or, to put it another way, did Amanda, Ron, or any other hotel staff member make any serious mistakes in dealing with Virgil or Sheila? If so, what were they?

2. Generally speaking, what are the essential security precautions hotel staff members should take when checking a guest into a hotel room?

3. Generally speaking, what are the essential security precautions hotel staff members should take when allowing guests access to safe deposit boxes?

Case Number: 3873CA

The following industry experts helped generate and develop this case: Wendell Couch, ARM, CHA, Director of Technical Services for the Risk Management Department of Bass Hotels & Resorts; and Raymond C. Ellis, Jr., CHE, CHTP, CLSD, Professor, Conrad N. Hilton College, University of Houston, Director, Loss Prevention Management Institute.

Appendix

Sample Room Notices

The following sample room notices are typical of most states' notices in that each contains information regarding its state's limited liability laws—sometimes including the wording of the actual law. Some of them also post room rates. The laws of these two states suggest the similarities and differences that can be found in such laws from state to state.

Texas

LIMITED LIABILITY LAW
BE IT ENACTED BY THE LEGISLATURE OF
THE STATE OF TEXAS

Article 4592—Liability for Valuables. Any hotel, apartment hotel or boarding house keeper, who constantly has in his hotel, apartment hotel or boarding house a metal safe or vault in good order and fit for the custody of money, jewelry, articles of gold or silver manufacture, precious stones, personal ornaments, or documents of any kind, and who keeps on the doors of sleeping rooms used by guests suitable locks or bolts and proper fastening on the transom and window of said room, shall not be liable for the loss or injury suffered by any guest on account of the loss of said valuables in excess of the sum of fifty dollars, which could reasonably be kept in the safe or vault of the hotel, unless said guest has offered to deliver such valuables to said hotel, apartment hotel or boarding house keeper for custody in such metal safe or vault, and said hotel, apartment hotel or boarding hotel or boarding house keeper has omitted or refused to deposit said valuables in such safe or vault and issue a receipt therefor; provided such loss or injury does not occur through the negligence or wrong doing of said hotel, apartment hotel or boarding house keeper, his servants, or employees and that a printed copy of this law is posted on the door of the sleeping room of such guest.

RATE POSTING
ROOM NO. _____

This room will accommodate _____ people during a capacity period and when the exclusive use of the room by one or more guests is demanded to the exclusion of other guests desiring accommodations, the full charge of $_____ will be made per day for such room.

During a period when it is necessary to utilize this room to its full capacity, the same will be assigned to one or more guests at the following rates:

    1 guest, $ _____   3 guests, $ _____

    2 guests, $ _____   4 guests, $ _____

    Posted _____ day of _____ 20 _____

New York

NOTICE TO GUESTS

A Safe is Provided in the Office for the Safekeeping of Money, Jewels, Ornaments, Bank Notes, Bonds, Negotiable, Securities, and Precious Stones Belonging to Guests.

DAILY RATE FOR ROOMS*

Single from	$_____	to $_____
Double from	$_____	to $_____
Extra Persons (each) from	$_____	to $_____

* * *

Charge for this Rental Unit:
Single $_____ Double $_____

MEALS*

Table d'hote Breakfast from	$_____	to $_____
Table d'hote Luncheon from	$_____	to $_____
Table d'hote Dinner from	$_____	to $_____

A la Carte as per menu

*SUBJECT TO APPLICABLE TAXES
GENERAL BUSINESS LAW—SECTIONS 200, 201, 203-a, 203-b, 206, 206-d

SECTION 200. SAFES; LIMITED LIABILITY. Whenever the proprietor or manager of any hotel, motel, inn, or steamboat shall provide a safe or safe deposit boxes in the office of such hotel, motel or steamboat, or other convenient place for the safe keeping of any money, jewels, ornaments, bank notes, bonds, negotiable securities, or precious stones, belonging to the guests of or travelers in such hotel, motel, inn or steamboat, and shall notify the guests or travelers thereof by posting a notice stating the fact that such safe or safe deposit boxes are provided, in which such property may be deposited, in a public and conspicuous place and manner in the office and public rooms, and in the public parlors of such hotel, motel, or inn, or saloon of such steamboat; and if such guest or traveler shall neglect to deliver such property to the person in charge of such office for deposit in such safe or safe deposit boxes, the proprietor or manager of such hotel, motel, or steamboat shall not be liable for any loss of such property, sustained by such guest or traveler by theft or otherwise; but no hotel, motel, or steamboat proprietor, manager or lessee shall be obliged to receive property on deposit for safe keeping, exceeding one thousand five hundred dollars in value; and if such guest or traveler shall deliver such property, to the person in charge of such office for deposit in such safe or safe deposit boxes, said proprietor, manager or lessee shall not be liable for any loss thereof, sustained by such guest or traveler by theft or otherwise, in any sum exceeding the sum of one thousand five hundred dollars unless by special agreement in writing with such proprietor, manager or lessee.

SECTION 201. LIABILITY FOR LOSS OF CLOTHING AND OTHER PERSONAL PROPERTY LIMITED. 1. No hotel or motel keeper except as provided in the forgoing section shall be liable for damage to or loss of wearing apparel or other personal property in the lobby, hallways or in the room or rooms assigned to a guest for any sum exceeding the sum of five hundred dollars, unless it shall appear that such loss occurred through the fault or negligence of such keeper, nor shall he be liable in any sum exceeding the sum of one hundred dollars for the loss of or damage to any such property when delivered to such keeper for storage or safe keeping in the store room, baggage room or other place elsewhere than in the room or rooms assigned to such guest, unless at the time of delivering the same for storage or safe keeping such value in excess of one hundred dollars shall be stated and a written receipt, stating such value, shall be issued by such keeper, but in no event shall such keeper be liable beyond five hundred dollars, unless it shall appear that such loss occurred through his fault or negligence, and such keeper may make a reasonable charge for storing or keeping such property, nor shall he be liable for the loss of or damage to any merchandise samples or merchandise for sale, unless the guest shall have given such keeper prior written notice of having the same in his possession, together with the value thereof, the receipt of which notice the hotel or motel keeper shall acknowledge in writing over the signature of himself or his agent, but in no event shall such keeper be liable beyond five hundred dollars, unless it shall appear that such loss or damage occurred through his fault or negligence; as to property deposited by guests or patrons in the parcel or checkroom of any hotel, motel or restaurant, the delivery of which is evidenced by a check or receipt therefor and for which no fee or charge is exacted, the proprietor shall not be liable beyond two hundred dollars, unless such value in excess of two hundred dollars shall be stated upon delivery and a written receipt, stating such value, shall be issued, but he shall in no event be liable beyond three hundred dollars, unless such loss occurs through his fault or negligence. Notwithstanding anything hereinabove contained, no hotel or motel keeper shall be liable for damage to or loss of such property by fire, when it shall appear that such fire was occasioned without his fault or negligence.

2. A printed copy of this section shall be posted in a conspicuous place and manner in the office or public room and in the public parlors of such hotel or motel. No hotel, motel or restaurant proprietor shall post a notice disclaiming or misrepresenting his liability under this section.

SECTION 203-A. HOTEL AND MOTEL KEEPER'S LIABILITY FOR PROPERTY IN TRANSPORT. No hotel or motel keeper shall be liable in any sum exceeding the sum of two hundred and fifty dollars for the loss of or damage to property of a guest delivered to such keeper, his agent or employee, for transport to or from the hotel or motel, unless at the time of delivering the same such value in excess of two hundred and fifty dollars shall be stated by such guest and a written receipt stating such value shall be issued by such keeper; provided, however, that where such written receipt is issued the keeper shall not be liable beyond five hundred dollars unless it shall appear that such loss or damage occurred through his fault or negligence.

SECTION 203-B. POSTING OF STATUTE. Every keeper of a hotel or motel or inn shall post in a public and conspicuous place and manner in the registration office and in the public rooms of such hotel or motel or inn a printed copy of this section and section two hundred three-a.

SECTION 206. RATES TO BE POSTED; PENALTY FOR VIOLATION. Every keeper of a hotel or inn shall post in a public and conspicuous place and manner in the office or public room, and in the public parlors of such hotel or inn, a printed copy of this section and sections two hundred and two hundred and one, and a statement of the charges or rate of charges by the day and for meals furnished and for lodging. No charge or sum shall be collected or received by any such hotel keeper or inn keeper for any service not actually rendered or for a longer time than the person so charged actually remained at such hotel or inn, nor for a higher rate of charge for the use of such room or board, lodging or meals than is specified in the rate of charges required to be posted by the last preceding sentence; provided such guest shall have given such hotel keeper or inn keeper notice at the office of his departure. For any violation of this section the offender shall forfeit to the injured party three times the amount so charged, and shall not be entitled to receive any money for meals, services or time charged.

SECTION 206-D. POSTING OF RATES OF VARIOUS TYPE ACCOMMODATIONS. In addition to other provisions in this article relating to posting of rates, every keeper of a hotel, motel or inn shall post publicly and conspicuously at the place maintained for the registration of guests so that it can be easily and readily seen and read by guests registering, a statement of the charges or rate of charges by the day indicating the standard rates for rooms or suites of different accommodations, and for meals furnished. The standard rates shall be that schedule of rates available to guests who do not qualify for special discounts or rate reductions.

Check-Out Time _____

REVIEW QUIZ

When you feel you have covered all of the material in this chapter, answer these questions. Choose the *best* answer.

1. Effective key control procedures include all of the following *except*:

    a. rotating locks to other parts of the property when there has been any known or suspected compromise.
    b. using keys that have the property's name, address, and logo on them, so the keys can be easily returned.
    c. performing an annual audit of all keys in the possession of employees.
    d. coding each room key to a master list at the front desk.

2. An emergency key opens:

    a. all guestroom doors.
    b. all of a property's doors.
    c. the secure key storage box.
    d. a guest's safe deposit box without the guest's key.

3. Security patrols are primarily responsible for:

    a. detecting and deterring security incidents.
    b. apprehending and arresting criminals.
    c. maintaining liaisons with local law enforcement agencies.
    d. establishing safe deposit box and key control procedures.

4. Which situation should a patrolling security officer investigate?

    a. a locked guestroom door
    b. non-guests loitering in the parking lot
    c. guests drinking in moderation in the property's bar
    d. guests arriving late in expensive cars

5. A property's statutory liability for the loss of a guest's valuables is usually limited by:

    a. the availability of in-room safes.
    b. the frequency of security patrols.
    c. effective lost and found procedures.
    d. signs pointing out the availability of a safe or safe deposit boxes.

6. Camille Jacobs checks into the Bayberry Lodge and requests a safe deposit box. After she completes the safe deposit box agreement card, Franco, the front desk agent, assigns her a box number, gets her signature, and issues her a key. Which step in the process did he forget?

    a. Franco should have asked Camille what she intended to put in the box.
    b. Franco did not ask to see a picture ID.
    c. Franco should have given Camille both keys.
    d. Franco did not forget anything.

REVIEW QUIZ *(continued)*

7. An item found in a guestroom should be:

   a. immediately sent to the address on the guest folio of the room's last occupant.
   b. held in the lost and found, or secured if the item is valuable.
   c. held at the front desk until the owner comes to claim it.
   d. discarded if not claimed within one week.

Answer Key: 1-b-C1, 2-a-C1, 3-a-C2, 4-b-C3, 5-d-C4, 6-b-C4, 7-b-C5

Each question is linked to a competency. Competencies are listed on the first page of the chapter. An answer reading 3-b-C4 translates to:

   3: the question number
   b: the correct answer
   C4: the competency number

Chapter 4 Outline

Losses Affecting All Departments
    Responding to Employee Theft
The Human Resources Department
    Exit Interviews
    Violence in the Workplace
    Alcohol and Drug Use and Abuse
The Engineering Department
The Rooms Division
    Front Service
    The Housekeeping Department
Purchasing and Receiving
Storage and Issuing
The Food and Beverage Department
    Spoilage and Pilferage
    Alcohol Storage, Issuing, and Service
    Point-of-Sale (POS) Systems
The Recreation Department
    Swimming Pools
    Health Clubs and Jogging Trails
Casino and Gaming Security
Report Writing and Recordkeeping
Special Guests and Events
    Guests with Disabilities
    VIP Guests
    Youth Groups
    Conventions, Meetings, and Exhibits

Competencies

1. Identify the variety of security concerns that affect each hotel department. (pp. 207–232)
2. Describe the security and safety issues for facilities with swimming pools, health/fitness services, and gaming areas. (pp. 232–240)
3. Identify the general types and uses of security reports and records. (pp. 240–243)
4. State the security concerns involved in serving guests with special needs. (pp. 243–246)
5. Explain the safety and security considerations for handling conventions, meetings, and exhibits. (pp. 246–249)

4

Departmental Responsibilities in Guest and Asset Protection

LODGING PROPERTIES MAY need to protect their guests and premises from a variety of risks and dangers. In meeting this goal, security and asset protection should be the responsibility of every employee. This chapter looks at the fact that the security responsibilities of employees may differ from department to department. Members of a specific department are often uniquely qualified to watch over those aspects of the operation within their department's area of concern.

The risks and dangers to guests and premises are not, however, a property's only security concerns. Every hotel and motel has assets it must protect as well. Asset protection procedures range from dealing with internal theft by employees and theft by guests to avoiding losses incurred through extending credit unwisely, establishing adequate computer safeguards, and more.

Despite the importance of asset protection, there is a tendency in many properties to concentrate primarily on security incidents relating to guests and the public on the premises. Little or no attention may be paid to internal security problems that can significantly erode profitability. Internal theft, for example, is a growing problem in many American businesses, and, unfortunately, the lodging industry has not been spared. It is particularly susceptible to internal theft since hotel and motel services and materials can often be readily exchanged in the community for cash or other services or used directly by the thief. High employee turnover and the physical expanse of many lodging establishments limit the ability of hotels and motels to effectively secure their operations against internal theft. There is a need for increased awareness of this problem and a concerted effort on the part of the management team to involve the security staff in controlling internal theft on a department-by-department basis. There must be strong management commitment to this aspect of the security program or it will not succeed.

Management should be aware of the security considerations involved in the operation of every department of its lodging establishment. Whether in a fully staffed, 1,000-room property or in a 60-room motel operated by an owner/manager, there should be a continuing audit of the functions in each department in order to protect the profitability of the property.

Losses Affecting All Departments

Asset protection is a crucial aspect of security for lodging establishments. Each property should examine the layout of its premises to determine how to more adequately protect the cashier location, receiving operations, and employee entrances, as well as other entrances not in the direct view of an observation center. Wherever there is a work process involving the assets of the property, attention should be given to protecting that function.

Before considering specific departments and their internal theft problems, we will review some losses that affect all departments. For example, losses may grow as the effectiveness of a property's system of accounting for its employees' time declines. How well do time clocks or sign-out sheets keep track of employee hours? Is a security staff member assigned to this function? Is the assignment rotated to prevent collusion? Does management insist that each employee sign out or clock out individually? There may be a major security problem if one employee is permitted to sign out or clock out for another individual or a group.

Hotels and motels that have a large number of part-time personnel may need to regularly verify that checks issued by the property are received by the individuals to whom they are addressed. In one case, a department head carried a number of part-time employees "on the books" who no longer worked for the hotel. In this instance, the collusion extended beyond the hotel and involved a teller at the bank who allowed a number of the former employees to cash checks made out to them.

Another type of crime is the use, usually by managers and supervisors, of gardeners, painters, and maintenance personnel to provide personal services on company time. When this happens, word of stolen services will spread to every employee on staff. Honest employees may then be tempted to "get in on the take."

Consider whether allowing executives and/or key staff members to receive free services from the dry cleaning and laundry departments is appropriate. Who monitors the exceptions? Who defines "executive" or "key staff member"? Consider establishing a no-exception rule that staff members must pay for dry cleaning and laundry services.

Another service with high theft potential is the long-distance phone call. When reviewing the bills, check and verify repeat numbers. Look for numbers with a 900 prefix, which are typically entertainment-oriented and include costly per-minute charges. Also, check unaccounted-for calls such as off-hour calls made from executive and administrative offices.

A no-exception policy on employee meals is another vital element in an internal control system. Some properties spot-check food facilities at times when meals are not normally provided to certain employees or categories of employees within the hotel or motel. Continuous monitoring may be necessary in instances where union contracts, or non-union agreements made at the time of employment, provide that certain classes of employees are not entitled to meals. A security person may monitor on an occasional basis to prevent collusion between food service personnel and other employees.

There may be advantages to monitoring the arrival and departure of a property's employees. Monitoring employees tends to discourage the unauthorized removal of the property's and guests' assets. If the design of a property permits, management may designate an employee entrance and exit. When separate employee entrances are feasible, they should be well lighted, adequately secured, and provided with round-the-clock security. The employee entrance may include

> ### Technology:
> ### A New Generation of Tools for Hospitality Security
>
> Proximity sensors can effectively monitor an employee's entrance or presence in any space of a property. The technology includes either infrared (IR) or radio frequency (RF) systems. The IR technology requires users to manually point the battery-operated IR transmitter at a receiving unit to establish the identity as a staff member authorized to enter the area. Failure to do so successfully would place the system in alarm. In other uses, it may record—rather than alarm—to substantiate a tour of patrol duty by a security officer.
>
> In the RF system, the proximity (the method by which a receptor unit recognizes entry to a secured location) is provided through radio frequencies that transmit to a receptor in the room or other secured area. The advantage of this system is that one is not required to hold a unit in hand; a badge or other transmitter on the person communicates approved entry by the individual. Although this system is more expensive, it eliminates the problem of incorrectly presented cards and the introduction of foreign materials into the card slot.
>
> The variety of proximity technologies permits a number of selections to meet specific and varied needs. Wiegand systems, bar codes, magnetic stripes, or smart chips permit a card to be encoded with more than a single technology. For example, a Wiegand system is one in which the card includes sets of embedded metal-alloy wires. The configuration of those wire sets determines the extent and use of the card within the proprietary encoding program for the facility. (This, of course, is merely another way to accomplish what may be accomplished through the use of cards containing "mag" stripes or smart chips.) A bar code might be added to the card to grant an authorized person access to a linen closet or liquor storage area.
>
> Thus, a single card with multiple systems may permit the employee to "clock in" when entering the employee entrance and enter only authorized areas throughout the work day; it may also serve as identification and authorization for meals or other services.

a security staff office from which the arriving and departing employees may be monitored.

Properties with large staffs may consider using some sort of employee identification to ensure that those people attempting to gain admittance to the property through the employee entrance are in fact employees. Some properties provide name and/or photo identification badges to the staff. Some organizations color-code identification by department. This allows for fast identification of employees, not only when they are arriving and departing, but also when they are (perhaps inappropriately) in areas outside of their departments. This means of quick identification can be very helpful to patrolling security officers as well as to any employee monitoring the entrance.

If possible, there should be a package room in which employees' packages may be checked and stored. The time clock or time sheets may be at this location and under the control of a security officer. In smaller properties where this is not feasible, an effort should be made to have employees pass a control point, such as the supervisor's or department head's office, to sign in and out.

Employees should be informed about what items they may bring onto or remove from the premises. To enforce this policy, management may establish a claim checking system for bringing items onto the premises and a parcel (or package) pass system for taking items off the premises. Employees bringing parcels onto the premises may be required to leave the parcels with a designated employee—for example, a security officer, department head, or entrance monitor—until they depart the premises. A parcel pass system includes a list of supervisors and managers who are authorized to issue passes for removing parcels from the premises. Such a pass system is helpful when employees purchase items from surplus or salvage. A parcel pass system should also include a list of the actual signatures of these authorized personnel for comparison. An employee wishing to leave the premises with any parcel (other than one brought onto the premises by the employee) should be required to present a parcel pass to the security officer or other appropriate employee. The pass should state the date, employee's name, parcel contents, and the signature of the employee's supervisor or department head. In cases in which the property being removed is not that normally found in the department for which the employee works (for example, a desk clerk removing cooking utensils), the signatures of the employee, his or her supervisor or department head, and the department head of the second department involved should be required. Employees should be informed of parcel control procedures when they are hired.

Restricting employee parking to a carefully selected area may also help control losses. The employee parking area should not be so close to the building that it allows employees to easily and quickly transfer stolen property to their cars. If possible, it should not be too near the food and beverage area or any unsecured doors with access to unsecured assets. From another perspective, it also should not take the best parking places away from guests. On the other hand, employee safety may be a consideration in choosing the employee parking area. It should not be located in a too-remote or essentially unprotected area.

With the expansion of concealed weapons laws in many jurisdictions, it is increasingly necessary for every property to enforce rules that may prohibit concealed weapons on the premises. Of course, any policies that restrict concealed weapons among employees, guests, or the general public should be reviewed thoroughly with legal counsel. Issues of liability involving firearms may be far-reaching and confusing. For example, an operation that does not allow guests to carry concealed weapons might be held liable if the guest leaves a gun in a vehicle that is subsequently stolen and the weapon is used in a fatal shooting. Special consideration must be given to the responsibility of the lodging operation if guns are to be received and stored on the premises.

Responding to Employee Theft

Different responses are available to management in dealing with assets lost through employee theft. Many properties state during the hiring interview or in the employee handbook that theft will be considered grounds for dismissal. A property's management may also decide to prosecute. Depending on the seriousness of

> **For Some Employees, Crime *Does* Pay**
>
> Studies conducted by the Department of Commerce, American Management Association, Joint Economic Committee of Congress, universities, and trade associations all conclude that losses from employee theft have a dramatic effect on the financial stability, profit level, and survival of most businesses.
>
> Several studies estimate that employee theft and dishonesty cost U.S. businesses between $60 and $120 billion per year, not including the billions spent on protecting against theft (guards, security systems, etc.). Most security experts agree that nearly every type and size of business is likely to experience some form(s) of employee theft and not realize the existence or extent of it. In fact, small and medium businesses are often more vulnerable to employee theft due to less of a separation of duties, less supervision/more autonomy, lack of controls/procedures/audits, and blind loyalty.
>
> Consider the following:
>
> - Opportunity to steal—not need—is the primary cause of employee theft.
> - A majority of employee theft goes undetected by management.
> - Employee theft is often committed in reaction to favoritism, unreasonable discipline, inconsistency, and other acts of poor or abusive supervision.
> - A majority of honest employees look the other way regarding employee theft and fail to report it.
> - Dishonest employees steal to the degree the system allows and don't stop until they are caught.
> - There is a direct correlation between drug abuse and employee theft.

Source: John Case & Associates

the offense, prosecution may result in high fines and/or imprisonment for former employees.

Whatever the decision, all employees should be treated equally under the rules. Making exceptions dilutes the effectiveness of the effort. Management should realize that if it allows a department head or supervisor to resign after being caught in criminal activity, the other employees will almost certainly hear of it, no matter how confidential the incident was intended to be. Such a policy may communicate to other employees the idea that the theft of time, materials, or services will not be severely punished. If lower-level employees are in fact severely punished while higher-level employees are not, the uneven treatment will be obvious. Care should be taken in applying disciplinary policies uniformly in order to avoid a claim of discrimination or an assertion of bad faith and unfair dealing. In some cases, collective bargaining agreements may govern disciplinary proceedings.

The Human Resources Department

The human resources function (often handled by a full-fledged human resources department in larger properties) faces security considerations even before an employee is hired. Since a property may be responsible for the acts of its employees, care should be taken to hire only the best people. Unfortunately, federal, state, and local regulations protecting the privacy of individuals often become an excuse for a failure to adequately screen job applicants. Such a failure can be disastrous. In August 1984, an Arizona jury awarded $1 million in compensatory damages and $5 million in punitive damages to the husband of a woman who was murdered by a motel employee. The defendant was held liable because it hired the murderer three days before the crime without performing any background check. The plaintiff claimed that if the motel had taken the time to check the applicant's personal references or past employers, it would have learned that the applicant had a long history of violence and arrests for aggravated assault and attempted rape. Instead, he was hired and put to work sweeping immediately following his interview.

Whatever the size of a hotel or motel, job application forms and hiring procedures should be developed with the advice of legal counsel. In this way, properties can guard against pre-employment inquiries that would leave them vulnerable to charges of discrimination by a rejected applicant and employment practices that might subject them to civil and criminal liability. If not prohibited by law, the following support screening systems may be considered:

- Criminal conviction check.
- Background check through professional investigators.
- Possible fingerprinting with submission to the appropriate law enforcement agency.
- Polygraph (lie detector) testing. Note, however, that the Employee Polygraph Protection Act of 1988 prohibits nearly all private employers from using polygraph tests as pre-employment or screening tools. One exception is for those job candidates applying for security officer positions. Consult legal counsel before using such a device.
- **"Honesty exams"**—tests prepared by outside organizations, administered at a hotel or motel, and returned to the source organization for evaluation.
- Credit check, particularly for any employee handling cash.
- **Bonding**—that is, taking out an insurance policy for protection from employee theft. Bonding allows for a more thorough background investigation. Bonding is usually provided through a blanket bond that specifies job classifications rather than individuals. For an additional premium, the policy may be endorsed to cover theft by and/or excess fidelity coverage (sometimes called "dishonesty insurance") on specific employees. This may be desirable for employees with significant access to the operation's assets.
- Department of Motor Vehicle check, particularly for employees involved in valet parking or in the operation of courtesy vehicles.
- An authorization form signed by the job applicant allowing access to job performance data from former employers. This will permit the source to provide full information without fear of violating privacy rights as established under federal, state, or local guidelines. Information asked of former employers may include the nature of the applicant's duties, his or her attendance and tardiness

> **Employee Screening**
>
> When filling positions that have direct guest contact, consider checking for prior criminal convictions. For example Thomas Davis, executive vice president of Hospitality Risk Controls Inc., notes, "I am not sure you would have a defense if you hired someone convicted of rape and didn't check his records—and then he went out and raped someone. But if you have an employee who checked out okay and then raped someone, I think you would have a case." Hoteliers are expected to take reasonable care in protecting guests; it is not reasonable to expect them to foresee and prevent every possible mishap or injury.
>
> If research needs are numerous, consider enlisting the services of a search company that specializes in providing background information, including past employment, driving records, and credit history. Such companies typically contact county courthouses in the counties where the prospective employee lived and check records dating back five to seven years.
>
> Background checks should occur before a person is hired. Otherwise, it may be considered discrimination to fire an employee based on past conviction information.

Source: *Hospitality Law*, LRP Publications. Used with permission.

record, a performance rating, the reason the employee resigned or was terminated, whether the employee is eligible for rehiring, an appraisal of the applicant's character, and other job-related information. (Note that Title VII of the Civil Rights Act of 1964, as amended by the 1972 Equal Employment Opportunity Act, applies to hiring practices. In addition, discrimination based on age or disability is covered under the Age Discrimination in Employment Act of 1967, the Rehabilitation Act of 1973, and the Americans with Disabilities Act of 1990. However, none of these laws prohibits the use of appropriate background investigations to screen applicants.)

Every application form should include a statement warning that any false information entered upon the form may result in immediate discharge. This is an important statement that is acceptable in most jurisdictions. (Be sure to check with local legal counsel.) It is helpful in overcoming the time-lag problem that most other screening techniques present.

In addition, there are several jurisdictions where state gambling commissions or local union organizations establish requirements for applicants and provide applicant certification.

Generally, the school record of a job applicant is not pertinent unless the individual is being moved into a supervisory or management training program. In that case, a request signed by the applicant authorizing access to school records is usually required. There is a cost assessed by the school for such data.

In a smaller property, where such a comprehensive screening process may not be possible, obtaining a formal application form and following up on the information provided is important. Obviously, an applicant with prior employment or criminal problems is unlikely to provide negative references. On the other hand, when significant gaps in the employment record occur, conduct an in-depth interview to explain those gaps.

It should be noted that, as a result of the Americans with Disabilities Act (1990), employment cannot be denied to a qualified applicant due to a disability. Over the years, the human resources departments of hospitality organizations have established a comprehensive set of job requirements for each position in the organization. This serves as the only acceptable method for determining the ability of a person with disabilities to function in any given work assignment. Safety is also a reasonable concern; employment may be denied to a disabled person if the requirements of a particular job would place that person or any other workers in danger of injury.

Finally, the application may be used to conduct a thorough interview with the applicant. If discrepancies are found, they should be carefully noted and verified; these may be the basis for rejection. Avoid derogatory entries on the application form, but be sure to document the reason for rejection and to file it with the application.

After a new employee is hired, the property should (when not prohibited by law) ask for appropriate identification to ensure that the applicant is in fact who he or she claims to be. Identification should be requested only *after* notification of hire to avoid the possibility of being accused of age discrimination by rejected applicants.

The human resources department plays many roles, though these can vary from property to property. Some properties use the department to train or help train new employees. With regard to security, the security department or employees in charge of the security function may assist in the training process of a new employee in order to emphasize the employee's role as an adjunct to the security staff. The employee should be instructed to promptly call the security office or another designated office or individual whenever a suspicious person, action, or condition is observed. This can be invaluable in extending the security presence throughout the hotel or motel.

Employee discipline is another issue that sometimes affects the human resources department. A property may need to discipline an employee for several reasons. Some of these reasons may be security-related, such as theft or some other infraction of the property's security rules. The human resources department itself generally will not discipline employees; such actions are usually left to the employee's department head or supervisor. It can, however, assist in developing discipline programs that help to ensure all employees are disciplined equally and fairly. The human resources department is sometimes asked to maintain records detailing why an employee was disciplined or terminated. If an employee or ex-employee challenges a disciplinary action, such records may be produced to justify the action taken.

Lodging properties should consult with counsel to determine termination procedures that will reduce or minimize subsequent claims by the terminated employee. When a union employee is involved, that employee may have rights under a collective bargaining agreement that are in addition to any rights he or she has under federal and state law.

The human resources department is also often responsible for keeping records listing any keys, equipment, uniforms, and other property of the hotel or motel issued to employees. The department compiles these records from information submitted by the appropriate management throughout the operation. When employees leave the organization for any reason, they should be required to return all keys, equipment, uniforms, identification cards, lockers, and so forth. Personnel records should be consulted to ensure that the departing employee has accounted for everything that the property issued to him or her.

Exit Interviews

Departing employees sometimes have things of interest to say. Though not widely used in the lodging industry, **exit interviews** can provide information relating to illegal activity on the property. The human resources director, security director, or general manager should conduct such interviews. The session should be informal and should be held on the final day of work. Allow sufficient time to obtain in-depth information. The executive should be ready to listen to complaints, indicate appreciation for the employee's time with the organization, and seek suggestions concerning how the employee's department might be improved. Subtle interviewing can lead to a discussion of problems in the department, including loss of services, time, and materials. Unfortunately, there are many functions within the hotel or motel for which employees are the best or only sources of information. If the employee is being dismissed, there is still value in a full discussion of the factors leading to the dismissal. If it appears that any elements in the dismissal could be adjudicated, such an interview may permit a delay of the dismissal for further investigation and review.

Violence in the Workplace

Recent years have seen a well-publicized increase in incidents of violence in the workplace. While most of the instances related to outside sources—a criminal during a robbery, an individual coming on-premises to commit an assault, or an irate guest or member of the public on the property—some related to problems with other workers or occurred as a result of being discharged.

In 1993, the National Safe Workplace Institute released a study valuing the cost of workplace violence at $4.2 billion annually. The institute estimated that in 1992, 111,000 violent incidents were committed in work environments, resulting in 750 deaths. Revisiting the subject in 1996, the Workplace Violence Research Institute conducted a survey that attempted to track the long-term financial effects of workplace violence; the new study suggested that the actual cost of workplace violence to businesses was closer to $35 billion.

Clearly, the human and financial costs are great. In an attempt to minimize them, many companies are taking a closer look at potential employees during the initial interview stage. A serious effort must be made to screen out individuals with violent inclinations from the work force. If the local jurisdiction permits the use of psychological testing in the hands of competent administrators, this should certainly be reviewed as an option by senior management. The use of a waiver on the part of the job applicant will also permit some questions that might uncover problems of a violent nature in the prior work assignment.

Some hoteliers enlist the services of outside firms to aid the screening process. According to Ben R. Furman, a former FBI agent and current president of Charlotte, North Carolina–based Rexus Corporation, conducting employee background checks has become a substantial part of his company's security business.

In addition to making such checks a standard element in the hiring process, Furman recommends establishing an in-house violence-prevention team that can work to develop policies and train supervisors and staff in risk management. Such a team might also identify specific jobs that involve a high risk of violence—for example, jobs involving direct contact with guests, access to weapons or other dangerous items, or minimal supervision. "Don't ignore an employee's history of confrontations, threats, or violence," Furman notes. "Liability and the risk of injury are greatest in those companies that bury their head in the sand."

It is most important that an organization establish the fact that there is no acceptance of behavior or activities that might lead to workplace violence. That focus must include situations that typically are mandated by federal or state law but which may be overlooked or "winked at" in the actual workplace. These areas include fair treatment without discrimination, sexual harassment, substance abuse or alcoholism, and the possession of firearms on the property at any time (unless required by some special assignments or local requirements).

Employee Assistance Programs. Every property, regardless of its size, should have an employee assistance program in place to deal effectively with violent incidents. Smaller properties likely will rely on off-site services, while larger properties may choose to offer on-premises resources as well. Consultants and other agencies within the community may assist in:

- Identifying problems and assessing risks before they result in violence
- Resolving employee-supervisor conflicts
- Providing stress management training
- Developing a written policy for handling workplace violence

Alcohol and Drug Use and Abuse

Of critical concern to the security of a lodging establishment is the use and abuse of drugs and alcohol by employees while on the premises. While employee effectiveness may be affected by the use of controlled substances away from the premises, the major concern is when the problem occurs on the premises of the hotel or motel.

Management should have a written policy clearly indicating specific actions to follow when it finds that employees are using or dealing in drugs on the premises. Providing for medical and psychological assistance is one possible policy. If drug use or drug dealing by employees will be considered a cause for legal action, that should be thoroughly explained to all employees.

Evidence of illegal drug activities may be discovered through locker inspections or by observing drug use or transactions. However, individual properties should consult with legal counsel to determine their rights and liabilities in connection with the inspection of employees' lockers. Inspections, if permitted by law, should always involve more than one individual and should be supervised by the human resources director. If the employee whose locker is being inspected is represented by a union, a union steward or other representative should accompany the management representative during the inspection process. If drugs are discovered, management should call the police and request that they take the appropriate actions (which will require securing a search warrant).

As is the case for many industries, the lodging industry may also face the problem of alcohol abuse among its employees. After reviewing the problem with legal counsel, management must decide whether to treat the problem with medical and psychological help or to take punitive actions such as dismissing the employee.

If assistance will be provided to employees, contact the various drug and alcohol programs within the community. Key staff members from the human resources and security departments should take any training available through these agencies to assist them in dealing with the problem effectively. Supervisors should also be involved, since they will probably be the first to notice their employees' drug- or alcohol-related problems. The security staff or other key staff members may provide in-house training sessions for supervisors. Review with legal counsel how support may be provided to the employee involved with drug or alcohol abuse, if that is management policy.

One cautionary note regarding dealing with an intoxicated employee: In the case of *Otis Engineering Corp. v. Clark* (1983), an employer in Texas sent home an employee who had become intoxicated while working a night shift. En route, the employee was involved in a two-car collision that took his own life and those of two women in the other car. The Supreme Court of Texas held that an employer who exercises control over an intoxicated employee has a duty to act in a reasonably prudent manner to prevent such an employee from causing an unreasonable risk of harm to others. Review with legal counsel how to best handle a situation of this kind. The related topic of liquor liability is discussed in more detail later in the chapter.

The Engineering Department

The engineering department plays an important role in the security of a property. In coordination with the security function, engineering maintains the security devices and systems on the property. Engineering should give high priority to any security or life-safety system or device in need of repair, maintenance, or replacement. In establishments where work orders are issued, the overprint "SECURITY PRIORITY" in red ink or security work orders printed on colored paper can be used to highlight urgency. Whenever a failure in the security systems or devices is detected, a work order form should be completed and immediately sent to the proper person for authorization and action. A copy of the work order form should also be provided to the security office for follow-up.

Engineering personnel may be called on to react to various emergencies endangering the safety or security of a property's guests or employees. For this reason, some properties that use radio communications on the premises put the engineering and security functions on the same frequency for at least certain periods of the day. When an emergency arises, this technique saves valuable time by allowing the dispatcher to notify security and engineering personnel with a single transmission.

Engineering personnel may play a crucial role in key control procedures. Depending upon the size of the property, the engineering department may have the key-making machine and key blanks under its direct responsibility. If so, close control should be maintained. The equipment, key blanks, and reserve keys should be kept secured. Only authorized engineering staff members should have access to the machine, the blanks, and the reserve keys.

Management should decide how many keys will be stored in the key rack and in reserve for any given guestroom. An audit and inventory of these room keys may also be helpful. No new keys should be issued without a formal requisition signed by an authorized person. Some organizations require authorization by the rooms manager, while others assign this responsibility to the security director, a resident manager, or another management employee. Whichever individual is designated, his or her signature should be required before the engineering department produces a key or purchases one from a contract locksmith. The engineering department should retain all requisitions for keys and should prepare and file a record of all keys duplicated.

Since hotel or motel maintenance requires equipment and materials that may also be used in homes or resold, it is important that strict controls over tools and materials be instituted. Tools should be issued only when they are signed out in a log or on an equipment check-out sheet. Similarly, a requisition should be drawn up for the materials required for a repair or maintenance job. Some properties require that the damaged or worn parts be returned upon completion of assignments. Unless a property is unusually large, tool storage cribs and tool crib clerks are rare. The supervisor or the chief engineer often controls the issue of tools. That individual is responsible for making sure tools are returned at the completion of a job.

In some properties the engineering staff is used for repair and maintenance functions off the premises for members of the management staff. This is legitimate only when the manager is also the owner of the lodging property (and therefore pays the engineering staff) or when owner or corporate approval has been given. Otherwise, the engineering department may be involved in the misappropriation of the organization's time, materials, and monies. If an employee is doing an off-the-job assignment on his or her own, the chief engineer should ensure that no materials are taken from the hotel or motel without proper authorization. There may be an agreement for the use of special tools, but these should be checked in and out through the regular tool log control. Purchase orders from the engineering department are usually authorized by the chief engineer and approved by the general manager or controller. In addition, the chief engineer or supervisor should determine which materials are necessary for an engineering or maintenance activity and then authorize the job requisition.

Unscheduled inventories should be conducted from time to time. Whenever practical, such an inventory should be accomplished through the accounting staff without the involvement of engineering personnel. Inventories and audits may uncover problems such as engineering and maintenance materials that are paid for but never ordered or received. For example, a fraudulent company using a post office box may bill a property $200 for light bulbs. Unless adequate controls and follow-up procedures are in place, the accounting office may pay the bill without verifying the purchase order or checking with engineering to ensure that the bulbs were in fact ordered and received. Coordination between the engineering, purchasing, and accounting functions can prevent this type of loss.

The Rooms Division

Front Service

Front service personnel are important allies of the security staff. The door attendant, bellstaff, valet parking attendants, and front desk staff continuously observe whoever arrives at or departs from the premises. Any suspicious activities or circumstances involving the guests or any member of the public entering the premises can be reported to security or another designated staff person by front service personnel.

Front desk personnel play a crucial role in key control, for example. Front desk clerks should never simply give room keys or cards to anyone who asks for them. Some sort of identification should be checked to ensure that the person requesting the key or card is the guest registered for that room. Additional protection is given to the arriving guest when the desk clerk announces the guest's room number quietly and privately. Also, when the layout of the lobby permits, the front desk may become the control center for the elevators and the entrance to the property. In a smaller property where there may be few or no uniformed service personnel, the front desk person may be the only staff member on the premises during the night hours. Under such circumstances, some properties limit access to the lobby and reception area. The decision of whether to admit someone is generally assigned to the front desk clerk. Access is sometimes controlled through the use of locks at the main entrance that may be released by remote control from the front desk.

The front desk may also serve as the command center in the event of an emergency such as a fire or flood. In many hotels and motels, there is always someone at the front desk and there is usually access to telephone service. In an emergency, on-premises security staff and/or the local police may be summoned as determined by established procedures or by management. An alternate location should be predetermined in the event that the front desk is disabled in the crisis.

Some (generally larger) hotels and motels find it desirable to locate the command center elsewhere, often in the telecommunications or PBX (private branch exchange) area. Some properties have designated a special extension number (for example, 66) for guests and staff members to use in an emergency. This number is monitored by the PBX operator and possibly also by security. This system may improve response capability in an emergency.

An aspect of emergency response is the capability for the guest to call 911 directly from the guestroom. Some properties have considered intercepting such calls and routing them through the hotel's switchboard. However, legal counsel usually will advise against such an action; should there be a delay in relaying an intercepted 911 message, the liability would be considerable. Rather, it is recommended that an effective liaison be developed between the establishment and the police, fire, and emergency medical service units in the community. In such a relationship, the emergency response unit would make a point of contacting the front desk en route to the room from which the 911 call had been made. Where such liaison has not existed, there have been embarrassing discrepancies in the management's listing of police calls versus those of the police department itself. If a hotel employee testifies in court that there were only 10 emergency calls during a given year, but the police then report that they had actually made 25 emergency calls, it may appear to the court and the jury that management really doesn't know what is going on—and apparently does not have an effective or coherent security program in place.

With regard to PBX procedures, the guest may be further protected by a policy of not allowing staff members to give the room numbers of guests or any other guest information to any callers. People calling from off the property may be connected to the appropriate guestroom without being told which room it is. Any individual inquiring in person about a guest may be asked to use the house phone to place the call to the guestroom. Generally, neither the front desk nor the PBX should give out guestroom numbers.

In protecting the guest, there are a number of simple security precautions that front service personnel can take. Some of these involve informing the guests of precautions the guests themselves may take. For example, when a guest arrives in his or her own vehicle, the front service staff (or, for that matter, appropriate signage or posted notices) may recommend that the guest take any removable units (tape/CD players, cellular telephones, and other electronic units) and lock them in the trunk. Also, they may suggest that articles be removed from the floor, seats, or window shelf and locked away. When valet service is provided, the valet should remove the key from the vehicle and secure it so that the vehicle cannot be removed by anyone except an employee. This is especially important when the vehicle is left at the front of the property before it is moved to the parking facility by the car valet. There have been incidents in which unattended vehicles have been stolen because the keys were available.

Luggage and other articles received by the door attendant should be receipted and moved to a secured area. Guests may then recover their belongings by presenting luggage receipt stubs at registration. Where such a system of control is not feasible, other methods for ensuring the safety and security of guests' luggage should be examined.

When the bellperson picks up the luggage from the secured area and joins the guest, usually at the room, he or she generally provides instructions on the lighting, radio, and television, and checks the ventilation. In addition to this standard information, the hotel or motel's management may consider having the bellperson review with the guest the use of all access control devices on the guestroom doors, connecting doors, sliding glass doors, and windows. The bellperson may also inform the guest of pertinent security information (such as the availability of safe deposit boxes and the telephone number to call during an emergency), point out or distribute the Traveler Safety Tips card (available from the American Hotel & Motel Association), point out the presence of any decals or notices posted in the room relating to guest security and the property's limited liability, and explain procedures for emergency evacuation.

Front office personnel also play a particularly important role in asset protection. The failure to collect payment for the products and services received by guests is usually a more significant source of loss than the theft of towels or ashtrays. Management should establish procedures that ensure that all charges made on the premises are promptly included on the guest's folio for proper billing. The use of computers and POS (point of sale) terminals can help the front office keep guest folios accurate. POS terminals immediately record any charge made by any guest anywhere on the property to his or her folio; lag time in updating the folio, which could allow the guest to check out without paying for all products and services received, is eliminated.

Also, by following the procedures established by management and the accounting department with respect to handling cash, checks, and credit requests, the front office can help keep the property from incurring losses through bad debts.

The Housekeeping Department

The housekeeping department also has a special responsibility for security, since its employees have direct access to the guestrooms and the guests' property. Consequently, careful screening of housekeeping personnel should be done during the hiring process.

Housekeeping personnel should receive instructions from the security department or the director of security regarding their role in the security of the property. Housekeeping staff should be instructed to promptly inform security personnel or another designated individual when guests or visitors are in unauthorized areas or are acting in an unusual or suspicious manner. The employee should not attempt to confront or detain such an individual. Instead, he or she should get to a phone—preferably behind a locked door—to notify security or the management office, which will take appropriate action. A policy on this procedure should be established following consultation with the appropriate department heads.

Housekeeping personnel are also an important element in a property's key control program. Management should consider issuing section master keys—whether metal keys or electronic cards—to the housekeeping staff that limit the staff's access to only those rooms for which they are responsible. Some properties establish a policy requiring that all master keys be issued and retrieved daily. Security personnel may verify that all keys are secured in a locked cabinet in the housekeeping area. A significant security advantage is obtained when using key

Exhibit 1 Security Checklist for Housekeeping Staff

- Deadbolt on corridor door and connecting room door
- Security chain on guestroom door
- Security bar and/or metal pin on glass sliding doors
- Stop devices on windows to limit access from outside the room, where windows may be opened
- Viewport (peephole), to verify that the unit has not been reversed so individuals in the corridor can look into the guest room
- Telephone
- In-room safe, secure and with no evidence of tampering

cards. Many systems record whose card was used to enter a room, as well as the time of entry.

Management should instruct room attendants to secure any key left in a guestroom after checkout. Such keys should never be placed on top of a housekeeping cart or anywhere else that may leave them vulnerable to theft. Some properties use housekeeping carts that have locked metal boxes to hold found keys. Other properties instruct their room attendants to carry found keys on their person. Room attendants finding keys should be instructed to turn them in in a timely manner.

Individuals who ask a room attendant to unlock a guestroom door for them (often stating that they have forgotten or lost their key) should be referred to the front desk. Legitimate guests may initially object to this response, but once they see it is part of a property's organized security effort, they likely will appreciate such a policy.

Guestroom access by the guest while the room is being serviced by the room attendant involves a critical decision as to whether the room is to be cleaned with the door open—and the housekeeping cart serving as a barrier to entrance—or with the door closed and locked. (A third alternative would be a team of two attendants cleaning the room with the door either open or closed.) Several investigative journalists with national broadcast media have focused on the ease with which one could gain access to a guestroom when the person was not even registered in the hotel. To help guard both the employees' safety and the guests' belongings, many properties now instruct their housekeepers to clean a guestroom with the door closed and locked. A sign that can be placed on the door informs the guest that the housekeepers would be happy to return later if the guest wishes to enter the room using a key. This helps properties avoid the problem of requiring the room attendant to serve as a security guard.

Housekeeping staff have opportunities to check security equipment to see that it is functioning properly. (See Exhibit 1 for a sample security checklist for housekeepers.) Inoperative access control devices such as locks, deadbolts, window latches, and so forth should be reported immediately. If the security of a room is being compromised by equipment failure, the engineering department should be informed so it can repair or replace the defective equipment. The front office may also need to be notified that the room is not secure, so that it will know not to rent the room until the problem has been corrected. Many properties have room attendants ensure that security decals or notices and other room postings are present as well. In the case of *Courtney v. Remler* (1983), a property's policy of having room attendants check for the presence of a security decal played an important part in establishing that the property had exercised reasonable care.

Staff should also take the time to check the room's furnishings for signs of wear, breakage, and stability—all with guests' safety in mind. Chairs with loose screws or broken springs should be noted and repaired or replaced before they can cause a guest injury. Torn or loose carpeting, which might cause a tripping accident, should be repaired. Interior door locks and door chain assemblies should be firmly attached and not missing any parts.

Linen rooms should have self-closing and self-locking doors, and the locks should be changed periodically. Storerooms and equipment rooms should have locks that are keyed differently from any other locks on the property. The availability of the keys should be strictly controlled. Room attendants' closets and all utility access doors should be locked at all times.

Since many items used in lodging properties have home-use or resale value, they may be stolen by both guests and employees. Such items include ashtrays, bath towels, tableware, china, glassware, sheets, pillowcases, blankets, bedspreads, and table linens. Linens often disappear through room service, while other items may be taken either during regular table or banquet service. Prompt removal of room service trays and equipment can help to control these losses. In addition, hotel and motel management should consider providing guests with two courtesy items to reduce the loss of towels. First, in properties with swimming pools, towel losses may be reduced by providing plastic bags for use with wet swim suits. Instead of wrapping the wet suits in towels to protect dry clothing in the suitcase, departing guests may place them in plastic bags provided by the property. Second, in facilities where vehicles may be parked adjacent to the guestroom, towels are sometimes used by guests to wipe condensation from the windows of the vehicle. Frequently, the towels are then thrown into the trunk for future use. Some properties have overcome this problem by providing specifically designed and marked paper or cloth towels as a courtesy item for wiping vehicle windows.

Asset control for the housekeeping department can be improved through an effective inventory program. It may even reveal that thefts by guests are not always as common as may be claimed. One hotel was suffering a sizable loss of sheets, pillow cases, and blankets. Room attendants claimed that guests were responsible for the thefts. Management questioned this assertion and changed the locks on the linen rooms. New key controls were also established requiring housekeepers entering the linen rooms for supplies to sign for a key and to return it immediately. Surprise inventories were taken several times a month. Losses eventually dropped by 80 percent. Consider weekly inventories of floor supplies

> **Housekeeping: Invasion of Privacy**
>
> Guests have a reasonable expectation of privacy in guestrooms, and that privacy should be protected. Consider the following case:
>
> A couple stayed in the honeymoon suite of the Canterbury Inn in Coralville, Iowa, on their engagement night in the summer of 1988. During the night, the couple heard noises behind the wall and thought it strange since there were no guestrooms near them, said their attorney Nestor Lobodiak.
>
> The noises emanated from behind the guestroom mirror. When the couple decided to investigate, they found that a section of drywall behind the mirror, approximately 8 x 8 inches, had been removed, and that they could see through the mirror from the back side—that it was, in fact, a two-way mirror.
>
> Lobodiak says the hole led to an adjoining attic space that was easily reachable from a housekeeping storage room below. The carts were stored there at night and all one had to do, he says, was "step up onto a cart, remove the cover, and pull up" into the attic space. While the existence of the mirror situation and the means for gaining access to the attic space were apparently well-known to the employees, the inn claimed that because its management was unaware, it could not be liable for damages.
>
> The case went to trial in July 1992. The jury found that the housekeeping supervisor was aware of the secret viewing area, and further found that because of her responsibilities, she should be considered in a management position. (There is also apparently a rule in Iowa that punitive damages may be awarded against a corporation only if there was knowledge of the wrong by someone at a management level.)
>
> The verdicts were a combined $300,000 in compensatory damages and $2 million each in punitive damages, for a total verdict of $4.3 million.

Source: *Hospitality Law,* LRP Publications. Used with permission.

and room set-ups, monthly departmental inventories, and quarterly accounting department inventories of the housekeeping department.

Laundry and Dry Cleaning. As noted earlier, it is usually advantageous for management to follow a policy of allowing no personal cleaning or laundry services for employees. Written policies should make it clear that cleaning and laundry services are provided only for uniforms required for the job assignment. Any violation of this policy may be considered theft of the property's services. Some organizations with large cleaning facilities may wish to institute a cleaning service for employees at a special rate; however, such services should be controlled and allow no exceptions to the established employee charges. Any policies regarding the use of laundry services should be uniformly applied.

Protection of the establishment's and guests' laundry items may be accomplished through the use of a careful receipt and identification system; a secured area for holding guest cleaning; thorough inventories of supplies; a control system for linens, uniforms, towels, and other company items; and an employee parcel pass program. These procedures will help ensure that employees do not remove items from the property except when they are authorized to do so.

Exhibit 2   Points for Asset Protection

- Maintain a division of duties.
- Fix responsibility in one individual.
- Limit the number of employees with access to assets.
- Keep cash banks and stores to a minimum.
- Have third-party employees perform surprise counts.
- Bond employees with access to cash, records, or stores.
- Schedule mandatory vacations and rotate employees.
- Conduct frequent external audits.
- Use cost-benefit analysis.

Purchasing and Receiving

Lodging properties must purchase a wide variety of products, supplies, and services in the course of daily operations. In small properties where the owner/manager is responsible for the purchasing function, there is less concern about theft. As properties get larger and more people become involved in purchasing, however, the chances of theft increase. Purchasing is one of the most difficult functions for security to monitor. Unless information on kickbacks or other forms of collusion between the purchasing agent and the vendor is available, it is difficult to prove that such an illegal relationship exists.

Theft can occur during the purchasing process in a number of ways—kickbacks, the use of fictitious companies, processing thefts, credit memo problems, intentional delivery invoice errors, quality substitutions, and more. Each of these problems can be prevented, or its incidence reduced, by using effective purchasing and payment procedures. Exhibit 2 offers several points for building in asset protection.

Kickbacks occur when the purchaser works in collusion with someone from the supplier's company. One type of kickback involves purchasing products at higher prices than normal with the added charge being split by the purchaser and the supplier's employee. To control this type of theft, management should regularly review invoices. If a seemingly inordinate number of products is being purchased from a single supplier, management may wish to investigate the situation. Management should also consider soliciting price quotations randomly to ensure that the prices it pays are competitive.

Dishonest purchasers may create fictitious companies that "sell" products to an operation and then bill the operation for the nonexistent goods. The checks for such products are usually sent to a post office box. To help combat this form of theft, management or appropriate accounting function employees should periodically review the company checks sent to suppliers. Unless the management is familiar with the supplier, it may wish to consider establishing a policy of not sending checks to companies with only post office box addresses.

> ## Division of Duties
>
> Division of duties, also referred to as separation of duties and segregation of duties, is the most important principle of internal control.
>
> It is a simple but powerful concept. Here's how it works: No one individual should have total control over any transaction. If there are two or more people involved with each transaction, it would take collusion (i.e., a conspiracy) between those two (or more) persons in order to falsify or otherwise change that transaction.
>
> One important way to implement the principle of division of duties would be to keep the custody of assets separate from the recordkeeping or accountability for those assets. In a hotel, cash handling is kept separate from bookkeeping. Front office cashiers, for example, have constant custody of large sums of cash. Why can't they simply take a handful? Because in a well-controlled operation, they have custody of the cash, but they do not have access to or control over the accountability for that cash. Their original bank, or float, is issued by another person who records the amount and shift time of that issue. The individual banks are also recorded in the general ledger by yet another person. The transactions that change the cashier's bank during the shift—such as revenue collections—may be posted by the cashier, but are likewise not under his or her total control. So, a cashier has custody and access, but cannot control the accountability. An income auditor may have access to the audit trail and accountability, but should not have access to the cash. As transactions get more complicated, more people are involved, making collusion more difficult.
>
> The essential preventive role that division of duties plays is that when several people are involved in a transaction (that is, no one person has complete control), collusion becomes a necessary condition to fraud or embezzlement. Collusion is a difficult and fragile process to achieve. When two or more people must collude to perpetrate a fraud, the probability of that fraud coming to fruition is far smaller than if one of the individuals had complete control.
>
> Division of duties, by itself, is not sufficient to prevent internal control problems. The division must be an effective one. If a hotel gives two relatives (or two lifelong friends) control over parts of a transaction, the separation may not be effective. Division of duties also can be expensive, and adding staff strictly for the sake of accomplishing it is generally not recommended.
>
> When operations are small, and effective division of duties may be difficult to cost-justify, management must assume more of the duties. If duties must be combined, such combinations should involve management personnel.
>
> Finally, division of duties should be combined with other principles to yield effective internal controls.

Processing thefts occur when suppliers request payment for an invoice more than once. The hotel or motel needs an effective internal control system to verify whether an invoice has already been paid or not. Likewise, the property must protect itself from delivery invoice errors—intentional or not—such as problems with arithmetic or short counts or weights.

Dealing with delivery invoice errors brings up an important point. A number of potential purchasing losses or thefts can be detected during receiving. For this reason, many properties choose to separate the purchasing and receiving functions. If a dishonest purchaser is allowed to receive products, he or she is much more able to hide any thefts.

The general manager may find it helpful to maintain a roster of sources for purchases made through the purchasing office. Occasionally reviewing that list with the purchasing director and the director of the department for which the purchases are made is also helpful. The general manager, chef, and food and beverage manager should also meet occasionally to review the price and quality of products purchased. Another element of control over certain purchases can be obtained by requiring multiple price quotations. For large purchases, management can insist on sealed bids and should participate in the bid opening and evaluation.

In properties that separate the purchasing and receiving functions, an effective system is needed to ensure that the employees receiving products know what the purchaser actually ordered. If receiving employees lack this information, they have no way of knowing whether everything that was ordered has been received. This may lead to various problems. For example, credit memo problems occur when receiving personnel sign delivery invoices for items not received. When products are not received either at all or in the required amount or number, a "request for credit memo" should be issued to reduce the original delivery invoice by the value of the items not delivered. If effective communication does not exist between the purchasing and receiving functions, credit memo problems may be due to oversight. They may also arise through collusion with a supplier's employee.

Quality substitutions are another problem that can be controlled during receiving. Quality substitutions occur when a price is quoted for the proper quality item, but a lower quality product is delivered. Receiving personnel should be qualified or trained to verify the quality of incoming products to ensure that the operation does not pay a high price for a low quality item. Quality substitutions do not necessarily lead a property to spend more than it had planned to spend, but they may lead to long-term losses due to guest dissatisfaction with the product. Dissatisfied guests tend not to return.

Relatively few hotels or motels have a formal receiving area that includes a dock, receiving office, and holding area for temporary storage. However, every property should designate an area for receiving materials in order to protect its assets. It is also helpful, regardless of size of the hotel or motel, to establish times for receiving goods and materials. This permits the supervisor to schedule an adequate number of staff members to receive, verify, and store the items. All materials should be weighed in and verified by count while the delivery person is still present so that delivery documents may be corrected if a discrepancy is found. When it is impossible to weigh or count the items when they are received, management should consider using a conditional receipt stamp which allows for a verification period. The receiving clerk should also check for damage or spoilage. This is of particular concern when foodstuffs are received.

In properties that do have a formal receiving platform, the platform should have a metal or other appropriate door that can be securely locked and which should be supplemented by an adjacent door for emergency exit. The emergency door may be alarmed and provided with panic hardware. The frames and doors in the receiving area should be metal, with concealed hinges and anti-shim protection at the lockset. Adequate lighting should be provided at all times. CCTV might also be used to monitor the receiving area.

Storage and Issuing

After items are received and verified, they should be immediately moved to locked storage. The hotel or motel's employees should move the items. If the receiving personnel are not available to move the items, the appropriate storage room supervisor should move the materials into storage. The supplier's delivery person should not be allowed to enter the property's storage areas. A copy of the receiving document should be given to the storeroom staff for further verification before the items are stored.

Storerooms may contain several thousand dollars' worth of a property's assets. Clearly, they must be secured. There are a number of security procedures which, when implemented, help protect stored assets. For example, the locking system for storage areas should be different from that for the guestrooms and public areas. This keeps employees who use master or section master keys in their normal duties (for example, room attendants) from having access to storerooms that they are not authorized to enter. A policy of limited access allows only authorized personnel to enter storage areas, which should be locked when not in use.

An important element in storeroom control is the use of effective inventory procedures. A **perpetual inventory** (which involves writing down all items as they are received for storage and issued from storage) could be kept for high value items. A **physical inventory** (which involves actually counting the items in a storage area) should be conducted from time to time. The perpetual inventory will reveal what *should* be in the storeroom. The physical inventory will reveal what actually *is* in the storeroom. Discrepancies may indicate a security problem.

In addition to departmental inventories, the accounting department should also conduct inventories at a frequency determined by management. Such inventories may vary from a weekly inventory of floor supplies and room set ups in housekeeping to an annual inventory of furniture and equipment. These inventories should be conducted by a team of personnel from accounting or a department other than the one being inventoried.

Nothing should be issued from storage without a requisition bearing an authorized signature. After-hour entrance to a storeroom should require a manager, supervisor, or security officer to accompany the employee needing to enter the locked storage facility. The key should be obtained from the front desk and should be logged. The individuals entering the storage area and the reason for entry should also be logged. An authorized requisition for the materials taken should be completed and left at the desk of the storeroom manager.

The Food and Beverage Department

Numerous technological developments have been adopted by the hospitality industry to improve or change existing control systems. In most instances, basic control processes have not been altered. Instead, technology has enhanced the accuracy, depth, and effectiveness of these processes, while reducing the labor involved.

Spoilage and Pilferage

Adequate checks in the receiving portion of the food service cycle can help stem loss due to spoilage and pilferage. Implementing a Hazard Analysis Critical Control Point (HACCP) program, which identifies critical points in the food-production cycle as they relate to food safety, will reveal points at which loss prevention controls may be most effective.

In addition to the HACCP system, there should be a continual review of spoilage. If frequent and excessive spoilage is reported, those responsible for the receiving process should evaluate product quality when it is delivered by the vendor; if substandard foods are arriving, receiving personnel should be empowered to refuse shipments or accept partial shipments. If the situation is chronic, a change in vendors may be warranted. In addition, storage equipment should be checked regularly for proper maintenance and temperature control. Many establishments maintain written temperature logs; electronic monitoring and control systems also are available that provide running temperature logs for refrigeration equipment. Other possible causes of spoilage include the following:

- An inordinate delay may have occurred during the transport of product from the receiving area to the storage area.
- Food may have been overpurchased, causing inventory levels to be too large.
- Staff members may be taking food and covering their tracks with a spoilage report.

Automated Purchasing Systems. Automated purchasing and inventory management systems allow for greater ease in auditing these aspects of the food service cycle and are a deterrent to theft and collusion. Some systems use electronic scanners to control the flow of product in and out of the receiving and storage areas of the hotel. The collected data is linked directly to inventory databases that track the flow of product through designated control points and prompt for reordering, comparing the amount of product available with preset par stock levels. Additionally, these systems assist in controlling product quality and food costs by issuing product based on production forecasts generated through the system by management.

By automating the receiving and requisition process, auditing may be performed in greater depth and with greater ease. By utilizing the data maintained by these systems and comparing theoretical cost information with actual data produced through physical inventories, proper control is maintained. The increased control and accuracy provided by such systems creates a higher level of confidence for management and a greater deterrent against pilferage.

Even an automated requisition system does not eliminate the need for signed requisitions and human oversight. On the contrary, no food product should ever leave a storage area without proper authorization. However, in an automated system, signatures often can be obtained through the system itself. For example, product requisitions initiated in the system by the executive chef will carry with them his or her user identification code; the system will not accept a requisition from an unauthorized user.

Such systems may allow for electronic interface with suppliers for the transmission of data related to the bidding process and order placement. These systems may also use data from the inventory management database to ensure proper product specifications and order amounts. In this process, the system compares vendor prices and suggests a vendor based on that comparison. This use of technology adds additional barriers to collusion between the purchasing staff and vendors. Collusion, once established, compromises the control system as well as profits and product quality, eventually leading to loss of food and beverage sales and profits. With this in mind, it is imperative that periodic audits of the purchasing process be conducted by management to enhance the control offered by these advanced systems.

Alcohol Storage, Issuing, and Service

Storage and Issuing. Alcoholic beverage storage and issuing demand extensive control. The food and beverage manager and hotel controller are often assigned the responsibility for ordering, receiving, storing, and issuing liquor as required.

Liquor requisitioned for a cash bar or hospitality bar in a suite or meeting room should be carefully monitored. Since the patron is eventually billed, food and beverage management must be able to provide an exact accounting for liquor consumed during the event. Technological developments in the area of beverage control allow for greater ease of monitoring this count. Some systems allow bartenders to control and count drinks poured through the use of electronically controlled spouts mounted on the liquor bottles themselves. Other systems, primarily used in large properties, dispense and monitor liquor served from a single, central location. These systems use a network of tubing to deliver the liquor to set locations within the property.

A supervisor or manager should also monitor the service at cash bars on the property. When a cash bar is used for a function, it is preferable for cashiers to sell tickets that are then exchanged for drinks. This makes verification of the drink sale easier than in a situation where the bartender must also collect payment and issue change. In the hotel lounge, however, the bartender is often responsible for all of these processes. In these instances, electronic control over liquor dispensing is often mandatory. Overpouring, underringing, brand switching, and nonringing of drink sales all threaten a good beverage control system. Many dishonest bartenders will go to great lengths to subvert the effectiveness of even the best control system. The key to eliminating such pilferage is to monitor all fluctuations in cash and bank reconciliation reports filed by bar staff and to watch very carefully the activities surrounding the sale of beverages in the hotel bar. This may be done by surveillance cameras. Another, more effective, method is to use a **spotter**. The spotter may be a contracted employee of the hotel or restaurant, or a "shopper" or spotter from an outside contract organization, who visits the bar, poses as a guest, and watches the activities of the bar staff. Spotters may be used when a problem is suspected or as a routine aspect of a good beverage control system.

Alcohol Service. Legislation in many states has created **dram shop acts** that generally create a *statutory*, as distinguished from common law, cause of action in favor of "[a]ny person who shall be injured in person, property, means of support or otherwise by any intoxicated person, by reason of the intoxication of any person" against "any person who shall, by unlawful selling to or unlawfully assisting in procuring liquor for such intoxicated person, have caused or contributed to such intoxication."[1]

Under many dram shop acts, a plaintiff must prove the following elements of the statutory cause of action: (1) an unlawful sale (2) of liquor or other alcoholic beverages (that is, beer or wine) (3) to an intoxicated person which (4) causes injury to another party. Under New York law, for example, "unlawful sale" refers to the law prohibiting the sale to minors, known habitual drunkards, or to intoxicated persons actually or apparently under the influence of alcoholic beverages.

Review this matter with your legal counsel to determine the best course of action for: monitoring the amount of liquor served to a patron; suggesting that a patron who appears to be intoxicated go home in a cab or remain at the premises overnight if he or she is not a registered guest in the hotel or motel; and handling the patron who insists he or she is not intoxicated and can drink more and/or drive without any difficulty. In these instances, consider contacting the local police. Carefully monitor the drinking age as mandated by the various states. Request appropriate identification in those instances when there is any question about the age of the patron. Food and beverage serving staff should be regularly reminded of their responsibilities under the state's alcoholic beverage control laws and related dram shop act.[2]

This is an area of liability that has seen a tremendous increase in the number of suits filed. Under a state's dram shop act, the potential liability of taverns, restaurants, and hotels and motels that serve alcoholic beverages is usually tremendous. The owners may be directly liable to the injured or deceased party or parties for various damages including medical expenses, property damages, damages for pain and suffering, support for spouse and dependents, lost wages, funeral expenses, and perhaps punitive damages.

Three samples will illustrate the potential exposure for liability under state dram shop statutes. A Minnesota restaurant was held liable for $207,097 in damages after it was found (despite its claims to the contrary) to have served alcohol to an intoxicated man who, after leaving, ran a stop sign and collided with the plaintiff's car, breaking her neck and causing permanent damage. In a Washington state case, a tavern was held liable for $450,000 in damages for allegedly serving approximately 19 drinks to a driver who then crashed into and killed someone. Finally, a Colorado bar was held liable for $15.4 million in damages after it served alcohol to an intoxicated, underage youth who then caused a car wreck that paralyzed a two-year-old boy.

Point-of-Sale (POS) Systems

Point-of-sale (POS) systems have replaced traditional cash registers in all major hotel operations. These computer-based systems allow for a very high level of control for a reasonable price in all areas where guest transactions are processed. The food and beverage department has gained the greatest benefit from this control.

Restaurant POS systems have eliminated the need for the cumbersome check control systems of the past. Checks no longer need to be issued to servers at the beginning of each shift. Control numbers no longer need to be recorded on lengthy and time-consuming check logs. The POS system maintains open guest checks in a database and assigns a check number based on the transaction number and the server's identification code. Management may then report on all transactions performed by a specific server for any given period of time. Other POS functions, such as open drawer alarms and keys that can be programmed for specific menu items or functions, give management more flexibility and greater reporting capabilities to track sales and control losses.

POS systems can interface with inventory management systems to trigger reorders of specific items by tracking the number sold over a specific period of time. For example, the system might be set up to track strip steak sales and inventory; once the system recognizes that the number sold has reached the predetermined reorder point, strip steaks are added to the requisition for the following day. This enhances production control, as the physical inventory level should match the POS report at the end of each shift or business day.

Transaction processing is the final area of technology that has seen marked improvement. Restaurant POS systems, as well as hotel property management systems (PMS), now have transaction processing and credit card approval as integrated features. At each transaction, the credit card is swiped through a reader that is attached to the POS or PMS. The system then obtains approval from the credit card company through a modem connected to the system's main computer. This integration of approval processing allows for a more efficient work flow as well as better integrated and more extensive reporting capabilities than were previously available.

The single caveat for hotel managers when addressing control through technology is to establish and review policy constantly. Technology certainly is helpful, but it is the policy and physical systems that determine how effective control functions will be in any operation. Extensive planning and research should be done before automating any system. And it should be remembered that sometimes a system is more effective in its manual state than it would be if automated.

The Recreation Department

Swimming Pools

Many guests find a property's swimming pool to be one of its more attractive features. Properties with swimming pools should, however, realize the potential safety hazards and liability associated with pools. Adhering to responsible pool practices will reduce the possibility of tragic accidents.

A property should be aware of all local and state laws and codes relating to such things as fencing off swimming areas, posting clear and concise pool instructions for pool users, employing lifeguards, following appropriate pool construction and maintenance procedures, keeping rescue equipment visible and readily available, posting accurate depth markings, and more. Consult legal counsel. Lawsuits filed against pool owners often cite one or more of the following issues: no fencing, inadequate fencing, unlocked gates, lack of safety equipment (such as a shepherd's hook or life ring), inadequate and/or inaccurate depth markings, poor pool maintenance, inadequate supervision, poor construction practices, and more. See Exhibit 3 for a comprehensive swimming pool safety checklist.

Be sure that all electrical lighting, connections, and equipment are protected by a ground fault circuit interrupter (GFCI), as this can prevent electrocution should there be a short or other electrical malfunction. (This is an OSHA mandate. Employees must be protected by a GFCI in any moist atmosphere where the employee might be in danger of shock or electrocution.) Ensure that lighting is adequate for persons approaching or leaving the pool area.

OSHA requires that an employee trained in first aid be present on each work shift. Have such an employee on call for any pool area incidents requiring immediate attention prior to the arrival of emergency medical personnel. Similarly, consideration should be given to having staff with knowledge of water rescue and cardiopulmonary resuscitation (CPR) on the premises and on call during pool operating hours. Of course, where the local jurisdiction mandates an attendant or lifeguard, such a person should have such knowledge.

The individual treating the pool with chemicals should be thoroughly trained to perform such functions. Have the employees trained through the National Spa & Pool Institute (NSPI). The NSPI regularly conducts training sessions on the basics of water chemistry and maintenance. Close the pool for daily cleaning; never permit guests in the vicinity of the pool during chemical treatment.

Install slip-resistant surfaces around the pool area—especially on the pool deck. Treat slippery tiles with an anti-slip coating, or install tiles containing slip-proof materials. Check with professionals for such treatments or materials.

Secure all pool ladders. Monitor the weather and clear the pool when threatening weather approaches. This is critically important when there is the threat of an electrical storm with the danger of lightning strikes in the open pool area.

Several recent tragic incidents involved pool drains. In one incident, a swimmer's hair became caught in a malfunctioning drain and, despite valiant rescue efforts, the individual drowned. In 1996, a 16-year-old New Jersey girl was held underwater by drain suction in a hot tub and drowned. In 1993, at the Medfield Area Recreation Club in Cary, North Carolina, five-year-old Valerie Lakey was in a wading pool whose drain cover had been pried off earlier in the day by other children. When she sat down, the resulting suction held her to the bottom of the pool and literally disemboweled her. Although the child survived, she must now take all nourishment intravenously and may require several organ transplants in the future. The Lakeys subsequently sued the pool's manufacturer, the pump's manufacturer, the county (which certified the pool), and the recreation club. After three years of lawsuits, the family finally received payments of $25 million from the pool's manufacturer (a record in North Carolina), $2.5 million from the county, $2.9 million from the pump manufacturer, and $500,000 from the club itself. This and similar judgments have led to the recommendation that an emergency switch be visible and readily accessible in the pool area to turn off the

Exhibit 3   Swimming Pool Safety Checklist

This checklist may seem extreme, but the source for each item is a real case in which the subject matter was the basis for liability on the part of the hotel.

Regulations

- Make sure your pool complies with all safety regulations for public pools.
- Be aware of all applicable state, county, and municipal regulations concerning the operation of your pool.
- Know whether a lifeguard is required. Even if a lifeguard isn't required by law, it's the surest step innkeepers can take to prevent tragedy and its enormous expense.
- If you use lifeguards part time, use them during the hours of greatest pool use.

Employees

- Instruct employees that when they enforce any pool rule, they must document it. That is tangible evidence you can take to court to defuse the usual arguments that pool areas are largely ignored by hotel employees.
- Have employees monitor the weather and clear the pool when threatening weather approaches.
- Be sure your employees prohibit alcohol-impaired guests from using the pool. This may be a difficult situation to handle, but it is essential; just like intoxicated drivers, intoxicated swimmers are far more prone to accidents.
- Instruct your employees to stop any rough-housing. Not only will this prevent accidents, but it's good public relations, since other pool users will be grateful.
- Have employees watch to make sure only registered guests use the pool. Also have them watch for prohibited material in the pool area.
- Police the pool area even when it is closed. Assume guests will try to use it outside of normal hours.
- Increase pool safety awareness during times of increased use.

Training

- Be certain that all lifeguards and pool attendants are certified and trained.
- Always have an employee who is trained in emergency first aid on duty when the pool is open.
- Provide an illustrated description of artificial respiration procedures with instructions that resuscitation should continue until help arrives.
- Make safety equipment immediately available. Have items that are required in your jurisdiction: life poles, ropes, life preservers, and so on.

Physical Checks

- Remove all diving boards and water slides.
- If you do retain a water slide, regularly check the water depth near the slide's release.

Exhibit 3 *(continued)*

- Make the division between shallow and deep ends obvious by means of ropes, floats, or coloring on the pool floor. A common source of trouble is when adults remove the rope dividing the shallow end from the deep end to swim laps. That rope rarely gets replaced, resulting in a dangerous situation.
- If appropriate, fence in the pool area to control access. Have self-closing and self-locking gates.
- Provide a pool telephone with clearly posted emergency numbers. This should be an outside line, not one to the front desk.
- Check to see whether the pool is adequately lit and whether the underwater lights work. Most hotel pools are open after dark, and underwater visibility has been a factor in many lawsuits.
- Make sure the lighting in the pool area is sufficient for passage. Many guests become relaxed around the pool and may not be safety-conscious.
- Install slip-resistant surfaces around the pool area.
- Test the water temperature. There have been cases of guests jumping into freezing cold water, resulting in shock and cardiac complications.
- Secure all pool ladders.
- Equip all wading pools for children with firmly attached drains, and inspect them regularly.
- Repair and clean the pool regularly.

Signage
- If you do not employ lifeguards, place a sign in a conspicuous spot informing all guests of that fact. The sign should also tell guests that they swim at their own risk.
- Display signs prohibiting all diving. Even if you don't have a diving board, the sign will prohibit diving from all sides of the pool. Be sure the signs have letters at least five inches high and that they are placed throughout the pool area.
- If you retain a water slide, post signs prohibiting head-first sliding.
- Correctly mark water depths in feet or meters.
- Display signs prohibiting glass or hard plastic containers in the pool area and enforce this rule.
- Display a sign prohibiting children from using the pool without adult supervision.
- Post and enforce pool hours.
- Post a notice requiring all swimmers to shower before using the pool.
- Prohibit alcoholic beverages in the pool area and post signs to that effect. Many major pool accidents are alcohol related.
- If your property has many international guests, write signs and markings in appropriate foreign languages, as well as in English.

Source: *Hospitality Law,* LRP Publications. Used with permission.

pump. Furthermore, dual drains, which reduce the suction at any given drain, are becoming more common.

A critical element in any hospitality facility is the establishment and implementation of an effective preventive maintenance program. Such a program should include a regular inspection ensuring that drain covers are held firmly in place (preferably with screws) and are not broken.

Even when not required by law in a particular property's jurisdiction, certain procedures may increase pool safety and reduce the likelihood of an accident that could result in the injury or death of a guest and liability on the part of the property. For example, fencing of a sufficient height around a pool may make it difficult for small children to climb over it. In the pool itself, some properties use float lines to separate the shallow and deep ends of the pool. (Such lines can also provide helpful handholds for swimmers who find themselves in distress.) Pool depth markings can appear on both the deck and the side of the pool above the water level in clearly visible characters. Properties may wish to mark pool depth in both feet and meters, especially if they have a large number of international guests. Depth markings should be accurate—many diving accidents occur in water that is shallower than marked.

Swimming pool signage should be posted around the pool area and written in letters large enough to be easily read. The signage might point out any number of instructions for pool users, though the instructions should be concise; guests might not read instructions that are too lengthy. Signage may point out, among other items determined by the property and the laws of its jurisdiction, the hours the pool is open; that the pool is for the use of registered guests only (if this is the case); that children should be accompanied by an adult; that users swim at their own risk; that running, horseplay, and diving (if appropriate) are prohibited; and either that the property has no lifeguard or (in properties that do have lifeguards) that swimming is not allowed unless a lifeguard is on duty (if this is the case).

Some properties do not serve alcohol at poolside and do not allow visibly intoxicated guests to use the pool. In addition, many properties keep glass out of the pool area.

When lifeguards are required or employed, some jurisdictions require them to be certified in rescue procedures.

Some properties inform guests who check in with children that children are not allowed to use the pool without parental supervision. Guests may be asked to sign a form indicating that they have read and understood the policy.

Police the pool area even when closed, and enforce the pool's posted hours of operation. Assume guests will try to use the facility other than during the pool hours. Increase pool safety vigilance during times of increased use.

Special groups, such as disabled persons, may require special assistance. The Americans with Disabilities Act (ADA) requires that there be special devices to assist guests with disabilities in using the pool. Seek professional advice in installing devices that will be effective and acceptable to the disabled community.

Special occasions, such as athletic competitions, prom nights, or other social events where out-of-town teams and visitors may be staying at the property, may also require special attention.

A concern of a different nature involves developing procedures for issuing and retrieving towels. Properties with pools (or, for that matter, with beach facilities) may lose a large number of towels if effective towel service procedures are not in place. Some properties have pool or beach attendants list all towels issued by guest name and room number; towel returns are then checked against this list.

Health Clubs and Jogging Trails

Health clubs and jogging trails are becoming increasingly popular. Many properties have installed or are installing exercise equipment for guest use. Properties that offer these services can take steps to reduce both the possibility of injuries to guests and the property's potential liability for such injuries.

Many properties with health clubs post a disclaimer and/or have guests sign a release stating that the guest is using the facilities at his or her own risk. Some jurisdictions, however, do not recognize such exculpatory agreements. Consult legal counsel.

In addition to containing a disclaimer stating that the guest is exercising at his or her own risk, signage in an exercise room may make a number of points:

- Guests should consult their physicians before exercising and follow their advice. Guests should not over-exercise.

- The improper use of exercise equipment can result in injury. Equipment should be used carefully and only for its intended purpose.

- If the room is not supervised, guests should not exercise alone.

- If the manufacturer of the equipment provides written instructions for its use, they should be posted and guests should be directed to read them.

- If the property has a minimum age requirement for the use of the exercise facilities, this requirement should be posted.

Guests sometimes do not know their limits. If the property has an exercise room attendant, guests may ask the attendant for advice concerning an appropriate exercise program. Professional advice in a fitness program should only be given by a qualified individual. An attendant should not be permitted to test a guest's heart rate and blood pressure and then recommend a program of physical exercise. If a guest suffers a heart attack while following the program, a property could face liability for the injury or death because the attendant was not medically qualified to assess the victim's overall health in recommending a physical fitness program. Guests should be urged to consult their physicians concerning whether they are physically able to meet the regimen of an exercise program.

If the property decides to offer aerobics classes, similar care for the guests' welfare should be taken. The instructor should be qualified to teach. He or she should not give any medical advice; participants should be advised to consult their personal physicians. Ideally, perhaps, the instructor will be an outside, independent contractor willing to insure against personal injury claims. Often, however, lodging properties allow employees to teach aerobics classes. Since an employer may be held liable for the acts of an employee acting within the scope of his or her employment, care should be taken to ensure that the employee is indeed qualified to teach such a class.

The lodging property is responsible for maintaining any equipment in the health club. The attendant (or other designated employee in properties that do not use an attendant) should check the equipment frequently to make sure that it is working properly and is safe for guest use. Properties that do not use an attendant sometimes place a telephone in the exercise room and post a number to call for assistance.

Properties offering saunas and hot tub whirlpools should post instructions for the use of these items. For example, guests with heart disease, high or low blood pressure, diabetes, or who are pregnant or under medication should be instructed not to use a whirlpool without a doctor's permission. People who fatigue easily should be requested not to use a sauna. Sauna and whirlpool companies or physicians may inform the property that users should not exceed a certain length of time of continuous use. This time limit may be posted for the guests' information. These sources can also indicate an appropriate temperature for saunas and whirlpools.

Other instructions might include directing guests to shower before entering a whirlpool. No pets should be allowed in the sauna or whirlpool. There should be no jumping or diving into a whirlpool. If children need to be accompanied by an adult, this can be noted.

It is critical that the unit and its water be maintained in a sanitary condition. Bacteria, viruses, or skin diseases may flourish in hot water if special cleaning and sanitizing are not provided on a continuing basis.

Jogging trails present a different potential problem. Many jogging trails leave the hotel or motel premises to wind their way through any number of areas not under the control of the property. Even trails that stay on hotel or motel property cannot always be perfectly maintained or protected from all possible hazards. For this reason, some properties choose not to post "recommended" or "approved" jogging trails for their guests. A property that does suggest jogging trails should tell its guests that it cannot guarantee the safety of anyone using the trail in any respect and that the guest assumes all risk. If rules and warnings are posted, guests should be told to heed them. If the property becomes aware of any specific dangers associated with a jogging trail (such as traffic problems, construction, or assaults), it should warn the guests of these known dangers. Failure to do so may result in liability.

Casino and Gaming Security

Casino and gaming facilities present additional challenges for protecting guests and employees. Many of these facilities are integrated with a large hotel, which may have as many as 5,000 or more rooms.

Many gaming operations are overseen by special state gaming commissions. Because of the commissions' requirements, gaming operations often are required to implement rigorous hiring procedures. This is a definite benefit for establishments that deal so openly with guest and operation assets. In addition, state gaming commissions typically require that there be armed, plainclothes state police officers on the casino floor. (It should be noted that 95 percent of a casino's own security officers are unarmed.)

The security function includes the casino as well as any guestrooms; meeting rooms; banquet, restaurant, and other food and beverage services; theme parks and attractions; and special amenities for "high rollers," which may include penthouse apartments, separate garden units, or other elaborate and sequestered accommodations.

A variety of crimes must be considered and planned for. What level of protection should be provided for big winners? What cooperative initiatives should be employed when the casino bank (cash cage or cash call window) becomes the target of gangs from neighboring metropolitan areas or when known criminals attempt to make the rounds of the local establishments? Larceny and pickpockets are continuing problems. Prostitution may be a problem. Parking-lot altercations, assaults, and the use of weapons are further concerns.

In coping with these potential incidents, the regulatory commissions are invaluable sources of information. They also can provide oversight for coordinating strategies. For example, when one gang took action against a casino bank, there was a cooperative venture involving the commission and casinos that overcame the gang's numerical superiority when it hit a facility and led to multiple arrests and resolution of the problem. It also led to construction requirements that included bars as part of the casino bank.

It is common practice to rotate security staff between the casino and hotel or other units. This protects against criminal collusion between the security staff and other staff members of the organization.

Surveillance capability and continuous monitoring are the hallmarks of gaming security. Contact between the surveillance facility and the "floor" should be uninterrupted, with security personnel watching the games for the rate of play and the amount played. They must also be alert to a dealer who may be compromised or tempted to collude with a player or players.

Surveillance is one of only two departments that typically does not report directly to the president/CEO of the property. The other department is internal audit. Both departments report to the audit committee of the board of directors. This is done to prevent white-collar and executive-level crime.

The advances in technology have become a double-edged sword. Counterfeiters have been able to so effectively duplicate tokens that it has become difficult for the "house" to detect counterfeit from legitimate tokens. The metal content, and the exact size, shape, indentations, weight, and so on are all readily achieved with the high-tech equipment and systems available to anyone with the purchase price.

Children under 18 are not allowed on the casino floor. As a result, they often are allowed to move through various areas of the property unattended, while their parents gamble. In May 1997, seven-year-old Sherrice Iverson was raped and murdered at a Nevada casino while her father, LeRoy, gambled. Ironically, LeRoy, his teenage son, and Sherrice had been told to leave another casino hours earlier because the father was not supervising his children. In the months following her daughter's death—and after a murder suspect already was in police custody—Sherrice's mother brought a wrongful death lawsuit against the casino, claiming that the resort bore some responsibility because it caters to adults with children (although minors are excluded from many areas of the casino). The hotel, the suit alleged, "purposely provides facilities and circumstances attractive to minors ... and to encourage parents to separate from their children." Notably, the lawsuit also contended that the casino's extensive security "creates an illusory impression of high security throughout the hotel." It appears that a visible security presence may actually be interpreted by some as a liability unless it is supplemented with clear, continually reinforced security messages aimed directly at guests.

The development of "family" attractions to supplement the casino and gaming facilities has involved the investment of hundreds of millions of dollars. This results in an increased number of minors in a property that includes both a large casino and a family attraction. The security officers must be trained in the effective handling of this security challenge.

Underage gambling is illegal and can compromise the gaming license for a casino. Any individual who seems to be underage must be requested to provide a valid proof of age. Senior management must consider alternative action for insuring the safety and security of the underage person who has just been directed from the casino floor and who has not been registered for any family program that may be available at the casino.

Finally, casino and gaming security personnel should be trained in CPR and basic first aid. In the late 1990s, the casino and gaming industry introduced the use of automatic external defibrillators (AEDs) for the treatment of sudden cardiac arrest. At properties equipped with such devices, security staff should be thoroughly trained in their use. "Good Samaritan" legislation has been enacted in several states and is under review in others to protect against litigation aimed at an individual who was properly trained and used the AED correctly but was unable to resuscitate the victim.

Report Writing and Recordkeeping

While the physical presence of security personnel may serve as a deterrent to some crime, the findings and observations of the personnel on patrol will contribute most effectively to the success of the security program when the information gathered on patrol is properly recorded and presented. Such reports may alert security and management officials to a security problem. For example, a patrolling security officer may note such things as burned-out lights, broken locks, or safety hazards. When such findings are communicated to management, the departments responsible for dealing with the problem may take appropriate steps.

Another value of an effective recordkeeping system is that it may help a property discover if a certain type of security incident is more prevalent than others. If this is the case, the property can focus attention on that particular problem. Also, records may be a great asset when a lawsuit is filed in response to an incident.

The more information available to a property about its security problems, the better equipped it will be to address and reduce them. Clearly, one way to learn more about security problems is to keep a detailed record of every incident that occurs. In this way, a history of security-related problem areas and a plan for action can be developed.

Because of the importance of report writing, many properties require their security personnel to possess good writing skills. The importance of neat, clear, concise, objective reports can be explained to security officers, who should realize that their reports may be used in the future by security investigators, law enforcement agencies, and management.

Of course, writing skills alone do not produce good reports. Security personnel need to be trained in how to file appropriate reports. They need to know the types of information to collect and report concerning the various situations they may face. They need to know the appropriate format in which to present the information and who should receive the information.

There are different types of reports that security officers may need to file. The most common is the **daily report (or shift report)**. This report details a security officer's patrols for the day or shift, noting anything out of the ordinary or anything calling for action of some kind. When a security incident occurs on the premises, an **incident report (or special report)** is called for. (See Exhibit 4.) Such reports may be filed for criminal acts such as assault, theft, robbery, embezzlement, fraud, and anything that has resulted in an arrest, and for problems such as guest or employee injuries or deaths, fires, and other safety incidents. Any incident involving the following circumstances should be thoroughly documented:

- A loss or injury to a guest, employee, or other person
- Damage to or destruction of a facility asset
- Any other situation or incident that management feels may be appropriate to document

A security incident report generally contains at least the following information:

- The time and date of the occurrence
- A narrative of the incident—what occurred, when, why, where, and by whom. Identify each person involved and list all witnesses and their addresses. In short, provide all the relevant facts that would assist another person in an investigation. Do not surmise or add subjective comments.
- The amount of the loss, if any
- The time the police were notified, if the incident involves the violation of a law
- The date of the report and its author's signature

Certain security records are confidential and should not be released to anyone. Generally speaking, guest and employee records are confidential by law, and as such should only be released, following review by a property's legal counsel, to an authorized person with a proper court order.

Developing a recordkeeping system that meets the needs of the organization may be of value in the event of litigation. A property may wish to acquire all police reports relating to the incident, along with the incident report. Appropriate file and backup storage capabilities are also important. Records, including records of

Exhibit 4   Incident/Loss Report

INCIDENT/LOSS REPORT	Time _____
	Guest _____ Room _____
	Employee _____ Dept. _____
	Other _____

(Please type or print)

Type of Incident/Loss (Fire, Theft, Disturbance, Etc.)
_____

Person Reporting Incident/Loss (Victim)
Name _____ Phone # _____
Address _____
City/State/Zip _____
Place of Employment _____ Phone # _____

Date & Time of Incident/Loss Date _____ Time _____
Date & Time Hotel Notified Date _____ Time _____
Description of Incident (Who, What, Where, When, Why) _____
_____
_____
_____
_____

Stolen Vehicle _____ | _____ | _____ | _____ | _____ | _____
                  Year   Make   Model   Color   Serial#   License#

Witness to Incident _____ Phone # _____
Value of Property _____
Were Police Notified? _____ By _____
Police Officer's Name & Badge No. _____ Report # _____

Action Taken
General Manager Notified   ☐ Yes ☐ No
Security Notified   ☐ Yes ☐ No
_____ Notified   ☐ Yes ☐ No

Person Taking Report _____
Position/Department _____
Home Phone # _____

daily security officer rounds and special logs, should be held for the length of time recommended by a property's local counsel. Such time intervals may vary from two to seven years.

The expanded use of computers within the lodging industry may be helpful in developing recordkeeping systems for security departments. Careful consideration should be given, however, to the possible security implications of using computers for this purpose. Security protocols should be in place to keep unauthorized individuals from viewing or altering restricted files. This is especially critical if the computer's information is accessible by another computer via either an internal intranet or an external connection to the Internet.

Special Guests and Events

Lodging properties often go out of their way to attract special guests and events. Events such as conventions, meetings, and exhibits are sought for the prestige and profits associated with them, although such events may also increase the potential for security incidents on the premises. In addition, individual properties seek to attract various specialized categories of guests and groups.

When a guest or a group needs or requests additional security, many properties include a clause in the contract stating that the individual or group will be charged for the additional cost. For example, the growth of terrorism may be a factor to consider when booking an individual or group that might attract terrorist actions. The property should evaluate its security preparedness when accepting any group that may involve special security risks. Appropriate agencies should be contacted, especially if the individual would be at a level that would involve the U.S. State Department.

In establishing security measures for special functions or events, the following suggestions might be considered with advice of legal counsel.

- Identify potential problems.
- Accomplish reference checks for groups. Check with prior hotels or convention centers where the group has held functions.
- Determine how to manage a problem group and its functions.

The prevention and containment suggestions for working with problem groups in Exhibit 5 may appear to be less-than-hospitable approaches to handling what could be quite profitable group business. However, these suggestions are for dealing with groups that are known for making trouble. They should not be applied to a respectable and reputable business association or corporation—although various steps could be implemented if incidents warrant them.

Some categories of guests have been recognized as having special characteristics that a lodging property may wish to address. Three of these special categories are guests with disabilities, VIP guests, and youth groups.

Guests with Disabilities

In 1990, the Americans with Disabilities Act (ADA) became law, changing the way in which U.S. businesses employ and serve people with disabilities. There are five

Exhibit 5   Working with Problem Groups

PREVENT:
- Restrict rooms availability.
    1. Do not allow single-night stays.
    2. Charge maximum rates (or time-limited group rates).
    3. Require a significant damage deposit.
    4. Where history and references will support it, deny room rental to some parties under authority of the Innkeepers' Law, which permits denial of occupancy based upon an innkeeper's concern that the presence of the denied individual would not be in the best interest of the property and its guests.
    5. Require credit cards.
    6. Require picture identification.
    7. Have the catering department handle all aspects of ballroom packages.
- Restrict access to hotel guests only.
- Make sure security/police officers maintain a strong, visible presence.
- React quickly when problems occur.

CONTAIN:
- Ask function leader/parents to sign a damage waiver.
- Require managers to be on duty.
- Restrict hotel access to guests only.
- Restrict guestroom floor access; limit the number of persons allowed in guestrooms.
- Have scheduled group functions/events.
- Require groups to police themselves by having their own security. Provide a roster of approved security contract organizations in the community—organizations with which you have a working relationship and whose management and staff may be trusted.
- Require photo identification wherever alcohol is served.
- Allow no outside liquor on the premises.
- Set "quiet hours" in advance and enforce them.
- React to potential problems swiftly and with authority.
- Restrict parking lot access.
- Explain to guests at check-in that eviction may occur if complaints are received.

titles to the law, but two are critical to the hospitality industry. Title I refers to employment issues and is administered by the Equal Employment Opportunity Commission. Title III addresses facility accommodations that affect all employees, guests, and the general public; this section is administered by the U.S. Department of Justice. (It should be noted that Title II—Public Services covers public transportation and includes courtesy van service that may be provided by a lodging facility. For example, all courtesy vans with seating for 17—16 passengers and a driver—must be wheelchair accessible. Additional requirements may apply as well; consult legal counsel.) ADA legislation has a definite impact on costs and includes a potential for litigation and fines. Title III permits action through civil suits when a disabled individual encounters a barrier to ready access. Should a civil penalty be awarded, it must not exceed $50,000 for the first violation or $100,000 for each subsequent violation.

According to the law, "readily achievable" changes must be made to "reasonably accommodate" guests before their arrival. "Readily achievable" has been interpreted as easy to accomplish and able to be provided without too much difficulty or expense. Consequently, what a major chain might achieve may not be achievable by an independent property of smaller size and lesser financial resources. Similarly, "reasonable accommodations" must be provided unless they create a significant difficulty or expense.

When constructing a new lodging establishment, architects should consult the U. S. Department of Justice, Civil Rights Division, for the current requirements. Government sources or knowledgeable consultants on disability accommodation should be involved whenever changes are considered within existing structures. For example, specific requirements for the minimum number of handicapped-accessible spaces in the parking lot, wheelchair-accessible rooms, rooms with roll-in showers, and hearing-impaired rooms should be verified.

As a result of ADA legislation, many properties now have rooms designed specifically for guests with disabilities. Such rooms should include switches, handles, and viewports that are at the correct height for wheelchair users, TDD (Telecommunications Device for the Deaf) equipment for guests with hearing and speech impairments, closed-captioned television, etc.

Emergency evacuation of people with disabilities is a primary concern for security personnel. This is a matter that must be reviewed with local fire authorities. In the event of fire, the fire department may prefer that they be met by a staff member with a full list of disabled persons on the property and their locations. In addition, fire alarms must provide a strobe light to alert those with impaired hearing. A public address system that includes guestrooms permits notice and instructions for guests with visual impairments.

Individual properties should consult with legal counsel with respect to any additional state or local laws that apply to serving guests with disabilities.

The Importance of Folio Information. Many properties develop methods by which the folios of disabled guests may be readily identified to ensure that prompt assistance is provided during an emergency. If an emergency leads to an evacuation of the property, employees may be sent to the rooms of disabled guests to offer assistance. All staff should be prepared to assist local fire and police with the evacuation of guests with wheelchairs, walkers, Seeing Eye dogs, and so on.

If the nature of the handicap is listed on the folio, employees will be better prepared to deal with situations that may arise. For example, if the guest is deaf, the employee will not presume that the room is empty simply because no one responds to knocking at the door. The employee may know to deliver written rather than verbal instruction. Similarly, an employee may offer an arm to a blind person. Some properties choose to give an appropriate key to employees going to assist disabled guests, just in case the guest cannot get to or open the door on his or her own.

VIP Guests

Special cooperation and liaison between all departments is critical when VIP guests are at a property. Coordination between front service, food service, sales, housekeeping, security, and the executive office is essential.

VIP guests may require additional security personnel. Some well-known figures may wish to keep a very low profile, and all staff should be instructed on how to appropriately respond to inquiring media and the general public. If the guest has a personal security staff, armed or otherwise, arrangements and accommodations may need to be made by the property and the local police. If the individual is controversial, the property may wish to request the assistance of the local police, the FBI, or some other authority. Properties expecting the arrival of a controversial guest may also want to review emergency evacuation and bomb threat procedures with their employees before the guest arrives.

Youth Groups

Depending upon the supervision provided by the adult leadership of a youth group, such a group may present a problem with vandalism and/or excessive noise that may disturb other guests. The security staff should develop a plan of action that will be of benefit to all parties—the group, the property, and the other guests. Planning and a close liaison with the adult leaders of the youth group will make a controlled group experience more likely. Properties may consider whether they wish to add an insurance premium or some other method of reimbursement to the guest group's contract to cover any property damaged through vandalism or pranks. However, individual properties should first consult with legal counsel to ensure that such conditions do not constitute age discrimination in jurisdictions where it is prohibited.

In addition to causing some security incidents, young people may in some cases be the targets of various types of criminal actions.

Conventions, Meetings, and Exhibits

Conventions, meetings, and exhibits are major functions that involve close cooperation among all departments and careful administrative attention. Assembling a large number of guests, exhibitors, and members of the general public also involves a number of special security considerations. The nature and number of guests and exhibits and the degree of public involvement may make it necessary to supplement the security staff. The sales department—which usually will be informed of any special group needs when the event is booked—can play an important initial role in coordinating the information that every other department will need to know in order to plan the most efficient and secure method of handling the convention, group, or exhibit.

Analyzing the nature of the group may also help in forecasting potential problems. Is the group controversial? Does the group include guests with special needs? Will there be a potential problem with alcohol consumption? If a school group is coming on tour, what is the ratio of adults to students? Have there been prior experiences with the group?

If exhibits are involved, the hotel or motel should determine its liability for them. Protection may be provided by the group or the property (depending on the stipulations of the contract and applicable law) from the time the exhibits arrive until they are dismantled and leave the premises. When special valuables are involved, such as an exhibition of jewelry, it may be advisable to require the exhibitors to provide additional contract security and to coordinate security with the local police. Properties doing this might consider obtaining a named insured agreement and a certificate of insurance. The contracts with exhibitors may also specifically note the exhibitors' responsibility for the receipt and shipment of their own materials.

An exhibit area should be secured when exhibitors and viewers are not present. It may be advisable to supervise cleaning personnel. Closed-circuit television (which is most useful in areas where there should be no motion) can, where available, be used to supplement the security effort when the exhibit area is closed.

Experience indicates that the heaviest loss of exhibits and exhibit materials occurs during shipment prior to installation at the assigned area and during the breakdown and shipment of exhibits to their next destination. A spot-check of empty containers and cartons as they are removed from the exhibit area during setup may deter or discover the attempted theft of exhibits. The contract with exhibit planners may include provisions for extra funds for securing exhibits during these critical periods.

Some properties suggest to exhibitors that they use some sort of badge system. Since a great number of extra personnel may be present, it may be difficult to distinguish between individuals who have a legitimate right to be on the premises and those who do not. If the hotel or motel has contracted to provide some of the extra personnel, the property may choose to use a badge system as a matter of policy.

One exit should be established for the control of hand-carried items removed by exhibitors from the exhibit area. The exhibit or convention manager may choose to place at this control point a list containing the signatures of persons qualified to remove hand-carried materials. A pass system under the control of the organization conducting the exhibition may also help increase security, even when the hotel or motel is directly involved in the setup, breakdown, and general security of the exhibits and the exhibit area.

When a convention or exhibit comes to a property, the convention or exhibit area is not the only area that may experience greater security problems. Perimeter, parking area, and guestroom incidents may also increase. Security personnel should be alert to people found in guestroom areas who seem to be loitering or present without a legitimate reason. (Remember that an unregistered person, unless the guest of a registered guest present at the time, is a trespasser.) If a person is a legitimate guest in need of helpful directions, a security officer can offer assistance; if the person is not a guest, he or she should be asked to provide identification and then escorted from the area.

Sometimes, meetings take place at lodging properties that require special security considerations. Such meetings, whether political or business, may call for lock changes just prior to the group's arrival, special identification for the attendees, and steps to help ensure that the business conducted in the meeting room cannot be overheard. Some meeting planners may ask that rooms next to the meeting room be left unoccupied; they may even choose to rent them simply for that purpose. Such groups may bring their own security personnel and equipment. When this happens, there should be clear communication beforehand between the group and the property about who is responsible for what. The local police may even become involved, depending on the importance and sensitivity of the meeting. "Sweeps" to debug the meeting room may be provided, along with other high-tech security measures.

Special Safety Considerations. Another aspect of convention, meeting, and exhibit management involves safety. The added construction and equipment used for some of these events may present a number of potential safety hazards.

Electrical outlets should be adequate for the power demands being made on them. Sufficient power and proper fuses should be used. Potential tripping hazards (such as electric wires and cables that run along the floor and platform areas, torn carpeting, and loose tiles) should be avoided. When it is impossible to provide overhead connections, wires can be placed in channels under carpeted areas in a manner that minimizes the heights of the ridge formed. Wires may be placed under carpeting with something to protect them from the damage that may be caused by people walking on them or by wheeled equipment moving over them.

Assembling platforms, daises, and podiums may also pose problems. Units that fit together to form a raised surface should form a rigid and interlocked platform surface. Where steps are required to reach the platform level, the steps should be secured to the side of the platform; a sturdy handrail may be provided. The Americans with Disabilities Act states that the platform or dais must be accessible by a ramp or lift. The ramp or lift should not block access to an aisle or the emergency exit.

Platform units should be constructed with adequate space requirements in mind. Platforms should have enough room to allow food servers (when appropriate) and members of the meeting to pass behind those seated without danger of falling from the platform or bumping the chairs of those seated.

A property may wish to perform periodic inspections of any chairs, tables, platforms, easels, and other equipment used for meetings. Since these items are constantly moved from room to room throughout the property, there may be an increased possibility for broken parts, slivers, and rough edges to develop. When water glasses are provided, the glasses should be inspected for chips or cracks. Broken and chipped glasses should be discarded.

A property should provide adequate, well-lighted exits that are properly marked and kept clear at all times. Platforms and exhibits should not block access to an exit. Draperies or decorations should not obscure the exit sign or exit access.

If any special flags or banners are used by a visiting group, they should be securely fastened. Employees should have access to safe ladders when installing these flags and banners. If the decorations are extensive and require an outside contractor who must use scaffolding, management should consider obtaining a special insurance certificate from the contractor that provides named insured protection, in the event of injuries to the contractor's employees, the property's employees or guests, or the public through the negligence of the contractor or his or her employees.

A property should ensure that adequate and appropriate fire extinguishing equipment is readily available. It should also consider reviewing the property's emergency evacuation plan for a convention or exhibit area with the management of the convention or exhibition. The potential for injury is likely to be reduced when all parties know in advance what to do and whose directions to follow in an emergency evacuation.

Endnotes

1. New York Gen. Oblig. Law SS 11-101.
2. For a detailed examination of the responsible service of alcohol, see *Controlling Alcohol Risks Effectively* (East Lansing, Mich.: Educational Institute of the American Hotel & Motel Association, 1993).

Key Terms

bonding—Insuring for protection from employee theft, usually provided through a blanket bond that specifies job classifications rather than individuals. For an additional premium, the policy may be endorsed to cover theft by and/or excess fidelity coverage on specific employees. This may be desirable for employees with significant access to the operation's assets.

daily report (or shift report)—Details a security officer's patrols for the day or shift, noting anything out of the ordinary or anything calling for action of some kind.

dram shop acts—Legislation establishing third-party liability for accidents involving intoxicated drivers. Such laws often hold that bartenders, servers, and owners can be jointly held liable if they unlawfully sell alcoholic everages to a minor or an intoxicated person who then causes injury to others.

exit interviews—Meetings conducted between the employer and an employee leaving the organization that attempts to identify the factors that have led to the employee's decision to leave.

honesty exams—Tests prepared by outside organizations, administered at a hotel or motel, and returned to the source organization for evaluation.

incident report (or special report)—Written when a security incident occurs on the premises.

kickbacks—Money or services paid to unethical employees who work in collusion with someone from a supplier's company. For example, higher-than-necessary prices may be charged by the supplier and approved by the hotel employee. Once the supplier is paid, the hotel employee and his or her contact in the supplier's company split the remaining money.

perpetual inventory—Keeping a list of all items as they are received for storage and issued from storage. This inventory will reveal what *should* be in the storeroom.

physical inventory—Counting all items in a storage area. This inventory will reveal what actually is in the storeroom.

processing thefts—Occur when suppliers request payment for an invoice more than once. A hotel or motel needs an effective internal control system to verify whether an invoice has already been paid or not.

spotter—A contracted employee of the hotel or restaurant or someone from an outside contract organization who visits a bar, poses as a guest, and watches the activities of the bar staff.

Review Questions

1. What are some of the losses likely to affect a hospitality operation?
2. How can hotels respond to employee theft?
3. What can the human resources department do to screen potential employees?
4. What is an exit interview? How can it be useful?
5. Should guests be able to make direct 911 calls from the guestroom? Why or why not?
6. What security procedures should housekeeping staff follow when cleaning a guestroom?
7. Why is "division of duties" considered the most important principle of internal control?
8. What steps can hotels take to make swimming pool areas more safe?
9. Why are accurate reports and records important to an operation's overall security/safety program?
10. What actions can a hotel take in response to a problem group that is already on-site?

Internet Sites

For more information, visit the following Internet sites. Remember that Internet addresses can change without notice.

ADA Requirements—Architecture/new construction
http://www.usdoj.gov/crt/ada/adahom1.htm

Equal Employment Opportunity Commission (EEOC)
http://www.eeoc.gov

IMI Data Search, Inc. (Employee Background Checks)
http://www.imidatasearch.com

National Spa & Pool Institute (NSPI)
http://www.nspi.org

Workplace Violence Research Institute
http://noworkviolence.com

Case Study

Soccer and Spice and Everything Chaotic

Michael Shepherd, the front desk manager at The Greenwood Hotel & Suites, caught up with Emily Gresch, the food and beverage manager, as they walked to the weekly staff meeting. They had both started at the 500-room full-service hotel on the same day six years ago. They'd remained friends, building a network of communication that helped their departments work together in new ways.

"So, Emily," Michael grinned, "which one of us do you think is in trouble—they've got the director of security in on this week's meeting."

"No kidding?" she asked. "I don't think I've seen Hannah at a meeting in the five years she's worked here. Maybe they're finally going to expand the electronic locking system to the employee areas and she's going to train us on it."

"If it's new equipment, it better be an upgrade to the point-of-sale system so we don't keep losing so much revenue on guests who don't tell our front desk agents that they ate at our $40 Sunday brunch buffet before checking out."

Michael held the door open for Emily as they arrived at the meeting room. They took their seats and after a few minutes of small talk, Jacob Kerr, the general manager, stood up and started the meeting. This was Jacob's second month at the property; he'd been transferred to The Greenwood from a similar sized property in a smaller town. He reviewed the sales and financial reports of the past week, then turned the meeting over to Samantha Zimmerman, the director of sales.

"I've got some good news and some bad news," Samantha began. Emily and Michael covertly exchanged amused glances—the sales director invariably tried to cushion any announcements of hardships on other departments with a glowing report of what wonderful work she'd done to increase the hotel's revenue.

"I've managed to bring back a group that is going to book 420 of our 500 rooms. They'll be here for two nights during our slow time and will be using our banquet services for at least one dinner. I was also able to sell them on a group rate that was only $30 off our rack rate, so our REVPAR will still be good."

"That sounds fantastic," Michael said.

"What's the bad news?" asked Emily.

The GM's lips twitched into a quirky smile, "The group is National Youth Soccer League and they're here for a rock concert, the Spice Girls, being held at the arena down the street."

Nearly every department head that had been with the hotel for longer than a year groaned. "Those are the folks that trashed the rooms last year," Ashley, the chief engineer, complained. "It took us almost a week to get all of our rooms back into rentable condition."

"We had to write off several rooms because they were signed for by teenagers who decided they weren't going to pay," said Matthew, the controller. "We never should have allowed a minor to register for a room—it's against our corporate policy. Minors can't be legally held to a contract."

"They also made a mess of the lobby," Michael said. "On Sunday morning they dropped all their luggage in the lobby and took off for breakfast. Our regular guests could barely get through to the check-out desk. Then one of the kids got angry when his bag was stolen."

"I seem to remember one of my room attendants telling me about this group," Brandon said. Brandon had assumed the position of executive housekeeper two months after the soccer group had last stayed at the hotel. "She told me that she found evidence of more than a dozen people staying in one room."

Samantha stood, bringing her fist down on the table. "Well, they weren't too thrilled with us either. I had to work really hard to get them to come back. It's a great piece of business, but we'll never get it again if we don't fix the problems that happened last time. Here's a list of the problems that the meeting planner said we needed to fix." Samantha walked around the table, giving everyone a sheet of paper. The list read:

- Several guests had items stolen from their rooms.
- The hotel was overcrowded.
- There was no parking in the hotel lot.
- The swimming pool was dirty.
- There was too much noise at night and the response from the front desk was unacceptable.
- There were too many kids that weren't a part of our group.
- There were funny smells coming from some of the rooms. We don't want our kids exposed to drugs.

"Of course the pool was dirty," muttered Ashley, the chief engineer. "Every kid and his 10 closest friends were using it. We should have shut it down or not let so many kids use it."

Hannah, who had been quietly taking notes throughout the meeting, stood up as the other department managers began to grumble. "I'm here at Jacob's request. Last year, the security staff did have to respond to a lot of problems with this group. But by the time we got involved things were out of control. This year, we are going to coordinate the security efforts among the departments to ensure that this group is taken care of and that The Greenwood continues to live up to its reputation as the place where guests get service that astounds."

"We're going to make sure our mistakes of last year are not repeated," Jacob said. "Which means that each of you will take responsibility for the security issues in your department. Hannah is going to assign responsibility and we'll evaluate the effectiveness of everyone's security plan after the event is over."

Hannah chewed on her lower lip, wishing Jacob hadn't taken the hard-line approach so early. "All of our departments can contribute to making sure that both our guests and the property are safe. We all have some great ideas on how to maintain security. Let's take a quick look at some of these issues and we can brainstorm ways to handle each of them. Then as each department develops its plan, I'll work with you to coordinate with other departments. Let's start with the room theft."

"Austin, the group's president, said that three different players had items taken from their rooms," Samantha said. "As I remember, one of those incidents involved a room attendant getting shoved against her cart while some punk grabbed a leather jacket in the closet and ran off with it. I think one of the other thefts also occurred while the room was being cleaned."

"There's an area with an easy solution," Ashley said. "Just have the room attendants close the door while they clean. I've never understood why the doors are left open anyway. We certainly don't have maintenance staff leave the door open when they work on the room."

"That's because you don't have to worry as much about your maintenance staff getting assaulted," Brandon said. "If you close the door, there's no way to tell if a room attendant is in trouble. Right now, a closed door with a room attendant cart in front of it is a warning sign."

"Perhaps you should adopt a team-based paradigm," suggested Madison, the human resources director.

"Come on, Madison," Brandon said. "You've interviewed these folks. If I put two of them in the same room, they'll be chattering the whole time. And with the door shut, they'll probably have the TV on the whole time so they don't miss their soaps."

Hannah raised her eyebrows, wondering if this attitude contributed to the high turnover among room attendants. "Does it really matter if they talk or watch TV?" she asked. "Just give them their room assignments and make sure they meet their quota of rooms and that the rooms are up to standard. Let them talk while they're cleaning."

"It is more productive to focus on outcome rather than process," Madison encouraged.

Brandon sighed, "I suppose I could test it for a week before the group checks in."

"So housekeeping will keep room doors shut," Hannah said. "That's a good start. Are there any other issues that we need to add to the list that Samantha passed out?"

"We need some sort of crowd control procedures," Michael said. "Last year we must have had a thousand people in the hotel, and they were all as rowdy as the crowd in Times Square on the eve of the millennium."

"We could put wrist bands on registered guests," suggested Megan. "If the only way they can get into the hotel is with an wrist band, that should control access to the property."

"We did use wrist bands last year," Emily said. "It didn't work."

"Actually, I think it could work," Michael said. "The problem was that we were giving away too many wrist bands. There was no control over how many wrist bands were issued. One of the valets told me that he saw some kids tossing them out the window to their friends—they must have found some way to slip them off their wrists—or they simply didn't go out into the lobby again once they were in the hotel."

"Let's order wrist bands that can be removed only if they're broken," Madison suggested.

"That's going to go over real well with my regulars," Michael said. "I've got three executives that come stay with us one night a week—they brought in $100,000 last year. I'm supposed to tell the CEO of a Fortune 500 company that she's got to wear a toe tag?"

"Here's another issue for you," Emily said. "Last year we must have had every pizza joint in the city delivering to our hotel. Not only did that hurt our food and beverage revenue, but we had delivery kids wandering the hotel. It can't be good security to have people wandering the halls when we have no way of keeping track of them."

"So let's just send them to the front desk, and have a front desk agent call the room and have someone come and pick the meal up," Megan said.

"That's a nice idea," Michael responded. "Except the guests usually will give their room number to the delivery people and they'll go right up to the room."

"Ah, but they won't be able to get in without wrist bands," Hannah said. "We'll just have the security people at the doors direct any delivery people to the front desk."

"Better make that the bell stand," Michael said. "They have a courtesy phone and can take care of it without disrupting check-ins. Besides, if the guest doesn't want to come down to the lobby, we could always have a bell attendant deliver it instead of the outside vendor."

"Good idea," Hannah said. "What other issues are there?"

"We've got to be more careful about minors abusing alcohol in their rooms," Emily said. "I can make sure my staff doesn't sell alcohol to minors, but last year they were bringing their own in."

"Anyone checking in with a cooler is going to be trouble," Ashley said. "I could tell there were a few drunken parties going on by the number of curtains that got used as bed sheets."

"We also need to limit the number of false alarms," Matthew said. "We got fined by the fire department last year because they had to respond to four false fire alarms that some kids decided to set off at all hours of the night."

"Why don't we just turn the alarms off during the event?" Brandon suggested.

"Perhaps because it would violate federal, state, *and* local law," Ashley shot back.

"Speaking of alarms," Hannah spoke up quickly. "We need to make sure that all of our emergency procedures are in place. Everyone needs to be clear on evacuation plans and how to handle medical emergencies. Madison, could you make sure there is a training checklist for all employees on our emergency response plans? Perhaps we could plan a drill for the week before the event."

By the end of the meeting, each department head had made an appointment with Hannah to set up security plans for the upcoming event. Samantha left to assure the meeting planner that the event would be the best ever.

Discussion Questions

1. What are the issues that each department's security plan needs to address?
2. What would be some of the responses to those issues?

Case Number: 3874CA

The following industry experts helped generate and develop this case: Wendell Couch, ARM, CHA, Director of Technical Services for the Risk Management Department of Bass Hotels & Resorts; and Raymond C. Ellis, Jr., CHE, CHTP, CLSD, Professor, Conrad N. Hilton College, University of Houston, Director, Loss Prevention Management Institute.

Case Study

Is It Getting Hot in Here?

Scenario #1: Why Train?

Rudy Jamison is the general manager of the newly remodeled Briarwood Inn. He is looking through the upcoming training schedule and sees that a fire extinguisher session is planned for the following month. Since the renovation brought the hotel up to current fire codes with the installation of a fully automated sprinkler system, Rudy doesn't feel the need for any additional expenses, like fire-related training sessions. When he announces at the weekly management meeting that he is canceling the session, everyone is shocked. The security manager tries to convince him that the training session is critical, but Rudy seems set in his ways and doesn't seem about to change his mind.

Scenario #2: Flaming Dessert

Lucas Romalin, a soon-to-be graduate of a local culinary arts program, was hired as a part-time server in the dining room of the Lancelot Lodge. When one of his tables ordered Bananas Foster, he was in his glory—he just loved the tableside flambé. He was a showman at heart, and enjoyed the reactions of guests when the flames leapt from the dessert cart. This particular table seemed to be in a partying mood, so Lucas doubled the amount of rum (he had also discovered the better the show, the bigger the tip!). However, this time, when he lit the match, the overabundance of alcohol and fumes caused the flame to burst upwards about three feet. Taken completely by surprise, Lucas stood momentarily stupefied as the drapes caught on fire. Then, in the ensuing commotion, Lucas tipped the burning dessert plate onto a guest's lap.

Scenario #3: Fire in the Guestroom

Julie, a seasoned front desk agent, is taking a breather in what otherwise has been a hectic morning. Then, this frantic call comes in from a guestroom: "There's a fire in my room—I dropped a cigarette into the wastebasket and it just caught on fire. Oh no! Now it's spreading to the drapes! What do I do?"

Scenario #4: Rags to Ruin

Gerrett Miller and Ronnie Jenkins still can't believe the hotel's entire laundry facility had been gutted from a fire the previous day.

"What do you think could have possibly caused this?" asks Ronnie.

"Well, my first instinct is always the lint traps. Those little devils will get you when you're not paying attention."

"No, it can't be that—we clean them between each load."

Gerrett paused, his mind searching for any plausible idea. Then it hit him. "What was the last load washed? It wasn't kitchen rags, by chance, was it?"

"As a matter of fact, it was. But I don't think that could be the reason. I mean, I did the same thing I always do—I put the rags straight into the washer and then the dryer. Then I set the timer and left. Nothing unusual there."

"I'm not so sure about that, Ronnie. I think we've found the problem."

Discussion Questions

1. *Scenario #1: Why Train?*

    How should the security manager go about convincing the GM to reinstate the fire extinguisher training session?

2. *Scenario #2: Flaming Dessert*

    What are the property's options for future flambés?

3. *Scenario #3: Fire in the Guestroom*

    What immediate instructions should Julie give the guest and what further action should Julie take?

4. *Scenario #4: Rags to Ruin*

    What was wrong with the laundering process Ronnie used and what needs to be changed?

Case Number: 3874CB

The following industry experts helped generate and develop this case: Wendell Couch, ARM, CHA, Director of Technical Services for the Risk Management Department of Bass Hotels & Resorts; and Raymond C. Ellis, Jr., CHE, CHTP, CLSD, Professor, Conrad N. Hilton College, University of Houston, Director, Loss Prevention Management Institute.

REVIEW QUIZ

When you feel you have covered all of the material in this chapter, answer these questions. Choose the *best* answer.

1. Which of the following statements is *true?*

   a. Employees guilty of theft should be prosecuted.
   b. Employee theft should result in immediate dismissal.
   c. All employees should be treated equally.
   d. Employees steal primarily because of personal need.

2. Bonding is:

   a. an access-limiting device.
   b. insurance against employee theft.
   c. a feature of various lock mechanisms.
   d. an inventory system.

3. The possibility of improper guestroom access may be reduced by:

   a. housekeeping personnel.
   b. front desk personnel.
   c. security officers.
   d. all of the above.

4. Which of the following statements is *false?*

   a. Only registered guests should be allowed to use a hotel swimming pool.
   b. The division between shallow and deep ends of the pool should be obvious.
   c. A pool telephone should connect to an outside line, not to the front desk.
   d. Pool safety is only a concern when the pool is officially open for use.

5. A security incident report should include all of the following *except:*

   a. the location of the general manager during the incident.
   b. the amount of loss involved.
   c. the signature of the report's author.
   d. the time the police were notified.

6. All of the following are guestroom changes implemented as a result of ADA legislation *except:*

   a. viewports at wheelchair height.
   b. a television remote control.
   c. available TDD equipment.
   d. wider doorways into guestrooms and bathrooms.

REVIEW QUIZ *(continued)*

7. Experience indicates that most thefts of exhibits occur:

    a. during the hour each day just before the exhibition opens.
    b. during the exhibition.
    c. during breakdown and shipment to the next destination.
    d. during the lunch hour, when security typically is lax.

Answer Key: 1-c-C1, 2-b-C1, 3-d-C1, 4-d-C2, 5-a-C3, 6-b-C4, 7-c-C5

Each question is linked to a competency. Competencies are listed on the first page of the chapter. An answer reading 3-b-C4 translates to:

  3: the question number
  b: the correct answer
 C4: the competency number

Chapter 5 Outline

Accounting Control Procedures
    Inventory Control
    Payroll Procedures and Concerns
    Sequential Numbering Systems
    Bank Deposits
Physical Protection of the Accounting Function
Cashiering Procedures
Establishing Credit Policies and Procedures
    Credit Cards
    Checks
    Denying Credit to a Guest
    Guest Registration and Check-out
Computer Security
    Accountability
    Auditability
    System Integrity
    Cost Effectiveness
    Ease of Implementation
    Policy Compliance
An Internal Audit Program

Competencies

1. Describe control procedures and physical protection for the accounting function. (pp. 261–264)

2. Identify security considerations for handling credit cards and checks. (pp. 265–271)

3. Demonstrate appropriate steps for denying credit to guests. (pp. 271–272)

4. Describe security concerns when handling reservations, registration, and check-out. (pp. 272–274)

5. Explain key issues affecting computer security in a hospitality environment. (pp. 274–280)

6. Describe the benefits and objectives of establishing an internal audit program. (pp. 280–283)

5
The Protection of Funds

WHETHER IN THE form of cash, credit card receipts, or incoming and outgoing checks, a lodging property regularly deals with substantial amounts of funds. If these monetary assets are not protected, profitability may be jeopardized.

Protecting funds is a primary responsibility of the accounting department, though other departments—particularly the front office—play important contributing roles in protecting certain financial assets.

The accounting department (or accounting function, in properties that do not have an actual accounting department) is responsible for overseeing the property's payroll, keeping careful records, and taking appropriate actions concerning accounts receivable and accounts payable. It also is typically at least partially (and sometimes solely) responsible for conducting inventories of the storerooms in the various departments of a property and for either overseeing or performing the purchasing and receiving functions. It also is sometimes responsible for working with management to establish the credit and cash handling policies for the business. Due to increasing dependence on computers for performing many of these tasks, computer security is another important concern of the accounting function.

Accounting employees play a significant role in protecting a property's financial assets. However, because of their central role in overseeing the financial transactions of every department and in discovering any theft of assets occurring on the premises, they themselves are often in a better position to embezzle assets than most other employees. For this reason, procedures need to be in place to make it difficult for accounting employees to abuse their position.

This chapter looks at how the accounting function protects the financial assets of a property and at certain procedures that may make the accounting function itself less susceptible to compromise.

Accounting Control Procedures

The accounting department, usually headed by a controller (or comptroller), relies on a number of procedural safeguards. Whenever possible, the various accounting functions should be handled by different staff members (in a smaller operation, it may not be economically feasible to provide the necessary staff). For example, all monies should be handled by one individual. Another member of the staff should process the bank deposit of monies. Bank reconciliation should never be completed by the same person who issues the bank deposit. Likewise, accounts receivable and accounts payable may be separate operations handled by different employees.

If purchasing and receiving are either overseen or performed by the accounting department, the same person should not be responsible for both functions (except when he or she is the owner/manager of a smaller property). This helps keep employees from misappropriating cash and charging the sums taken to false accounts.

Inventory Control

Inventory control is often coordinated through the accounting department. Although some departments perform inventories of their supplies for their own benefit, major inventories should not be conducted by department heads or supervisors for their own departments. Better control is obtained when the inventory staff comes from outside the department.

Equipment inventory control may be enhanced through the use of serial numbers marked on the manufacturer's plate on many pieces of equipment. Consider implementing a system for permanently marking other items that do not carry a manufacturer's identification number. The markings should be a matter of record within the accounting office for inventory purposes and for identification when stolen items are recovered. With the increasing tendency to avoid placing logos or other identification attractive to "collectors" on hotel and motel goods, it is sometimes difficult to positively identify recovered property so that the police can release it to the hotel or motel. Some properties have solved this problem by sewing a colored thread into the corner of a hem or other appropriate place on linens, blankets, towels, and so forth, which permits the identification and recovery of stolen goods. A number of computer-based inventory control programs are available and should be considered.

Payroll Procedures and Concerns

The payroll process should be coordinated by as large a staff as may be required in relation to the number of employees and frequency of paydays. Master payroll files should be routinely matched with master personnel files to ensure that everyone on the payroll is currently employed by the property. Payroll theft may occur when someone either creates a fictitious employee or continues to carry an employee on the payroll who has departed. Unclaimed wages of departed employees may also be stolen.

Payrolls may be padded when employees claim to have worked more hours than they actually did. This problem can be lessened or eliminated through the use of an effective timekeeping system. The possibility of collusion in this type of theft may also be lessened by separating the timekeeping and check distribution duties. There should be a payroll verification with photo identification every six months.

Other concerns include keeping pay records in a secure storage area and providing appropriate physical security for payroll checks. Protection for *all* accounting records may be enhanced through the use of fire- and theft-resistant facilities. Computer controls such as keeping a separate record of on-premises computer data at an off-premises site should also be considered.

Sequential Numbering Systems

All order forms, blank checks, invoices, and other forms required for a specific function in the hotel or motel should be provided in a sequential numbering system. Every number should be accounted for, including voids and the reasons for any voids. Any variation from sequential control may allow an employee to misuse a purchase order, invoice, or check for his or her personal advantage. Check writing or printing equipment and signature plates or stamps should be secured. Except in an operation run by an on-premises owner/manager, there should be a two-signature requirement on all checks.

Bank Deposits

Bank deposits are frequently handled by a member of the staff in smaller properties. Larger properties, on the other hand, often have their bank deposits picked up by an armored car service. In both instances, every effort should be made to avoid either a typical pattern of pick-up by the outside service or a routine of an individual, route, and time of delivery to the bank by a member of the accounting department. When feasible, the member of the accounting department should be accompanied by another member of the property's staff. While security staff would seem logical for this assignment, an employee accompanied by a uniformed (and, in most cases, unarmed) security officer might be an equally vulnerable but more obvious target.

If a property uses an armored car service, that service should provide a list containing personnel signatures and photo IDs for verification purposes. When the armored car arrives to pick up a bank deposit, the property has the personnel sign for the deposit. The property then compares the signatures and photo ID with those on its list to ensure that they match *before* turning the deposit over.

Physical Protection of the Accounting Function

The accounting function, especially as it relates to the cashier, should be carefully protected. If at all possible, the general cashier and accounting offices should be located away from the public and guest areas of the property. Heavy-duty doors and locks should be installed in these areas. A silent alarm is advisable, particularly in the cashier area, where a significant amount of money may be kept.

Consider adding an alarm to the general cashier's safe. In all cases where combination locks are used on safes, the combinations themselves should be made available only to those employees who have an absolute need for such information. Whenever an employee who knows the combination leaves or is terminated or reassigned, the combination should be changed. Recorded combinations and the specific facilities to which they refer should be kept in a secure, double-locked box. Access to this box should be restricted to the controller and general manager jointly. Periodic rotation of locks and combinations may also be considered.

If feasible, a contract money pick-up service may be used. Following the preparation of monies for banking, they may be stored in a drop-safe that can only be opened by the armored car pick-up staff. When banking is handled by the staff of the hotel or motel, the on-premises drop-safe should have an alarm and access should be limited to only authorized employees.

Cashiering Procedures

The cashiering function is a critical aspect of accounting and requires special controls. For example, the amount of cash available in a cash register should be limited by establishing a cash bank for use by cashiers at the front desk and at food and beverage and other sales outlets under the direct control of the hotel. Under such a system, each cashier is given the smallest amount of cash that will still allow the cashier to transact business normally. The cashier becomes responsible for this cash and for all the cash that is added to this starting amount by sales during the cashier's workshift.

The cashier should be instructed to close the cash register drawer between each transaction. If an employee works with an open cash register drawer, he or she may not record a transaction or may later ring up only a portion of it and then steal the extra money when closing out the drawer at the end of the shift. Occasionally, a member of the audit team within the accounting office or a supervisor should conduct an unscheduled audit of the register.

Ideally, only one person should have access to each cash drawer. Multiple users of a cash drawer make it difficult, if not impossible, to determine responsibility for any shortages.

All transactions should be immediately recorded upon payment. This is particularly important in beverage service. Failure to enter the payment right after the drink is mixed, served, and paid for may lead to the misappropriation of funds by bartenders and beverage servers. If a guest check is used to record drinks, each drink should be written down on the check as it is served. In establishments without computerized point-of-sale controls, bar server's drinks also should be **redlined** by the bartender, a practice that involves underlining the last drink listed on the check to verify that the drink has been served. In this way, the check cannot be used to serve free drinks or to enable servers to pocket the monies from a duplicate order.

A policy should be established regarding the placement of currency during a cash transaction. Generally speaking, the employee should not place currency on the register ledge; doing so may make it easier for a thief to grab the money and run. Some organizations recommend that the money be placed in the cash drawer, but above the clip, until the transaction is completed. This can be helpful when a guest claims to have presented a bill of higher denomination than was actually presented. If the bill is under the clip, it is difficult to prove what denomination was actually received.

Cashiers should be instructed to complete any transaction in process before changing currency into different denominations for guests. This procedure helps deal with con artists who request different denominations of bills continually, making change requests until the cashier becomes so confused that he or she gives away more money than was received. Each request for a variation in denomination should be handled as a new, rather than as a continuing, transaction.

Establishing Credit Policies and Procedures

Whether a property has 20 rooms or 2,000 rooms, it needs a sound credit policy. Such policies will vary from property to property because each hotel and motel deals with a different location, clientele, and so forth. Each property must choose credit policies that best meet its needs. Remember, however, that one of a lodging property's needs is to provide hospitality. While a credit policy must be sufficient to protect the property, it should not so inconvenience or insult guests that it drives them away.

Credit policies may be chosen or set in a number of ways. Properties that belong to a large corporation might be expected to tailor the corporate credit policy to fit the individual property's needs, services, and type of guest. Sometimes the general manager of a property will determine the policy. Other properties have a credit committee or accounts receivable team that establishes or reevaluates policy. Depending on the size of an operation and the number of employees it has, its committee could consist of the general manager, controller, credit manager, front office manager, resident manager, director of sales, food and beverage manager, catering manager, and anyone else that an organization thinks should be involved. If a property already has too many bad debts on its books, its committee might be asked to study six months' worth of bad debts. Working together, the members of the committee may discover both where the property's present policy is weak and how to make it stronger.

After a property determines a tentative credit policy, it should consult with its local counsel to ensure that the policy does not violate any state or local laws.

Whether the policy a property decides to follow is corporate, committee written, or established by the general manager, it should be introduced to and understood by front office personnel—and everyone else who has anything to do with credit at the property—before it is implemented. The finest credit policy will not prevent losses due to bad debts if it is poorly implemented.

Credit Cards

Unfortunately, the illegal use of credit cards has become big business in the crime community. Credit card fraud may involve the use of stolen, counterfeit, and altered cards. Even when a patron offers a legitimate credit card, a property may be stuck with a bad debt if it does not follow the procedures for accepting the card that have been established by the credit card company. Special care should always be exercised by all employees who may be presented with credit cards. Employees should be trained (and retrained as necessary) about the restrictions and requirements of the individual cards that their property accepts.

In addition to meeting the credit card companies' requirements, employees will need to be trained to meet their property's requirements. Exhibit 1 offers a list of general guidelines for preventing credit card fraud. In addition, many of the following procedures meet the requirements of both the property and the credit card company.

When a guest presents a credit card, the employee responsible for handling the transaction should immediately check both the signature block—to ensure that

Exhibit 1   Ten Guidelines for Preventing Credit Card Fraud

1. Avoid imprinting credit cards on hotel registration cards, folios, forms, and other paperwork to which hotel staff members may have access.
2. Protect guests' credit card information by putting it in a sealed envelope in a secure place.
3. Tighten security regarding the storage and recording of hotel guests' credit card information. Only authorized staff members should have access to such information.
4. Use electronic data-capture machines that enter information directly into the computer, thereby reducing hotel personnel's access to that data.
5. Destroy documents containing credit card information, including unsigned credit card slips and computer printouts.
6. Restrict access to photocopying machines, especially during the night, and locate the machines in open, busy, and well-lit areas.
7. Install closed-circuit television cameras in areas where guest information is kept, so that if it is determined that cards have been compromised, evidence may exist to begin tracking down those responsible.
8. Educate staff members to take fraud seriously and to report any suspicious actions or incidents to hotel security or law-enforcement agencies.
9. Review security procedures and devise operational systems to discover and prevent white-collar crime.
10. Cooperate with credit card companies, police, and agencies seeking to prevent counterfeiting.

the card is signed—and the expiration date. If the date has expired, that fact should be pointed out to the guest so that another means of payment can be arranged. Credit card companies will not honor expired cards. The penalty for accepting one may be a bad debt loss to the property for the entire amount charged. A benefit of the advance of electronic technology is the instantaneous and inconspicuous computer validation of a credit card.

Computer verification will not reveal the fraud when an illegal card holder presents a card before the legal holder has noticed and reported the card lost or stolen. Nonetheless, verifying the card by electronic authorization for acceptance of the card will generally protect the property from loss if the use of the card later proves fraudulent. Employees receiving electronic authorization should note the authorization number on the guest's credit card voucher and perhaps even on the guest's **folio**.

If the card proves, after verification, to be invalid, the employee should follow the established procedures of the property and the individual card company. Most properties ask employees to alert either the credit manager or general manager, who will handle the situation. In the case of a stolen card, security personnel might also be asked to be readily available. The federal government has made the fraudulent use of credit cards a criminal offense. However, lodging properties should be wary of detaining guests they suspect of theft or fraudulently avoiding payment of their bills. Such detention, especially if unjustified or improperly instituted, might open the property to suits for false imprisonment and slander, depending on the circumstances of the case and state laws. Hotels and motels should check with their own counsel before establishing any procedures for detaining guests suspected of credit card fraud or other wrongdoing. Some properties insist that credit card companies indemnify them against such lawsuits. The holder of a stolen credit card will usually leave when it is realized the card is under special scrutiny.

Even when authorization is granted, credit card companies generally require that certain procedures be followed to reduce the possibility of the fraudulent use of cards before they are reported missing. The employee accepting the card should compare the signature on the card with the signature on the voucher or registration card and match the name of the person presenting the card with the name on the card. If the employee is suspicious, he or she should ask for additional identification. Many properties routinely ask all guests to provide positive identification during registration. If a credit card voucher is signed by someone other than the legal card holder (for example, the holder's spouse or offspring), the credit card company will not pay if the legal holder contests the charge.

Making excessive charges or exceeding the hotel's established **floor limit** (the specific amount of credit per card that individual properties are allowed by credit card companies) is infrequent due to the use of computerized control systems, including point-of-sale (POS) systems. An account that is nearing an established limit is reviewed with the credit card company electronically, without involving the guest. The guest would only be involved should an increase in limit be denied, in which case the guest should be called into the office of the credit manager or other designated representative of the hotel. The hotel should then make the phone available for the guest to speak with the credit card company representative.

Some properties also set their own high balance limit for guests. Such properties usually check their guests' balances at least once a day. Computerized properties may perform this task twice a day. When it occurs once a day, it usually is carried out during the night audit. The auditor, who is responsible for balancing the guest folios, lists on a high balance report the name, room number, and balance for those guests who have exceeded the established limit. The next morning, management studies the night auditor's report, checks individual folios to discover guests' payment plans, and makes decisions about which guests must be contacted to settle part or all of their bills before being allowed to charge any more services.

Some computerized establishments program their computers to indicate the moment the guest goes one cent over (for example) $100 less than the credit card floor limit or $50 less than the high balance limit. For instance, if the floor limit for a particular credit card is $500, the credit manager will be informed as soon as a guest has spent $400.01; the manager can then keep an eye on the account so the property will be ready to get authorization on the account from the credit card company.

Some properties also train personnel such as front office cashiers, housekeepers, room service staff, and so forth to alert the management when a guest is spending wildly, tipping excessively, or charging even small items like a pack of cigarettes to his or her room number. All personnel who accept charges to a room number may quickly confirm electronically the legitimacy of a registered guest to avoid allowing others to use services for which they can never be billed. Some organizations provide a special guest identification card, passport, key, or other device to confirm that an individual is a registered guest. In properties that keep some guests on a cash basis, employees should be informed of, or trained to find out for themselves, which guests are not allowed to charge. A verification call for services charged to the room will cover this situation; the accounting or front desk departments can immediately confirm that the guest can or cannot charge to the room account.

Management should also determine in advance the dollar level at which an interim bill will be presented to a guest on an extended stay. This especially applies to resort properties where guests are often present for a week or two. It is also applicable during conventions or meetings where food and beverage charges may be significant, particularly for the host.

Lodging establishments may consider reserving a specified amount of credit in a guest's credit card account to ensure payment for services rendered, but they must be aware of local laws regarding such procedures. Thus, if a guest comes into a property planning to stay eight days, and the property knows that the anticipated charges will exceed the authorized floor limit, the property may wish to reserve the amount of the anticipated charges in the guest's credit card account. But if the guest then decides to leave earlier than planned, his or her credit is now tied up. Laws vary from state to state, but in some states, the property is obligated to notify the credit card company to release the unused credit that had been authorized. In New York, for example, a property may only request such a reserve of credit if it informs the guest beforehand of the amount it wishes to reserve and obtains the guest's consent. Moreover, after final charges have been determined, it must promptly communicate with the credit card company to request the release of any credit previously reserved that is greater than $25 above the charges actually billed. Local counsel should approve a property's policy before it is instituted.

Checks

During registration, guests should be asked to indicate how they plan to settle their accounts. Initially, this is a function of the front desk clerks, but if the guest indicates that payment will be by check, the credit manager may need to be notified. A number of check services and computerized check guarantee programs are available and should be reviewed as possible backup for a decision to accept checks. (Properties contemplating the use of such a service should ask the service for proof from the Federal Trade Commission that it complies with the Fair Credit Reporting Act.) These services are available around the clock and can be an invaluable aid to the lodging industry. Smaller properties, however, might find the cost of such programs prohibitive and discover that their own well-thought-out check cashing policies can adequately serve their particular needs.

Both the cashier and the credit manager must deal with guest identification when a check is presented for cash or services. Acceptable identification includes:

- current driver's license
- valid passport with photo ID

- credit card with laminated photograph and signature
- identification cards—such as those issued by the armed services, police departments, and some businesses—that include a photograph, a physical description, and a signature

The U.S. Small Business Administration recommends not accepting the following unless they are accompanied by a valid driver's license: social security cards, business cards, club or organization cards, bank books, work permits, insurance cards, learner's permits, letters, birth certificates, library cards, unsigned credit cards, or voter registration cards.

It is important to note that the property has no obligation to accept a check, regardless of whether the check is valid. However, a property cannot practice illegal discrimination in refusing to accept checks. Employees should never be instructed to refuse checks on the basis of race or gender, for instance. Such refusal may be a violation of local, state, or federal discrimination laws.

Management should also define a policy on prosecution in the event of a returned check. Usually, upon re-submission a check returned for insufficient funds will clear. If it does not, few banks will accept the check a third time. The next step is to contact the individual who wrote the check and request immediate payment. A property should review with counsel the laws covering actions to seek recovery in its community. If, after repeated attempts, the property cannot collect, it may wish to consider prosecution. Generally speaking, it may be to the hotel or motel's advantage to establish a reputation for following up on bad checks and other guest or patron fraud. If a property becomes known as lax in its collection efforts, credit and income problems may sharply increase.

Reputable collection agencies provide an alternative to tying up staff time and effort in following up on bad checks or other guest accounts in arrears. While a percentage of the sums collected goes to the agency, that amount is generally less than the expense incurred by direct involvement of the property's staff.

Where the establishment accepts personal checks, electronic check verification (by subscription to various services) has become the favored method for check authorization. The popularity of the automated teller machine (ATM) has sharply reduced the request for check cashing privileges. Where the property has a policy of accepting personal checks, there are several questions to consider:

- Are checks accepted for room and taxes only?
- Are checks accepted for food, beverages, gift shop purchases, or other similar items or services?
- Will a check verification service be used for each transaction?
- Are checks drawn on foreign bank accounts acceptable?
- Will payroll checks, government checks, travelers checks, money orders, or second- and third-party checks be accepted?

In addition, under what circumstances will a check be cashed to accommodate a frequent guest? (As an aspect of hotel "frequent stay" programs, a check cashing privilege is often provided, up to a specified limit.) Are there other circumstances under which this privilege might be extended to a guest who is not a frequent guest? Regardless of the situation in which this check cashing privilege is offered, the amount of the check should be entered on the computer folio to avoid exceeding the "house limits" on accepted checks.

When a property accepts an advance payment by check from a guest who decides to leave the property earlier than planned, the property should not write a refund check unless the bank verifies that the guest's check has cleared. If the property still has the check, it should return it to the guest and ask for another check for the actual amount of the bill. Many properties do not refund cash for goods or services when the original payment was by check.

Checks written for payment of the guest's bill should be made out to the property, not to cash. On the other hand, if the property allows guests to write checks in return for cash, the checks should be made out to "cash," not to the property. This procedure will keep a guest who writes a check for cash from claiming that the property accepted the check as payment for the room and services.

Many properties choose not to accept second- or third-party checks. Second-party checks are checks made out to the guest presenting the check. Third-party checks are checks made out to someone who has then signed the check over to the guest presenting the check. The hotel or motel accepting such a check may experience collection problems if the maker of the check stops payment. When properties that do accept second-party checks receive a check that has already been endorsed, they should have the guest sign the check again and then compare the signatures.

There are a number of things that front office personnel and cashiers should know and keep in mind when dealing with checks. A real check should have a perforation on at least one side and should state the name, branch, city, and state where the bank is located. A government check will have a distinct watermark and thread embedded within the paper. A payroll check usually has the name of the employer printed on it. In most instances, "payroll" is also printed on the check. The employee's name is printed by a check writing machine or typed. In metropolitan areas, properties often choose not to cash a payroll check that is hand printed, rubber stamped, or typewritten, even if it appears to be issued by a local business and drawn on a local bank.

Employees should not accept illegible checks or checks with erasures or overwritten amounts. Checks should be signed in ink in the presence of the property's employee. The guest's signed name should conform to the name as it appears on the face of the check. Checks that are marked "For Deposit Only," "For Collection," or with similar terms should not be accepted.

Employees should not accept checks from guests without identification. When identification is offered, employees should ensure that all signatures, photo IDs, and/or physical descriptions match the person offering the identification. If a property requires its employees to write identifying information on the check (such as a driver's license number), the information should be written on the face of the check; bank stamps and clearinghouse imprints will often make any entries on the reverse of the check illegible.

Most authorities recommend against accepting post-dated checks. A check should not be accepted if it is not dated at all; some authorities also suggest not accepting checks more than 30 days old. The written and numerical amounts on the check should agree. Some properties do not cash checks from intoxicated persons.

Studies have shown that checks numbered 400 and below are statistically more likely to bounce than checks with higher numbers. Similar studies report that people who intentionally write bad checks most often write them in the $25 to $40 range.

Almost every check a property will ever see has a series of magnetic ink characters (numbers) starting at or near the lower left corner on the face of the check. On a good check, no light will reflect from these numbers when the check is tilted to the light. If the light reflects, the check was not printed by a bank and is very likely fraudulent. With the increasing sophistication of reproduction processes, checks may be reproduced that are extremely difficult to recognize as phony. Nonetheless, the numbers on many of such copies will be shiny. Employees finding such checks should run a finger across the front. If the print smears, the check is fraudulent. Watermarks and paper quality should also be considered when judging the validity of the check being presented.

A property should also be alert for counterfeit travelers checks. Travelers check companies can inform a property how to spot fraudulent checks. To confirm the authenticity of an American Express Travelers Cheque, for example, an employee should wet the tip of a finger and rub the moistened finger tip over the surface of the check across the denomination on the back *left* side. If it smears, it is legitimate. This is the *only* part of the check that should smear.

Denying Credit to a Guest

If a property checks a guest's credit properly, it greatly reduces the likelihood of subsequent trouble. But when a property has found a guest's credit to be poor or otherwise insufficient, how does it inform the guest of this fact?

When speaking to a guest about his or her credit, the hotel or motel employee should realize that more than money is involved. The guest may perceive his or her dignity, pride, even self-respect to be under attack. The employee should be as diplomatic as possible. His or her voice and manner should be friendly and calm, no matter how belligerent the guest is. This section contains a few tips on how to deal with this difficult task. They should be modified as necessary to fit the situation at hand, the guest involved, and the property's own philosophy.

When a credit card company will not allow a guest to charge a purchase to a card, the employee should not state this fact in a voice loud enough to be overheard by anyone other than the affected guest. The employee should not refer to the card as "bad" or "worthless." He or she should not ask the guest to leave the premises immediately or either threaten to or actually telephone the police. Instead, the employee should quietly ask the guest to step into an office or other area out of earshot of others; once there, the guest should be informed that further use of the credit card has not been approved by the card company. If the guest asks what that means, the employee is not obligated to explain a credit card company's policy. The property could, however, offer the use of its telephone so that the guest can speak with a credit card company representative to clear up the matter. The

Exhibit 2 Sample Confirmation Notice Credit Explanation

[Personalize with your property's name and/or logo.]

OUR CREDIT REQUIREMENTS

We are very pleased you have chosen to stay at _____. To make your stay totally pleasurable, we would like you to know our credit policies:

1. **Credit Cards.** We accept the following credit cards: [Name those your property accepts.] When you check in, we will take an imprint of your card to establish credit and expedite your check-out.
2. **Direct Billing** [for companies only]. If you wish to have your account billed directly to your firm, we must have a letter of authorization at least _____ day(s) prior to your arrival.
3. **Cash.** We are also happy to have you choose to pay cash in any part of our hotel. We will ask that you pay room charges and tax in advance.
4. **Checks.** [State your property's policy.]

We look forward with pleasure to serving you.

---

employee should also allow the guest a chance to explain or to provide another means of payment.

When a guest insists on presenting a check that, due to hotel/motel policy, cannot be cashed, the employee may note the availability of an ATM in the lobby of the hotel or in another nearby location.

Guest Registration and Check-out

Reservations. Most guests make reservations through telephone contacts or electronically (via faxes, e-mail, or the Internet). When confirming the reservation, a number of properties send an explanation of their credit policy to their future guests. Exhibit 2 is an example of such a mailing. Properties using such explanations will need to alter the exhibit to fit their particular needs and policies.

If a property requires a deposit to hold a room for a late arrival, it should ensure that the guest knows when that payment is due. If the property will accept a check for this deposit, it should consider allowing enough time for the check to clear before the guest's arrival.

Registration. Lodging services cannot be reclaimed by the property if the customer decides to leave without paying. When checking in, guests should be required to make acceptable payment arrangements. Certain registration procedures can reduce the potential for later problems.

If a property has its guests manually fill out its registration cards, it should require them to *print* the information legibly. If there are illegible numbers or words, the room clerk should ask the guest to state the information aloud. The clerk should then print the clarification next to the guest's writing. The clerk should also make certain that the guest signs the card. If the property pre-prints

Exhibit 3 Format for Credit Policy Given to Cash-Paying Guests

---

[Personalize with your property's name and/or logo.]

OUR CREDIT POLICY

To our guests:

We are glad you are staying at _____ and would like you to know our credit policy for guests paying cash.

[State policy.]

Of course, if you have a major credit card, you may use it in the dining room, gift shop, etc.

We hope you enjoy your stay with us.

---

guest information on registration cards, guests should verify the information and sign the card. Walk-ins (that is, people arriving without reservations) will of course have to complete their registration cards by hand.

Many properties use registration cards that ask for quite a lot of information—for example, both home and business telephone numbers, home and business addresses, make of car, license plate number, and more. The purpose of getting so much information is to make it easier to find the guest if there are later collection problems.

Front desk personnel should be trained to verify the completeness of registration cards. For example, if a guest does not write "Avenue," "Street," "Boulevard," "Drive," or so forth after the street address, the clerk should ask for this information and complete the address. When possible, the property should compare the guest's actual automobile license plates with what he or she has written on the registration card.

When guests pay room charges and tax in advance, a property will need to decide whether it will require them to make a deposit toward telephone, valet, laundry, and other services provided by the property. Properties not requiring such a deposit may explain courteously to the guests that they should be certain to stop at the desk when they check out so that they can pay any accumulated charges. Some properties use telephone systems that can be programmed not to allow long-distance calls from rooms rented by such guests.

Lodging properties should consider developing policies regarding guests wishing to pay cash. For example, many properties require payment in advance for such guests for at least the first night. The guests may also be informed that they are on a cash basis at the property. Some properties choose to print a written statement of the property's credit policy for cash-paying guests that may be given to them at registration. Exhibit 3 is a sample format for such a document. When cash-paying guests check in, there should be a procedure that will notify the property's various departments of this fact. In order to identify cash-paying guests quickly, some properties mark their folios "Paid in Advance," "Cash Only," or with some similar designation.

Checking Out. If reservation and/or check-in procedures have been handled carefully and guests' high balances have been monitored each day, checking out is in most cases a very simple procedure. Generally, guests appear at the front desk to return their room keys and report that they are checking out. The cashier should always ask whether a guest has had any late charges (telephone calls, breakfast or room service charges, and so forth). An increasing number of properties eliminate some of the doubt about late charges by using computers and POS terminals that record charges instantaneously to the guest folios. The cashier then presents the totaled bill, allows the guest to review it, and accepts payment (usually by the method determined during registration) or, if appropriate, reminds the guest that he or she will be direct-billed.

In an effort to expedite the check-out process, bills may be placed under the door on the morning of check-out, or the billing information may be available via the television. The guest may call a special telephone number or, using an interactive TV connection, check out of the room. The key may be left in the room, and the guest may leave the property without standing in line at the front desk. However, care must be taken that charges and other guest information are not compromised through failure to place the guest check sufficiently under the door to avoid recovery by an unauthorized person who may have criminal intent.

With the increasing popularity of alternative methods of checking out, some security and legal advisers have questioned whether the lack of a signature might negate the transaction as a viable contract. The trend toward charging for changing the length of intended stay without advising the property in advance has resulted in obtaining a signature at check-in. At that time, the guest must verify the number of nights by signature and the room rate by initial. Although there has not been a court test, it seems probable that a court would recognize the signature on the agreement to the dates of lodging as a commitment to pay for that stay at the initialed rate.

Computer Security

The rapid advance of computer technology in recent years has given the lodging industry another security concern. Illegal entry into the computer of a hotel or motel can greatly threaten the organization's financial stability. Fires, natural disasters, and hardware theft can result in damaged or irretrievably lost data.

Each lodging operation should regularly conduct a complete risk assessment of all computer systems to uncover specific areas of vulnerability. This is an assessment of the risk associated with the loss of each and all systems as well as all data stored on those systems. This assessment should be repeated annually or as new systems are brought online and legacy systems are replaced.

A strong information technology security program will cover a number of key areas, including:

- Accountability in management

- System auditability
- Integrity of systems and data
- Cost effectiveness
- Ease of implementation
- Policy compliance

Accountability

The structure and resources of lodging organizations usually require that one person carry the responsibility for overall computer system security. In many properties this is either the controller or the director of management information systems (MIS). However, every user must be held accountable for protecting the information resources of the property and the corporation. Sharing system or file access passwords or providing other information that could allow unauthorized access to a property's systems is equivalent to company sabotage or theft. It becomes important, therefore, to limit access to information and systems to those users who require such access to perform their assigned duties.

Auditability

It is the responsibility of the designated systems security officer of the property to maintain awareness of when users are accessing information, what they are accessing or modifying, and when and how unauthorized attempts to access a system are being made.

The use of unique passwords is one acceptable method of authorizing use and protecting computer data. When a property uses passwords, it should strongly encourage employees to avoid writing them down. Any master list of passwords—whether on paper or electronic—should be protected from unauthorized access. Some properties choose to change passwords at random; some computer systems prompt for new passwords at regular intervals. Passwords of employees who have left or been transferred or terminated may be held in reserve for a suitable length of time before being reissued to other employees; some properties permanently delete the passwords of such persons from the system.

In order to maintain an audit trail and monitor system usage, system administrators in conjunction with the security officer in the property should activate access, violation, and modification logs that track password use. Access logs provide an electronic record of each attempt to log on to a system. Violation logs record who attempted to violate system or file-level security, and modification logs record user information on all files that have been modified. In some systems, it is possible to have such logs activate an alarm when data gathered in the log fall outside established parameters. Such notification allows the system administrator the opportunity to locate the source of the potential security risk.

System Integrity

There is not a security plan or system for computers that is 100 percent foolproof. In fact, many information technology (IT) managers say, "You do the best you can.

After that, if someone really wants to get into a system, they will get in." Unfortunately, this is true. Since such access can happen from within a property or from the outside, it is important to take measures to prevent "hacking" into a system on both fronts. It is the responsibility of the appointed systems security officer to perform due diligence as it relates to system integrity, keeping the system continuously operational without data loss or security incident.

The level of security available on a particular system in most cases begins with the operating system. For example, Microsoft's Windows 95 and Windows 98 are desktop operating systems designed primarily for home and small-business computer users; they offer less security than Windows NT and Novell Netware, which are network operating systems.

Computer Viruses. Computer viruses are destructive computer programs that can "infect" a computer and damage data files, system files, and applications. Viruses can replicate themselves and can be transmitted as hidden files or programs from one computer to another. Viruses are most often transmitted when users carry a floppy disk from computer to computer, copying files to and from the disk without considering whether or not they might contain a computer virus. An infected disk may invisibly transmit the virus to each computer that reads the disk. This in turn infects one computer after another. The second and much more effective (and malicious) way viruses are spread is over the Internet. Internet mail attachments are notorious for carrying computer viruses. These programs are attached to e-mail messages and then sent to numerous users. The unsuspecting user then opens the mail and carelessly infects the computer with a virus.

The most effective way to prevent the spread of computer viruses is to use a computer program that "inoculates" a machine and its data against the threat of viruses. These programs work as virus shields, scanning files for known computer viruses as they are opened or run. If a virus is detected, it is immediately cleaned from the system. Additionally, these programs can be set up to periodically scan the entire computer for viruses. Virus protection programs are extremely effective when installed on a server and used in a local area network (LAN). In this situation, any data that is stored on the server can be scanned and cleaned on a regular basis. Because new "strains" of computer viruses are constantly being developed and circulated, virus-protection software should be updated regularly to ensure the best protection possible. Some vendors now make such software updates available for easy downloading from their Web sites.

Internet Connectivity. When computers have access to the Internet as well as corporate and local area networks, it is important to protect data from unauthorized distribution over the Internet. It is especially critical to control Internet access centrally in any property where computers are connected to the hotel LAN and to the Internet via a modem. Anytime there is a modem on a PC, there is the possibility for unauthorized transmission of data from the network, out of the hotel, via the modem. It is more secure to provide Internet access via the network so that a firewall can be put in place to protect the hotel's data and systems. **Firewalls** are communications filters that allow only authorized access and data transmission to and from a network.

Access Restrictions. The more people that have access to a computer, the greater the possibility for compromised security. Implementing certain access restrictions can help to maintain system integrity.

One type of restricted access involves the creation of different levels of authorization for access to different levels of information. Such systems limit the information available to employees to only those areas necessary for the performance of their jobs. Front desk staff, for example, would be limited to computer access relating to the check-in and check-out functions only.

In some hotels, it may be necessary to limit the time periods during which computers may be accessed. This can be managed through the user rights and privileges aspect of a network operating system. For example, users may be granted access to the network only between 9:00 A.M. and 5:00 P.M. This prevents access to data when there is no network administrator available to monitor data activity.

Embezzlement. Embezzlement is a major crime against which computers should be protected. With a little knowledge of programming, it is fairly easy to set up dummy accounts in order to embezzle money. Funds may be directed to such accounts for long periods of time before being detected. The use of passwords and restricted levels of access help to safeguard a property's assets, but it is not possible to completely eliminate the potential for someone to bypass these safeguards. Security systems can only make it difficult for unauthorized persons to gain access to the computer; authorized personnel may be in positions of authority that allow them access to important restricted information which they use for illegitimate purposes.

There are a number of ways to reduce the potential for embezzlement by computer. Some involve the same procedures used for preventing embezzlement of any sort. For example, there should be a **separation of duties**. The computer programmer should not also be the computer operator. This separation of duties prevents the programmer from building loopholes into the program to permit access later for personal profit. Also, the computerized check writing operation should be separated from the department that authorizes checks, in order to keep false data from resulting in actual cash payments. A single individual should not be able to generate a payment. Some properties use a mandatory vacation policy to ensure that every employee's work—including that of potential embezzlers with access to the computer—is periodically reviewed by someone else (that is, the employee who substitutes for the vacationing employee).

Outside computer services. Perhaps somewhat surprisingly, protection from computer embezzlement and fraud may sometimes be enhanced through the use of outside computer services. Although this practice involves revealing internal information to persons outside the organization, the people seeing it will generally have little personal use for it—especially if the service is well organized and conscious of the security requirements of its clients. Employees within outside computer services seldom have the opportunity to gain the familiarity with a lodging property that is needed to effectively embezzle its assets. This is especially true when the lodging property assigns different computer responsibilities to more than one outside computer service. Contrast this with the situation in which corrupt or potentially corrupt internal employees have such detailed knowledge of the workings of the property that they are relatively well equipped to embezzle in ways that are hard to detect.

Of course, care should be taken in selecting an outside service. A property choosing a service should ensure that the service has an effective internal security program. This involves not only protecting the confidentiality of the information entrusted to the service, but also taking adequate precautions against hazards such as fire, flood, vandalism, civil disturbances, power blackouts, and more. The service also should be financially sound; services that are not may be more susceptible to the temptation to misuse their positions of trust. Also, there is the potential for records and documents to be tied up indefinitely if the service goes bankrupt.

Physical Access to Servers. The server room or main computer room in a property should be secured in a separate area from other operations, protected by adequate locks and double-door entry. All movement of personnel into the area should be controlled, and access should be granted only to those who work with the network. A log should be maintained in computer operating areas detailing any stoppages and any resulting problems. Such records should be maintained and reviewed regularly by supervisory personnel.

Physical Protection of the Computer. Computer security involves more than protecting against fraud or vandalism. The computer itself should be maintained and protected from numerous hazards that could temporarily or permanently incapacitate it.

The greatest danger is fire. Computer rooms should be constructed of fireproof or fire-resistant materials. Sprinkler systems may be useful, although flooding is not good for computers either. Systems that use special gases that rapidly extinguish fires are available, but they are expensive to maintain. Review the local fire code requirements; some jurisdictions mandate water sprinkler systems in addition to or in place of chemical systems. Employees should be trained in how to react quickly and effectively to a fire in the computer room or a fire that may threaten the computer room. Because simple overheating can also be a problem, computer rooms are often air conditioned.

Properties also should take measures to protect against power failures that may disrupt computer functions. One strategy is to route all computer equipment through an uninterrupted power supply (UPS) unit. Common IT problems such as electrical outages should have recovery procedures detailed in a disaster handbook. These procedures should provide step-by-step instructions on how to maintain critical systems using backup power facilities and how to recover any transactions that were in process when the outage occurred.

Computer equipment, although increasingly affordable, is still coveted by many unscrupulous individuals. It is therefore paramount that desktop equipment be secured in place to prevent theft. Anti-theft systems include those that can be used to mount equipment to a base that is then secured to a desk or the floor, cable and lock systems, and systems that use fiber-optic cable and an integrated alarm system.

Finally, every hotel should develop a comprehensive disaster recovery plan that includes procedures for recovery from both natural disasters and premeditated, malicious attacks on critical information systems.

Data Backup. It is most important that all critical data on a hotel's network be backed up each day. Additionally, critical report information should be printed at regular intervals in case of emergency or system outage. For instance, room occupancy and guest information should be printed regularly (for each shift) so that room status can be determined in the event of the system going down.

Physical backup on tape, high-capacity disk, or recordable CD/DVD should be performed daily and stored off-site in the event of fire or theft of system equipment or data. In some instances, corporate policies will govern backup procedures and the storage of backup media. Otherwise, each property should develop adequate procedures that meet the needs of that property.

Cost Effectiveness

While cost effectiveness is important, it also is important to gain the commitment from senior management to invest in the appropriate level of resources to protect the information systems of the property. In all cases, the level of resources allocated to securing data should be directly proportional to the value of the data to the organization. Systems in student computer labs, for example, may hold data that can be easily replaced or reinstalled; therefore, data security is not a high priority. However, an organization with irreplaceable proprietary business information might use data encryption on all file transmissions, implement redundant data storage, and manage all security procedures closely; the financial life of the organization may depend upon it.

Ease of Implementation

Data and system security should be relatively easy to implement. An overly complex system may be underutilized or incorrectly set up because it is too difficult to work with, thereby compromising system intergrity. A system should be flexible enough to assign access to system resources and information as needed without using extensive IT staff resources. Frequently, network operating systems allow system administrators to grant company-wide access by user type. Many hotel property management systems allow for the assignment of user rights by job function: the front office manager would have additional rights to those granted to the reservationist or the guest services representative that works the front desk. These are easily implemented user parameters that are controlled by the application or by the system software.

Policy Compliance

In addition to a well-designed security plan, complete with policies and procedures related to accountability, auditability, cost effectiveness, and ease of implementation, IT managers must be concerned with general safeguards against unauthorized access to data and continuous system operation.

Additional policies and procedures may be set to ensure data security. Password protection of system and file access is a classic example of a basic security parameter. However, once a password is revealed, it is useless as a security parameter. It is therefore important to implement policy associated with password management. The severity of the policy depends on the needs of the organization. For example, requiring users to change their password daily on a restaurant POS system would be counterproductive. However, implementing the same policy in the accounting department might be considered prudent, especially when any personnel with system administrative privileges leave the organization.

Computer security involves many aspects of the computer system. It is important that IT managers or the responsible party at the hotel property consider all aspects of computer security. Additionally, security managers should communicate to other hotel employees the importance of security and their role in the effectiveness of the overall security of the hotel's information systems.

An Internal Audit Program

Internal auditing has been defined as being the eyes and ears of an operation's owners or management.

An **internal audit** is an independent appraisal function set up in a hotel or motel to examine and evaluate the adequacy and effectiveness of the establishment's internal control system and its overall performance. The auditing process offers a general manager analyses, appraisals, recommendations, counsel, and information concerning his or her hotel's operation. Internal auditors examine every phase of the operations to ensure that all company assets are properly recorded and safeguarded and that company operations are conducted in an efficient and businesslike manner. To be effective, the auditing process must span departments, encompassing financial activities and such areas as food and beverage, engineering, marketing and sales, and human resources.

Internal auditors are responsible for performing the following tasks:

- Determining that company policies are followed
- Determining that internal controls are adequate
- Suggesting improvements in practices and procedures to obtain increased efficiency or to lower operating costs
- Detecting fraud or manipulation of records
- Determining that all laws are obeyed

The internal auditor is ever watchful for any activity or failure that could cause a company to become party to a lawsuit or be subject to punitive action by a government agency. Exhibit 4 offers further details about the responsibilities of an internal auditing program.

Management has two options when it comes to obtaining an objective, analytical review of a specific operation. The internal audit team may be made up of company personnel assigned to that task, or the hotel can outsource the internal

Exhibit 4 Statement of Responsibilities of Internal Auditing

The purpose of this statement is to provide in summary form a general understanding of the responsibilities of internal auditing. For more specific guidance, readers should refer to the Standards for the Professional Practice of Internal Auditing.

Objective and Scope

Internal Auditing is an independent appraisal function established within an organization to examine and evaluate its activities as a service to the organization. The objective of internal auditing is to assist members of the organization in the effective discharge of their responsibilities. To this end, internal auditing furnishes them with analyses, appraisals, recommendations, counsel, and information concerning the activities reviewed. The audit objective includes promoting effective control at reasonable cost. The members of the organization assisted by internal auditing include those in management and the board of directors.

The scope of internal auditing should encompass the examination and evaluation of the adequacy and effectiveness of the organization's system of internal control and the quality of performance in carrying out assigned responsibilities. Internal auditors should:

- Review the reliability and integrity of financial and operating information and the means used to identify, measure, classify, and report such information.
- Review the systems established to ensure compliance with those policies, plans, procedures, laws, regulations, and contracts which could have a significant impact on operations and reports, and should determine whether the organization is in compliance.
- Review the means of safeguarding assets and, as appropriate, verify the existence of such assets.
- Appraise the economy and efficiency with which resources are employed.
- Review operations or programs to ascertain whether results are consistent with established objectives and goals and whether the operations or programs are being carried out as planned.

Responsibility and Authority

The internal auditing department is an integral part of the organization and functions under the policies established by senior management and the board. The purpose, authority, and responsibility of the internal auditing department should be defined in a formal written document (charter). The director of internal auditing should seek approval of the charter by senior management as well as acceptance by the board. The charter should make clear the purposes of the internal auditing department, specify the unrestricted scope of its work, and declare that auditors are to have no authority or responsibility for the activities they audit.

Throughout the world internal auditing is performed in diverse environments and within organizations which vary in purpose, size, and structure. In addition, the laws and customs within various countries differ from one another. These differences may affect the practice of internal auditing in each environment. The implementation of the Standards for the Professional Practice of Internal Auditing, therefore, will be governed by the environment in which the internal auditing department carries out its assigned responsibilities. Compliance with the concepts enunciated

(continued)

Exhibit 4 *(continued)*

> by the Standards for the Professional Practice of Internal Auditing is essential before the responsibilities of internal auditors can be met. As stated in the Code of Ethics, members of The Institute of Internal Auditors, Inc. and Certified Internal Auditors shall adopt suitable means to comply with the Standards for the Professional Practice of Internal Auditing.
>
> **Independence**
>
> Internal auditors should be independent of the activities they audit. Internal auditors are independent when they can carry out their work freely and objectively. Independence permits internal auditors to render the impartial and unbiased judgments essential to the proper conduct of audits. It is achieved through organizational status and objectivity.
>
> The organizational status of the internal auditing department should be sufficient to permit the accomplishment of its audit responsibilities. The director of the internal auditing department should be responsible to an individual in the organization with sufficient authority to promote independence and to ensure a broad audit coverage, adequate consideration of audit reports, and appropriate action on audit recommendations.
>
> Objectivity is an independent mental attitude which internal auditors should maintain in performing audits. Internal auditors are not to subordinate their judgment on audit matters to that of others. Designing, installing, and operating systems are not audit functions. Also, the drafting of procedures for systems is not an audit function. Performing such activities is presumed to impair audit objectivity.
>
> *The Statement of Responsibilities of Internal Auditing* was originally issued by The Institute of Internal Auditors in 1947. The current Statement, revised in 1997, embodies the concepts previously established and includes such changes as are deemed advisable in light of the present status of the profession.

Courtesy of The Institute of Internal Auditors.

auditing function to professionals trained in the art of analyzing records, controls, and procedures.

According to a survey conducted by the Institute of Internal Auditors, the primary reason why hoteliers consider outsourcing is the perception of reduced costs. However, internal audit directors generally expressed the opinion that as a permanent employee the internal auditor develops a better understanding of organizational methods, and can provide improved responsiveness and loyalty to the company's goals and vision. Outside contractors, such as CPA firms, rely on standardized checklists that apply to traditional operations. Internal auditors, because they are involved in the day-to-day operations, are more familiar with the unique internal workings of the organization and are able to tailor their approach accordingly. In addition, because of their greater intimacy with the inner workings of their hotel's systems, staff auditors may be better equipped to detect fraud and protect the operation's resources. On the other hand, staff auditors also will have close ties with others in the hotel, which may impair their ability to be wholly unbiased and honest. As a result, the hotel may be given a less-than-accurate appraisal, and significant problems may go unaddressed. Clearly, there are strengths and weaknesses of either approach to the internal audit function that must be weighed.

Individual auditors may report to an audit committee, which may in turn report to the chief financial officer. If an outside agency is employed, that agency also would report to the chief financial officer.

Key Terms

firewalls—Communications filters on networked computer systems that allow only authorized access and data transmission to and from the network.

floor limit—The maximum amount of credit per credit card that is allowed by the sponsoring credit card company. Such companies may refuse payment for charges that exceed this limit, unless prior approval of the specific charges is sought. It is up to the hotel to know and observe the floor limit established by each credit card company.

folio—A statement of all transactions affecting the balance of single account.

internal audit—The organizational plan, methods, and measures adopted by a hospitality operation to safeguard its assets, check the accuracy and reliability of its accounting information, promote operational efficiency, and ensure adherence to the operation's policies and procedures.

redlined—When the last drink listed on a check is underlined (typically in red) to verify that the drink has been served. Redlining helps to prevent the check from being used to serve free drinks or to enable servers to pocket the monies from a duplicate order.

separation of duties—An element of internal control systems in which different personnel are assigned the different functions of accounting, custody of assets, and production. The purpose is to prevent and detect errors and theft.

Review Questions

1. Why should accounting functions be handled by different staff members?
2. What are some of the typical cashiering procedures?
3. What precautionary steps can employees take when presented with a credit card?
4. What forms of guest identification are acceptable when a check is presented for cash or services?
5. What is a second- or third-party check, and why do many properties choose not to accept them?
6. What questions must a property consider when accepting personal checks?
7. How should a guest's credit be denied, when necessary?
8. Why are incomplete or illegible guest registration records a problem?

9. What key areas are covered by a strong information technology security program?

10. What tasks are internal auditors responsible for performing?

Internet Sites

For more information, visit the following Internet sites. Remember that Internet addresses can change without notice.

Amerisafe Industries, Inc.
http://www.ameriworld.com/btv/index.htm

Hospitality Financial and Technology Professionals
http://www.hftp.org

The Information Systems and Control Association and Foundation
http://www.isaca.org

The Institute of Internal Auditors
http://www.theiia.org

Case Study

Points of Internal Control at the Eastwick Resort

Scenario #1—Purchasing

Percy Purveyor, a hotel supplier, sat opposite the general manager of the Eastwick Resort, Guy Thorpe. Percy was meeting with him to satisfy his curiosity—and to air a grievance.

"I've been in business in this area for a few years now, Guy, and I know my competitors' products and prices well. Your property has been using Electrotel products all its life, and I know for sure that my goods are of better quality than theirs. Our price ranges are pretty close. I'm dying to know what kind of discount they're giving you to make you so faithful to them all this time."

"Discount? None but the usual one for the volume we purchase," said Guy.

"Not even a discount for timely payment?"

"Well, yes, that too, but those are the only two. Why are you so surprised?"

"That makes Electrotel's deal with you even worse. My volume discount and discount for timely payment are even better than theirs, and my rates are still comparable—for a better product." Percy leaned back and looked thoughtfully at Guy. "Your purchasing agent shows only a hint of interest when I make a pitch; it seems like he's just not listening. None of my solid arguments for considering my company's products reach him. It boggles my mind that someone could consistently choose a clearly inferior series of products at higher prices. Has your customer base changed to warrant lower-end products?"

Guy bristled. "Certainly not. This remains a property for the business traveler and upscale leisure market."

Percy shrugged. "It was just a thought. Your purchasing policies mystify me."

"I have noticed that our property lags behind comparable ones in purchasing efficiency," mused Guy. "By more than five thousand dollars some months. I'll tell you what: Let's meet again at the end of the month and talk about your products some more. Between now and then, there's some research I'd like to do."

Scenario #2—Check Cashing

The Eastwick Resort received two returned checks from the bank this week. One was a personal check for $250 that was dated March 18, and the hotel had tried to cash it March 17; and the other was a corporate check for $1,000.

The corporate check looked valid, with two signatures by financial officers and "Travel" in the memo space. When hotel staff called the corporation, they found that the check was indeed valid but only for authorized corporate agents, and the guest the hotel had hosted was not authorized.

Furthermore, the guest tricked the hotel into giving him almost $860 in cash by saying that though the corporation had prepaid his expenses for a week-long stay, he was going to leave after one night and would like to be reimbursed for the difference.

Scenario #3—Payroll

Almost all the housekeeping staff at the Eastwick Resort are part-time employees, and turnover is high. Recently, payroll expenses have increased significantly, but the general manager believes that the actual number of employees has dropped. When Guy Thorpe calls in his housekeeping manager, Jay, even Jay doesn't know for sure how many room attendants currently are (and should be) on the payroll. Some are on leave for various reasons, some have made it unclear whether they still want to work for the property, and so on. "We may have ghosting going on—someone could be setting up fictitious employees on the payroll and collecting their 'wages,'" Guy tells Jay.

Scenario #4—Linen Loss

The housekeeping department at the Eastwick Resort has been losing six to eight sheets per week. Jay and his assistant normally take inventory monthly, but they started taking it weekly when they noticed losses. Jay decided that the volume of loss is too high and too consistent to be attributable to guest theft, so he turns his attention to employees.

Scenario #5—Room Charges

Celia Sly has just treated several of her close friends to a hearty lunch at the Eastwick Resort's restaurant. When the server presents the check, Celia asks her to charge it to room 213. The server agrees to take care of it.

Scenario #6—Cash Drawers

The restaurant at the Eastwick Resort has been trying a new system of distributing cash drawers. In an effort to promote cooperation and to create an atmosphere of trust with and among its employees, it has made all three cashiers on a given shift responsible for all three cash drawers the restaurant uses. Managers hoped that cashiers would develop team spirit and that they might prevent other cashiers from stealing. This system worked fine at first, but recently, the cash drawers have been short by a total of about $20 after every shift. The cashiers have become suspicious of each other and have complained loudly to managers.

Discussion Questions

1. For each scenario, what policies and procedures could be implemented to prevent the type of loss concerned? What can managers do to deal with the situation before them?
2. Which of the scenarios would require action from the security department and which would require action from other departments?
3. Suppose that the Eastwick Resort's profit goal was twelve percent. If the operation managed to recover none of its losses from the events described above, how much would the operation have to achieve in sales to recoup its losses? Use the figures given below:

Scenario #1 Purchasing	$5,000/month × 12 months =	$60,000
Scenario #2 Check Cashing	$250 + $1,750 + $50 in fees =	$ 2,050
Scenario #3 Payroll	$200 in stolen wages per week × 52 weeks =	$10,400
Scenario #4 Linen Loss	$65 in lost sheet value per week × 52 weeks =	$ 3,380
Scenario #5 Room Charges	$85 meal × 52 weeks =	$ 4,420
Scenario #6 Cash Drawers	$20 × 14 shifts/week × 52 weeks =	$14,560

Case Number: 3875CA

The following industry experts helped generate and develop this case: Wendell Couch, ARM, CHA, Director of Technical Services for the Risk Management Department of Bass Hotels & Resorts; and Raymond C. Ellis, Jr., CHE, CHTP, CLSD, Professor, Conrad N. Hilton College, University of Houston, Director, Loss Prevention Management Institute.

REVIEW QUIZ

When you feel you have covered all of the material in this chapter, answer these questions. Choose the *best* answer.

1. There should be a two-signature requirement on all checks issued by a lodging property *except*:

    a. those made out to "Cash."
    b. for payroll checks.
    c. for those signed by the owner-manager.
    d. when the employee signing the check is highly trusted.

2. Which of the following is *least* likely to lessen internal loss at cash registers?

    a. register audits
    b. recording all transactions upon payment
    c. assigning one person per register
    d. cashier applicant screening

3. Electronic verification of credit cards generally:

    a. guarantees that the card's presenter is the legitimate owner.
    b. requires the card's presenter to wait a long time.
    c. protects the property from loss if the card later proves fraudulent.
    d. involves checking the expiration date and signature block.

4. If a credit card proves to be invalid, hotel staff should:

    a. invite the guest into a private room to discuss his or her credit situation.
    b. follow the property's and card company's established policies.
    c. inform the guest that he or she cannot/will not be allowed to stay at the hotel.
    d. privately telephone the police.

5. When should payment arrangements be made between the guest and the property?

    a. when checking in
    b. when making a reservation
    c. at check-out
    d. at any point during the guest's stay

6. Computer passwords should be:

    a. written down near the computer.
    b. very hard to memorize.
    c. permanent and unchanging.
    d. unique.

REVIEW QUIZ *(continued)*

7. Internal auditors are primarily responsible for:
    a. prosecuting those who attempt to defraud the hotel.
    b. preparing annual tax documents.
    c. determining that all laws are obeyed.
    d. explaining downturns in a hotel's business.

Answer Key: 1-c-C1, 2-d-C1, 3-c-C2, 4-b-C3, 5-a-C4, 6-d-C5, 7-c-C6

Each question is linked to a competency. Competencies are listed on the first page of the chapter. An answer reading 3-b-C4 translates to:

   3: the question number
   b: the correct answer
  C4: the competency number

Chapter 6 Outline

Developing an Emergency Management Program
Bombs and Bomb Threats
Fire
Hurricanes
    Hurricane Watch
    Hurricane Warning
    Waiting
    Direct Hit
    Conclusion
Tornadoes
Floods
Earthquakes
Blackouts
Robberies
Medical and Dental Emergencies
Terrorism
    Sabotage
    Kidnappings and Hostage Situations
    Riots and Civil Disturbances
Media Relations
    What to Tell the Media
    Dealing with Group Disturbances

Competencies

1. Describe the role of an emergency management plan. (pp. 291–295)
2. Demonstrate knowledge of safety and security measures for responding appropriately to a variety of emergency situations, including bombs, fires, hurricanes, tornadoes, floods, earthquakes. (pp. 295–305)
3. Implement procedures for handling blackouts, robberies, medical and dental emergencies, terrorist acts, and civil disturbances. (pp. 305–316)
4. Outline a viable media relations response in the event of an emergency situation. (pp. 316–321)

6

Emergency Management and Media Relations

AT FIRST GLANCE, emergency management may seem a subject area alien to the concept of hospitality; yet, in today's society, emergency preparedness is an important element in a lodging establishment's ability to provide for guests and the public. As with any segment of administration and operations, there must be a commitment on the part of the property's management to emergency preparation, management, and recovery.

This chapter will discuss programs at the property level to deal specifically with a wide variety of emergency situations, including bomb threats, fires, hurricanes, tornadoes, floods, earthquakes, blackouts, robberies, emergency medical incidents, and terrorism. It then will explore constructive ways of working with the media and public relations to successfully recover from an emergency and rebuild a positive reputation.

Developing an Emergency Management Program

Emergency or contingency planning is an important element in the security of a lodging establishment. The degree of emergency preparation that is feasible will vary from property to property. Management should consider: What resources, equipment, and staff members are to be directed to such a program? Will community or governmental agencies be involved in achieving an acceptable program? Where will the control center be located? Who will be in charge? What is the order of command to cover situations when the top members of management may be unable to assume leadership roles? Questions like these are relevant to emergency management planning.

In developing an emergency (or contingency) plan for a hotel or motel, management should consider the following items:

- The potential for various types of emergencies to occur
- Liaison possibilities with other hotels and motels in the community; service organizations (Red Cross, Salvation Army, etc.); local agencies, including police and fire authorities; and local utility companies
- Personnel needs, availability, and skills
- Equipment, supply, and communications needs
- Training opportunities to prepare the staff for an emergency

- Opportunities for emergency preparedness and simulated emergency drills at the community level

Remember that each property is different. As with so many other aspects of the successful operation and administration of a hotel or motel, the emergency program must be developed on an individual basis.

An initial step might be the formation of an executive-level committee within the property to help establish the emergency plan. This executive-level committee may include all department heads in addition to the general manager, assistant managers, and resident manager. In a small property, such a committee could include the owner and/or manager and at least one or two additional key personnel.

Once formed, the committee could begin by identifying the possible emergencies for the particular area and property. The following emergencies and any others that may be appropriate to a given property may be reviewed to determine whether any could affect the hotel or motel: bomb threats or bombings, fire, hurricane, tornado, flood, earthquake, blackout, blizzard, ice storm, kidnapping, hostage situation, medical or dental emergency, sniper, workplace violence, riot and civil disorder, mudslide, contaminated water supply, food poisoning, elevator emergency, lightning, forest fire, hazardous materials spills. Of course, some emergencies will be unique to a single operation and therefore impossible to predict.

After deciding which events are likely to occur, an effort can then be made to determine which local agencies will provide support in the event of an emergency. Such agencies may provide resources and backup prior to, during, and after an emergency, which can be coordinated with the individual property's program. The 10 regional offices of the Federal Emergency Management Agency (FEMA) establish programs under direction of the national FEMA office. On the Internet, the offices of FEMA maintain a continuing reporting service on various emergencies within the regions, along with various resources to assist an individual property and its community in meeting the emergency. The programs provide an ongoing coordinated effort to prepare the general public for emergency situations. Finding such support "before the fact" is the difference between having a written plan and active planning.

The support of neighboring properties may also be a factor in an emergency. One example of cooperation among lodging properties themselves was reported by the Dallas County Hotel/Motel Association. When smoke was observed rising from the Quality Inn—Market Center from a two-alarm fire, it brought an immediate response from neighboring hotels. The Loews Anatole Hotel sent two security men equipped with radios to the fire scene to relay any emergency needs. At the Holiday Inn—Market Center, the guests evacuated from the Quality Inn were referred to a "command room" set up in a banquet hall for shelter, information, and new housing assignments. The Executive Inn housed most of the evacuated guests. In addition, the DuPont Plaza volunteered its laundry facilities to help out. Many other hotels in the area offered their help throughout the night.

A number of other local organizations can be contacted and included, if possible, in the emergency plan. Consider including the American Red Cross, the Salvation Army (or a similar organization with emergency housing, clothing, and feeding capabilities), civil defense or an integrated emergency management systems office, local utilities, the volunteer fire department, the water department, full-time police and fire departments, the weather forecasting service, National Guard units, the building inspector's department, various service organizations (such as Lions, Rotary, Sertoma), and fraternal organizations (such as Masons, Shriners, Knights of Columbus).

Another critical element in the development of an emergency response plan is the assessment of the property's personnel. Inventory the skills of staff members and find out whether any employees are certified in first aid, lifesaving (water rescue), or cardiopulmonary resuscitation (CPR); or skilled in carpentry, electrical work, plumbing, mechanical work, or food preparation under emergency conditions (for example, preparing food over a wood fire).

After this information has been compiled, emergency program planners may ask themselves various questions about the possible circumstances that may be faced at the hotel or motel during an emergency. What staff will be available if a natural disaster involves the whole community? How many of the staff will be able to reach the hotel or motel? Will it be possible for staff members with special skills to reach the hotel or motel? What will be the on-site alternative be if skilled staff persons are unable to reach the property? Are there provisions for key staff to bring family members with them to avoid having to cover responsibilities in two different locations? Is there a plan for handling an emergency when only one key staff member is on duty? What backup is feasible and how soon can backup be provided? Can cooperative agreements be arranged in advance with other hotels and motels in the area?

As a result of thinking about such questions, management can then consider the formation of emergency response teams. Generally, the composition of an emergency response team will vary according to the nature of the emergency. Management should consider staff and material needs on an emergency-by-emergency basis. A natural disaster that affects the entire community puts the hotel or motel into a different position than a fire, bomb threat, or hostage situation on the premises. The concentration of effort by the local fire and police authorities will be entirely different when responding to a single emergency at a hotel than it will be when responding to a community-wide problem, such as a flood or tornado.

In structuring an emergency response team, the following elements should be addressed:

- Consider establishing responsibilities by department for appropriate response by the staff within the department.
- Consider establishing a command center with a pre-arranged chain of command; the front desk and PBX (or phone facility at the front desk in the smaller property) can serve as that command center. If the front desk is put out of commission as a result of an emergency, alternative command centers might be set up in the executive offices, security director's office, or chief engineer's office.

- In a community-wide emergency, the property itself may have to provide technical, mechanical, and even fire-fighting capability. Consider defining and assigning to specific personnel such responsibilities as food service, housing, laundry, first aid, and construction repair as required by the nature of the particular emergency.

- It should be clearly explained to staff members that there is a single designated spokesperson for the hotel or motel. All employees should understand that they are not to talk to reporters or camera operators.

A review of equipment needs, including special equipment needs, should also be undertaken. Some possible equipment and supply needs include:

- Emergency lighting (including flashlights and candles with protective containers); auxiliary generators with reserve or alternative fuel supplies; sump pumps for relieving flooding problems; and emergency communication equipment (CBs, two-way radios).

- Food and water reserves. Consideration should be given to menu alternatives for times when cooking facilities are minimal or totally unavailable.

- Gas, battery, or manually operated tools for use in the event of power failure; tools for cutting, lifting, and moving debris in the event of building collapse due to flooding, wind, or earthquakes.

- Shutters for covering glass surfaces.

- Bedding, cots, and bed linens, if the property is designated as a housing center in a community-wide incident.

A program that is tailored to deal with a variety of emergencies is more effective if in writing (OSHA mandates that the fire emergency program be in writing). The written plan should be flexible, but should also provide enough information and detail that each employee knows what his or her responsibilities are in the event of an emergency.

Once written programs are developed, they should be disseminated. How will all members of the staff be trained in their individual roles in implementing the emergency action plan? Investigate first aid, CPR, lifesaving, and emergency response training opportunities within the community. Do not limit the training to management and supervisory personnel. The more trained staff present, the more likely an effective response will be provided in an emergency. Some properties may want to consider expanding the training to permit key members of the property's staff to participate at the community level in emergency-preparedness drills and in simulated exercises.

As mandated by OSHA, fire drills and rehearsals must be conducted. Many lodging operations have full fire drills during the day or on an early evening shift. All guests are advised of the drill and may even be invited to participate to a limited degree. For example, they may be requested to go to the nearest exit, but not to use the exit stairway to leave the floor. Guest involvement is an opportunity for employees to actually direct guests in a simulated emergency evacuation.

Community rehearsal for a natural disaster provides an opportunity to deal realistically with a number of people—establishing emergency shelters or converting existing accommodations to provide for a large number of people, administering first aid for simulated injuries, and meeting any other requirements connected with a specific emergency. Properties interested in a community-wide exercise should advise local police, fire, and emergency management authorities of their interest. Some hotels or motels may wish to volunteer their premises for housing, feeding, etc., as part of the community plan if the property is not directly affected by the emergency.

Finally, properties should consider incorporating an inspection and maintenance program for equipment assigned for emergency use. During the 1977 blackout in New York City, for example, a large hospital had to resort to the emergency battery backup for life-support systems. Reportedly, an effective maintenance program for auxiliary equipment was not in place; as the auxiliary equipment went online, it failed. Only the availability of units from the fire and police department made it possible to sustain life-support capabilities.

On-premises sessions with local authorities may also be considered. They could evaluate the operation as an integral part of the community emergency action plan.

Bombs and Bomb Threats

Procedures for responding to bombs and bomb threats at a hotel should be considered for inclusion in the property's emergency plans. The plan should be in writing, and a command center and alternate command centers should be identified. Staffing for such an emergency is critical to the success of the program. As previously noted, an analysis of the assignment of personnel and alternates is necessary to cover absences or incidents that occur when a minimal number of staff may be present.

There is a need for a continuing review of this problem at a national level. For example, during 1995 there were 1,562 bombings that involved improvised explosive devices, 406 bombings that involved improvised incendiary devices, and property damage in excess of $105 million.

Review Exhibit 1 for help in establishing a similar checklist for use in your particular hotel or motel. All staff members who are most likely to receive a bomb threat by phone should have copies. That may include switchboard staff members and personnel in the executive offices, security office, and front desk area.

The people who receive the bomb threat should be instructed not to use a radio or beeper system; the electrical impulse may cause certain types of bombs to detonate. Rather, they should contact the general manager, manager-on-duty, or the security department on a regular telephone or hardwired intercom so that the situation can be quickly assessed and the appropriate authorities (police, fire, bomb squad) notified.

The individual should also be instructed to obtain as much information as possible from the caller. Suggested questions are noted in Exhibit 1. In addition, the individual receiving the call should listen closely for voice characteristics and

Exhibit 1 Sample Bomb Threat Checklist

1. Date: _____ 2. Origin of call:
   Time of call: _____   Local _____ Long Distance _____
   Time caller hung up: _____   Internal _____
3. Exact words of caller: _____
   _____

   (CONTINUE ON BACK IF NECESSARY)

4. Ask the following, if possible:
   a. When is the bomb set to go off? _____
   b. What kind of bomb is it? _____
   c. Where did you place the bomb? _____
   d. Why did you place the bomb? _____
   e. What is your name and address? _____
   _____

   f. What does the bomb look like? _____

5. Caller: Male _____   Female _____   Adult _____   Child _____
             Age _____   Suspect _____

6. Speech: Slow _____   Excited _____   Disguised _____   Rapid _____
             Loud _____   Accent _____   Normal _____   Sincere _____
             Drunk _____ Deep _____   Soft _____   Nasal _____

7. Have you received a bomb threat before?   Yes _____   No _____
8. Do not discuss call with other employees.
9. Immediately notify the following: General Manager
                                        Manager-on-Duty
                                        Security
10. Person taking call: Name _____
                        Department _____
                        Home Phone # _____

background noises so this information can be provided to the appropriate authority to help in its investigation.

Local police should be called immediately after receipt of a bomb threat. As the police are called, some properties will begin a search of the premises. Engineering, security, and housekeeping supervisory personnel are often the source for members of a search team. These staff members work throughout the entire property and are likely to notice suspicious items or changes in the arrangement of equipment, furnishings, or other articles that might indicate the presence of a bomb. The scope of the search will depend on the information provided by the caller. However, the members of the team should not touch, handle, or move any suspicious object they might find.

While the search is in progress and before the police arrive, management will have to decide whether to evacuate the property. The policy in this regard should be carefully reviewed by top management with the advice of legal counsel. If the caller specified the bomb's placement, management may decide to evacuate only those areas surrounding the alleged location of the bomb. If the caller did not specify the bomb's placement and an evacuation is deemed necessary, some properties will limit the evacuation to public areas within the establishment, since guests may be safer in their rooms than they would be passing through public areas during an evacuation. This is one of the most difficult decisions for management to make. Unfortunately, there is no "rule of thumb." Even when the police arrive, they may leave the decision to evacuate to management, although they may make recommendations.

A single evacuation team with alternate escape routes mapped out can meet most of the emergency evacuation needs of a lodging establishment. Since the team usually includes the same members, they should receive training in the various alternate strategies employed depending on the nature of the emergency.

If, in spite of every effort, a bomb does explode on the premises, the response plan should include procedures for emergency medical service, evacuation of the injured to a medical facility, an emergency search of the bomb site and removal of structural elements which may have trapped individuals at the time of the explosion, and debris removal and repairs to return the hotel or motel to operational status. Remember, local authorities may need time to examine the bomb site. Prior knowledge and permission from the authorities may be required before repair work can begin.

Fire

Written plans must be formulated for possible fire emergencies. The OSHA standard for "Means of Egress"[1] mandates that employee emergency plans and fire prevention plans shall include:

1. Emergency escape procedures and emergency escape route assignments
2. Procedures to be followed by employees who remain to operate critical hotel/motel operations before they evacuate
3. Procedures to account for all employees after emergency evacuation procedures have been completed
4. Rescue and first aid duties for those employees who are to perform them
5. The preferred means of reporting fire and other emergencies
6. Names or regular job titles of persons or departments who can be contacted for further information or explanation of duties under the plan

Staffing for a fire emergency is an important consideration. A property should carefully evaluate its needs and realistically establish appropriate responses and emergency teams. Emergency team members may come from various parts of the property. The team's general responsibilities may include evaluating the situation when a fire is reported, extinguishing small fires if this can be done safely, assisting the fire department, maintaining calm and order with guests and employees, and assisting in any necessary evacuation. The task of maintaining calm and order among the guests involves establishing procedures for communicating with them. Survivors of some hotel fires have voiced concerns over the lack of information available at the time about the fire and what they should do.

As part of a property's emergency action plan, OSHA requires an employer to designate and train a sufficient number of persons to assist in the safe and orderly evacuation of employees. In addition, the plan must be reviewed with each employee covered by the plan when it is initially developed, whenever the employee's responsibilities or designated actions under the plan change, and whenever the plan itself is changed. Although OSHA requirements are not directed to the public or guests, they undergird the hotel or motel's program for emergency evacuation of guests and the public, as well as employees.

Two important points concerning the nature of fires and injuries due to fires need to be made. First, there are three main classes of fire that a lodging property should prepare for. Class A fires involve ordinary combustibles such as wood, paper, and cloth. Class B fires involve flammable liquids and grease, paints, oils, and so forth. Class C fires involve electrical equipment. (Class D fires involve combustible metals and are rare in a hotel environment. Class K fires, involving cooking oils and grease, are a particular concern for hotels with food and beverage operations.) Although a fire can begin with any single type of fuel source, it can and most often does spread to fuel sources in other classes. For example, an electrical fire near an open can of paint and a bag of old rags can become an "ABC" fire in a matter of seconds. Each class of fire requires a specific type of extinguishing agent. A property should inform its employees of where its fire extinguishers are located and train them in how to use the type or types of fire extinguishers available on the premises.

The second point is that most injuries and deaths are caused by the smoke and gases that are released during a fire and not by the actual flames. Keeping close to the floor increases the chance for survival of people caught in a fire. If it is necessary to move through or into a smoke-filled room, the person doing so should place a wet towel over his or her head and mouth, if possible; the towel will act as a filter, making breathing easier.

Fires may start in various ways. One cause of fire is arson. It is difficult to establish a profile of a typical arsonist as their motives vary. Tragic fires may be started out of spite; fires have been started by discharged employees and by persons evicted from a property's bar or lounge. Fatal fires have also been traced to individuals with psychological and physiological problems. Within legal limits, every effort should be made to screen new employees to avoid employing an arsonist.

When a fire occurs, there should be immediate action. The fire alarm should be sounded to alert guests and employees of the fire, and the fire department should be immediately notified. Employees should learn the location of fire alarm boxes and how to operate them *before* an emergency occurs. Some alarms send an automatic alarm signal to the local fire department, but a follow-up telephone call may still be advisable to confirm that the fire department has indeed received the alarm. Anyone in immediate danger should be evacuated from the area if possible.

It is sometimes said that the first five minutes of fire fighting may be worth more than the next five hours of fire fighting. Once a fire has been discovered and reported, the time that passes while awaiting the arrival of the fire department may be crucial. During this period, prompt and effective action by trained personnel on the scene may contain or extinguish the fire. Of course, personnel should be trained not to take risks that unnecessarily endanger themselves or others; it may be beyond the ability of the staff to fight some fires.

After a fire has occurred, a property may ask for a fire report that discusses what is known about the fire and any damage or injury it caused. A sample fire report is shown in Exhibit 2. The form should be developed and adapted to meet your specific needs.

Review your fire protection program and capabilities with local fire authorities and remain current on local code changes that may apply to your lodging facility. Fire protection requirements specified by the Occupational Safety and Health Act should be carefully reviewed for compliance.

Some communities require the fire authority to review and approve emergency fire programs for the property. Some fire departments have the capacity to assist in training hotel or motel employees in fire emergency procedures. Working relationships with the fire authorities can be very helpful.

Hurricanes

Hurricanes present both water and wind damage problems for hotels and motels (see Exhibit 3). According to the National Hurricane Center in Miami, a hurricane produces a "storm surge" that precedes the hurricane. This surge of water causes a tide averaging 22 feet above the mean low-water level. The hurricane itself brings winds in excess of 75 miles an hour. Consequently, a property should take precautions to minimize the potential for damage in such an event.

The National Hurricane Center has established an information system to notify people about the threat of a hurricane. The first step is the declaration of a hurricane watch.

Hurricane Watch

When the National Weather Service issues a hurricane watch for an area, it indicates that a hurricane is on its way and may be a threat over the next few days. This should be the first signal to "batten down the hatches."

At this stage, there are no physical signs of impending bad weather. Properties may wish to begin preparing the premises. Anything outside that is mobile—such as lounges, tables, chairs, trash cans, small planters, umbrellas, and guestroom patio furniture—may be removed and stored inside the building.

Provisions may be made for an ample supply of duct tape, which could be used to prevent seepage around doors and to "X" over large sections of glass in

Exhibit 2 Sample Fire Report

This report must be completed for ALL fires regardless of the dollar loss and forwarded to the appropriate management.

Date _____   Time fire was discovered _____
Time fire department was notified _____
Name of person notifying fire department _____
Guest name & room number _____
Manager—describe exactly what happened _____

_____

Where did fire start? _____
What burned? _____
Fire damage: Building _____
             Contents _____
Number and kind of portable extinguishers used _____
Did sprinkler system operate? _____
Did dry chemical or CO_2 system operate? _____
Action taken by fire brigade _____

Action taken by fire department (including time of response) _____

Injuries: Employee _____
     Guest _____
Name and phone number of fire department office/investigator _____

---

public areas, as may be necessary. A number of Masonite sections cut to window size may be helpful, with an ample supply of 2-by-4 braces for securing any shutters to the window areas. This material is also useful for the temporary repair of broken doors or windows.

A supply of caulking may be needed for sealing all solid doors at ground level. It may also be used for leaks that might develop around windows. Sandbags may be necessary to protect against water intrusion and can be purchased in the quantity necessary for the property.

Each property should be equipped with a supply of waterproof flashlights for outside and inside use in the event of a power failure. Candles and appropriate holders, with windguards if possible, should also be on hand.

All key personnel should be instructed to be on call if the storm should worsen. They in turn may arrange for people in their departments to also be available, if necessary. Consider having department heads bring their families to the

Exhibit 3   Hurricane Scale and Effects on Property

Category	Definitions and Effects
ONE	*Winds 74–95 mph:* No real damage to building structures. Damage primarily to unanchored mobile homes, shrubbery, and trees. Also, some coastal road flooding and minor pier damage.
TWO	*Winds 96–110 mph:* Some roofing material, door, and window damage to buildings. Considerable damage to vegetation, mobile homes, and piers. Coastal and low-lying escape routes flood two to five hours before arrival of center. Small craft in unprotected anchorages break moorings.
THREE	*Winds 111–130 mph:* Some structural damage to small residences and utility buildings with minor amount of wall failures. Mobile homes are destroyed. Flooding near the coast destroys smaller structures, with larger structures damaged by floating debris. Terrain continuously lower than five feet above sea level may be flooded inland eight miles or more.
FOUR	*Winds 131–155 mph:* More extensive wall failures with some complete roof structure failure of small residences. Major erosion of beach areas. Major damage to lower floors of structures near the shore. Terrain continuously lower than 10 feet above sea level may be flooded, requiring massive evacuation of residential areas inland as far as six miles.
FIVE	*Winds greater than 155 mph:* Complete roof failure on many residences and industrial buildings. Some complete building failures with small utility buildings blown over or away. Major damage to lower floors of all structures located less than 15 feet above sea level and within 500 yards of the shoreline. Massive evacuation of residential areas on low ground within 5 to 10 miles of the shoreline may be required.

This data from the National Oceanic and Atmospheric Administration (NOAA) provides the Saffir/Simpson Hurricane Scale by which the storm's intensity is measured.

premises. Besides being a safety measure, it will relieve employees of the added worry of their families in addition to their property responsibilities.

During a hurricane watch, guests should be informed that any removal of furniture is being done as a precaution. The hurricane could change direction and move out to sea, at which point the watch would be removed and everything could return to normal. If the hurricane remains on an endangering path, however, and the storm begins to intensify, the watch will be removed and a "hurricane warning" will be posted.

Hurricane Warning

As storms reach "hurricane warning" intensity, there is usually a rather noticeable change in weather, with increased winds, possible showers, and darkening skies. At this point, the storm may be considered a serious threat and constant monitoring of forecasts should begin. It is also likely at this time that government agencies for the locale may recommend complete evacuation of the area.

Following the devastating hurricanes during the 1990s, the policy of staying to protect the property from storms and looters has been reassessed. For example, in 1992 Hurricane Andrew demolished property valued at $25 billion and left 200,000 persons homeless. FEMA's relief costs exceeded $1.8 billion. The tragically destructive Hurricane Mitch in 1998 left more than 9,000 persons dead and entire communities wiped out.

Although there recently has been an increase in ordered evacuations by local, state, and federal agencies, there continues to be a reluctance in some jurisdictions to issue such a mandate, as the storm may divert in the last hours before an anticipated direct hit; the economic and political fallout could be considerable. Properties in the direct path of a destructive storm cannot minimize damage by the presence of a few persons or even the entire staff. The possible risk to life of staff required to remain in an establishment must be reviewed by senior management in consultation with community emergency service agencies.

Measures should be taken to rearrange all high-cost foodstuffs. Dry goods should be removed from low-lying storage areas to a higher level in the property. If there is insufficient storage for frozen items on a higher floor, frozen foods should be relocated to the highest shelves in the present freezers. During a power outage, the doors to all refrigerators and freezers should not be opened. Frozen and refrigerated foods will remain at a safe temperature for a period of 12 to 14 hours.

During a warning, the hurricane may still veer away from the coast and reduce any possible danger. If, however, the storm continues to intensify and heads directly for the coastline, the Weather Sevice will begin to announce the time and with what intensity the hurricane is expected to hit.

Thomas E. Drabek, Ph.D., Department of Sociology, University of Denver, has conducted a significant study of the disaster evacuation behaviors of hotel guests and other tourists and transients in areas that are involved in a disaster evacuation, whatever the disaster might be. Dr. Drabek has found through post-disaster interviews and screenings that there is a breakdown in communications to the guest, tourist, or transient. They become quite apprehensive as they do not have any idea what is going on, what options they might have, or what the property plans to do for them. Disaster planning for the lodging establishment should include specific instructions as to how the non-staff persons on the property are to be kept advised of the property's status and its total disaster and possible evacuation plan.[2]

Waiting

With only hours left until the storm hits, the final flood precautions should be taken. Sandbags can be put in place, limited-access doors caulked, windows taped, and temporary repair lumber made accessible.

If the Civil Defense authorities have designated the property as a Civil Defense Shelter, it is not necessary to evacuate guests. All that can be done at this time is to reassure people and keep a close watch on the storm's progress.

Direct Hit

If the forecasts for the hurricane continue to become more severe and it becomes inevitable that the hurricane will strike the area, everyone should be moved into the hallways on each floor above the third floor, as an initial wave surge can be 20 to 25 feet high. The center core of the building is the safest place to be if glass should break and water begins to rise. An ample supply of chairs, blankets, pillows, and candles can be made available on each floor.

The employees should be concerned with the welfare of the guests and with immediately responding to any emergency situations that arise. From this point on, it is a matter of "sitting it out."

Conclusion

After the hurricane passes, an immediate evaluation of the damage must be made and procedures for clean-up established. Normal operation should be resumed as quickly as possible.

Tornadoes

Tornadoes involving properties at inland or lake locations may generally be met within the framework of the program developed for withstanding a hurricane. Frequently, tornado action will occur as an aftermath of a hurricane's movement from the ocean or gulf onto land. In all instances, being prepared and having a plan are of vital importance. Assigning duties to personnel is an important part of planning, and it will be more successful if done without the pressure of an impending emergency. Attention should be given to the protection of lives on the property.

If possible, a shelter can be established in a basement area, tunnel, underground parking facility, or other below-grade location removed from glass windows, doors, or panels. When selecting a shelter, avoid locations in the building where there is a long-span roof (such as over a convention or meeting room), a covered swimming pool, or an atrium-style lobby.

Maintain a battery-operated radio in operative condition. In a tornado emergency, the radio might provide the only communication with the outside.

Floods

Recent years have seen significant and extensive flooding throughout the contiguous United States. In such instances, a full evacuation is ordered and there is no opportunity to implement an emergency plan. However, for most other flood situations, the following suggestions are relevant.

Properties located in areas where floods occur should have an emergency plan for use in the event of a flood. All necessary pump equipment should be accessible and in working order. All supplies required for caulking, barricading, and related protection should be stored in such a way that they are available for immediate use. Telephone numbers for emergency supplies, information, and assistance should be conspicuously posted and updated when necessary.

When a property is warned of a possibility of flooding, the general manager should be immediately notified. He or she should verify the report by calling the local Civil Defense agency or the police. If the possibility of flooding is verified, the general manager can then contact those employees involved in flood emergency control.

The general manager, or his or her designee, may then assume responsibility for coordinating all departments in flood control procedures. Consider the following plan of action if there is a danger of flooding.

The front desk, which may serve as the communications link to outside agencies, can make all employees and guests aware of the possible emergency, evacuate rooms as needed, and relocate guests moved from rooms in endangered areas. The housekeeping department can attend to guests on lower levels of the property and supply necessary materials, such as old bedspreads, to be used for sealing smaller openings to prevent water seepage.

The engineering and maintenance department can at this time issue to appropriate employees any foul-weather gear on hand; set up a large flood-control pump; load a van with emergency flood control equipment (door barriers, sandbags, caulking guns); install any additional standby sump pumps; verify the working condition of gas-operated pumps; check the operation of any emergency generators; clear the basement of any objects that may get lost, damaged, or that could clog sump pumps; and test the operation of flood emergency warning lights. Additional measures may include erecting flood-control barriers when water reaches the barrier marking-stake and notifying guests via posted bulletins and oral instructions to move vehicles to higher ground, wherever possible.

The security department should secure the property and assets of the establishment and move as much as possible to a secured location away from the anticipated flood level. It should also patrol guest areas, reassure guests, assist as needed in relocating guests to upper floors of the property, and coordinate activities on the premises with those of local authorities, as necessary.

Earthquakes

Management should investigate whether an earthquake is likely to occur in the community where the hotel or motel is located. Where such a danger exists, planning might include:

- Establishing a command center and assigning personnel to emergency response teams as previously discussed.
- Supplying the center with portable radios and additional batteries.
- Keeping first aid supplies on hand for use by trained staff members.
- Establishing food and water reserves.
- Keeping appropriate wrenches available for turning off gas and water valves. The security staff as well as the engineering staff should know the location and proper method for turning off such utilities.

- Providing flashlights and extra batteries. Schedule an occasional maintenance check to be sure flashlights and batteries are operative.

A general recommendation during an earthquake is to suggest that employees and guests remain indoors and get under a substantial piece of furniture, such as a desk or table. A door frame may also provide some protection. Individuals should be instructed to stay away from windows and to find an inside location where there is minimal danger of being struck by falling objects, such as books from shelves or stored items from shelves in storerooms or display areas. Shelf units or other items of furniture that might tip and injure a person should be anchored to the floor or to a wall.

If staff or guests are outside the building, suggest the advisability of getting to an open area and staying away from buildings and overhead power lines.

As stated earlier, security, engineering, and housekeeping personnel frequently compose a search team. Following an earthquake, they should immediately check for any personal injuries and provide appropriate first aid until medical assistance can be obtained or the victims can be safely moved to a medical facility. The team should also check for spills or leaking water, gas, or chemical containers on the premises that could result in physical harm, fire, or explosion. Toilet facilities should not be used until the integrity of the sewage system is verified.

Food and water supplies should be inspected and necessary steps taken to protect such supplies for use during the emergency. Where refrigeration has been interrupted, consider preparing as much of the food as possible with the use of outdoor cooking equipment such as grills or charcoal broilers.

The property should take appropriate steps to prevent injuries from broken windows, doors, curtain walls, and so forth. Employees should be careful around shelving, doors to storage areas, and closets where materials may have piled up against the door, creating a hazard.

Any pre-arranged program with local agencies and authorities should be implemented. If the property has sustained minimal damage, it may serve as an emergency center for the community. Communication by messenger, two-way radio, ham radio, or CB radio can keep the hotel or motel in contact with local authorities and the community.

Blackouts

Guests, employees, the property, and the assets of the hotel or motel and its guests may all become involved in a blackout. Security should be a consideration in the plan of action when the power fails.

Battery-operated emergency lighting should be considered. In larger establishments, the feasibility of an emergency generator should also be reviewed. With or without that lighting capability, the security staff or other management staff must be ready, with flashlights as a light source, to secure the monies and negotiable items on the premises.

As necessary, security personnel should work with the engineering department and local police and fire authorities in freeing guests or employees from

> **The Opryland Hotel's Blackout Solution**
>
> In 1998, the 2,883-room Opryland Hotel purchased two locomotive engines to obtain the diesel capability for generating power. This supplements four generators that provide additional auxiliary power. This combined capacity allows management to meet most, although not all, of the power needs of the large hotel, convention, and entertainment complex. It also permits Opryland to benefit from an "economy surplus power" rating from the Nashville Electric Service. Usually this rating is provided to heavy industry within a community. To avoid a brownout or blackout, the utility may call upon Opryland to go on-line with its auxiliary system during a time of excessive peak demand throughout the Nashville power grid.
>
> While this co-generation aspect of operations is not usually a consideration within the context of loss prevention management, this can affect the bottom line in a positive way—with payback in around five years. It also permits a large facility to continue functioning when the balance of the community may be in a brownout or blackout. More important to the community is the fact that the shift of power need might actually avert a brownout or blackout condition on the Nashville grid.

stalled elevators. Management should consider providing auxiliary equipment for light and communication to a stalled elevator. Ideally, emergency generators will provide sufficient power to move elevator cars to the next floor for evacuation. If feasible, sufficient power may be generated to maintain the services of one car during a blackout.

It is most important to have patrols operating during a blackout to reassure guests and staff and to minimize any acts of vandalism or sabotage on the premises. The potential for looting should be recognized and a plan of action formulated to deal with such incidents. Give special attention to the fire hazard from candles provided for emergency use in the guestrooms. Candles should be used with appropriate holders or windguards.

If sufficient security staff is available, perimeter patrols should be increased, especially at access points. Consider whether access may be reduced to a single location at the main entrance of the property. Where courtesy cars and employees' personal vehicles are on the premises, such vehicles could be strategically located to temporarily provide perimeter lighting.

Robberies

Unfortunately, because lodging properties typically have at least some cash on the premises, cashiers are sometimes confronted by armed robbers. While it is easy to tell cashiers to be calm, suggestions concerning their behavior during a robbery will help them respond as reasonably as possible under the circumstances. Cashiers should comply with a robber's demands and make no sudden movements that might be perceived by the robber as an attempt to thwart the crime. Cashiers should not do anything to jeopardize their lives or the lives of other persons. Amateur criminals may be extremely nervous, and professional criminals may have little regard for others; in either case, unexpected actions or a lack of cooperation might cause a weapon to be used.

Management should consider having a silent alarm in the cash drawer that may be activated when a predetermined packet of bills is removed from a certain clip. Generally, the serial numbers of the bills in this packet are recorded and the bills are not used in regular business transactions. When complying with a robber's demand for money, the cashier removes this packet of money with the rest of the money. No comment should be made; the cashier should not offer unsolicited information to the robber. The cashier should avoid the appearance of setting off an alarm.

A property's management should consider developing a robbery description form to meet its needs (see Exhibit 4). Whether or not such a form is used, the cashiers and other employees should observe the robber carefully, noting physical characteristics such as height, weight, build, color and length of hair, eye color, facial hair, complexion, scars, tattoos, piercings, clothing, and anything unusual. Attention should also be given to the voice and mannerisms of the robber and to the type of weapon he or she is using.

If it can be done without danger, employees should try to observe the robber's direction of escape and the type and license number of the escape vehicle (if any). If the robber leaves behind any evidence such as a note, the cashier should carefully set it aside for the police. Similarly, employees should refrain from touching, and assist in preventing others from touching, articles or places the robber may have touched or evidence he or she may have left from which fingerprints may be taken.

As soon as possible following the incident, the property should notify the police.

Medical and Dental Emergencies

Lodging properties need to face the possibility of guests becoming seriously ill, accidentally injured, or even dying. The security staff should be ready to deal appropriately with any of these unfortunate incidents. Management should consider a policy for dealing with such problems. It should review with legal counsel and the insurance company an appropriate response to medical emergencies. It should also review with legal counsel the applicability of "good Samaritan" laws, which protect, within limits, passersby who try to help.

The Occupational Safety and Health Act requires that a trained first-aider be present on each workshift in all hotels and motels, unless those properties have ready access to medical services on the premises or in close proximity. This may prove helpful in incidents involving guests, as the staff member trained in first aid will have some knowledge of how best to assist the guest. An important point is that first-aiders will have a better idea of what *not* to do in certain situations.

The property should review with legal counsel the local regulations regarding calling an emergency medical service (EMS). This is important, for a guest may decline assistance and then later sue a property for its failure to provide appropriate aid. If legal counsel advises calling an EMS, the trained first-aider on staff should make the guest comfortable and only provide first aid assistance if a

Exhibit 4 Sample Robbery Description Form

1. Male or Female _____
2. Approximate Age _____
3. Race and Nationality _____
4. Height _____
5. Weight _____
6. Build _____
7. Color and length of hair _____
8. Color of eyes _____
9. Facial Hair:
    A. Beard _____
    B. Mustache _____
    C. Goatee, etc. _____
10. Tattoos _____ Piercings _____
11. Complexion—light, dark, etc. _____
12. Speech—accent, impairments, etc. _____
13. Clothing worn:
    A. Hat _____
    B. Shirt _____
    C. Coat or jacket—length and color _____
    D. Trousers—color and style _____
    E. Shoes _____
14. Outstanding physical characteristics—limp, deformities, etc. _____
15. Description of vehicle, if used _____
16. License number _____
17. Direction of escape _____
    WITNESS NAME _____
    _____
    _____

life-threatening condition or situation exists (severe bleeding, poisoning, and loss of consciousness due to choking or another condition affecting the ability of the guest to breathe). Cardiopulmonary resuscitation (CPR) training may also be valuable in helping a guest who may be having a heart attack. (See Exhibits 5, 6, and 7 for information relating to choking, how to get medical help fast, and CPR techniques.) The arrival of the EMS staff shifts responsibility to them for proper transportation to a medical facility. Except in major community-wide emergencies, property employees should never move a guest to a medical facility in anything other than an ambulance.

Exhibit 5 When Someone Is Choking

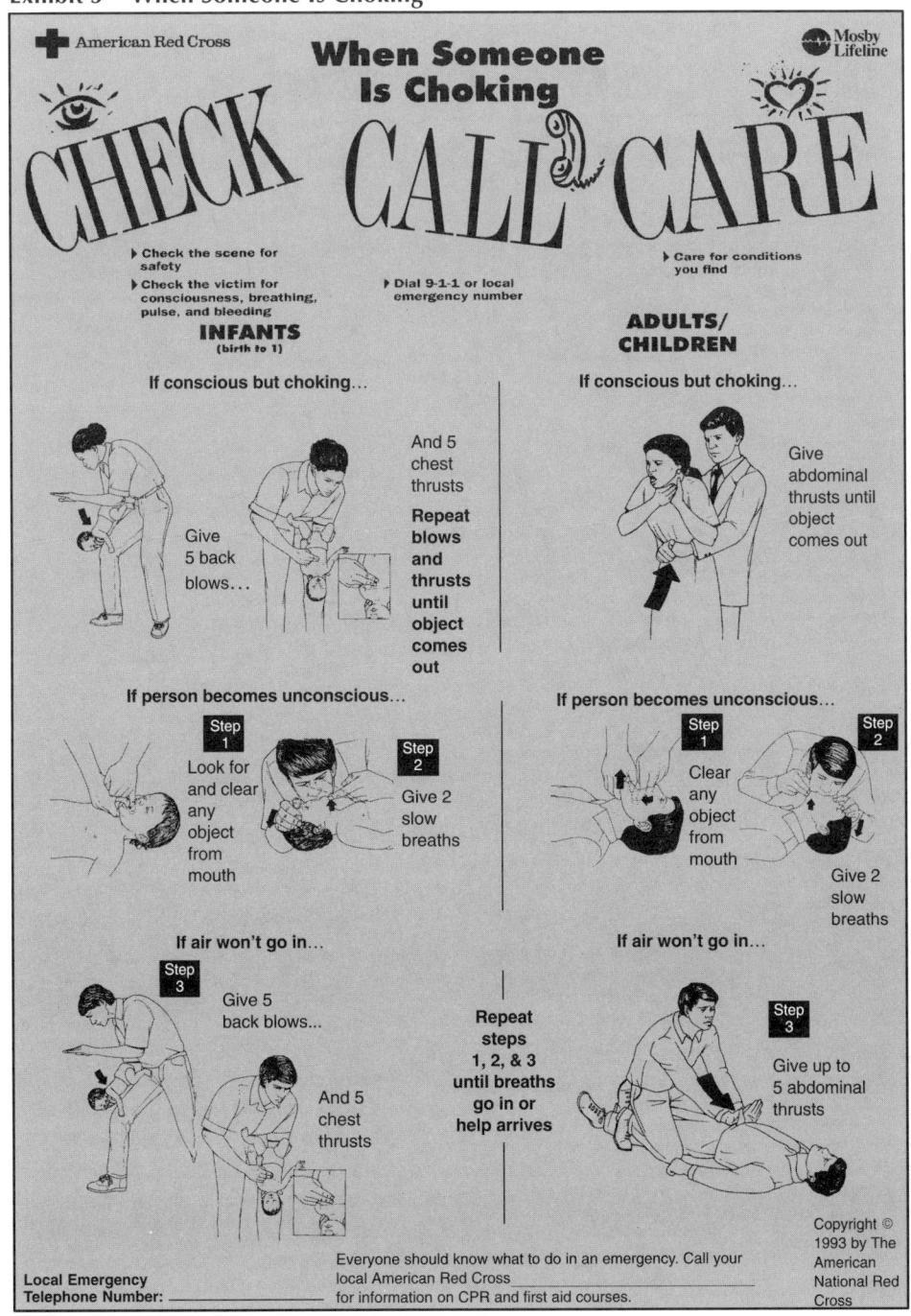

Courtesy of the American National Red Cross

Exhibit 6 How to Get Medical Help Fast

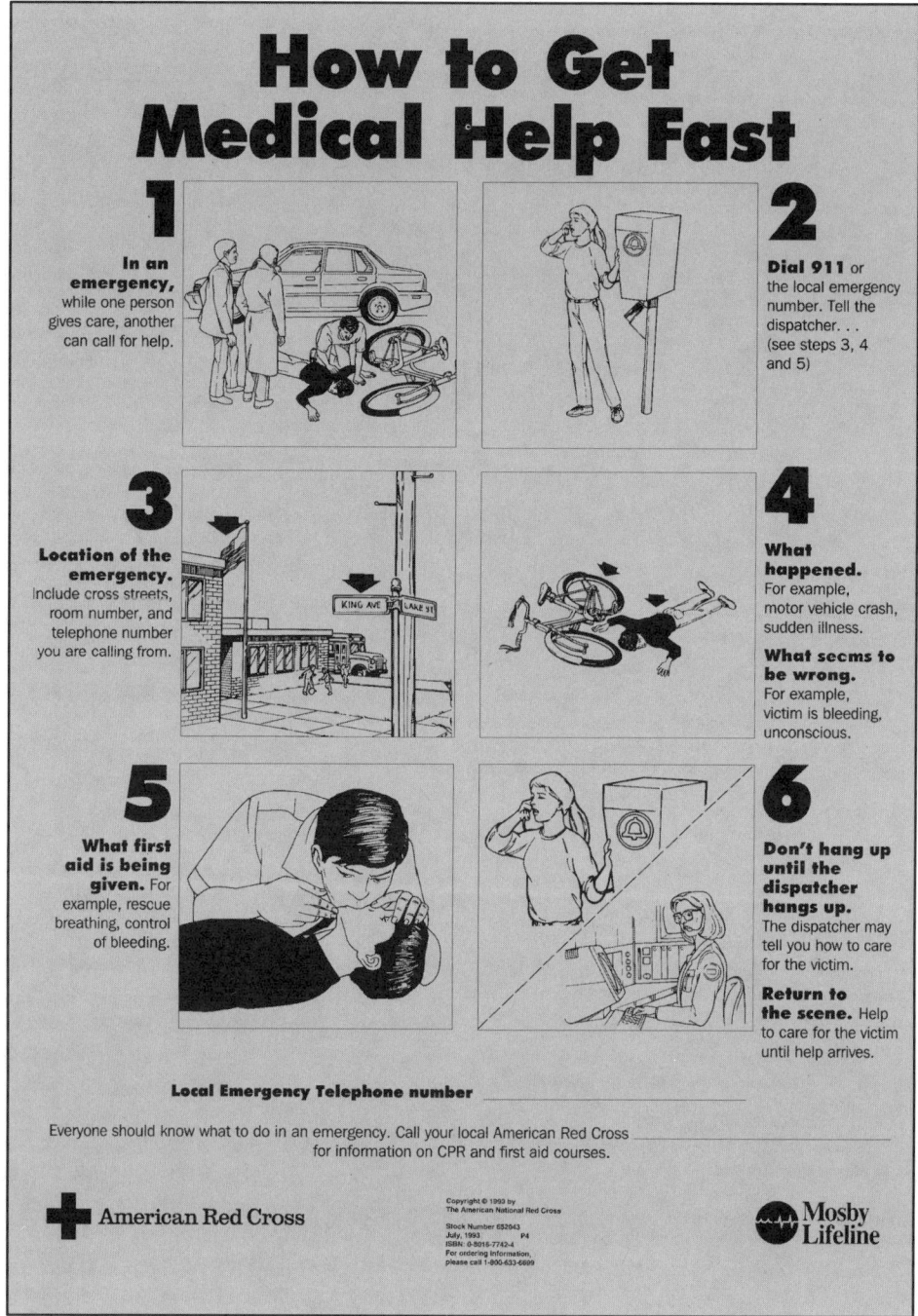

Courtesy of the American National Red Cross

Emergency Management and Media Relations   311

Exhibit 7   Adult Lifesaving Steps

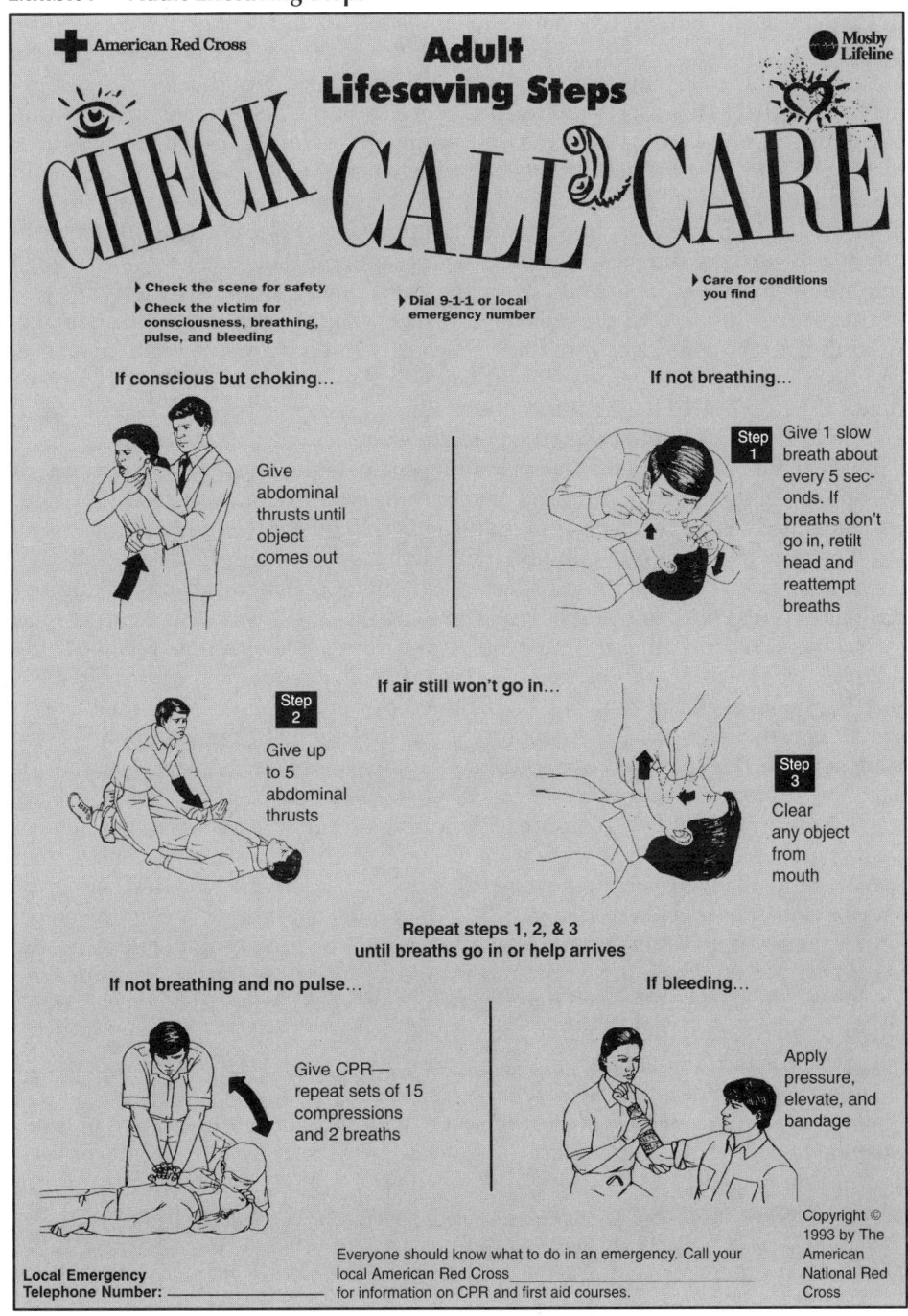

Courtesy of the American National Red Cross

When a property chooses to offer medical and dental services to guests through the use of house physicians and dentists, it should ensure that those house physicians and dentists are qualified. In *Stahlin v. Hilton Hotels Corporation*,[3] a guest, while hurriedly dressing in the room of the defendant hotel in Illinois, got his foot tangled in his shorts and fell backward, banging his head against the wall. The injury caused some pain and a large bump. His roommate called the hotel later that evening to report that the guest had a large bump on the back of his head and was vomiting. The hotel responded by sending up a woman who claimed to be a licensed practical nurse to offer assistance and medical help. She was, in fact, unlicensed. She did not diagnose a serious injury, although the guest was suffering a subdural hematoma. As a result, when the guest finally did seek the services of a doctor, it was too late to prevent major surgery and permanent brain damage. According to the court, this could have been prevented if an immediate diagnosis had been made. The hotel was found liable to the guest for $210,000. The court stated that the hotel had no duty, under Illinois law, to provide medical aid or assistance in this case, but that if the hotel did come forward to offer medical help, it must exercise reasonable care in providing such medical assistance. The hotel, in the opinion of the court, had volunteered to come forward and supply medical aid, but had failed to supply a competent person to administer the medical aid.

For reasons relating to liability, many hotels and motels, instead of offering house personnel, keep lists obtained from legitimate local medical and dental associations of physicians, dentists, and medical facilities to allow guests to make their own choices. When a guest is incapacitated and does not have a close relative at the premises, the decision should be made by a responsible member of management staff on premises at that time or by a paramedic or other trained personnel.

In coordination with the property's top management and its food service management, the security or medical staff should consider a plan of action for dealing with food poisoning incidents.

A property should also consider developing procedures for advising callers of a guest's illness and/or hospitalization. Usually, the police will provide information about incidents in which they are involved. An emergency medical service or a hospital may be less likely to notify the family or business associates of the guest. Rather than simply saying a guest has checked out or providing details as to the nature of an illness or injury, PBX and front desk personnel should consider the following: advise the caller that the guest was moved to a hospital due to a sudden illness or injury; provide the name and number of the hospital and attending physician, if possible; and connect the caller with any friend, relative, or associate of the guest if such a person is available.

It is important for the director of security or another representative of management to record any known facts or circumstances relating to an illness or accidental injury. If possible, the property should obtain statements from any witnesses to an accident. It should carefully examine the accident site, noting the condition of stairs, floor surfaces, carpeting, or any other factor involved in the accident. Any number of questions may be asked. Was the guest wearing shoes with worn heels, clogs, slippers, sandals, or other footwear that may not provide adequate protection for the foot or which reduces the guest's stability? Were there physical disabilities or limitations that might have been a factor in the accident? What was the weather? Had moisture from rain or snow been tracked into the area where the accident occurred? Was too much or too little lighting involved? Management should record any statements made by the guest and, if possible, photograph the area. Employees in the area of the accident should be instructed not to speak to the guest about whether the guest or the property is at fault. Until all the facts are known, management should make no statements and draw no conclusions.

Properties should review with the police or the coroner the appropriate response in the event of the death of a guest. Generally speaking, the police should be called immediately and the room secured until their arrival. Neither the body nor any personal effects should be touched. The police usually take charge and provide instructions on handling the guest's personal effects. If instructed to prepare the guest's possessions for removal, an inventory should be made and retained as a matter of record in case survivors later raise questions as to the items turned over to the police. Careful records should be made regarding the death, including when the guest was last seen by the staff, the time of discovery, and any data provided by the police, coroner, or other authorities.

Terrorism

Terrorism is a growing worldwide problem that may affect any number of lodging properties, perhaps especially properties and chains with operations overseas. Terrorist acts can include bombings, arson, kidnappings, hostage situations, rioting and civil disorders, and almost any act calculated to achieve some sort of political or ideological objective. We have already discussed procedures for dealing with bombings and fires. This section will look at sabotage, kidnapping and hostage situations, and riots and civil disorders. We will focus on these acts in relation to terrorism, though clearly these tactics may be used by people other than terrorists (for example, kidnappers who merely seek a ransom).

With the international holdings of many hotel corporations, special attention should be given to the executive's safety while visiting foreign lodging properties. The best advice to the executive is to keep a low profile. Consider the following points: American embassies and consulates will advise any American citizen or business representative who requests information on possible terrorist threats in foreign countries; traveling executives may wish to avoid types of cars or actions that might identify them as American, rich, or important; potential victims of terrorist acts should make all necessary emergency financial arrangements for dependents, and designate an individual or office to contact in the event these plans must be implemented. Updated overseas security advisories are available on the Internet from the Bureau of Diplomatic Security at http://www.ds.state.gov.

Sabotage

Sabotage is a terrorist technique that can be guarded against in a number of ways. Some of these involve simply adhering to sound security procedures. For example, security personnel should thoroughly investigate anything unusual or abnormal on the premises. Employees alert to security concerns may deter a potential saboteur or discover attempted sabotage before any damage has occurred.

Effective personnel procedures may also be useful. It is essential to perform a thorough pre-employment reference check of all applicants. Suspicious background information may be elicited and questionable candidates weeded out through the use of pre-employment personality tests. The employer must realize, however, that such checks will not catch all types of dangerous individuals, because in some cases the applicants are highly intelligent and well aware of how to give the "right" answers in order to get hired.

Another security tactic that may prevent sabotage is dispensing equipment and supplies under a very strict accounting procedure. Double sets of signatures can be required for obtaining certain materials and equipment. Two persons can be required to unlock a door to a restricted area. This team approach discourages unauthorized use of materials or presence in an area. Collusion between the potential saboteur and another employee would be necessary for the destructive act to be carried out.

Saboteurs may attempt to destroy a property's equipment and machinery, especially that related to its power supply. Electric cabinets and motor rooms should be locked. These facilities should be restricted to authorized personnel only. Employees using equipment should check it before starting work. This may reveal sabotage before any injuries or destruction actually takes place.

Kidnappings and Hostage Situations

Executives and their families are particularly vulnerable to terrorist kidnappings. Few are ready to meet the situation without an emotional or physical reaction, least of all children.

Potential kidnapping victims can be told of certain protective tactics in advance. Past kidnappings indicate that kidnappers generally keep victims under surveillance for substantial periods of time in order to discover travel patterns and arrange a suitable time and place for the crime. Unpredictability is one of a potential victim's best weapons, as is being discreet on the telephone (which may be tapped) when discussing information concerning travel plans. When preventive actions fail and a kidnapping occurs, kidnapping victims should:

1. Remain calm and be alert to situations which they can use to their advantage.

2. Not attempt to fight back or struggle physically. No matter how reasonable their captors may appear to be on the surface, they cannot be trusted to behave normally and their actions may be unpredictable.

3. Comply with the instructions of their abductors as fully as possible.

4. Mentally note the time spent in transit, direction, distances, speeds, landmarks along the way, special odors, and distinctive sounds and voices—even when blindfolded.

5. Mentally take note of the characteristics of their captors, including their habits, surroundings, speech mannerisms, and what contacts they make.

6. Not expect a good opportunity for escape. No attempt should be made unless it has been carefully calculated to ensure the best possible odds for success.
7. Not provoke their captors. They may be unstable and react irrationally.
8. Request special medicines or medical attention immediately if they have a disease or physical condition that requires treatment.
9. Try to establish some kind of rapport with their captors.

Lodging property officials, staff, and guests may also be subject to being held hostage on the premises. Many of the suggestions concerning kidnapping victims also apply when dealing with terrorists taking hostages. Some properties have chosen to train certain key staff members at the local and, when appropriate, corporate levels in hostage negotiation. It has been found in some cases that terrorists will refuse to negotiate with the police or a government negotiator; instead, they compel the staff to negotiate.

Every property must determine for itself the likelihood of its being the target of terrorist acts. Depending on the property and its location, the likelihood may be remote. On the other hand, international chains with a large number of properties may find the possibility to be great enough to warrant concern and advance planning. A corporate contingency plan for dealing with kidnappings and hostage situations might necessitate determining which members of the corporate staff should go to an emergency site. Operations, security, insurance, fire protection, safety, communications, and public relations officers are all possible candidates for an initial corporate response team. As stated earlier, there should be only one official spokesperson for the property.

Riots and Civil Disturbances

Two aspects of terrorism that should not be overlooked are riots and civil disturbances. Management should develop a feasible plan of action that will be implemented whenever a riot or civil disturbance occurs within reasonable distance of the lodging property. Such a disturbance cannot be ignored, even if it originates at some distance from the establishment.

Perimeter protection should be focused primarily on buildings rather than the grounds. Basement and ground-level windows should be secured, as should all entrances except the main entrance to the lobby, which should be protected by security throughout the duration of the emergency. Check for tunnels and utility connections to the property to prevent unwanted access.

Properties should consider installing fire-retardant wood or metal shutters on windows. This is especially helpful in the event of fire bombing efforts by rioters. A roof security detail may also be considered for neutralizing fire bombs that may be thrown onto the roof or other elevated surfaces.

If at all possible, properties should keep unwanted individuals out of the hotel or motel. If forced entry is made, an effort may need to be made to negotiate for the safety of guests and employees. Preparation for the responsibility of such negotiations should be coordinated with local authorities and legal counsel. This is especially important if a hotel or motel representative is to assume the role of negotiator.

Cash on hand should be reduced at the initial warning of a riot or civil disorder. If possible, monies should be moved by armored car to a bank.

A plan for food rationing might be considered. If guests and employees are trapped on the premises, a plan for feeding would be helpful. Alcoholic beverages should be secured during the emergency and should not be served.

If possible, vehicles may be protected by moving them into a secured area on the property or to a location away from the property and the riot or civil disorder.

Security staff may be supplemented by personnel from other departments to provide a security presence throughout the property. Patrols of each floor on a continuing basis may be required throughout the emergency.

Media Relations

Emergencies and bad news involving a hotel or motel may negatively affect the public's perceptions of a property. While good news is often forgotten, bad news may create a lasting memory, and its effects on business may be devastating. Effective media relations can help to minimize these effects.

Public relations plays an important part in an emergency response program. The ties between public relations and security may be critical. Unless instructed by management, the security director should not meet with the media, but may serve as a resource for the public relations director and staff as they prepare a statement for the designated property spokesperson.

What to Tell the Media

In handling emergencies and bad news with regard to public and media relations, management should exercise discretion based on the circumstances and the nature of business operations and policies. Both management and employees should know how to address the media *before* an emergency occurs.

The American Hotel & Motel Association produces a very fine *Crisis Communications Management* training video and workbook. Featuring live interviews with general managers and veteran journalists, this video can help hoteliers learn the basic steps needed to prepare for—and recover from—disastrous situations.

Every property should consider preparing its own public relations manual (with advice of legal counsel) and educate employees on the proper procedures to follow. Once a manual has been printed, it should be distributed to supervisory personnel. Then, all employees should be informed of the property's policy regarding communications with the news media. In addition, employees may be reminded of the manual's key elements from time to time. Exhibit 8 offers 10 steps to consider when preparing a media relations policy.

This section does not (nor could it) present a comprehensive media relations policy for all properties to follow. However it does discuss points that all hotels and motels might consider in preparing their own crisis communication manuals.

Exhibit 8 Establishing an Emergency Media Relations Policy

A media relations policy, also known as a crisis communications plan, explains the principles, policies, and goals that will drive a property's interactions with the media. Following are 10 steps that will show management to be responsible, competent, and cooperative in a time of emergency.

1. All facts and statements will be released through a single, designated spokesperson.
2. All company employees will be told to refer all questions to the designated spokesperson.
3. All public statements must be truthful.
4. Information will be shared as soon as it becomes available and can be confirmed.
5. A reasonable effort will be made to answer all questions.
6. The media will be allowed access to the hotel property except for areas:
   - Where the safety of reporters, guests, or employees would be compromised
   - Where security of valuables would be jeopardized
   - Declared off-limits by investigators
7. Whatever the nature or cause of the crisis, management will publicly express concern for the victims for any harm, loss, or inconvenience caused by the crisis.
8. Management will publicly acknowledge its intention to cooperate with all investigating authorities and, if necessary, to conduct its own study of the incident.
9. Employees and management will cooperate with the authorities and refer the media to them.
10. Never speculate.

Adapted from *Crisis Communications: Guidelines for the Lodging Industry*, American Hotel & Motel Association.

- The owners or management of the property should contact their attorneys for advice on whether any statement should be made to the media. The property may wish to ask counsel to help in preparing such a statement, so that neither legal rights nor the outcome of future litigation are jeopardized.
- Before answering any questions about an incident, a property should quickly and accurately determine the facts surrounding the incident.
- If a property and its attorneys decide that communication with the press is appropriate in the given situation, *there should be only one spokesperson for the property*. The spokesperson should be fully briefed on responses to any questions that may arise and should be instructed not to deviate from the prepared response. A fairly popular technique of some media reporters is to seek out and interview people, including employees, whom the incident affects or who saw the incident, instead of or in addition to interviewing the organization's spokesperson. All employees should be notified and reminded through their department heads or supervisors that they should not respond to reporters'

inquiries, but rather should refer all inquiries to management or the official spokesperson. The owner, the manager, and the appointed spokesperson should be available to respond to such referrals.

- Reporters should not be allowed to wander unescorted through the property to check damage or to interview guests and witnesses, especially if there has been a fire, explosion, or other event which may have caused structural damage.
- If possible, communications to the media should be made at a scheduled news conference so that all reporters receive the same information at the same time.

In the event of a serious incident at a property, all media inquiries should be referred by management or the appointed spokesperson to the appropriate investigating authorities (for example, the police or fire departments).

Responding to reporters' questions with "No comment" is never acceptable. It creates the perception that facts are being hidden and may move an investigative reporter into creating unnecessary and misleading reporting of an incident. All questions should be answered by the official spokesperson. In order to avoid "No comment," some properties find it preferable to explain why no comment can be made. For example, in the event of a fire or suspected arson, the inquiries should be referred to the fire chief. The property spokesperson should explain that he or she is unable to comment on the cause of the fire because it is under routine investigation by the fire department, which will release its own findings.

If there are casualties resulting from an incident, news inquiries should be referred to the fire chief, police chief, and local hospitals for confirmation. The names of victims or supposed victims should not be released to the media by the hotel or motel. Rather, such information comes from the investigating authority after notification of next of kin.

When the news media request immediate estimates from management on the extent of physical damage to the property, they may be informed by the spokesperson that any quick assessment of the extent of damages could only be a guess. Newspersons can be truthfully told that the property's insurance company investigators have been notified and that the dollar amount of damage will have to be determined by them.

There may be any number of details concerning some incidents that the property may wish to tell authorized investigators, but not the media. These details will obviously vary from incident to incident. For example, a property that has been robbed may choose not to inform the media of the exact amount of money taken or whether any cash was overlooked by the robbers. It may not discuss the types of alarm systems it uses (or whether it uses any at all) and if they functioned properly. It may withhold the identity of any witnesses who can accurately describe or identify the criminals.

Suicides, bombings, and irrational actions of unstable people may happen, on rare occasions, in a hotel or motel. Properties faced with such occurrences should immediately contact legal counsel regarding their proposed statements to the media. It may be appropriate for the spokesperson to request in those cases that the name of the property not be mentioned by the media, since lodging industry

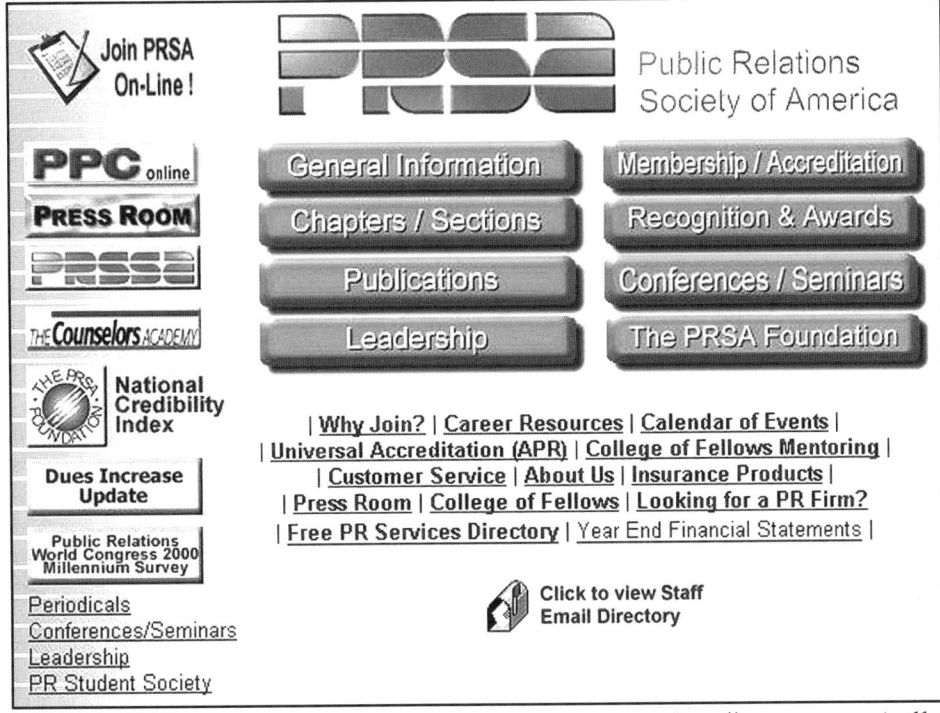

Organizations such as the Public Relations Society of America (http://www.prsa.org) offer a variety of resources, networking, and professional development opportunities for anyone who works regularly with the media to create and maintain a positive corporate image.

experience and psychological studies have shown that when a depressed or disturbed person learns of this type of activity, he or she may be drawn to the same place to commit a similar deed. The media can be asked to refer to the property as "a downtown hotel" or "a motel north of town," for example.

When possible, management or the spokesperson can describe the positive actions taken in coping with an emergency to ensure ongoing guest services and comfort. This information and cooperation may result in more sympathetic media coverage. Reporters may subsequently be more inclined to report only the facts, avoiding the temptation to sensationalize because of an uncooperative spokesperson. Also, efforts to accommodate displaced or inconvenienced guests are positive news that the property may use to combat any negative inferences which the public might draw from the emergency, regardless of its cause. The Las Vegas Palace Station Hotel & Casino made such a positive publicity effort when lightning and heavy thunderstorms caused major property damage in the summer of 1998. The initial press release, available the day following the incident, presented the situation clearly and straightforwardly:

> Early this morning, a portion of the casino roof collapsed during a heavy thunderstorm that struck the Las Vegas Valley. The collapsed area impacted approximately 25 percent of the 85,000-square-foot casino. In

addition to the roof collapse, the storm also knocked out all electrical power within a 10-square block area of Palace Station and sent floodwater through several entrances of the casino.

A few hours following this incident, a four-alarm fire broke out in a building facade at the top of the hotel tower. Damage was confined to the outside of the building at the roof. The Las Vegas Fire Department attributed the fire to lightning or rain that short-circuited wiring atop the hotel tower. It was extinguished approximately 30 minutes later while hotel security personnel evacuated approximately 2,200 guests. Injuries were minor in both incidents.

The 21-story hotel tower is fully functional with the exception of the rooms on the 21st floor that underwent more substantial smoke and water damage. The casino portion of the facility is currently closed as the company evaluates its alternatives.

The press release went on to include a quote from the property's Executive Vice President and Chief Financial Officer Glenn C. Christenson: "We are fortunate that none of our guests or team members suffered any serious injuries.... We are working with our insurance representatives, construction consultants, and engineers to determine the extent of damages, a realistic timetable for repairs, and when we can completely re-open." The next day's follow-up release announced the re-opening of several gaming facilities and four restaurants.

According to Director of Corporate Communications Jack Taylor, the key is to have "a good plan—and stick to it. Whenever you are offering any product to the public, you have to be prepared for anything that could occur. We developed our communications plan over five years ago; as our company grew, we found we needed to expand our crisis management strategies. Today, we have a written plan on the shelf at every one of our properties." That plan enabled the Palace Station to take swift action on the day of the emergency. "We had TV crews live on every side of the hotel. Our crisis response team hit the ground running, and we literally did a news conference in the parking lot. We had to act extremely quickly to make sure everyone was 'on the same page,' getting the same information. Your messages must be continuous, consistent, and accurate."

Once Taylor and his department felt the press releases had run their course, they turned to paid advertising. "Once the news aspect runs out, ads can step in and play a key role in communicating your message." The property also prepared a video news release to distribute to local media that had covered the original crisis, showing off the improvements and repairs and the hotel's series of re-opening celebrations. They also brought one of the local TV news crews back to the property for a walk-through with the city's fire chief, who explained how well-prepared the hotel was and how smoothly the emergency had been handled.

Dealing with Group Disturbances

Problems involving group disturbances might include picketing or aggressive activity by organizations critical of the property's hiring or employment policies; consumer groups taking issue with one or more of the property's services; political groups protesting the presence of a controversial guest; and more.

The bad publicity associated with such disturbances can be aggravated when the group has informed the media of its intentions ahead of time. This means reporters, television cameras, and photographers may be on the scene before the property is aware of what is happening.

Once the property is aware of what is happening, it can prepare a statement to make to the media with regard to the demonstration. It should be approved by legal counsel, if possible, and should be brief, factual, and as objective as possible. Also, the property should consider notifying the police.

If the group disturbance is well organized and members have contacted the media in advance, it is quite likely that they will have prepared their own written information to release to the media. A property is justified in asking for a copy of this material from either the media or the protesting group. This may help in the preparation of the property's statement. If the property cannot obtain this information, either in writing or orally from a group leader, it is reasonable for its spokesperson to respond to media questions by saying that the property cannot comment on something about which it knows nothing.

Endnotes

1. Occupational Safety and Health Standards, Subpart E—Means of Egress. Code of Federal Regulations, Title 29, Chapter XVII, Part 1910, Subpart E; Revised as of July 1, 1979; Amended as 45 FR 60703—September 12, 1980. Section 1910.38 Employee emergency plans and fire prevention plans.
2. Thomas E. Drabek, "Disaster Evacuation Behavior: Tourists and Other Transients," (Boulder, Colo.: Institute of Behavioral Science, University of Colorado, 1996).
3. 484 F.2d 580 (7th Cir. 1973).

Review Questions

1. What are the different types of emergencies lodging operations might have to deal with?
2. Why is emergency planning an important element in lodging security?
3. What items should management consider when developing an emergency management program?
4. What are the categories of hurricanes and what are the effects of each category?
5. What are some typical precautions to take, regardless of the type of emergency?
6. How should medical emergencies be handled?
7. Should a property offer medical service through the use of house physicians and assistants? Why or why not?
8. When preventive actions fail and a kidnapping occurs, what are some things kidnap victims should do?
9. How do media relations play a part in the emergency response system?
10. What should be included in a property's media relations policy?

Internet Sites

For more information, visit the following Internet sites. Remember that Internet addresses can change without notice.

American Red Cross
http://www.redcross.org

Bureau of Diplomatic Security
http://www.ds.state.gov

The Crisis Coalition
http://www.crisiscoalition.com

Federal Emergency Management Association (FEMA)
http://www.fema.gov

Hart Media (Media Training/Crisis Communication)
http://www.hartmedia.com

International Association of Business Communicators
http://www.iabc.com

National Fire Protection Association (NFPA)
http://www.nfpa.org

National Oceanic and Atmospheric Administration (NOAA)
http://www.noaa.gov

National Safety Council
http://www.nsc.org

Opryland Hotel
http://www.opryhotel.com

Overseas Security Advisory Council
http://www.ds.state.gov/osacmenu.cfm

Public Relations Society of America (PRSA)
http://www.prsa.org

The Salvation Army
http://www.salvationarmy.org

Case Study

Terrorist on the Telephone

PBX Operator Carolee Tomlinson glanced at the clock. "Noon," she thought as the phone rang with yet another call. She was eager to help the caller and leave for a very well-deserved lunch break. It seemed everything at the Northpoint was especially hectic today. It was the first day of the hotel's first large convention since a major renovation project was completed. With over 1,000 nationally respected guests on site, everyone wanted to make the best impression possible.

"Thank you for calling the Northpoint Hotel. How may I direct your call?"

"There's a bomb at your hotel."

Carolee gulped. "I beg your pardon, sir?"

"Your hearing better improve fast unless you want to see a lot of people get blown up."

She took a deep breath and tried to keep her nerves under control as she reached for the Northpoint's printed list of bomb-threat procedures. "I'm sorry, sir, we seem to have a bad connection. If you're on a cell phone, it might be best to—"

"I'm not on a cell phone, I'm in a ph—" He stopped. "Just listen. There's a bomb in your hotel and you'd better do something about it."

"What time is it going to go off?" Carolee asked, reading from the bomb-threat checklist.

"Forty-five minutes from now."

"12:45," she said, taking notes.

"That's what I said."

"Where is it?"

"Why don't we just say that's for me to know and you to find out. More fun that way, don't you think?"

"What kind of bomb is it?"

"The kind that sends a very, very loud message." The caller laughed, and Carolee noted the sound of traffic in the background.

"Why are you doing this?"

"You've got a lot of nerve, asking me that. I think it's time all those so-called scientists came face-to-face with the fact that there are some things they just can't fix. Maybe they won't keep thinking they can play God with people's lives."

The convention, Carolee thought. The Cancer Research Society of America. Who in the world could possibly hold a grudge against cancer researchers? And then Carolee remembered something. "Is this Dale?"

The line went dead.

Carolee glanced up at the clock. It was 12:07. Amazing how quickly your whole world can change, she thought as she dialed the police. After informing them of the threat, she notified the property's general manager, Marisa Hingle.

Marisa quickly appeared at Carolee's workstation. "What was your impression of the caller?" she asked.

Carolee reviewed her notes from the conversation. "It was a man, no accent to speak of. I think he was calling from a phone booth; I heard traffic in the background."

"No location or description of the device?" Marisa asked.

"He just said it would send a very loud message," Carolee paused. "You know, I think it was Dale Edgar. The caller specifically said he wanted to get back at our conference attendees because they were 'playing God with people's lives.' I know Dale's wife died of cancer about two weeks after he quit to care for her, and I sort of recognized his voice. But I didn't really know him well, so I don't know if it's something he's really capable of or whether he's just bluffing."

"Thanks, Carolee," Marisa said as she hurried away, glancing at her watch. "No matter who it was, we're taking every precaution. Make the evacuation call now."

For the Northpoint Hotel, "every precaution" meant an evacuation and a complete search of the property for any packages, luggage, or other devices that looked suspicious, out of place, or unclaimed.

Carolee referred to her bomb-procedures sheet again and dialed into the public-address system that goes into all of the rooms in the hotel.

"We apologize for this inconvenience," Carolee read over the PA, "but an emergency situation has arisen. We must ask that you evacuate the premises immediately, taking with you your valuables and personal belongings, and proceed to the park located across the street from the hotel. Please use the stairwells, if necessary. Do not use the elevators. Thank you. Safety code 319."

"Safety code 319" was the Northpoint's code for a bomb threat, which every staff member at the hotel would recognize. Even as people were beginning to hurry out of the conference rooms and guestrooms, hotel staff were assembling in their assigned areas.

The food and beverage and sales managers began moving through the seminar rooms and meeting spaces being used by the conference attendees. Room attendants checked linen closets and other storage areas to be sure they were indeed locked and that there were no signs of suspicious activity. Engineering employees worked their way through the mechanical rooms, checking all equipment for anything that looked unusual.

Marisa and her staff were standing at the entrance ushering guests into the parking lot when three police cars screeched down the driveway. The Channel 10 news van and a car from the *Suburban Sun-Sentinel* were close behind. Marisa knew that once the call went out over the police bands it would only be a question of "when," not "if," the news media would arrive. She also knew that herding 1,000 eminent doctors and scientists across the street and into the park was bound to create images too intriguing for the TV broadcasters and newspaper photographers to ignore. She searched the growing crowd for the hotel's director of public relations and the property's designated spokesman, Roger Carr.

Discussion Questions

1. Did the general manager make the right choice in evacuating over 1,000 guests to the park? What factors influenced her decision?

2. Based on this year's experience, should the Northpoint Hotel take any steps to prepare for bomb threats against this convention group in future years? If so, what steps might they take?

3. What points might Roger Carr make when he makes a statement to the local media? When should that statement occur?

Case Number: 3876CA

The following industry experts helped generate and develop this case: Wendell Couch, ARM, CHA, Director of Technical Services for the Risk Management Department of Bass Hotels & Resorts; and Raymond C. Ellis, Jr., CHE, CHTP, CLSD, Professor, Conrad N. Hilton College, University of Houston, Director, Loss Prevention Management Institute.

REVIEW QUIZ

When you feel you have covered all of the material in this chapter, answer these questions. Choose the *best* answer.

1. An emergency plan should include all of the following *except:*

    a. personnel availability and skills.
    b. communications needs.
    c. an analysis of past emergencies at the property.
    d. a list of liaison possibilities.

2. A hotel's in-house bomb search team often consists of members from which departments?

    a. engineering, security, and housekeeping
    b. security, food and beverage, front office
    c. front office, housekeeping, engineering
    d. housekeeping and engineering only

3. Class B fires involve:

    a. electrical equipment.
    b. flammable liquids.
    c. wood, paper, or cloth.
    d. explosive gasses.

4. A hurricane watch means:

    a. conditions are right for a hurricane to form.
    b. a hurricane is on its way.
    c. evacuation procedures should get underway immediately.
    d. the same thing as a hurricane "warning."

5. According to the Occupational Safety and Health Act, at least one hotel employee _____ should be present on each work shift.

    a. who can speak a foreign language
    b. with security guard experience
    c. with first aid training
    d. who can lift 75 pounds

6. In what situation should a hotel spokesperson use the phrase "No comment"?

    a. when speaking with antagonistic reporters
    b. when the speaker wishes to keep some facts private
    c. when the information is none of the reporter's business
    d. never

REVIEW QUIZ (continued)

7. Holding a press conference after an on-premises emergency will help to ensure that:

    a. reporters will print or broadcast the information you want.
    b. guests have all of the information they need.
    c. the property's message is not misrepresented or misquoted.
    d. all reporters receive the same information at the same time.

Answer Key: 1-c-C1, 2-a-C2, 3-b-C2, 4-b-C2, 5-c-C3, 6-d-C4, 7-d-C4

Each question is linked to a competency. Competencies are listed on the first page of the chapter. An answer reading 3-b-C4 translates to:

   3: the question number
   b: the correct answer
   C4: the competency number

Chapter 7 Outline

The Risk Management Process
    Identification of Risk
    Assessment of Potential Losses
    Selection of Proper Risk Management Instruments
    Studying the Plan and Implementing Decisions
Contributions of Risk Management to a Business
    Pre-Loss and Post-Loss Contributions
    Direct and Indirect Contributions
Insurance
    Insurance Purchase
    Industry Regulation
Commercial Package Policy
    Commercial Property Coverage
    Commercial Crime Coverage
    Boiler and Machinery Coverage
    Inland Marine Coverage
    Commercial General Liability Coverage
    Commercial Automotive Coverage
Additional Types of Coverage
    Flood Coverage
    Umbrella Coverage
    Legally Mandated Coverage
Claims Management
Establishing a Safety Committee
    The Value of Communication
    The Roles of the Safety Committee
    Safety Committee Duties

Competencies

1. Define risk management and outline the steps in the risk management process. (pp. 329–334)

2. Identify the contributions of risk management to a business in terms of pre- and post-loss contributions, direct and indirect contributions, insurance, insurance purchase, and industry regulation. (pp. 334–339)

3. List and describe the types of coverage found in commercial package policies and in additional types of coverage available to lodging properties. (pp. 339–348)

4. Demonstrate the proper procedures used for managing claims. (pp. 348–350)

5. Describe the roles and duties of a safety committee. (pp. 350–353)

7

Risk Management and Insurance

BEFORE GUESTS, EMPLOYEES, and business partners can be impressed by outstanding service, they need to perceive they have a secure and safe environment. Understanding these issues will result in effective hospitality industry management; the results will be enhanced security and safety levels for customers and employees, provided in ways which are cost efficient and integrated into all elements of daily operations.

Risk management is the protection of corporate assets through the identification, determination, and management of the risks a corporation faces. The goal of the risk management process is to achieve the most economical treatment of risk issues. As hospitality corporations have grown in size, the field of risk management has developed to provide a dedicated and knowledgeable managerial approach to the variety of security and safety issues which arise. The complexity and number of risk issues warrant this type of management. In addition, smaller operations that rely more on contract (as opposed to in-house) risk management services need to be knowledgeable purchasers of these services.

The Risk Management Process

The four steps in the risk management process are identification of risks, assessment of potential losses, selection of proper risk management instruments, and studying the plan and implementing decisions (see Exhibit 1).

The goal of the early stages of risk management is to reduce to "acceptable levels" the company's exposures to risk. This doesn't mean these are the lowest levels achievable nor that they are economically the most advantageous; it does mean that the survival of the hotel is not threatened as a result. With the logical approach of risk management, businesses can avoid potentially catastrophic levels of loss and keep the overall cost of risk at reasonable economic levels.

Identification of Risk

The risk management process begins with an **identification of risk** that involves not only the assets of the hotel that may be subject to loss, but also the relevant perils that may increase the probability and severity of loss.

Standardized checklists, walk-through audits, and balance sheets can assist in identifying **physical assets**. All such assets should be identified and their value established. Various options exist to establish value, including cost, book value

Exhibit 1 The Risk Management Process

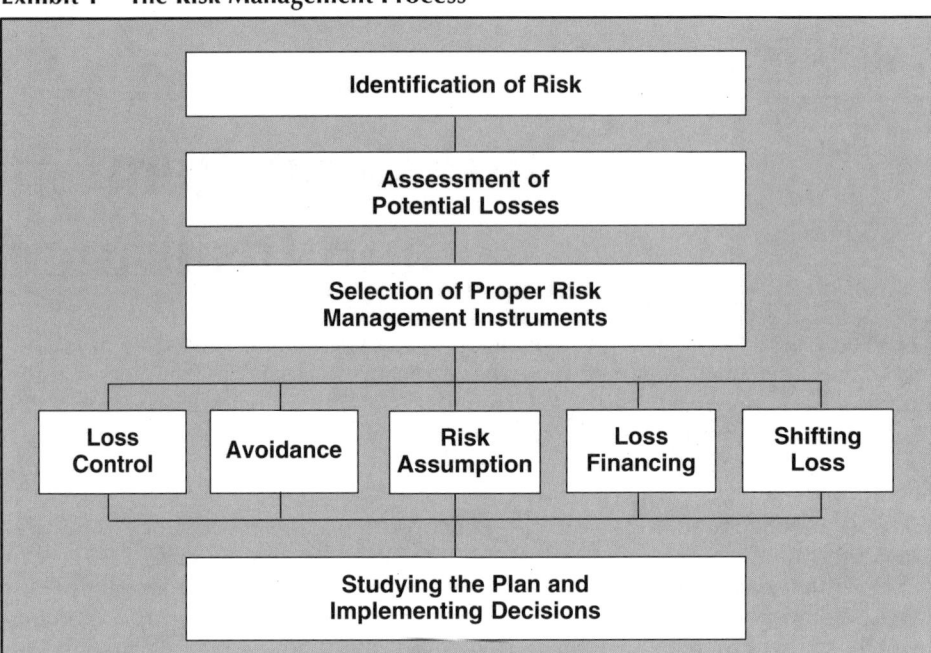

(cost less depreciation), and replacement cost. Consideration of possible losses of cash and receivables should also be part of the property analysis.

Hospitality firms also have a major investment in people. The **people asset** is at risk in several ways. Some people, such as the owner or a world-renowned chef, might be particularly critical to the ongoing success of the business. Their injury or death could severely affect the business. Other individuals, although possibly less critical to the business, are still subject to injury or illness that, could lead to operating difficulties and increased costs for insurance or workers' compensation programs.

Businesses also need to recognize the potential risk to profits—and their predecessor, income. For example, a hotel subject to a fire may not only lose physical assets and have physical injuries to employees; it is also likely to experience a loss of income (and profits) during the time necessary to rebuild and reopen following the fire. Income losses during this time could be severe enough to threaten the hotel's survival even if physical and people related losses are fully compensated.

Perils and Hazards. Once the assets of a hotel are identified, the next step is to determine what factors might contribute to potential losses of these assets. The factors that might *cause a loss* are referred to as **perils;** the factors that might *create or increase the chances of loss* are known as **hazards**. Fire, for example, is a peril common to all hospitality businesses. Failure to regularly and properly clean the ductwork in kitchen ventilating equipment is a hazard resulting from poor maintenance procedures.

Peril identification is relatively straightforward. A major challenge occurs when new perils are recognized or when the perception of perils on the part of the community changes. For example, in the 1970s, the discovery of the *legionella* bacteria in a hotel cooling tower resulted in the introduction of a new peril associated with the operation of this and similar equipment. As far as physical assets are concerned, the peril of global climate change in the twenty-first century is clearly on the minds of those operating low-lying coastal resorts.

While peril exposure is widespread—and in some instances almost unavoidable—the hospitality manager can do a great deal to manage hazards. For example, good maintenance practices in cooling tower operation can reduce or eliminate the *legionella* risk associated with cooling towers (the hazard).

Assessment of Potential Losses

Once the risk management process has identified perils and hazards, it is necessary for the manager to engage in two activities: the assessment of potential losses and the determination of risk comfort levels. The **assessment of potential losses** process can be relatively straightforward, especially for smaller operations. The maximum potential losses, or costs, can be defined by the value of the property, the amount of a day's receipts when considering theft losses, the legal system (for example, limits on innkeeper's liability for guest belongings), and, in the short run, the cost of the insurance premium. Determination of liability losses represents a larger uncertainty for both smaller and larger operations.

For larger operations existing in multiple locations, the assessment of potential losses becomes more complicated. It involves the consideration of severity of losses (What is the magnitude of potential losses?), along with the frequency of these losses (How often are they expected to occur?), coupled with the complexity of dealing with the issues for multiple locations.

Having assessed potential losses, the hospitality manager (or owner) must then make some decisions related to **risk comfort levels**, or the view of risk to be taken by the business. Management's risk-related comfort level involves the question of how much risk is too much risk. The answers will vary depending on individual differences. Some investors are averse to risk and choose secure investments, while others invest their funds in highly speculative ventures where the potential returns (and potential losses) are much greater. In some instances, a false comfort level—caused by ignorance—results in an unknowing assumption of risk. This is a very dangerous situation; ideally, the comfort level has been achieved via clear knowledge on the part of management of what is at risk, the factors that place these items at risk, and the probability and likely cost of a loss.

Many companies have saved untold sums by looking past first impressions to seriously weigh all of the risk-related variables at stake. One franchisor was considering offering a franchise to a large and successful hotel in a major U.S. market. It appeared to be a sound business decision—the hotel had existing contracts providing a large base business, an excellent location, and, overall, was a very attractive business venture—yet the franchisor ultimately walked away from the deal due to risk issues! Why? The hotel did not have a sprinkler system installed (as an existing building, the code stated it did not need to comply with the same standards as new construction) and the owner was unwilling to install such a system. The franchisor felt it could not jeopardize itself by having a major hotel fly its flag without sprinklers. The risk was too great.

Selection of Proper Risk Management Instruments

After identifying the risks an organization is exposed to, the manager or owner must determine how to handle those risks. One important way to deal with risks is via loss control. Risks can also be avoided completely in some instances, insured, self-insured, or passed on contractually to another party (other than an insurance company). It is often the case that responses to certain combinations of perils and hazards involve a combination of actions, including loss control, avoidance, risk assumption, loss financing, and shifting of loss.

Loss Control. **Loss control** involves actions to reduce the frequency and/or the severity of the various losses which can occur. Loss control requires excellent knowledge of perils and how they may affect the hotel. For example, in order to deal with loss control regarding fires, managers need to understand key issues associated with fires in terms of origin, physical characteristics, spread, and elements of interactions with physical assets and human beings. Knowledge is also required of various hazards which increase the hotel's risk; such knowledge would include the role physical structure and design plays in creating fire hazards, as well as the contribution of operating techniques to increasing this risk.

Loss control professionals recognize that actions to address loss control may involve either or both the reduction of frequency and the reduction of severity. Some risk issues lend themselves to both actions while others are affected by only one. Loss control activities during the past decades, for example, have reduced both the frequency and severity of hotel fires. And while no risk manager can reduce the potential frequency of a hurricane at a given location, actions by managers can reduce the severity of losses that occur when the hurricane hits.

Loss control actions are sometimes grouped into those involving physical factors and those involving human behavior. Loss control involving physical factors focuses on the elimination or reduction of unsafe physical conditions through redesign or modification of the physical elements themselves—such as the installation of electronic locking systems. Instructing housekeeping staff about guestroom security procedures deals with human behavior. Actions involving physical factors are visible evidence of loss control and may not rely upon a significant ongoing managerial effort as do human behavior actions. Physical modifications may continue to function long after employee training about risk is forgotten. However, not all risks can be managed by physical measures.

Avoidance. **Avoidance** is taking a preventive loss control action because the risk associated with a certain activity is unacceptable or because the action necessary to avoid the risk is so readily achievable that it would be foolish not to do so. Removing diving boards from swimming pools is an attempt at avoidance of personal injury. Not serving alcohol at events where minors might be present would be another avoidance activity relating to liability. It is also possible that avoidance might be undertaken for activities other than those having unacceptable risks. For example, the purchasing of pre-cut chicken parts by a hotel restaurant eliminates the potential for cuts to employees preparing the product for cooking. This avoidance tactic possibly results in a more economical way of doing business, with the economics driven, in part, by reductions in workplace injury costs.

Risk Assumption. **Risk assumption** means that few or no loss control actions are taken because the risk associated with a certain activity is very low. While this may mean the potential costs are low and no loss control action is considered warranted, it could also mean the nature of the risk is such that no action can be taken. For example, we probably take little loss control action related to the common cold. We also take little loss control action related to a meteor striking our property. In the first instance, although the frequency is high, the severity is slight; in the second instance, the severity is very high but the frequency is, fortunately, very low. In both instances, risk is assumed.

Assumption still requires some method of financing. However, because of the small level of various assumed risks, the expenses in these areas may not even be accounted for as risk-related expenses. Towels stolen from guestrooms, for example, may only show up as linen shortages, and the cost of replacement may be treated the same as towels discarded due to wear or damage.

Loss Financing. Even when loss control efforts are applied, risk—and therefore loss—is generally not eliminated. There needs to be some means available to pay for the loss, and insurance, or **loss (risk) financing**, is a very common method. (Insurance will be discussed in greater detail later in the chapter.)

Those involved in hotel operations, especially at the department head level, may find themselves relatively uninvolved in insurance purchases. Hotel owners make the insurance decisions for much of the property using their own criteria of risk and often linking coverage with other properties they may own. For larger companies, insurance decisions are made at the corporate office because of the economies of such purchases and because risk issues and insurance purchases are best dealt with for the company as a whole rather than individually. Finally, the language of insurance can be daunting and viewed as relatively arcane to property-level management without exposure to this area.

Despite the remoteness of the insurance purchase decision from the duties of most managers, managers should not assume that they can get by without any knowledge of insurance. Knowledge of the fundamentals of insurance and claims management will benefit managers in their business careers. First, as prospective managers are receiving their education they do not know what the future holds. Those with entrepreneurial goals will quickly find themselves as owners, making insurance decisions for their personal business ventures. Even those without immediate goals of ownership will find themselves representing owners requiring insurance knowledge.

Shifting Loss. **Shifting loss** is an attempt to shift the risk from one party to another by legal contract. This involves a number of common business activities such as contractual agreements (including leasing and subcontracting). In addition, risk is often transferred via clauses in other contracts (examples being hold-harmless agreements, indemnity agreements, and requirements for insurance purchases). Since both parties to contracts will be attempting to shift risk to the other, awareness of risk issues in contracts is an important element of a good risk management program. The provisions of various laws of innkeeping at the state level limit the potential loss of hotels—transferring this to the person who has the loss. For example, if the Hollyhock Hotel hires Joe's Plumbing and Joe drops a wrench and injures himself, the hotel would not be held liable.

Studying the Plan and Implementing Decisions

Each of the risk management practices discussed should be integrated into a comprehensive risk management plan for the property. Prior to its implementation, the plan should be studied by management and legal consultants. Management should be comfortable with the specific actions which are outlined for loss control and avoidance, the levels of risk assumption that are made, the proposed levels of insurance, and the approaches outlined to shift loss. Legal consultants should review the proposed activity in light of existing labor agreements and contracts and for general legal compliance. At this point, the real work of risk management begins—that of implementing the proposed decisions.

In large corporations, there is a full-time risk management department that helps guide the implementation process. It brings particular skills to this process in areas such as loss prevention training programs, knowledge of the insurance marketplace, and the details of insurance purchase. Smaller operations may find some of this responsibility is in the hands of consultants and insurance agents or brokers. However, even with a strong corporate staff, much of the responsibility for implementation lies in the hands of unit managers. For example, it is the unit managers who ensure that security policies are understood and followed. These managers are also in a position to provide feedback to the risk management department when elements of the program are difficult to incorporate. The implementation of any plan also requires appropriate adjustments to local conditions and situations. For example, due to local regulations regarding security guard qualifications and training, it may not be financially possible for a hotel to have its own guard force—even if the corporate policy disallows contract service.

One potential problem with risk management efforts is neglect. Once actions are implemented and success is achieved, it is sometimes easy to neglect ongoing fine tuning and re-training to keep the program successful. The result is that loss-producing situations recur—along with additional costs. Risk management is ongoing, not a "do it and forget it" effort.

Contributions of Risk Management to a Business

When exploring the benefits of risk management for a hospitality operation, discussions should include contributions which exist pre- and post-loss, as well as those contributions which are both direct and indirect.

Pre-Loss and Post-Loss Contributions

Pre-loss risk management contributions involve the following elements.

The Economy of Preparing for Loss. This should be a natural outgrowth of the "identification of risk" element of the risk management process. By implementing risk management techniques, companies are able to minimize the cost of risk—the combined costs of losses incurred, insurance, and risk management measures to reduce losses.

Reduced Anxiety. By having a risk management program in place, management can be assured that losses will not be catastrophic, consequently allowing them to focus on the business itself. This provides an overall reduction in anxiety for the hotel's owners, managers, and employees.

Meeting Externally Imposed Obligations. A well-run risk management program will ensure these obligations—ranging from government regulations to contractual requirements—are not only met, but that it is done in an economical manner.

Post-loss risk management contributions include the following elements.

The Survival of the Business. In the face of major catastrophic events, it is possible that hotels without sufficient risk management programs may be unable to sustain themselves. It is not unusual, for example, for an independent restaurant to be forced out of business by a major fire. In other instances, certain events may result in a slow strangulation of the business due to negative public perceptions.

Continued Operation. Effective risk management programs will ensure that continued operation is not inhibited by failure to have a backup supplier of products.

Stable Earnings. Risk management is particularly important when dealing with the financial community and outside investors. Even if a hotel can, in the long run, survive a series of hits, the resulting erratic earnings that may occur can cause a lowered rating in the financial community which could jeopardize continued operation, growth, and even survival.

Continued Growth. Unless a hotel can regroup and rebuild—sometimes both literally and figuratively—in the aftermath of catastrophic events, its ability to achieve continued growth can be seriously impaired.

Social Responsibility. This can be thought of as the hotel's contributions to the general welfare of society. Via payrolls and benefits, employees make a living and receive medical and other care. The physical facilities of the hotel and its profits are a source of tax revenue for the community. If a hotel can recover quickly from property damage that could potentially affect the local economy or successfully avoid laying off staff, society will experience the benefits.

Direct and Indirect Contributions

A **direct contribution** of risk management is the reduction in expenses due to losses. Though straightforward, this may be problematic at times. Since the result is cost avoidance, risk management professionals can find their efforts unappreciated (if not unknown) since their value comes in the form of money *not* spent, while they continue to have funds expended to run the risk management program.

An **indirect contribution** of risk management generally follows the elements of pre-loss and post-loss contributions with one significant addition: risk management programs can provide a potential advantage in terms of relationships with suppliers, customers, and employees. One example is employee productivity and retention; companies with a safe workplace not only have reduced workers' compensation costs but could also experience higher job satisfaction and lower employee turnover.

Insurance

Correct decisions regarding insurance purchases can help properties minimize their financial expenses due to losses, reducing not only the monetary cost of loss, but the potential anxiety and worry which may accompany uncertainty regarding the ability to survive these losses. Insurance providers can be highly beneficial in reducing potential losses as well, thereby further enhancing corporate survival and reducing potential anxiety and worry associated with these losses. Finally, knowledge of insurance can assist in securing the correct coverage at a reasonable cost, controlling the cost of risk financing while still providing the coverage needed. Insurance may be purchased by companies in order to provide funds to pay for losses resulting from natural disasters, workplace injuries, and other events which may be encountered in the course of business, such as auto accidents, theft, and liability claims.

Insurance Purchase

The purchase of insurance involves both risk transfer and risk sharing. **Risk transfer** occurs when all or part of the financial costs of a loss are transferred from the insured to the insurer, who is typically in a stronger financial position to pay the loss than the insured. This transfer of risk has an identifiable cost: premium payments and, if a claim is made, deductible payments. **Risk sharing**, or **pooling**, occurs when the group policy holders agree to share the risk costs of the group via a payment by all to a fund shared by the group. Consider this simple example. Assume that 1,000 farmers in Nebraska agree that if any farmer's home is damaged or destroyed by a fire, the other members of the group will indemnify, or cover, the actual costs of the unlucky farmer who has a loss. Assume also that each home is valued at $100,000, and, on average, one home burns each year. In the absence of insurance, the maximum loss to each farmer is $100,000 if the home should burn. However, by pooling the loss, it can be spread over the entire group, and if one farmer has a total loss, the maximum amount that each farmer would have to pay is only $100 ($100,000 ÷ 1,000). In effect, the pooling technique results in the substitution of an average loss of $100 for the actual loss of $100,000.

Also inherent in an insurance purchase may be an element of risk retention, since many insurance policies will require the payment of a deductible by the insured. In some instances the policies may only cover losses in excess of certain amounts (in effect a deductible, but generally not called so).

Viewed from a risk standpoint, the company purchasing insurance can be thought of as trading off a potentially large, unpredictable cost for a generally smaller but highly predictable cost. And, while the unpredictability of loss for a single business can be high, insurance combines the losses of a large number of firms into a group that is large enough that losses become much more predictable. For example, the potential losses due to a fire at an individual hotel could be as much as the entire building itself or as little as no damage. And, the probability of a fire at an individual hotel is very low. The combination is a potentially large and highly unpredictable loss at the individual hotel level. However, the total number of hotel fires in the U.S. and the total property losses from those fires are relatively predictable from one year to the next. Insurance takes advantage of this fact and allows all hotels to pay a relatively small amount of money (the premium) to cover the losses of a relatively small group of hotels (those with fires).

Not all possible risks are insurable, for a variety of reasons. Insurance scholars indicate there are four key prerequisites for an insurable risk.

- There must be a sufficiently large number of roughly similar exposure units to make the losses reasonably predictable. The large number of units argument is a result of the laws of probability providing higher levels of predictability as the number of units grows.

- The loss produced by the risk must be definite and measurable. The need for a definite and measurable loss is necessary in order to determine the amount of money that needs to be paid in premiums.

- The loss must be accidental and unintentional. Providing insurance for a loss that could be a decision of the insured would obviously open the door for fraud. For example, insurance payments are not made when a building is burned down by a person who insures the building.

- The loss must not be catastrophic. Avoiding insuring of catastrophic losses (i.e., to a large number of the insured units at the same time) is necessary if the financial viability of the insurer is to be sustained. One example here is the exclusion of damages "due to acts of war" from insurance policies. Such damage could be so widespread and so unpredictable that insurance could clearly not be written to provide coverage.

When contemplating the purchase of insurance there are a number of options available. While most insurance is purchased from private insurance companies, some insurance, such as workers' compensation coverage or flood insurance, is available from public (governmental) sources.

Private insurance purchases may be from **stock insurers** (a corporation owned by stockholders who participate in the profits and losses of the insurer) or **mutual insurers** (a corporation owned by the policyholders). There are many additional forms of these types of insurers as well. Blue Cross and Blue Shield and health maintenance organizations (HMOs) are types of insurance that provide medical coverage. Insurance companies themselves purchase insurance through **reinsurers**, firms that transfer potential risk from a single insurance company to a number of insurance companies.

The purchase of insurance is done through agents or brokers. **Agents** legally represent the insurer and have the authority to act on the insurer's behalf. Agents

> ### What to Seek in a Broker
>
> Your broker should be from an organization large enough to meet your insurance needs, but small enough to develop a relationship providing the equivalent of an on-staff insurance manager. At least you'll get your calls returned and reasonable on-site assistance as needed.
>
> The company should have other lodging industry business. Avoid becoming the guinea pig for a broker's excursion into the world of lodging industry insurance. Ask for references and discuss what services have been provided to your peers by this broker. In further screening, ask these questions:
>
> - Regardless of the size of your property, does the broker have sufficient staff to provide on-site review of insurance needs?
> - Is the broker, through its staff or through the loss prevention staff of an insurance company, able to provide safety, security, and claims services?
> - What's the claims service record? Will you or your broker be involved in the discussion of proposed settlement offers?
>
> After selecting a broker or agent, you're responsible for issuing a broker or agent-of-record letter. Such a letter may be expanded to note anticipated services, inspections, claims handling, and other items mutually agreed upon. However, this should be a separate document so an unencumbered broker or agent-of-record letter is available to an insurance company. This letter of agreement, on your letterhead, authorizes the insurance brokerage or agency to solicit insurance coverage in your behalf. With advice of counsel, this may include:
>
> - Cancellation procedures. Spell out the time frame following notice of cancellation by either party.
> - Exclusivity. Just as you wish your broker or agent to shop the market for a better insurance coverage and premium, so should you shop for a broker or agent to do the best possible job for you. Since the most effective broker-client relation is based upon mutual trust and cooperation, an exclusive broker-of-record document is advisable. Should such a relationship degenerate, the cancellation procedure (noted above) will permit designation of a replacement broker or agent.

Source: Raymond C. Ellis, Jr., "Smart Insurance Buys: Strong Thread in Insurance Lifeline," *Lodging*, April 1990, p. 31.

will normally issue a binder which is temporary evidence that insurance exists until a policy is issued. **Brokers** legally represent the insured. A broker solicits applications for insurance and then attempts to place the coverage with an appropriate insurer; upon acceptance, the policy is issued. Brokers are active in many aspects of insurance, often providing specialized services and focusing on specific forms of insurance coverage.

Industry Regulation

Purchasers of insurance, whether through an agent or broker, want to be sure that the company providing the insurance is legitimate and has the financial capability to cover losses. The government recognizes this and provides a rather extensive regulatory system of state insurance departments that provide oversight on the operation of insurance companies. Besides legislation applying to all firms, insurance companies must comply with industry-specific legislation at both the state and federal level. The National Association of Insurance Commissioners (NAIC) provides general guidance and communication regarding insurance issues.

An insurance purchase decision should include consideration of the insurer's rating. Ratings involve a review of the insurer's financial exposures, the income from premiums, and the various assets of the firms. A.M. Best Company and Standard and Poors (among others) provide ratings of insurers. Ratings firms use letter grades to rate companies. Be sure to understand the meaning of the letters since an "A" from one company may be the top grade while at another it may be somewhat less than the top. With insurance purchasing, you not only "get what you pay for," you also "pay for what you get." To be sure you have adequate coverage at a reasonable cost, it is important to correctly specify your needs when contacting insurance providers. Exhibit 2 outlines the importance of insurance specifications.

Given the potential complexities of decisions regarding coverage and the costs of coverage, some operations may opt for participation in **group coverage**. Groups exist for all types of properties (luxury, independent, ski resorts), as well as for state associations. Most large hotel chains purchase group coverage for their hotels rather than allowing each to negotiate coverage individually. Benefits of purchasing insurance in this manner include lower prices and rate stability. The larger number of participants in the group provides a more predictable loss base and therefore more predictability in pricing of premiums. And purchasing groups focusing on the industry itself will provide opportunities to customize the policies to the specific needs of the industry. For example, ski resorts purchasing insurance from a ski industry group should have lower costs and more available and specific coverage for ski lift–related incidents.

Commercial Package Policy

A common way to provide property coverage is through purchase of a **commercial package policy (CPP)**. The CPP has common provisions suitable for various business types, but can also be modified to cover the needs of a specific business. The CPP also includes coverage for various liability exposures. Combining property and liability exposures in a single package can result in lower insurance costs and a coverage which has fewer gaps (and fewer possible difficulties in determining coverage if a loss occurs). The CPP contains two or more forms of insurance coverage that may include:

- Commercial property coverage
- Commercial crime coverage
- Boiler and machinery coverage
- Inland marine coverage
- Commercial general liability coverage
- Commercial automotive coverage

Exhibit 2 The Importance of Insurance Specifications

The single most important document in arranging a competitive and comprehensive insurance program is the specifications that are submitted to the insurance company. This document should be composed of the following sections:

Corporate History
It is important that the underwriters are given a clear picture of your company, it's past as well as what is being planned for the future.

Exposures
Depending on the coverage you are applying for, full disclosure of your current exposures, such as sales, payroll, vehicles, property values real and personal by location, loss of income potential, rental value, rental expense, etc., should be provided. In addition to your current exposures, your exposures for the past three to five years are also an intricate part of the underwriting process. As a subsection to exposures, you will need to supply the construction, occupancy, and protection information (COPE) on all locations.

Loss Information
Three to five years of detailed loss history by coverage is required. A separate report on large losses with more complete detail should also be included.

Program Design
It is always better to outline the type of program you feel will best suit the needs of your company than to let the underwriters dictate one which will not accomplish the goals you have set forth. You need to indicate the type of limits, deductibles, and cash flow options you wish to see in this section. You also need to outline the parameters for claims reporting and loss control engineering requirements.

Safety and Management Programs
From an underwriter's point of view, management's commitment to safety has a direct bearing on the extent of losses he may expect in the course of the policy year. If possible, include any and all safety manuals, employee training information, company guidelines, etc. If this is not practical, identify the types of programs in place and offer to make the manual or personnel available upon inspection.

Contingent Exposures/Contractual Obligations
You will need to provide detail on contractual obligations that may go outside of the general coverage parameters. You will also need to identify those contingent exposures which could affect you, but for which you do not have direct control. (Concessionaires and vendors who come onto your property.)

As stated at the outset, this is a very important document. It can also be somewhat intimidating. It is important that you and your broker, in partnership, assemble it and are in agreement as to its contents. Full disclosure of all possible exposures as well as past and current loss history eliminates any misunderstanding with the underwriters and will allow for a mutually beneficial relationship.

Source: George Kearon and Carey O'Connor, *The BottomLine*, April/May 1997, p. 14. Used with permission.

The components of the CPP include a **common policy declarations component** and a **common policy conditions component.** The declarations component involves an identification of the insured, the property insured, policy period, summary of coverage, and premium. The conditions component includes statements regarding transfer provisions, rights of the insurer to conduct property inspections and surveys—as well as examination of books and records—and cancellation and change provisions.

There are many aspects of the CPP and its coverage that should be carefully reviewed with the insurance broker or agent. The purpose of this discussion is to provide an introduction to the CPP; details of specific insurance policies and coverage options are beyond the scope of this chapter.

Commercial Property Coverage

Commercial property coverage commonly includes building and personal property components. The building includes physical structures, machinery, and equipment that are permanently installed, such as light poles and mailboxes. Equipment used to maintain or service the building such as floor buffers and fire extinguishing equipment is also included. Personal property includes property of the insured (such as furniture and fixtures), as well as personal property of others in the care, custody, or control of the insured.

A variety of additional coverage can be included which expands the property coverage. For example, additional coverage can be purchased for a fire department service charge, debris removal, and building ordinance coverage which includes increased costs of construction coverage. "Traditional fire insurance policies exclude the additional costs to bring property up to code standards," notes Ralph Korn, an Arizona-based risk-management consultant. Hoteliers should make certain they guard against the following hidden costs: demolition of the undamaged portion of your building (if required by law), reconstruction of the part not destroyed, and additional construction costs to bring a new building into compliance with codes.[1]

Extensions of coverage can also be purchased. A building insurance extension, for example, includes new structures on the premises or newly acquired buildings at other locations—insured automatically up to a specified limit and time. Other provisions of commercial property coverage include deductibles, coinsurance, and valuation. **Coinsurance** is a provision of some policies that requires the insured to carry insurance equal to a specified percentage of the property's value—or receive less than full reimbursement for a loss. Exhibit 3 shows coinsurance calculations to determine the insurance amount to be paid on a claim. **Valuation** establishes the rules for which a property is valued at the time of a loss. A **causes of loss form** identifies the specific types of perils (fire, lightning, etc.) which are covered under the policy; an earthquake is one peril which isn't covered in the basic insurance.

Business owners also generally purchase **business income (extra expense) coverage**. This coverage recognizes that property damage and other events may result in loss of business income, and that certain expenses may continue during the recovery period. Well-structured business income coverage can mean the difference between the survival and death of the business. Specifically, it is designed to cover the loss of business income, expenses that continue during the shutdown period, and extra expenses because of a direct physical loss to insured property.

Exhibit 3 Coinsurance Calculations

Failure to insure property up to proper coinsurance levels (typically 80 or 90 percent of the property's value) is the most common problem encountered in property insurance policies. If your operation is underinsured, the insurance company will penalize you by paying less than the face amount on your policy.

To determine the insurance amount to be paid on a claim:

$$\frac{\text{Amount of insurance carried}}{\text{Amount of insurance required}} \times \text{Actual loss} = \text{Amount to be paid}$$

Example 1:

The replacement value of your property is $111,000 and your policy requires you to insure to at least 90 percent (or about $100,000), but you only insure $80,000. You sustain $40,000 in fire damages. How much would you recover?

$$\frac{\$80,000}{\$100,000} \times \$40,000 = \$32,000$$

The unreimbursed $8,000 would come out of your own pocket.

Example 2:

You insure the required $100,000. You sustain $40,000 in fire damages. How much would you recover?

$$\frac{\$100,000}{\$100,000} \times \$40,000 = \$40,000$$

This formula is not perfect, however. It doesn't work if you have insured to the required amount but sustained a *complete* loss. In that instance, you would only recover the amount to which you had insured—in this case, $100,000. Because you only insured to $100,000, you would incur $11,000 in unreimbursed damages. It is for this reason that experts recommend insuring to full value—that way you always get paid 100 percent of your loss.

Abridged from Phillip M. Perry, "Don't Let Your Fire Insurance Go Up in Smoke," *Restaurants USA*, October 1997.

The loss of business income provision of these policies involves the net profit or loss that would have been earned plus continuing normal operating expenses, including payroll. The coverage also includes extra expenses incurred (such as rental of substitute equipment), action of civil authority (such as denial of use of a facility due to rioting), and extended business coverage (recognizing that a period of time may be required to fully recover from the event). Business owners should investigate the potential value to the firm of various optional coverages including the maximum period of indemnity, monthly limit of indemnity, agreed value, and extended period of indemnity. Finally, business owners should be aware of coinsurance provisions in their policies which require minimum amounts of insurance coverage and function similar to coinsurance provisions for property insurance.

Exhibit 4 Types of Crime Insurance Available

- Form A—Employee Dishonesty
- Form B—Forgery or Alteration
- Form C—Theft, Disappearance, and Destruction
- Form D—Robbery and Safe Burglary
- Form E—Premises Burglary
- Form F—Computer Fraud
- Form G—Extortion
- Form H—Premises Theft and Robbery outside the Premises
- Form I—Losses of Safe Deposit Boxes
- Form J—Securities Deposited with Others
- Form K—Liability for Guests' Property—Safe Deposit Box
- Form L—Liability for Guests' Property
- Form M—Safe Depository Liability
- Form N—Safe Depository Direct Loss

Commercial Crime Coverage

Commercial crime coverage recognizes that the assets of the firm include cash and other securities and that these are potentially at risk from the acts of people. Besides concern about the loss of cash and securities of the operation itself, potential liability for guests' property in safe deposit boxes is a concern of lodging operations. Exhibit 4 lists a variety of available crime insurance types.

Boiler and Machinery Coverage

Boiler and machinery coverage applies to many types of equipment including boilers, refrigerating systems, engines, turbines, and generators that are not covered under the property component of the CPP coverage. With the critical nature and large quantity of such equipment that may be present in hotels, resorts, and even some restaurants, it is important to consider the value of this coverage. The insurance can be purchased to include not only direct losses to the equipment, but also losses to items such as business income, spoilage, and extra expenses to maintain operation (such as renting a piece of portable equipment).

Inland Marine Coverage

Inland (and ocean) marine coverage may seem like unnecessary insurance for most hotels or restaurants. However, inland marine coverage provides protection for goods shipped on land. Operations that take title to goods (such as furniture and equipment for a renovation) at the time of shipment from the supplier may wish to purchase inland marine coverage. Any property relying on shipment of materials or supplies by water (e.g., an island resort) may also wish to consider marine coverage.

Are You Getting Your Insurance Premium Dollar's Worth?

The insurance premium you pay each year for your property, liability, workers' compensation, and other business coverage includes a commission, unless you have agreed to pay your agent or broker a fee for services. That commission or fee entitles you to a good deal of service. Some of those services are listed here:

1. Insurance without Gaps
2. Competitive Quotes
3. Explanation of Coverages Available/Provided
4. Timely Delivery of Policies and Endorsements
5. Claims Reporting and Monitoring
6. Periodic Loss Reports
7. Loss Prevention/Loss Control Assistance

1. Insurance without Gaps

The most important service you deserve from your professional insurance person (agent or broker) is a thorough analysis of your insurable exposures to loss or claims. To accomplish this, he or she must have clear and complete understanding of your business and everything for which your business is responsible through ownership, contract, or lease. Without this information, your insurance professional cannot do the best job for you. For instance, if you have a warehouse where you store furniture, supplies, and computers, then you have an exposure to a liability loss for injury or damage to someone else, as well as an exposure for loss or damage to your property. Or, if one of your employees uses his or her car to take deposits to the bank, then your business has a "non-owned auto" liability exposure and an exposure to loss of the deposit through off-premises holdup or robbery.

Once your agent or broker knows what's involved in your business activities, he or she needs to design an insurance program that has no gaps or uninsured exposures. You may not choose to buy insurance for all your exposures, but it should be your choice: when you choose not to buy insurance for an aspect of your risk, you are essentially "self-insuring" that exposure. Consider whether or not you could stay in business if you have a loss under that self-insured risk.

2. Competitive Quotes

Around 60 to 90 days before your policies expire, it pays to reinvest time in your renewal. On your own, ask others in your industry about their insurance and jot down the names of preferred insurers. Spend time with your agent or broker to bring him or her up to date on what is going on in your business, as well as what services you expect regarding your renewal. Mention the "preferred insurers" of which you have heard, and ask your agent to include them in the competitive process. You should get quotes from two or three insurance companies on each policy, but you may not want to do this every year. Compare coverage as well as price to be sure you know what you are selecting. Ask what is excluded from each quote to see what's covered.

(continued)

3. **Explanation of Coverages Available/Provided**

   Even "plain English" insurance policies need translation into lay terms to spell out what is covered when and for how much. Your insurance professional should help you understand what coverages and options are available, what is being recommended, and what are the trade-offs. Once you have purchased insurance, you need an explanation of what you bought and how to use it, when and if the need arises.

4. **Timely Delivery of Policies and Endorsements**

   Once you order policies, your insurance professional should receive them from the insurance company, review, and deliver them within 60 days. Hold on to your expired policies, especially those covering auto and general liability. If years from now you get notice of a claim for something that occurred in the expired year, you still have coverage under the old policy if it was on an "occurrence" form (most liability coverages *are* on this form).

5. **Claims Reporting and Monitoring**

   When a loss occurs, getting it correctly and promptly reported to the insurer is very important. Your broker or agent can review your claim and help provide all the pertinent information. If it is a loss to your property, your broker can facilitate with the claims adjuster for payment from the company. For claims involving injury or damage to others, monitoring is needed to assure that claims are closed as promptly and favorably as possible. Your broker can provide that service.

6. **Periodic Loss Reports**

   Your broker or agent can also obtain loss runs or consolidated reports of all claims you have had which make up your loss history. This is often needed if you choose to change insurers in the future. Providing competing insurers complete loss experience can determine whether or not you get favorable quotes on your insurance premiums.

7. **Loss Prevention/Loss Control Assistance**

   Finally, the best way to improve your claims experience and "appeal" to an insurer as a profitable client is to have an effective loss prevention and/or loss control program in place. Loss prevention requires that fire and life safety issues, security precautions, industrial hygiene issues, and safety procedures be intertwined in management's philosophy and practice. The expertise needed to assist you in developing a loss prevention/loss control program to fit your operation can be obtained from your agent, broker, or insurance company. The insurers recognize that helping you *prevent* claims protects their bottom line, so they do want to help. Some agents and brokers have safety professionals on their staff for you to use.

   Should you find that you are not getting all you deserve for your insurance premium dollar, just discuss your concerns with your broker or agent. If, for any reason, your current insurance professional is unwilling to provide the services described, there are many others around who would jump at the chance to serve you and your business.

Source: Sherry Z. Terao, *Risk Management Bulletin*, AH&MA Risk Management Committee, April 1994.

Commercial General Liability Coverage

Businesses can incur legal liability for a variety and growing number of reasons. Providing coverage for such liability is an important decision since these liabilities can be for large sums of money. The **commercial general liability (CGL)** policy addresses the various sources of loss exposure of business firms and the various types of losses which may be incurred.

Premises and operations coverage involves legal liability that can arise out of ownership and maintenance of the location where the firm does business. This would include slips and trips by guests as well as guests who are injured due to the collapse of a chair.

Products liability coverage involves injury to guests or damage to their property from defective products. While hotels may not think they produce "products," food produced for a banquet or wedding reception could receive coverage under this option.

Completed operations coverage involves liability losses that occur away from the premises and arise out of the insured's product or work after the insured has relinquished possession of the product or the work has been completed. Hospitality operations certainly want this sort of coverage to exist for those doing work on or in their property as well as for the manufacturer of products they purchase. Contractual liability coverage is desired if liability has been assumed from another party by written or oral contract.

Contractual liability coverage concerns instances where the business incurs some legal liability as a result of a contract with another firm. A common element of coverage would exist for leased space where the lease agreement calls for the lessee to assume liability for use of the property. As a general rule, liability assumed under a contract is not covered unless specifically stated.

Contingent liability coverage addresses the potential liability which can occur as a result of the work of independent contractors. While the business is generally not legally liable for work done by contractors, there are some circumstances when liability does exist. An example would be when the work done by the contractor is inherently dangerous—such as may be involved with some types of construction or demolition activities.

A number of liability loss exposures require the purchase of additional insurance coverage (or may not be insurable). Among the excluded loss exposures are items such as liability of directors and officers, liquor liability, pollution, war, and employer related practices. Where available, separate coverage for these may be purchased.

Insurance purchasing should not be a "do it and forget it" activity. Good record keeping is essential. Information about major items acquired (cost, date of purchase, description), copies of insurance policies (including expired policies), financial records, and correspondence related to insurance and claims should all be stored in a safe location. This may mean storage off the hotel property, since you may need this information the most following a fire or other disaster at the property.

Commercial Automotive Coverage

Commercial automotive coverage provides a combination of liability and physical damage coverages. Physical damage coverage can include collision coverage, comprehensive coverage (loss from any cause *except* collision or overturn), and specified causes-of-loss coverage (only losses from specified perils are covered). Hotels which provide valet services—or even parking lots—should consider the purchase of **garage coverage** which provides liability, parking attendant, and physical damage coverage.

Additional Types of Coverage

Flood Coverage

Flood insurance began as a federal government insurance program developed to provide coverage for a difficult to insure class of properties—those located in flood prone areas. This has subsequently been broadened to allow private insurers to sell insurance that is underwritten by the federal program. Flood insurance provides low-cost coverage from damage resulting from the overflow of inland or tidal waters, the unusual or rapid accumulation of runoff, or mudslides which are proximately caused by flood.

Umbrella Coverage

Umbrella coverage provides insurance above and beyond that of other underlying coverages. The concept behind this coverage is that several of the hospitality firms may be jeopardized by potentially catastrophic liability judgments (or in some instances, property losses). Umbrella coverage could be written for as little as a few million dollars for a small firm to several hundred million for a large firm.

Legally Mandated Coverage

While some insurance is optional, some coverage is legally mandated. Some coverage is mandated for all operations, such as automobile insurance, while other insurance is the result of contracts signed related to the operation, such as a franchise agreement.

Insurance coverage required by contracts can exist in a variety of forms and for a variety of coverages. Franchise agreements require coverage for a variety of things during the lifetime of the franchise, including insurance during construction, comprehensive-commercial general liability coverage during operation, workers' compensation and employer's liability insurance (also usually required by law), property insurance, and business interruption insurance. Management agreements are also likely to include insurance provisions.

Workers' Compensation. The most common and possibly costly type of legally mandated insurance is **workers' compensation**. This insurance exists to provide a source of benefits for workers who are injured in the workplace. Coverage includes medical expenses, disability payments, survivor's death benefits, and rehabilitation benefits. Disability payments involve a replacement of income lost as a result

> **Providing Workers' Compensation**
>
> Workers' compensation insurance may be provided by state programs, private insurance, or self-insurance.
>
> Firms utilizing state programs may be doing so because of their small size or high risk characteristics. Private insurance coverage is commonly purchased with a large number of insurers providing the coverage. (In some states, private insurance for workers' compensation is not permitted and is instead provided from a monopoly state fund.) It is also possible to purchase workers' compensation insurance through industry organizations.
>
> The uniform classification and rating system that state programs and private insurance rely upon as their pricing basis is developed by the National Council on Compensation Insurance (NCCI). Using this system as a starting point, the actual base premium rates are then established by state governments. A variety of modifications to this base rating method are available, especially for larger firms. These modifications—which include experience rating, participating or dividend plans, retention programs, and retrospective rating plans—move the cost basis of the workers' compensation from a fixed rate per dollar of payroll (varied for type of job) to a cost based more on the overall claim level experienced by the business itself.
>
> Some larger companies may elect to self-insure. Where allowed by state law, firms can receive approval to provide workers' compensation coverage from their own cash flows. These firms may hire outside administrators to manage these programs or they may handle them internally.

of the injury. The disability may be total or partial, temporary or permanent. A critical element of the workers' compensation system is that no determination of fault by the employer is necessary. Workers' compensation insurance may be provided by state programs, private insurance, or self-insurance.

Employers' Liability Insurance. Besides workers' compensation, firms are likely to want to purchase **employers' liability insurance**. While workers' compensation insurance provides employers with coverage for claims from the injured employee, claims from other parties (such as a spouse) as a result of the injury are not covered. There are also other circumstances when a workplace injury covered by workers' compensation can result in a potential liability for the employer. For example, the employee may sue a third party and this third party may sue the employer. Employers' liability insurance provides coverage for a large number of these circumstances.

Other legally mandated insurance coverage may be provided by separate policies, by inclusion in other policies, or by the government itself.

Claims Management

In spite of vigorous efforts to reduce the possibility of a loss, losses do happen. This can be an injury to a guest or an employee or loss of or damage to guest or hotel property. Before any of these occur, the hotel should have clearly established the **claims management** process, or the procedures that will be used to manage claims.

This should include proper documentation, procedures regarding the incident, and settlement policies. Some of these claims may be filed with the insurance company for reimbursement, while others may be assumed at the property level or charged against a corporate insurance account.

Proper documentation of incidents is an important step in claims management. Use of a standardized reporting form at the property level helps to ensure proper documentation. There may be different forms or components of the same form used depending on the nature of the incident. Incidents involving injury to guests may require information that is much different than that involving a robbery or assault. Prompt capture of this information is critical since transient hotel guests and employee turnover make data gathering too long after the fact very difficult.

Another key element of good claims management involves proper procedures regarding the incident itself. Showing a proper level of concern on guest claims—without overtly indicating or accepting responsibility—requires training for employees and management. Ignoring the guest's concerns at the time of the incident can turn a simple slip into a major claim. The same is true for prompt care and concern related to employee injuries.

A strategy is needed in settling claims. Do you want to fight every claim that is made, only those which are potentially significant, or none of them? Keep in mind that insurance companies will have their own approaches to claims that may be different from yours. Discussion and coordination with the insurance providers can help to align their claims management methods with the hotel's. Decisions about legal services in relation to claims are also potentially important. Some firms will elect to allow the insurance company's counsel to represent them in the claims process unless the dollar amount is particularly great or the claim involves something particularly damaging to the company's reputation (such as a food-related liability claim in a restaurant).

Many property-related claims will involve only the property and the insurance company. The insurance company includes information in its policies that defines the responsibilities of the insured when making a claim. The first step is prompt notification of the insurer that a potential loss has occurred. The insurance company will then investigate the claim. Their interests include whether the policy was in effect when the loss occurred, whether the policy covered the peril that caused the loss, and whether the type of loss was covered by the policy. The insured may be asked to substantiate the loss that is claimed. For example, if a property is decorated with historical photos and furnished with antiques, documentation of this may be required. If loss of business income is claimed, financial records will need to be provided for documentation.

With the introduction of centralized claims management centers in larger chain operations and similar services from insurance providers, incident reporting is sometimes done online via computer connections or via phone. Prompt reporting of incidents is critical to prompt and cost effective settlement of claims.

Finally, it must be recognized that claims reporting is mandatory for injuries serious enough to warrant workers' compensation claims. Since the potential seriousness is not always known at the time of an injury, a log for minor injuries (initially requiring only first aid) is also recommended. Proper procedures will vary by state due to the nature of the workers' compensation process.

Establishing a Safety Committee

Establishing a safety committee is one way properties can help to ensure the effectiveness of their safety programs. In addition, by having employees assist in establishing safety policies, reviewing accidents, recommending corrective action, and participating in safety inspections and other related safety functions, safety committee involvement is also a valuable means for creating property-wide acceptance of safety programs.

The Value of Communication

One of the purposes of the safety committee is to bring management and staff together in a cooperative effort to improve the safety and health of workers. Therefore, it makes good business sense to include representatives from the ranks of management as well as line-level employees. Managers and staff can meet together to discuss their unique and common concerns regarding safety. The safety committee thereby becomes a forum for achieving mutual solutions.

A safety committee will succeed only if it requires management's participation; managers should not make the mistake of assuming that the existence of such a committee removes them from all involvement. Yet, at the same time, it is important that the safety committee not be dominated by management in general—or by any other individual. To help avoid such a situation, it is worth devoting meeting time to establishing ground rules and techniques for decision making that promote consensus.

Management representatives and the committee chair will be the primary conduits of communication between the safety committee and the hotel. Committee members are the primary communicators with other staff. For everyone to feel well-represented and appropriately informed, it is important that communication occur in both directions.

Many properties find it helpful to establish a written operating policy prior to creating a safety committee. Such a policy establishes the committee's mission, guidelines for membership, member duties, and general procedures for handling a variety of safety issues. Exhibit 5 is an example of a generic policy that may be adapted to suit an individual property's needs.

The Roles of the Safety Committee

Ideally, the safety committee is a genial and open forum for management and staff to communicate safety-related concerns. The benefits of such communications may be substantial. Every hazard the committee identifies and helps to eliminate means significant potential savings in accident costs. The safety committee can serve as a valuable problem-solving group that addresses workplace conditions, morale, and quality. By developing solutions, the safety committee improves the company's competitive advantage.

Exhibit 5   Sample Safety Committee Policy

Introduction

[Hotel Name] is committed to accident prevention in order to protect the safety and health of every employee. Injury and illness losses due to hazards often are needless, costly, and preventable. To prevent these losses, a joint management/staff safety committee will be established. Employee involvement in accident prevention and support of safety committee members and activities is necessary to ensure a safe and healthful workplace.

Purpose

The purpose of our safety committee is to bring staff and management together in a nonadversarial, cooperative effort to help our operation promote and maintain a safe and healthful workplace.

Organization

There will be at least two management representatives to the safety committee. One employee representative from each department will also be selected or encouraged to volunteer as a safety committee member. Managers and employees are encouraged to volunteer as members of the committee.

Safety committee members will serve a continuous term of at least one year. Length of membership will be staggered so that at least one experienced member is always serving on the committee.

Membership in the committee will be considered professional development and added to each participant's performance appraisal.

Responsibility

The safety committee has the following responsibilities:

1. Meet regularly to discuss safety and health
2. Communicate with employees and the employer
3. Identify hazardous conditions and unsafe work practices
4. Recommend strategies to eliminate hazards

Recommendations

Written recommendations concerning potential hazards will be submitted by the safety committee to management. Management will respond to recommendations according to the following schedule:

Identified Hazard	Severity of Injury	Response
Fatal	Fatality	Immediate
Serious	Serious physical harm	Immediate
Minor	Minor injury	14 days
Administrative	Not applicable	30 days

(continued)

Exhibit 5 *(continued)*

Procedures

The committee's plan of action requires procedures by which the committee may successfully fulfill its role. Procedures developed should include:

- Meeting date, time, and location
- Election of chairperson and recorder
- Order of business
- Records

Duties of each member should include:

- Reporting unsafe conditions and practices
- Attending all safety and health meetings
- Reviewing all accidents and near-accidents
- Recommending ideas for improving safety and health
- Setting an example by working safely
- Completing assignments
- Effectively representing employee safety interests

Summary

Only the planning and effective leadership of management and the safety committee can build a program that lasts. The safety committee should be an effective problem-solving team, providing guidance and leadership in safety and health matters.

The committee also provides an excellent arena for employees to improve their professional skills in communications, human relations, problem solving, meeting management, and analysis. Since supervisors and managers should be informed about occupational safety and health, the safety committee is a natural "school" of preparation for future company managers. In fact, some companies make safety committee involvement a prerequisite for managerial advancement.

Safety Committee Duties

Safety committee meetings should be scheduled regularly, with a consistent meeting time established. Avoid postponements, as they tend to reduce the effectiveness of the committee and employee involvement. Follow a set agenda (a sample is provided in Exhibit 6) and keep minutes of the meetings. A chairperson and recorder should be chosen from the committee membership.

Chairperson. Typically, a chairperson's responsibilities are to:

- Prepare agendas for meetings.
- Arrange for the meeting room.
- Notify members of scheduled meetings.
- Distribute the agendas.

Exhibit 6   Sample Safety Committee Meeting Agenda

1. Call to order/roll call.
2. Review minutes of last committee meeting.
3. Review results of periodic workplace safety inspections.
4. Review accident investigations. When appropriate, submit suggestions to management for the prevention of future incidents.
5. Review reports of alleged hazardous conditions.
6. Submit recommendations to assist in the evaluation of employee suggestions.
7. Agree on a time and place for next committee meeting.

- Delegate responsibilities.
- Make assignments.
- Preside over and conduct the meetings.
- Enforce committee ground rules.
- Communicate with hotel management.
- Report the status of recommendations.

Safety Committee Recorder. Include the following responsibilities in any written committee guidelines for the safety committee recorder:

- Assist the chairperson with the agendas.
- Record minutes of the meetings.
- Distribute and post the minutes.
- Assume chairperson's duties if necessary.

Safety Committee Members. Safety committee members should expect to:

- Receive suggestions, concerns, and reports from other staff.
- Present staff suggestions, concerns, and reports to the committee.
- Report back to staff on their suggestions, concerns, and reports.
- Attend all safety committee meetings.
- Receive training on safety and health subjects.
- Review injury and illness reports.
- Monitor safety and health programs and systems.
- Set a good example by working safely.
- Conduct safety inspections.
- Make recommendations for corrective action.
- Assist in communicating committee activities to all employees.

Endnotes

1. Phillip M. Perry, "Don't Let Your Fire Insurance Go Up in Smoke," *Restaurants USA*, October 1997.

Key Terms

agents—Legal representatives of the insurer who have the authority to act on the insurer's behalf. Agents will normally issue a binder which is temporary evidence that insurance exists until a policy is issued.

assessment of potential losses—The maximum potential losses, or costs, that can be defined by the value of the property, the amount of a day's receipts (when considering theft losses), the legal system, or the cost of the insurance premium.

avoidance—Not engaging in an action because the risk associated with it is unacceptable.

boiler and machinery coverage—Insurance that applies to equipment including boilers, refrigerating systems, engines, turbines, and generators that are not covered under the property component of the CPP coverage. It can include not only direct losses to the equipment, but also losses to items such as business income, spoilage, and extra expenses to maintain operation (such as renting a piece of portable equipment).

brokers—Legal representatives of the insured who solicit applications for insurance and then attempt to place the coverage with an appropriate insurer. Brokers are active in many aspects of insurance, often providing specialized services and focusing on specific forms of insurance coverage.

business income (extra expense) coverage—Insurance that recognizes that property damage and other events may result in loss of business income, and that certain expenses may continue during the recovery period.

causes of loss form—Identifies the specific types of perils (fire, lightning, etc.) which are covered under an insurance policy.

claims management—Process and actions to be taken when an event occurs that may result in a loss.

coinsurance—A provision of some policies that requires the insured to carry insurance equal to a specified percentage of the property's value—or receive less than full reimbursement for a loss.

commercial automotive coverage—Insurance that provides a combination of liability and physical damage coverages, including collision coverage, comprehensive coverage, and specified causes-of-loss coverage.

commercial crime coverage—Insurance that recognizes that the assets of the firm include cash and other securities and that these are potentially at risk from the acts of people.

commercial general liability (CGL)—An insurance policy that addresses the various sources of liability loss exposure of business firms and the various types of losses which may be incurred.

commercial package policy (CPP)—A common way to provide property coverage, the CPP includes coverage for various property loss exposures.

commercial property coverage—Insurance that includes building and personal property components.

common policy conditions component—An insurance component that includes statements regarding transfer provisions, rights of the insurer to conduct property inspections and surveys—as well as examination of books and records—and cancellation and change provisions.

common policy declarations component—An insurance component that involves an identification of the insured, the property insured, policy period, summary of coverage, and premium.

completed operations coverage—Insurance that involves liability losses that occur away from the premises and arise out of the insured's product or work after the insured has relinquished possession of the product or the work has been completed.

contingent liability coverage—Insurance that addresses the potential liability that can occur as a result of the work of independent contractors.

contractual liability coverage—Insurance that concerns instances where the business incurs some legal liability as a result of a contract with another firm.

direct contribution—A reduction in the risk management expenses resulting from losses.

employers' liability insurance—Insurance that provides coverage for claims from other parties (such as a spouse) as a result of a workers' compensation injury.

flood insurance—Insurance that provides low-cost coverage from damage resulting from the overflow of inland or tidal waters, the unusual or rapid accumulation of runoff, or mudslides which are proximately caused by flood.

garage coverage—Insurance that provides liability, parking attendant, and physical damage coverage.

group coverage—Insurance that allows large chains to purchase coverage for all their hotels rather than allowing each to negotiate coverage individually; benefits include lower prices and rate stability.

hazards—Factors that might create or increase the chances of a loss.

identification of risk—Identifying not only the assets of the hotel that may be subject to loss, but also the relevant perils and hazards that may increase the probability and severity of loss.

indirect contribution—A reduction in losses due to secondary relationships with suppliers, customers, and employees in the marketplace.

inland (and ocean) marine coverage—Insurance that provides protection for operations that take title to goods at the time of shipment from the supplier.

loss control—The actions taken to reduce the frequency and/or the severity of losses.

loss (risk) financing—The use of insurance (in various forms) to cover the costs of risk.

mutual insurers—A corporation owned by the policyholders.

people asset—A hotel's financial investment in its employees.

perils—Factors that might cause a loss of assets.

physical assets—A hotel's financial investment in its property.

pooling (risk sharing)—A provision of insurance in which the group policy holders agree to share the risk costs of the group via a payment by all to a fund shared by the group.

premises and operations coverage—Insurance that involves legal liability that can arise out of ownership and maintenance of the location where the firm does business.

products liability coverage—Insurance that involves injury to customers or damage to their property from defective products.

reinsurers—Insurance firms that transfer potential risk from a single insurance company to a number of insurance companies.

risk assumption—Taking few or no loss control actions because the risk associated with a certain activity is very low or the assumed risks have small financial costs.

risk comfort level—The degree of risk that is acceptable to a hospitality business.

risk management—The protection of corporate assets through the identification, determination, and management of the financial risks a corporation faces.

risk sharing (pooling)—A provision of insurance in which the group policy holders agree to share the risk costs of the group via a payment by all to a fund shared by the group.

risk transfer—A provision of insurance that transfers the risk associated with policy-covered losses from the insured to the insurer.

shifting loss—An attempt to shift risk from one party to another by legal contract.

stock insurers—A corporation owned by stockholders who participate in the profits and losses of the insurer.

umbrella coverage—Insurance that provides insurance above and beyond that of other underlying coverages.

valuation—Establishing the rules for which a property is valued at the time of a loss.

workers' compensation—The most common type of legally mandated insurance, it exists to provide a source of benefits for workers who are injured in the workplace. Coverage includes medical expenses, disability payments, survivor's death benefits, and rehabilitation benefits.

Review Questions

1. What are the basic steps in the risk management process?
2. What is the difference between a hazard and a peril?
3. What is one common form of loss financing?
4. What is risk transfer? What is risk sharing?
5. Why do many hotels and motels purchase a commercial package policy?
6. How can properties far from marine areas benefit from inland marine coverage?
7. What is the purpose of workers' compensation insurance?
8. When should properties establish claims management procedures?
9. Who typically should participate in a property's safety committee?
10. What duties should safety committee members expect to perform?

Internet Sites

For more information, visit the following Internet sites. Remember that Internet addresses can change without notice.

A.M. Best Company
http://www.ambest.com/

American Hotel and Motel Association (AH&MA)
http://www.ahma.com

American Insurance Association
http://www.aiadc.org/

American Risk and Insurance Association (ARIA)
http://www.aria.org

Blue Cross and Blue Shield
http://www.bluecross.com/

Business Insurance Magazine
http://www.businessinsurance.com/

Claims Magazine
http://www.claimsmag.com/

Insurance Information Institute
http://www.iii.org

Insurance News Network
http://www.insure.com/

Insurance Online
http://www.insure.net/

Insurance Services Office
http://www.iso.com

National Council on Compensation Insurance (NCCI)
http://www.ncci.com/index.html

National Fire Protection Agency
http://www.nfpa.org

Occupational Safety and Health Administration (OSHA)
http://www.osha.gov

Risk & Insurance Magazine
http://www.riskandinsurance.com/

Risk and Insurance
Management Society, Inc.
http://www.rims.org

RiskINFO
http://www.riskinfo.com/

RiskNet Risk Management Systems
http://www.integral.com/risknet.asp

RiskNet: Safety Forum
http://www.rnsf.com

RISKWeb
http://www.riskweb.com/

Self-Insurance Institute of America, Inc.
http://www.siia.org/

Standard & Poors
http://www.standardandpoors.com/

Case Study

Slipping Up—A Committee Catches Careless Acts

"Our mission is to provide a safe environment for employees, guests, and visitors and to ensure that the same accident never happens twice," said Abigail, the safety committee chair and executive housekeeper of the Seven Bungalows Resort. The resort boasted 1,500 rooms spread over 200 acres of tropical beach. The property catered to vacationers by pampering them with fine food, state-of-the-art fitness facilities, luxurious linens, skillful massage artists, and spacious rooms with awe-inspiring views.

It was 9 A.M. on a Tuesday morning and the safety committee had gathered for its monthly meeting. The top item on the agenda for the hour-long meeting was the orientation of two new members—Ryan, a laundry supervisor, and Brianna, the executive administrative assistant for the chief financial officer.

Around the table were the other members of the committee: Victoria from the front office; Jack, the executive chef; the dining room's maître d', Rachel; Jennifer, the banquet manager; the human resources representative, Tony; and Joseph the security director. Each of them had been on the safety committee for a minimum of a year. A few, such as Abigail and Joseph, had been on it since its inception eight years ago.

"Victoria, why don't you explain to Ryan and Brianna the four functions that we serve as a security committee," Abigail suggested.

Victoria smiled as if the two were VIP guests and pointed to the orientation packet in front of them. "You'll find it all in your booklets, but in brief, we fulfill four very important purposes. First, we emphasize prevention by working together to identify hazards in each of our departments through safety inspections. Second, we are all conduits of safety information to and from this committee and our respective departments. Third, we act to create an awareness of safety issues in the hotel. Finally, we investigate accidents as they occur."

"Most of the hazard identification has been done," Jack said. "But new hazards are constantly being created and oftentimes the procedures we've put in place to protect people get bypassed. We'll show you how to do an inspection, what to look for, and what constitutes a hazard. After this meeting is over, you can accompany me as I do my weekly inspection of the kitchen. Abigail will then work with you to develop checklists for each of your areas."

"The things you find on your inspection can help you fulfill our second purpose," Abigail said. "You can let us know what hazards we need to deal with, and you can let your co-workers know what hazards exist and why certain safety precautions exist. This also helps create a greater awareness of safety at the resort. What sort of things come immediately to mind when you think about the safety information that all employees need to know?"

"Well, certainly the Material Safety Data Sheets for all the chemicals in the laundry," Ryan answered. "OSHA requires that everyone know where an MSDS is for each chemical. They're also very useful for knowing what sort of personal protective equipment should be worn when handling each chemical. I know I use them a lot."

"Good," Abigail said. "What about you, Brianna? What sort of safety information do the administrative employees need to know?"

"That's a tough one, and one I've been thinking about since I was asked to be on the committee. There just aren't a lot of hazards in the office—unless you count paper cuts," Brianna said, ending with a chuckle.

"Actually, you might be surprised at the hazards an office can present," Victoria said. "Two years ago, I would have agreed with you. But there are little things that people forget about when they're in a hurry that have the potential to cause great harm. File cabinets with a lot of files need to be secured so they don't tip over. People leave drawers open and then trip over them. Worse, you see people standing on chairs with wheels to reach things on shelves. Those are just a few of the hazards that your department might have to deal with."

"You're right," Brianna said, nodding thoughtfully. "Just yesterday our accounting clerk was cussing because she had tripped on a dangling mouse cord."

"It's the accident investigation aspect that we're going to concentrate on today," said Joseph, the security director. "It's the duty that requires the greatest amount of observation and judgment on your part—and also the duty that can be most critical in helping prevent any accident from occurring more than once. When investigating a scene, you want to look for unsafe acts and unsafe conditions. Unsafe conditions can be corrected by making a physical change to the process or area, usually through the generation of a work order. Unsafe acts must be corrected with additional training or by changing the way that the job is done."

Tony opened up his folder and handed Ryan and Brianna a blank accident investigation form. "We're going to do a miniature case study. It's one that we've put together based on an accident that actually happened a few years ago at the resort—and one that is the type that could happen any day. We'll describe the accident and then discuss the sorts of questions that you should ask when you arrive at the scene. You can then practice filling out the sheet based on the described scenario."

"The scenario starts with you getting a call to the banquet department," began Rachel. "One of the servers from the Sea Urchin Lounge was drafted to help with a banquet after she finished her eight-hour shift at the lounge. She's fallen and is complaining of leg and back pains."

Jennifer picked up the story. "You arrive on the scene. She's in a back-of-the-house hallway sitting on the floor, leaning up against the wall. One of the server assistants is picking up the dishes that fell off the tray that the server, we'll call her Jasmine, was carrying. Another employee is drying a spot of water on the floor. What sort of things are you going to look for right away? Ask questions and we'll answer according to what you see."

"How many dishes was she carrying?" Brianna asked.

"A lot. Without taking time to count them, you can tell that the large tray was pretty full and she was probably carrying around 35 pounds of dirty dishes," Jennifer responded.

"Thirty-five pounds?" Ryan asked. "Was her vision obstructed?"

"Probably," Jennifer said. "That's a question that you'll have to ask her directly, but you think it likely."

"Should she have been carrying the tray? If she was going down a hallway, then it was probably some distance to be carrying a tray of dirty dishes. They can be awkward to carry. Shouldn't she have been using a cart of some type?"

"Very good. She was carrying the tray for about 300 feet when she fell," Abigail said. "What else do you look for?"

"What about her shoes?" asked Brianna. "Are they in good shape, are they working shoes?"

"Her heels are very worn—she's worked in them for a long time. You can even see the nails on her heel," Rachel said. "You also notice that there's the sheet to a pat of butter that is sticking to one of her shoes."

"Should she really have been working? Did she get a rest after her eight-hour shift? Maybe she's fatigued."

"What is the lighting like?" Ryan asked.

Joseph responded, "The lights are on, but you notice that two of the fluorescent tubes have burned out and things are a little dimmer than they should be."

"What about the surface of the floor?" Brianna asked. "Is it carpet? Tile? Is it level or is it a ramp?"

"And how close to the door was she when she fell? Is there any chance that she might have been hit by the door?"

The questions continued as the safety committee worked their way through the case, guiding the two new members into fully exploring the scene.

Two weeks later, Ryan had just finished programming the dilution levels for the new detergent they were using for table linens. He grabbed his clipboard to record the amounts when he noticed that Morgan, a new laundry attendant, was pouring bleach into the spotter at a table in the middle of the laundry room—and that she was wearing neither gloves, goggles, nor an apron.

Just as he was about to call out to her, Kyle, another laundry attendant who was pulling out a cart filled with dirty guestroom towels, backed into Morgan. She stumbled forward and the bleach she was pouring splashed into her eyes.

Discussion Questions

1. What factors contribute to the effectiveness of the safety committee of Seven Bungalows Resort?
2. Based on the description of the laundry incident, list the observations and questions that would provide information for completing an accident investigation form.
3. What items would go on an accident report checklist?

Case Number: 3877CA

The following industry experts helped generate and develop this case: Wendell Couch, ARM, CHA, Director of Technical Services for the Risk Management Department of Bass Hotels & Resorts; and Raymond C. Ellis, Jr., CHE, CHTP, CLSD, Professor, Conrad N. Hilton College, University of Houston, Director, Loss Prevention Management Institute.

REVIEW QUIZ

When you feel you have covered all of the material in this chapter, answer these questions. Choose the *best* answer.

1. The risk management process begins with the identification of risk. What two types of assets must be identified at this stage?

    a. business and people
    b. physical and people
    c. interior and exterior
    d. perils and hazards

2. Factors that might create or increase the chances of loss are known as:

    a. poor maintenance.
    b. physical assets.
    c. perils.
    d. hazards.

3. Which of the following is *not* a benefit of purchasing group coverage?

    a. lower prices
    b. no negotiation necessary
    c. rate stability
    d. customized policies

4. If a guest slips on a patch of ice and sues the hotel, which type of commercial general liability coverage would be necessary to cover the losses which may be incurred?

    a. premises and operations coverage
    b. product liability coverage
    c. completed operations coverage
    d. contingent liability coverage

5. Umbrella coverage:

    a. provides a combination of liability and physical damage coverages.
    b. is designed to cover the loss of business income because of a direct physical loss to an insured property.
    c. provides insurance above and beyond that of other underlying coverages.
    d. is legally mandated.

6. When managing claims, the first step is to:

    a. complete and file all necessary documentation.
    b. contact legal counsel.
    c. promptly notify the insurer of potential loss.
    d. meet with the accounting department to arrange payment.

REVIEW QUIZ (continued)

7. Which of the following statements regarding safety committee meetings is *false?*
    a. They are not necessary if there are no immediate problems.
    b. They should follow a set agenda.
    c. They should be scheduled regularly.
    d. Someone should record the minutes of the meeting.

Answer Key: 1-b-C1, 2-d-C1, 3-b-C2, 4-a-C3, 5-c-C3, 6-c-C4, 7-a-C5

Each question is linked to a competency. Competencies are listed on the first page of the chapter. An answer reading 3-b-C4 translates to:

  3: the question number
  b: the correct answer
  C4: the competency number

Appendix:

A Guide to OSHA Regulations for the Lodging Industry

The following material has been excerpted from

A Guide to Occupational Safety and Health Standards Compliance for the Lodging Industry

Edited by Raymond C. Ellis, Jr., CHE, CHTP, CLSD

Used with permission.

A Guide to OSHA Regulations for the Lodging Industry

THE OCCUPATIONAL SAFETY and Health Act of 1970 was designed as a method "to assure so far as possible every working man and woman in the Nation safe and healthful working conditions and to preserve our human resources" in business establishments throughout the United States. Enacted on December 29 1970, implementation of the legislation began at various dates during 1971. Standards pertaining to various chemical and toxic substances continue to be under development and review.

This broad legislation adopted many existing standards promulgated by the American National Standards Institute, the National Fire Protection Association, and other nationally recognized standards organizations. Although the Act was designed to protect employees, the multiple use of the same premises by employees, the public, and guests may result in protection for guests and the public as well.

Posting requirements, recordkeeping requirements, and many of the myriad rules and regulations in interpretation of the Standards apply to lodging properties. These include requirements involving walking and working surfaces, means of egress, occupational health and environmental controls, hazardous materials, personal protective equipment, medical and first aid, fire protection, materials handling and storage, machinery and machine guarding, welding, cutting and brazing, and electrical equipment and systems. We will consider a number of aspects of the law, although we often will not be able to present here all of the detailed information contained in the complete Standards.

Federal regulations in recent years have exempted employers with ten or fewer full-time and part-time employees per calendar year from the recordkeeping and reporting requirements, except the obligation to report fatalities or multiple hospitalization accidents and the obligation to maintain a log of occupational injuries and illnesses. Exempt employers, however, are required to make reports when notified in writing by the Bureau of Labor Statistics that they have been selected to participate in a statistical survey of occupational injuries and illnesses.

In any study of OSHA compliance, it is necessary to recognize the need for a full understanding of the Act by senior management. Consequently, our review will indicate those areas in which the senior management is the ultimate decision-maker as to the appropriate response by the lodging facility to the OSHA requirements.

Following that review, this guide will focus on the compliance with the requirements of OSHA on a department-by-department basis. Naturally this will be a bit repetitious as similar aspects of the Law will, of necessity, appear in the compliance requirements for most of the departments in one form or another.

STATE PLANS (Part 1902)

The Act includes the opportunity for state-approved plans, rather than administration of the Occupational Safety and Health Act by the federal establishment. Hotel organizations with properties located in a number of states are aware that there are states which receive grant monies from OSHA for the administration of OSHA through the state-approved plans. This may result in differences in administration of the Act by the state versus the federal OSHA. Generally, any conflict in such administration or interpretation of the Act can be resolved at the federal level. The following states and territories have state-approved plans (New York and Connecticut cover state and other government agencies only):

- Alaska
- Arizona
- California
- Connecticut
- Hawaii
- Indiana
- Iowa
- Kentucky
- Maryland
- Michigan
- Minnesota
- Nevada
- New Mexico
- New York
- North Carolina
- Oregon
- Puerto Rico
- South Carolina
- Tennessee
- Utah
- Vermont
- Virgin Islands
- Virginia
- Washington
- Wyoming

As noted above, the states have a certain latitude in interpretation and application of the requirements under the Act. Consequently, there may be times when properties in the same chain are encountering different applications of a specific mandate under the Act. One stipulation by the national office of OSHA is that the requirements under the Act must be at least as stringent as those at the national level.

Where there appears to be an interpretation that is "off the wall," contact the federal OSHA office with jurisdiction for the area in which the property is located (visit: http://www.osha.gov/oshdir/area.html for area offices).

INSPECTIONS, CITATIONS, AND PROPOSED PENALTIES (Part 1903)

AUTHORITY FOR INSPECTION

Compliance Officers are authorized to enter *without delay* and at reasonable times any establishment to inspect and investigate during regular hours any place of employment, and all pertinent conditions, structures, machines, apparatus, devices, and equipment; and to review records required by the Act. Representatives of the Department of Health, Education and Welfare, and of the state shall also be authorized to conduct similar inspections and investigations.

EMPLOYEE COMPLAINTS

Any employee or employee representative may request an inspection if it is felt that there is a violation of the OSHA mandates on the property. The complaint may be sent to the Area Director or to a Compliance Safety and Health Officer. The identity of the complainant is never given by OSHA to the employer or senior management. If the Area Director considers the complaint to have merit, an inspection will be ordered. Such an inspection is normally limited to matters specified in the complaint. A general inspection can be implemented based upon the specific complaint by an employee, but usually is not. If it is decided the request has no merit, the Area Director will directly contact the complainant and note that there is no basis for an inspection. This decision may be challenged and would then receive a review and final decision by the Regional Administrator. That decision is not subject to further review.

Should the employer learn the identity of the complainant and take adverse action relative to the individual's employment or assignments, this would place the management in violation of the Act and subject to penalties.

WHEN ADVANCE NOTICE OF INSPECTION IS PERMISSIBLE

Advance notice of an inspection may not be given unless there is an imminent danger which should be corrected as quickly as possible. Even though the property may correct such a condition, the inspection would still proceed and penalties may be assessed. If there is a situation in which it is determined that it would be better to conduct the inspection after regular business hours, or there is the need for special preparations for the inspection, pre-notice may be provided. If representatives of employee groups, or the employer or appropriate employees to aid in the inspection process must be notified, then a pre-notice may be given. Finally, if the Area Director (OSHA) determines that a more effective and efficient inspection could be accomplished through pre-notice, it will be issued through that office. Advance notice will usually not be given more than 24 hours before the inspection and is rarely given.

REFUSAL TO PERMIT INSPECTION

The employer has the right to refuse admission of the Compliance Safety and Health Officer. However, the Compliance Safety and Health Officer may then obtain a court order authorizing such an inspection. Since this may involve expensive litigation, it is not recommended that the employer deny entry to the inspector. In the event of objection to inspection or refusal to permit inspection of any portion of an establishment, the official representative will endeavor to learn the reason for such refusal and must report the refusal and reason to the Area Director. The matter will further be referred to the Regional Administrator and Regional Solicitor for appropriate action, including compulsory process, if necessary. A Supreme Court decision in May 1979 supported the need for a search warrant where admission was refused by an employer.

RECEPTION OF THE COMPLIANCE SAFETY AND HEALTH OFFICER

The responsibility for receiving the Compliance Safety and Health Officer (CSHO) is obviously that of senior management or the employer. This should not be a function relegated to one of the departments within the property. The employer would certainly want representation from the departments, as appropriate. It is advised that consideration be given to including the chief engineer and the human relations director as part of the team that would accompany the Compliance Safety and Health Officer on the tour of inspection. If at all possible, the general manager should also be a member of that inspection team. The compliance officer may limit the size of the accompanying party if it is felt that the size would hinder the inspection.

INSPECTION PROCEDURES

Upon arrival, the Compliance Safety and Health Officer must present credentials confirming that he or she is an authorized inspector. If compliance officers are on premises as the result of an employee complaint, they will provide that information but will not divulge the name of the complainant. They must explain the nature and purpose of the inspection and generally cover the scope of the inspection. They should indicate the records that they wish to review; but this does not preclude a request for additional records should the ongoing inspection process indicate the need for such data. They are entitled to take photographs and environmental samples. They may also privately question any employer, owner, operator, agent, or employee of the establishment.

REPRESENTATIVES OF EMPLOYERS AND EMPLOYEES

A representative of the employer and a representative designated by the employees may accompany the Compliance Officer. Additional employer or employee representatives may accompany him where such additional representatives will further aid the inspection.

The Compliance Officer shall have authority to resolve all disputes as to who is the representative authorized by the employee. If there is no authorized employee representative, the Compliance Officer shall consult with a reasonable number of employees concerning matters of safety and health in the workplace.

If in the judgment of the Compliance Officer, a third party not employed by the employer (such as a safety engineer or industrial hygienist) is reasonably necessary to the conduct of an effective inspection, such a party may accompany the Compliance Officer to the inspection.

QUESTIONING OF EMPLOYEES

In a property with union representation, the union steward or other designated union representative will be part of the inspection team. Where no union representation exists, the Compliance Safety and Health Officer may question as many employees in private as may be felt necessary to obtain full information. Under those circumstances there may not be an employee accompanying the inspection party.

EXIT CONFERENCE

At the conclusion of the inspection, the Compliance Officer shall confer with the employer or designated representative and informally advise him or her of any apparent safety or health violations evidenced during the inspection. At this conference, the employer shall be afforded an opportunity to provide to the Compliance Officer with any pertinent information regarding conditions in the workplace. Representatives of the employees will also be given the opportunity for an exit conference. These conferences may be held jointly or separately.

IMMINENT DANGER

If, in the process of an inspection, it is determined that an imminent danger exists, the inspector will advise the employer and employees of this danger. The Act requires that the inspector recommend civil action to restrain the conditions or practices leading to the imminent danger situation. Even though the employer may immediately remove the conditions or practices resulting in the imminent danger, the employer may be subject to citation and proposed penalties. While it is unlikely that an imminent danger situation would occur in a lodging establishment, a chemical spill or leak in a chemical system on the premises could result in such a condition.

DE MINIMIS VIOLATIONS

A de minimis violation has no direct or immediate relationship to safety or health. It is one of those administrative devices that leaves the employer asking why it was issued at all. Essentially it is advisory, and there will be no fine assessed. An example of a de minimis citation relates to a lodging establishment that had failed to indicate where the employees should gather by department after an emergency evacuation. It is logical that such instruction should be provided as it would assist in determining whether all employees of a given department had been safely evacuated from the building, but it is not directly mandated by the Act.

CITATIONS

Citations are issued by the Area Director based upon a review of the inspection report. The Director may further review the citations with the Regional Solicitor to cover the various legal aspects of the citations that are being issued through the area office. The citation will specify the nature of the violation and the pertinent provision of the Act. Citations must be issued with reasonable promptness. If the citation results from an employee's request for inspection, a copy of the citation will also be provided to the employee or an authorized representative of the employee, or employees. No citation may be issued after the expiration of six months following the inspection and identification of an alleged violation. There must be a recommended reasonable period of time for abatement of the violation.

PROPOSED PENALTIES

The Area Director shall determine the amount of any proposed penalty, giving due consideration to the appropriateness of the penalty with respect to the employer and the history of previous violations, and shall notify the employer of any proposed penalties relating to the OSHA inspection. Appropriate penalties may be assessed even though the employer immediately abates, or initiates steps to abate, such alleged violations. If you, as employer, wish to contest the citation before the

Review Commission, you must do so within 15 working days following receipt of the proposed penalty. If there is no intention to contest the penalty, the payment must be made within the limits indicated on the OSHA document.

POSTING OF CITATIONS

The employer must post a copy of the unedited citation immediately upon receipt. It should be posted at or near the place of the alleged violation. The citation must be posted until the violation is abated, or for three working days, whichever is later. Even if you do file a contest, the citation still must be posted. However, the law does permit the employer to also post a copy of the notice of contest along with the citation. That notice will indicate the reason for the contest and specific steps that have been taken to abate the violation. De minimis violations need not be posted.

INFORMAL CONFERENCES

Within the 15-working-day period, the employer, employee, or employee representative may request an informal conference which will normally be conducted by the Area Director. If the challenge is able to be resolved in that conference, there will be no representation to the Review Commission and the agreed action will be taken by the employer to resolve the citation and proposed penalty. At the discretion of the Area Director, either party may be included in a hearing that has been brought by the other party. Any party may be represented by counsel. The informal conference does not change the limitations of the 15 working days, and the employer must decide to request an informal conference as soon as possible if there is a matter for challenge. Otherwise, the time will lapse and the employer may be in violation of the citation and proposed penalties because formal notice of contest will not have been filed in a timely manner. The earlier the informal conference, the more time the employer will have to file a formal contest within the allocated time. An informal conference should be requested to discuss any citations received.

PETITION TO MODIFY THE ABATEMENT DATE

An employer may file a petition for modification of the abatement date if circumstances do not permit completion within the abatement period. The petition must include information as to what has been done to accomplish abatement and the reason or reasons for an inability to meet the limits of the abatement period. (For example, it is impossible to meet the abatement deadline due to delay in shipping and receiving of a special part or an item of equipment.) Such a petition must be received by the Area Director no later than the close of the working day following the date on which abatement was to have been completed. Furthermore, a copy of the petition must be posted for 10 days in a conspicuous place at or near the violation site for the information of the employees at the property in question.

FAILURE TO CORRECT A VIOLATION WHICH HAS BEEN CITED

If a follow-up inspection indicates that the employer has failed to correct an alleged violation that has been cited, the Area Director will consult the Regional Solicitor. If it is determined that additional penalties are warranted, notice will be provided to the employer by registered mail or through personal delivery by the Compliance Safety and Health Officer. The correction period on the new violation begins with the entry of a final order by the Review Commission. Again, the right of contest is available to the employer and follows the same time constraints as noted above.

EMPLOYER AND EMPLOYEE CONTEST BEFORE THE REVIEW COMMISSION

As noted previously, the notice of contest must be given within 15 working days following receipt of a citation or notice of proposed penalty. An important additional item of information is that the employee or an employee representative may also file a written notice with the Area Director indicating that the time for abatement of the violation is unreasonable. Of course this may be either favorable or unfavorable to the employer depending upon whether they are challenging the abatement period as too long or too short. The 15-working-day limitation for filing will also apply to the employee or employee representative.

CONTRACTOR AND MULTI-EMPLOYER CONCERNS

Since many lodging establishments contract for various maintenance, construction, and repair functions, it should be noted that the property management assumes an OSHA compliance responsibility if this is not carefully defined in the contract. The contract must specify the responsibility of the contractor to comply with all OSHA requirements that apply to the contractor's particular function on the property.

Not only must you provide the contractor with information on your hazard communication, tagout/lockout, and confined space programs, but the contractor should provide full data on chemicals that will be brought on the premises as well as ensuring that proper ladders, scaffolds, personal protective equipment, and any other items of equipment will be in accord with the OSHA requirements.

The contract and lease agreement for leaseholders on the premises should also define those areas of OSHA responsibility assumed by those individual organizations. All applicable aspects of OSHA for the other employers on the property must be reviewed so you are assured of their compliance.

OSHA VIOLATIONS BECOME A MAJOR FINANCIAL CONSIDERATION

Effective March 1, 1991, penalties for violations for standards promulgated under OSHA were substantially increased. The same categories of violations established in 1970 still apply, but the penalties for such violations have increased sevenfold. In the category of "serious" and "other than serious" violations, fines have increased from $1,000 to $7,000.

A willful violation, in which evidence shows that the employer committed an intentional and knowing violation of the Act, is increased from $10,000 to $70,000. Since the fine may apply to each incident rather than to a class of incidents, a minimum mandatory penalty of $5,000 will apply per violation. For example, the category of "water on the floor" would not be the single designation for five incidences of water on the floor, but could become five distinct violations with a minimum fine of $25,000.

Failure to abate a violation beyond a date agreed upon by the employer and OSHA will result in a daily fine of $7,000 until compliance is achieved.

Repeated violations are to be treated in the same manner as willful violations with a fine of up to $70,000.

The term "egregious" is appearing more frequently in OSHA citations and is the multiplier mentioned above where five "water on the floor" incidents would be cited and fined as five violations rather than the prior practice of one citation, "water on the floor," covering all such incidents detected during an OSHA inspection. Egregious is defined as flagrant.

The message is loud and clear. Make sure the property is complying with all of the applicable OSHA Safety and Health standards. Failure to do so could prove to be disastrously expensive. It could also lead to criminal charges where negligence on the part of management resulted in a fatality or multiple serious injuries. This could result in significant fines and imprisonment.

RECORDING AND REPORTING OCCUPATIONAL INJURIES AND ILLNESSES (Part 1904)

EMPLOYER RESPONSIBLE FOR REPORTING

Again, the employer is designated as the responsible person for the implementation of a system to record any job-related injury or illness. While this function will be assigned to human resources or some other office that may be indicated by the general manager, the responsibility ultimately is that of the general manager or the employer. The recordkeeping requirements are the same for the states with approved programs as for federal OSHA.

LOG NO. 200 FORM

In all establishments with 11 or more employees, the Log No. 200 Form must be maintained. The reverse of the Log form has full instructions on those incidents that should be recorded. Recordability is established when a case results from a work accident or from an exposure in the work environment that results in a death, an illness, or an injury. In order to be recorded, the injury must result in medical treatment, other than first aid; or loss of consciousness; or restriction of work or motion; or an injury that requires transfer to another job.

There are five steps in the decision process as to whether the incident is recordable:

1. Determine whether a case occurred—that is, whether there was a death, illness, or injury.

2. Establish that the case was work-related—that it resulted from an event or exposure in the work environment.

3 Decide whether the case is an injury or illness.

4. If the case is an illness, record it and check the appropriate illness category on the log.
5. If the case is an injury, decide if it is recordable based on a finding of medical treatment, loss of consciousness, restriction of work or motion, or transfer to another job.

The following considerations are involved in the evaluation process and the actual completion of a Log entry:

Date of injury or onset of illness: For occupational injuries, enter the date of the work accident which resulted in injury. For occupational illnesses, enter the date of the original diagnosis or illness, or, if absence from work occurred before diagnosis, enter the first day of absence attributable to the illness which was later diagnosed or recognized.

Injury or illness with lost workdays: Any injury which involves days away from work, or days of restricted work activity, or both, must be recorded since it always involves one or more of the criteria for recordability.

Lost workdays/days away from work: Enter the days away from work (consecutive or not) on which the employee would have worked but could not because of occupational injury or illness. The number of lost workdays should not include the day of injury or onset of illness or any days on which the employee would not have worked even though able to work. For any employees in a part-time category, it may be necessary to estimate the number of lost workdays. Estimates of lost workdays shall be based upon prior work history of the employee AND days worked by employees, not ill or injured, working in the department and/or occupation of the ill or injured employee.

Lost workdays/days of restricted work activity: One should enter the number of workdays (consecutive or not) on which because of injury or illness:
- The employee was assigned to another job on a temporary basis, or
- The employee worked at a permanent job less than full time, or
- The employee worked at a permanently assigned job but could not perform all duties normally connected with it.

The number of lost workdays should not include the day of injury or any days on which the employee would not have worked even though able to work.

Injuries or illnesses without lost workdays must pass the test for recordability before being entered upon the Log.

The informal policy of entering every work-related injury or illness for ease of recordkeeping is self-defeating as it does not permit comparison with any figures released for general industries, or specifically for the lodging industry. It could also present a false picture of a property with an extremely poor record should a Compliance Officer inspect the premises.

Special reference should be made to the total columns for the Log. If an employee's loss of workdays is continuing at the time the totals are summarized, estimate the number of future workdays the employee will lose, add that estimate to the workdays already lost, and include this figure in the annual totals. No further entries are to be made with respect to such case in the next year's log.

Definitions:

Occupational injury is any injury such as a cut, fracture, sprain, amputation, etc., which results from a work accident or from an exposure involving one single incident in the work environment. (Note: Conditions resulting from animal bites, such as insect or snake bites or from one-time exposure to chemicals, are considered to be injuries.)

Occupational illness of an employee is any abnormal condition or disorder, other than one resulting from an occupational injury, caused by exposure to environmental factors associated with employment. It includes acute and chronic illnesses or diseases which may be caused by inhalation, absorption, ingestion, or direct contact. The Log contains a listing of various occupational illnesses and disorders which should be referenced in a review of the reverse of the Log No. 200 form.

Finally, **medical treatment** includes treatment (other than first aid) administered by a physician or by registered professional personnel under the standing orders of a physician. Medical treatment does NOT include first aid treatment (one-time treatment and subsequent observation of minor scratches, cuts, burns, splinters, etc., which do not ordinarily require medical care) even though provided by a physician or registered professional personnel.

WORKER'S COMPENSATION FIRST REPORT OF INJURY FORM OR OSHA NO. 101 FORM

Each incident logged must have a backup report on file with the Log. The "first report of injury " form, which must be filed with the worker's compensation carrier, is acceptable and saves the necessity of filling out additional report forms.

If such a form is not used, it will be necessary to complete an OSHA No. 101 form for the purpose of backup. Either form must be filed within six days of the incident. Such data may be maintained by computer as long as there is print-out capability on site should a Compliance Safety and Health Officer request the information during an inspection. At locations where the "master" log is maintained at corporate headquarters, the location must be able to produce a log covering its experience complete and current to a date within 45 calendar days.

ANNUAL SUMMARY

A summary sheet of the OSHA Log No. 200 forms must be completed at the end of each calendar year. The summary sheet must include:

- Calendar year covered
- Company name
- Establishment name if different from company designation
- Establishment address

- Certification signature, title, and date. The employer is required to certify that the report is true and complete.

The prior year's summary sheet of the OSHA Log No. 200 forms must be posted for the month of February in a location available to all employees. It may be removed on the first of March and filed away. It should be retained with substantiating documents for five years. The file from six years ago may be discarded.

ACCESS TO RECORDS

Upon request, the employer must make available OSHA records for inspection and copying by any representative of the Secretary of Labor or the Secretary of Health, Education and Welfare; or any state with an approved plan or any employee, former employee, or their authorized representative. Such copying must be accomplished in a reasonable manner and at reasonable times.

REPORTING OF FATALITY OR MULTIPLE HOSPITALIZATION INCIDENTS

Within eight hours after the death of an employee from a work-related incident or the inpatient hospitalization of three or more employees as the result of a work-related incident, the employer shall orally report the fatality/multiple hospitalization by telephone or in person to the nearest Area Office of the Occupational Safety and Health Administration (OSHA), or by using the OSHA toll-free central phone number (1-800-688-9889).

This requirement also applies to each fatality or hospitalization of three or more employees which may occur within 30 days of the actual incident. Exception: If the employer is unaware of the incident, that employer must report within eight hours after learning of such an incident.

Each report shall include:

- Establishment name
- Location of incident
- Time of the incident
- Number of fatalities or hospitalized employees
- Contact person
- Phone number
- A brief description of the incident

FALSIFICATION, OR FAILURE TO KEEP RECORDS OR REPORTS

Any employer who knowingly falsifies records or fails to maintain required records may be punished with a fine of not more than $10,000, or by imprisonment for not more than six months, or both.

REVISION OF LOG FORMS BY OSHA

During the period of preparation of this guide, OSHA was conducting public hearings on the development of a new format for the Log. The American Hotel & Motel

Association, state associations, and other media sources will announce such a change. At such time, the establishment should introduce the new Log form and any changes in recordkeeping and recordability that may be instituted.

CHANGE OF OWNERSHIP

The employer is responsible for only that part of the year in which the establishment was actually owned. However, the employer must maintain any records received in the transfer for the five-year period, noted above, or for the 30 years required under medical monitoring. (This occurs when an employee is exposed to a health hazard such as Hepatitis B, a chemical spill, etc. In such cases, the employer must retain the records for the 30-year period even though the individual may no longer be employed at the establishment.)

PETITIONS FOR RECORDKEEPING EXCEPTIONS

There is a petition process for the employer who wishes to maintain records in a different manner from that required under the Law. Reference should be made to 29 Code of Federal Regulations, Ch. XVII (7-1-94 Edition), Section 1904.13, if there is any interest in such action.

SMALL EMPLOYERS

An employer with no more than 10 employees at any time during the calendar year need not comply except for the reporting of fatalities and multiple hospitalization incidents. The employer may also be required to maintain records if notified by the Bureau of Labor Statistics that the employer has been selected to participate in a statistical survey of occupational injuries and illnesses.

BUREAU OF LABOR STATISTICS FOR THE LARGER PROPERTY

The property with 11 or more employees may also be notified by the Bureau of Labor Statistics of the U.S. Department of Labor that the reports are to be provided for the upcoming year. This is the only time the establishment must provide Log data to the government.

RULES OF PRACTICE FOR VARIANCES, LIMITATIONS, VARIATIONS, TOLERANCES, AND EXEMPTIONS UNDER OSHA (Part 1905)

Part 1905 of the Act provides techniques for an employer to seek relief from those aspects of the Act that are difficult, if not impossible to achieve. Perhaps the practices developed by the employer and staff have provided as safe a method for accomplishing a task as that which would be achieved through a more difficult and expensive approach mandated under the Act. Whatever the basis for a request for relief, the Act does permit such an option. The sections are technical and will certainly require the involvement of your counsel. It is recommended that should such action be contemplated, attention be given to 29 Code of Federal Regulations, Ch. XVII (7-1-94 Edition), Part 1905, Subparts A through E.

The section referenced above will provide a full disclosure of the potential for time and expense in attempting to obtain relief from any given requirement under the Act.

CONSULTATION AGREEMENTS (Part 1908)

Part 1908 covers the program of consultation which assists the employer in complying with OSHA. Several of the following objectives and services are presented in this Part:

- The program was devised to assist the employer on-site or by phone or correspondence in establishing effective occupational safety and health programs; and to prevent work-related injuries and/or illnesses.
- Such assistance may be provided through education and training of employers, supervisors, and other groups of employees as necessary to ensure safe working locations and practices.
- While on-site consultation will not result in citations or penalties for violations, the employer must make any corrections that may be required to remove a violation. That action and commitment by the employer "may serve as the basis for employer exemption from certain OSHA enforcement activities." Both the federal OSHA and states with approved programs provide this service. (See http://www.osha.gov/oshdir/consult.html for the roster of consultant offices for both federal OSHA and states with approved programs.)
- A protocol for the on-site consultation is quite specific, and the employer is advised to discuss this in detail with the consultant before scheduling such a meeting. You are reminded that it will be necessary to correct any violations. Should it be determined that a "serious" hazard exists, an abatement period will be established. At this point, you, as employer, are under the same requirements as under a formal inspection except that there is a recommendation (not a requirement) that you post the violation at the site of the hazard and there will be no penalties unless there is failure to comply with the abatement agreement. You are further advised that the consultant is required to notify the OSHA enforcement office should there be a failure to provide correction of any hazards in a timely manner. This, of course, would move the situation from a consultative to a compliance and penalty stage. In either instance, you would be subject to follow-up inspections to verify abatement.
- It must also be noted that the consultant has the right to question or discuss safety-related matters with any of the employees seen during the course of a tour of the property. The consultant will encourage the employer to allow participation by employees or employee representatives in the inspection tour and consultative activities to the fullest extent practicable.

Current data may be obtained at http://www.osha.gov/oshprogs/consult.html.

A CLOSER LOOK AT THE BEWILDERING WORLD OF OSHA STANDARDS FOR THE LODGING INDUSTRY (Part 1910)

Similar to those responsibilities under the inspection and recordkeeping aspects of the Occupational Safety and Health Act, there are many mandates under the standards section of the Act that require special attention by the EMPLOYER. Once, again, the designation of EMPLOYER figures prominently in the implementation of the Law. While one may be unhappy with the implications, one cannot quarrel with the concept that it should be the full responsibility of the employer for the safety of all functions taking place under his or her responsibility.

In the following pages we shall look at most of the applicable standards under the Act and attempt to note, in an easily understandable format, exactly what you as EMPLOYER must do. As previously noted, this may be a bit repetitious as requirements at the property level will specifically affect each department within that property with similar mandates.

SUBPART C—GENERAL SAFETY AND HEALTH PROVISIONS (1910.20)

- **MEDICAL RECORD ACCESS:** The main thrust of this section is to ensure the availability of relevant exposure and medical records to employees, their representatives, or the Assistant Secretary (OSHA).

- **EMPLOYEE EXPOSURE RECORD:** If, for example, there was a chlorine leak in a tank that provided chlorination for a large pool, or series of pools on a property, all employees who were exposed to those fumes would come under a medical monitoring program. An employee exposure record would be established. They would have follow-up examinations at least at an annual interval. Also, the records for such employees must be retained for 30 years, even though they may have left years earlier than the 30-year period. Such records would be accessible, as noted above. Other sources would include environmental monitoring, biological monitoring, and material safety data sheets.

- **WHAT EMPLOYEE MEDICAL RECORDS INCLUDE:** any record concerning the health status of an employee which is made or maintained by a physician, nurse, or other health care personnel or technician. Such records may include the medical and employment questionnaires or histories (including job description and occupational exposures); medical examinations, X-rays, and all biological monitoring not described as an "employee exposure record"; medical opinions, diagnoses, progress notes, and recommendations; first aid records; descriptions of treatments and prescriptions; and employee medical complaints.

- **MEDICAL RECORDS NOT SUBJECT TO ACCESS INCLUDE:** physical specimens, health insurance claims records, records created solely in preparation for litigation which are privileged from discovery under the applicable rules of procedure or evidence, and records concerning voluntary employee assistance programs (alcohol, drug abuse, or personal counseling programs).

- **RULES OF ACCESS:** The employer must provide records in a reasonable time, place, and manner. If the employer cannot provide reasonable access within 15 working days, the employer must indicate the reason for the delay and the earliest possible time that the records will be available.

  A copy of the record is to be provided without cost to the employee or employee representative; or the necessary mechanical copying facilities will be made available at no cost to the employee or employee representative for copying the record; or the record may be loaned for a reasonable time for copies to be made away from the premises.

  An original X-ray, at the employer's discretion, may be restricted to on-site inspection or may be made available on a temporary loan.

  The employer shall not charge for the initial request or for additional data that has been added since the initial request.

  Previously requested data may be made available on a repeat request at a reasonable charge reflecting a non-discriminatory, administrative cost. (This may cover search and copying expenses but may not include overhead expenses.)

- **EMPLOYEE INFORMATION:** At the time of employment and at least annually thereafter, the employer must inform current employees concerning the existence, location, and availability of medical records as reviewed in this section; the person or persons responsible for maintaining and providing access to the records; and each employee's rights of access to these records. The employer will maintain a copy of this section and appendices and make copies readily available, upon request, to employees.

- **TRANSFER OF RECORDS:** Whenever an employer goes out of business, the records shall be transferred to the successor employer. The successor employer shall receive and maintain these records.

  Where there is no successor organization, the employer shall notify employees of their rights to access to records at least three (3) months prior to the last day of business.

  Those records required to be maintained for thirty (30) years where there is no successor employer may be transferred to the Director of the National Institute for Occupational Safety and Health (NIOSH) if so required by a special occupational safety and health standard. Or, the employer may inform the Director of NIOSH in writing of the impending disposal of records at least three (3) months prior to such disposal.

APPENDIX TO THE MEDICAL RECORDS ACCESSIBILITY STANDARD

A non-mandatory sample authorization letter is provided for your information and for the information of your employees. (See Exhibit 1.)

Exhibit 1 Non-Mandatory Sample Authorization Letter

I, _____ (full name of employee), hereby authorize _____ (individual or organization holding the medical records) to release to _____ (individual or organization authorized to receive the medical information) from my personal medical records:

_____

(Describe generally the information desired to be released.)
I give my permission for this medical information to be used for the following purpose:

_____

but I do not give permission for any other use or re-disclosure of this information. (NOTE: Several extra lines are provided so that you can place additional restrictions on this authorization letter if you want to. You may, however, leave these lines blank. On the other hand, you may want to (1) specify a particular expiration date for this letter (if less than one year); (2) describe medical information to be created in the future that you intend to be covered by this authorization letter; or (3) describe portions of the medical information in your records which you do not intend to be released as a result of this letter.)

_____

_____

Full name of Employee or Legal Representative

Signature of Employee or Legal Representative

Date of Signature

SUBPART D—WALKING-WORKING SURFACES (1910.21–1910.32)

THE EMPLOYER'S RESPONSIBILITIES: The employer is fully responsible for providing a workplace that fully meets the requirements of this standard. This necessitates that the employer provide adequate and safe walking and working surfaces throughout the property. This includes the floor surfaces throughout the establishment as well as all working surfaces.

The employer is further challenged to provide special protection or facilities in the following categories: floor openings or holes, handrails, platforms, runways, toeboards, wall openings or holes, stairs (including the riser, the nose or nosing), and the tread with its width and run (horizontal distance from one leading edge to the leading edge of an adjacent tread).

There is a comprehensive section on ladders. Basically, it is the responsibility of the employer and management to provide a safe ladder, maintain it in the best possible working order, and supervise so that the proper ladder is used for the task at hand. There is no official OSHA label, but manufacturers are permitted to indicate that the ladder has been constructed according to OSHA requirements. The standard covers every conceivable ladder from stepstools to fixed ladders that extend up a chimney or from one level of rooftop service penthouses to another level.

Scaffolds are also referenced and may be found in use in some larger establishments. Again, the standards are quite detailed and, when followed, will provide maximum safety in the use of a scaffold if the condition of the unit is maintained and the staff uses the scaffold in the approved manner.

1910.22 GENERAL REQUIREMENTS

- Housekeeping: All places of employment, passageways, storerooms, and service rooms shall be kept clean, orderly, and in a sanitary condition.

- The floors shall be maintained in a clean and as dry as possible condition.

- Where wet processes are used, drainage shall be maintained, and mats, false floors, or platforms should be provided where practicable.

- To facilitate cleaning, all work areas shall be kept free from protruding nails, splinters, holes, or loose boards.

- Aisles and passageways shall be kept free and in good repair with no obstruction across or in any aisles that could create a hazard. Safe clearances shall be allowed throughout the work area for movement of mechanical or wheeled equipment. Permanent aisles and passageways shall be appropriately marked.

- Covers and guardrails shall be provided to protect against the hazard of falling into an unprotected opening.

- Floor load protection: Rooms or other areas must display approved signage indicating the safe floor load for storage or safe numbers of people in a place of public accommodation. Such loads will be approved by authority having jurisdiction for the place in which the facility is located.

1910.23 GUARDING FLOOR AND WALL OPENINGS AND HOLES

- Protection for floor openings shall be provided on all stairways with a railing constructed to standard. With the exception of the entrance, the railing shall be provided on all exposed sides. Infrequently, stairways in aisleways or other traffic areas may have a hinged floor-opening cover and removable standard rails.

- Every ladderway floor opening or platform shall be guarded by a standard railing with a standard toeboard on all exposed sides other than the entrance with the protection of a swinging gate or offset to prevent walking directly into the opening.

- It is rare for hatchways or chute floor openings to be found in a hospitality facility. If present, they must be guarded by a standard hinged floor-opening cover with appropriate railings and toeboards.

- Every skylight floor opening and hole shall be guarded by a standard skylight screen or a fixed standard railing on all exposed sides.
- Infrequently used pits, trapdoors, manhole openings, temporary floor openings, or floor holes must be guarded by floor-cover protection, with railings and toeboards as required. When in use, the opening must be attended or removable railings must be provided.
- Where doors or gates open directly on a stairway, the equivalent of a 20-inch platform must be provided to allow for the swing of the door.
- Protection for wall openings or holes must be provided if there is a drop of more than 4 feet. Such protection may include a rail, roller, picket fence, half-door, or equivalent barrier. Every window wall opening at a stairway landing, floor, platform, or balcony from which there is a drop of more than 4 feet and where the bottom of the opening is less than 3 feet above the standing surface shall be guarded by standard slats, standard grill work, or a standard railing. A standard toeboard shall be provided where the window opening is below the standing surface.
- Where there is a hazard of materials falling through a wall hole, a standard toeboard or an enclosing screen of solid construction must be provided.
- Open-sided floors, platforms, and runways that are 4 feet or more above adjacent and lower working areas must be guarded by a standard railing and toeboard wherever persons pass below, or where there is moving machinery or equipment for which falling items could create a hazard.

Stairway Railing and Guards Require:

- Flights of stairs with four or more risers shall have handrails.
- Stairways of less than 44 inches having both sides enclosed shall have at least one handrail, preferably on the right hand descending.
- Stairways of less than 44 inches with open sides should have at least one railing on the open side.
- Stairways of less than 44 inches and open on both sides must have two handrails.
- Stairways of more than 44 inches but less than 88 inches require railings on each side whether open or closed.
- On stairways 88 inches or more in width, one stair rail is required on each side, open or closed, and a center rail approximately at the midway position.
- Winding stairways will be provided with a railing that will prevent walking on all portions of the treads having a width less than 6 inches.

Railings, Toeboards, and Cover Specifications:

- A standard railing includes a top rail, intermediate rail, and posts. A nominal vertical height of 42 inches is required. Top rail shall be smooth surfaced

(Editorial comment: It has been found that the maintenance of railings in a light color and in a clean condition will more likely be a used rail than one in dark colors with the potential for an unseen buildup of grease and dirt.) Top and intermediate rails should end so the rails do not overhang the terminal posts to avoid a projection hazard.

- A stair railing shall be constructed similar to the above but shall not be more than 34 inches nor less than 30 inches from the upper surface of the top rail to the surface of the tread at its forward edge.

- Wood railing posts should be of at least 2-inch by 4-inch stock spaced not to exceed six feet; the top and intermediate rails shall be at least 2-inch by 4-inch stock. If a top rail is made of two right-angle pieces of 1-inch by 4-inch stock, posts may be placed on 8-foot centers, with 2-inch by 4-inch intermediate rail.

- Pipe railings, posts, and top and intermediate railings shall be at least $1^1/_2$ inches nominal diameter, with posts spaced not more than 8 feet apart on center.

- Structural steel railings, posts, and top and intermediate rails shall be of 2-inch by 2-inch by $^3/_8$-inch angles or other shapes of equivalent bending strength, with posts not more than 8 feet apart on center.

- The anchoring of the railings, posts, and rails, whatever the material, shall be capable of withstanding a load of at least 200 pounds in any direction at any point on the top rail.

- A standard toeboard shall be 4 inches nominal height from its top edge to the level of the base surface. It shall be secured in place with not more than $^1/_4$ inch of space above the base level. It may be made of a substantial material, either solid or with openings not greater than 1 inch. If materials are stored where the toeboard does not protect against falling objects, paneling or other protective screening must be provided.

- A handrail shall be mounted directly on a wall or partition by means of a bracket attached so as to avoid any obstruction to a smooth top and sides. It should be of rounded or other shape that will provide an adequate handhold for grasping to prevent a fall. The ends of the rail shall be positioned to avoid a projection hazard. There must be a clearance of at least 3 inches between the handrail or railing and any other object. Spacing of brackets shall not exceed 8 feet.

- Floor-opening sites must have trench, conduit covers, and manhole covers able to support a rear axle load of at least 20,000 pounds. All hinges, handles, bolts, or other parts shall be flush with the floor and cover surface.

- Skylight screens shall be of such construction and so mounted as to withstand a load of 200 pounds applied perpendicularly at any one area on the screen. The construction should prevent flexing of the screen that would break the glass in the skylight. Grillwork construction should have openings no more than 4 inches long. Slatwork should have openings no more than 2 inches apart but with length unrestricted.

- All other barriers for wall openings shall be able to support a load of at least 200 pounds at any point other than upward. Wall opening grab bars must not be less than 12 inches in length and shall have at least three inches clearance; and must also pass the minimum 200-pound test. This similar test applies on all wall opening screens.

1910.24 FIXED INDUSTRIAL STAIRS

Fixed industrial stairs within the hospitality industry will usually be "back-of-the-house," or "behind the scenes." Where applicable, the following requirements apply:

- Stair strength must carry a load five times the normal live load-never less than 1,000 pounds
- The minimum stair width is 22 inches
- Angle of stairway rise is between 30 and 50 percent
- Stair treads shall be reasonably slip-resistant, and the nosings shall be of non-slip finish with uniform rise height and tread width
- Stairway platform shall be no less than the width of a stairway and a minimum of 30 inches in length in the direction of travel
- Standard railings shall be provided on all open sides of exposed stairways and platforms and shall be provided on at least one side in enclosed stairways, preferably right side descending
- Vertical clearance of at least 7 feet measured from the leading edge of the tread must be provided

1910.25 PORTABLE WOODEN LADDERS

This standard prescribes construction, care, and use of common types of portable wooden ladders.

Care of Ladders:

- Maintained in good condition at all times with tight joints; all metal parts securely attached and all moving parts working freely.
- Metal bearings of locks, wheels, pulleys, etc. shall be frequently lubricated.
- Frayed or badly worn rope shall be replaced.
- Safety feet and other auxiliary equipment shall be kept in good condition.
- Ladders shall be inspected frequently and defective ladders shall be withdrawn from service for repair or destruction and tagged or marked as "Dangerous—Do Not Use!"
- Rungs should be kept free of grease and oil.

- Wooden ladders should never be painted as the paint could cover up flaws in the ladder.

Use of Ladders:

- Portable rung and cleat ladders should be used so the pitch from the top of the ladder to the foot of the ladder is one quarter the working length of the ladder. The ladder shall be placed to prevent slipping or it shall be lashed or held in position. Ladders shall not be used in a horizontal position as platforms, runways, or scaffolds.
- Unless specified for multiple use and so constructed, ladders are not to be used by more than one person at a time.
- Portable ladders must be securely placed before use.
- Ladders must not be used in front of doors opening toward the ladder unless the door is blocked open or guarded.
- Ladders shall not be placed on boxes, barrels, or other unstable bases to obtain additional height.
- Ladders with any broken parts shall not be used, and improvised repairs shall not be made.
- Short ladders shall not be spliced together to provide longer sections.
- Ladders made by fastening cleats across a single rail shall not be used.
- Ladders shall not be used as guys, braces, or skids, or for other than intended purposes.
- Other than on a platform stepladder, the top rung shall not be used as a step.
- On two-section extension ladders, the following minimum overlap is required:
    - Three feet up to and including 36 feet in length
    - Four feet over 36 feet up to and including 48 feet
    - Five feet over 48 feet up to and including 60 feet
- Portable rung ladders will be used only with the metal reinforcement on the underside.
- No ladder shall be used to access a roof level unless it extends 3 feet above the support contact at that roof.
- Middle and top sections of window cleaner's ladders should not be used for a bottom section unless provided with safety shoes.
- Nonslip bases must be provided on all ladders where there is the hazard of slipping. This should not substitute for safe placement, lashing, or holding of the ladder.
- The bracing on the back legs of a ladder are not for climbing.

1910.26 PORTABLE METAL LADDERS

Care of Ladders:

- Ladders must be maintained in good usable condition always.
- If a ladder tips, it must be inspected for dents, bends, or excessively dented rungs. Check all rung connections, hardware connections, and rivets for shear.
- If used under oily or greasy conditions, clean with a solvent or steam-clean.
- Remove damaged ladders from service and mark, "Do Not Use!" Do not return them to service until they are repaired by maintenance or the manufacturer.

Use of Ladders:

- Follow the rule of placing the base of the ladder a distance equal to one-fourth the working length of the ladder to achieve the proper angle.
- The ladder is limited to use by one person only. The 200-pound load applies.
- The ladder base section must have a secure footing.
- The top of the ladder must be properly secured.
- A climber must face the ladder when ascending or descending.
- Ladders must not be tied or fastened together to provide long sections unless manufactured for that purpose.
- A ladder should not be used as a brace, skid, guy, or gangway, or in any other manner than intended for the ladder.

1910.27 FIXED LADDERS

- All fixed ladders must be regularly inspected and treated to resist rust and corrosion. Similar care must be provided for wooden ladders to avoid decay. The installation of extensive fixed ladders is limited within the hospitality industry. For further information if such an installation is on the premises, reference should be made to the Code of Federal Regulations, Section 1910.27.

1910.28 SAFETY REQUIREMENTS FOR SCAFFOLDING

- Scaffolds shall not be loaded in excess of rated capacity. Again, scaffolding is not a regular activity within the lodging industry, and in-depth information should be obtained from the Code of Federal Regulations, Section 1910.28, if scaffolding is in use at your property.

1910.29 MANUALLY PROPELLED MOBILE LADDER STANDS AND SCAFFOLDS (TOWERS)

This applies to mobile work platforms (including ladder stands but not including aerial ladders) and rolling (mobile) scaffolds (towers).

The use of mobile tubular welded frame scaffolds or mobile tubular welded sectional folding scaffolds is limited within the lodging industry. Generally, this equipment will be brought on the premises by a contractor. It is recommended that the contract include the stipulation that the scaffolding, its installation, and its use be in compliance with OSHA requirements as specified in Code of Federal Regulations 1910.29.

1910.30 OTHER WORKING SURFACES

In larger lodging installations, dockboards (bridge plates) may be used in receiving or convention receiving areas. The portable and powered dockboards must be strong enough to sustain a rated load and must be capable of being secured so as to not slip out of position when in use.

GENERAL REQUIREMENTS

- **Housekeeping**—The employer must keep all places of employment, passageways, storerooms and service rooms in a clean, orderly, and sanitary condition.
- **Floors**—The floors in all areas shall be maintained in a clean and, insofar as possible, a dry condition. Where wet processes are used, drainage must be maintained and false floors, mats, platforms, or other dry standing places should be provided where practicable.
- **Aisles and passageways**—These must be wide enough for intended traffic and must be kept clear and in good repair with no obstruction that could create a hazard. Permanent aisles and passageways should be appropriately marked.
- **Covers and guardrails**—Protection must be provided on any floor or wall opening where an employee (or guest in the instance of a public area) might be in danger.
- **Floor Load Protection**—In all public areas and back-of-the house work and storage areas, the loads approved by the building official for that jurisdiction must be posted.

(Where there is a special concern for any aspect of this regulation, reference should be made to 29 Code of Federal Regulations, Ch. XVII [7-1-94 Edition], Subpart D—Walking-Working Surfaces, Sections 1910.21 through 1910.32.)

SUBPART E—MEANS OF EGRESS (1910.35–1910.40)

MEANS OF EGRESS: This comprehensive standard requires direct employer and senior management involvement. It is necessary that the property have a continuous and unobstructed way of exit travel from any point in the building or structure to a public way. The means of egress must have three separate and distinct parts: the way of exit access, the exit, and the way of exit discharge. When an exit is protected from other parts of the building, the separation shall have at least a one-hour fire resistance rating when the building is three stories or less. The separation must have at least a two-hour fire resistance rating if the structure is four or more stories in height. Again, this is a technical area in which the building architects, the building department for the local jurisdiction, and the authority having jurisdiction for the fire code (usually a local fire chief) will quickly inform you as to whether you are in compliance. As employer, owner, owner-manager, or manager, you should be aware that you are responsible for:

- Width and capacity of means of egress.
- Maintenance of floor load capacity throughout the structure.
- Provision of doors that open out to permit egress from a place of assembly.
- Elimination of mirrors on exit doors or in the vicinity of the door that could cause confusion on the part of the individual making an emergency exit.
- Maintenance of exterior ways so they are free from ice and snow or any other obstruction.
- Ways of exit wherein a dead end is not in excess of 20 feet.
- Headroom and changes in elevation.
- Provision of fail-safe alarmed exit doors. (If they fail to operate normally, they will open under an emergency system override.)
- Ensuring that furnishings and decorations do not obstruct exits, access thereto, egress therefrom, or visibility thereof.
- Where required, all automatic sprinkler systems and fire alarm signaling systems shall be maintained for immediate response capability.
- Ensuring that all passageways, stairways, or doors that are not part of an exit be so marked with notice such as, "Not an Exit." Other specific warnings might include: "To Basement," "Storeroom," "Linen Room," etc.
- Provision of appropriate signage with proper size and lighting to clearly define the way of exit, the exit, and the way of exit discharge.

EMPLOYEE EMERGENCY PLANS AND FIRE PREVENTION PLANS

The employer is responsible for providing an emergency evacuation program that will instruct each employee as to exactly what role is to be played in the event of an emergency evacuation. Normally, this requirement applies to employees only in most business functions where there is not a significant group of non-employees present. Obviously, any evacuation program in a lodging establishment must include a plan for the evacuation of guests, and patrons of meetings, and food-service or beverage-service facilities.

The emergency plan must include:

- Emergency escape procedures and emergency escape route assignments.
- Procedures for employees who must close down functions before evacuating.
- Procedures for ensuring that all persons are evacuated and accounted for. This will be more difficult in accounting for the public and guests but can be more exacting in determining whether all staff has been safely evacuated.

- Rescue and emergency medical assistance (usually provided through a call to 911).
- The preferred means of reporting a fire or other emergency.
- Designation by department and position as to *who is in charge* under the plan.

The plan must be in writing for establishments with more than 10 employees. It must be maintained at the workplace and be available for employee review.

The employer must establish a training program:

- Initially train a cadre of employees who will implement the program on-site.
- Review the program with each employee when the plan is initially developed; whenever the employee's assignment under the emergency program is changed; or whenever the plan is changed.
- The employer shall provide training upon initial assignment.
- A copy of the written program shall be maintained in the workplace and shall be made available for employee review.
- For detailed requirements of this standard, reference should be made to 29 Code of Federal Regulations, Ch. XVII (7-1-94 Edition), Sections 1910.35–1910.40.

SUBPART F—POWERED PLATFORMS, MANLIFTS, AND VEHICLE-MOUNTED WORK PLATFORMS (1910.66–1910.70)

Larger lodging properties may have some powered equipment, especially for building maintenance. A portion of the standard is provided for general information. For greater detail, reference should be made to 29 Code of Federal Regulations, Ch. XVII (7-1-94 Edition), Sections 1910.66–1910.70, with appendices.

1910.66 POWERED PLATFORMS FOR BUILDING MAINTENANCE

This covers powered platform installations permanently installed and dedicated to interior or exterior building maintenance of a specific structure or series of structures. This does not refer to suspended scaffolds (swinging scaffolds) used to service buildings on a temporary basis nor to suspended scaffolds used for construction. These are respectively referenced in Subpart D of this part and under Subpart L of 29 Code of Federal Regulations, Part 1926. Building maintenance includes, but is not limited to, such tasks as window cleaning, caulking, metal polishing, and reglazing.

1910.67 VEHICLE-MOUNTED ELEVATING AND ROTATING WORK PLATFORMS

This includes any vehicle-mounted device, telescoping or articulating or both, which is used to position personnel. This type of device may be found within the lodging industry to assist in relamping, the hanging of decorations, and other necessary maintenance or repair functions in high-ceiling spaces within a facility.

1910.68 MANLIFTS

In rare instances there may be manlifts in resort-related amusement park towers for staff only. They may also be found in multistory parking facilities. However, they are the exception rather than the rule for the industry, and reference should be made to this section only as it may be necessary.

SUBPART G—OCCUPATIONAL HEALTH AND ENVIRONMENTAL CONTROL (1910.94–1910.100)

VENTILATION

Essentially, this standard refers to manufacturing processes involving abrasive blasting. However, the standard does provide regulations on the use of grinding wheels. Since many properties will have a grinding wheel in the maintenance and engineering operations area, the employer must be aware of his or her responsibility. Full details may be obtained through reference to 29 Code of Federal Regulations, Ch. XVII (7-1-94 Edition), Sections 1910.94 through 1910.100. Special reference on the use of the grinding wheel is in Section 1910.94. Spray booths are also covered in this section. Again, such units may be found in the larger properties, and the standard should be referenced in order to provide full compliance with the highly technical and specific requirements of the law.

OCCUPATIONAL NOISE EXPOSURE

Section 1910.95 under the Code of Federal Regulations, noted above, should be carefully reviewed. Again, this is a standard that is highly technical and requires professionally trained persons to assist in implementing such a program for your property. When information indicates that any employee's exposure may equal or exceed an eight-hour time-weighted average of 85 decibels, the employer must develop and implement a monitoring program. Based upon an employee complaint, a bar-lounge facility with a "live" band was cited and fined and ordered to maintain the music decibel level at a more acceptable level. Reduction in decibel level by the band and a rest interval within each hour helped to address the time-weighted requirement in this instance. Review those operations that have a continuous noise present and study ways in which that noise level and intensity might be reduced. Where such conditions exist, it will be necessary for the employer to:

- Monitor the work area in order to identify those employees who should attend a hearing conservation program and to enable the employer to select the proper hearing protectors.
- Notify all employees exposed at or above an eight-hour time-weighted average of 85 decibels of the results of the monitoring.
- Establish and maintain an audiometric testing program as specified in Section 1910.95 above.

In support of this audiometric program, a number of states provide an OSHA On-Site Consultation service. Consult the local OSHA office in your area for the contact on the audiometric consultation service for your location (see http://www.osha.gov/oshdir/consult.html).

SUBPART H—HAZARDOUS MATERIALS (1910.101–1910.120)

This is a wide-ranging and comprehensive standard that deals with many aspects of the use of hazardous chemicals in the workplace. The variety and diversity of chemicals used in the lodging industry make it impossible to provide more than a cursory review of the width and breadth of the standard. Where your property has a specific installation that comes under the control of the standard, reference should be made to 29 Code of Federal Regulations, Ch. XVII (7-1-94), Sections 1910.101 through 1910.132. The following section is emphasized for your review:

The employer must determine that all compressed gas cylinders under the property's control are in a safe condition insofar as can be determined by visual inspection. All such units must be properly secured by chain or strap when stored or in use.

OUTDOOR CONTAINER STORAGE AND OUTDOOR PORTABLE TANK STORAGE

In recent years the Environmental Protection Agency has introduced regulations that moved the entire nation from underground to aboveground storage facilities. Since many properties have such tanks, your special attention is called to those regulations in Section 1910.106 in the Code of Federal Regulations reference noted above.

STORAGE AND HANDLING OF LIQUEFIED PETROLEUM GASES

Since liquefied petroleum (LP) gas is used in many lodging establishments, special attention should be given to Section 1910.110 of this standard. It is highly technical and will require qualified engineers and installers. The employer is charged with the responsibility for ensuring that all requirements in the selection, installation, use, and maintenance of LP gas facilities are in accord with this standard.

HAZARDOUS WASTE OPERATIONS AND EMERGENCY RESPONSE

The possibility of a hazardous waste problem increases as there are more and more tank trucks that are parking in areas surrounding hotels and motels along major interstate roads and highways. It is the responsibility of the employer to meet with the appropriate authorities in the community for the handling of such an emergency. Police, fire, local emergency planning offices, and the Environmental Protection Agency are but a few of the agencies that should be contacted for establishing a response capability. Section 1910.120 of the standard provides detail in this regard. It would seem most appropriate for the property not to establish a clean-up team, but to integrate a chemical spill emergency with the emergency evacuation program for the property. Of course, a minor spill might involve trained staff to clean up such a spill. However, even in a minor spill where the employee may be exposed to toxic fumes, the employee must be fitted with a totally encapsulating chemical-protective suit and individually fitted respiratory mask and tank at a cost that is in the thousands of dollars. Again, we suggest emergency evacuation and the call for professionals from within the community.

MINIMUM ILLUMINATION INTENSITIES IN FOOTCANDLES

A chart appears in this standard that is of special interest to the lodging industry. There are incidents resulting in litigation where the intensity of lighting is an important factor. Generally, the court has concurred with the specification that from one to one and a half foot-candles evenly distributed throughout a parking area would be acceptable. Many times an expert witness will testify that he or she was able to read a newspaper at the normal reading distance in an area of the parking lot. That has always satisfied the court

Now we have a differing and higher intensity requirement stipulated in a Federal Code. The following is recommended in this standard:

Footcandles	Area of Operations
3	Excavation and waste areas, accessways, active storage areas, loading platforms, and refueling areas
5	General site area (this would probably include parking lots)
10	General shops (e.g., mechanical and electrical rooms, active storerooms, employee living quarters, locker or dressing rooms, dining areas, and indoor toilets and workrooms)
30	First aid areas and offices

TOILET FACILITIES

Another code requirement is "buried" in this same standard. With the number of toilet facilities available in a lodging establishment, there is usually not a problem with the number of commodes or urinals available. However, if there are locations away from the public areas of the property (laundry, engineering, and housekeeping departments back-of-the-house, for example), the following facilities must be provided:

Number of Employees	Minimum Number of Facilities
1–15	One
16–35	Two
36–55	Three
56–80	Four
81–110	Five
111–150	Six
Over 150	One per each 40 additional employees

In facilities for men only, urinals may be substituted for water closets except that the number of water closets will not be reduced to less than two-thirds of the minimum specified.

In the 1–15 category, the standard permits a unisex installation. Where toilet rooms will be occupied by no more than one individual at a time, can be locked from the inside, and contain at least one water closet, separate toilet rooms for each sex need not be provided.

SUBPART I—PERSONAL PROTECTIVE EQUIPMENT (Part 1910.132–1910.140)

GENERAL REQUIREMENTS

Protective equipment, including personal protective equipment for eyes, face, head, and extremities; protective clothing; respiratory devices; and protective shields and barriers shall be provided, used, and maintained in a sanitary and reliable condition. Such equipment will be indicated wherever it is necessary to provide the employee with special protection due to the hazardous aspects of the work assignment.

All personal protective equipment shall be of a safe design and construction for the work to be performed. The employer is charged with the responsibility of determining those hazards present in the job assignment which might be corrected or alleviated through the use of appropriate personal protective equipment. It should be noted that even if the personal protective equipment (PPE) is provided by the employee (highly unlikely in the lodging industry), the employer still has the responsibility to ensure its adequacy, including proper maintenance and sanitation of such equipment. All PPE must meet the standards as established under the American National Standards Institute or other national authorized standards-making organizations.

TRAINING

Each employee shall be trained to know at least the following:

- When PPE is necessary
- What PPE is necessary
- How to properly put on, remove, adjust, and wear PPE
- The limitations of PPE
- The proper care, maintenance, useful life, and disposal of PPE

The employer shall verify that each affected employee has received and understood the required training through a written certification that contains the name of each employee trained, the date(s) of training, and the subject of certification.

EYE AND FACE PROTECTION

Each affected employee shall use appropriate eye or face protection when exposed to eye or face hazards from flying particles, hot liquids, acids, or caustic compounds (these are used in cleaning by housekeeping or kitchen workers), dust from overhead cleaning and dusting activities, and the many other exposures encountered in the day-to-day assignments for many of the staff of a lodging establishment.

The following requirements must be considered by the employer:

- Eye protection with side protection must be provided whenever there is the danger of particles or objects entering from the side during the normal work procedure.
- When an employee wears prescription lenses, the prescription must be incorporated in the eye protection; or the protective glasses must accommodate the wearing of the prescription eyeglasses without disturbing the proper position of the prescription lenses or the protective lenses.

It is unlikely there will be many, if any, assignments requiring filter lens protection against radiant energy. If the engineering and maintenance staff does any welding work, this requirement does apply. Refer to 29 Code of Federal Regulations, Ch. XVII (7-1-94 Edition), Section 1910.132.

Employers will provide eye and face equipment that will fully meet the nature of the hazard that might be encountered by the employee while on a particular work assignment. Such equipment must:

- Provide adequate protection against the hazard
- Be reasonably comfortable
- Fit snugly and must not interfere with movements of the worker
- Be durable
- Be capable of being disinfected
- Be easily cleanable
- Be kept clean and in good repair

RESPIRATORY PROTECTION

The employer is charged with the responsibility of eliminating those conditions that contaminate the breathing air with harmful dusts, fogs, fumes, mists, gases, smokes, sprays, or vapors. In normal cleaning operations, employees in the lodging industry may be exposed to any or all of the above. The work requirements must be carefully reviewed so that adequate protection is provided. Of course, it is most satisfactory if it is possible to engineer the situation so that none of the above hazards will be a problem. Use of less toxic materials is also a "step in the right direction."

When engineering controls are not feasible, such as in dusting overhead on guestroom furniture and furnishings, a dust mask may be the best solution to the problem. The cost of a full respirator with full oxygen supply through a cylinder or air compressor is in the vicinity of $2,000. In larger properties where there are chemicals used from bulk tanks (such as chlorine for chlorinating of water supply for spas, Jacuzzis, and swimming pools), it will be necessary to have full respiratory capability with the fitting and specific assignment of respirators to employees. This may be restricted to specific engineering staff covering a 24-hour period. If it is necessary to provide such respiratory protection, reference should be made to 29 Code of Federal Regulations, Ch. XVII (7-1-94 Edition), Section 1910.134.

HEAD PROTECTION

The employer must assess the work assignment to determine whether any employee is in danger of injury to the head from objects falling from above; or from injury due to restricted access to crawl spaces and closed areas where overhead pipes and projections might also cause injury to the head. If the establishment has electricians on staff, protective helmets designed to reduce electrical shock hazard shall be provided.

FOOT PROTECTION

This is one area of protection that becomes a major concern within the lodging industry. The costs can become significant, and with the levels of turnover, the property is hard-pressed to comply and yet stay in business. The requirements for the employer are quite specific. Each affected employee shall wear protective footwear when working in areas where there is a danger of foot injuries due to falling or rolling objects, or objects piercing the sole, and where such employees' feet are exposed to electrical hazards. A review of the foot injuries for the establishment is beneficial in the development of a foot protection program. To address the problem of the economics of shoe purchase for a work force with heavy turnover, some corporations have set up a "safety shoe program" and partially subsidize the purchase of such shoes with the employee paying a reasonable portion of the cost. New style lines in safety shoes with the safety toe protection are not easily identified as a special shoe and may be worn as a regular, comfortable shoe both on and off the job. The editor is unaware of any instance wherein OSHA has required the underwriting and establishment of a footwear program within a lodging establishment.

ELECTRICAL PROTECTIVE EQUIPMENT

The employer shall provide insulating blankets, matting, covers, line hose, gloves, and sleeves made of rubber to meet requirements set in 29 Code of Federal Regulations, Ch. XVII (7-1-94 Edition), Section 1910.137. It would be unusual for a lodging facility to require this level of equipment as it would more likely be provided to a contract electrical service or utility. If there is a remote location where full electrical services are required as part of staff, then reference should be made as noted above.

HAND PROTECTION

Employers shall review the need for hand protection on the various work assignments in the lodging establishment. Protection should be provided when employees' hands are exposed to hazards such as those from skin absorption of harmful substances; severe cuts or lacerations; severe abrasions; punctures;

chemical burns; thermal burns; and harmful temperature extremes. OSHA has cited and fined for employees working in housekeeping, food service, and kitchen cleaning operations where hand protection had not been provided by the employer. As noted under the Bloodborne Pathogens section (pages 418–428), this mandate becomes critical in several of the departments of a hotel or motel.

SUBPART J—GENERAL ENVIRONMENTAL CONTROLS (1910.141–1910.150)

SANITATION

- All places of employment shall be kept as clean as possible at all times during the working process.
- Where wet processes are used, special action should be taken to provide false floors, mats, platforms, or other dry standing places.
- Every work floor and passageway shall be kept free from protruding nails, splinters, loose boards, and unnecessary holes and openings.
- Receptacles for solid or liquid waste or refuse must be leakproof and must be easily cleaned and sanitized. Unless it is possible to maintain a sanitary condition without a cover, a solid, tight-fitting cover will be provided.
- All sweepings, solid or liquid waste, and garbage must be removed at regularly scheduled intervals to maintain maximum sanitary conditions on the premises.
- Vermin shall be controlled through a continuing and effective extermination program.
- Potable water shall be supplied in all places of employment for drinking, washing of the person, cooking, washing of foods, washing of cooking or eating utensils, washing of food preparation or processing areas, and personal service rooms.
- In the rare instances where potable water may be provided (for example, on a resort property distant from the main buildings), it must be provided in a closed container with a tap, and a common drinking cup is not permitted.
- Nonpotable water that may be used for firefighting purposes must be clearly marked as such. It must be indicated that such water cannot be used for drinking, laundry, food preparation and cleaning, or any other personal use. The system must be developed to prevent backflow or backsiphoning of such waters into the potable system.
- The requirements for toilet facilities are the same as those provided under Subpart H, page 392.
- Washing facilities shall include lavatories with hot and cold running water or tepid running water. Hand soap or similar cleansing agents shall be provided. Individual hand towels of cloth or paper will be provided. Warm air dryers or individual sections of continuous clean toweling are also acceptable. One

shower, where required, shall be provided for each 10 employees of each sex, or a numerical fraction thereof. Body soap or other appropriate cleaning agents, and individual clean towels will be provided. Showers shall be supplied with hot and cold water feeding a common discharge line.

- Change rooms will be supplied whenever it is required for employees to change clothing for uniforms or other special attire. The change rooms will be equipped with storage facilities for street clothes and separate facilities for the required uniform or special clothing worn by the employee while on duty.
- When clothing is provided by the employer, it will be cleaned as required, between shifts and will be dry before reuse.
- No employee shall be allowed to consume food or beverages in a toilet room or in any area exposed to toxic substances. Food or beverages should not be stored in such areas.
- All employee food facilities and operations must be operated and maintained in a hygienic manner.

SAFETY COLOR CODE FOR MARKING PHYSICAL HAZARDS

The color RED shall be the basic color for identification of the following:

- Fire protection equipment and apparatus.
- Danger will be indicated in red, as in the use of safety cans or other portable containers of flammable liquids. A yellow band with clearly identified letters or stenciled letters on the container should specify the contents.
- Red lights shall be provided at barricades.
- Danger signs shall be painted red.
- Emergency stop bars on equipment such as flatwork ironers shall be red.
- Stop buttons or electrical switches where letters or other markings appear, used for emergency stopping of the equipment, shall be in red.
- The color yellow shall be the basic color for designating caution and for marking physical hazards such as striking against, stumbling, falling, tripping, and "caught in between." This color has been used to advantage on stairs in both back-of-the-house stairways and fire stairwells. The marking in yellow of the nosing of the top and bottom step of each flight highlights the beginning and ending step of each flight and assists in preventing stairway falls or tripping. Consideration should be given to painting the metal or wooden stair railings in a light color (not necessarily in yellow), as it has been found there is a greater inclination for individuals to grasp the railing if it has a light color and appears to be clean. Similarly, a dark or dirty-appearing railing is less likely to be grasped, and there are more stair falls under such circumstances.

SPECIFICATIONS FOR ACCIDENT PREVENTION SIGNS AND TAGS

These specifications are intended to cover all safety signs except those designed for streets, highways, railroads, and marine regulations. They do not apply to bulletin boards or to safety posters that are used for a lodging establishment safety program.

Classification of signs according to use:

- **Danger signs** shall not vary in the type of design of signs posted to warn of specific dangers and radiation hazards. All employees shall be instructed that danger signs indicate immediate danger and that special precautions are necessary.
- **Caution signs** shall be used only to warn against potential hazards or to caution against unsafe practices. All employees shall be instructed that caution signs indicate a possible hazard against which proper precautions should be taken.
- **Safety instruction signs** shall be used where there is a need for general instructions and suggestions relative to safety measures.

SIGN DESIGN

- Signs shall have rounded or blunt corners and shall be free from any irregular surfaces that could cause injury. The ends or heads of bolts or other fastening devices shall be located in such a way that they do not constitute a hazard.
- **Danger signs** shall use the colors red, black, and white in an opaque, glossy finish.
- **Caution signs** shall have yellow backgrounds, and the panel shall be black with yellow letters. Any letters used against the yellow background shall be black in an opaque, glossy finish.
- **Safety instruction signs** shall have a standard background of white, and the panel green with white letters. Any letters used against the white background shall be black in an opaque, glossy finish.
- **Slow-moving vehicle signs** consist of a fluorescent yellow-orange triangle with a dark red reflective border. The yellow-orange triangle is a highly visible color for daylight exposure. The reflective border defines the shape of the fluorescent color in daylight and creates a hollow red triangle in the path of motor vehicle headlights at night. This is more likely to be found in a resort setting where mowers and other special vehicles that operate at less than 25 mph. are used and must move on public roads on occasion.
- **Sign wording:**
  - Must be easily read and concise.
  - Must contain sufficient information to be easily understood.
  - Must make a positive rather than a negative suggestion.
- **Biological hazard signs**: The impact of the bloodborne pathogen standards on the lodging industry has made this an important symbol. This sign shall be used to signify the actual or potential presence of a biohazard and to identify equipment, materials, or combinations thereof that contain or are

contaminated with viable hazardous agents that are harmful to an individual's well-being.

ACCIDENT PREVENTION TAGS

This applies to all accident prevention tags used to identify hazardous conditions and provide a message to employees with regard to hazardous conditions or to meet specific tagging requirements of other OSHA standards.

- The *major message* of a tag should be very specific and concise. For example: "High Voltage," "Close Clearance," "Do Not Start," or "Do Not Use," or a corresponding pictograph used with a written text or alone.

- The *signal word* includes that portion of the tag's inscription that contain key words that will capture the employee's immediate attention.

- Use: Tags are to be used as a means to prevent accidental injury or illness to employees who are exposed to hazardous or potentially hazardous conditions. Tags are to be used until such time as the identified hazard is eliminated or a hazardous operation has been completed. Tags need not be used where signs, guarding, or other positive means of protection are being used.

GENERAL TAG CRITERIA

Tags shall contain a signal word and a major message.

- The signal word shall be either "Danger," "Caution," "Biological Hazard," "BIOHAZARD," or the biological hazard symbol.

- The major message shall indicate the specific hazardous condition or the instruction to be communicated to the employee.

- The signal word shall be readable at a minimum distance of five feet or such greater distance as may be warranted by the hazard.

Biohazard

- The tag's major message shall be presented either in pictographs, written text, or both.

- The signal word and the major message shall be understandable to all employees who may be exposed to the identified hazard.

- All employees shall be informed as to the meaning of the various tags used throughout the workplace and what special precautions are necessary.

- Tags shall be affixed as close as safely possible to their respective hazards.

- Danger tags shall only be used in major hazard situations where there is danger of death or serious injury.

- Caution tags shall be used in minor hazard situations where there is lesser threat of serious injury, but a potential for injury, nevertheless.
- Warning tags may be used to represent a hazard level between "Caution" and "Danger."
- Biological hazard tags shall be used to identify the actual or potential presence of a biological hazard, and the symbol design shall conform to the design shown above.

PERMIT-REQUIRED CONFINED SPACES

An amazing number of confined spaces may be present within a lodging establishment. This does not cover confined spaces such as the narrow space between a row of files and a wall. Rather, it covers those locations where the space may have its own atmosphere with a minimum of airflow or oxygen. A couple of examples are the boiler where a maintenance person is going into the unit to clean out potash, and a heating oil storage tank where it is necessary to get into the tank to clean out the sludge before refilling the tank for the winter season.

A key aspect of the confined space rule involves the written program for spaces that require permits. Under the rules, the employer must ensure that the "permit-required confined spaces program" includes the following elements:

- A written program to prevent unauthorized entry
- Procedures and practices for safe entry, including the testing and monitoring of conditions in the space
- Responsibilities of the attendant who must be stationed outside permit spaces during an entry
- Procedures to summon rescuers and prevent unauthorized personnel from attempting rescue
- A system for preparing, issuing, using, and canceling entry permits
- Procedures for concluding entry operations and canceling entry permits
- Proper equipment needed to test, monitor, and ventilate the space, as well as communications, rescue, and personal protective equipment

CONFINED SPACE PERMIT SYSTEM MUST INCLUDE THE FOLLOWING 15 PIECES OF DATA

- Permit space to be entered
- Purpose of entry
- Date and duration of entry
- List of authorized entrants
- Names of current attendants
- Name and signature of entry supervisor who authorized entry
- Lists of hazards in the permit space

- Measures to isolate permit space and to control hazards
- A statement of acceptable entry conditions
- Results of tests, initialed by the person(s) who did them
- List of rescue and emergency services and means to summon them, including communication procedures for attendants and entrants
- Required equipment, such as respirators or alarms, and any other necessary information. Any additional permits, such as for hot work (welding, etc.)
- Contractors also come under this rule, and the employer must make sure that contractors are aware that the workplace has confined spaces that may be entered only with a permit, according to the OSHA ruling
- It is also required that the employer apprise the contractors of hazards associated with any potentially hazardous confined space and the procedures used
- The contractor and employer must coordinate their operations when entering a permit space, and contractors must be debriefed after work has been completed in the space

Employers with such confined spaces should refer to 29 Code of Federal Regulations, Ch. XVII (7-1-94 Edition), Section 1910.146, for a detailed coverage of requirements under this standard.

THE CONTROL OF HAZARDOUS ENERGY (LOCKOUT/TAGOUT)

This standard covers the servicing and maintenance of machines and equipment in which the unexpected energization or start-up of the machines or equipment, or release of stored energy, could cause injury to employees. This standard will not apply to the normal operations of machines or equipment except when:

- An employee is required to remove or bypass a guard or other safety device.
- An employee is required to place any part of the body into an area on a machine or piece of equipment at the point of operation during the actual machine operation cycle.
- The regulation will not apply to work with cord- and plug-connected equipment where the plug is under the direct control of the employee performing the work.

TYPICAL MINIMAL LOCKOUT/TAGOUT SYSTEM PROCEDURES

- **General:** Lockout is the preferred method of isolating machines or equipment from energy sources. To assist employers in developing a procedure which meets the requirements of the standard, however, the following simple procedure may be used where there is a single power source. For more complex systems, a more comprehensive procedure will need to be developed, documented, and utilized.
- **Purpose:** This procedure establishes the minimum requirements for the lockout or tagout of energy-isolating devices. It will be used to ensure that the

machine or equipment is isolated from all potentially hazardous energy, and locked out or tagged out before employees perform any servicing or maintenance activities where the unexpected energization, start-up, or release of stored energy could cause injury. (List your type(s) and magnitude(s) of energy hazards.)

- **Responsibility**: Appropriate employees shall be instructed in the safety significance of the lockout (or tagout) procedure. (List name(s)/job title(s) of employees authorized to lockout or tagout.) Each new or transferred affected employee and other employees whose work operations are or may be in the area shall be instructed in the purpose and use of the lockout or tagout procedure. (List name(s)/job title(s) of affected employees and how to notify them.)
- **Preparation for lockout or tagout:** Make a survey and identify all isolating devices to be certain which switch(es), valve(s), or other energy-isolating devices apply to the equipment to be locked or tagged out. More than one energy source (electrical, mechanical, or others) may be involved. (List type(s) and location(s) or energy-isolating means.)

SEQUENCE OF LOCKOUT OR TAGOUT SYSTEM PROCEDURE

- Notify all affected employees that a lockout or tagout system is going to be utilized and the reason for it. The authorized employee shall know the type and magnitude of energy that the machine or equipment utilizes and shall understand the hazards thereof.
- If the machine or equipment is operating, shut it down by normal stopping procedure (depress stop button, open toggle switch, etc.).
- Operate the switch, valve, or other energy-isolating device(s) so that the equipment is isolated from its energy source(s). Stored energy (such as that in springs, elevated machine members, rotating flywheels, hydraulic systems, and air, gas, steam, or water pressure, etc.) must be dissipated or restrained by methods such as repositioning, blocking, bleeding down, etc. (List type(s) of stored-energy methods to dissipate or restrain.)
- Lockout and/or tagout the energy-isolating devices with assigned individual lock(s) or tag(s). (Method(s) selected: i.e., lock, tags, additional safety measures, etc.)
- After ensuring that no personnel are exposed, and as a check on having disconnected the energy sources, operate the push button or other normal operating controls to make certain the equipment will not operate. CAUTION: Return operating control(s) to the "neutral" or "off" position after the test.
- The equipment or machine is now locked out or tagged out.

RESTORING MACHINES OR EQUIPMENT TO NORMAL PRODUCTION OPERATIONS

- After servicing and/or maintenance is complete and equipment is ready for normal production operations, check the area around the machines or equipment to ensure that nothing is exposed.

- After all tools have been removed from the machine or equipment, guards have been reinstalled, and employees are in the clear, remove all lockout or tagout devices. Operate the energy-isolating devices to restore energy to the machine or equipment.

PROCEDURE INVOLVING MORE THAN ONE PERSON

In the preceding steps, if more than one person is required to lockout or tagout equipment, each person shall place his/her own personal lockout or tagout device on the energy-isolating device(s). When an energy-isolating device cannot accept multiple locks or tags, a multiple lockout or tagout device (hasp) may be used. If a single lock is used to lockout the machine or equipment, the lock's key should be placed in a lockout box or cabinet that allows the use of multiple locks to secure it. Each employee will then use his/her own lock to secure the box or cabinet. As each person no longer needs to maintain his/her lockout protection, that person will remove his/her lock from the box. (List name(s), job title(s) of employees authorized for group lockout or tagout.)

BASIC RULES FOR USING LOCKOUT OR TAGOUT SYSTEM PROCEDURE

All equipment shall be locked out or tagged out to protect against accidental or inadvertent operation when such operation could cause injury to personnel. Do not attempt to operate any switch, valve, or other energy-isolating device that it is locked out or tagged out.

The following lockout (or tagout) procedure is suggested for establishing your compliance with the intent of this law:

Entry No.	Description
1.	Name of company
2.	Type(s) and magnitude(s) of energy and hazards
3.	Name(s), job title(s), of employees authorized to lock out or tagout
4.	Name(s), job title(s) of affected employees and how to notify
5.	Type(s) and location of energy-isolating means
6.	Type(s) of stored energy, methods to dissipate or restrain
7.	Method(s) selected, i.e., locks, tags, additional safety measures, etc
8.	Type(s) of equipment-check to ensure disconnections
9.	Name(s), job title(s) of employees authorized for group lockout/tagout

LOCKOUT OR TAGOUT PROCEDURE

For in-depth detail on the lockout/tagout regulations, refer to 29 Code of Federal Regulations, Ch. XVII (7-1-94 Edition), Section 1910.147, the control of hazardous energy (lockout/tagout).

SUBPART K—MEDICAL AND FIRST AID (1910.151–1910.153)

The employer shall ensure the ready availability of medical personnel for advice and consultation on matters of work health.

In the absence of an infirmary, clinic, or hospital in near proximity to the workplace which is used for the treatment of injured employees, a person or persons shall be adequately trained to render first aid. First aid supplies approved by the consulting physician shall be readily available.

Where the eyes or body of any person may be exposed to injurious corrosive materials, suitable facilities for quick drenching or flushing of the eyes and body shall be provided within the work area for immediate emergency use.

The employer's attention is especially called to the drench and flush facilities noted above. There have been a number of citations within the lodging industry for failure to have "eye stations" in the event of eye injury from some of the corrosive cleaners used in kitchen cleaning, engineering, and housekeeping. Such stations must have dedicated plumbing to avoid mixing-valve failures or nonpotable water backup problems. A reasonable number of such stations should be considered for installation in back-of-the-house locations readily accessible to employees most likely to encounter such eye injuries. Drench shower requirements have generally been met through the multitude of showers available throughout the property. However, it may be necessary to make such a drench facility available to kitchen workers or engineering and maintenance staff as they do not have the ready access to the showers a room attendant would.

SUBPART L—FIRE PROTECTION (1910.155–1910.165)

There is an extensive section of this standard that establishes the requirements for a fire brigade. The concept of the brigade as compared with an emergency fire response team on premises is the difference in training and equipment. The brigade will attain the capability of a volunteer fire department and will fight structural as opposed to incipient fires. (An incipient fire is a fire, for example, that is just getting started on an upholstered piece or in a wastebasket.) If your location is in a resort or rural area or you are otherwise remote from a fire service with a resultant significant delay in response time due to distance, you may have to consider the fire brigade option. Under those circumstances, you are advised to review 29 Code of Federal Regulations, Ch. XVII (7-1-94 Edition), Section 1910.156. This provides information on the special training schools and locations, and the special personnel protective equipment required for a brigade member as compared with an emergency response team member.

Under the Act, it is permissible to make a management decision to immediately evacuate the premises and to not attempt to fight the fire at all. This usually is not an option open to lodging establishments due to the responsibility for guests and the public that may be on the premises. Obviously, failure to fight or contain the fire could seriously affect the ability to evacuate the premises.

PORTABLE FIRE EXTINGUISHERS

Some jurisdictions will permit the elimination of fire extinguishers in a fully sprinklered facility. This section permits the omission of extinguishers where a standpipe and fire-extinguishing suppression system is properly installed and maintained. However, consideration should be given to the use of extinguishers as this would permit the fighting of incipient fires rather than waiting for a fire to generate enough heat to activate an automatic sprinkler head.

The employer has the responsibility of:

- Providing portable fire extinguishers mounted, located, and identified so as to be readily available to the employee.
- Ensuring that the extinguishers are approved by a reputable national testing organization.
- Ensuring that the extinguishers are maintained in a fully charged and operable condition.
- Providing fire extinguishers for employee use based upon the classes of anticipated workplace fires and on the size and degree of hazard which would affect their use.
- Placing extinguishers for Class A (wood, cloth, paper) fires so that the greatest distance for access by an employee is 75 feet or less.
- Placing fire extinguishers for Class B (flammable liquids, gases, oils, greases) fires so that the greatest distance for access by an employee is 50 feet or less.
- Placing fire extinguishers for Class C (electrical) fires on the basis of the appropriate pattern for the existing Class A or Class B hazards, at electrical cabinets and rooms and at intervals appropriate to the size of the property, not to exceed 75 feet, preferably less.
- Inspecting, maintaining, and testing all portable fire extinguishers in the workplace.
- Providing an annual maintenance check; monthly visual inspections; and hydrostatic testing of the canister as required under the law. This should be contracted with a reputable fire service company in the community. There are technical aspects of the standard that are better handled by professionals. If the decision is to handle this in-house and with testing organizations, reference should be made to 29 Code of Federal Regulations, Ch. XVII (7-1-94 Edition), Section 1910.157.
- Training of employees in the correct and effective use of fire extinguishers in extinguishing incipient fires. Here, again, it is recommended that consideration be given to training all employees so that time is not lost while awaiting the arrival of a fire emergency team on the premises. Of course, the fire department should be immediately notified plus notice given to the property's emergency response group. The Act permits special training of a fire team as noted above, but the editor still urges consideration of training all employees.

STANDPIPE AND HOSE SYSTEMS

Where such systems are in place, the employer has responsibility to ensure that they are properly installed, maintained, and ready for emergency use. The Act does not mandate that these systems be installed but does require that they be properly used by employees trained in their use. Review with the local fire authorities the connections and hoses that are in place on the premises. Generally the fire service will not use the hoses on the premises but will use the heavy duty equipment brought to the fire scene by the fire department. The employer is charged with the responsibility of providing water in a sufficient amount to supply 100 gallons per minute for a period of at least 30 minutes.

The employer shall ensure that hose systems are inspected at least annually and after each use.

AUTOMATIC SPRINKLER SYSTEMS

Automatic sprinklers installed in workplaces are not mandated, but OSHA is specific on installation, maintenance, and use responsibilities. The section requires that the system be installed according to design with the necessary discharge capabilities, densities, and water flow characteristics for effective coverage of a given workplace site. This is fully covered under the National Fire Protection Association Standard 13 or 13-R, which applies to the installation of sprinkler systems in the lodging industry. The section requires that the employer protect the system against freezing, exterior surface corrosion, and mechanical damage. A water-flow alarm system must be in place for any premises with more than 20 sprinkler heads.

FIXED EXTINGUISHING SYSTEMS, GENERAL

Again, there is no mandate for the installation of fixed extinguishing systems. Rather, there is a concern that the employer ensure the safety of the employees relative to the system and the effectiveness of the system as established through installation, maintenance, and use. The employer must ensure that the employee not be placed in a situation where the system operates before the employee is able to move to a place of safety. The employer must ensure the presence of an alarm system which will provide such a safeguard for the employee. The employer is also charged with the responsibility of training employees to inspect, maintain, operate, or repair fixed extinguishing systems and annually review their training to keep them up-to-date in the functions they are to perform. Automatic detection equipment shall be approved, installed, and maintained. The employer shall ensure that at least one manual station is available for activation of the system and will also provide personal protective equipment needed for immediate rescue of employees trapped in a hazardous atmosphere created by an agent discharge. Finally, the employer must provide a pre-discharge employee alarm that is capable of being perceived above ambient light or noise levels before the system discharges.

FIXED EXTINGUISHING SYSTEMS, DRY CHEMICAL

The employer is responsible for ensuring that the system is compatible with any foams or wetting agents used in conjunction with the dry chemical. Again, a predischarge alarm must be provided with sufficient time for the employee to safely exit the area before the chemical discharges.

FIXED EXTINGUISHING SYSTEMS, GASEOUS AGENT

The standard requires the employer to ensure that the system is properly installed, maintained, and used. Since the use of halon is being affected by the concern for atmospheric damage by this chemical, the employer must provide protection against whatever substitute chemical may be installed. A pre-discharge alarm is to be provided for the employee that will permit safe evacuation of the area before the system discharges. The employer must also assure that no unprotected employees enter the area during a discharge of the chemical agent.

FIXED EXTINGUISHING SYSTEMS, WATER SPRAY, AND FOAM

The employer shall ensure that foam and water spray systems are designed to be effective in at least controlling fire in the protected area or on protected equipment. The employer shall further ensure that drainage of water spray systems is directed away from areas where employees are working and that no emergency egress is permitted through the drainage path.

OTHER FIRE PROTECTION SYSTEMS

FIRE DETECTION SYSTEMS

The employer is responsible for the integrity of all automatic fire detection systems from installation, maintenance, and use through restoration of systems when either tested or in alarm status. The employer must ensure that the servicing, maintenance, and testing of fire detection systems, including cleaning and necessary sensitivity adjustments, are performed by a trained person. The employer must also ensure that the alarm is designed to operate in time to control or extinguish a fire. There is an interesting requirement that the alarm not be delayed for longer than 30 seconds. This should be reviewed by management with the local fire authorities, and an emergency action plan must be installed and shared with all employees to meet the requirements of this standard whenever it is necessary to delay the "full alarm" beyond this 30-second limit.

EMPLOYEE ALARM SYSTEMS

The employee alarm system must be correctly installed, maintained, and used to alert employees for an appropriate emergency response. The alarm must be capable of being perceived above ambient noise or light levels. Tactile devices may be used to alert employees who would not otherwise be able to recognize the audible or visual alarm. The employer will fully explain to all employees the employee alarm system, its activation, and the expected employee response to the alarm. The employer shall ensure that all employee alarm systems are maintained in operating condition except when undergoing repairs or maintenance. The employer shall ensure that the servicing, maintenance, and testing of employee alarms are done by trained persons who can make sure the alarm system stays in a reliable and safe condition. Manual stations for operation of the systems must be unobstructed, conspicuous, and readily accessible.

SUBPART M—COMPRESSED GAS AND COMPRESSED AIR EQUIPMENT (1910.166–1910.171)

While there is no direct application of this standard to the lodging industry, and this standard particularly applies to air receivers, the employer should be aware that all cylinders should be properly stored and maintained, and that particular attention should be given to the maintenance of gages and valves. All safety valves should be regularly tested to determine whether they are in good operating condition. There would be no violation or citation under this section, but it provides an opportunity to give a reminder for safe storage and use of compressed gas cylinders utilized on a lodging premises.

SUBPART N—MATERIALS HANDLING AND STORAGE (1910.176–1910.190)

Where mechanical handling equipment is used, sufficient clearances must be provided in all areas through which such equipment must move. Aisles and passageways shall be kept clear and in good repair, with no obstruction across or in aisles that could create a hazard. Permanent aisles and passageways shall be appropriately marked. This, of course, applies to "back-of-the-house" locations, although some public areas might be tastefully marked to control traffic flow that involves both the public and employees. Again, aspects of this standard may assist in the movement of wheeled equipment such as luggage carts and food units that are usually hand-operated.

Storage of materials in the stockroom and other storage areas shall not create a hazard. Materials must be properly stored in tiers in such a manner that they will not slide nor collapse. Storage areas shall be kept free from accumulation of materials that constitute hazards from tripping, fire, explosion, or pest harborage.

This standard contains a significant section on servicing multi-piece and single-piece rim wheels. If your property has large vehicles such as trucks, tractors, trailers, buses, or off-road machines, reference should be made to this section: 29 Code of Federal Regulations, Ch. XVII (7-1-94 Edition), Section 1910.177. This provides a standard for the safe "changing of tires" on such equipment. This standard does not apply to the servicing of rim wheels used on automobiles, or on pickup trucks and vans utilizing automobile tires or truck tires designated "LT."

Powered industrial trucks are also included in this standard. Again, the use of fork trucks, tractors, platform lift trucks, motorized hand trucks, and other similar industrial trucks powered by electrical or internal combustion engines is limited to very few lodging establishments. Where such equipment is used, reference should be made to Code of Federal Regulations, Ch. XVII (7-1-94 Edition), Section 1910.178.

SUBPART O—MACHINERY AND MACHINE GUARDING (1910.211–1910.222)

This has special relevance to the lodging industry. Over the years there have been numerous injuries due to the failure to use the guard or the conscious effort to bypass the guard to make the operation of the equipment easier, according to the employee's claim. A comprehensive section of the standard deals with grind wheels. These would be found in the maintenance and engineering department, if on the property at all. It is required that the grind wheel be guarded and that the work rest be adjusted close to the wheel with a maximum opening of one-eighth inch to prevent the work from becoming jammed between the wheel and the rest. General requirements for machines note that guards should be affixed to all machines when practical and possible. Care must be taken that a guard does not in itself create a hazard. The point of operation is the focus of any guarding effort. Special devices should be used to provide additional protection, even though a guard may be present. For example, a pushstick may be provided for pushing short pieces of materials through saws. Care must be taken that the pushstick does not become engaged with the saw blade, causing injury to the hand from the stick rather than from the blade of the saw. These special hand tools for placing and removing material shall be used to keep the operator's hand out of the danger zone, but are not to be used in lieu of an appropriate guard.

A special note concerning the guarding of fan blades: There have been serious accidents in the lodging industry in which an employee has lost fingers or severely injured a hand in the blades of a fan. When the edge of the blade is less than seven (7) feet above the floor or a working surface, the blades shall be guarded. The guard shall have openings no larger than one-half $1/2$ inch.

There is a comprehensive section dealing with woodworking machines. Should the property have a maintenance department wherein such machinery is extensively used, reference should be made to 29 Code of Federal Regulations, Ch. XVII (7-1-94 Edition), Section 1910.213, woodworking machine requirements.

Similarly, reference should be made to the above CFR under Section 1910.219, mechanical power-transmission apparatus, when there are large machine, engine, and boiler rooms and facilities. Wherever there are shafts (whether horizontal, vertical, or inclined) that could catch clothing or a body part, adequate guarding must be provided. This requirement also applies to flywheels, belts, pulleys, cranks, connecting rods, and power-transmission apparatus located in basements. Gears, sprockets, chains, hand-operated gears, friction drives, keys, setscrews, and other projections also require adequate guarding. Collars and couplings, clutches, cutoff couplings, and clutch pulleys, when within seven (7) feet or less of the floor or working surface, must be enclosed by a stationary guard. The engine room must have a guardrail, preferably with a toeboard-especially where employees may be working at a level lower than walkways or ramps where other employees may be passing by or working.

SUBPART P—HAND- AND PORTABLE-POWERED TOOLS AND OTHER HAND-HELD EQUIPMENT (1910.241–1910.247)

Most of the hand- and portable-powered tools and other hand-held equipment deal with explosive-actuated fastening tools, high-velocity tools, and low-velocity piston tools. Again, there is a section dealing with the use of grinding machines with a focus on portable units. If your property has such tools, consult 29 Code of Federal Regulations, Ch. VXVII (7-1-94 Edition), Section 1910.241, for an in-depth review of the standards that apply.

For other tools, such as portable drills, trimmers, etc., the following rules apply. Each employer shall be responsible for the safe condition of tools and equipment used by employees, including tools and equipment that may be supplied by employees.

Compressed air should not be used for cleaning purposes except where the pressure has been reduced to less than 30 pounds per square inch (30 p.s.i.) and then only when effective chip-guarding and personal protective equipment is provided. Again, this type of operation will rarely be found in a lodging establishment.

The guarding of portable tools is a critical part of this standard, and every effort should be made to ensure that the proper guards are provided and used. The above-referenced Code of Federal Regulations should be reviewed under Section 1910.243 for details on the guarding that is required. Generally, the manufacturer will provide such a guard, and an appropriate guard should be requested whenever ordering such portable equipment. Pay special attention to switches and controls. A constant pressure switch or control will deactivate the unit when pressure is released. A lock-on device may be permitted if a turnoff can be accomplished through a single motion of the same finger or fingers. This, of course, addresses the problem of repetitive motion injuries that could occur through the required constant pressure on a tool that is causing vibration or trauma from impact. Grounding is indicated with reference to the requirements set forth in Subpart S-Electrical, pages 38 and 39 in this guide. There should be a routine inspection by the employee before using any portable equipment to ensure that it is operating properly, has a guard in place, and is effectively grounded. Grounding is of particular importance where an employee may be gardening with cutters, trimmers, etc., while standing on damp ground or dew-soaked grass.

Power-lawnmower regulations will apply to many lodging establishments. The items of critical importance to lodging management include walk-behind, riding-rotary, and reel power lawnmowers, all of which must comply with American National Standards Institute requirements. The rules do not apply to a walk-behind mower which has been converted to a riding mower by the addition of a sulky; nor does it apply to flail mowers, sicklebar mowers, or mowers designed for commercial use.

Appropriate guarding must be in place whenever the equipment is in use or is being serviced. The guard may be removed after power is off and secured in an off position in order to permit proper servicing of cutting blades and any other moving parts normally guarded during operation. Warning instructions shall be affixed to the mower where guards must be removed in order to affix a catcher assembly. This warning will state that the mower is not to be used without either the catcher unit or guard in position. Verify that the manufacturer has provided appropriate grass discharge openings and guarding. The word "Caution" shall be placed near the discharge opening.

The blade must stop rotating within 15 seconds of shutoff, and the maximum tip speed of any blade shall not exceed 19,000 feet per minute.

On walk-behind rotary mowers, appropriate guarding shall be provided. A bar that can only be removed by special tools will be across the discharge area. Mowers may have a swingover handle; but in those instances, full guarding must be provided at both "leading edges." The handle must be fastened in such a manner that it cannot be unintentionally uncoupled while in operation. Deadman controls will be provided, and wheel-drive disengaging controls shall move in the opposite direction from the unit's motion in order to disengage the drive. Detailed information may be obtained from 29 Code of Federal Regulations, Ch. XVII (7-1-94 Edition), Section 1910.243.

SUBPART Q—WELDING, CUTTING, AND BRAZING (1910.251–1910.257)

These functions may occur in large facilities, but generally this activity will be handled through contract labor. Reference should be made to 29 Code of Federal Regulations, Ch. XVII (7-1-94 Edition), Sections 1910.251–1910.257. You are reminded of the extreme danger from fires due to welding and cutting functions. Usually there will be contract labor providing such service. The contract should cover the responsibility of the contractor to provide maximum fire protection safety and to ensure that there is adequate comprehensive/general-liability insurance and workers' compensation insurance in order to adequately protect your property and bottom line against litigation. If your property does have welding capability in the engineering and maintenance department, it is suggested that you refer to the above 29 Code of Federal Regulations entry.

SUBPART R—SPECIAL INDUSTRIES (1910.261–1910.275)

Among the several special industries represented in this standard, there are two of concern to the lodging industry.

BAKERY EQUIPMENT (1910.263)

- All gears, regardless of location, must be completely enclosed.
- Sprockets and V-belt drives located within 8 feet, 6 inches from the floor shall be completely enclosed. If lubrication of the machinery must be accomplished while the machine is in motion, fittings must be placed so as to prevent the employee from reaching into any dangerous part of the machine when

lubricating it. Note: Other sections of the Act specify less than 7 feet overhead as the limit for protection as compared with the 8 feet, 6 inches noted above. "Completely enclosed" is the key difference in what otherwise appears to be contradictory levels.

- All hot water and steam pipes must be insulated as necessary to protect employee from contact.
- Mixers must be fully guarded with all electrical controls located so as to be in full view of the operator while the bowl is in the open position. Of these controls, only the stop switch may be duplicated. Safety devices must be provided that will engage both hands of an operator while the bowl is more than one-fifth open and which will prevent the agitator from starting when in that one-fifth open position. A full enclosure is required when the agitator is in motion. Bowl-locking devices shall be of a positive type which require the attention of the operator for unlocking. Devices shall be made available for moving bowls weighing more than 80 pounds, with contents, into and out of the mixing position on the machine. Much of the other referenced equipment refers to a commercial bakery operation. If the bakery operation in your facility is into such heavy, production-oriented equipment, reference should be made to 29 Code of Federal Regulations, Ch. XVII (7-1-94 Edition), Section 1910.263. Two general safety rules from this standard remind that all door locks shall be operable from both within and outside the cooler and floors shall be maintained in a nonslip condition.
- Ovens must be located so that a fire or explosion will not expose groups of persons to possible injury. Sections of the oven such as doors must be restrained so that they will not strike employees near the oven should an explosion occur. For this reason ovens shall not adjoin lockers, lunch or sales rooms, main passageways, or exits.
- Emergency stop buttons shall be provided near the operator station.
- Main shutoff valves must have manual as well as automatic capability in the event of an emergency, and must be so located that they would be accessible in the event of fire or explosion.
- All oven piping shall be tested to be gastight.
- On electrical heating equipment, a main disconnect switch or circuit breaker shall be provided and the system must provide for a lockout or tagout when the equipment is being cleaned or serviced.
- All safety devices on ovens shall be inspected at intervals of not less than twice per month by an authorized and qualified employee and not less than once per year by a manufacturer's representative.
- Gas pilot lights shall be protected, and failure of any gas pilot shall automatically shut off the fuel supply to the burner. Electric spark ignition must be integrated so that failure of either electricity or gas will automatically cut off both energy sources. Special devices must be in place to avoid buildup of any explosive mixtures within an oven. This includes safety shutoffs in fuel lines.

These devices must be tested twice monthly. Such a valve can only be reopened manually and must be arranged so that it cannot be locked in an open position by external means. One manually operated fuel shutoff valve shall be provided to each oven and must be ahead of all other valves in the system. Where blowers supply combustion air, the safety shutoff valve shall be interlocked so that it will close in case of air failure.

- Duct systems in ovens that operate under pressure shall be tested for tightness in the initial start of the oven and also at intervals no more than six months apart.

LAUNDRY MACHINERY AND OPERATIONS (1910.264)

- All washing machines, drying tumblers, and shakers (clothes tumblers) shall be provided with a means for holding open the doors or covers of inner and outer cylinders while being loaded or unloaded. An exception is any shakeout or conditioning tumblers where the clothes are loaded into an open end of a revolving cylinder.

- All steam and hot water pipes within 7 feet of the floor or working platform must be insulated. Where pressure-reducing valves are used, one or more relief or safety valves shall be provided on the low-pressure side of the reducing valve, in case the piping or equipment on the low-pressure side does not meet full initial pressure requirements.

- Markers and others handling soiled clothes shall be warned against touching the eyes, mouth, or any part of the body on which the skin has been broken; and they shall be cautioned not to touch or eat food until their hands have been thoroughly washed.

- Employees shall be properly instructed as to the hazards of the job and the safe practices to overcome such hazards.

- No safeguard, safety appliance, or device attached to any laundry machinery shall be removed or rendered ineffective except when making immediate adjustments or repairs. Such items shall be immediately replaced upon completion of such repairs or adjustments.

SUBPART S—ELECTRICAL (1910.301–1910.399)

This is a highly technical standard, and it is recommended that a licensed electrician be hired on staff or used under contract. Reference should be made to 29 Code of Federal Regulations, Ch. XVII (7-1-94 Edition), Sections 1910.301 through 1910.399. Four major sections apply:

- Design safety standards for electrical systems
- Safety-related work practices
- Safety-related maintenance requirements
- Safety requirements for special equipment

Under general requirements, the following items should be considered:

- All electrical equipment must meet rigid standards of examination, installation, and use. Suitability and mechanical strength and durability must be ensured.
- Electrical insulation; heating effects under conditions of use; arcing; classification by type, size, voltage, current capacity, and specific use; and other safety factors must be considered.

Some specifics for your information:

- Electrical equipment may not be used if it does not contain the manufacturer's name, trademark, or other descriptive marking. Other markings shall provide voltage, current, wattage, or other ratings as necessary.
- Identification of disconnecting means and circuits is of particular interest to the lodging industry. Each disconnecting means must be identified for each motor or appliance under control of that device. It must be legibly marked to indicate its purpose unless arranged so that this is self-evident. Each service, feeder, and branch circuit at its disconnecting means or overcurrent device shall be marked as above. This means all panel boards in use throughout the lodging industry should have the legend as to exactly what each switch controls.
- All live parts must be guarded against accidental contact and should be limited to authorized persons only. Doors to electric equipment rooms and panels should be marked "DANGER" and should restrict entry to authorized staff only.
- Adequate work space must be provided in front of electric equipment according to voltage and a chart contained in the aforementioned Code of Federal Regulations.
- Systems must be grounded. This also pertains to appliances, electric tools, and any other electrical equipment. All equipment connected by cord and plug is also under this requirement. Ground fault detection and relaying shall be provided to automatically de-energize any electrical device or system which may have developed a ground fault.
- Reference should be made under the previously noted Code of Federal Regulations to Section 1910.305 for requirements on wiring methods, components, and equipment for general use. The standard addresses both permanent and temporary wiring. Your attention is called to the mandate that lamps for general illumination shall be protected from accidental contact or breakage.
- Protection shall be provided by elevation of at least 7 feet from normal working surface or by suitable fixture or lampholder with guard. (Especially check for fluorescent tube guarding.)
- Lighting fixtures, lampholders, lamps, and receptacles may have no live parts normally exposed to employee contact. However, rosettes and cleat-type lampholders and receptacles located at least 8 feet from the floor may have exposed parts.

- Fixtures in wet or damp locations must be approved for that purpose and shall be so constructed and installed that no water can enter any part of the fixture and its connections.
- Appliances, other than those in which the current-carrying parts at high temperatures are necessarily exposed, may have no live parts normally exposed to employee contact. The appliance must have a disconnect capability and shall be marked with its rating in volts and amperes or volts and watts.
- On all electrical items, the disconnect means must be evident except where it is remote from the unit, in which case the standard on lockout/tagout protection will apply (covered previously under lockout/tagout, pages 402–404).
- Reference should be made to Section 1910.306 on specific-purpose equipment and installations, such as electric signs and outline lighting, elevators, dumbwaiters, escalators, moving walks, warning signs, data processing systems, and air conditioning systems.
- Emergency power systems must have separate circuit wiring entirely independent of all other wiring and equipment. Where emergency lighting is necessary, the system shall be so arranged that the failure of any individual lighting element, such as a burning out of a light bulb, cannot leave any space in total darkness.
- Fire-protective signaling systems and communication systems are also covered under this section. Normally, these installations are made by the manufacturer or a special contractor. Specify in that contract that installation must not only meet Electrical Code, but must also meet the requirements of OSHA.
- Safety-related work practices establish categories of qualified and unqualified persons. This distinguishes between employees trained in avoiding electrical hazards and those with little or no training in this regard.
- Training will be guided by the requirements in the standard. There will be additional requirements for the unqualified person with concern for familiarity with basic electrical safety requirements in addition to the more advanced rules noted under this standard.

Specifically, safety-related work practices shall be employed to prevent electric shock or other injuries from either direct or indirect electrical contacts. As noted above, the lockout/tagout standard will apply here with specific reference to electricity as the energy source. Full implementation of the lockout/tagout standard will meet the requirements of this electrical standard. The numerous technical and assignment-specific mandates make it advisable to refer to Section 1910.333, selection and use of work practices, under the previously noted Code of Federal Regulations.

SUBPART Z—TOXIC AND HAZARDOUS SUBSTANCES (1910.1000–1910.1500)

There are several sections within this subpart that are of particular interest to the hospitality industry: asbestos, lead, benzene, bloodborne pathogens, formaldehyde, and hazard communication. If there are other quantities of other chemicals about which there may be some question, it is recommended that 29 Code of Federal Regulations, Ch. XVII (7-1-94 Edition), Part 1910, Subpart Z, Sections 1910.1000 through 1910.1500, be reviewed. Lead (1910.1025), benzene (1910.1028), and formaldehyde (1910.1048) are substances that require special handling. If these are present in any quantity, careful attention should be paid to the instructions in the referenced sections. We shall pay particular attention to asbestos, bloodborne pathogens, and hazard communication as areas in which there is more general involvement by a greater number of properties in the lodging industry.

ASBESTOS (1910.1001)

There has been a recent focus on asbestos by OSHA with citations and fines issued against lodging establishments, even though the main thrust of the revised regulations has been directed toward construction and brake repair activities. If there are any questions as to the possibility of asbestos installations on the premises (and that can include anything from insulation and fire-protective spraying of steel structural members to asbestos floor tiles), a professional air-sampling should be obtained. Revised in August 1994, with an effective date of October 11, 1994, the permissible exposure limits (PELS) are based upon time-weighted average (TWA) limits. Under this mandate, an employer must ensure that no employee is exposed to an airborne concentration of asbestos in excess of 0.1 fiber per cubic centimeter of air in an eight-hour time-weighted average as specified under the regulation's air-sampling methods.

This is a highly technical section and should be reviewed in its entirety if asbestos is present on the premises. Mandates cover respiratory protection with the required training program, respirator fit testing, and protective work clothing and equipment. Mandates also cover the removal and storage of contaminated items and their cleaning or replacement. Further requirements specify changing-room and hygiene practices and the program of communication of the hazards to the employees through signage and training.

BLOODBORNE PATHOGENS (1910.1030)

PURPOSE

The Hospitality Industry Exposure Control Plan is designed to eliminate or minimize employee exposure to bloodborne pathogens that may be encountered in the workplace. Bloodborne pathogens are defined as pathogenic microorganisms that are present in blood and can cause disease in humans. These pathogens include, but are not limited to, Hepatitis B Virus (HBV) and Human Immunodeficiency Virus (HIV), which causes AIDS.

SCOPE

The Exposure Control Program complies with OSHA 29 Code of Federal Regulations, Section 1910.1030. It ensures that employees are effectively informed concerning potential and existing workplace health hazards and the protective measures necessary to reduce exposure.

The Exposure Control Plan consists of the following sections:

- Exposure Determination
- Methods of Compliance
- Hepatitis B Vaccination and Post Exposure Evaluation
- Communication of Hazards to Employees
- Information and Training

EXPOSURE DETERMINATION

Review all job classifications to determine which jobs pose a reasonable risk of exposure to bloodborne pathogens. An exposure incident may result from non-intact skin, eye, mucous membrane, or contact with blood or other potentially infectious material. OSHA defines potentially infectious materials to include blood and human body fluids that the Center for Disease Control recommends handling with "universal precautions."

All employees in the following job classifications may have occupational exposure to bloodborne pathogens:

- Hotel nurses and/or physicians
- Emergency response personnel
- Security and safety staff
- Lifeguards

Some employees in the following job classifications may have occupational exposure to bloodborne pathogens:

- Foodservice personnel
- Housekeeping personnel

- Laundry personnel
- Maintenance personnel

The following is a list of tasks and procedures in which occupational exposure may occur:

- Cleaning cuts and abrasions
- Treating burns
- Administering CPR
- Laundering linens
- Removing contaminated linens and towels from guestrooms
- Cleaning vomitus from food service areas
- Clearing blocked toilet

NOTE: All occupational bloodborne pathogen exposure incidents (including needlestick injuries, lacerations, or splashes) must be recorded on OSHA Log No. 200 if the incident results in: (1) medical treatment (e.g., immune serum globulin, Hepatitis B vaccine, or other prescribed medical treatment); or (2) diagnosis of possible seroconversion (possible exposure to contaminated blood). In the instance of seroconversion, only the injury, such as "needlestick," shall be recorded, not the serologic status of the employee.

To address confidentiality concerns, OSHA has amended 29 Code of Federal Regulations, Section 1904.7, to require that when a log or supplemental record contains information related to bloodborne pathogens, the employer must ensure that personal identifiers are removed prior to granting access to the record.

METHODS OF COMPLIANCE

Engineering and work practice controls shall be used to eliminate or minimize employee exposure. The following work practice controls must be adhered to in order to minimize exposure to bloodborne pathogens.

HANDWASHING

Employees must wash their hands and any other skin surface with soap and water and/or flush mucous membranes with water immediately following contact with blood and other potentially infectious materials. Hands must be washed immediately or as soon as possible after removal of gloves or other protective equipment. Washing facilities should be designated for those employees not in close proximity to a wash basin by virtue of work assignment; for example, a room attendant has at least one wash basin readily accessible most of the work day.

Contaminated Needles and Other Contaminated Sharps

Contaminated needles shall not be bent, recapped, or removed. The breaking or shearing of a needle is prohibited. All needles and other sharps (such as broken glass) must be disposed of immediately by being placed in a sharps container that is:

- Closeable
- Puncture resistant
- Leakproof on sides and bottom
- Fluorescent red-orange in color
- Labeled with a BIOHAZARD symbol

The containers must be located as close as possible to the immediate area where sharps are likely to be found. It is recommended that consideration be given to establishing an emergency response team that would be called upon when a room obviously is contaminated with needles, blood and/or body fluids on surfaces and in towels, bedding, etc. OSHA Health Compliance has agreed to this approach and it reduces the cost of personal protective equipment as well as the cost of the Hepatitis B vaccination. Such a team would have the "sharps container" as part of the response equipment. However, it must be remembered that the room attendant (maid) must be provided with gloves and eye and face protection for use while cleaning the bathroom area. A dust mask should be provided to supplement the eye and face protection when the room attendant is using any powdered cleaners or doing any overhead dusting or cleaning.

Other Regulated Waste Containment

This regulation is related to the health care industry, but has application to the lodging industry in the instance of bedding and towels that are heavily contaminated with blood or body fluids. Usually these items would be dry by the time staff arrives to clean a room. Of course, an emergency situation in which an individual is bleeding could confront staff with a different problem. In that situation, it would be necessary to have a container that provides the same protection as the sharps container mentioned above.

Usually, the bedding and/or towels would be placed in a plastic bag (red-orange in color) and marked with the BIOHAZARD symbol. Whether the laundry is done in-house or at a commercial laundry, this sealed bag would provide the conveyance to the laundry and alert it to the special handling that is necessary.

Laundry

Contaminated laundry should be handled as little as possible. Employees who have contact with contaminated laundry must wear protective gloves, face and eye protection, and a dust mask to protect against particulate of dried blood and body fluids that become airborne when bedding and towels are removed from the BIOHAZARD bag.

A special wash formula, which contains stabilized chlorine, must be used when processing contaminated laundry. If there is a daily volume of contaminated laundry, it may be advisable to dedicate a machine for contaminated laundry only.

Otherwise, the contaminated laundry could be in the final run of the day for one of the machines using the special wash formula noted above.

Work Practices

The following activities are prohibited in work areas where there is reasonable likelihood of occupational exposure to bloodborne pathogens (this applies more in health care than in lodging):

- Eating
- Drinking
- Smoking
- Applying cosmetics or lip balm
- Handling contact lenses

Significantly Contaminated Items

Again, the material must be placed in a container that provides the following protection:

- Must be leakproof
- Must be red-orange in color and bear the BIOHAZARD symbol
- Must be capable of complete closure before being shipped

This becomes medical waste and should not be disposed of with your regular garbage and waste. Since it is unlikely the property will have significant quantities of heavily contaminated items, it may be possible to work out an arrangement with a local clinic or hospital which serves the property's staff and guests, as may be required. Otherwise, a local medical or health care facility should be contacted for information on a licensed waste removal vendor. Be sure the waste is being moved to a licensed site to avoid future cleanup problems under an EPA initiative.

Personal Protective Equipment

As previously noted, personal protective equipment must be provided to employees "at risk" of coming into contact with items contaminated with bloodborne pathogens. Such equipment includes:

Gloves. Disposable gloves should be a standard component of emergency response equipment and should be donned by personnel prior to initiating any routine or emergency tasks in which there is the possibility of exposure to blood or other body fluids.

- Disposable (single use) gloves shall be replaced as soon as practical when contaminated, torn, or punctured.
- Disposable (single use) gloves shall not be washed or decontaminated.
- Utility gloves may be decontaminated for re-use if the integrity of the glove has not been compromised. (Gloves may be decontaminated in a solution of

1/4 cup of household bleach to a gallon of water or U.S. EPA chemical germicide that has a label claim of tuberculocidal activity.) If they are cracked, peeling, torn, punctured, etc., they must be discarded.

- While wearing gloves, avoid handling personal items such as combs or pens that could become soiled or contaminated. Before removing the gloves, wash the gloved hands with soap and water to reduce the transfer of contaminants to the hands as the gloves are removed. Then thoroughly wash your ungloved hands.
- If an employee is allergic to the gloves that are normally provided, the facility must provide an alternative. This might include hypoallergenic gloves, glove liners, powderless gloves, or simply changing to another brand of gloves.

Masks, Eye Protection, and Face Shields. Depending upon the level of exposure, the following eye, nose, and mouth protective equipment should be used:

- Goggles
- Chin length face shields
- Glasses with solid side shields
- Dust mask to cover mouth and nostrils in a particulate environment

Prescription glasses may be used as protective eyewear as long as they are equipped with solid side shields that are permanently affixed or of the "add-on" type. If the protective eyewear is chosen over the use of a face shield, the eyewear must be worn in combination with a mask to protect the nose and mouth (dust mask).

Overalls, Aprons, or Uniforms. Appropriate protective clothing such as overalls, aprons, and uniforms or similar outer garments shall be worn in occupational exposure situations. The type and characteristics will depend upon the task and degree of exposure anticipated.

Appropriate personal protective equipment is to be accessible and will be issued by the property. Kits should be at designated locations so that employees may readily access them as needed.

- The property shall clean, launder and/or dispose of personal protective equipment in accordance with the Exposure Control Plan and at no cost to the employees.
- The property will repair or replace personal protective equipment as needed at no cost to employees.
- If a garment is penetrated by blood or other potentially infectious materials, it shall be removed immediately or as soon as possible.
- All potentially contaminated personal protective equipment shall be removed prior to leaving the work area. When removed, it shall be placed in an appropriately designated area or container for storage, washing, decontamination, or disposal.
- All employees who might be exposed must use appropriate protective equipment.

Housekeeping

- All equipment and working surfaces shall be decontaminated after contact with potentially infectious materials. Note: Chemical germicides that are approved for use as "hospital disinfectants" and are tuberculocidal when used at recommended dilutions can be used to decontaminate surfaces where blood or body fluids are present.
- All pails, wastebaskets, or other receptacles where contaminated materials may have been placed should be fully decontaminated.
- Broken glassware which may be contaminated shall not be picked up directly by hand. It must be cleaned up using mechanical means such as a brush and dustpan, or tongs.
- Bedding and towels that are contaminated will be carefully removed by an attendant wearing the appropriate protective equipment as previously noted. Where a mattress is directly involved, it should be removed and cleaned before returning it to service. A similar procedure will apply to any upholstered pieces in the guestroom or public area of the establishment.

HEPATITIS B VACCINATION

After determining those work assignments in which an employee may be at risk from bloodborne pathogens, the property must offer the Hepatitis B vaccination series at no cost to the employees in Job Classification 1 within 10 days of work placement. Other employees in Job Classification 2 may also be offered the vaccination series unless there has been a determination to follow the use of an emergency response team plan (see page 420). In such an instance, the series would be provided to the response team members only. The employee may decline the vaccination; in that case, a Hepatitis B Vaccine Declination Form (Exhibit 2) must be signed and made part of the employee's personnel records. The employee also may decline the series if the series has previously been administered and the employee is immune.

The form permits the employee to change his or her mind. He or she would be eligible for the series at a later time at no expense to the employee.

If exposed to an incident involving a needle or contact with contaminated surfaces or materials, the employee should immediately report the exposure and should be referred to a doctor. A medical decision will be made whether a gamma globulin and Hepatitis B vaccination series should be immediately initiated. Such an incident places that employee under a continuing review and monitoring program, and it will be necessary to maintain records on that employee for 30 years (even if the individual leaves the employ of the company at some point). Refer to Subpart C—General Safety and Health Provisions, pages 379–381.

Post-Exposure Evaluation and Follow-Up

Following an exposure incident, an employee will be offered a confidential medical evaluation and follow-up at no cost to the employee. The evaluation shall include at least the following:

Exhibit 2   Hepititis B Vaccine Declination Form

I understand that due to my occupational exposure to blood or other potentially infectious materials I may be at risk of acquiring Hepatitis B virus (HBV) infection. I have been given the opportunity to be vaccinated with Hepatitis B vaccine, at no charge to myself. However, I decline Hepatitis B vaccination at this time. I understand that by declining this vaccine, I continue to be at risk of acquiring Hepatitis B, a serious disease. If in the future I continue to have occupational exposure to blood or other potentially infectious materials and I want to be vaccinated with Hepatitis B vaccine, I can receive the vaccination series at no charge to me.

_____   _____
Employee Signature   Witness

_____   _____
Employee Name Printed   Date

OR

I decline the Hepatitis B vaccination at this time because I have previously received the complete Hepatitis B vaccination series, or antibody testing has revealed that I am immune, or the vaccine is contraindicated for medical reasons.

_____   _____
Employee Signature   Witness

_____   _____
Employee Name Printed   Date

- Documentation of the exposure incident.
- Assessment of work practices and protective clothing used at the time of the exposure and the reason for failure of the practices and equipment, if that was the case.
- Identification and documentation of the source individual unless infeasible or prohibited by law. (Some lodging chains have made it policy to follow up with the guest if a carelessly discarded needle was involved in the exposure incident. Frequently it will be learned that the needle had been used by a diabetic.

This, of course, does not automatically ensure that the guest does not have HIV or HBV.)

- An effort should be made to have the source person undergo a blood test. This becomes a very sensitive issue and should be carefully reviewed with counsel. The Act is focused upon an employee situation and does not, therefore, have applicability to the non-employee. In a health care situation, there is greater likelihood of full knowledge of the blood condition of the patient, or the easy capability of obtaining a blood sample as a routine medical procedure.
- When data on the source person is obtained, this must be provided to the employee without divulging the name of the source person.
- The exposed employee's blood shall be collected as soon as feasible and tested after consent is obtained. Should the employee consent to baseline blood collection but not to HIV serological testing, the sample will be preserved for 90 days. If the employee decides to have the HIV evaluation done within the 90 days, it will be performed as soon as feasible.
- Post-exposure treatment should be provided in accord with U.S. Public Health Service recommendations.
- Counseling will be provided at no cost to the employee, as will the evaluation of reported illnesses that may be related to the exposure incident.

Management will provide the evaluating physician with the following data:

- A copy of OSHA 29 Code of Federal Regulations, Section 1910.1030
- The employee's duties that relate to the exposure incident
- Documentation of the exposure incident in full detail
- Results of the source individual's blood testing, if available
- All relevant employee medical records

The person responsible for medical records will provide the employee with the physician's written report within 15 days of completion of the evaluation. The report will be strictly limited to:

- Whether HBV vaccination is needed or if the employee has begun receiving such vaccinations
- Confirmation that the employee has been fully informed of all results
- Confirmation that the employee has been informed of any medical conditions related to the exposure incident and further evaluation and treatment that may be required

COMMUNICATION OF HAZARDS TO EMPLOYEE—LABELS AND SIGNS

Warning labels shall be affixed to any containers holding contaminated materials for any reason. The labels shall include the symbol at right. These labels shall be fluorescent orange or red-orange with letters or symbols of a contrasting color.

Required labels shall be attached as close as possible to the container by string, wire, adhesive, or other method that prevents loss or unintentional removal. Red or red-orange bags may be substituted for labels.

INFORMATION AND TRAINING

All employees with potential occupational exposure to bloodborne pathogens shall participate in a training program. This includes part-time and temporary employees. The training will be given during working hours and at no cost to the employees. (The editor suggests that there be a general session in which ALL employees receive an explanation of the program and what should be done if an accidental needle-stick incident occurs. The in-depth session should be directed to the employees at risk by virtue of job assignment.)

Training Shall Be Provided As Follows:

- At the time of initial assignment where the employee may be at risk
- Within 10 days of assignment and annually thereafter
- The Exposure Control Plan must be reviewed with new employees during the orientation program
- Additional training shall be provided when changes, such as modification of tasks or procedures, affect the employee's occupational exposure
- Material appropriate in content and vocabulary to educational level, literacy, and native language of employees shall be used for all required training

The Bloodborne Pathogen Training Program Shall Include the Following Elements:

- An accessible copy of the requirements of the standard and an explanation of its contents
- A general explanation of the nature and symptoms of HBV and HIV bloodborne diseases
- An explanation of modes of transmission of bloodborne pathogens
- An explanation of the Exposure Control Plan and the means by which the employee can obtain a copy of the written plan
- An explanation of the appropriate methods for recognizing tasks and other activities that may involve exposure to blood, body fluids, or other infectious materials
- An explanation of the use and limitations of methods to prevent or reduce exposure, including appropriate engineering controls, work practices, and personal protective equipment
- Information on the types, proper use, location, removal, handling, decontamination, and disposal of personal protective equipment

- An explanation as to the basis for selection of personal protective equipment
- Information on the Hepatitis B vaccine, including information on its efficacy, safety, method of administration, the benefits of being vaccinated, and the fact that the vaccine and vaccination will be offered free of charge
- Information on the appropriate actions to take and persons to contact in an emergency involving blood or other potentially infectious materials
- An explanation of the procedure to follow if an exposure incident occurs, including the method of reporting the incident and the medical follow-up that will be made available
- Information on the post-exposure evaluation and follow-up that the organization is required to provide for the employee following an exposure incident
- An explanation of the signs and labels and/or color coding required by regulations
- An opportunity for an interactive question-and-answer period with the person conducting the training session (instructors must be thoroughly conversant with the materials covered in the training session)

Training Records Shall Include the Following:
- The dates of the training sessions
- The contents or a summary of the training sessions
- The names and qualifications of persons conducting the training
- The names and job titles of all persons attending the training sessions

Training records shall be maintained for three years from the date on which the training occurred.

COMPLIANCE MONITORING

Strategies that can be used to monitor compliance with this regulation include the following:

- Accident/injury reports
- Accident and near-miss investigations
- Evaluation of education and training programs
- Observing employee performance
- Self-audits

HAZARD COMMUNICATION (HAZCOM) (1910.1200)

In May 1988 a major safety responsibility for instructing employees on the use of hazardous chemicals became effective. While many chemical compounds are used in many households, OSHA differentiates between the exposure of a room attendant on a daily basis as compared with the occasional use within a household. Consequently, some cleansers and chemical cleaners are considered a hazardous chemical under the Act. The hazard communication requirements became effective May 23, 1988.

According to the Act, every property should have:

- A list of hazardous chemicals and chemical compounds in use at the property
- A material safety data sheet (MSDS) library
- A written hazard communication program
- Labeling
- Training for employees

Since the application of the HAZCOM program to the lodging industry, the list of the most frequently cited standard violations found during inspections of lodging establishments consistently include:

- Failure to have a written HAZCOM program
- Failure to have a training program
- Failure to maintain an MSDS library
- Failure to provide labels on all hazardous chemicals in use on the property

A LIST OF HAZARDOUS CHEMICALS AND CHEMICAL COMPOUNDS IN USE AT THE PROPERTY

- Review all purchases for the past year.
- Perform a physical inventory.
- Identify unlabeled containers, if possible. Arrange for proper disposal if no longer used. If in quantity, obtain professional assistance to avoid violating EPA disposal requirements.
- Dispose of obsolete or surplus materials.
- Be especially aware of items purchased locally through "petty cash" by maintenance staff. The retailer is not required to provide an MSDS for the products; but you as a commercial user have the responsibility for obtaining such information, even if it necessitates writing to the manufacturer as listed on the product label.
- List materials by department with specific location of the basic supply.
- Establish daily or regular use amount of each item.

- Determine the maximum amount stored. Is the supply a danger because of quantity? Could smaller amounts be maintained without affecting economic or operational considerations?
- Determine toxicity, flammability, and other health hazards.
- Establish limits of exposure. How long may an employee use a product in a given work period? Is there a cumulative effect from continued exposure? If so, is there protective equipment which will permit unlimited product use by an employee?
- Is proper protective equipment available? Where face masks are needed, are they correctly fitted and properly maintained, and are employees trained in their use? With the cost of a full oxygen mask in excess of $1,000, such equipment should definitely be under full control as to storage, maintenance, and use.

ESTABLISH AN MSDS LIBRARY

- Obtain a material safety data sheet for each hazardous chemical in use on the premises. Check with your supplier to assist in obtaining this data from the manufacturer.
- Collect the MSDSs in one location.
- Obtain assistance in "translating" the chemical and side-effects data into an understandable form for the employees.
- There should be two master files on MSDS data. One is to be retained by the individual assigned that responsibility. The other should be at the front desk for reference by any fire, police, or utility response service unit.
- In addition, a collection of MSDS data must be provided in each department with data on those chemicals used by that department's employees (i.e., housekeeping, maintenance, stewards, food and beverage, etc.). The "library" must be readily accessible to all employees on a 24-hour basis.
- The responsible employee will maintain files in current status and will be sure MSDS data is available on all new products. Training in use of new products will be coordinated if another person has the training responsibility.
- It is suggested that the master file in the possession of the responsible staff person contain a section covering discontinued chemicals or chemical compounds where a given product maintains a trade name but has a change in the chemical makeup. Employee exposure to chemicals could become the basis for action against the employer under the workers' compensation or other sections of OSHA. Possession of those records would be invaluable in adjudicating such claims.

WRITTEN HAZARD COMMUNICATION PROGRAM

Each lodging establishment must have a written hazard communication program. This information must be shared with those employees handling the hazardous materials. It shall be based upon the list of hazardous chemicals in use and the MSDS files.

It shall specify the individuals responsible for:

- Hazardous chemical list
- MSDS files
- Label program
- Training

LABELING

This is a critical section of the requirement. Many labels are so technical that they are impossible for the hotel/motel employer or the employee to understand. "Translation" should be obtained from a qualified source as quickly as possible. Generally, where an employee draws a small portion of a chemical product from bulk for daily use in a smaller container, it is not necessary to transfer a label to this smaller quantity, as it is assumed the chemical will be fully used during the work shift. It is only when such materials are not returned to the original bulk container or used in the course of the day that a label is required. Again, a coordinator should handle this matter and provide the necessary follow-up and training.

Although the above daily-use exemption is permitted from an operating point of view, it is suggested that consideration be given to labeling all containers. There will obviously be instances where more is taken than necessary for the day's assignments and the employee fails to take the time to return the surplus materials to the bulk storage. The container is put on the shelf in the linen room and soon there is a collection of unidentified containers. It is better to label all containers.

Labels Must:

- Identify the material in the container.
- Provide the manufacturer's name, address, phone number, and special emergency phone number (if available).
- List appropriate hazard warnings.
- Be in English. (It makes good business sense to translate into the language of any large employee groups any information that would be more readily understood in their native language. Of course, the English portion should also be maintained.)
- Not be in conflict with requirements of the Department of Transportation, Environmental Protection Agency, or the Consumer Product Safety Commission.

Employer Labels

When necessary to draw chemicals from bulk, a label must be provided for the smaller spray bottle or container. As in the other labeling requirements, the chemical identity should be listed with appropriate hazard warnings for the employees' protection. This should include an emergency phone number for the manufacturer and for local emergency medical services.

TRAIN THE EMPLOYEES

The following elements are basic to the development of an effective HAZCOM training program:

- Who will train?
- How will non-routine aspects of chemical use be covered? Once a quarter, or semi-annually, etc.?
- What data is to be made available?
  - Requirements of standards
  - Jobs requiring the use of listed hazardous chemicals
- Where will the program be presented, and what will its availability be?
  - Based upon required hazardous chemicals list
  - Based upon in-house copies of MSDSs for the chemicals
- Training content
  - Physical and health hazards:
    - Chemical groups
    - Specific chemicals
  - Methods and observations for detection of release of hazardous chemicals:
    - By visual appearance
    - By odor
    - Identifying places on the premises where chemicals are used (released)
    - Chemical monitoring methods
  - Measure for:
    - Work practices
    - Emergency procedures
    - Personal protective equipment
    - Engineering controls
  - Explanation of programs to employees:
    - Labeling
    - How to obtain and use MSDSs
- Have records confirming:
  - Who was trained and when

- That the training has been reviewed to afford the necessary updates, deletions, presentations to new employees, refreshers, etc.
- That employees know:
  - Where the MSDS files are located and how to use them
  - Labeling requirements in relation to products used regularly by employees
  - The appropriate protective equipment for the chemical product in use (and actually use the protection as required)

SOURCES

Check for state requirements; currently, 23 states and jurisdictions have right-to-know laws. These laws mandate knowledge of hazardous substances being used in the workplace. Both the state and federal requirements must be met, particularly when one may be more stringent than the other. The most stringent code always applies.

Local organizations may have programs available. Be sure the program focuses on the hotel/motel need and is in an understandable and reasonably applicable format.

HAZARD COMMUNICATION AND COMPLIANCE KIT

OSHA has published *Hazard Communication—A Compliance Kit*. Properties interested in obtaining this publication may obtain it by contacting:

SUPERINTENDENT OF DOCUMENTS
U. S. Government Printing Office
Washington, DC 20402-9325
(202) 512-1800
MasterCard/Visa accepted; fax completed form to (202) 512-2250

Obtain information and order electronically via: GPO Access, Superintendent of Documents home page: http://www.gpo.gov/su_docs/

The cost of the publication is $18. The reference number is 029-016-00147-6. It takes six to eight weeks to fill orders.

OSHA INFORMATION SOURCE

Questions on OSHA health standards may be referred to: (202) 219-8036

Questions on OSHA safety standards may be referred to: (202) 219-8031

OSHA's World Wide Web site is: http://www.osha.gov

WORKPLACE VIOLENCE

DIMENSIONS OF WORKPLACE VIOLENCE IN THE HOSPITALITY INDUSTRY

Workplace violence in the hospitality industry comes from several sources:

- Guests or the public
- Criminals
- Employees
- Relatives or "friends" of employees

There are approximately one million violent crimes per year with one-tenth of that total involving handguns.

According to a report from a National Alert issued by the National Institute of Safety and Health (NIOSH) in 1993, the following problems plague the employees of the hospitality industry. Employees frequently:

- Must handle money in public areas
- Work alone with no back-up available
- Are assigned to late-night or early morning hours
- Work in high-crime areas

Robbery is involved in four out of every five workplace murders.

Fast-food outlets are becoming a favorite target because criminals can "hit" them for about $500, as compared with $200 in a convenience store.

A national insurance company's survey for 1993 noted that:

- 15 percent of American workers have been physically assaulted during their work career
- Of these attacks, one in six involved a lethal weapon
- In one of the years surveyed, one in four employees was attacked, threatened, or harassed while on the job

For the period from 1980 through 1989, NIOSH recorded 7,603 homicides, or an average of 750 murders per year. A Department of Labor study verified 1,004 workplace homicides in 1992. This led to the category of "epidemic" being assigned to the tragedy of homicides in the workplace. Homicides have become the number-one cause of death for women in the workplace, accounting for 41% of work-related fatalities in the period 1980–1989.

NIOSH has made some recommendations for addressing the problem of violence in the workplace. These include:

- Make high-risk areas visible to more people
- Install adequate external lighting
- Use drop safes to minimize cash on hand

- Carry small amounts of cash
- Post signs announcing that limited cash is on hand
- Install silent alarms
- Install surveillance cameras
- Increase the number of staff on duty
- Provide training in conflict resolution and nonviolent response
- Instruct workers to avoid resistance during a robbery
- Provide bulletproof barriers or enclosures
- Have police check on employees routinely (but not on a schedule)

Moving from the focus on workplace violence through criminal activity, let us turn to the continuing problem of workplace violence from co-workers, or relatives or "friends" of employees. In this situation, the violent individual is known to most, if not all, of the individuals involved. The most usual cause of a violent reaction by an employee is a termination, which brings a tremendous sense of insecurity to most people. As an employee begins to mentally and emotionally review the experience of termination, an attitude of "getting even" becomes primary to some individuals. These individuals tend to find scapegoats for their present situation. While there is rarely validity to the belief of some former employees that other employees must have provided negative information that led to their termination, that becomes the center of these individuals' thought processes. A supervisor or manager may also be blamed. Some individuals who feel they were unfairly "picked on" by a representative of management begin to develop an urgent desire to "get even."

It becomes critically important at the workplace that there be a special sensitivity on the part of employees and supervision to any signs that might indicate the possibility of violent behavior on the part of an employee. Just as there are "community watch programs" and a Traveler Safety Campaign (a program that provides information to travelers through public service announcements, videotapes, and information-card handouts), so must there be an "awareness program" instituted for employees, so they can be sensitive to early indications of potential violence by other employees. Such a program is not intended to set up a "spy network" or "undercover operation." Rather, it should be a program in which an employee's anonymous report to a designated member of management should initiate a follow-up to verify the validity of the employee's concerns.

Some signs to watch for include:

- The individual who is "going to get even"
- The employee with a more-than-usual interest in and fascination with guns
- Substance abuse and alcoholism
- The individual who complains that "everyone is out to get me"

In further development of a team approach, it is important that the employees feel comfortable with reporting signs of violence that they have been trained to recognize through workshops conducted by professionals. In turn, supervisors must be trained to appropriately respond to any reports received from employees.

Such workshops should include topics on:

- Conflict resolution.
- Dealing with stress in the workplace.
- The policies of the company concerning substance abuse and alcoholism.
- The policy concerning the provision of an Employee Assistance Program (EAP) or other similar treatment protocol. The role of security should be defined, since this area may be felt to be the concern of human resources only.
- The violence dimension certainly establishes the need for a cooperative effort.
- Awareness training for sensitivity to signs of aggression or violence.
- Expanding the communications skills of all levels of employees and supervisors.
- Availability of counseling sessions.
- How to deal with difficult people; this would include guests, the general public, and the employees.

The hospitality industry, along with other business and industry groups throughout the nation, is challenged to develop an environment in which the employees will be willing to confide their fears and concerns without fear of ridicule or intimidation. Supervisors and managers must also recognize that the inability to prevent an employee from seeking vengeance is not a reflection on their ability to supervise or manage. On the other hand, senior management must be aware of the fact that inappropriate supervisory "heckling and harassing" of an employee could be basic to the actual problem at the work site, and must be prepared to address that problem should it be evidenced in the investigation of a potential violent act by an employee.

Gang violence can be a problem in the workplace. With the many entry-level jobs within the hospitality industry, groups of (usually) male employees in their teens and early twenties can put the property at risk for gang violence. The usual indicators of violence on the part of a single employee are rarely elements in gang activity. Among clear indicators may be similar dress styles or certain jewelry. Police authorities may have a gang liaison group within the police department that would be a major source for assistance in preventing gang violence on the premises. The premises, by the way, also include the parking lot, where certain situations could lead to "shoot-outs" that involve innocent guests and other bystanders if the situations are not controlled from the outset.

It is most important that an organization establish the fact that there is no acceptance of behavior or activities that might lead to workplace violence. That focus must include situations which are generally mandated by federal or state law, but may be overlooked or "winked at." These areas include discrimination and unfair treatment, sexual harassment, substance abuse or alcoholism, and the possession of firearms on the property at any time, unless required by some special assignments or local requirements.

Screening, which has been emphasized in other sections of this guide, is certainly of major concern in any consideration of workplace violence. A serious effort must be made to screen the individual with such inclinations from the work force. If the local jurisdiction permits the use of psychological testing in the hands of competent administrators, this should certainly be reviewed as an option by senior management. The use of a waiver on the part of a job applicant will also permit questions that might uncover information about problems of a violent nature in the applicant's prior work experience.

One of the more difficult dimensions of violence in the workplace is in the "jilted lover" who comes on the premises without warning to kill an employee and/or his or her new lover. Again, this becomes a part of sensitivity and awareness training. If employees know of this change in a relationship, and some concern is indicated by one or both of the new lovers in the "love triangle," this information should be shared with management and special efforts should be made to provide protection against a tragic incident. In such a case, the "jilted" individual may not be known to many of the employees at the site, and that individual would have free access to many areas of the hospitality facility. Tragically, any guest or employee could intercept the object of the individual's murderous intent without anyone being alerted to the trouble until the gunshots are heard.

According to a research project by the Defense Personnel Security Research Center (PERSEREC) entitled *Combating Workplace Violence*, there is no exact method to predict when a person will become violent. One or more of these warning signs, however, may be displayed before a person becomes violent, but these signs *do not* necessarily indicate that an individual *will* become violent. A display of these signs should trigger concern because they are usually exhibited by people experiencing problems. The signs are:

- Irrational beliefs and ideas
- Verbal, nonverbal, or written threats or intimidation
- Fascination with weaponry and/or acts of violence
- Expression of a plan to hurt himself or others
- Externalizing blame
- Unreciprocated romantic obsession
- Taking up a lot of a supervisor's time with behavior or performance problems
- Fear reaction among co-workers/clients
- Drastic change in belief systems
- Displays of unwarranted anger
- New or increased source of stress at home or work
- Inability to take criticism
- Feelings of being victimized

- Intoxication from alcohol or other substances
- Expressions of hopelessness or heightened anxiety
- Productivity and/or attendance problems
- Violence towards inanimate objects
- Steals or sabotages projects or equipment
- Lack of concern for the safety of others

OSHA has issued papers regarding violence within the health care and retail industries. The focus of the retail industry articles has been fast food restaurants and convenience stores without specific focus on the lodging industry. It would appear that ultimately OSHA will begin to cite violations under the OSHA General Duty Clause where it is determined that the employer did not make a reasonable effort to protect the employee against violent acts.

Index

A

accident prevention signs, 137
accounting
 alarms, 263
 control procedures, 261–263
ADA. *See* Americans with Disabilities Act
alarm systems, 130–133
 considerations for, 132
 contact, 131
 control center, 130
 local, 131
 remote, 131–132
 safety, 132–133
 silent, 131
alcohol
 automated dispensing and monitoring, 230
 dram shop acts, 231
 storage, issuing, and service, 230–231
American Red Cross, 292–293, 309–311
Americans with Disabilities Act (ADA), 214
 legislation, 243–245
 viewport requirements, 145
armored car service, 263
arrests, citizen's, 12, 21–22
arson, 298
asset protection, 4–5, 207–249
 claim checking system, 210
 concealed weapons, 210
 employee identification, 209
 employee meals, 208
 employee parking, 210
 employee theft, 210–211
 engineering, 217–219
 food and beverage, 228–232
 front office, 221
 human resources, 211–217
 important points, 225
 internal control system, 208–211
 long-distance charges, 208
 recreation department, 232–238
 rooms division, 219–224
assets, vulnerability of, 5–6
automated purchasing systems, 229–230
avoidance, 332–333

B

bank deposits, 263
Banks v. Hyatt Corporation, 108–119, 174
biometrics, 142
blackouts, 305–306
bloodborne pathogens, 419–428
boiler and machinery coverage, 343
Boles v. La Quinta Motor Inns, 129
bombs and bomb threats, 295–297, 322–324
 sample checklist, 296
Boston Tremont Hotel, 103
Bureau of Diplomatic Security, 313
business income coverage, 341–342

C

carbon monoxide detectors, 135
cash payment policies, 273–274
cashiering
 function, 264
 special controls, 264
casino and gaming security, 238–240
 internal audit, 239
 surveillance, 239
CCTV. *See* closed-circuit television
checking out, settling accounts, 274
checks
 accepting, 268–271
 check guarantee programs, 268
 identification, 268–269
 policy acceptance questions, 269–270
 refusing, 269
 traveler's, 271
 verification, 270–271
citizen's arrests, 12, 21–22
Civil Defense, 302
civil disturbances, 315–316
claims management, 348–350
closed-circuit television (CCTV), 123–125
 dummy cameras, 123
 expert tips, 126
 features, 124–125
 limited use, 123
 placement, 123
coinsurance, 341–342
 calculations, 342
commercial
 automotive coverage, 347
 crime coverage, 343
 general liability coverage, 346
 package policy, 339–347
 property coverage, 341–342
communication systems, 125–127
compensatory damages, 29
computer security 274–280
 data backup, 279
 embezzlement, 277
 fire, 278
 firewalls, 276
 Internet, 276
 outside services, 277–278
 passwords, 275
 policy compliance, 279–280
 restricted access, 277
 system accountability, 275
 viruses, 276
computer systems, risk assessment, 274
Connie Francis case, 30–31
contact alarms, 131
contingency (emergency) plan, 291–295
conventions, 246–249
 safety hazards, 248–249
Courtney v. Remler, 146–154, 223
CPTED. *See* Crime Prevention Through Environmental Design
credit, denying, 271–272

credit cards, 265–268
    floor limit, 267
    high balance limit, 267
    illegal use of, 265
    preventing fraud, 266
    procedures for acceptance, 267
    verification, 266
credit policy, establishing, 265
    procedures, 265
    reservations, 272
Crime Prevention Through Environmental Design (CPTED), 104–107
    parking facility security features, 121
Crisis Communications Management (training video), 316
crisis communications policy, 317

D

damages
    compensatory, 29
    punitive, 29
Department of Drug Enforcement Administration (DEA), 178–179
    field divisions, 178
directed verdict, 29–30
disabilities, guests with, 243–246
division of duties, 226
dram shop acts, 231
drug dealing, 177–179
    illegal drug manufacture, 178–179

E

earthquakes, 304–305
EEOC. *See* Equal Employment Opportunity Commission
electronic access systems, 167–169
embezzlement, 277
emergencies
    adult lifesaving steps, 311
    choking, 309
    cooperation with other properties, 292
    getting medical help, 310
    identifying, 292

media relations, 316–321
medical and dental, 307–313
press releases, 319–320
social organization, 292–293
emergency
    equipment, 294
    evacuation, 297, 302
    inspection and maintenance program, 295
    response teams, 293–294
emergency plan
    assessing staff skills, 293
    development, 291–295
    executive-level committee, 292
employee
    alcohol and drug use, 216–217
    assistance programs, 216
    discipline, 214
    screening, 213
employers' liability insurance, 348
Equal Employment Opportunity Commission (EEOC), 244–245
exhibits, 246–249
    safety hazards, 248–249
exit interviews, 215

F

face recognition, 142, 143
Federal Emergency Management Agency (FEMA), 292, 302
fire
    arson, 298
    classes of, 135–136, 298
    computer security, 278
    decrease in hotels, 32
    drills, 294
    emergencies, 297–299
    extinguishers, 135–136
    Life Safety Code, 134
    sample report, 300
firewalls, 276
floods, 303–304
    insurance coverage, 347
floor limit, 267
food and beverage
    automated purchasing systems, 229–230

spoilage and pilferage, 229–230
foreseeability, 28
forms, self-inspection, 107
Fortney v. Hotel Rancroft, Inc., 60–63
front service
    command center, 219
    guest recommendations, 220

G

Garzilli v. Howard Johnson's Motor Lodges, Inc., 30–31
glass protection, 122
"Good Samaritan" legislation, 240
group disturbances, media relations, 320–321
guestroom security, 4, 137–146
    AAA deadbolt specification, 139
    ADA viewport requirements, 145
    biometrics, 142
    electronic locking systems, 139–140
    locks, 139
    secondary access-limiting devices, 142–143
    viewports, 143–145

H

Hazard Analysis Critical Control Point (HACCP) program, 229
hazards, identifying, 330–331
health clubs and jogging trails, 237–238
health emergencies, 307–313
hostage situations, 314–315
Hotel and Motel Fire Safety Act of 1990, The, 133
hotel fires, decrease of, 32
hotel security, societal concerns, 31–32
housekeeping
    guestroom access, 222
    inventory program, 223
    security checklist, 222
human resources, hiring procedures, 212–213
hurricanes, 299–303

speeds and effects on
property (chart), 301
warning, 301–302
watch, 299–301

I

identification of risk, 329–331
incident reports, 241
infrared radiation detection, 132
inland marine coverage, 343
innkeeper laws, 24–28
innkeeper's statutes, safe deposit box, 180–181
in-room safes, 186
in-room security
    floor plans, 146
    information cards, 146
    on-premises programs, 145
Institute of Internal Auditors, 282
insurance
    brokers, 338
    employers' liability, 348
    group coverage, 339
    legally mandated coverage, 347–348
    prerequisites for an insurable risk, 337
    ratings, 339
    regulation, 338–339
    risk sharing (pooling), 336
    risk transfer, 336
    services, 344–345
    specifications, 340
    umbrella coverage, 347
    workers' compensation, 347–348
insurers
    mutual, 337
    stock, 337
internal audit, 280–283
    statement of responsibilities, 281–282
    tasks, 280
inventories, unscheduled, 219
inventory control, 262

K

key control, 4, 165–167
    annual audit, 167
    basic questions concerning, 169
    employees' role, 167
    front service, 219

housekeeping, 221–222
    levels of keying, 165
    procedures, 218
    safe deposit box, 182
kickbacks, 225
kidnapping, 314–315
King v. Trans-Sterling, Inc., 168
Kraaz v. La Quinta Motor Inns, Inc., 169–173

L

LAN. *See* local area network
Las Vegas Palace Station Hotel & Casino, 319–320
laundry and dry cleaning, 224
law enforcement, liaison with, 7–8
legal cause, 29
Life Safety Code, 134
lifesaving steps, adults, 311
lighting
    appropriate, 120
    emergency, 121
    engineer, 120
    outdoor, 120
local alarms, 131
local area network (LAN), 276
locks
    AAA deadbolt specifications, 139
    electronic, 139–140
    guestroom, 137, 139
Lodging Security Officer Training Program, 19
loss
    assessing of potential losses, 331–332
    control, 332
    financing, 333
    shifting, 333–334
lost and found procedures, 186–191

M

Malone et al. v. Courtyard by Marriott Limited Partnership et al., 93–98
Matt et al. v. Days Inn of America, Inc., 80–85
means of egress, 297
media relations, 316–321
    establishing a policy, 317
    group disturbances, 320–321
medical emergencies, 307–313

meetings, 246–249
    safety hazards, 248–249
microwave detectors, 131

N

National Hurricane Center, 299
National Safe Workplace Institute, 215
National Weather Service, 299
negligence, 29
Nordmann v. National Hotel Company, 127–129

O

Occupational Safety and Health Act/Administration (OSHA), 132–133, 178
    bloodborne pathogens, 419–428
    fire emergency, 294, 297
    means of egress, 297
    medical emergencies, 307
    regulations, 367–438
    safety alarm requirements, 132–133
    swimming pools, 233
    workplace violence, 434–438
Opryland Hotel, 138, 306
Orlando Executive Park, Inc. v. P.D.R., 65, 70–80, 174
Otis Engineering Corp. v. Clark, 217

P

parking areas, 121
patrols, 174–176
    as crime deterrent, 174
    pattern of, 174
    primary functions, 174
    special training, 176
payroll procedures, 262
peepholes. *See* viewports
perils, identifying, 330–331
perimeter
    barriers, 120
    control, 4, 104–125
    establishing, 119–120
Peters v. Holiday Inns, Inc., 55–60, 121, 174

Phillips Petroleum Co. v. Dorn, 60–61, 63–65
photoelectric light beam, 132
physical security, 104–125
  checklist, 105–106
  glass protection, 122
  lighting, 120
  parking areas, 121
  perimeter barriers, 120
  self-inspection form, 107
point-of-sale (POS) systems, 231–232
police. *See* law enforcement
problem groups, 244
prostitution, 177
proximate cause, 29
public relations, 316–321
Public Relations Society of America (PRSA), 319
punitive damages, 29
purchasing and receiving, 225–228

R

radio frequency (RF) fields, 131
reasonable care, 3, 28
recordkeeping, 240–243
recreation department, swimming pools, 232–237
registration
  cards, 272–273
  security concerns, 272–273
Reichenbach v. Days Inn of America, Inc., 65–70
remote alarms
  infrared radiation detection, 132
  microwave detectors, 131
  photoelectric light beam, 132
  radio frequency (RF) fields, 131
  seismic detector, 132
reports
  sample incident and loss, 242
  types of, 241
  writing, 240–243
riots and civil disturbances, 315–316
risk
  assumption, 332–333
  comfort levels, 331
  financing, 333
  sharing (pooling), 336
  transfer, 336
risk assessment, computer systems, 274
risk management
  assessing potential losses, 331–332
  direct and indirect contributions, 335–336
  identifying risk, 329–331, 335
  implementation, 334
  perils and hazards, 330–331
  pre-loss and post-loss contributions, 334–335
  process (chart), 330
robberies, 306–307
  sample description form, 308
Robertson v. Sixpence Inns of America, Inc., 86–93
room communications, interactive cable television, 145
Rosier v. Gainsville Inns Associates, Ltd., 141–142

S

sabotage, 313–314
safe deposit box
  access procedures, 184–185
  innkeeper's statutes, 180–181
  key control, 182
  limited liability notices, 199–202
  procedures, 179–186
  sample agreement form, 188
  sample policy, 187–189
  special or unusual access, 185–186
safes, in-room, 186
safety alarms, OSHA requirements, 132–133
safety committee
  agenda sample, 353
  chairperson's duties, 352–353
  establishing, 350–353
  members' roles, 350–353
  policy sample, 351–352
  recorder's duties, 353
safety equipment, 133–137
  accident prevention signs, 137
  carbon monoxide detectors, 135
  fire extinguishers, 135, 136
  smoke detectors, 134
  sprinkler systems, 135–137
safety programs, 145
Salvation Army, 292–293
security
  computer, 274–280
  guidelines, 4–5
  publications about, 17
  records, 4
  training for, 15–24
security equipment
  selecting, 103–104
  uses and limitations, 103
security officers
  arming, 13–14, 20
  authority, 20–23
  citizen's arrests, 21–22
  contract, 11–12
  decisions regarding, 10
  in-house, 12
  interrogation by, 22
  off-duty police, 12, 19–20
  personnel issues, 12–14
  scheduling, 14–15
  screening of, 12–14
  searches by, 22
  staffing, 8–15
  supervision, 14–15
  training program, 19
  uniforms, 9–10
  use of force by, 22–23
security program, 4–15
  developing, 4–6
  elements of, 4
  implementing, 6–15
  managing, 4–5
  requirements, 6
  team concept, 23–24
seismic detectors, 132
separation of duties, embezzlement, 277
sequential numbering systems, 263
serial numbers, for inventory control, 262
signs
  accident prevention, 137
  swimming pool, 236
smoke detectors, 134
special guests and events, 243–249
spoilage and pilferage, 229–230
spotter, 230
sprinkler systems, 135–137

Stahlin v. Hilton Hotels Corporation, 312
Stardust Hotel, 168
state statutes, 24–28
storage and issuing, 228
summary judgment, 29
surveillance, 122–125
    closed-circuit television, 123–125
    equipment, 122
    patrols, 174–176
swimming pools, 232–237
    National Spa & Pool Institute (NSPI), 233
    OSHA guidelines, 233
    regulations, 233
    safety checklist, 234–235
    signage, 236

T

telephones, in-room, 145

terrorism, 313–316, 322–324
tornadoes, 303
Traveler Safety Tips, 25, 221
traveler's checks, 271

U

U.S. Small Business Administration, 269
umbrella coverage, 347
unauthorized persons, 176–178
Understanding Hospitality Law, 24–28

V

Vacation Village v. Burns International Security Service, 19

valuation, 341
viewports, 143–145
VIP guests, 246
vulnerability, 5–6

W

Wenninger v. Motel 6, Inc., 44–55, 174
workers' compensation insurance, 347–348
workplace violence, 215–216, 434–438
Workplace Violence Research Institute, 215

Y

youth groups, 246